P9-CKS-591

| PAGE 42 | ON THE ROAD | YOUR COMPLETE DESTINATION GUIDE
In-depth reviews, detailed listings
and insider tips |

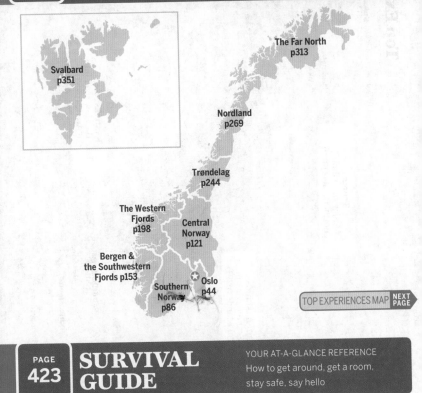

Svalbard p351

The Far North p313

Nordland p269

Trøndelag p244

The Western Fjords p198

Central Norway p121

Bergen & the Southwestern Fjords p153

Southern Norway p86

Oslo p44

TOP EXPERIENCES MAP NEXT PAGE

| PAGE 423 | SURVIVAL GUIDE | YOUR AT-A-GLANCE REFERENCE
How to get around, get a room,
stay safe, say hello |

Directory A–Z

THIS EDITION WRITTEN AND RESEARCHED BY

**Anthony Ham,
Stuart Butler, Miles Roddis**

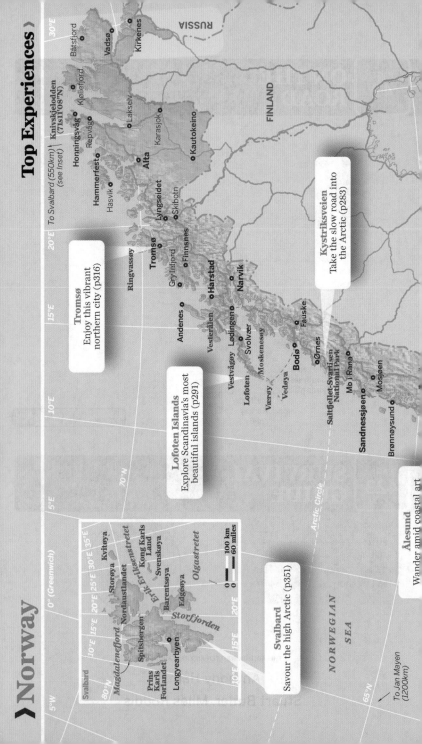

› Norway

Top Experiences ›

Tromsø
Enjoy this vibrant northern city (p316)

Lofoten Islands
Explore Scandinavia's most beautiful islands (p291)

Kystriksveien
Take the slow road into the Arctic (p283)

Svalbard
Savour the high Arctic (p351)

Ålesund
Wander amid coastal art

To Svalbard (550km) (see inset)

Knivskjelodden (71s11′08″N)

RUSSIA

FINLAND

Båtsfjord
Vadsø
Kirkenes
Kjøllefjord
Honningsvåg
Repvåg
Lakselv
Hammerfest
Hasvik
Karasjok
Alta
Lyngseidet
Skibotn
Kautokeino
Tromsø
Ringvassøy
Gryllefjord
Finnsnes
Harstad
Andenes
Narvik
Vesterålen
Løsdingen
Svolvær
Fauske
Vestvågøy
Lofoten
Moskenesøy
Bodø
Værøy
Ørnes
Vedøya
Saltfjellet-Svartisen National Park
Mo i Rana
Mosjøen
Sandnessjøen
Brønnøysund

Arctic Circle

Svalbard
80°N
Kvitøya
Storøya
Nordaustlandet
Erik Eriksenstretet
Kong Karls Land
Spitsbergen
Prins Karls Forlandet
Svenskøya
Barentsøya
Longyearbyen
Edgeøya
Olgastretet
Storfjorden

Magdalenefjord

NORWEGIAN SEA

To Jan Mayen (1200km)

0 — 100 km
0 — 60 miles

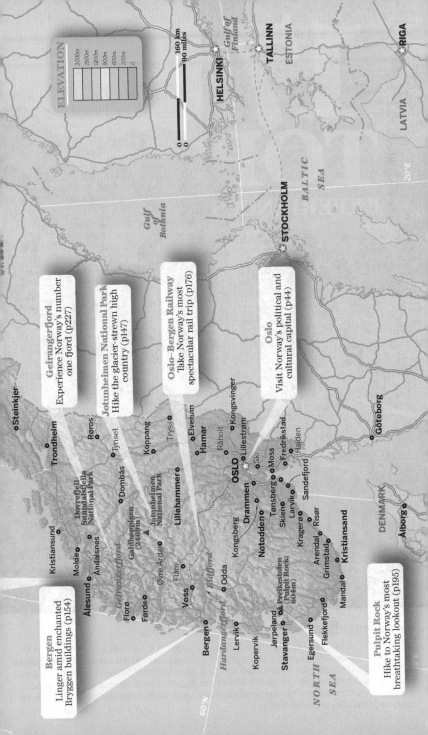

Bergen
Linger amid enchanted Bryggen buildings (p154)

Geirangerfjord
Experience Norway's number one fjord (p227)

Jotunheimen National Park
Hike the glacier-strewn high country (p147)

Oslo–Bergen Railway
Take Norway's most spectacular rail trip (p176)

Oslo
Visit Norway's political and cultural capital (p44)

Pulpit Rock
Hike to Norway's most breathtaking lookout (p195)

ELEVATION

3000m
1500m
1200m
900m
600m
300m
0

160 km
90 miles

0

HELSINKI

Gulf of Finland

TALLINN
ESTONIA

RIGA
LATVIA

20°E

BALTIC SEA

STOCKHOLM

Gulf of Bothnia

Steinkjer

Trondheim

Røros
Tynset
Koppang
Trysil
Elverum
Hamar
Råholt
Kongsvinger
Lillestrøm
OSLO
Ski
Moss
Fredrikstad
Halden
Sandefjord
Göteborg

Kristiansund
Molde
Andalsnes
Ålesund
Florø
Førde

Geirangerfjord

Galdhøpiggen
(2469m)

Dovrefjell–
Sunndalsfjella
National Park
Dombås

Jotunheimen
National Park
Lillehammer

Øvre Årdal
Flåm
Voss

Sognefjord

Odda
Kongsberg
Drammen
Notodden
Tønsberg
Skien
Larvik
Kragerø
Arendal
Risør
Grimstad
Kristiansand

Bergen

Hardangerfjord

Lervik
Kopervik
Jørpeland
Stavanger

Preikestolen
(Pulpit Rock;
604m)

Egersund
Flekkefjord
Mandal

NORTH SEA

DENMARK

Ålborg

Pulpit Rock
Hike to Norway's most breathtaking lookout (p195)

60°N

17 TOP EXPERIENCES

Geirangerfjord

1 The 20km chug along Geirangerfjord (p227), a Unesco World Heritage Site, must rank as the world's loveliest ferry journey. Long-abandoned farmsteads still cling to the fjord's near-sheer cliffs while ice-cold cascades tumble, twist and gush down to emerald-green waters. Take it from Geiranger and enjoy the calm as you leave this small, heaving port or hop aboard at altogether quieter Hellesylt. Prime your camera, grab a top-deck open-air seat and enjoy what's literally the only way to travel its secluded reaches.

ofoten Islands

Few visitors forget their first sighting of the Lofoten Islands (p291), laid out in summer greens and yellows, their razor-sharp peaks poking dark against a clear, cobalt sky. In the pure, exhilar- ing air, there's a constant tang of salt and, in the villages, more than a whiff of cod, that giant of e seas whose annual migration brings wealth. A hiker's dream and nowadays linked by bridges, e islands are simple to hop between, whether by bus, car or – ideally – bicycle.

Hurtigruten Coastal Ferry

3 So much more than merely a means of getting around, the iconic Hurtigruten coastal ferry (p439) takes you on one of the most spectacular coastal journeys anywhere on earth. On its daily journey between Bergen and Kirkenes, it dips into coastal fjords, docks at isolated villages barely accessible by road, draws near to dramatic headlands and crosses the Arctic Circle. In the process, it achieves in five or six days what would take months on land: it showcases the entire length of Norway's most glorious coast.

GZS/IMAGEBROKER

Northern Lights

4 There is no more uplifting natural phenomena than the aurora borealis, or northern lights (p387). Visible throughout the long night of the Arctic winter from October to March, they dance across the sky in green or white curtains of light, shifting in intensity and taking on forms that seem to spring from a child's vivid imagination. While there's no guarantee that the northern lights will appear at any given time, if you are lucky enough to see them, it's an experience that will live with you forever.

ANDERS BLOMQVIST

Hiking the Jotunheimen

5 The high country of central Norway ranks among Europe's premier summer destinations. Although there are numerous national parks criss-crossed by well-maintained hiking trails, it's Jotunheimen National Park (p147), whose name translates as 'Home of the Giants', that rises above all others. With 60 glaciers and 275 summits over 2000m, Jotunheimen is exceptionally beautiful and home to iconic trails such as Besseggen, Hurrungane and those in the shadow of Galdhøpiggen, Norway's highest peak. Jotunheimen's proximity to the fjords further enhances its appeal.

Bryggen, Bergen

6 Set amid a picturesque and very Norwegian coastal landscape of fjords and mountains, Bergen lays a strong claim to being one of Europe's most beautiful cities. A celebrated history of seafaring trade down through the centuries has bequeathed to the city the stunning (and Unesco World Heritage–listed) waterfront district of Bryggen (p154), an archaic tangle of wooden buildings. A signpost to a history at once prosperous and tumultuous, the titled and colourful wooden buildings of Bryggen now shelter the chic boutiques and traditional restaurants for which the city is famous.

JAN STRØMME

RALPH HOPKINS

Svalbard

7 The subpolar archipelago of Svalbard (p351) is a true place of the heart. Deliciously remote and yet surprisingly accessible, Svalbard is Europe's most evocative slice of the polar north and one of the continent's last great wilderness areas. Shapely peaks, massive icefields (60% of Svalbard is covered by glaciers) and heartbreakingly beautiful fjords provide the backdrop for a rich array of Arctic wildlife (including around one-sixth of the world's polar bears, which outnumber people here), and for summer and winter activities that get you out amid the ringing silence of the snows.

Kystriksveien Coastal Route

8 The lightly-trafficked coastal route (p283) through Nordland is for those with leisure to savour its staggering beauty. You might well not have time for the full 650km but a sample is all but mandatory if you're progressing northwards. It's not one to be rushed. The frequent ferry hops offer compulsory, built-in breaks and stunning seascapes, while both inland glaciers and accessible offshore islands – such as Vega, famous for its eider ducks, or Lovund, home to 200,000 puffins – are seductive diversions.

Oslo–Bergen Railway

9 Often cited as one of the world's most beautiful rail journeys, the Oslo–Bergen rail line is an opportunity to sample some of Norway's best scenery. After passing through the forests of southern Norway, it climbs up onto the horizonless beauty of the Hardangervidda Plateau and the continues down through the pretty country around Voss and on into Bergen. En route it passes within touching distance of the fjords and connects (at Myrdal; p176) with the incredibly steep branch line down to the fjord country that fans out from Flåm.

Pulpit Rock

10 As lookouts go, Preikestolen (Pulpit Rock; p195) has few peers. Perched atop an almost perfectly sheer cliff that juts out more than 600m above the waters of gorgeous Lysefjord, Pulpit Rock is one of Norway's signature images and most eye-catching areas. It's the sort of place where you'll barely be able to look as travellers dangle far more than seems advisable over the precipice, even as you find yourself drawn inexorably towards the edge. The hike to reach it takes two hours and involves a full-day trip from Stavanger.

Wildlife-Watching

11 Norway is the last refuge for some of Europe's most intriguing wildlife (p390). While you may stumble upon polar bears (in Svalbard only), Arctic foxes, reindeer and other species during your explorations of the Norwegian wild, dedicated safaris in the Norwegian interior will take you within sight of the otherworldly musk ox (pictured), as well as the rather loveable elk (moose). Along the coast, Norway's bird life is abundant and filled with interest, while whale-watching outings are a staple of the Nordland coast, especially around Lofoten and Vesterålen.

ADA/IMAGEBROKER

NEV/IMAGEBROKER

Dog-Sledding

12 There's no finer way to explore the Arctic wilderness than on a sled pulled by a team of huskies (p33). Blissfully free from engine noise and the din of modern life, accompanied by a soundtrack of yelping dogs and the scrape of the sled across the snow, dog-sledding (from half-day excursions to multi-day expeditions) takes you out into the trackless world of Norway's far north and allows you to immerse yourself in the eerily beautiful light of the Arctic winter.

Stave Churches

13 All over southern and central Norway you'll come across wooden stave churches. They come in all forms, from the monumental to the pocket-sized and cute, but no matter what form they take there's something about them that will stir up hazy memories of childhood. For the stave churches of Norway, many of which come surrounded in stories of trolls, are without doubt the very definition of fairy-tale churches, and none more so than the spectacular Heddal Stave Church (p110).

HAN/IMAGEBROKER

Art Nouveau in Ålesund

14 Snug, tidy Ålesund (p230) owes much of its charm to a devastating fire that ripped through its wooden structures a century ago, destroying everything except the jail and a church. From its ashes rose a brand-new town, mostly of stone and mostly designed by young Norwegian architects who had trained in Germany. Strongly influenced by the Jugendstil (art nouveau) movement of the time, they designed buildings rich in ornamentation, with turrets, spires, gargoyles and other fanciful elements based on local motifs.

RICHARD CUMMINS

Sami Culture

15 Snowmobiles have ousted sleds and nowadays only a minority of Sami live from their reindeer herds or coastal fishing. But the Sami culture (p404), transcending the frontiers of Norway, Sweden and Finland, lives on and strong. The affairs of the Norwegian Sami are regulated by the Sami Parliament, its building a masterpiece of design in mellow wood. And Sami identity lies secure in the language and its dialects, traditions such as the *joik* (a sustained, droned rhythmic poem), and handicrafts such as silversmithing and knife making.

Tromsø

16 Tromsø (p316), a cool 400km north of the Arctic Circle, is northern Norway's significant city with, among other superlatives, the world's northernmost cathedral, brewery and
botanic garden. Its busy clubs and pubs – more per capita than in any other Norwegian town – owe
much to the university (another northernmost) and its students. In summer, Tromsø's a base for
round-the-clock, 24-hour daylight activity. Once the first snows fall, the locals slip on their skis or
snowshoes, head out of town and gaze skywards for a glimpse of the northern lights.

RICHARD CUMMINS

Oslo

17 Oslo (p44) is reinventing itself. This is a city aiming to become nothing less than a world-
renowned centre of culture. It's already bursting at the seams with museums and top-notch
art galleries, but now it's got itself a brand-new, glacier-white opera house that could make even
Sydney envious. This is only the start of a project that will transform the city's waterfront over the
next decade and in the process make Oslo one of the most happening cities in Scandinavia.

welcome to
Norway

Norway is a once-in-a-lifetime destination and the essence of its appeal is remarkably simple: this is one of the most beautiful countries on earth.

Stirring Landscapes

The drama of Norway's natural world is difficult to overstate. Impossibly steep-sided fjords of extraordinary beauty cut gashes from a jagged coastline deep into the interior. The fjords' fame is wholly merited, but this is also a land of glaciers, grand and glorious, snaking down from icefields that rank among Europe's largest. Elsewhere, the mountainous terrain of Norway's interior resembles the ramparts of so many natural fortresses, and yields to rocky coastal islands that rise improbably from the waters like apparitions of childhood imaginings. And then, of course, there's the primeval appeal of the Arctic. Such landforms provide a backdrop for some of Europe's most charismatic wildlife – polar bears (in Svalbard), reindeer and musk oxen to name just three – and the setting for many a picturesque wooden village. Together they lend much personality, if any were needed, to what is an astonishing topographical story.

The Call of the Wild

In Norway experiencing nature is very much an active pursuit, and Norwegians' passion for exploring their natural world has created one of Europe's most exciting and varied adventure-tourism destinations. Some activities may only be for the young, energetic and fearless, but most – such as world-class hiking, cycling and white-water rafting in summer; dog-sledding, skiing and snowmobiling in winter – can be enjoyed by anyone of reasonable fitness. On our travels we've encountered 93-year-old snowmobilers and whole families with young children racing down rapids. Whether you're here in summer when the options are more varied, or in winter for the soul-stirring spectacle of the northern lights, these activities are both reason alone to visit and an exhilarating means of getting away from the crowds and close to nature.

Scandinavian Sophistication

The counterpoint to so much natural beauty is found in the country's vibrant cultural life, which celebrates local traditions and draws in the best from around the world. Norwegian cities are cosmopolitan and brimful of architecture that showcases the famous Scandinavian flair for design through the ages. At the same time, a busy calendar of festivals, many of international renown, are worth planning your trip around.

Worth the Expense

And yet if one topic above all others dominates conversations among travellers to Norway, it's the formidable cost of travel here. Make no mistake: Norway is one of the most expensive countries on earth, which is yet another reason why saving up to come here is akin to planning the trip of a lifetime. But is it worth it? Absolutely: Norway will pay you back with never-to-be-forgotten experiences many times over.

need to know

Currency
» Norwegian kroner (Nkr)

Language
» Norwegian

When to Go

Longyearbyen
GO mid-Jun–mid-Aug, Dec–Feb

Tromsø
GO mid-Jun–mid-Aug, Dec–Feb

Trondheim
GO Jun–Aug

Warm summers, cold winters
Mild summers, cold winters
Polar climate

Bergen
GO Jun–Aug

Oslo
GO Jun–Aug

High Season
(mid-Jun–mid-Aug)

» Accommodation and transport often booked out in advance

» Accommodation prices at their lowest

» No guarantees with the weather – can be warm and sunny or cool and rainy

Shoulder
(May–mid-Jun & mid-Aug–Sep)

» A good time to travel, with generally mild, clear weather and fewer crowds

» Accommodation prices can be high, except on weekends

» Book accommodation well ahead for festivals

Low Season
(Oct–Apr)

» Can be bitterly cold

» Many attractions are closed

» March is considered high season in Svalbard

» Accommodation prices high, except on weekends

Your Daily Budget

Budget less than
€120

» Dorm beds: €21-45

» Huts or cabins: from €45

» Doubles in B&Bs/guesthouses: from €62/87

» Excellent supermarkets and cheaper lunch specials

» Book ahead for *minipris* tickets

Midrange
€120–200

» Double room in midrange hotel (weekends and mid-June to mid-August): €90-175

» Lunch or dinner in decent local restaurant

» Car rental: from €75 per day

Top end over
€200

» Double room in top-end hotel: €175 and up

» Lunch and dinner in decent local restaurants

Money

» ATMs widely available. Credit cards accepted in most hotels, restaurants and shops.

Visas

» Generally not required for stays of up to 90 days (not required for members of EU or Schengen countries). Some nationalities need a Schengen visa.

Mobile Phones

» Local SIM cards are widely available and can be used in most international mobile phones. Mobile coverage in all but wilderness areas.

Driving/ Transport

» Drive on the right; steering wheel is on the left side of the car. Good train network in south and centre of country; buses elsewhere.

Websites

» **Fjord Norway** (www. fjordnorway.com) Focused on Norway's star attractions.

» **LonelyPlanet.com** (www.lonelyplanet.com/ norway) Destination information, hotel bookings, forums etc.

» **Norway.com** (www. norway.com) Links to tourist information with a practical focus.

» **Norway Guide** (www.norwayguide.no) A rundown on Norway's top attractions.

» **Visit Norway** (www. visitnorway.com) Norwegian Tourist Board site ranging from the practical to the inspirational.

Exchange Rates

Australia	A$1	Nkr5.92
Canada	C$1	Nkr5.96
Europe	€1	Nkr7.98
Japan	¥100	Nkr7.24
New Zealand	NZ$1	Nkr4.57
UK	UK£1	Nkr9.41
USA	US$1	Nkr5.99

For current exchange rates see www.xe.com.

Important Numbers

There are no area codes in Norway.

Directory assistance	☏180
International access code	☏00
Norway country code	☏47
Ambulance	☏113
Police	☏112

Arriving in Norway

» **Gardermoen International Airport, Oslo**

Buses: Flybussen airport buses (www. flybussen.no) go to the centre of Oslo (one-way/return €17.50/29.50); one to four hourly from 4.05am to 9.50pm; 40 minutes

Trains: Airport Express Trains (www.flytoget. no) go to the centre of Oslo (€21); up to six hourly from 4.18am to midnight; 22 minutes

Taxis: €75 to €110; 30 minutes to one hour to the centre, depending on traffic

KEEPING COSTS DOWN

The prices for hotels (and just about everything else) in Norway can be a real shock to the system, but there are some strategies for keeping travel costs at a reasonable level. The period from mid-June to mid-August is the best time to visit the country: although the crowds can be off-putting, hotel prices can be 40% less than for the rest of the year. In most accommodation types, a buffet breakfast is included in the room price – turn breakfast into your main meal of the day – while in many restaurants, discounted lunchtime specials also enable you to eat well without spending too much. Picking up your rental car in neighbouring Sweden can also reduce costs, while those travelling by train should plan ahead and book online for heavily discounted *minipris* fares.

if you like...

Fjords

Norway's epic landscapes rank among Europe's most varied and beautiful, but the sheer drama of the fjords is alone worth the effort of coming to this remarkable country. Here, cliffs plunge down to barely populated shorelines and vertiginous waterfalls drop from impossible heights while isolated farms occupy seemingly inaccessible pockets of green.

Geirangerfjord Iconic Norwegian fjord that inspires even when viewed alongside crowds and cruise ships (p227)

Nærøyfjord Unesco World Heritage–listed fjord region of extraordinary beauty (p203)

Lysefjord A near-perfect fjord watched over by the world-famous Pulpit Rock (p195)

Magdalenefjord, Svalbard Quite simply one of the most beautiful places on earth and worth the considerable effort to reach (p364)

Hardangerfjord Stunning network of fjords with lovely fjord-side villages (p176)

Lofoten Islands Trollfjord and Vestfjorden are high points of these islands' stirring natural beauty (p291)

Hiking

Norway's extensive network of national parks makes this one of Europe's premier hiking destinations. From hiking the high country of central Norway to the sweeping panoramas of the Arctic North, from traditional trails to the gravitas of walking atop glaciers, Norway is a dream destination for those eager to explore the wilderness step by step.

Jotunheimen National Park Stunning network of trails amid glaciers and Norway's highest peaks (see the boxed text, p148)

Rondane National Park Shapely peaks and plenty of trails to escape the crowds (p142)

Hardangervidda National Park A vast upland plateau with reindeer and glacier hikes a possibility (see the boxed text, p151)

Saltfjellet-Svartisen National Park One of the best places for glacier hikes just inside the Arctic Circle (p276)

Aurlandsdalen Classic four-day trek from source to sea (p204)

Lysefjord Hike to some of Norway's most spectacular lookouts (p195)

Winter Activities

The alter ego to Norway's world-famous summer attractions is its extraordinary range of winter activities. Many of these take place in the Arctic North, with dog-sledding, snowmobiling and skiing the marquee attractions. Apart from allowing you to try new modes of transport, these activities take you beyond inhabited regions and add a new dimension to your experience of Arctic and sub-Arctic Norway.

Dog-sledding & snowmobiling, Svalbard Head off into Norway's most beautiful frozen wilderness (p358)

Dog-sledding, Karasjok Get a lesson from a husky master just outside the Sami capital (p347)

Reindeer- and dog-sledding, Tromsø Arctic trails close to the Swedish border (p317)

Snowmobiling, Kirkenes Explore the Pasvik Valley by day or moonlight alongside the Russian border (p341)

Skiing, Lillehammer Ski the downhill runs used during the 1994 Winter Olympics (p129)

King crab safaris, Kirkenes Arguably Norway's strangest (and most delicious) winter 'sport' (p341)

If you like...contemporary architecture
that encapsulates the Arctic North,
Tromsø's Arctic Cathedral (p316) and
the Sami Parliament in Karasjok (p347)
perfectly evoke ice-bound Arctic forms

Stave Churches

There is no more appealing Norwegian architectural style than the stave church. These fantastical structures evoke Norway's medieval past with dark-wood walls rising to turrets and ornamental flourishes, at times suggesting seemingly mythical creatures, at others the prow of a Viking ship. Most churches are found in Norway's fjord regions and the close-up intricacy of detail and the pleasing aspect of the whole is often offset by a stunning location.

Heddal Stave Church, Notodden An astonishing flight of architectural fancy (p110)

Urnes Unesco World Heritage–listed church on the shores of a fjord (p211)

Lom Perfectly sited structure where valleys meet (p145)

Borgund One of the best-preserved examples, with a medieval wooden bell tower (p206)

Fantoft Stave Church, Bergen Poignantly reconstructed church that burned to the ground in 1992 (p162)

Ringebu A lovely little church set on a wooded hillside (p144)

Stordal Hybrid church unusual for being more spectacular on the inside (p226)

Wildlife

Polar bears, whales, reindeer, musk ox, Arctic fox, elk (moose)...Norway is home to some of Europe's most charismatic wildlife and although populations are small, most are readily accessible to even casual wildlife-watchers. Prolific bird species make Norway one of the most important birdwatching destinations in northern Europe.

Svalbard Home to a checklist of Arctic wildlife, including polar bears, Arctic foxes, reindeer and bird life (p354)

Dovrefjell-Sunndalsfjella National Park Track down bird life and musk ox on safari from Oppdal or Dombås (see the boxed text, p140)

Hardangervidda National Park Home to around 7000 wild reindeer, Norway's largest herd (p150)

Gjesvær Remote and rewarding with millions of seabirds (p334)

Stø Whale-watching expeditions with birds and seals thrown in (p306)

Evje Set out on the trail of elk in the southern Norwegian interior (see the boxed text, p118)

Femundsmarka National Park Rich bird life and musk ox close to Røros and the Swedish border (p137)

City Life

The counterpoint (and gateways) to stunning natural landscapes, Norway's cities are also worthy destinations in their own right. Set for the most part against picturesque backdrops, these urban centres invariably overflow with museums and large student populations who bring much life and personality to often-pedestrianised streets. Each also has at least one architectural landmark of singular beauty and all allow you to sample the best of local and international cuisine and bars that capture that suave Scandinavian spirit.

Bergen Norway's prettiest and most cosmopolitan city (p154)

Trondheim A fine cathedral, culinary excellence and a buzzing student population (p245)

Ålesund Art nouveau architecture and a lovely coastal setting (p230)

Tromsø Vibrant student town deep in the Arctic (p316)

Stavanger Museum-rich port city with an engaging old quarter (p188)

Oslo Norway's cultural and political capital (p44)

GRANT DIXON

>> The switchback roads of Trollstigen (p223)

Villages

Norway's cities may make a lot more noise, but this is a country first and foremost of small isolated settlements that have, for centuries, been the lifeblood of Norwegian existence. Almost invariably built of wood, these villages are found across the country – with the exception of the far north, due to the devastation wrought during WWII – from fishing villages or fjord-side hamlets to former mining settlements deep in the interior.

Røros Unesco World Heritage–listed former mining settlement with splendid wooden buildings (p132)

Å A gloriously preserved Lofoten fishing village (p301)

Sogndalsstrand One of the prettiest wooden villages along Norway's southern coast (p105)

Nyksund Once abandoned fishing village transformed into an artists colony (p306)

Utne Charming fjord-side village with Norway's oldest hotel (p182)

Undredal One of Sognefjorden's loveliest villages, with fewer crowds than most (p203)

Nusfjord An artsy Lofoten village that captures the islands' spirit (p299)

Scenic Drives

Norwegian ingenuity in taming a challenging landscape and connecting even the remotest settlements has bequeathed some extraordinarily beautiful roads. Eighteen are designated as National Tourist Routes (see p445), but even these only scratch the surface.

Sognefjellet Road, Jotunheimen National Park Breathtaking route across the roof of Norway (p147)

Kystriksveien Coastal Route Norway's premier coast road, especially between Stokkvågen and Storvik (p285)

Trollstigen The 'Troll's Ladder' is a dizzying succession of steep hairpin bends between fjords (p223)

Snøvegen Short but nervewrackingly steep trail with unrivalled views over fjords (p204)

Rv815, Lofoten Islands Takes you through the dramatic landscapes for which Lofoten is famous (see the boxed text, p299)

Gamle Strynefjellsvegen Among the loveliest drives in western Norway (see the boxed text, p219)

Ulvik to Odda, Hardangerfjord Hugs the fjord shoreline with some fine vistas (p176)

Viking History

Ruling over Norway (and much of Europe) for five centuries, the Vikings provide many of Norway's most picaresque historical tales (see p369). Their primary strongholds were the coastal inlets all along the southern and southwestern Norwegian coast; it was from here that they launched their longships in their quest for world domination and to here that they returned with the spoils of victory.

Stiklestad Scene of an epic 11th-century battle that forever changed Viking history (p257)

Kaupang Archaeological ruins with the traces of a 9th-century Viking town (p90)

Karmøy island A Viking festival and fine Viking-themed museums (p187)

Balestrand Intriguing Viking archaeology site in fjord country (p207)

Tønsberg Norway's oldest town, with Viking-era grave mounds (p87)

Eidfjord Easily accessible Viking grave mounds on a small plateau above the fjord (p178)

Lindesnes Viking canal, historical centre and rock paintings in the deep south (see the boxed text, p104)

month by month

Top Events

1. **Moldejazz**, July
2. **Bergen International Festival**, May
3. **Northern lights**, January or February
4. **Extreme Sports Festival**, June
5. **Sami Easter week**, March

January

Despite bitterly cold temperatures, January is a popular time for snowmobiling, dog-sledding and the northern lights in the magical half-light of the polar night. By the end of January, the sun has returned to mainland Norway.

Northern Lights

The aurora borealis, one of the natural world's most astonishing phenomena, is reason enough to visit northern Norway in winter. Combining the experience with more earthbound festivities, visit Tromsø in late January for the Northern Lights Festival (p319).

Midwinter Jazz

Deep in the months-long Arctic night and quite possibly the world's northernmost jazz festival, Svalbard's Polar Jazz festival (p358) serves as a rhythmic reminder that life continues even in the depths of the polar winter. Usually held in late January or early February.

February

Generally Norway's coldest month, February is ideal for viewing the northern lights, winter activities and joining two celebrations that capture the spirit of the Norwegian winter. Booking ahead is recommended, especially in northern Norway.

The Sami Winter

No-one endures the Arctic winter quite like the Sami, the indigenous inhabitants of Norway's north, and, during Sami Week (p319) in early February, they transform Tromsø's main street into the scene for the national reindeer sledge championship.

Rørosmartnan

Norway's largest winter festival in Røros (p134) dates back centuries and runs from Tuesday to Saturday in the second-last week of February. It's the perfect tonic for the long Norwegian winter with cultural programs, markets and live entertainment.

March

Days are lengthening as Norway awakes from its reluctant slumber with a full program of festivals (either celebrating winter's end or traditional Norwegian activities). It's one of the most popular months for visiting Svalbard.

Sami Easter Week

Easter among the indigenous Sami people in Kautokeino (p349) sees celebrations to mark the end of the polar night, with weddings, reindeer racing, the Sami Grand Prix (actually a *yoik* – a rhythmic-poem contest) and other traditional events.

Vinterfestuka

Throughout its long winter, Narvik looks forward to this week-long festival (p279) of cultural events with music, local food and people scanning the horizon for the sun. In addition to the sun-welcoming component, the festival honours the hardy souls who built the northern railway.

⭐ Here Comes the Sun

The inhabitants of Longyearbyen in the high-Arctic archipelago of Svalbard must withstand the winter darkness longer than any other Norwegians. It should come as no surprise, therefore, that their week-long Sunfest (p358), in early March, is celebrated with special fervour.

⭐ Winter's-End Dog-Sledding

Alta's Borealis Alta winter festival (p326) in March has concerts and other cultural events aimed at saying good riddance to winter. The festival also marks the beginning of Europe's longest dog-sled endurance race, the epic Finnmarksløpet.

April

April has surprisingly few festivals of note and represents something of a breathing space before the end-of-winter celebrations and action-packed Norwegian summers. The weather is improving and few tourists are around.

🍷 Food & Wine in Stavanger

Stavanger is a port city *par excellence* and its culinary culture is one of Norway's most varied. In mid-April, the local love of food and wine takes on special significance with the Stavanger Vinfest (p191).

May

By May, Norway has a real spring in its step: the weather's warming up, Norway's renowned music festivals get under way and tourists have yet to arrive in great numbers.

⭐ Constitution Day

On 17 May the country becomes engulfed in a wave of patriotism during Norway's most popular nationwide festival. It's celebrated with special fervour in Oslo (p63), where locals descend on the Royal Palace dressed in the finery of their native districts.

☆ Night Jazz Festival (Nattjazz)

Norway's calendar is replete with world-renowned jazz festivals and this fine Bergen festival (p164) in late May is one of the happiest, with serious jazz to be heard as the city's large student population gets into the swing.

⭐ Bergen International Festival

One of the biggest events on Norway's cultural calendar, this two-week Bergen festival (p164), beginning in late May, showcases dance, music and folklore presentations. In a typically Bergen twist, it's at once international and a return to the city's roots.

☆ Northern Blues & Soul

Close to the end of May or in early June, Alta's blues and soul festival (p326) is a worthy prelude to the summer-long program of music festivals. Held in the far north, it draws a respected international cast of bands.

June

The main tourist season begins in earnest and it's always worth booking ahead for accommodation. Some of Norway's best festivals take place and the weather can be mild and clear, although poor weather is possible.

⭐ Viking Festival

Often considered to be Norway's Viking heartland, Norway's southwest resonates with sites attached to an altogether more epic past. In early or mid-June, Karmøy island (p187) provides a focal point for this fascinating history, and stages Viking feasts, processions and saga evenings.

⭐ Middle Ages Festival

Locals in period costume and Gregorian chants in the glass cathedral of Hamar are the highlights of this popular local festival (p130). Held in June, it provides an alternative slant on the long-distant Norwegian past in a fantastic setting.

👁 Midnight Sun Marathon

A midnight marathon could only happen in Norway, and Tromsø is the place to try the world's northernmost 42km road race (p319). It's held in June and is possibly the only marathon in the world where the participants are still straggling in at 5am.

Extreme Sports Festival

Adventure junkies from across the world converge on Voss (p174) in late June for a week of skydiving, paragliding, parasailing and base jumping; local and international music acts keep the energy flowing.

July

July is the peak tourist season throughout most of Norway with the year's best weather and cheapest prices for hotels. Tourist sights can be crowded and we strongly recommend advance reservations for accommodation.

Kongsberg Jazz Festival

Kongsberg's Jazz Festival (p109), Norway's second largest, begins in early July, lasts four days and pulls in some of the biggest international names. As it precedes the Moldejazz festival, this is a great season for jazz-lovers.

Mountain Festival

In early July, Åndalsnes hosts what could be northern Europe's largest gathering of mountaineers and rock-climbers, swapping stories and inching their way up the sheer cliffs. The Norsk Fjellfestival (p224) has a full program of folk events to liven up the evenings.

All Things Aquatic

In the second week of July, Fredrikstad takes to the water with its Glomma Festival (p79), with bathtub regattas for seafaring wannabes and veteran sailing ship exhibitions. There are also ritual duels and concerts.

Moldejazz

Norway has a fine portfolio of jazz festivals, but Molde's version (see the boxed text, p237) in mid-July is the most prestigious. With 100,000 spectators, world-class performers and a reputation for consistently high-quality music, it's easily one of Norway's most popular festivals.

St Olav Festival

This nationwide commemoration of Norway's favourite saint in late July is celebrated with special gusto in Trondheim (p252), with processions, medieval markets, Viking dress-ups, concerts and a local food festival. In Stiklestad (p258) the saint is celebrated in a prestigious five-day pageant.

August

August is the scene of musical festivals across all genres. The weather should still be fine and cheaper high-season prices continue, although in some cases only until the middle of the month. Book ahead.

Rauma Rock

If Norway's regular diet of jazz and blues festivals doesn't suit your musical tastes, Central Norway's largest musical gathering is held in Åndalsnes (p224) over two days in early August, with everything from indie to hard rock.

Notodden Blues Festival

This outstanding blues festival in early August offers proof that even smaller Norwegian towns play their part in the country's festival obsession. You'll find it in nondescript Notodden (p110); it draws a massive international crowd.

International Chamber Music Festival

Most Norwegian music festivals cater more to a young and energetic audience, but Stavanger in early August provides an antidote with this stately festival (p191); some concerts take place in the architecturally distinguished Stavanger Cathedral.

Nordland Music Festival

The combining of diverse musical genres appears to be the only unifying theme when Bodø (p288) celebrates 10 days of music from symphony orchestras to jazz trios, folk groups and rock bands. It's held from early to mid-August.

Oslo International Jazz Festival

A worthy member of Norway's coterie of terrific jazz festivals, this one takes over Oslo (p63) for six days of live music in August. It's so popular that many locals plan their summer holidays to be back in town for this event.

☆ Voss Blues & Roots Festival

If you're around the western fjords in late August, head for Voss (p174) and one of Norway's better music festivals. It serves as something of a last farewell to summer, adding an especially festive feeling to proceedings.

★★ Norwegian Film

The highlight of the year for Norway's small but respected film industry, the Norwegian International Film Festival (p186) in Haugesund showcases innovative new works and coincides with the national film awards. It's held in mid- to late August.

September

The crowds have largely disappeared, but so have most of the cheaper summer deals; in some areas, many hotels and restaurants actually close down. In short, a quieter but often more expensive time to visit.

★★ Dyrsku'n Festival

Seljord's premier annual festival (p117) centres on Norway's largest traditional market and cattle show and is one of the best ways to get a feel for traditional Norwegian culture. Held in the second week of September, it attracts 60,000 visitors annually.

October

Summer is a distant memory and by the end of the month the months-long polar night begins in Svalbard. Temperatures have begun to drop and business travellers far outnumber those travelling for pleasure.

☆ Lillehammer Jazz Festival

This former Olympic city farewells the now-distant summer with the last major jazz festival (p125) of the Norwegian year; like any ski town, Lillehammer rocks (so to speak) during festival time, which is sometimes late September but more often October.

★★ Bergen International Film Festival

Arguably Norway's most important film festival (p164), Bergen becomes a film-lover's paradise with subtitled movies in cinemas across the city in mid- to late October. Unlike Haugesund's August film festival, the focus is resolutely international.

★★ UKA

Norway's largest cultural festival (p252) means three weeks of concerts, plays and general celebration led by Trondheim's 25,000-strong university student population. It takes place in odd-numbered years, beginning in October and not stopping until well into November.

☆ Svalbard Blues

Svalbard doesn't bother with festivals in summer: the endless sunlight is reason enough to be happy. In late October, with the long polar night just around the corner, Longyearbyen hosts a well-regarded blues festival (p358), with scheduled concerts and improvised jam sessions.

itineraries

Whether you've got six days or 60, these itineraries provide a starting point for the trip of a lifetime. Want more inspiration? Head online to lonelyplanet. com/thorntree to chat with other travellers.

10 Days
Norway in Microcosm

❯ After a couple of days exploring the many galleries and museums of **Oslo**, take the scenic Oslo–Bergen railway, one of the most spectacular rail journeys on earth. From Oslo, the line climbs gently through forests, plateaus and ski centres to the beautifully desolate **Hardangervidda Plateau**, home to Norway's largest herd of wild reindeer and numerous hiking trails. At Myrdal, take the Flåmsbana railway down to **Flåm**, from where fjord cruises head up the incomparable **Nærøyfjord**. Travel via Gudvangen, sleep overnight in **Stalheim**, and then continue on to **Voss**, where thrill-seekers love the easily accessible activities on offer.

Voss serves as a gateway to the splendid scenery of **Hardangerfjord**, where **Ulvik** and **Eidfjord** stand out among Norway's most worthwhile fjord-side towns. Away to the south, **Stavanger** is one of Norway's most appealing cities and a base for trips to **Lysefjord**, including the walk up to the dramatic Preikestolen (Pulpit Rock).

A boat journey along the coast takes you to beautiful **Bergen**, with its stunning timbered houses and cosmopolitan air.

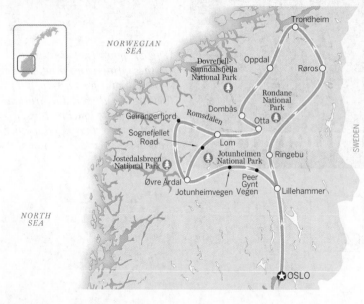

Two Weeks
The Heart of Norway

❯ The dramatic high country of central Norway is simply spectacular and, provided you're willing to rent a car for part of the time, it offers some unparalleled opportunities to explore the region's quiet back roads; serious cyclists could also follow many of the same routes for a slower, but spectacular, journey.

A short train or bus ride from **Oslo**, **Lillehammer** hosted the 1994 Winter Olympics and it remains one of central Norway's most pleasing spots, with a wealth of Olympic sites and a lovely setting. Continuing north, **Ringebu** has one of Norway's prettiest stave churches, but having a car enables you to take the quiet Rv27, which draws near to the precipitous massifs of the **Rondane National Park**, before continuing northeast to Unesco World Heritage-listed **Røros**, one of Norway's most enchanting villages, with painted timber houses and old-world charm. From Røros, it's an easy detour north to **Trondheim**, a delightful coastal city with a stunning cathedral, large student population and engaging cultural scene.

Turning to the south, head past **Oppdal** and **Dombås**, gateways to the **Dovrefjell-Sunndalsfjella National Park**, which is a base for musk-ox safaris in summer. From Dombås, consider a side-trip by train or down the E136, which leads through the heart of **Romsdalen** with its sheer rock walls. Returning to the main road south, head to **Otta**, where the E15 branches west to **Lom**, a lovely wooden town with a gorgeous stave church at the confluence of two steep valleys. The E15 continues deep into the fjord country to **Geirangerfjord**, perhaps the king of all Norwegian fjords. Twist down through the network of fjords to Stryn, Olden and Fjærland, gateway towns to the dramatic glacial scenery of the **Jostedalsbreen National Park**.

Travel southeast to Sogndal, then northeast along the shores of pretty Lustrafjord and up onto the **Sognefjellet Road**, which leads through the extraordinarily beautiful **Jotunheimen National Park** with its wonderful hiking trails, soaring peaks and countless glaciers. One of the most scenic roads in northern Europe, Sognefjellet Road warrants driving its length, even as far as Lom, and then returning as far as Turtagrø. From there, head up a scenic road to **Øvre Årdal**, then twist your way across to the **Jotunheimvegen** scenic road, and then to another, the wonderfully quiet **Peer Gynt Vegen**, and back down to Lillehammer.

Two Weeks
The Norwegian Coast

❯ The coastline between Trondheim and the Lofoten Islands is magnificent, taking you across the Arctic Circle and following a shoreline fissured with deep inlets, shadowed by countless offshore islands and populated by quiet fishing villages that are the lifeblood of coastal Norway. You'll need a car to make the most of this route, although travelling aboard the Hurtigruten coastal ferry, even for just a leg or two, is another fine way to travel in a much shorter time frame.

Begin in **Trondheim** and linger for a couple of days in one of Norway's most agreeable cities. Heading north, via **Hell**, stop off in **Stiklestad**, a site of great historical significance for Norwegians. Then it's on to **Rørvik** on the coast, where a fascinating multimedia display is the perfect introduction to coastal life.

The Rv17 travels north to picturesque **Brønnøysund**, and don't miss the offshore detour to the fascinating, Unesco World Heritage–listed island of **Vega**. Back on the mainland, the extraordinary **Kystriksveien coastal route** hugs the coastline. Another candidate for Norway's most spectacular drive, this road passes an estimated 14,000 islands. It can be slow going with all the ferries and inlet-hugging stretches of road, but it is unquestionably worth it. The entire route could be done in a couple of days, but four or five is far more enjoyable. Factor in time as well for a detour to the **Saltfjellet-Svartisen National Park**, home to Norway's second-largest icefield and accessible glacier tongues. The most beautiful section of the Kystriksveien route is between Stokkvågen and Storvik, and it's along this section that you'll cross the **Arctic Circle**.

Bodø has much to recommend it, but its primary appeal is as the gateway (by ferry) to the **Lofoten Islands**. Unlike any other landscape in Norway, the Lofoten could easily occupy a week of your time, although it can be experienced much more rapidly for those in a hurry. All the islands and villages are worth visiting, but on no account miss **Å**, a charmingly preserved village at the southern tip of Moskenesøy. Like Lofoten but with far fewer visitors, **Vesterålen** is wild and beautiful and worth a day or two, including summer whale-watching off **Stø**, before you head on to journey's end at **Narvik**.

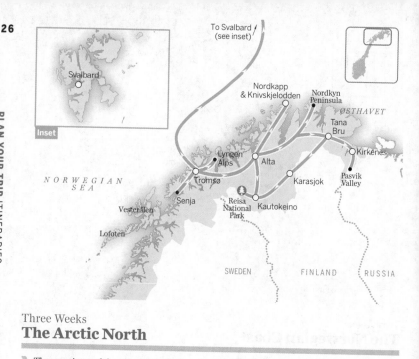

Three Weeks
The Arctic North

> The mystique of the extreme north has drawn explorers for centuries. Here is a horizon-less world seemingly without end, a frozen wilderness that inspires the awe reserved for the great empty places of our earth.

Tromsø, arguably Norway's liveliest medium-sized town, is a university town par excellence. Its Polar Museum captures the spirit of Arctic exploration; its Arctic Cathedral wonderfully evokes the landscapes of the north while the surrounding peaks host a wealth of summer and winter activities. Tromsø is also an ideal base for excursions inland to the **Lyngen Alps**, which are rugged and supremely beautiful with many glaciers and craggy summits. You could also visit **Senja** for a day, but it's far better to stay overnight to truly embrace the quiet of northern Norwegian nights.

Heading east, the rock carvings of **Alta** should also not be missed, and the same can be said for **Nordkapp**, although for different reasons: as far north as you can go in Norway without setting out to sea, Nordkapp is high on novelty value, if somewhat overwhelmed by visitors. Forsake the crowds and instead hike out to neighbouring **Knivskjelodden**, Norway's true north. Further east, the **Nordkyn Peninsula** has much to explore and nearby **Tana Bru** is one of the best places in the world to go salmon fishing. **Kirkenes** and the neighbouring **Pasvik Valley**, close to the Russian border, have loads of summer and winter activities, including the unusual king crab safaris.

Next, head to Inner Finnmark, the heartland of the Sami people. **Karasjok** is the undisputed capital of Sami Norway, filled with fascinating sites of Sami patrimony and opportunities for winter dog-sledding and cross-country skiing, and summer hiking. Further west, **Kautokeino** is another long-standing centre of Sami culture, and its museum is an ideal place to provide cultural context to your visit. Hiking in the **Reisa National Park** is a possibility, but only for the seriously fit.

And no exploration of the Arctic North would be complete without **Svalbard**. Return to Tromsø and catch a flight deep into polar regions where the Svalbard archipelago is one of Europe's last great wildernesses. This old whaling centre supports a rich array of Arctic wildlife, including reindeer and polar bears, not to mention epic glaciers, icebergs and icefields.

Outdoor Activities

Best Cycle Route

Rallarvegen
Location: Finse to Flåm
Season: mid-Jun–mid-Aug

Best Extreme Sport

Para-bungee jumping
Location: Voss
Season: May-Sep

Best Salmon Fishing

Tana Bru
Location: Eastern Finnmark
Season: mid-Jun–mid-Aug

Best Glacier Hike

Hardangerjøkulen
Location: Hardangervidda Plateau
Season: mid-Jun–mid-Aug

Best Hike

Besseggen
Location: Jotunheimen National Park
Season: mid-Jun–mid-Aug

Best Dog-Sledding

Engholm's Husky
Location: Karasjok
Season: Dec-Mar

Best Winter Skiing

Olympic ski slopes
Location: Lillehammer
Season: Dec-Mar

Planning Your Trip

When to Go

Norway has two major – and radically different – seasons for activities. Outside these periods, you'll probably find that the operators have simply shut up shop and, in many cases, followed their passion elsewhere in the world wherever the weather suits.

The summer season – when signature activities include hiking, kayaking, white-water rafting and the high-thrill pursuits that usually have 'para' attached as a prefix (namely parasailing etc) – most reliably runs from mid-June until mid-August. That's when there are enough travellers around to ensure regular departures and hence a wider range of options that suit your schedule. Depending on the weather, many operators, however, open in May and remain open until the middle or end of September.

Winter – when skiing, snowmobiling and dog-sledding take over – usually runs from December (or late November) until late February or early March.

What to Take

There are few requirements for most summer activities and operators who organise white-water rafting, kayaking, parasailing and other similar 'sports' will provide the necessary equipment.

The major exception is hiking. Most hikers head out onto the trail under their own steam, but even those who plan on joining

PERSONAL HIKING-EQUIPMENT CHECKLIST

Summer

☐ Sturdy hiking boots; if you're heading to Svalbard, knee-high rubber hiking boots are recommended

☐ A high-quality sleeping bag – even in summer, the weather can turn nasty at short notice

☐ Warm clothing, including a jacket, jersey (sweater) or anorak (windbreaker) that can be added or removed, even in summer

☐ A bed sheet – most huts charge extra for bedlinen

☐ A sturdy but lightweight tent

☐ Mosquito repellent

☐ A lightweight stove

☐ Airline-style sleeping mask for light-filled Norwegian summer nights

☐ Membership of Den

Norske Turistforening (DNT; see p30)

☐ Good topographical maps (see p430)

Winter

☐ Warm boots (ideally with a thick insulation of wool) big enough to wear double socks and to move your toes inside

☐ At least one long underwear top and bottom (not cotton, but preferably underwear made of polypropylene)

☐ Multiple pairs of light synthetic (polypropylene) socks and heavy wool socks (again, not cotton)

☐ Flannel or polypropylene shirts

☐ Trousers for walking, preferably made from breathing waterproof (and windproof) material such as Gore-Tex

☐ Fleece sweater

☐ Windproof and waterproof jacket with hood and big enough to let you wear a lot of clothes underneath

☐ One knitted, fur or fleece hat (such as a balaclava) to protect your face and another windproof one to cover your head and ears

☐ Long woollen scarf

☐ Woollen mittens and windproof and waterproof mittens

☐ Air-filled sleeping pad

☐ Arctic-strength sleeping bag filled with synthetics or down; only necessary if you're likely to be sleeping out overnight

☐ Swiss Army knife

☐ Torch (flashlight) with extra batteries or headlamp

---

an organised hike will usually need to bring their own equipment.

In winter, you won't need much in the way of equipment for most of the activities – skis etc can be rented at ski stations and there are no special requirements for snowmobiling or dog-sledding – but see the checklist for what you will need to bring.

Activities

Visiting Norway is inspirational in a way that few destinations in the world can match. The fresh air of the Norwegian wilderness lends itself perfectly to a range of activities-based exploration; Norway is one of the world's premier wilderness destinations and it has a world-class adventure industry to match. Just about anything's possible and each of the following activities is covered in the relevant regional chapters. This chapter contains an overview to whet your appetite and get you planning.

For more on wildlife-watching opportunities, see p390, while safaris to track down the legendary king crab are on p341. Norway's extensive network of national parks is covered on p395.

Summer

Summer is undoubtedly the most popular time for visiting Norway and, if you do, there are numerous opportunities to wed an appreciation of Norway's wild beauty to a true sense of adventure.

Cycling

Whether you're keen for a two-wheeled amble around the flat shoreline of your favourite fjord or a serious cyclist with your sights set on the ultimate Norwegian challenge, Norway won't disappoint. For the practicalities of cycling and bicycle hire in Norway, turn to p439.

For the ambler, many tourist offices, some hotels and most bicycle shops rent out bicycles for casual cyclists, while Trondheim has taken this to a whole new level with free bicycles; for details see the boxed text, p256. Oslo (p60) is another city with excellent cycling options.

Cycling Resources

For the serious cyclist, there are some extraordinary routes that the world cycling community raves about. See the Top Five boxed text for some of our favourites or the following list of useful resources:

Bike Norway (www.bike-norway.com) An excellent website with descriptions of some of the better long-distance cycling routes. It also sells online nine different cycling maps, some with route descriptions, for Nkr120 to Nkr260, although not all are available in English; click on 'Brochure' on its home page.

Syklistenes Landsforening (☎22 47 30 33; www.slf.no, in Norwegian; 3rd fl, Storgata 3, Oslo) The main contact point for Norway's cycling clubs and useful for information on long-distance cycling routes and tunnels. It also sells *Sykkelruter i Norge* (Nkr120); it's only available in Norwegian, but the English-text *Sykkelguide* series of booklets with maps are available for Nkr125 each and include Lofoten, Rallarvegen, the North Sea Cycleway from the Swedish border at Svinesund to Bergen, and other routes.

Tourist offices Most tourist offices offer advice (and sometimes maps) on cycling trails in their local area.

For National Tourist Routes, see the boxed text on p445.

Extreme Sports

Norway is gaining traction as a favoured destination for thrillseekers thanks to its combination of highly professional operators and spectacular settings. Those who either have

TOP FIVE CYCLING EXPERIENCES

» Sognefjellet Rd, through the **Jotunheimen National Park** (p147)

» The exhilarating descent from Finse down to the shores of Aurlandsfjorden Flåm along the **Rallarvegen** (see the boxed text, p152)

» **Lofoten** (p291) with its leisurely cycling through some wonderful, rugged scenery

» Across the **Hardangervidda Plateau** near Rjukan (see the boxed text, p115)

» The steep and spectacular **SnøVegen** route above the fjords (see the boxed text, p204)

no fear or would simply love a bird's-eye view of some of Europe's most spectacular country have numerous possibilities, although they're almost exclusively centred on the the fjord region in the western part of the country.

Voss in particular is arguably Norway's adventure capital and one of the world epicentres for extreme sports. Devotees of high-speed airborne pursuits converge on this lovely town in late June for the **Extreme Sports Festival** (www.ekstremsportveko.com).

Some of the best places to get the adrenaline flowing:

» **Voss** (see the boxed text, p173) Paragliding, parasailing, a 180m-high bungee jump from a parasail (which claims to be Europe's highest bungee-jump) and skydiving.

» **Rjukan** (p114) Norway's highest land-based bungee jump (84m), located in the southern Norwegian interior.

» **Kjeragbolten, Lysefjord** (p197) Base jumping from the sheer cliffs of Lysefjord close to the famous chock-stone of Kjeragbolten.

Fishing

Norway's rivers and lakes have drawn avid anglers since the 19th century and salmon-fishing is the undoubted star attraction. Norway's salmon runs are still legendary and, in June and July, you can't beat the rivers of Finnmark. In addition to salmon, 41 other fish species inhabit the country's 200,000 rivers and lakes. In the south, you'll find the best fishing from June to September, and in the north, in July and August. In Svalbard, the best fishing holes are well-kept secrets, but Arctic char inhabit some rivers and lakes. The 175-page book *Angling in Norway*, available from tourist offices for Nkr185, details the best salmon- and trout-fishing areas, fees and regulations, of which there are many.

Regulations vary between rivers but, generally, from mid-September to November, fish under 20cm must be thrown back. At other times between August and May, the limit is 30cm. Fishing is also prohibited within 100m of fish farms, or cables and nets that are anchored or fastened to the shore, while fishing with live bait is illegal.

Anyone over 16 who wishes to fish in Norway needs to purchase an annual licence (Nkr220 for salmon, trout and char and Nkr110 for other fish), which is sold at post offices. To fish on private land, you must also purchase a local licence (Nkr60 to Nkr400

WEATHER WARNING

Always check weather and other local conditions before setting out cross-country. This applies whenever traversing any exposed area, but is particularly an issue for hikers and cross-country skiers (two Scottish cross-country skiers died after being caught in snow and freezing fog in March 2007 on the Hardangervidda Plateau despite, according to some reports, being warned by local experts not to set out). The only months that favourable conditions can be *almost* guaranteed for hiking are July and August. Even then, you should always be prepared for sudden inclement weather and stay aware of potential avalanche dangers, which are particularly rife in Jotunheimen but are a possibility anywhere in Norway's high country. Also, never venture onto glacial ice without the proper equipment and experience. And trust the advice of locals, who understand the conditions better than even the most experienced out-of-town hikers – if they say not to go, don't go.

per day), which is available from sports shops, hotels, campsites and tourist offices. Some areas require a compulsory equipment disinfection certificate (Nkr110).

Fishing Spots

There's fishing to be found throughout Norway, but the following are some of the best:

» **Tana Bru** (p337) Legendary salmon fishing.

» **Saltstraumen Maelstrom** (p290) Popular fishing where two fjords collide.

» **Moskenesøy** (p300) Deep-sea fishing off the Lofoten islands.

» **Gjesvær** (p334) Expeditions near Nordkapp.

» **Tromsø** (p317) Ice fishing in winter.

Glacier Hiking

There's something about glaciers that inspires wonder, and one of Norway's most memorable summer pastimes is glacier walking. This is, however, an activity that comes with a word of warning: walking atop glaciers is a potentially perilous undertaking and you should only set out on such a venture with an experienced local guide. Among our favourite places for a glacier hike are the following:

» **Hardangerjøkulen glacier on Hardangervidda** (see p151) Said by some to be Norway's most breathtaking glacier hike.

» **Folgefonna National Park** (p183) One of Norway's largest icefields, with glacier hikes at various points around the perimeter.

» **Nigardsbreen** (p214) The pick of the accessible glaciers in the Jostedalsbreen area.

» **Saltfjellet-Svartisen National Park** (p276) Some of Europe's lowest-lying (and hence easily accessible) glacier tongues just inside the Arctic Circle.

» **Svalbard** (p357) With 60% of Svalbard covered by glaciers, there are plenty of opportunities here, including close to Longyearbyen.

Hiking

Norway has some of Europe's best hiking, including a network of around 20,000km of marked trails that range from easy strolls through the green zones around cities, to long treks through national parks and wilderness areas. Many of these trails are maintained by Den Norske Turistforening and are marked either with cairns or red Ts at 100m or 200m intervals.

The hiking season runs roughly from late May to early October, with a much shorter season in the higher mountain areas and the far north. In the highlands, the snow often remains until June and returns in September, meaning that many routes are only possible in July and August.

Hiking Resources

Den Norske Turistforening (DNT; Norwegian Mountain Touring Club; ☏22 82 28 22; www.turist foreningen.no; Storgata 7, Oslo) is the Norwegian hiker's best friend and it's an important resource for anyone heading out on the trail. Its various chapters maintain a network of around 460 staffed and unstaffed mountain huts and lodges throughout the country. For more details, see p425.

If you're going to do lots of hiking, it's certainly worth joining DNT – annual membership for adults/19–26-year-olds/students/seniors costs Nkr530/295/295/410, with reduced rates for school-age children and family members of DNT members. Membership entitles you to seven *Fjell og Vidde* magazines as well as discounted rates at DNT huts; the *DNT Yearbook* costs an extra

Nkr50. DNT also sells hiking maps and topographic sheets (see p430).

There are many excellent hiking books. Erling Welle-Strand's 1993 *Mountain Hiking in Norway* includes itineraries, sketch maps and details on huts. More recent is Constance Roos' *Walking in Norway* (2003) and *Walks and Scrambles in Norway* by Anthony Dyer et al (2006). A good choice for avid hikers is *Norwegian Mountains on Foot* by DNT, which is the English edition of the Norwegian classic *Til Fots i Fjellet*.

Hiking Routes

The list of possibilities for hiking in Norway is almost endless, but if we had to list our top 10, it would be the following:

» **Jotunheimen National Park** (see the boxed text, p148) The doyen of Norwegian hiking destinations, with countless routes and incomparable high country.

» **Rondane National Park** (p142) Less-crowded trails than those of Jotunheimen, but arguably as beautiful.

» **Hardangervidda Plateau** (see the boxed texts, p151 and p115) Trails criss-cross this magnificent plateau, the home of reindeer.

» **Aurlandsdalen** (p204) Historic four-day hike following ancient trading routes from Geiteryggen to Aurland.

» **Trollstigen** (p224) Some wonderful treks through the dramatic Trollstigen range.

» **Dovrefjell-Sunndalsfjella National Park** (p140) Wildlife- and bird-rich park with the Knutshøene massif as a centrepiece.

» **Stabbursdalen National Park** (p336) Roadless park with tracks through glacial canyons and the world's northernmost pine forest.

» **Reisa National Park** (p350) Demanding 50km route through the remote reaches of Inner Finnmark.

» **Saltfjellet-Svartisen National Park** (p276) Icecaps and treeless uplands lend these trails an epic Arctic quality.

» **Trollheimen** (p138) Rolling mountains and high-altitude lakes make for memorable walking.

Kayaking

With all the hype surrounding hiking, white-water rafting and extreme summer sports, Norway's kayaking possibilities rarely receive the attention they deserve. And yet the chance to take to the water is a wonderful way to experience Norway's waterways without doing so in the company of countless other travellers aboard cruise ships and tourist boats.

Kayaking Resources

To find out more about the Norwegian paddling scene, contact **Norges Padleforbund** (📞21 02 98 35; www.padling.no), which has lists of kayaking operators and routes in Norway, although that section of the website is only in Norwegian.

Kayaking Destinations

Norway's premier kayaking sites are clustered around (although by no means restricted to) the western fjords and there are numerous operators offering guided kayaking

ALLEMANNSRETTEN

Anyone considering camping or hiking in Norway should be aware of *allemannsretten* (every man's right, often referred to as 'right of access'). This 1000-year-old law, in conjunction with the modern Friluftsleven (Outdoor Recreation Act), entitles anyone to:

» camp anywhere for up to two days, as long as it's more than 150m from a dwelling (preferably further and out of sight);

» hike or ski across uncultivated wilderness areas, including outlying fields and pastures (except in fields with standing crops and close to people's houses);

» cycle or ride on horseback on all paths and roads; and

» canoe, kayak, row and sail on all rivers and lakes.

However, these freedoms come with responsibilities, among the most important of which are the prohibition against fires between 15 April and 15 September and the requirement that you leave the countryside, any wildlife and cultural sights as pristine as you found them.

excursions. It's also possible in many places to rent kayaks and the accompanying equipment from fjord-side campsites and tourist offices. Other good places for sea kayaking are found along the Nordland coast (including in Lofoten, Vesterålen, Narvik and Mo i rana), Langøya and Svalbard.

Top kayaking destinations include the following:

» **Jostedalen** (p215) Guided kayaking and hiking trips that get up close with a glacier.

» **Svalbard** (p358) Difficult to imagine a more dramatic backdrop for your paddle.

» **Langøya, Vesterålen** (p305) Introductory and more advanced courses around the time of 170km Arctic Sea Kayak Race in July.

» **Voss** (see the boxed text, p173) One- to three-day kayaking trips on gorgeous Nærøyfjord.

» **Flåm** (p199) Takes you away from the crowds on one of Norway's prettiest but busiest fjords.

» **Geiranger** (p227) Coastal kayaking trips from a spectacular Geiranger base.

» **Lustrafjord** (p210) Four-hour kayaking tours on this lovely arm of Sognefjorden.

Rock Climbing & Mountaineering

Norway's astounding vertical topography is a paradise for climbers interested in rock, ice and alpine pursuits. In fact, outside the Alps, Norway is probably Europe's finest climbing venue, although Norway's climatic extremes mean that technical climbers face harsh conditions, short seasons and strict restrictions. The western fjords region in particular is all the rage among serious climbers.

Climbing Resources

For general information on climbing in Norway, contact **Norsk Tindeklub** (☎41 20 80; www.ntk.no, in Norwegian).

In addition to the rock climbers' classic *Climbing in the Magic Islands* by Ed Webster, which describes most of the feasible routes in Lofoten, look for *Ice Fall in Norway* by Sir Ranulph Fiennes, which describes a 1970 sojourn around Jostedalsbreen. The more practical *Scandinavian Mountains* by Peter Lennon introduces the country's finest climbing venues.

Climbing Destinations

The most popular alpine venues in Norway include the following. Ice climbers should head to Rjukan (p114).

» **Trollveggen or Romsdalshorn, Åndalsnes** (p224) Norway's prime climbing routes. Åndalsnes also hosts a very popular mountaineering festival, Norsk Fjellfestivalen, in early July.

» **Lyngen Alps** (p324) Remote climbing and mountaineering but only for the experienced and self-sufficient.

» **Uskedalen** (p185) A well-guarded but much-celebrated secret in the world climbing community, close to Rosendal.

» **Henningsvær, Lofoten** (p297) Site of a good climbing school that organises expeditions on the islands' vertiginous rock walls.

Skiing

Although primarily a winter activity, skiing is possible year-round in Norway if you know where to look. Numerous cross-country trails remain snow-bound throughout the year, while there are a number of summer ski centres that allow both cross-country (Nordic) and downhill skiing. These include the following:

» **Stryn Summer Ski Centre** (see the boxed text, p219) Norway's largest 'sommar skisenter' with good cross-country and downhill trails.

» **Folgefonn Sommar Skisenter** (p183) A well-regarded centre high on the icefields of the southwestern fjord region.

» **Galdhøpiggen Summer Ski Centre** (p149) At 1850m above sea level but still in the shadow of Norway's highest peak, this is one of the prettiest places to ski at any time although it's inaccessible in the depths of winter.

White-Water Rafting

The cascading, icy-black waters and white-hot rapids of central Norway are a rafter's paradise during the short season from mid-June to mid-August. A number of reputable operators offer trips, primarily in central Norway. These range from short, Class II doddles to Class III and IV adventures and rollicking Class V punishment. Most are guaranteed to provide a thrill, and the rates include all requisite equipment and waterproofing.

Norges Padleforbund (☎21 02 98 35; www.padling.no) provides a comprehensive list of rafting operators in Norway.

The best places to go rafting include the following:

» **Heidalen, Sjoa** (p143)

» **Setesdalen, Evje** (see the boxed text, p118)

» **Drivadalen, Oppdal** (see the boxed text, p138)

» **Voss** (see the boxed text, p173)

» **Jostedalen** (p215)

Winter

Unlike in other countries where snowfalls create chaos and bring life to a halt, Norway remains very much alive and active throughout the long winter months. Skiing is the most popular winter activity (both as a leisure pursuit and a means of getting around), while snowmobiling serves a similar purpose in the far north and on the subpolar archipelago of Svalbard. Dog-sledding is another major drawcard.

Dog-Sledding

Norway's Sami have not traditionally used dog-sledding as a means of getting around, but indigenous peoples in Greenland and Siberia have done so for centuries and it readily transfers to the Norwegian wilds. This is easily our favourite winter activity because it enables you to experience Arctic and sub-Arctic wilderness areas by slowing you down to a pace that suits the quiet beauty of the terrain free from engine noise, quite apart from being one of Norway's most environmentally sound means of getting around.

Expeditions can range from half-day tasters to multiday trips with overnight stays in remote forest huts. With most operators, you'll have the option (depending on the number of travellers in your group) of *mushing* your own sled (after a brief primer course before setting out) or sitting atop the sled and watching the world pass by as someone else urges the dogs onwards.

In addition to the possible expeditions listed here, there are long-distance endurance dog-sled races where you can see how the professionals do it. They are the **Femundlopet** (www.femundlopet.no), which starts and ends in Røros in early February, and the 1000km-long **Finnmarkslopet** (www.finnmarkslopet.no), which starts and ends in Alta in March and traverses the length of the far north in between.

Dog-Sledding Destinations

Although most of the dog-sledding possibilities are to be found in Norway's high Arctic, Røros, in central Norway, is another option.

» **Karasjok** (p347) Wonderful short and long expeditions run by Sven Engholm (who has won the Finnmarkslopet a record 11 times) and his team.

» **Svalbard** (p358) The most spectacular landscapes bar none that can be reached by husky.

» **Alta** (p329) Three-hour excursions to five-day expeditions not far from Alta.

» **Røros** (p134) From a few hours to a few days in one of Norway's coldest corners.

» **Tromsø** (p317) Up to four-day treks from Kvaløya island, south of town, with reindeer-sledding also possible.

» **Kirkenes** (p341) Mostly short-haul excursions but longer options are possible.

Skiing

'Ski' is a Norwegian word and thanks to aeons-old rock carvings depicting hunters travelling on skis, Norwegians make a credible claim to having invented the sport. Interest hasn't waned over the years and these days it's the national pastime.

Cross-Country Skiing

Most skiing is of the cross-country (Nordic) variety, and Norway has thousands of kilometres of maintained cross-country ski trails. However, visitors should only set off after closely studying the trails/routes (wilderness trails are identified by colour codes on maps and signposts) and ensuring that they have appropriate clothing, sufficient food and water, and emergency supplies, such as matches and a source of warmth. You can either bring your own equipment or rent on site.

Most towns and villages provide some illuminated ski trails, but elsewhere it's still worth carrying a good torch, as winter days are very short and in the north there's no daylight at all in December and January. The ski season generally lasts from early December to April. Snow conditions vary greatly from year to year and region to region, but February and March, as well as the Easter holiday period, tend to be the best (and busiest) times.

Downhill Skiing

Norway has dozens of downhill winter ski centres, although it can be an expensive pastime due to the costs of ski lifts, accommodation and the après-ski drinking sessions. The spring season lasts longer than in the Alps and the snow is better quality, too.

Skiing Resources

For general information on skiing in Norway, contact DNT (p30) or visit the excellent website **Norske Spor** (Skiing in Norway;

THE TELEMARK MANOEUVRE

The Telemark region of Norway has lent its name to the graceful turn that has made Nordic (cross-country) skiing popular around the world. Nordic ski bindings attach the boot at the toes, allowing free movement of the heel; to turn, one knee is dropped to the surface of the ski while the other leg is kept straight. The skis are positioned one behind the other, allowing the skier to smoothly glide around the turn in the direction of the dropped knee.

www.skiingnorway.com). The **Norwegian Tourist Board** (www.visitnorway.com) also publishes the useful annual *Skiing in Norway* brochure.

Skiing Destinations

Norway's better and more popular skiing locations include the following:

» **Lillehammer** (p129) The chance to ski the downhill slopes used in the 1994 Winter Olympics.

» **Trysil** (p131) The largest network of trails in the country, with something to suit every standard and style.

» **Holmenkollen, Oslo** (p61) Has 2400km of cross-country trails, many of them floodlit.

» **Geilo** (p151) The Oslo–Bergen railway line leaves you within sight of the ski lifts.

» **Voss** (see the boxed text, p173) Good trails in the Stølsheimen Mountains high above Voss.

» **Hovden** (p120) A popular winter resort in the southern Norwegian interior.

» **Karasjok** (p347) Cross-country skiing in the far north.

Snowmobiling

While snowmobiling may have its critics as a less-than-environmentally-sound means of getting around, life for many in the high Arctic would simply not be possible in winter without the snowmobile. For the traveller, snowmobiling also enables you to get much further than is possible with dog-sleds and into areas that would not otherwise be possible.

Most operators allow you to ride as a passenger behind an experienced driver or (usually for an additional charge) as the driver yourself; for the latter, a valid driving licence may be required. Some places also offer night tours, often on the pretext of getting away from the city lights in order to see the aurora borealis.

Snowmobiling Destinations

Snowmobiling is generally restricted to the far north and Svalbard. Possibilities include the following:

» **Svalbard** (p358) Norway's premier snowmobiling location, with trails taking you deep into the main Spitsbergen island of this extraordinary place; in keeping with Svalbard's status as a protected wilderness area, there are some restrictions on where you can go.

» **Kirkenes** (p341) Day and night trips into the beautiful Pasvik Valley wedged between Finland and Russia.

» **Alta** (p329) One of the largest snowmobile operators in mainland Norway.

» **Tromsø** (p317) Some good trails close to Norway's northern capital.

Snowshoeing

Like most winter activities, strapping on a pair of snowshoes is a time-honoured way of getting around in snowbound regions and one that has morphed into a popular winter activity. That said, in our experience snowshoeing is something of a novelty to try for short distances rather than longer excursions – it can be exhausting and it takes a long time to get anywhere.

Throughout the Arctic North, hotels and operators who organise other winter activities rent out snowshoes and some also organise expeditions in **Narvik**, **Lofoten** and **Tromsø** (p317).

Tour Operators

Norwegian Tour Operators

Norwegian tour operators offering activities and adventure expeditions are covered throughout this guidebook – the page numbers listed in the preceding pages of this chapter will take you to many of these operators. Although it is sometimes possible to simply turn up and join a tour, we always recommend that you make contact in advance, especially during the peak summer and winter seasons, to make sure that you don't turn up and find that all available places have been taken or that the departures don't fit within your travelling schedule.

International Tour Operators

Many companies outside the country offer adventure- or activities-based tours to Norway. In most cases, tours are all-inclusive: the cost of your tour includes all accommodation, airfares, the cost of the activities and in *some* cases equipment. In short, what you lose in flexibility you gain in convenience. As always, shop around with local operators to check whether you'll also be saving any money – as a general rule, you're unlikely to save much, if anything.

The following list of reputable international operators offering adventure-based travel is not exhaustive but instead represents a starting point for seeing what is available.

Arcturus Expeditions (www.arcturusexpeditions.co.uk) UK operator specialising in Arctic boat cruises but with at least one dog-sledding option.

Borton Overseas (www.bortonoverseas. com) US company specialising in adventure travel with dozens of Norwegian tours, including hiking, cycling, cross-country skiing and a full range of winter options.

Exodus (www.exodus.co.uk) Cross-country skiing and trips to Svalbard.

Go Fishing Worldwide (www.gofishing worldwide.co.uk) Salmon fishing on a range of Norwegian rivers.

High & Wild (www.highandwild.co.uk) Allows you to join the April reindeer-herding migration of the Sami by snowmobile.

Norway Direct (www.norwaydirect.com) Dog-sledding, snowmobiling, rock-climbing, white-water rafting and more.

Responsible Travel (www.responsibletravel. com) Not an operator as such but a handy collection of sustainable tours in Norway, including many with an activities focus.

Tangent Expeditions International (www. tangent-expeditions.co.uk) Greenland specialist with well-organised ski and mountaineering trips to Svalbard.

Wilderness Journeys (www.wilderness journeys.com) Sea-kayaking around the World Heritage–listed Vega archipelago.

Travel with Children

Best Regions for Kids

Oslo
Green parklands in abundance and a large array of museums, many with an interactive component, make this one of Europe's more child-friendly cities.

Central Norway
Lillehammer's (sometimes-interactive) Winter Olympic sites may appeal, as will activities around Røros and safaris that set off in search of elk (moose) and musk ox.

Bergen & the Southwestern Fjords
Bergen and Stavanger have numerous child-oriented attractions, while elsewhere there are boat trips on the fjords, interactive museums, water-based activities and the occasional Viking landmark.

Nordland
Whale-watching is the main draw here with ample opportunities on Lofoten, Vesterålen and nearby.

The Far North
Primarily winter activities such as dog-sledding thrill travellers of any age, while the northern lights are something the kids will never forget.

Norway is a terrific destination in which to travel as a family. This is a country that has become world famous for creating family-friendly living conditions and most hotels, restaurants and many sights are accordingly child-friendly. It's worth remembering, however, that the old parental adage of not trying to be too ambitious in how far you travel is especially relevant in Norway – distances are vast and, such is the terrain, journey times can be significantly longer than for equivalent distances elsewhere.

Norway for Kids

Domestic tourism is often organised around the assumption that many Norwegians will be travelling as a family, with everything from hotels to museums more than willing to not only accommodate children but make sure they have a good time.

Museums

Some of Norway's museums will immediately appeal to children (such as natural history museums), but even where the subject matter is more adult in focus, some museums have interactive exhibits and/or children's play areas with toys and activities. And in summer (especially July), numerous museums with a historical focus organise programs for children, with games, activities, and staff dressed up in period costumes.

On a practical level, most attractions allow free admission for children up to six years of age and half-price (or substantially discounted) admission for those aged up to 16. Family tickets are available at many of Norway's sights.

Theme Parks

Dotted around the country are some terrific theme parks that allow you to pass a day on rides and in themed pavilions; the focus is usually local in character, with trolls and other mythical Norwegian creatures recurring themes. Regional tourist offices usually have brochures for such places. Larger towns and some coastal regions also have excellent aquariums.

Activities & Wildlife-Watching

Adventure tourism is one of Norway's major attractions, and there are a whole range of activities that kids can enjoy, although obviously the older your children, the wider the range of possibilities. For young travellers, wildlife safaris in search of whales, elk and musk ox are a terrific option. Dog-sledding is also possible in Svalbard, the far north and around Røros.

For older children, you may be surprised at what can be accomplished, from short hikes to kayaking and family white-water-rafting trips, and even some of the higher-octane thrills around Voss may be possible for travellers as young as 10 or 12.

Children's Highlights
Museums

» Viking Ship Museum, Oslo – reconstructed Viking ships

» Kon-Tiki Museum, Oslo – guaranteed to inspire the inner explorer

» Zoological Museum, Oslo – stuffed Arctic wildlife

» VilVite, Bergen – terrific interactive science centre with lots of buttons

» Arkeologisk Museum, Stavanger – Viking-themed activities in summer

» Norsk Oljemuseum (Petroleum Museum), Stavanger – one of Norway's most interactive museums

» Children's Museum, Stavanger – wonderful indoor playground for younger kids

» Nordvegen Historiesenter, Karmøy island – part museum, part Viking farm

» Norwegian Glacier Museum, Fjærland – hands-on exhibits of Norway's icefields

» Norsk Luftfartsmuseum, Bodø – ideal for the aeroplane enthusiast

Theme Parks

» Kristiansand Dyrepark – outstanding zoo and funfair in Norway's far south

» Hunderfossen Familiepark – water rides, wandering trolls and fairy-tale palaces

» Atlanterhavsparken (Atlantic Ocean Park) – one of northern Europe's best aquariums

» Bergen Akvariet – fantastic aquarium that you can reach by boat

» Lofotakvariet, Kabelvåg – seals, sea otters and other marine creatures

» Olympic sites, Lillehammer – everything from simulators to bobsled runs

» Senjatrollet, Senja – the world's biggest troll, with accompanying attractions

» Polar Zoo, Setermoen – an excellent animal park with Arctic species

Activities

» White-water rafting – family-friendly trips in Sjoa and elsewhere

» Dog-sledding – possible from Røros in central Norway to Svalbard in winter, with sleds on wheels in summer

» Skiing – year-round skiing at centres used to catering for kids, including Lillehammer, Trysil and, in summer, Stryn

» Kayaking – shorter family-friendly trips in Voss, Svalbard and the fjords

Wildlife-Watching

» Whale-watching – see the giants of the sea off the Nordland coast

» Musk-ox safaris – search for this otherworldly beast in central and southern Norway

» Elk safaris – free-range moose in southern and central Norway

» Reindeer and arctic foxes, Svalbard – often seen within Longyearbyen itself

» Polar bears, Svalbard – just hope you don't see one at close quarters!

Other Highlights

» The myths of Seljord – troll-rich country home to Selma the Serpent

» Midnight sun – endless days have huge novelty appeal

» Northern lights – one of the natural world's most mysterious phenomena

Planning

As you'd expect, children's products such as baby food, infant formulas, soy and cow's milk and disposable nappies (diapers) are widely available in Norway (in supermarkets, pharmacies and more expensive convenience stores), but they're much more expensive than back home. You may want to bring a reasonable supply in order to keep costs down.

When to Go

Easily the best time to travel in Norway with children is the main tourist season that runs from mid-June to mid-August – this is when hotels offer the best deals for families, all sights and attractions are open and the weather is more conducive to a happy family holiday.

If you've come to Norway for the northern lights or activities such as dog-sledding, don't be put off by the bitterly cold weather. It's all about coming prepared with the appropriate clothes (Norwegian families don't hide in their homes for 10 months of the year!) and winter can be a magical time to be here.

Accommodation

Hotels, hostels, campsites and other accommodation options often have 'family rooms' or cabins that accommodate up to two adults and two children. Although many hotels do have larger, dedicated family rooms, other places simply squeeze in cots and/or extra beds when space allows, always for an additional fee. The best hotel deals are to be found in summer, or on weekends throughout the year.

One hotel chain that makes a special effort to cater for families from mid-June to mid-August is **Thon Hotels** (www.thonhotels.no), where family rooms can cost as little as Nkr1090 – stunning value by Norwegian standards. Most Thon Hotels also have a small children's play area and nice touches such as children's check-in steps. Other hotels, particularly larger chains, may offer similar summer deals.

Restaurants

Even in some upmarket restaurants, children will be made to feel welcome and, as a result, Norwegians are often seen eating out as a family group. Many restaurants offer children's menus with smaller portions and prices to match. And most of those that don't are willing to serve a smaller portion if you ask.

The high cost of meals can mean it's a challenge in Norway to ensure that your children eat well, but the general availability of hot dogs, hamburgers and pizzas do provide a fall-back option in case of emergency. Supermarkets are also good if you're stocking up for a family picnic and many have pre-made meals. Most restaurants have baby-change areas and a limited number of high chairs.

Transport

Norway's impressive public transport system is at once a comfortable means of getting from A to B and – given the variety, which spans trains, buses, tourist boats and ferries – may also carry considerable appeal for children.

On trains and buses, children under four generally travel for free (although they won't have a seat), while those aged between four and 15 (16 on the Hurtigruten coastal ferry) pay 50% of the adult fare.

Car-rental firms hire out children's safety seats at a nominal cost, but it's essential that you book them in advance, especially in summer and on weekends when demand is high.

Regions at a Glance

Oslo

Museums & Galleries ✓✓✓
Architecture ✓✓
Activities ✓✓

Norway's Cultural Home

If it happened in Norwegian history, there's probably a museum in Oslo dedicated to the event, from the Vikings to Thor Heyerdahl and beyond. Some of the towering icons of national culture have wall space here as well.

Beautiful Buildings

Oslo's growing architectural reputation was cemented with the opening of the award-winning Opera House in 2008, but there's plenty more to turn the head, from a 14th-century fortress to the distinctive parliament and town hall.

The Great Outdoors

Oslo's inhabitants like nothing better than to escape the pressures of city life and take to the stands of green that surround the city. Much of the activity coalesces around the Holmenkollen Ski Jump and the Nordmarka woodland.

p44

Southern Norway

Festivals ✓✓
Villages ✓✓
Landscapes ✓

Festivals

The summer tourist season draws Norwegians to the southern coast in droves. Yes, they come partly for the beaches, but some of Norway's most popular festivals and celebrations of coastal life also loom large.

Seaside Hamlets

Southern Norway's seaside villages showcase the white-washed timber architecture for which the region is famous.

Beyond Fjords

Coastal inlets of the kind that once sheltered Vikings are the topographical mainstay of the south, but there's drama aplenty in Jøssingfjord, the rolling hills of Setesdalen and the peak of Gausta.

p86

Central Norway

Hiking ✓✓✓
Wildlife ✓✓✓
Architecture ✓✓

Hikes

Jotunheimen National Park has the most celebrated trails, although the parks of Hardangervidda and Rondane are every bit as good.

Wildlife

There aren't many places where it's easier to see three signature species of the north: wild reindeer roam the Hardangervidda Plateau, the musk ox inhabits two central Norwegian national parks and the humble elk (moose) is easy to see.

History in Wood

Two stave churches (at Lom and Ringebu), the mining town of Røros and Lillehammer's Maihaugen Folk Museum take you on a journey through Norwegian architectural history.

p121

Bergen & the Southwestern Fjords

Fjords ✓✓✓
Villages ✓✓✓
Cities ✓✓✓

Fantastic Fjords
Spectacular Hardangerfjord, its shorelines carpeted in fruit trees, is far less trammelled by tourists than the fjords further north. To the south, Lysefjord is picture-perfect with two iconic vantage points: Pulpit Rock and Kjeragbolten.

Timeless Hamlets
Some of Norway's prettiest villages – Ulvik, Eidfjord and Utne to name just three of Hardangerfjord's small settlements – are at once worthy destinations in their own right and front-row seats for stunning fjord country.

Beautiful Bergen
There is no more picturesque city in northern Europe than Bergen, with its harbourside district, mountainous backdrop and vibrant cultural life.

p153

The Western Fjords

Fjords ✓✓✓
Activities ✓✓✓
Architecture ✓✓

Best Fjords
Norway's western fjords region – home to Geirangerfjord, as well as Nærøyfjord, Aurlandsfjorden and the other vertiginous tributaries of the vast Sognefjorden – is one of the most beautiful places on earth.

Ice-Bound
Take to the water in a kayak or hike up a mountainside, but the main drawcard here is the chance to venture onto the glacier tongues of the epic Jostedalsbreen icefield.

Stave Churches & Art Nouveau
Norway's prettiest stave churches – including Stordal, Kaupanger, Borgund and Urnes – are set against a postcard-perfect backdrop of fjords and mountains. To the northeast, art nouveau Ålesund is magnificent.

p198

Trøndelag

Hiking ✓✓
Cities ✓✓
History ✓✓

Sacred Path
Few Norwegian hiking trails resonate so strongly with the sacred. The Pilgrims' Way is an ancient pilgrimage trail with Trondheim as its goal. The Bymarka wilderness also contains fine trails.

Terrific Trondheim
A worthy rival to Bergen for the title of Norway's most agreeable city, Trondheim boasts excellent museums, a thriving culinary and cultural scene and a slew of architecturally distinguished buildings.

Medieval Echoes
Trondheim's 12th-century Nidaros Cathedral is Scandinavia's largest medieval building. To the northwest, Stiklestad marks the site of St Olav's martyrdom and one of the most significant battles in Viking history.

p244

Nordland

Scenery ✓✓✓
Islands ✓✓✓
Nature ✓✓✓

Enter the Arctic
Whether you choose the snaking Kystriksveien or the Arctic Highway, there are no finer passages into the Arctic anywhere in the world.

Jagged Coast
More than 14,000 islands sit offshore from the Nordland coast. The Vega archipelago consists of low-lying skerries; Vesterålen is wild and untrammelled, while Lofoten is arguably Europe's most spectacular island chain.

Whales & Glaciers
Nordland's coastal landscapes are the scene for Norway's best whale-watching possibilities, notably at Stø, Andenes, Narvik and Henningsvær. Inland, Saltfjellet-Svartisen National Park is Norway's second-largest icefield.

p269

The Far North

Activities ✓✓✓
The Sami ✓✓✓
Landscapes ✓✓✓

Arctic Winter

While the rest of Norway hibernates for winter, the far north takes to the snow aboard snowmobiles, skis and sleds pulled by teams of huskies.

Sami Homeland

The indigenous Sami are Arctic Norway's most enduring human inhabitants and their emergence from centuries of persecution and an extreme climate is celebrated most powerfully in Karasjok and Kautokeino, now proud bastions of Sami culture.

Coast & Cathedrals

From the remote national parks of the interior to the coastal splendours of Senja, the Lyngen Alps and Nordkapp, Norway's high-Arctic landscapes inspire travellers and architects alike.

p313

Svalbard

Activities ✓✓✓
Landscapes ✓✓✓
Wildlife ✓✓✓

Year-Round Adventure

Dog-sledding and snowmobiling in winter, hiking, cruises and kayaking in summer – there's not much you can't do here.

Frozen Wilderness

Svalbard's natural beauty – ice-bound for much of the year – defies superlatives. Much of the archipelago ranks among Europe's most beautiful wilderness areas, with mountainous ramparts, epic icefields and lonely fjords.

Arctic Wildlife

Here be polar bears. And walrus. And whales, reindeer, Arctic fox and more than 160 bird species. Svalbard offers a rare opportunity to see the inhabitants of this accessible slice of the polar north.

p351

Look out for these icons:

 TOP CHOICE Our author's recommendation

 A green or sustainable option

FREE No payment required

See the Index for a full list of destinations covered in this book.

On the Road

Oslo

Includes »

Best Places to Eat

» Feinschmecker (p66)

» Punjab Tandoori (p67)

» Baltazar (p66)

» Markveien Mat & Vinhus (p68)

» Fishermen's Coop (p67)

» Smia Galleri (p69)

Best Places to Stay

» Ellingsens Pensjonat (p63)

» Grims Grenka (p63)

» Gamlebyen Gjestegaarder (p79)

» Grand Hotel (p64)

Why Go?

To the rest of the world, Norway is where Mother Nature has created one of her finest works of art. Against such a wonderful natural canvas, it's easy to forget that man can also be artistic, and many a visitor has been left surprised to discover that Oslo is home to world-class museums and galleries to rival anywhere else on the European art trail.

But even here Mother Nature has managed to make her mark, and Oslo is fringed with forests, hills and lakes awash with opportunities for hiking, cycling, skiing and boating.

Add to this mix a thriving cafe and bar culture, top-notch restaurants, nightlife options ranging from opera to indie rock, and a large and visible immigrant community who add their own colourful touch to the city and the result is a thoroughly intoxicating place in which to forget about the fjords for a while.

When to Go

Oslo

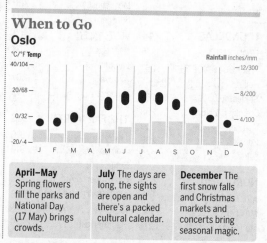

April–May
Spring flowers fill the parks and National Day (17 May) brings crowds.

July The days are long, the sights are open and there's a packed cultural calendar.

December The first snow falls and Christmas markets and concerts bring seasonal magic.

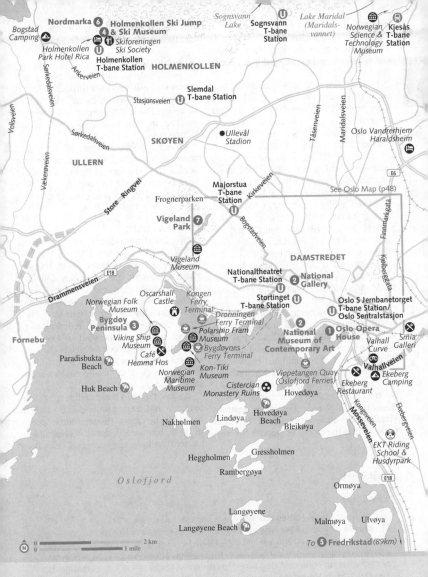

Oslo Highlights

❶ Sing like a soprano in the new **Oslo Opera House** (p46)

❷ Scream with delight at seeing *The Scream* in the **National Gallery** (p47), and see how today's artists shape up in the **National Museum of Contemporary Art** (p47)

❸ Examine the ships and charts of the Viking Ship,

Kon-Tiki and Polarship Fram Museums on **Bygdøy Peninsula** (p56)

❹ Conquer your fear of heights from the summit of **Holmenkollen Ski Jump** (p59)

❺ Stroll the fortress walls and explore the quirky boutiques of Fredrikstad's charming **Gamlebyen** (p78)

❻ Pick summer blueberries and go winter skiing in Oslo's **Nordmarka** (p60)

❼ Reconsider parenthood while looking at the works of Gustav Vigeland at **Vigeland Park** (p55)

❽ Eat your way around the world in the city's Norwegian and ethnic **restaurants** (p65)

History

The name Oslo is derived from the words *Ás*, the Old Norse name for the Norse Godhead, and *lo*, meaning 'pasture', yielding roughly 'the fields of the gods'.

The city was originally founded in 1049 by King Harald Hardråde (Harald Hard-Ruler; see p372), whose son Olav Kyrre (Olav the Peaceful) set up a cathedral and a corresponding bishopric here. In the late 13th century, King Håkon V created a military presence by building the Akershus Fortress (Akershus Festning; see p49) in the hope of deterring the Swedish threat from the east. After the mid-14th-century bubonic plague wiped out half of the country's population, Norway united with Denmark, and from 1397 to 1624 Norwegian politics and defence were handled from Copenhagen. Oslo slipped into obscurity, and in 1624 it burned to the ground. It was resurrected by King Christian IV, who rebuilt it on a more easily defended site and renamed it Christiania, after his humble self.

For three centuries, the city held on as a seat of defence. In 1814 the framers of Norway's first constitution designated it the official capital of the new realm, but their efforts were effectively nullified by Sweden, which had other ideas about Norway's future and unified the two countries under Swedish rule. In 1905, when that union was dissolved and Norway became a separate kingdom, the stage was set for Christiania to flourish as the capital of modern Norway.

It reverted to its original name, Oslo, in 1925 and the city has never looked back.

◉ Sights

Oslo's main street, Karl Johans gate, forms a ceremonial axis westward through the heart of the city to the Royal Palace. Most sights, including the harbour front and Akershus Fortress, are within a 15-minute walk of Karl Johans gate.

Whether you're artistic or literary, a peacenik or a history enthusiast, an explorer or an athlete, chances are there is a museum in Oslo tailor-made for you. Most are clustered around the city centre, on Bygdøy Peninsula or near Vigeland Park.

CENTRAL OSLO

TOP CHOICE **Oslo Opera House**   OPERA HOUSE
(Den Norske Opera & Ballett; Map p52; ☎ 21 42 21 21; www.operaen.no; Kirsten Flagstads plass 1; admission to foyer free; ☺foyer 10am-11pm Mon-Fri, 11am-11pm Sat, noon-10pm Sun) Hoping to transform the city into a world-class cultural centre, the city fathers have embarked on a massive waterfront redevelopment project (which is scheduled to last until 2020), the centrepiece of which is the magnificent new Opera House, a creation likely to become one of the iconic modern buildings of Europe.

Designed by Oslo-based architectural firm Snøhetta and costing around €500 million to build, the Opera House, which opened in 2008, has been designed to resemble a glacier floating in the waters off Oslo. It's a

---

OSLO IN...

Two Days

Start your day at the **National Gallery** for a representative dose of artwork by Edvard Munch. Afterwards, in **Aker Brygge** try an alfresco, pier-side lunch of peel-and-eat shrimp from one of the local fishing boats. Take a ferry from here to Bygdøy Peninsula, and spend your afternoon learning about the exploits of Norway's greatest explorers at the **Polarship Fram** or **Viking Ship Museums**. On day two head to the breathtaking new **Oslo Opera House** (timing your visit to coincide with one of the guided tours), after which you can take a look at all that's cool and modern at the **National Museum of Contemporary Art**. In the afternoon explore the medieval **Akershus Castle**, and learn how to make the world a better place at the **Nobel Peace Center**.

Four Days

If you have a couple of extra days, wander among the bold, earthy statues at **Vigeland Park** and consider launching yourself off the enormous **Holmenkollen Ski Jump**, although it's probably better to content yourself with a virtual attempt in the nearby simulator. The energetic might also spend a day walking, skiing or biking in the **Nordmarka**; otherwise simply make a lazy day trip to pretty **Fredrikstad**.

subtle building that at first doesn't look all that impressive, but give it time and it'll leave you spellbound. Impressive at any time, it's probably at its most magical in the winter when snow provides it with a gleaming coat and the surrounding harbour fills with sparkling sheets of ice.

Before venturing inside be sure to walk up onto the roof, which was designed to act as a 'carpet' of sloping angles and flat surfaces. It's a symbolism that obviously works because Norwegians love to sprawl out across it on sunny days and sunbathe. Also, don't miss 'playing' the **musical rods** that sit both up on the roof and near the entrance. Floating just offshore of the Opera House is Monica Bonvicini's **She Lies**, a three-dimensional interpretation of Caspar David Friedrich's 1823–24 painting *Das Eismeer* (The Sea of Ice). As the tides rush in and out of the harbour, the steel and glass sculpture spins and twists, which gives the viewer a constantly changing perspective on the sculpture.

The main entrance to the Opera House is purposely small and unimpressive, which serves only to add to the sense of vastness that greets you on entering the main foyer (the windows alone are 15m high and flood the foyer with light). Aside from the windows, the other dominating feature of the foyer is the **Wave Wall**. Made of strips of golden oak, the wall curves up through the centre of the foyer and provides access to the upper levels of the building. Opposite the wave wall, green lights create playful patterns on the wall (and make the toilets and coat room they hide the most artistic you will ever visit!).

Also in the foyer is a **restaurant** (mains Nkr230, set menus Nkr395), serving suitably modern and arty takes on old Norwegian classics.

To see more of the building's interior, you will have to join one of the infrequent guided tours. These run in **English** (Nkr100; ☺2pm daily mid-Apr–Aug, 2pm Fri-Sun Sep–mid-Apr) and **Norwegian** (Nkr100; ☺noon daily) and take you into some of the building's 1100 rooms. The guide will explain much of the artistic symbolism of the building and reveal something of life behind the scenes at the Opera House. In high season it's a good idea to book a space on a tour in advance.

While wandering around the building, it can be easy to forget that it's not just there to serve as eye candy for tourists, and that its prime role is to act as a showcase for top-notch opera and ballet performances. Upcoming performances are listed on the website and ticket prices vary from Nkr100 to Nkr1000.

Eventually the ongoing waterfront redevelopment will see the Munch Museum and the National Library relocated to sites close to the Opera House, although neither is likely to be completed during the lifetime of this book.

National Gallery   ART GALLERY
(Nasjonalgalleriet; Map p52; www.nasjonal museet.no; Universitetsgata 13; adult/child Nkr 50/free; ☺10am-6pm Tue, Wed & Fri, 10am-7pm Thu, 11am-5pm Sat & Sun) One of Oslo's major highlights is the National Gallery. It houses the nation's largest collection of Norwegian art, including works from the Romantic era and more-modern works from 1800 to WWII. Some of Edvard Munch's best-known creations are on display, including his most renowned work, *The Scream* (see the boxed text, p59). There's also an impressive collection of European art with works by Gauguin, Picasso and El Greco, and impressionists such as Manet, Degas, Renoir, Matisse, Cézanne and Monet.

For more on Edvard Munch, see p413.

**National Museum of
Contemporary Art**   MODERN ART
(Museet for Samtidskunst; Map p52; www.nasjonal museet.no; Bankplassen 4; adult/child Nkr 50/free; ☺11am-5pm Tue, Wed & Fri, 11am-7pm Thu, noon-5pm Sat & Sun) Featuring the National Gallery's collections of post-WWII Scandinavian and international art is the National Museum of Contemporary Art. Some of the 3000-piece collection is definitely an acquired taste, but it does provide a timely reminder that Norwegian art didn't cease with Edvard Munch. There are frequent cutting-edge temporary exhibitions. The in-house cafe is also worthy of praise.

Nobel Peace Center   MUSEUM
(Fredssetner; Map p52; www.nobelpeacecenter.org; Brynjulf Bulls plass 2; adult/child Nkr80/free, free with Oslo Pass; ☺10am-6pm mid-May–Aug) Norwegians take pride in their role as international peacemakers, and the Nobel Peace Prize is their gift to the men and women judged to have done the most to promote world peace over the course of the previous year. This state-of-the-art museum celebrates the lives and achievements of the winners with an array of digital displays intended to

Oslo

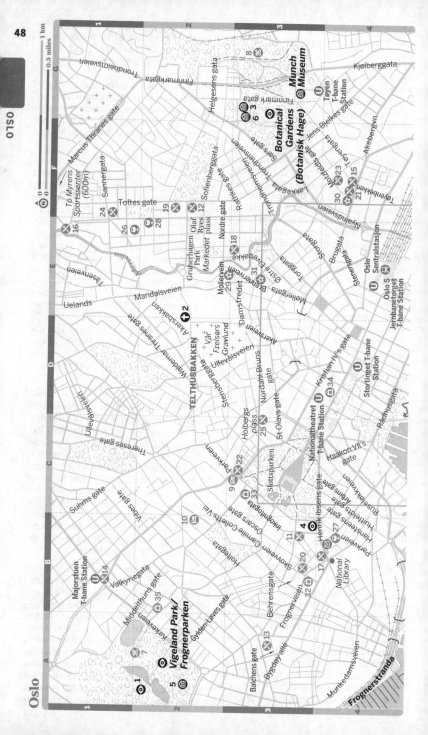

offer as much or as little information as the visitor desires. Don't miss the Nobel Book on the 2nd floor or the movie theatre streaming films on the history of the prize and its winners (see p56). There are frequent changing exhibitions focusing on different aspects of the prize and its winners. Recent exhibitions have detailed the struggle against apartheid in South Africa and the pros and cons of the controversial awarding of the 2009 prize to US President Barack Obama.

Akershus Castle & Fortress   CASTLE

Strategically located on the eastern side of the harbour, dominating the Oslo harbour front, are the medieval castle and fortress, arguably Oslo's architectural highlights.

When Oslo was named capital of Norway in 1299, King Håkon V ordered the construction of Akershus to protect the city from external threats, but it has been extended and modified and had its defences beefed up a number of times since.

When Oslo was rebuilt after a devastating fire in 1624, the city, renamed Christiania, was shifted to the less vulnerable and more defensible site behind the protective fortress walls. By 1818 the need for defence had been superseded by the need for space and most of the outer rampart was destroyed to accommodate population growth. From 1899 to 1963 it underwent major renovations, and nowadays the parklike grounds serve as a venue for concerts, dances and theatrical productions – a far cry from its warlike origins and a welcome departure from its grim history. Note, however, that this complex remains a military installation and may be closed to the public whenever there's a state function.

In the 17th century, Christian IV renovated **Akershus Castle** (Akershus Slott; Map p52; adult/child Nkr65/25, free with Oslo Pass; ☉10am-4pm Mon-Sat, 12.30-4pm Sun May-Aug, shorter hr rest of yr; guided tours 11am, 1pm & 3pm Mon-Sat, 1pm & 3pm Sun) into a Renaissance palace, although the front remains decidedly medieval. In its dungeons you'll find dark cubbyholes where outcast nobles were kept under lock and key, while the upper floors contained sharply contrasting lavish banquet halls and staterooms.

The castle chapel is still used for army events, and the crypts of King Håkon VII and Olav V lie beneath it. The guided tours are led by university students in period dress, and while not compulsory they do offer an entertaining anecdotal history of the place that you won't get by wandering around on your own.

Entry to the expansive **fortress** (Akershus Festning; Map p52; admission free; ⊘6am-9pm) is through a gate at the end of Akersgata or over a drawbridge spanning Kongens gate at the southern end of Kirkegata. After 6pm in winter, use the Kirkegata entrance.

The **Akershus Fortress Information Centre** (Map p52; ⊘9am-5pm Mon-Fri, 11am-5pm Sat & Sun mid-May–mid-Aug, closes 1hr earlier rest of yr), inside the main gate, has an exhibit recounting the history of the Akershus complex. Staff also offer guided tours of the castle grounds on request. At 1.30pm you can watch the changing of the guard at the fortress.

Also within the fortress complex, adjacent to a memorial for resistance fighters executed on the spot during WWII, is the **Norwegian Resistance Museum** (Norges Hjemmefront Museet; Map p52; www.nhm.mil.no; adult/child Nkr50/free, free with Oslo Pass;

⊘10am-5pm Mon-Sat, 11am-5pm Sun Jun-Aug, shorter hr rest of yr). The small but worthwhile museum covers the dark years of German occupation, as well as the jubilant day of 9 May 1945 when peace was declared. Artefacts include underground newspapers, numerous maps and photographs and, most intriguingly, a set of dentures that belonged to a Norwegian prisoner of war in Poland, and were wired to receive radio broadcasts.

Astrup Fearnley Museum   MODERN ART
(Astrup Fearnley Museet; Strandpromenaden 2; www.afmuseet.no) The museum reopened in September 2012 at a new site in Tjuvholmen, in a building specially designed by architect Renzo Piano. Check the website for up-to-date information.

Damstredet   OLD TOWN
The quirky 18th-century wooden homes of the Damstredet district and the nearby Telthusbakken are a nice change of pace from

the modern architecture of the city centre. Once an impoverished shanty town, Damstredet has become a popular residential neighbourhood for artists. To get there, walk north on Akersgata and turn right on Damstredet gate. Telthusbakken is a little further up Akersgata, also on the right. On the way, you'll pass **Vår Frelsers Gravlund** (Map p48), the graveyard where Ibsen, Munch and Bjørnstjerne Bjørnson are buried.

Stenersen Museum
MODERN ART

(Stenersenmuseet; Map p52; Munkedamsveien 15; adult/child Nkr45/25, free with Oslo Pass; ☺11am-5pm Wed & Fri-Sun, 11am-7pm Tue & Thu) This museum of Modernism, Realism and avantgarde art contains three formerly private collections of works, dating from 1850 to 1970, by Norwegian artists. The museum and much of the art, which includes works by Ludvig Karsten and Amaldus Nielsen, were a gift to the city by Rolf E Stenersen. There's free admission between October and April.

Ibsen Museum
MUSEUM

(Ibsen-Museet; Map p52; www.ibsenmuseet.no; Arbins gate 1; adult/child Nkr85/25, free with Oslo Pass; ☺guided tours hourly 11am-6pm mid-May–mid-Sep, shorter hr rest of yr) Housed in the last residence of Norwegian playwright Henrik Ibsen (see p409), the Ibsen Museum is a must-see for Ibsen fans, as are his birthplace of Skien (p111) and Grimstad (p96), where the eminent playwright spent his formative years. The study remains exactly as he left it, and other rooms have been restored to the style and colours popular in Ibsen's day. Visitors can even glance into the bedroom where he uttered his famously enigmatic

---

LOCAL KNOWLEDGE

THE NORWEGIAN RESISTANCE: 'NEVER AGAIN!'

The day the German army marched into Oslo – April 9, 1940 – Gunnar Sønsteby watched it parade down Karl Johans gate, mounted his bicycle and disappeared into the woods to join the resistance.

At the time, there wasn't really anything to join. After 125 years of peace, Norwegians watched bewildered as their country was occupied in less than 60 days and their king and cabinet were forced into exile. But by the end of the war, there were 40,000 homespun resistance soldiers, 60 underground newspapers and the Norwegian *hjemmefront* (resistance) could take credit for some of the war's most successful acts of sabotage.

These actions came at a cost. Over 50,000 Norwegians were arrested for political reasons during WWII, not a small number for a country of only three million, and 9000 were sent abroad. Of these, 1400 Norwegians, half of them Jewish, would never return.

With that in mind, we posed a few questions about the resistance to Ivar Kraglund, director at Oslo's Resistance Museum.

If resistance fighters had to escape, where did most of them go? Almost 50,000 people escaped to Sweden, some on their own and others with guides. Once there, many received military training. By the end of the war, there were 13,000 Norwegians who had been trained in Sweden and who were carrying Swedish weapons.

Did any famous acts of sabotage take place? The most important attack was on the heavy water plant at Vemork in 1943 (see p111). It is probably one of the most famous sabotage attacks of WWII, and the museum has the only remaining water cell from the factory that I know of.

And what happened to Gunnar Sønsteby? He became the leader of the 'Oslo gang' and one of Norway's most famous resistance fighters. He's probably best known for his attack on the registration offices in 1944, which made it impossible for the Germans to send Norwegian recruits to the front.

What other reminders of the resistance are there in Oslo? In addition to the Resistance Museum, keep an eye out for the haunting, grey Victoria Terrasse near Oslo centre, which was commandeered by the Gestapo. At the time, it was known as the *skrekken hus* (house of fear). And a little further on, at Solli plass (Map p52), there's a bronze statue of Sønsteby and his bicycle.

As told to Kari Lundgren

Central Oslo

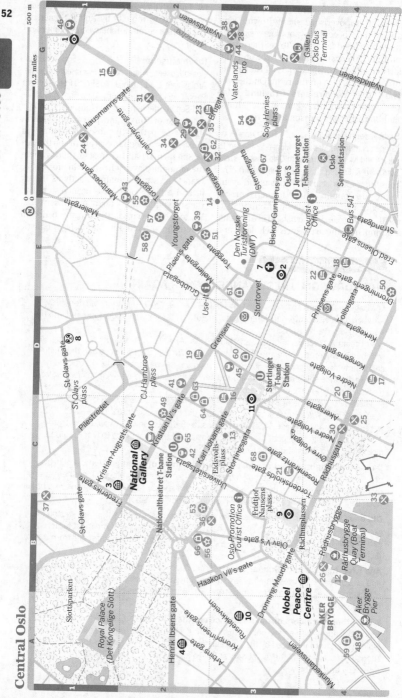

0.2 miles

500 m

Slottsparken

Royal Palace
(Det Kongelige Slott)

St Olavs gate

Frederiks gate

St Olavs gate

Pilestredet

St Olavs
plass

St Olavs gate

Kristian Augusts gate

Nationaltheatret T-bane
Station

National
Gallery

CJ Hambros
plass

Henrik Ibsens gate

Arbins gate

Kronprinsens gate

Ruseløkkveien

Haakon VII's gate

Olav V's gate

Oslo Promotion
Tourist Office

Dronning Mauds gate

Nobel Peace
Centre

AKER
BRYGGE

Aker Brygge Pier

Rådhusbrygge
Quay (Boat
Terminal)

Rådhusbrygge

Munkedamsveien

Karl Johans gate

Universitetsgata

Eidsvolls-
plass

Stortingsgata

Rosenkrantz gate

Tordenskiolds gate

Fridtjof
Nansens
plass

Rådhusplassen

Kristian IV's gate

Grensen

Stortinget
T-bane Station

Nedre Vollgate

Øvre Vollgate

Øvre Vollgate

Nedre Vollgate

Akersgata

Rådhusgata

Stortorvet

Grubbegata

Pløens gate

Møllergata

Torggata

Use-It

Youngstorget

Den Norske
Turistforening
(DNT)

Bishop Gunnerus gate

Mariboes gate

Møllergata

Calmeyers gate

Hausmanns gate

Akersgata

Torggata

Storgata

Steneragata

Prinsens gate

Dronningens gate

Tollbugata

Kirkegata

Kongens gate

Nedre Vollgate

Fred Olsens gate

Nylandsveien

Akerselva

Nylandsveien

Vaterlands
bro

Soya Henies
plass

Oslo S
Jernbanetorget
T-bane Station

Tourist
Office

Oslo
Sentralstasjon

Bus 541

Strandgata

Galleri
Oslo Bus
Terminal

Nylandsveien

last words 'Tvert imot!' ('To the contrary!'),
before dying on 23 May 1906.

FREE **Historical Museum**   MUSEUM
(Historisk Museet; Map p52; www.khm.uio
.no; University of Oslo, Frederiks gate 2; adult/child
Nkr50/free; ⊙10am-5pm Tue-Sun mid-May–mid-
Sep, shorter hr rest of yr) The Historical Museum
is actually three museums under one roof.
Most interesting is the ground-floor **National
Antiquities Collection** (Oldsaksamlingen),
which has displays of Viking-era coins,
jewellery and ornaments. Look out for
the 9th-century **Hon treasure** (2.5kg), the
largest such find in Scandinavia. A section on
medieval religious art includes the doors and
richly painted ceiling of the Ål stave church
(built around 1300). The second level has an
Arctic exhibit and the Myntkabinettet, a collection of the earliest Norwegian coins from
as far back as AD 995. The second level and
top floor hold the **Ethnographic Museum**,
with changing exhibitions on Asia, Africa
and the Americas.

FREE **Oslo Cathedral**   CATHEDRAL
(Domkirke; Map p52; Stortorvet 1; admis-
sion free; ⊙24hr) Dating from 1697, the Oslo
Cathedral has just been reborn following on
from several years of intensive renovations.
The highlights of a visit are the elaborate
stained-glass windows by Emanuel Vigeland (brother of Gustav) and painted ceiling (completed between 1936 and 1950).
The exceptional altarpiece, a 1748 model of
the Last Supper and the Crucifixion by Michael Rasch, was an original feature of the
church (from 1700), but it was moved all
over the country before being returned from
Prestnes church in Majorstue in 1950. The
organ front and pulpit were both part of the
original construction. Occasional concerts
(Nkr150) are held in the church.

The **bazaar halls** (Basarhallene; Map
p52), around the back of the church, date
from 1858 and are currently used by summer handicraft sales outlets and cafes.

FREE **Oslo Rådhus**   TOWN HALL
(Rådhus; Map p52; www.rft.oslo.kommune
.no; Fridtjof Nansens plass; free admission; ⊙9am-
6pm, guided tours 10am, noon & 2pm) This
twin-towered town hall, completed in 1950
to commemorate Oslo's 900th anniversary,
houses the city's political administration.
Something of an Oslo landmark, its red-
brick functionalist exterior is unusual, if
not particularly attractive. It's here that
the Nobel Peace Prize is awarded on 10
December each year (see p56).

Central Oslo

FREE **Stortinget** PARLIAMENT BUILDING

(Map p52; www.stortinget.no; Karl Johans gate 22; admission free; ⊙guided tours in Norwegian & English 10am, 11.30am & 1pm Mon-Fri 24 Jun-21 Aug) Built in 1866, Norway's yellow-brick parliament building is one of Europe's more charming parliaments. If you find yourself really hooked on Norwegian political debate, you can tune into live action through the Stortinget website.

FROGNERPARKEN & VIGELAND PARK

TOP CHOICE Vigeland Park PARK

(Map p48; ⊙yr-round) The centrepiece of Frognerparken is an extraordinary open-air showcase of work by Norway's best-loved sculptor, Gustav Vigeland. Statistically one of the top tourist attractions in Norway, Vigeland Park is brimming with 212 granite and bronze Vigeland works. His highly charged work ranges from entwined lovers and tranquil elderly couples to contempt-ridden beggars. His most renowned work, *Sinataggen* (the 'Little Hot-Head'), portrays a London child in a mood of particular ill humour.

It's a great place to visit in the evening after other sights have closed.

FREE Oslo City Museum MUSEUM

(Oslo Bymuseet; Map p48; www.oslomu seum.no; Frognerveien 67; admission free; ⊙11am-4pm Tue-Sun, closed last week Dec until mid-Jan) Near the southern entrance to Vigeland park lies this museum. Housed in the 18th-century Frogner Manor (built on the site of a Viking-era manor), it contains exhibits of minor interest on the city's history.

Frognerparken itself attracts Oslo locals with its broad lawns, ponds, stream and rows of shady trees. On a sunny afternoon it's ideal for picnics, strolling or lounging on the grass.

To get here, take tram 12 to Vigelandsparken from the city centre.

Vigeland Museum MUSEUM

(Map p45; www.vigeland.museum.no; Nobels gate 32; adult/child Nkr50/25, free with Oslo Pass; ⊙10am-5pm Tue-Sun Jun-Aug, shorter hr rest of yr) For an in-depth look at Gustav Vigeland's work, visit the Vigeland Museum, opposite the southern entrance to Frognerparken. It was built by the city in the 1920s as a home and workshop for the sculptor in exchange for the donation of a significant proportion of his life's work, and it contains his early collection of statuary and monuments to public figures, as well as plaster moulds, woodblock prints and sketches. When he died in 1943, his ashes were deposited in the tower and the museum was opened to the public four years later. Guided tours are available (in English), with prior notice, from Nkr800 per group. In addition to the works of Vigeland the museum also has a changing schedule of modern art. Free admission from October to April.

GUSTAV VIGELAND

The sculptor Gustav Vigeland (1869–1943) was born to a farming family near Mandal, in the far south of Norway. As a child and teenager he became deeply interested in Protestantism, spirituality, woodcarving and drawing – a unique combination that would dominate his life's work. In 1888 Vigeland secured an apprenticeship to sculptor Brynjulf Bergslien. The following year he exhibited his first work at the State Exhibition of Art. It was the break he needed, bringing his talents to national and international attention.

In 1891 he travelled to Copenhagen and then to Paris and Italy, where he worked with various masters; he was especially inspired by the work of French sculptor Auguste Rodin. When his public grants ran out he returned to Norway to make a living working on the restoration of the Nidaros Cathedral in Trondheim and producing commissioned portraits of prominent Norwegians.

In 1921 the City of Oslo recognised his talents and built him a spacious studio in which to work; it's now a museum.

The highlight of Vigeland Park is the 14m-high granite *Monolith*, which crowns the park's highest hill. This incredible production required three stone carvers working daily from 1929 to 1943 and was carved from a single stone pillar quarried from Iddefjorden in southeastern Norway. It depicts a writhing mass of 121 detailed human figures, both entwined with and undermining each other in their individual struggle to reach the top. The circle of steps around it supports rows of stone figures. The figures, together with the pillar, have been interpreted in many ways: as a phallic representation, the struggle for existence, yearnings for the spiritual spheres and transcendence of cyclic repetition.

Leading down from the plinth bearing this column is a series of steps that support sculptures depicting people experiencing the full range of human emotions and activities. The numerous sculptures dominating the surrounding park carry the artist's themes, from the realistic to the ludicrous.

THE WORLD'S MOST PRESTIGIOUS PRIZE

Most Nobel prizes – physics, chemistry, medicine, literature and economics – are awarded every October in Stockholm, but the most prestigious prize of all, the Peace Prize, is reserved for Oslo. In his will in 1895, Alfred Nobel, the Swedish founder of the prize and the inventor of dynamite, instructed that the interest on his vast fortune be awarded each year 'to those who, during the preceding year, shall have conferred the greatest benefit on mankind'.

It is unclear why Nobel chose Norway to administer the Peace Prize, but whatever the reason, it is a committee of five Norwegians, appointed for six-year terms by the Norwegian Storting (parliament), that chooses the winner each year. Their meetings, held in a room of the Nobel Institute that is decorated with the pictures of winners past, from Mother Teresa (1979) to Mikhail Gorbachev (1990) and Al Gore (2007), are closed-door affairs presided over by the chairman of the Norwegian Nobel Committee, professor Ole Mjøs. Meetings are also attended by the institute's director, Geir Lundestad. Appointed director in 1990, Lundestad filled us in on some prize history and discussed his pet project – the new **Nobel Peace Center** (p47).

What's the difference between being nominated and short-listed for the Peace Prize? Anyone can be nominated, from President George Bush to Madonna, and this often causes a huge outcry, but there is a big difference between being nominated and being selected as the winner! We start from almost 200 candidates in February. The list is cut down to 30, then five, and the rest of the time is spent focusing on the qualifications of the candidates on the shortlist.

Is the committee ever criticised for being too secretive? The committee is transparent, but it is true that the list of nominees is closed for 50 years and no minutes are kept, though some of the members keep notes, which they have made public.

How has the nature of the prize changed while you've been director? The definition of peace has slowly broadened to include elements that reflect the changing world. Human rights, for example, was initially a very controversial interpretation when it [the prize] was given in 1960 to South African activist Albert Lutuli. The environment was added as a road to peace in 2004 and there is always pressure to widen the definition further.

Describe the ideal candidate? Many see the prize as a declaration of sainthood, but winners are often just more or less ordinary people who have tried to do something useful for peace. Their efforts have been heroic, but they are all very different. At the same time, they share a vision and they have the courage to carry it out.

What is special about the new Fredssetner? The new Peace Center is where we tell the story of all the laureates. It is the most electronically advanced museum in Oslo and the idea is that people can choose to learn as much or as little as they want to find out. It is up to you.

As told to Kari Lundgren

BYGDØY PENINSULA

The Bygdøy Peninsula (Map p45) holds some of Oslo's top attractions. You can rush around all the sights in half a day, but allotting a few extra hours will be more rewarding.

Although only minutes from central Oslo, Bygdøy maintains its rural character. The royal family has a summer home here, as do many foreign ambassadors and Oslo's most well-to-do residents.

Ferry No 91 (☎23 35 68 90) operates from early April to early October, making the 15-minute run to Bygdøy (adult/child Nkr40/20, free with the Oslo Pass) every 20 minutes from 8am to 8.45pm in summer; earlier final departures the rest of the year. Note that the above prices are for ticket purchase onboard the boat. If you buy your tickets from one of the kiosks on the departure jetties the prices are lower (adult/child Nkr26/13, or a 24-hour pass is Nkr70/35 per adult/child). Keep an eye out for the king's ship KS *Norge* on the ride over, as well as the king's and queen's royal yacht clubs

(Kongen and *Dronningen)*, which face one another on either side of the Frognerkilen.

The ferries leave from Rådhusbrygge 3 (opposite the Rådhus) and stop first at Dronningen ferry terminal, from where it's a 10-minute walk to the Norwegian Folk Museum and a 15-minute walk to the Viking Ship Museum. Beyond the ships it's a further 20 minutes' walk to Bygdøynes, where the Kon-Tiki, Polarship Fram and Norwegian Maritime Museums are clustered; the route is signposted and makes a pleasant walk. Alternatively, the ferry continues to Bygdøynes. You can also take bus 30 to the Folk Museum from Jernbanetorget T-bane station, next to Oslo S.

TOP CHOICE **Viking Ship Museum** VIKING MUSEUM
(Map p45; www.khm.uio.no; Huk Aveny 35; adult/child Nkr60/30, free with Oslo Pass; ⊙9am-6pm May-Sep, shorter hr rest of yr; ⬛) Even in repose, there is something intimidating about the sleek, dark hulls of the Viking ships *Oseberg* and *Gokstad* – the best preserved such ships in the world. There is also a third boat here, the *Tune,* but only a few boards and fragments remain. All were built of oak in the 9th century. The ships were pulled ashore and used as tombs for nobility, who were buried with all they expected to need in the hereafter: jewels, furniture, food, servants, intricately carved carriages and sleighs, tapestries and fierce-looking figures. Some of these items are also displayed in the museum. All three ships were excavated from the Oslofjord region between the end of the 19th century and the start of the 20th.

The impressive 22m-long *Oseberg,* buried in 834, is festooned on prow and stern with elaborate dragon and serpent carvings. The burial chamber beneath it held the largest collection of Viking Age artefacts ever uncovered in Scandinavia, but had been looted of all jewellery. As daunting as the ship appears, it was probably only ever intended as a royal pleasure craft. The sturdier 24m-long *Gokstad,* built around 890, is the finest remaining example of a Viking longship, but when it was unearthed its corresponding burial chamber had also been looted and few artefacts were uncovered. In addition to the three ships, the museum has recently put on display some of the skeletons found alongside the boats.

Norwegian Folk Museum FOLK MUSEUM
(Norsk Folkemuseum; Map p45; www.norskfolkemu seum.no; Museumsveien 10; adult/child Nkr100/25, free with Oslo Pass; ⊙10am-6pm mid-May–mid-

Sep, shorter hr rest of yr) Norway's largest open-air museum and one of Oslo's premier attractions is this folk museum. The museum includes more than 140 buildings, mostly from the 17th and 18th centuries, gathered from around the country, rebuilt and organised according to region of origin. Paths wind past old barns, elevated *stabbur* (raised storehouses) and rough-timbered farmhouses with sod roofs sprouting wildflowers. The Gamlebyen (Old Town) section is a reproduction of an early-20th-century Norwegian town and includes a village shop and an old petrol station; in summer (daily except Saturday) you can see weaving and pottery-making demonstrations. Another highlight is the restored stave church, built around 1200 in Gol and shifted to Bygdøy in 1885. Little people will be entertained by the numerous farm animals, horse and cart rides, and other activities (some of which cost extra).

The exhibition hall located near the main entrance includes exhaustive displays on Norwegian folk art, historic toys, national costumes (including traditional clothing used for weddings, christenings and burials), domestic and farming tools and appliances, as well as visiting exhibits. However, the most interesting exhibition focuses on the life and culture of the Sami. It examines their former persecution and looks at how they have adapted to life in a modern Norway. Temporary exhibitions are often hosted and these can be as varied as church art or 1950s pop culture. Sunday is a good day to visit, as folk music and dancing is staged at 2pm (in summer).

ℹ️ **OSLO PASS**

The **Oslo Pass** (adult 1/2/3 days Nkr240/340/430, child Nkr100/120/160), sold at the tourist office, is one popular way of cutting transport and ticket costs around the city. The majority of the city's museums are free with the pass, as is public transport within the city limits (barring late-night buses). Other perks include restaurant and tour discounts. Note that if you are planning on just visiting city-centre museums and galleries, many of which are free, it can actually work out more expensive to buy an Oslo Pass than not to!

As most of the exhibits are outdoors, it makes sense to go on a nice day!

Polarship Fram Museum
MUSEUM

(Map p45; www.fram.museum.no; adult/child Nkr60/25, free with Oslo Pass; ☺9am-6pm Jun-Aug, shorter hr rest of yr) Nature is often the best architect. Which is why, when the well-known shipbuilder Colin Archer was asked to design a ship whose hull could withstand the crush of polar ice, he looked no further than an egg for inspiration (this oval design means that when ice is contracting against it the boat is pushed up and onto the ice rather than being merely crushed by it like other ships). Launched in 1892, the *Polarship Fram*, at the time the strongest ship ever built, captained by both Fridtjof Nansen and Roald Amundsen, spent much of its life trapped in the polar ice. From 1893 to 1896 Nansen's North Pole expedition took the 39m schooner to Russia's New Siberian Islands, passing within a few degrees of the North Pole on their return trip to Norway.

In 1910 Amundsen (see p376) set sail in the *Fram* (meaning 'forward'), intending to be the first explorer to reach the North Pole, only to discover en route that Robert Peary had beaten him to it. Not to be outdone, Amundsen turned the *Fram* around and, racing Robert Falcon Scott all the way, became the first man to reach the South Pole. Otto Sverdrup also sailed the schooner around southern Greenland to Canada's Ellesmere Island between 1898 and 1902, travelling over 18,000km.

You're allowed to thoroughly explore the ship, peek inside the cramped bunkrooms and imagine life at sea. In addition, there are detailed exhibits complete with maps, pictures and artefacts that bring the various expeditions to life, from Nansen's attempt to ski across the North Pole to Amundsen's discovery of the Northwest Passage and the fateful rescue attempt that ended in his disappearance.

Kon-Tiki Museum
MUSEUM

(Map p45; www.kon-tiki.no; Bygdøynes; adult/child Nkr60/25, free with Oslo Pass; ☺9.30am-5.30pm Jun-Aug, shorter hr rest of yr; ▮) A favourite among children, this worthwhile museum is dedicated to the balsa raft *Kon-Tiki*, which Norwegian explorer Thor Heyerdahl sailed from Peru to Polynesia in 1947. The museum also displays the totora reed boat *Ra II*, built by Aymara people on the Bolivian island of Suriqui in Lake Titicaca. Heyerdahl used it to cross the Atlantic in 1970. For a full run-down on the life of this extraordinary explorer, see p91.

Norwegian Maritime Museum
MARITIME MUSEUM

(Map p45; www.norsk-sjofartsmuseum.no; Bygdøynesveien 37; adult/child Nkr60/free; ☺10am-6pm mid-May–Aug, shorter hr rest of yr) The author Roald Dahl once said that in Norway everyone seems to have a boat, and there is no better place to explore that theory than at the Norske Sjøfartsmuseum. The museum depicts Norway's relationship with the sea, including the fishing and whaling industries, the seismic fleet (which searches for oil and gas), shipbuilding and wreck salvaging. The highlight for many is a 20-minute film with footage of the Norwegian coastline.

GRÜNERLØKKA AREA

Munch Museum
ART MUSEUM

(Munch-museet; Map p48; www.munch.museum.no; Tøyengata 53; adult/child Nkr75/40, free with Oslo Pass; ☺10am-6pm Jun-Aug, shorter hr rest of yr) Fans of Edvard Munch (1863–1944) won't want to miss the Munch Museum, which is dedicated to his life's work and has most of the pieces not contained in the National Gallery. The museum provides a comprehensive look at the artist's work, from dark (*The Sick Child*) to light (*Spring Ploughing*). With over 1100 paintings, 4500 watercolours and 18,000 prints and sketching books bequeathed to the city by Munch himself, this is a landmark collection. There's free admission between October and April. To get here, take bus 20 or the T-bane to Tøyen, followed by a five-minute signposted walk.

Botanical Garden
GARDENS

(Botanisk Hage; Map p48; Sars gate 1; admission free; ☺7am-9pm Mon-Fri, 10am-5pm Sat & Sun mid-Mar–Sep, shorter hr rest of yr) Oslo's 15-acre Botanical Garden features over 7500 plants from around the world. There are also plants from the Oslo fjords, including four that are almost extinct in nature. However, most visitors don't actually care what the plants are and just content themselves with lolling about under a tree!

Natural History Museum
MUSEUM

(Naturhistorisk Museum; Map p48; www.nhm.uio.no; Sars gate 1; adult/child Nkr50/25; ☺11am-4pm Tue-Sun) Under the trees of Oslo's Botanical Garden, the university's Natural History Museum comprises two different museums: the **Zoological Museum**, which as you might guess is stuffed full of stuffed (excuse

PLEASE DON'T STEAL THE ARTWORK...

On 12 February 1994, the day of the opening ceremony of the Winter Olympics in Lille-hammer, Norwegians woke to the news that arguably the nation's most prized cultural possession, *The Scream,* by Edvard Munch, had been stolen from the National Gallery in Oslo. There was nothing high-tech about this deeply embarrassing incident – a patrolling police officer discovered the theft (carried out by breaking a window and using wire cut-ters) when he found a ladder propped up against the gallery wall. In place of the painting was a note: 'Thanks for the poor security'.

The nation was appalled, even more so when the authorities received a ransom de-mand of US$1 million from people with ties to the anti-abortion movement. A Lutheran minister who had helped plan anti-abortion protests during the Olympics claimed that the painting would be returned if Norwegian national TV broadcasted a graphic film showing a foetus being aborted.

Finally, after almost three months, the Norwegian police discovered four fragments of the painting's frame in the northern Oslo suburb of Nittedal. Within days, Edvard Munch's masterwork, which was painted on fragile paper, was found undamaged in a hotel in As-gardstrand, about 60km south of Oslo. Three Norwegians were arrested and the country breathed a huge collective sigh of relief.

Fast-forward 10 years. On 22 August 2004, two masked, armed men walked into the Munch Museum, threatened a guard, took another version of *The Scream* (Munch paint-ed four versions) as well as another Munch masterpiece, *The Madonna,* and made off with them in a getaway car, all within five minutes and in front of startled gallery visitors. No alarms went off, the police took 15 minutes to arrive and, astonishingly, the paintings were uninsured (gallery officials claimed that the paintings were simply priceless).

Finally, two years and nine days later, the police recovered both paintings and today the bristling security around these works of art provides a somewhat ironic, after-the-fact reminder to keep your hands to yourself.

the pun) native wildlife. Adjacent to this is the **Geological-Palaeontological Museum**, which contains displays on the history of the solar system and Norwegian geology, as well as examples of myriad minerals, meteorites and moon rocks. The palaeontological sec-tion includes *Ida,* the world's oldest com-plete primate fossil. In addition you can ogle a 10m-long iguanodon skeleton and a nest of dinosaur eggs. The admission fee also allows you to get green-fingered with the tropical plants inside the greenhouses.

FREE **Gamle Aker Kirke** CHURCH (Map p48; Akersbakken 26; admission free; ⊙noon-2pm Mon-Sat) This medieval stone church, located north of the centre on Akersbakken, dates from 1080 and is Oslo's oldest building. Take bus 37 from Jernbanetorget to Akersbakken, then walk up past the churchyard.

GREATER OSLO
Holmenkollen Ski Jump & Museum
SKI JUMP & MUSEUM
The **Holmenkollen Ski Jump**, perched on a hilltop overlooking Oslo, offers a panoramic

view of the city and doubles as a concert venue. During Oslo's annual ski festival, held in March, it draws the world's best ski jumpers.

The **Ski Museum** (Map p45; www.skiforenin gen.no; Kongeveien 5; adult/child Nkr90/45, free with Oslo Pass; ⊙9am-8pm Jun-Aug, shorter hr rest of yr) leads you through the 4000-year history of Nordic and downhill skiing in Norway. There are exhibits featuring the Antarctic expeditions of Amundsen and Scott, as well as Fridtjof Nansen's slog across the Greenland icecap (you'll see the boat he constructed from his sled and canvas tent to row the final 100km to Nuuk). Recently redone exhibits on the 2nd floor cover the more modern aspects of skiing and include a glimpse of the royal family on skis.

Admission to the Ski Museum includes a visit to the **ski-jump tower**. Part of the route to the top of the tower is served by a lift, but you're on your own for the final 114 steep steps. Outside, the **ski-jump simula-tor** (adult/child Nkr50/35) is good for a laugh, but don't try it if you have a weak stomach. To get to the museum, take T-bane line 1 to Holmenkollen and follow the signs uphill.

At the time of research the entire complex was closed for renovations, but it is due to reopen before this book hits the shelves.

Nordmarka
FOREST

The woodland north of the Holmenkollen Ski Jump, known as Nordmarka (Map p77), is a prime destination for hiking, mountain biking, sledding and skiing. It's also the geographical centre of the city, which must make Oslo, quite appropriately, about the only capital in the world to have a wild forest at its heart! For skiers, there is **Tryvan Vinterpark**, Oslo's largest skiing area with 14 slopes and six lifts. In the summer, the **Tryvannstårnet observation tower** is a good place to start a hike or a bike trip. The 118m-tall tower is no longer open for visitors, but the view from its base is still fantastic. Make sure to take a container for picking blueberries in summer. From the Holmenkollen T-bane station, take the scenic ride to the end of the line at Frognerseteren and look for the signposted walking route.

Henie-Onstad Art Centre
MODERN ART

(Henie-Onstad Kunstsenter; Map p77; www.hok.no; Høvikodden; adult/child Nkr80/30; ☺11am-7pm Tue-Fri, 11am-5pm Sat & Sun) This private art museum contains works by Joan Miró and Pablo Picasso, as well as assorted impressionist, abstract, expressionist and modern Norwegian works. From Jernbanetorget, take bus 151 to Høvikodden.

🏃 Activities

Avid skiers, hikers and sailors, Oslo residents will do just about anything to get outside. That's not too hard given that there are over 240 sq km of woodland, 40 islands and 343 lakes within the city limits.

Climbing

The best local climbing is on the pre-bolted faces of Kolsåstoppen, which is accessible on T-bane line 3 to Kolsås. Otherwise, there's the largest indoor climbing wall in the Nordic countries at **Myrens Sportssenter** (Map p48; ☏23 22 67 67; www.myrenssportssenter .no, in Norwegian; Sandakervn 24; adult/child from Nkr100/70; ☺9am-11pm Mon-Thu, 9am-9pm Fri, 10am-6pm Sat, 10am-8pm Sun).

Cycling

Mountain bikers will find plenty of trails on which to keep themselves occupied in the Oslo hinterland. The tourist office has free cycling maps, with *Sykkelkart Oslo* tracing the bicycle lanes and paths throughout the city, and *Idrett og friluftsliv i Oslo* covering the Oslo hinterland. It also has a pamphlet called *Opplevelsesturer i Marka,* which contains six possible cycling and/or hiking itineraries within reach of Oslo.

Two especially nice rides within the city (which are also suitable to do on an Oslo city bike) are along the Akerselva up to Lake Maridal (Maridalsvannet; Map p45; 11km) and in the woods around Bygdøy (Map p45). The trip to Maridal will pass several waterfalls and a number of converted factories at the edge of Grünerløkka and cross several of Oslo's more unique bridges, including the Anker, or *eventyr* (fairy-tale), bridge.

Cyclists should be sure to stop for coffee and a waffle at **Hønse-Louisas Hus** (Map p48; Sandakerveien 2; ☺11am-6pm). This can also be done on foot by taking the T-bane to Kjesås and following the path back into the city. Cycling, or walking, around Bygdøy is far more pastoral and provides ample opportunity for swimming breaks. There is a bike rack in front of the Norwegian Folk Museum. For more serious cycling, take T-bane line 1 to Frognerseteren and head into the Nordmarka.

For Norway-wide cycling information and for more detailed maps for the Buskerud region (the area surrounding Oslo), contact **Syklistenes Landsforening** (Map p52; ☏22 47 30 30; www.slf.no, in Norwegian; Storgata 23c; ☺10am-5pm Mon-Fri). It is a local club and not really set up for tourists, but members are happy to help if they can. Ring the bell 10m to the right of the door if it looks closed.

Hiking

A network of 1200km of trails leads into Nordmarka from Frognerseteren (at the end of T-bane line 1), including a good trail down to Sognsvann lake, 6km northwest of the centre at the end of T-bane line 5 (Map p45). If you're walking in August, be sure to take a container for blueberries, and a swimsuit to cool off in the lake (bathing is allowed in all the woodland lakes around Oslo except Maridalsvannet and Skjersjøen lakes, which are drinking reservoirs). The pleasant walk around Sognsvann itself takes around an hour, or for a more extended trip, try hiking to the cabin at **Ullevålseter** (www.ullevalseter .no, in Norwegian; ☺closed Mon), a pleasant old farmhouse that serves waffles and coffee. The round trip (about 11km) takes around three hours.

The Ekeberg woods to the southeast of the city centre (take bus 34 or 46 from

Jernbanetorget) to **Ekeberg Camping** (Map p45) is another nice place for a stroll. During the summer weekends, it's a popular spot for riding competitions and, more recently, cricket matches. There is an Iron Age heritage path through the woods, and for a piece of architectural history don't miss the **Ekeberg Restaurant** (Map p45), one of the earliest examples of functionalism. On the way down, stop at the **Valhall Curve** (Map p45) to see the view that inspired Edvard Munch to paint *The Scream*.

Avid hikers may want to stop by the **DNT office** (Map p52; 40 00 18 68; www.turist foreningen.no; Youngstorget 1; 10am-4pm Mon-Wed & Fri, 10am-6pm Thu, 10am-2pm Sat, open 1hr earlier May-Sep), which maintains several mountain huts in the Nordmarka region and can provide information and maps covering longer-distance hiking routes throughout Norway.

Ice-Skating

At the **Narvisen outdoor ice rink** (Map p52; Karl Johans gate) you can skate for free whenever it's cold enough to freeze over (around November to March). Skates can be hired from the ice rink for around Nkr50.

Skiing

Oslo's ski season is roughly from December to March. There are over 2400km of prepared Nordic tracks (1000km in Nordmarka alone), many of them floodlit, as well as a ski resort within the city limits. Easy-access tracks begin at the end of T-bane lines 1 and 5. The **Skiservice Centre** (22 13 95 04; www .skiservice.no; Tryvannsveien 2), at Voksenkollen station, one T-bane stop before Frognerseteren, hires out snowboards and Nordic skis. The downhill slopes at **Tryvann Vinterpark** (40 46 27 00) are open in the ski season. **Skiforeningen** (Ski Society; Map p45; 22 92 32 00; www.skiforeningen.no; Kongeveien 5) can provide further information on skiing options, or check out www.holmenkollen.com.

Swimming
ISLANDS & BEACHES

When (or perhaps, if) the weather heats up, there are a few reasonable beaches within striking distance of central Oslo. Ferries to half a dozen islands in the Oslofjord region leave from Vippetangen Quay, southeast of Akershus Fortress. Boats to Hovedøya and Langøyene are relatively frequent in summer (running at least hourly), while other islands are served less often. The last ferry leaves Vippetangen at 6.45pm in winter and 9.05pm in summer.

The southwestern shore of otherwise rocky Hovedøya (Map p45), the nearest island to the mainland, is popular with sunbathers. The island is ringed with walking paths to old cannon emplacements and the 12th-century **Cistercian monastery ruins**.

South of Hovedøya lies the undeveloped island of Langøyene (Map p45), which has superb swimming from rocky or sandy beaches (one on the southeastern shore is designated for nude bathing). Boat 94 will get you there.

The Bygdøy Peninsula has two popular beaches, **Huk** (Map p45) and **Paradisbukta** (Map p45), which can be reached on bus 30 from Jernbanetorget to its last stop. While there are some sandy patches, most of Huk comprises grassy lawns and large smooth rocks ideal for sunbathing. Separated into two beaches by a small cove, the beach on the northwestern side is open to nude bathing. If Huk seems too crowded, a 10-minute walk through the woods north of the bus stop leads to the more secluded Paradisbukta.

SWIMMING POOLS

Oslo has two outdoor municipal swimming pools: **Frognerbadet Swimming Pool** (Map p48; 23 27 54 50; Middelthuns gate 28; mid-May–mid-Aug) in Frognerparken (entry via Middelthuns gate); and **Tøyenbadet Swimming Pool** (Map p48; 23 30 44 70; Helgesens gata 90), which is near the Munch Museum. Entry costs the same for both pools (adult/child Nkr78/37).

Tours

The best Oslo tours offer juicy cultural and historical morsels (or a boat trip), while also giving visitors the flexibility to explore at their leisure.

OSLO FOR CHILDREN

After the long, dark winter nights, the arrival of spring and summer brings masses of baby carriages out onto the streets (we wonder if there is a connection between said long, dark nights and the amount of children in Oslo...). Despite this, Oslo is not one of Europe's more child-friendly cities, as many of the sights and restaurants are aimed squarely at adults, and it can sometimes feel as if children are tolerated more than welcomed. Note also that most of the museums and galleries insist on making you use one of their own baby carriages – something guaranteed to please every parent who has just managed to get their little darling off to sleep!

Despite this, you can still visit Oslo with children and enjoy the experience. Most Oslo parents will tell you that the best activities are often the simplest and free. There are no rules against climbing the statues at Frognerparken, for example, or chasing your little sister around the garden's 3000m mosaic labyrinth. The park also has one of the city's best playgrounds. Nearer the centre, the cannons and fortifications at Akershus Fortress are great for sparking the imagination.

More-organised summer activities include taking an hourly **Thomas Train City Tour** (www.thomastoget.com; adult/child/under 3yr Nkr70/30/free; ◷11am-5pm Mon-Sat mid-Jun-Aug) or the twice-hourly **Oslo Toget** (www.oslotoget.no; adult/child/under 3yr Nkr70/30/free; ◷10am-9pm Mon-Sat mid-Jun-Aug), which is another cheerfully painted open-air train. Both do a loop around the city centre. Tours begin every half-hour in front of the Paléet shopping centre (Map p48) and Aker Brygge shopping complex (Map p52). There's a Christmas train in December.

For a more rural experience, try the **EKT Riding School and Husdyrpark** (EKT Rideskole and Husdyrpark; Map p45; ☎22 19 97 86; www.rideskole.no, in Norwegian; Bekkelagshøgda 12; pony rides Nkr170) in the Ekeberg forest southeast of the city centre. There are sheep, goats, pigs and rabbits, as well as Norwegian fjord ponies. Take tram 19 towards Ljabru to Sportsplassen and walk 15 minutes uphill until you reach the farm. The **Norwegian Folk Museum** (p57) also has regular events geared towards children. For something more slippery, most kids will love meeting the snakes and lizards (as well as the odd monkey) at the **Oslo Reptilpark** (Map p52; www.reptilpark.no, in Norwegian; St Olavs gate 2; adult/child Nkr100/70, free with Oslo Pass; ◷10am-6pm Apr-Aug).

In the winter, try sledding down the 'legendary' **Korketrekkeren** (corkscrew) toboggan run. The 2km-long track drops 255m and began its life as a bobsledding run for the 1952 Olympics. Sleds can be rented at the **Akerforeningen** (www.akeforeningen.no, in Norwegian; adult/child from Nkr80/50; ◷9am-9pm Mon-Sat, 10am-6pm Sun during winter), next to the Frognerseteren restaurant. To get here, take the T-bane to Frognerseteren and follow the signs downhill.

A popular rainy day distraction is the **Norwegian Science & Technology Museum** (Norsk Teknisk Museum & Telemuseum; Map p45; www.tekniskmuseum.no; Kjelsåsveien 143; adult/child Nkr80/40, free with Oslo Pass; ◷10am-6pm mid-Jun–mid-Aug, shorter hr rest of yr) near Lake Maridal, which has Norway's first car and tram, water wheels, clocks and enough gadgetry to keep the whole family busy for a few hours at least.

Finally, **TusenFryd** (Map p77; www.tusenfryd.no, in Norwegian; Vinterbro; height over/under 120cm Nkr265/216; ◷10.30am-7pm mid-Jun–Sep, shorter hr rest of yr), an amusement park 10km south of the city, is enormously popular with kids from all over the Buskerud region. The park offers carousels, a fantasy farm and an excellent wooden rollercoaster, which creates zero gravity 12 times each circuit. You'll find it just off the E6. The Tusen-Fryd bus (bus number 546; Nkr60) departs from the corner of Fred Olsens gate and Prinsens gate (Map p52) roughly hourly between 10am and 4pm.

City Sightseeing BUS TOUR
(www.citysightseeing.no; ◷May-Sep) Oslo's version of the hop-on, hop-off phenomenon. Tickets cost from Nkr150/80 per adult/child, are valid for 24 hours, and cover the overwhelming proportion of city sights, which you can explore at your own pace. The tourist office has a list of stops that this tour company goes to.

Oslo Promenade
WALKING TOUR

(www.guideservice.no; adult/child Nkr100/free; ☉5.30pm Mon, Wed & Fri Jun-Aug) Another tour option is to go on a 1½-hour evening city walk starting from in front of the Rådhus (town hall). The guides are knowledgeable and entertaining, making this a good option for getting an insider's view of Oslo.

Båtservice Sightseeing
BOAT TOUR

(Map p52; www.boatsightseeing.com; Pier 3, Rådhusbrygge) For a more comprehensive package, or if you want to get out on the water, try Båtservice Sightseeing, which does a whole array of watery tours aboard either a traditional wooden schooner or a more up-to-date motor boat. Some tours are also combined with bus rides. Prices set sail from Nkr170.

✯✯ Festivals & Events

Oslo's most festive annual event is surely the 17 May **National Constitution Day** celebration, when Oslo residents, whose roots spring from all over Norway, descend on the Royal Palace dressed in the finery of their native districts. For details on all upcoming events in the city, take a look at www.visitoslo.com.

Other Oslo festivals of note include the following:

Inferno Metal Festival
MUSIC

(www.infernofestival.net; ☉late Apr) This festival lets the dark lords of heavy metal loose on the good people of Oslo.

Norwegian Wood Festival
MUSIC

(www.norwegianwood.no; ☉Jun) Oslo plays host to dozens of music festivals but this is one of the bigger ones. The 2010 event saw Van Morrison as one of many performers.

Oslo International Jazz Festival
JAZZ

(www.oslojazz.no; ☉Aug) Jazz and Oslo's long summer evenings go well together. This festival brings big names to the city.

Oslo Opera Festival
OPERA

(www.operafestival.no; ☉Sep) Live opera fills the concert halls and even the streets of Oslo for three weeks in September.

Oslo World Music Festival
MUSIC

(www.osloworldmusicfestival.no; ☉early Nov) It's not just the West that can make music. The rest of the planet's diverse rhythms are showcased at this world-music festival, which also includes lots of child-friendly events.

🛏 Sleeping

Oslo has plenty of accommodation, including a growing number of small B&Bs, which offer more character than the chain hotels. However, compared to many other parts of Europe, standards are generally fairly low.

OSLO

TOP CHOICE **Ellingsens Pensjonat**
PENSION €

(Map p48; ☎22 60 03 59; www.ellingsenspensjonat.no, in Norwegian; Holtegata 25; s/d Nkr480/670, with shared bathroom Nkr400/580) Located in a quiet, pleasant neighbourhood, this homey pension offers one of the best deals in the capital. The building dates from 1890 and many of the original features (high ceilings, rose designs) remain. Rooms are bright and airy, with refrigerators and kettles, and there's a small garden to lounge about in on sunny days. There's no exterior sign, but it's the big white house. It's a popular place, so reservations are a must in the summer.

TOP CHOICE **Grims Grenka**
DESIGN HOTEL €€€

(Map p52; ☎23 10 72 00; www.grimsgrenka.no; Kongens gate 5; s/d from Nkr1395/1595; P�) Oslo's answer to the exclusive, cosmopolitan experience offered by boutique hotels in London and New York, Grims Grenka has minimalist, modern rooms, a hipster rooftop bar, an Asian-fusion restaurant and

---

DON'T MISS

THE GREENEST FESTIVAL?

Music festivals aren't renowned for their green credentials, but the **Øya Festival** (www.oyafestivalen.com; ☉Aug), the largest rock and indie music festival in Norway, is an exception to the rule. The four festival stages are powered through renewable energy, all rubbish is recycled, and maybe most impressively, the sewage generated by the 16,000 festival goers is converted into bio-fuel and used to power the buses that take people to and from central Oslo and the festival grounds.

The Øya Festival attracts some of the biggest names in the rock and indie scene, with performers at the 2010 festival including the Flaming Lips, Air, LCD Soundsystem and Paul Weller as well as nearly 200 other bands. In addition there are all the normal festival sideshows.

is, without doubt, one of the most exciting hotels in Oslo.

Cochs Pensjonat
HOTEL €

(Map p48; ☑23 33 24 00; www.cochspensjonat.no; Parkveien 25; s/d from Nkr580/780, with shared bathroom Nkr480/680; 🛜) Opened as a guesthouse for bachelors in the 1920s, the very good value Cochs has sparsely furnished, clean rooms, some of which have kitchenettes. It's ideally located behind the Royal Palace. The rooms at the back overlooking the Slottsparken are especially spacious. There is a luggage room. The hotel offers a discounted breakfast buffet at a coffee shop around the corner for Nkr65.

P-Hotel
HOTEL €€

(Map p52; ☑80 04 68 35; www.p-hotels.com; Grensen 19; s/d Nkr795/995; @🛜) In addition to offering some of the best prices in central Oslo, the P-Hotel has comfortable if slightly dull rooms with decent bathrooms. Breakfast, which is put in a bag and delivered to your door, is included. There are tea- and coffee-making facilities in the rooms. This hotel couldn't be much more central.

Thon Hotel Astoria
CHAIN HOTEL €€

(Map p52; ☑24 14 55 56; www.thonhotels.com; Dronningens gate 21; s Nkr760-1110, d Nkr1025-1375; 🛜) This might be marketed as a Thon 'budget' hotel, but if it weren't for the slightly smaller than normal bathroom and the lack of a minibar or pay TV, there would be nothing to distinguish this hotel from some much more expensive options. It's well positioned close to the train station, but the only nearby parking is on the street.

Anker Hostel
HOSTEL €

(Map p52; ☑22 99 72 00; www.ankerhostel .no; Storgata 55; 6-/8-bed dm with bathroom Nkr220/210, r from Nkr580; P@🛜) This huge traveller-savvy hostel boasts an international atmosphere, spick-and-span rooms, laundry, luggage room, kitchens (some rooms also contain kitchens) and small bar. Breakfast costs an extra Nkr55, linen Nkr50 and parking Nkr175 per 24 hours. The location isn't very scenic, but it's convenient, with Grünerløkka and the city centre only a five-minute walk away.

Grand Hotel
HISTORIC HOTEL €€€

(Map p52; ☑23 21 20 00; www.grand.no; Karl Johans gate 31; s Nkr1395-2160, d Nkr1495-2260; P@🛜☀) Brimming with period character, the regal Grand Hotel has long been considered the benchmark of true elegance in

Oslo. The rooms are beautifully appointed and classy without being overdone. If you book early enough, some fantastic bargains are available.

Anker Hotel
BUDGET HOTEL €€

(Map p52; ☑22 99 75 00; www.anker-hotel.no; Storgata 55; s/d from Nkr790/990; P@🛜) Owned by the same people as the neighbouring Anker Hostel, this could be described as a 'budget business hotel' and the plain and simple rooms are perfect for those who feel a bit too old for the hostel. A reasonable breakfast is included.

Oslo Budget Hotel
BUDGET HOTEL €

(Map p52; ☑22 41 36 10; www.budgethotel.no; Prinsens gate 6; s Nkr499-599, d Nkr599-799; @🛜) Don't expect any fancy frills, but otherwise this place does what it says on the label and provides cheap, clean and central accommodation that most guests find to their liking. The more expensive 'standard' rooms come with attached bathrooms, while the budget rooms have shared bathrooms. A fairly measly breakfast is Nkr59 extra; you're better off going to a nearby cafe or bakery.

Thon Hotel Spectrum
CHAIN HOTEL €€

(Map p52; ☑23 36 27 00; www.thonhotels.com; Brugata 7; s Nkr660-1110, d Nkr925-1375; @🛜) Bright purple sofas and equally purple flowers adorn the reception area, and the comfortable and well-priced rooms are noteworthy for their huge windows and fairly small bathrooms. Sadly, staff don't exactly rush forward to help guests.

Perminalen Hotel
HOSTEL €

(Map p52; ☑23 09 30 81; www.perminalen.no; Øvre Slottsgate 2; dm with bathroom Nkr370, s/d Nkr620/840; 🛜) Perminalen has a barracks feel, but tidy rooms and a central location make up for the sterile, dormitory atmosphere. Prices include linen and a simple breakfast, which you can eat outside in the summer.

Rica Victoria Hotel
CHAIN HOTEL €€€

(Map p52; ☑24 14 70 00; www.rica-hotels.com; Rosenkrantz gate 13; s Nkr895-1845, d Nkr900-1845; P@🛜) This straightforward business hotel, located between Aker Brygge and Karl Johans gate, is more used to hosting businessmen than tourists, but if you snag a room during a special offer then you won't be disappointed. It has a few converted rooms for guests with disabilities.

One of the cheapest ways of staying in Oslo, and one that promises a much more personable stay than anything a hotel can offer, is to take a room in one of the city's handful of B&Bs. **B&B Norway** (www.bbnorway.com) is an online source of information that lists many of Norway's better-established B&Bs. The tourist office can also point you towards some options (but only if you visit in person).

The following are a few possibilities, but do note that none of these properties have been individually checked by our authors.

Den Blå Dør B&B (☑22 19 99 44; Skedsmogata 7; s/d Nkr400/550) Breakfast Nkr50.

Mary's Bed and Breakfast (☑22 92 17 71; kjell.pedersen@chello.no; Jerpefaret 15b; s/d Nkr400/700)

Anna's Place (☑67 58 92 68; annasplacenorway@hotmail.com; Myrveien 2b, Jar; tw Nkr800)

Blue Room (☑66 84 90 10; tmamen@attglobal.net; Neåsen 11c, Nesbru; s/d Nkr700/900)

B&B Poppe (☑22 23 70 66; midoripoppe@msn.com; Carl Kjelsens vei 15; s/d Nkr250/500; ⊘closed Jul)

Frogner Guestroom (☑22 55 21 30; www.baktruppen.org/frogner_guestroom.html; Baldersgate 11a; s/d Nkr500/700)

Høvik B&B (☑41 77 33 42; linejen2@online.no; Granalleen 44, Høvik; per person Nkr375-500)

If you're still lucky enough to be under 26, **Use-It** (Map p52; ☑22 41 51 32; www.use-it.no; Møllergata 3), the Oslo Youth Information Service, will also help with bookings at hostels and private homes; there's no minimum stay and bookings are free.

GREATER OSLO

Holmenkollen Park Hotel Rica

HISTORIC HOTEL €€

(Map p45; ☑22 92 20 00; www.holmenkollenparkhotel.no; Kongeveien 26; r Nkr695-1135; ❗@❷❀) Founded in 1891 as a sanatorium by Dr Ingebrigt Christian Lund, this castle-like hotel offers luxury, history, great views and, all things considered, a very reasonable price. If that weren't enough, you also get a vast breakfast buffet, complete with organic produce.

Oslo Vandrerhjem Haraldsheim   HOSTEL €

(Map p45; ☑22 22 29 65; www.haraldsheim.no; Haraldsheim-veien 4; dm from Nkr245, s/d Nkr470/625, with shared bathroom Nkr415/540, all incl breakfast; @) A pleasant, if hard to find, hostel 4km from the city centre. It has 24-hour reception and 268 beds, mostly in clean four-bed dorms. There are kitchen and laundry facilities. Linen costs Nkr50. Take tram 12, 15 or 17, or bus 31 or 32 to Sinsenkrysset, then walk five minutes uphill.

Ekeberg Camping   CAMPGROUND €

(Map p45; ☑22 19 85 68; www.ekebergcamping.no; Ekebergveien 65; 4-person tent with/without car Nkr260/180; ⊘1 Jun-1 Sep; ❗) Nestled on a scenic knoll southeast of the city, Ekeberg Camping provides one of the best views over Oslo. It can get seriously crowded, and facilities (kitchen, laundry, convenience store and showers) aren't as well maintained as they could be. Take bus 34 or 46 from Jernbanetorget to Ekeberg Camping (10 minutes).

Bogstad Camping   CAMPGROUND €

(Map p45; ☑22 51 08 00; www.bogstadcamping.no; Ankerveien 117; tent with/without car from Nkr260/180, cabins Nkr440-1285; ⊘yr-round; ❗) Located at the edge of the Nordmarka, Bogstad Camping is ideal for enjoying the Oslo outdoors. However, as one of northern Europe's largest campsites, it can get very busy. The facilities include showers and communal kitchen, and there is a nearby kiosk and restaurant. It's 9km north of the city centre. To get here, take bus 32 from Oslo S (about 30 minutes).

✕ Eating

In the past, going to a restaurant in Oslo meant parting with great wads of cash for very little that could be called good food. Luckily, this began to change in the late '90s, and though costs are still high, today there are plenty of places to choose from. If you're after a healthy meal that won't break the bank, the secret is to think Asian and African. Oslo is full of decent Indian,

Thai, Vietnamese, Ethiopian and Somalian restaurants where a proper meal normally costs about half that of a standard Norwegian restaurant.

For the ultimate snack try a *polse* (hot dog) in a *lumpe* (potato cake) for Nkr18 or a waffle with sour cream and strawberry jam.

OSLO

TOP CHOICE **Feinschmecker**   GOURMET €€€

(Map p48; ☎22 12 93 80; www.feinschmecker.no, in Norwegian; Balchens gate 5; set menus Nkr695) If you're starting to think Norwegian food is all about burgers and pizzas, this absolutely sublime restaurant, with its modern take on old Norwegian dishes, will quickly make you change your mind. The crayfish soup and lamb with wild mushrooms are out of this world. Despite the quality of the food and the high prices, the atmosphere is surprisingly laid-back. Book ahead.

TOP CHOICE **Baltazar**   ITALIAN €€€

(Map p52; ☎23 35 70 60; www.baltazar.no; Dronningens gate 27; mains Nkr250-325, set menus from Nkr595; ☉dinner Mon-Sat) Located in the bazaar halls of the cathedral, Baltazar serves up sublime Italian classics with a thoroughly modern twist. It's one of those places where the food is as much art as something to eat. There's also a good wine list. During the summer (when the owners are in Lucca, Italy), the main restaurant is closed and lunch is served at Trattoria Cappuccino, in the leafy courtyard behind the cathedral.

Rust   INTERNATIONAL €

(Map p48; ☎23 20 22 10; Hegehaugsveien 22; snacks & light meals Nkr36-59, mains Nkr119-129) On a small side street lined with cafes and restaurants, Rust is bright, colourful and 100% modern Oslo. It has plenty of outdoor seating and loads of blankets for when it gets cold. Good for a quiet cocktail, burgers, hearty salads or tapas late into the night.

Café Sara   PUB FOOD €€

(Map p52; ☎22 03 40 00; Haumanns gate 29; mains Nkr119-180; ☉11am-2.30am) Despite the light and airy name, this is a dark but warm English-style pub serving a hearty mix of Norwegian and British dishes as well as pizzas and Tex-Mex. The house special is a meat stew with corn, rice and potatoes – perfect for a cold winter's night. Tuesday is Girls Beer Night and is something of a well-known lesbian get-together.

Café Skansen   MEDITERRANEAN €€

(Map p52; ☎24 20 13 11; www.cafeskansen.no, in Norwegian; Rådhusgata 32; pasta & salad mains Nkr90-180) One of the new wave of sophisticated cafes and restaurants currently taking Oslo by storm. As in many such places, this one looks south to the Mediterranean for style and taste – and on sunny summer days its outdoor terrace does indeed feel very far from the popular images of a frozen Norway.

Theatercafeen   TRADITIONAL €€€

(Map p52; ☎22 82 40 50; Stortingsgata 24/26; small dishes Nkr98-154, mains Nkr190-318) A favourite with Norwegian families during Christmas and on 17 May, the Theatercafeen, located directly across from the National Theatre, presents Norwegian classics in posh Viennese surroundings. Favourites include the reindeer steak with mushrooms and whortleberries. At the time of research,

GAY & LESBIAN OSLO

Oslo is a liberal, gay-friendly city in an already liberal country, which makes for a relaxed gay/lesbian scene. Favourite watering holes include the mixed scene at **Elsker** (Map p52; Kristian IV's gate 9), meaning lover in Norwegian, which has a 'kind of Eurovision schläger-musical profile', according to local Øyvind Gjengaar; and the dark basement at **London Pub** (Map p52; www.londonpub.no; CJ Hambros plass 5; cover charge Nkr40), Oslo's oldest gay bar. The parties at **Stratos** (Map p52; www.stratos.as, in Norwegian; Youngstorget 2; cover Nkr100-150) are also popular.

At the end of June, don't miss **Skeive Dager** (www.skeivedager.no, in Norwegian), Oslo's Gay Pride week complete with a parade, art exhibits, concerts and other events. Girls Beer Night at **Café Sara** (Map p52; ☎22 03 40 00; Haumanns gate 29) every Tuesday evening is a good place for lesbians to meet up.

For more information, the *Streetwise* guide published by Use-It (p73) has a 'Gay Guide', which covers cafes, pubs, clubs, bookstores and activities. Or for a truly insider scoop, ask someone to translate the weekly guide from *Blikk* (www.blikk.no), Oslo's gay and lesbian magazine.

it was closed for renovations but was expected to reopen shortly.

Pizza da Mimmo
ITALIAN €€
(Map p48; ✎22 44 40 20; Behrensgate 2; pizza around Nkr150) Despite the vast quantity of pizza places in Oslo, and Norway in general, actually getting a decent, authentic Italian pizza remains something of a challenge. This family-run basement restaurant serves what is arguably the best pizza in Oslo and is justifiably popular; book ahead on weekends.

Gates of India
INDIAN €€
(Map p48; ✎22 69 09 33; www.gateofindia.no, in Norwegian; Bogstadveien 66a; lunch specials Nkr149, mains Nkr150-200; ⊙3-10pm Mon, 3-11pm Tue-Sat, 2-10pm Sun) Upstairs across from the Majorstuen T-bane station, Gates of India is a little pricey, but for scrumptious subcontinental flavours in a fairly refined atmosphere, it's hard to beat. The service is slow.

Grand Café
NORWEGIAN €€
(Map p52; ✎23 24 20 18; Karl Johans gate 31; mains Nkr120-275) At 11am sharp, Henrik Ibsen would leave his apartment on Drammensveien (now Henrik Ibsens gate) and walk to Grand Café for a lunch of herring, beer and one shot of aquavit (alcoholic drink made from potatoes and caraway liquor). His table is still here. Don't worry, though, there's more than herring on the menu. Take your pick from reindeer, Arctic char and mussels and chips.

Tullins Café
INTERNATIONAL €
(Map p52; ✎22 20 46 16; Tullins gate 2; snacks & light meals Nkr69-108) This dimly lit cafe offers a little bit of everything, from salads and burgers to pasta and stir-fry dishes. It's a favourite among students.

Taste of the Far East
ASIAN €
(Map p52; ✎22 20 56 28; Bernt Ankersgate 6b; lunch menu Nkr88; ⊙1pm-midnight) As the name suggests, it's light and healthy Thai and Vietnamese curries, soups and noodles at this popular restaurant.

Japo Sushi
JAPANESE €
(Map p48; ✎22 55 55 11; Frognerveien 1; lunch menus Nkr100) Given that Norwegians cheerfully down pickled herring for breakfast, it shouldn't be too surprising that Oslo has some good sushi. Japo is one fast option of many.

AKER BRYGGE
Aker Brygge, the old shipyard turned trendy shopping complex west of the main harbour,

has a **food court** (⊙11am-10pm) with various eateries and waterside restaurants.

If the weather is nice, the local meal of choice is peel-and-eat shrimp, eaten dockside with a fresh baguette, mayonnaise and just a touch of lemon. **Fishermen's Coop** (Map p52; Rådhusbrygge 3/4; ⊙7am-5pm Tue-Sat; shrimp per kg Nkr120), during summer, is a good place to buy shrimp, or, on Thursdays, keep an eye out for one of Norway's richest men, Kjell Inge Røkkes, who can be found selling shrimp from his boat *Trygg*.

People & Coffee
INTERNATIONAL €
(Map p52; www.peopleandcoffee.com, in Norwegian; Rådhusgata 21; mains Nkr59-140, lunch specials Nkr139; ⊙breakfast & lunch) Much more than a mere coffee shop, this friendly place offers one of the city centre's best-value lunch deals with hot, filling meals such as chilli con carne, soups that are just the ticket on a cold winter's day, salads and the best carrot cake we have had in Oslo (and we've tried a lot!).

Solsiden
SEAFOOD €€€
(Map p52; ✎22 33 36 30; Søndre Akershus Kai 34; starters Nkr125-155, mains Nkr185-295; ⊙May-Sep) Solsiden means 'sunny side' in Norwegian, which explains why this place is so popular among sun-craving locals. Located inside a grey warehouse, and often overlooked by massive cruise ships, on the opposite side of Pipervika from Aker Brygge, Solsiden serves up some of the city's best seafood and has an ideal view over the fjord.

AROUND OSLO S & GRØNLAND

TOP CHOICE Punjab Tandoori
INDIAN €
(Map p48; ✎22 17 20 86; Grøn-landsleiret 24; mains Nkr70-85) Full of the richness and flavours of the north of the subcontinent, this simple canteen-style affair serves spot-on curries that would stand out in India let alone Oslo. It's a real neighbourhood institution for the local Asian community and Norwegians in the know.

Mama Africa
ETHIOPIAN €
(Map p52; ✎96 65 05 99; Galleriet Oslo, Scweigaardgt 12; mains Nkr109-139; ⊙3-11pm) With walls adorned with tourist posters proclaiming the wonders of Ethiopia and a cool, jazzy African soundtrack on the stereo, this is a perfect place in which to try *injera* and *wat*. Despite the fact that it's a tamed-down version of what you'd find in the mountains of Ethiopia, we still guarantee you've never eaten anything like this before. Oh, and that's

DON'T MISS

CAFES

Fact: unaided by Starbucks, Norwegians drink more coffee per capita than any other nationality. And while most coffee drinking happens at home, preferably alongside waffles, in Oslo there is a good selection of coffee bars. Most cafes offer toothsome open-faced sandwiches to snack on, topped with *gulost* (yellow cheese) or mayonnaise and shrimps. *Boller* (raisin rolls) and *skolebrød* (pastry with vanilla cream filling) are also popular. The following are just a few of our favourites.

Kaffebrenneriet (Map p52; www.kaffebrenneriet.no; Universtetsgata 1; ⊙7am-7pm Mon-Fri, 9am-5pm Sat, 10am-5pm Sun) Opposite the National Gallery, this relaxed cafe has dozens of different types of coffee (including packets to take away), cakes, yoghurts and other tasty snacks. All of which make it a great place to refuel before an assault on the gallery.

Zagros Café (Map p52; Storgata 34; ⊙10am-6pm Mon-Sat, noon-8pm Sun) Kick back on a sofa and argue with yourself about which of the sweet and rich honey-coated Indian or Middle Eastern cakes on sale will go best with your strong Italian coffee.

Stockfleths (Map p52; Lille Grensen) Founded in 1895, the award-winning Stockfleths is one of Oslo's oldest coffee shops. It also serves thick slices of wholegrain bread with brown cheese, a favourite Norwegian snack.

Åpent Bakerei (Map p48; ☑22 04 96 67; Inkognito terasse 1; ⊙7.30am-5pm Mon-Fri, 8am-3pm Sat) A neighbourhood cafe that serves coffee in deep, cream-coloured bowls and has unbeatable breads and pastries. A freshly baked roll topped with homemade *røre syltetøy* (stirred jam) and enjoyed on the bakery's patio makes for one of Oslo's best and least expensive breakfasts.

---

not a tablecloth, that's the *injera,* and yes, you do eat it! It's on the 1st floor of the Galleriet Oslo, above the bus station.

Teddy's Soft Bar　　　RETRO AMERICAN €
(Map p52; ☑22 17 36 00; Brugata 3a; light meals from Nkr85; ⊙lunch & dinner Mon-Sat) The jukebox in the corner gives Teddy's Soft Bar a flavour of 1950s USA. It's something of a local institution that has scarcely changed in decades. It's rumoured to have the best burgers in town as well as that other 1950s America favourite – milkshakes.

Salaama Restaurant　　　SOMALIAN €
(Map p48; ☑41 55 59 62; Motzfeldtsgata 5; mains Nkr50-80) What did you do today? Oh, I went to some little Somali joint I know and had a typical Somali breakfast of *canjeero iyo beer,* which is fermented bread mixed with liver and spices.

Mithas the Sweethouse　　　SWEETS €
(Map p52; ☑22 17 03 03; Grønland 2a) A couple of the delectable Iranian sweets that fill the glass counters here are the perfect end to a meal at the nearby Punjab Tandoori.

Red Sea Star　　　ERITREAN €
(Map p52; Storgata 45; mains Nkr89; ⊙1-11pm Tue-Fri, 3-10pm Sat) Wrap your lips around

some *kai wat* or spicy food at this friendly Eritrean-run place.

GRÜNERLØKKA AREA

Oslo's Greenwich Village, while always lively and frequented by a well-dressed, youthful crowd, is especially pleasant in the summer when life spills out onto the sidewalks from the numerous cafes, bars and restaurants around Olaf Ryes plass.

TOP CHOICE **Markveien Mat & Vinhus**

MODERN NORWEGIAN €€€
(Map p48; ☑22 37 22 97; Torvbakkgt 12; mains Nkr240-290, 3 courses Nkr495) With a hint of truffle oil or a dash of dill, the cooks at Markveien make Norwegian cooking unforgettable. The restaurant focuses on using local seafood and meat, as well as organic produce, to create its delectable dishes. You shouldn't miss the house specials of either lamb or crayfish.

Dr Kneipp's Vinbar　　　INTERNATIONAL €€
(Map p48; ☑22 37 22 97; Torvbakkgt 12; mains Nkr115-300) If you're not in the mood for the formal dining room of Markveien Mat & Vinhus, slide into one of the dark wooden booths at Dr Kneipp's next door for finger food with a strong Spanish and Italian flavour or a sumptuous dessert (the cheesecake

is legendary), not to mention an amazing 400-strong wine list. Another plus for the place is the super-friendly staff.

Sult   MODERN NORWEGIAN €€
(Map p48; ☑67 10 99 70; www.sult.no; Thorvald Meyers gate 26; lunch mains Nkr99-139, dinner menu Nkr355) Sult has a polished green-and-black colour scheme and perfectly captures the Grünerløkka vibe with an imaginative menu replete with superb fish and pasta dishes often using local and organic ingredients. It's always packed, so get here early and wait for a table in the attached bar appropriately called Tørst (meaning 'thirsty').

Bistro Brocante   FRENCH €€
(Map p48; ☑22 35 68 71; Thorvald Meyers gate 40; lunch specials Nkr59-129, starters Nkr96-102, mains Nkr192-199) This informal French-inspired cafe serving simple French snacks and typical bistro dishes (dinner only) has some fantastic salads, quiches and even coq au vin. The outdoor tables are at a premium in summer.

Fru Hagen   INTERNATIONAL €€
(Map p48; ☑22 38 24 26; Thorvald Meyers gate 40; mains Nkr118-137) The low-key and always full Fru Hagen (Mrs Garden) serves sandwiches and burgers, all with a healthy side portion of vegetables. The juicy vegie burger is well worth scoffing. Its location facing Olaf Ryes plass also makes it good for people-watching.

Mucho Mas   MEXICAN €€
(Map p48; ☑22 37 16 09; www.muchomas.no; Thorvald Meyers gate 36; burritos from Nkr145) What it lacks in authenticity, Mucho Mas more than makes up for in cheese and portion size. The full Mexican repertoire is on offer, including tacos, nachos and burritos (which are enormous); all dishes are offered in meat or vegetarian versions. Well-priced beer helps put out the fire.

Hotel Havana   DELI €
(Map p48; Thorvald Meyers gate 38; ⊙10am-6pm Mon-Fri) International deli with everything from French cheese to Belgian chocolates. The chorizo and manchego sandwiches (Nkr55) are an especially good bet, and coffee is also served (of course!).

VÅLERENGA & EKEBERG

TOP CHOICE **Smia Galleri**   MODERN NORWEGIAN €€€
(Map p45; ☑22 19 59 20; Opplandsgata 19; mains Nkr185-230) Smia Galleri is one of those places Oslo residents are so fond of they almost hate to share it. The leafy patio is perfect on summer afternoons and there's jazz on Thursday evenings. If the restaurant has it, try the rhubarb crumble with wild strawberry sorbet. It takes about 15 minutes to get here: from Oslo S, take bus 37 towards Helsfyr T-bane station and get off at Vålerenga.

DON'T MISS

AFRICA IN OSLO

Oslo, as you'll quickly notice, has a large south Asian and African immigrant community. Many of these Africans are refugees who've fled civil war, internal strife or political repression in Somalia, Ethiopia and Eritrea. This has led to a flurry of Ethiopian and Somalian restaurants opening up in certain neighbourhoods of the city, and for something really different, you shouldn't miss the opportunity to eat out in one of these restaurants. We guarantee you'll never have tasted anything quite like Ethiopian food!

We cornered Issak Abdi and Sugaal Rashid, two refugees from southern Somalia, and asked them where and what to eat in order to get a flavour of the tastes of the Horn of Africa. Here are their suggestions.

Salaama Restaurant in Grønland is a good place to try Somalian food. In Somalia we eat a lot of rice and spaghetti, but you should try *suqaar*, which is strips of meat with onions and spices. Or try the rice and fish; the fish is cooked in a very special way that makes it delicious.

For Ethiopian food a favourite place is **Mama Africa**, near the city centre. It has a very relaxing atmosphere and is a romantic place to go. It serves *injera* but a favourite is *special tibs*, which is brought to the table still cooking. It makes us feel like we're still in Africa. And you must try the coffee. Ethiopian coffee is the best in the world.

Red Sea Star is also good, but it's expensive. It's an Eritrean restaurant, but there is no real difference between that and Ethiopian food.

ATTENTION SELF-CATERERS & HOME DRINKERS

Anyone aged over 18 can buy beer at Oslo supermarkets until 8pm from Monday to Friday and 6pm on Saturday. For wine or spirits, you'll have to be at least 20 years old and visit the **Vinmonopolet** (Map p52; Oslo City Shopping Centre; ⊘10am-5pm Mon-Wed, 10am-6pm Thu, 9am-6pm Fri, 10am-2pm Sat). There are a number of other branches throughout the city.

The Grønland district and the backstreets east of Storgata are brimming with inexpensive ethnic supermarkets where you'll find otherwise unavailable items such as fresh herbs and African, Asian and Middle Eastern ingredients. One such place is the excellent **Nor Brothers** (Map p52; Storgata 34; ⊘8am-10pm Mon-Sat), which also has a fruit and veg section that surpasses any of the big supermarkets for quality and price. **Grønland Bazaar** (Map p48; Tøyengata 2) is a Middle Eastern–themed shopping centre, while **Rimi Supermarket** (Map p52; Storgata 32; ⊘8am-10pm Mon-Sat) is a standard all-purpose grocery chain; another branch can be found at Oslo S.

Ekeberg Restaurant NORWEGIAN €€€
(Map p45; ☎23 24 23 00; www.ekebergrestauranten.com; Kongsveien 15; mains Nkr220, set menus from Nkr375) An early example of functionalist architecture, the 1929 Ekeberg Restaurant once attracted long lines of spectators eager to be seen enjoying a beer outside this angular, painfully white, nonconformist building. After falling into disrepair in the 1980s, the restaurant was renovated and reopened with a classy menu and a slick bar. If nothing else, go for the view.

HOLMENKOLLEN AREA
Frognerseteren Restaurant NORWEGIAN €€€
(☎22 92 40 40; www.frognerseteren.no; mains Nkr145-345; ⊘11am-10pm Mon-Sat, 11am-9pm Sun) There are three good reasons to visit Frognerseteren: the apple cake, the view and the building. The apple cake (Nkr98) is billed as the best in Oslo and the view, from over 400m above sea level, is as good as it gets. As for the building, with dragon heads and enough wood trim to rival the most ornate Swiss chalet, it is the epitome of the Viking revival style popular in the 1860s.

BYGDØY PENINSULA
The Bygdøy Peninsula (Map p45) doesn't have a lot to offer hungry museum goers aside from a couple of highly overpriced cafes in or around the museums. Generally we'd recommend taking a picnic lunch with you. There is, however, one exception.

Café Hemma Hos MODERN NORWEGIAN €€
(Map p45; ☎22 55 62 26; www.cafehemmahos.no; Fredrikborgsveien 16; mains Nkr165-190) The owners of the Café Hemma Hos, close to the Viking Ship Museum, know there is more to culinary life than hot dogs and stale sandwiches, and have created an oasis of good food in a sea of tourist traps. Sit out in the pleasant gardens and choose from a menu that includes pickled herrings, crayfish and a variety of tapas.

Drinking & Entertainment
The tourist office's free monthly brochure *What's On in Oslo* lists current concerts, theatre and special events, but the best publication for night owls is the free *Streetwise*, published annually in English by Use-It.

Bars & Clubs
Going out in one of the world's most expensive cities requires a bit of skill, but high prices certainly don't keep the locals at home. Quite the opposite: Oslo is more vibrant, busy and nonchalantly proud of its up-and-coming status than ever. And the manageable size of the city makes it easy to figure out where to be on any given night.

Note that many Oslo nightspots have an unwritten dress code that expects patrons to be relatively well turned out – at the very least, don't show up in grubby gear and hiking boots. For most bars and clubs that serve beer and wine, you must be over 18 years of age, but many places, especially those that serve spirits, impose a higher age limit. On weekends, most Oslo nightspots remain open until at least 3am.

Beer prices for half-litres typically range from Nkr50 to Nkr65, but for those travellers watching their kroner, some places (usually grim and inhabited by wary elbow-on-the-bar locals) charge as little as Nkr30. **Stargate** (Map p52; Grønland 2; half-litre Nkr36) is a decent (well OK, maybe cheap is a better word than decent) and central dive.

The city's best neighbourhood bar scene is along Thorvald Meyers gate and the surrounding streets in Grünerløkka. The Youngstorget area has some of the most popular places close to the city centre, while the Grønland neighbourhood has a more alternative feel.

Tea Lounge
BAR

(Map p48; www.tealounge.no; Thorvald Meyers gate 33b; ⊙11am-1am Mon-Wed, 11am-3am Thu-Sat, noon-3am Sun) During the bright and cheerful daylight hours, this split-personality bar is a teashop with a superb range of brews and a chilled-out soundtrack, but in the dark of night it transforms itself into one of the hippest bars in Oslo, with a list of cocktails to suit.

Bar Boca
BAR

(Map p48; Thorvald Meyers gate 30) Squeeze into what is quite possibly the smallest bar in Oslo and you'll find that you have slid back in time to the 1960s. It's retro cool and has a cocktail selection as great as its atmosphere.

Fish Og Vilt
CLUB

(Map p52; Pløens gate 1) DJs rock the crowd in the covered backyard of this bar-club, which boasts an impressive selection of beers and cocktails. It's a popular central spot, and on a Monday night it's really the only place worth considering.

Palace Grill
BAR

(Map p48; Solli gate 2) The well-heeled crowd of Oslo West can be found sipping cocktails at the New Orleans–style courtyard bar here. It's also an excellent restaurant.

Villa
CLUB

(Map p52; www.thevilla.no; Møllergata 23; ⊙Fri & Sat) With arguably the best sound system in the city, this is a die-hard house and electro music club. In addition to Friday and Saturday, it's also open on some Thursdays.

Süd Øst
BAR

(Map p52; Trondheimsveien 5; ⊙11am-midnight Mon & Tue, 11am-1am Wed & Thu, 11am-2am Fri & Sat) Has an outdoor terrace for summer sun seekers.

Robinet
BAR

(Map p52; Mariboes gate 7) To the north of the Youngstorget square, this tiny, retro bar is packed with musicians and media types.

Dattera Til Hagen
BAR

(Map p52; Grønland 10) The back garden of this bar is especially busy in the summer.

Onkel Donald Kafé-Bar
BAR

(Map p52; Universitetsgata 26) Another popular central location.

Live Music
Oslo has a thriving live-music scene – it's said that the city hosts around 5000 gigs a year. Keep your ear to the ground in summer to hear about outdoor concerts at Vigeland Park – a weird and wonderful venue.

The city's largest concert halls, **Oslo Spektrum** (Map p52; www.oslospektrum.no; Sonja Henies plass 2) and **Rockefeller Music Hall** (Map p52; www.rockefeller.no; Torggata 16), once a bathhouse, host a wide range of artists and events.

TOP CHOICE Blå
JAZZ MUSIC

(Map p48; www.blaaoslo.no, in Norwegian; Brenneriveien 9c; admission Nkr100-150) It would be a pity to leave Oslo without checking out Blå, which features on a global list of 100 great jazz clubs compiled by the savvy editors at the US jazz magazine *Down Beat*. As one editor put it, 'To get in this list means that it's quite the club'. Sometimes it veers into other musical styles such as salsa, and when there's no live music, DJs get the crowds moving.

Mono
ROCK MUSIC

(Map p52; www.cafemono.no, in Norwegian; Pløens gate 4) An upbeat place, Mono is the rock club of choice with the cool and beautiful of Oslo. It's known for managing to book the best up-and-coming indie bands.

DON'T MISS

THE HOUSE OF LITERATURE

If you like books, you really shouldn't miss Oslo's shrine to the printed word, **Litteraturhuset** (House of Literature; Map p48; www.litteraturhuset.no; Wergelandsveien 29). The promotion of literature is at the core of everything it does – there are frequent workshops, talks and debates. Perhaps of equal interest is the in-house **cafe** (⊙10am-12.30pm Mon-Tue, 10am-3.30pm Wed-Sat, noon-8pm Sun), which serves pasta, salads and soups tasty enough to attract the odd princess from the neighbouring Royal Palace. There's also a well-stocked bookshop, a bar and frequent screenings of art-house films.

Gloria Flames ROCK MUSIC
(Map p48; www.gloriaflames.no, in Norwegian; Grønland 18) In Grønland, Gloria Flames is a popular rock bar with frequent gigs and a roof-terrace bar during daylight hours.

Theatre
See also Oslo Opera House (p46) for information on catching a world-class opera or ballet performance.

National Theatre THEATRE
(Nationaltheatret; Map p52; www.nationaltheatret.no, in Norwegian; Stortingsgata 15) Norway's showcase theatre, with its lavish rococo hall, was constructed specifically as a venue for the works of Norwegian playwright Henrik Ibsen, whose works are still performed here.

Black Box ALTERNATIVE THEATRE
(Map p52; www.blackbox.no; Stranden 3) An exciting calendar of alternative dance and theatre takes place at the cafe-style Black Box in the Aker Brygge complex.

MS Innvik ALTERNATIVE CULTURE
(Map p52; ✆22 41 95 00; www.msinnvik.no, in Norwegian; Langkaia) A car ferry turned theatre and world-music concert venue, MS Innvik offers, culturally, the polar opposite to the highbrow entertainment of the next-door Opera House. See the website for a rundown of what's taking place each week. To get here, take the footbridge over the E18 south of the central station.

Hausmania ALTERNATIVE CULTURE
(Map p48; www.hausmania.org; Hausmannsgate 34) Run by a group of alternative artists, this equally alternative cultural centre consists of galleries and work spaces, down-and-dirty bar-club (admission Nkr50; ⊙Fri & Sat), theatre, skate hall, graffiti wall and vegan cafe.

Cinema
Saga Kino CINEMA
(Map p52; ✆22 83 23 75; Stortingsgata 28) The six-screen Saga Kino cinema shows first-run movies, including Hollywood fare, in their original language; the entrance is on Olav V's gate.

Filmens Hus CINEMA
(Map p52; ✆22 47 45 00; www.nfi.no; Dronningens gate 16) Filmens Hus screens old classics and international festival winners most days.

🔒 Shopping
Oslo excels in upmarket shopping and there are many fine shops on Grensen and Karl Johans gate. For art, try the galleries on Frognerveien, for exclusive boutiques head to Hegdehaugsveien or Skovveien and for funky shoes or T-shirts go no further than Grünerløkka.

Oslo City Shopping Centre (Map p52; www.oslocity.no, in Norwegian; Stenersgata) and the more glamorous **Glasmagasinet Department Store** (Map p52; www.glasmagasinet.no, in Norwegian; Stortorvet 9) are good for mainstream shopping.

TOP CHOICE Nomaden BOOKSHOP
(Map p48; www.nomaden.no, in Norwegian; Uranienborgveien 4; ⊙closed Sun) This is a classic travel bookshop where the shelves are bursting with guides, maps and travel literature that will have you dreaming of your next holiday in no time.

Vestkanttorget Flea Market FLEA MARKET
(Map p48; Amaldus Nilsens plass; ⊙10am-4pm Sat) If you're happy with pot luck and sifting through heaps of junk, take a chance here. It's at the plaza that intersects Professor Dahls gate, a block east of Vigeland Park, and it's a more than pleasant way to pass a Saturday morning.

Norli BOOKSHOP
(Map p52; www.norli.no, in Norwegian; Universitetsgata 20-24; ⊙closed Sun) The largest bookshop in Norway stocks a good range of foreign-language titles as well as numerous Lonely Planet guidebooks.

Husfliden TRADITIONAL CLOTHING
(Map p52; Rosenkrantz gate 19-21) Husfliden is a large shop selling quality Norwegian clothing and crafts. It is also a popular place to buy a *bunad* (national costume).

Hassan og Den Dama CLOTHES, JEWELLERY
(Map p48; www.dendama.com; Skovveien 4) One of many boutiques on Skovveien, this shop has clothing, shoes and jewellery produced by Scandinavian as well as international designers.

Ark Bokhandel BOOKSHOP
(Map p52; www.ark.no, in Norwegian; Øvre Slottsgate 23-25; ⊙closed Sun) This shop has a good English-language and stationery section; branches around town.

Norway Designs CLOTHES, JEWELLERY
(Map p52; www.norwaydesigns.no, in Norwegian; Stortingsgata 28) Features designer clothing and beautiful glassware, stationery and watches within a stone's throw of the National Theatre.

Heimen Husflid
CLOTHING

(Map p52; www.heimen.net, in Norwegian; Rosenkrantz gate 8) Clothing and crafts.

Unique Design
CLOTHING

(Map p52; Rosenkrantz gate 13) Good for sweaters.

Information

Emergency

Ambulance (✆113)

Fire (✆110)

Police (✆112; Hammersborggata 10)

Internet Access

Almost all hotels and hostels in Oslo provide wi-fi access (although it's not always free) and some also have computers with internet for guest use. Many bars and cafes also have free wi-fi for those who are eating or drinking there.

Arctic Internet Café (Oslo S; per hr Nkr40-60; ☺9am-11pm) Located on the 1st floor of Oslo S station.

Infittelecom Internett Cafe (Dronningens gate 22; per hr Nkr30; ☺9am-11pm)

International Sidewalk Express (Oslo S; per 1½hr Nkr29; ☺24hr) A large internet cafe inside the Oslo S train station next to the west exit (same exit as the tourist office).

Use-It (Møllergata 3; free access; ☺9am-6pm Mon-Fri Jul & Aug, 11am-5pm Mon-Fri Sep-Jun)

Laundry

A Snarvask (Thorvald Meyers gate 18; ☺10am-8pm Mon-Fri, 8am-3pm Sat)

Billig Vask & Rens (Ullevålsveien 15; ☺8am-9pm Mon-Fri, 8am-3pm Sat)

Left Luggage

Oslo S and the bus station have various sizes of lockers. Those under the age of 26 can also leave luggage for free at the Use-It centre.

Medical Services

If you're pressed for time (and not worried about the expense), the Oslo Kommunale Legevakten clinic has a list of private doctors it recommends.

Jernbanetorget Apotek (Fred Olsens gate) A 24-hour pharmacy opposite Oslo S.

Oslo Kommunale Legevakten (Oslo Emergency Clinic; ✆22 93 22 93; Storgata 40; ☺24hr) Casualty and emergency medical clinic.

Money

There are banks with ATMs throughout the city centre, with a particular concentration along Karl Johans gate. The tourist office and post office in Oslo S exchange money (into Norwegian kroner only) at a less advantageous rate (usu-

ally 3% less than banks). **Forex** (www.forex.no; Fridtjof Nansens plass 6 & Oslo S; ☺9am-6pm Mon-Fri) is the largest foreign-exchange service in Scandinavia.

Post

Main post office (Map p52; cnr Prinsens gate & Kirkegata) As well as this main office, you'll also find convenient post office branches at Solli plass (Map p48), Oslo Sentralstasjon (Oslo S; Map p52) and on Grensen (Map p52).

Telephone

Telekort card phones and coin phones are found throughout the city. Coin phones take Nkr1 to Nkr20 coins, but you'll need at least Nkr5 for a local call. Faxes can be sent from post offices.

Telehuset (Haakon VII gate 1; ☺10am-6pm Mon-Thu, 10am-5pm Fri, 10am-4pm Sat) If you want a SIM card for your mobile phone.

Tourist Information

Den Norske Turistforening (DNT; Norwegian Mountain Touring Club; Map p52; ✆22 82 28 22; www.turistforeningen.no; Storgata 3; ☺10am-5pm Mon-Wed & Fri, 10am-6pm Thu, 10am-2pm Sat, open 1hr earlier in summer) Provides information, maps and brochures on hiking in Norway and sells memberships, which include discounted rates on the use of mountain huts along the main hiking routes. You can also book some specific huts and pick up keys.

Oslo Promotion Tourist Office (Map p52; ✆81 53 05 55; www.visitoslo.com; Fridtjof Nansens plass 5; ☺9am-7pm Jun-Aug, 9am-5pm Mon-Sat Apr, May & Sep, shorter hr rest of yr) Located just north of the Rådhus. Look out for its useful *Oslo Guide* or the monthly *What's On in Oslo* (both are available at all tourist offices in and around the city as well as at many sights and hotels).

Tourist Office (Map p52; ✆81 53 05 55; Jernbanetorget 1, Oslo S; ☺7am-8pm Mon-Fri, 8am-8pm Sat & Sun May-Sep, 7am-8pm Mon-Fri, 8am-6pm Sat & Sun Oct-Apr) Easy to find under the glass Trafikanten tower in front of the Oslo S; handles Oslo-specific questions, sells the Oslo Pass and bike passes, and can help find hotels, hostels and B&Bs with rooms available.

Use-It (Map p52; ✆24 14 98 20; www.use-it .no; Møllergata 3; ☺9am-6pm Mon-Fri Jul & Aug, 11am-5pm Mon-Fri Sep-Jun) The exceptionally helpful and savvy Ungdomsinformasjonen (Youth Information Office, better known as Use-It) is aimed at, but not restricted to, backpackers under the age of 26. It makes (free) bookings for inexpensive or private accommodation and provides information on anything from current events to hitching possibilities.

ⓘ Getting There & Away

Air

Oslo Gardermoen International Airport (Map p77; ☎91 50 64 00; www.osl.no) opened in October 1998 and has a motorway and high-speed rail link to the city centre. For details of international services, see p435.

Domestic flights also depart from here and include services (with sample one-way fares) to Bergen (Nkr370), Stavanger (Nkr320), Tromsø (Nkr430) and Trondheim (Nkr370).

KLM, Widerøe, SAS Braathens and Ryanair also operate 'Oslo' services to/from Torp Airport, some 123km southwest of Oslo, and the new Rygge airport, around 60km southeast of the centre.

Boat

For details of international ferries, see p436.

Ferries operated by **DFDS Seaways** (Map p45; www.dfdsseaways.com; Vippetangen 2) connect Oslo with Denmark from the Vippetangen Quay off Skippergata. Bus 60 stops within a couple of minutes' walk of the terminal.

Color Line Ferries (Map p48; www.colorline .no; Color Line Terminalen, Hjortnes) runs to/from Kiel (Germany); boats dock at Hjortneskaia, west of the central harbour. Take tram 13 from Oslo S, bus 33 or the Color Line bus, which leaves from platform 7 of the central bus terminal one hour before boat departures.

Bus

Long-distance buses arrive and depart from the **Galleri Oslo Bus Terminal** (Map p52; Schweigaards gate 8, Galleri Oslo); the train and bus stations are linked via a convenient overhead walkway for easy connections.

Nor-Way Bussekspress (www.nor-way.no) has the biggest range of services. International services also depart from the bus terminal.

Car & Motorcycle

The main highways into the city are the E6 from the north and south, and the E18 from the southeast and west. Each time you enter Oslo, you must pass through (at least) one of 19 toll stations and pay Nkr25.

Hitching

Hitching is never completely safe so we don't recommend it, but if you do choose to hitch out of Oslo, it's generally best to take a bus or train to the outskirts of the city and start hitching from there.

To hitch to Bergen, take bus 161 to its final stop and wait beside the E16 towards Hønefoss. For Trondheim, take T-bane line 5 (direction: Vestli) to Grorud and wait beside Rv4, which connects

to the E6. For the south coast and Stavanger, take bus 32 to the Maritim petrol station. For general information, see p444.

Train

All trains arrive and depart from Oslo S (Map p52) in the city centre. It has **reservation desks** (☉6.30am-11pm) and an **information desk** (☎81 50 08 88, press 9 for service in English) that provides details on routes and timetables throughout the country.

There are frequent train services around Oslofjord (eg Drammen, Skien, Moss, Fredrikstad and Halden). Other major destinations include Stavanger via Kristiansand, Bergen via Voss, Røros via Hamar, and Trondheim via Hamar and Lillehammer.

For details of international schedules and prices, see p438.

ⓘ Getting Around

Oslo has an efficient public-transport system with an extensive network of buses, trams, underground trains (T-bane) and ferries. In addition to single-trip tickets, day and transfer-able eight-trip tickets are also available. Children aged four to 16 and seniors over 67 years of age pay half price on all fares.

The Oslo Pass (see p57) includes access to all public-transport options within the city, with the exception of late-night buses and trams. Bicycles can be carried on trams and trains for an additional Nkr11. The automatic fine for travelling without a ticket is a rather punitive Nkr750.

Trafikanten (☎177; www.trafikanten.no; Jernbanetorget; ☉7am-11pm) is located below Oslo S tower and provides free schedules and a public-transport map, *Sporveiskart Oslo*.

To/From Gardermoen International Airport

Flybussen (www.flybussen.no) is the airport shuttle to Gardermoen International Airport, 50km north of Oslo. It departs from the bus terminal at Galleri Oslo three or four times hourly from 5.10am to 9.50pm. The trip costs Nkr140/240 one-way/return (valid one month) and takes 40 minutes. **Flybussekspressen** (www.flybussekspressen.no) connects Gardermoen with Majorstuen T-bane station (Nkr180) and other places, one to four times hourly.

FlyToget (www.flytoget.no) rail services leave Gardermoen airport for Oslo S (Nkr170, 19 minutes) every 10 minutes between 4.18am and midnight. Every second train continues onward to the National Theatre and stops south of there, terminating at Asker. In total contrast to Norwegian road-traffic speeds, this train pelts along at 210km/h making it, apparently, the fastest airport train in the world. In addition, most northbound **NSB** (www.nsb.no)

intercity and local trains stop at Gardermoen (Nkr110, from 26 minutes, hourly but fewer on Saturday).

To/From Torp Airport

To get to/from Torp Airport (Map p77) in Sandefjord, 123km southwest of Oslo and serviced by Ryanair and Wizzair among others, take the **Torp-Expressen** (www.torpekspressen.no; single adult/child Nkr190/100, return adult/child Nkr320/200) bus between Galleri Oslo bus terminal and the airport (1½ hours). Departures from Oslo leave 3½ hours before scheduled departures, and leave from Torp 35 minutes after flights arrive. Although the service operates primarily for Ryanair and Wizzair passengers (the bus will wait if the flight is delayed), passengers on other airlines may also use it. At other times, you'll need to take the hourly Telemarksekspressen bus (or a taxi; from Nkr190, 10 minutes) between the airport and Sandefjord train station from where there are connections to Oslo (trains also stop at Torp station from where a free shuttle takes you to the airport).

To/From Rygge Airport

To get to/from Oslo's newest airport, Rygge, in Moss, 60km southeast of Oslo and serviced by Ryanair and Norwegian among others, take the **Rygge-Expressen** (www.ryggeekspressen.no; single adult/child Nkr130/70, return adult/child Nkr230/140) bus between Galleri Oslo bus terminal and the airport (one hour). Departures from Oslo leave three hours before scheduled departures, and leave from Rygge 35 minutes after flights arrive. Trains also run from Oslo (Nkr139, 50 minutes) to the airport roughly hourly.

Bicycle

The best place to rent bicycles is the **Skiservice Sykkelutleie** (☎22 13 95 00; www.skiservice.no, in Norwegian; Tryvannsveien 2; per day Nkr350) in the Nordmarka. To get there by public transport, take T-bane 1 towards Frognerseteren and get off at the Voksenkollen station (the second-last stop).

One alternative if you don't plan on going too far is **Oslo Citybike** (www.oslobysykkel.no), a network of bikes that cyclists can borrow for up to three hours at a time from bicycle stands around the city. Access cards (Nkr80) can be purchased from the tourist office and last for 24 hours, but bikes must be exchanged or returned to a rack within three hours or you will lose your deposit (Nkr500 for losing the card and a whopping Nkr3500 if you lose the bike!). They're convenient and well maintained. The system is closed between midnight and 6am.

For ideas on where to cycle, see p60.

Boat

Ferries to the Oslofjord islands sail from Vippetangen Quay (see p61). For details of ferries to Bygdøy, see p56.

Boats connect Oslo with Drøbak (boat 602; Nkr100, 1½ hours, once daily) and other Oslofjord stops en route: Ildjernet, Langåra and Håøya (which is a holiday spot offering fine swimming and camping). It departs from Aker Brygge pier, but exact departure times vary depending on the day. Ask either at the pier or the tourist office.

Bus & Tram

Bus and tram lines lace the city and extend into the suburbs. There's no central local bus station, but most converge at Jernbanetorget in front of Oslo S. Most westbound buses, including those to Bygdøy and Vigeland Park, also stop immediately south of the National Theatre.

The frequency of service drops dramatically at night, but on weekends, night buses N12, N14 and N18 follow the tram routes until 4am or later; there are also weekend night buses (201 to 218). These services are called Nattlinjer and cost Nkr45 per ride (no passes are valid).

Tickets for most trips cost adult/child Nkr26/13 if you buy them in advance (at 7-Eleven, Narvesen and Trafikanten) or adult/child Nkr40/20 if you buy them from the driver. A day pass costs Nkr70/35 per adult/child.

Car & Motorcycle

Oslo has its share of one-way streets, which can complicate city driving a bit, but the streets are rarely as congested as in most other European cities.

Metered street parking, identified by a solid blue sign with a white 'P', can be found throughout the city. Payment (up to Nkr44 per hour) is usually required from 8am to 5pm Monday to Friday, and until 3pm Saturday. At other times, parking is free unless otherwise posted. The city centre also has 16 multistorey car parks, including those at Oslo City and Aker Brygge shopping centres; fees range from Nkr70 to Nkr200 per 24-hour period.

Note that the Oslo Pass includes parking at all municipal car parks; instructions for display come with the pass.

Taxi

There are taxi stands at Oslo S, shopping centres and city squares, but any taxi with a lit sign is available for hire. Otherwise, phone **Norgestaxi** (☎08000) or **Oslo Taxi** (☎02323), but note that the meter starts running at the point of dispatch! Oslo taxis accept major credit cards.

T-Bane

The six-line Tunnelbanen underground system, better known as the T-bane, is faster and extends further from the city centre than most city bus lines. All lines pass through the Nationaltheatret, Stortinget and Jernbanetorget (for Oslo S) stations. Ticket prices are the same as for the buses and trams.

AROUND OSLO

Drøbak

POP 11,500

Once Oslo's winter harbour, Drøbak is a cosy little village by the water's edge, home to enough clapboard timber buildings to warrant a day trip from the capital.

The helpful **tourist office** (☑64 93 50 87; Hanegata 4; ⊙8am-6pm Mon-Fri, 10am-4pm Sat & Sun Jun-Aug) by the harbour has a wealth of information on Drøbak, including *Walks Around Drøbak* (free) to assist your rambling through the village.

In town, there are several small eateries around the pretty Torget Sq and along nearby Storgata.

⊙ Sights

Drøbak is known as Oslo's 'Christmas town' and is renowned for its public decorations. There's also a Christmas shop, **Tregaardens Julehus** (www.julehus.no; Torget 4; ⊙10am-5pm Mon-Fri, 10am-3pm Sat Mar-Oct, longer hr rest of yr), which has a Father Christmas postbox for kids.

Saltvannsakvarium (www.akvarium.net, in Norwegian; Havnegata 4; adult/child Nkr40/15; ⊙10am-7pm May-Aug, shorter hr rest of yr) is a small aquarium that is full of bubble-faced local fish. It can also lay claim to the title of the world's only *lutefisk* (dried and salted white fish) museum. Well, we suppose somewhere has to! Not far away, the small **Drøbak Båtforenings Maritime Samlinger** (Kroketønna 4; adult/child Nkr20/free; ⊙11am-7pm May-Aug) is a museum of maritime paraphernalia.

Not to be missed is the imposing **Oscarsborg fortress**, which lies on an offshore island and dates back to the 1600s. It was the Oscarsborg batteries that sank the German warship *Blücher* on 9 April 1940, an act that saved the king and the Norwegian government from being captured. The fort museum was renovated in 2005, and open-air concerts and complete operas are held here during the summer. There is even a hotel, spa and restaurant on the island if you want to extend your stay. **Ferries** (www.oscarsborgfestning.no) to the island (adult/child Nkr70/50, five minutes) depart around 24 times daily from the harbour year-round.

ⓘ Getting There & Away

The hourly bus 541 travels between Oslo and Drøbak (Nkr65, one hour). Alternatively, in July you can travel by boat (see p75).

The new tunnel from Drøbak under Oslofjord to the other side charges Nkr55 each way for a car (motorcycles free).

Drammen

POP 62,600

Drammen is an industrial centre of more interest to businesspeople than tourists. With heavy port machinery and factories, it hardly jumps out at you as being worth a stop. It does, however, have a couple of quirky elements: Drammen was the start of the Royal Rd to Bergen, and it was the original home of the potato alcohol aquavit, which may warrant a detour. The **Drammen Turistkontor** (☑32 21 64 50; www.drammen.no/drammen_turistkontor_as; Bragernes Torg 6; ⊙9am-6.15pm Mon-Fri, 10am-3pm Sat yr-round, 10am-3pm Sun 21 Jun-Aug) can provide further information.

⊙ Sights & Activities

Drammen has several buildings of note, all of which are clustered in the old centre around the main thoroughfare, Bragernes Torg: the historic **Stock Exchange** (Bragernes Torg), which now houses a somewhat less historic McDonald's; the restored **Rådhus** (Engenes 1), the town hall, which was a former courthouse and jail; the **fire station** (Bragernes Torg), now a bank; the lovely **Drammen Theatre** (Gamle Kirkeplass; ⊙events only), built in 1870, burned down in 1993 and reopened in 1996; and the Gothic-style **Bragernes church** (Bragernes Torg), built in 1871.

ⓘ Getting There & Away

Trains run to Oslo every 30 minutes (Nkr91, 37 minutes) and buses depart once or twice every hour (Nkr60, 35 minutes).

Around Drammen

Another interesting excursion will take you to Åmot, where the **Royal Blåfarveværk** (www.blaa.no; ⊙11am-6pm Jul–mid-Aug, shorter

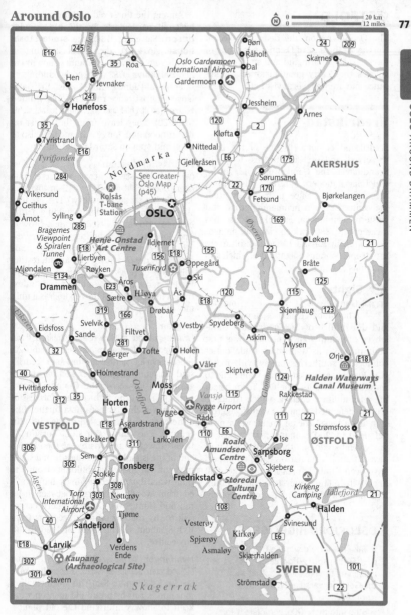

hr rest of yr) was established by King Christian VII in 1773 to extract cobalt for the production of blue pigments for the glass and porcelain industries. There are a number of sights of interest within the complex, including the **cobalt works** (adult/child Nkr75/free), the **manor house** (adult/child Nkr50/free), the **cobalt mines** (adult/child Nkr110/50) and a **museum** (adult/child Nkr55/free).

Various combinations of joint tickets are available.

ØSTFOLD

The Østfold region, the detached slice of Norway to the east of Oslofjord, is a mix of forest, pastoral farmland and small seaside villages that carry great historical significance and are well worth visiting.

Fredrikstad

POP 72,760

Fredrikstad is home to one of the best-preserved, and prettiest, fortress towns in Scandinavia: the Gamlebyen (Old Town), which has a modern waterfront district just across the water. Once an important trading centre between mainland Europe and western Scandinavia, Fredrikstad also has a cathedral (1880), which contains stained-glass work by Emanuel Vigeland; bizarrely, the steeple contains a lighthouse, which still functions at night.

⊙ Sights

TOP CHOICE **Gamlebyen**   OLD TOWN
The timbered houses, moats, gates and drawbridge of the Fredrikstad Gamlebyen are simply enchanting. It was first built in 1663; as a primary trade outlet connecting southern Norway with mainland Europe, Fredrikstad was vulnerable to waterborne assaults. The Old Town began life as a military enclave, which could be readily defended against Swedish aggression and attacks. The perimeter walls, once defended by 200 cannons, now consist of grassy embankments that make for a very pleasant stroll. The narrow, cobbled streets have been similarly preserved and are still lined with picturesque 17th-century buildings, many of which remain occupied today.

OSLOFJORD HIGHLIGHTS

» Take the ferry down the Oslofjord past **Oscarsborg Fortress** (p76), imagining the fateful shots that sank the German warship *Blücher* on 9 April 1940

» Step into the 1700s, complete with cannons and duels, during a historical re-enactment in the **Gamlebyen** at Fredrikstad

» Gasp for breath after a spring dip in the Oslofjord during a visit to the **Hvaler Skerries** (p82)

Among the finest old buildings in town, look out particularly for the **old convict prison** (Salveriet; 1731); the **stone storehouse** (1674–91), the oldest building in Gamlebyen and now a ceramics showroom; and **Balaklava** (1783), a historic building.

From mid-June to mid-August, the Gamlebyen tourist office runs one-hour **guided tours** (adult/child incl free entry to all sights Nkr95/20). They leave from the tourist office at noon and 2pm weekdays, and also at noon and 4pm on Saturday and Sunday.

Fredrikstad Museum   MUSEUM
(www.ostfoldmuseet.no; combined ticket with Isegran adult/child Nkr50/20; ⊙11am-4pm mid-Jun–mid-Aug, shorter hr rest of yr) The Fredrikstad Museum is housed in a building dating back to 1776 and is well worth a browse. The downstairs area houses temporary exhibitions, while upstairs you'll find scale models of the Old Town and an interesting collection of relics from three centuries of Fredrikstad's civilian, military and industrial activities. Also on the top floor is a military museum.

Isegran   ISLAND, MUSEUM
(www.isegran.no, in Norwegian; combined ticket with Fredrikstad Museum adult/child Nkr50/20; ⊙noon-5pm Tue-Sun mid-Jun–mid-Aug) Fredrikstad Museum has another section on Isegran, an islet across the Glomma. Norse sagas mention the 13th-century fortress of Isegran, which later became a further line of defence against Sweden in the mid-17th century. The **ruins** of a stone (originally wood) tower remain visible at the eastern end of the island. It's also the site of a small museum on local boatbuilding (from the time when boats were lovingly handcrafted from wood). Boats run between Isegran and Gamlebyen or the modern centre (Nkr6). By road or on foot, access is from Rv108, about 600m south of Fredrikstad city centre.

Hvalfanger (Whaling) Museum   MUSEUM
(Tolbodgaten; admission Nkr10; ⊙noon-4pm Wed-Sun Jun, Sat & Sun Aug-Sep) This small whaling museum is run by proud old men only too keen to show you around the old photos, the formidable whaling guns once used in the Antarctic, and the even more formidable penis of a blue whale. No English is spoken and all labels are in Norwegian.

Kongsten Festning   FORT
On what was once called 'Gallows Hill' stands the flower-festooned Kongsten Fest-

ning (Kongsten Fort). Dating from 1685, it once served as a lookout and warning post for the troops at nearby Gamlebyen. Although it can get overrun on summer weekends, this otherwise lonely and appealingly unkempt spot is a fun place at which you can scramble around the turrets, embankments, walls and stockade, or just sit in the sun and soak up the quiet. The silence is occasionally broken on summer evenings when the grounds host concerts. It's a 10-minute walk southeast of the Gamlebyen drawbridge (turn off Torsnesveien at Fredrikstad Motell & Camping).

✦✦ Festivals & Events

Glomma Festival   CONCERTS, FOOD
(www.glommafestivalen.no) The Glomma Festival runs over two weeks in early July. The first week is dedicated to culinary delights and the second week features musical performances, ritual duels, a 'bathtub regatta' for creative vessels and a veteran-sailing-ship exhibition. It's a very popular festival, so book ahead for accommodation.

🛏 Sleeping

GAMLEBYEN & SARPSBORG

[TOP CHOICE] Gamlebyen Gjestegaarder
BOUTIQUE HOTEL €€
(☎69 32 20 20; www.gamlebyengjestegaarder.no; Smedjegaten 88; s/d Nkr995/1195; @) Don't gasp, but this is one of those rare Norwegian beasts – an affordable hotel with character and style! Housed in the renovated former artillery barracks, the rooms might be small but they all differ from one another. Some have opted for a classic look and others are bright, bold and new. Whichever style you go for, all have rain showers in the bathrooms.

Gamlebyen Gjestegaarder Guesthouse
BUDGET HOTEL €
(☎69 32 20 20; www.gamlebyengjestegaarder.no; Smedjegaten 88; s/d Nkr495/595; P@) This is the pick of the town's budget crop and has well-maintained rooms that have had a little bit of love shown to them. There are common bathrooms only, and not many of those either. There's a kitchen for guest use or you can pay Nkr100 extra for breakfast. It's run by the same people as the Gamlebyen Gjestegaarder.

Tuneheimen Vandrerhjem   HOSTEL €
(☎69 14 50 01; www.sarpsborgvandrerhjem.no; Tuneveien 44; dm from Nkr275, s with/without bathroom Nkr545/465, d with/without bathroom

Nkr750/670, all incl breakfast; P) The nearest youth hostel to Fredrikstad is near Tunevannet lake, 1km from Sarpsborg, which is in turn a 14km bus ride from Fredrikstad. Linen costs an extra Nkr65; there is an open kitchen or you can buy dinner for Nkr125.

Fredrikstad Motell & Camping
CAMPGROUND €
(☎99 22 19 99; www.fredrikstadmotell.no in Norwegian; Torsnesveien 16-18; tent with/without car Nkr170/110, motel s/d Nkr400/500, cabins Nkr800; P) This multifaceted but largely uninspiring place, in the grounds of Kongsten Fort, is nonetheless good for its proximity to the Old Town. From the centre, take any bus (eg 362) headed for Torsnes.

NEW TOWN

Hotel Victoria   HISTORIC HOTEL €€
(☎69 38 58 00; www.hotelvictoria.no, in Norwegian; Turngaten 3; s/d mid-Jun–mid-Aug & Sat-Sun Nkr895/1020, Mon-Fri rest of yr Nkr1240/1365; @🛜) This place has had a recent makeover and has common areas full of period trimmings and sturdy, old-fashioned rooms, some of which have views to the trees and the flowers of the neighbouring park. The staff are exceptionally helpful and friendly, and if you book through the Fjord Pass system, you can get a substantial discount.

Hotel Valhalla   HISTORIC HOTEL €€
(☎69 36 89 50; www.hotelvalhalla.no, in Norwegian; Valhallsgate 3; s Nkr695-750, d Nkr895-1090; P@) High on a hill overlooking the town, but within easy walking distance of the centre, this lovely old wooden house has comfortable, tidy rooms and good views. It also has rooms in a new neighbouring block that mainly have IKEA to thank for their furnishings. They do, though, have little kitchens for self-caterers. To get here, walk to the northern end of Storgata and then, turning right, follow the hotel signs up the hill.

🍴 Eating

GAMLEBYEN
The Old Town is stuffed like a tin of sardines with places to eat.

Café Balaklava   INTERNATIONAL €€
(☎69 32 30 40; Færgeportgata 78; mains Nkr135-230; ⊙noon-9pm) Café Balaklava is a charming, well-run place that devotes time and care to preparing meals that vary from pasta and burger-style standards to barbecued

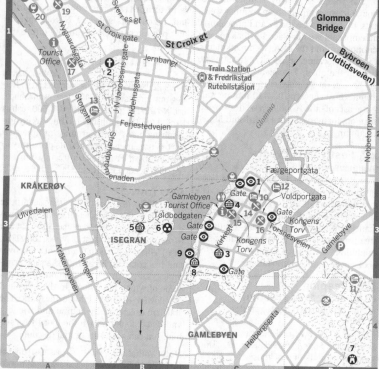

steaks or gently baked trout cooked in wine and herbs. There's a pleasant outdoor patio, which becomes a bustling hub of activity during the summer months.

Zwart Cafe
CAFE €
(Kirkegt 27; teas & coffees Nkr20-30, cakes Nkr30; ⊙11am-10pm Mon-Fri, 10am-10pm Sat, noon-10pm Sun) For a light lunch or afternoon tea and cake (homemade chocolate cake anyone?), this cute cafe in the corner of the main square is the bee's knees. It also pieces together some very pleasing salads.

Major-Stuen
TRADITIONAL €€€
(☎69 32 15 55; Voldportgata 73; starters Nkr110, mains Nkr255-295; ⊙noon-10pm) This fine place specialises in Norwegian dishes cooked in the sort of slow and old-fashioned manner that guarantees a good meal. There's a formal indoor dining room or a much more informal garden area out the back.

Lille Frederik
SNACKS €
(Torvgaten; mains around Nkr80-100; ⊙11am-10pm Mon-Fri, 10am-10pm Sat, noon-10pm Sun) For burgers, snacks and coffee, cosy little Lille Frederik is just the place. It's hugely popular in summer, when snackers descend on the outdoor tables like seagulls, and queues can be long. Steak and chips for Nkr99 is a good deal and the ice creams have hordes of fans.

NEW TOWN
The Fredrikstad waterfront between Storgata and the water is lined with all manner of restaurants and bars, most with pleasant outdoor terraces ideal for a summer's afternoon or evening.

Thai Restaurant
THAI €€
(☎69 30 81 81; Nygaardsgata 33; mains Nkr130-190) No prizes for guessing what sort of cuisine comes steaming out of the kitchens here. Though it may not be imaginatively

Fredrikstad

named, this restaurant offers perfectly spiced curries. Your body will thank you for giving it rice rather than another hotdog.

Mother India INDIAN €€
(📞 69 31 22 00; Storgata 20; mains Nkr140-195; ⏰ 3-11pm Mon-Thu, 3pm-midnight Fri & Sat, 2-10pm Sun) This atmospheric Indian restaurant gets the thumbs up from locals and travellers alike for its attractive decor and authentic Indian dishes. It's at the northern end of Storgata.

Restaurant La Riveria SEAFOOD €€
(📞 69 33 86 88; Storgata 13, Engelsviken; lunch special Nkr98, mains Nkr125-249; ⏰ 11am-10pm Mon-Thu, 11am-11pm Fri-Sat, noon-10pm Sun) This red clapboard building has a summer terrace, a waterfront setting and fair-priced seafood dishes (the lunch specials are great value). It's on the waterfront just off Storgata.

Pizzanini INTERNATIONAL €€
(📞 69 30 03 00; Storgata 5; pizzas Nkr109-299, pastas Nkr169; ⏰ noon-1am Sun-Thu, noon-2am Fri & Sat) When other restaurants stand empty, this place always buzzes, due in part to its young vibe and extensive, well-priced menu.

🍷 Drinking

The following have breezy outdoor tables in summer.

Oasen Food & Lounge BAR
(Storgata 20; ⏰ 3pm-3am Wed-Fri, noon-3am Sat) Beside the waterfront, chilled beats fill the air here. The terrace is perfect for lazy summer evening drinks. There are a couple of similar places nearby.

Bar Oscar LIVE MUSIC
(Storgata 5; ⏰ noon-1.30am Sun-Thu, noon-2.30am Fri & Sat) With a buzzy vibe, Bar Oscar offers cover bands from 10.30pm Wednesday (free) and from 11.30pm Friday and Saturday (cover charge from Nkr60).

ℹ️ Information

The **Gamlebyen tourist office** (📞 69 30 46 00; www.opplavfredrikstad.com; Tøihusgata 41; ⏰ 9am-5pm Mon-Fri, 11am-4pm Sat & Sun mid-Jun–mid-Aug, shorter hr rest of yr), in Gamlebyen is complemented in the summer by the smaller **tourist office** (📞 69 39 65 00; Dampskipsbrygga 12; ⏰ 8am-8pm 15 Jun-15 Aug) at the marina.

ℹ️ Getting There & Away

Intercity buses arrive and depart from the Fredrikstad Rutebilstasjon at the train station. Bus 2450 and 2460 run to/from Sarpsborg (Nkr30, 25 minutes, twice hourly). Nor-Way's Oslofjordekspress has one to seven daily services between Oslo and Fredrikstad (Nkr155, 1¼ hours), with most buses continuing to Hvaler; there are also regular **Flybussekspressen** (www.flybussekspressen.no) services from Fredrikstad to Oslo Gardermoen International Airport (Nkr170, 2¼ hours, every hour or two).

Fredrikstad lies on the **NSB** (www.nsb.no) rail line between Oslo and Göteborg. Trains to/from Oslo (Nkr182, one hour) run about 10 times daily, and also go to Sarpsborg and Halden, but note that southbound international trains require a mandatory seat reservation.

ℹ️ Getting Around

To cross the Glomma to Gamlebyen, you can either trek over the high and hulking Glomma bridge or take the ferry (adult/child Nkr10/5, two minutes), which shuttles across the river Glomma to the main gate of Gamlebyen regularly between around 5.30am and midnight (exact times depend on the day).

Around Fredrikstad

HVALER SKERRIES

Norwegian holidaymakers and artists love the Hvaler Skerries, an offshore archipelago of 833 forested islands and islets guarding the southern entrance to Oslofjord. The main islands of **Vesterøy**, **Spjærøy**, **Asmaløy** and **Kirkøy** are connected to the mainland by a toll road (Nkr55) and tunnel. Bus 365 (Nkr58) runs all the way from Fredrikstad to Skjærhalden, at the far end of Kirkøy.

Hvaler **tourist office** (☑69 37 50 00; Skjærhalden; ☺8am-3.30pm mid-Jun–mid-Aug) can point you in the direction of the numerous sights dotted around the islands. There are a couple of other seasonal tourist offices scattered around the islands.

Above the coastline of Akerøy island, accessible only by ferry (taxi boat) from Skjærhalden, clings a well-preserved 17th-century coastal **fortress**, renovated in the 1960s. Admission is free and it's always open.

The mid-11th-century **stone church** (Skjærhalden; ☺noon-4pm Jul, noon-4pm Sat 2nd half of Jun & 1st half of Aug) on Kirkøy is one of the oldest in Norway. The church hosts a week-long music and arts festival in July.

The tourist office has a list of fully equipped private houses and chalets in the Hvaler Skerries, which are available for between Nkr450 and Nkr800 per day.

All year, the M/S *Hollungen* and M/S *Hvalerfergen II* sail roughly every hour from Skjærhalden and through the Hvaler Skerries (Nkr35, one hour). Alternatively, you can sail with the scheduled tour ferry **M/S Vesleø II** (www.hvalerfjordcruise.no, in Norwegian) between Skjærhalden, Koster (Sweden) and Strömstad (Sweden) from mid-June to mid-August for Nkr130/95 per adult/child return.

ROALD AMUNDSEN CENTRE

The renowned explorer Roald Amundsen, who in 1911 was the first man to reach the South Pole, was born in 1872 at Hvidsten, midway between Fredrikstad and Sarpsborg. Although the family moved to Oslo when Roald was still a small child, the family home in Hvidsten, which was the base for a small shipbuilding and shipping business, is now the **Roald Amundsen Centre** (museum & guided tour adult/child Nkr40/10; ☺11am-5pm Sat & Sun, guided tours noon & 2pm 21 Jun-23 Aug), which is dedicated to the man's life and expeditions. Standing surrounded by these quiet fields of southern Norway, it seems perhaps not so surprising that Amundsen set off to seek adventure so far from home. The centre is signposted about 11km east of Fredrikstad, along the Rv111 towards Sarpsborg.

STOREDAL CULTURAL CENTRE

This **cultural centre** (www.storedal.no, in Norwegian; Storedal; adult/child Nkr35/free; ☺10am-4pm Tue-Fri, noon-5pm Sun 20 May-Aug) is 11km northeast of Fredrikstad. King Magnus the Blind was born here in 1117; he took the throne at 13 years of age and earned his nickname at 18 when he was blinded by an enemy in Bergen. A later owner of the farm, Erling Stordahl, who was also blind, developed a monument to King Magnus, as well as a centre dedicated to the blind and other people with disabilities.

The most intriguing feature is the *Ode til Lyset* (Ode to the Light), a 'sound sculpture' by Arnold Haukeland and Arne Nordheim, which, using photo cells and a computer in the farmhouse, transmutes the slightest fluctuations in natural light into haunting, ever-changing music. To get here, follow Rv110 east for about 9km from Fredrikstad; the centre is 2.1km north of the main road.

BORGARSYSSEL MUSEUM

This excellent Østfold county **museum** (www.ostfoldmuseet.no, in Norwegian; Gamlebygaten 8, Sarpsborg; adult/child Nkr40/free; ☺10am-4pm Tue-Fri, noon-5pm Sat & Sun Jun-Aug) lies in the town of Sarpsborg (14km northeast of Fredrikstad). The open-air display contains 30 period buildings from various parts of the country and includes a vast collection of cultural art and artefacts. It also has a **herb garden**, a **petting zoo** and the **ruins** of King Øystein's St Nikolas church, constructed in 1115 and destroyed by the Swedes in 1567. From Fredrikstad, trains and buses run frequently to Sarpsborg.

OLDTIDSVEIEN

People have lived and worked in the Østfold region for thousands of years, and numerous examples of ancient stone works and rock paintings lie along the Oldtidsveien (Old Times Way), the old sunken road between Fredrikstad and Sarpsborg. At Solberg, there are three panels with around 100 figures dating back 3000 years. At Gunnarstorp are several 30m-wide **Bronze Age burial mounds** and several **Iron Age standing stones**. The site at Begby includes well-preserved renditions of ships, men and animals, while Hunn has several **stone circles** and a series of **burial mounds** dating from 500 BC to AD 800. The **rock paintings** at Hornes clearly depict 21 ships complete with oarsmen. The sites are signposted off the E6, just south of Sarpsborg, but they may also be visited on a long day walk or bike ride from Fredrikstad.

Halden

POP 28,100

The soporific border town of Halden, at the end of Iddefjord between steep rocky headlands, possesses a hugely significant history as a cornerstone of Norwegian defence through centuries of Swedish aggression. With a pretty little harbour filled with yachts, a looming fortress rising up behind the town and a sprinkling of decent restaurants, this place makes a worthwhile detour.

The Halden **tourist office** (☑69 19 09 80; www.visithalden.com; Torget 2; ◉9am-4.30pm Mon-Fri mid-Jun–mid-Aug, 9am-3.30pm Mon-Fri rest of yr), just off Torget, has some useful information. In summer, there is a second office at the fortress, **Infosenter** (◉10am-5pm mid-May–Aug).

History

Halden served as a garrison during the Hannibal Wars from 1643 to 1645. From 1644 it was fortified with a wooden stockade. In the 1658 Roskilde Treaty between Sweden and Denmark, Norway lost its Bohuslän province (and Bohus fortress), and Halden was left exposed as a border outpost requiring heavy defences. When attacks by Swedish forces in 1658, 1659 and 1660 were scarcely repelled, the need for better fortification became apparent, resulting in the fortress, which was begun in 1661.

In the midst of it all, in 1659 and 1716, the Halden resistance resorted to fire to drive out the enemy, a sacrifice honoured with a mention in the Norwegian national anthem, which includes the lines: '...we chose to burn our nation, lest we let it fall'. The fires also serve as a centrepiece for a museum in the fortress on the town's history.

Further attacks from the Swedes continued into the 19th century. In the first few years of the 20th century, Fredriksten Fortress was armed with increasingly powerful modern cannons, turret guns and howitzers. However, this firepower was removed during the 1906 negotiations for the dissolution of the Swedish-Norwegian union and the town nestled into life as a quiet seaside village.

◉ Sights

Fredriksten Fortress & Museums

FORTRESS, MUSEUMS

(Fredriksten Festning; www.halden.museum.no, in Norwegian; adult/child incl all museums Nkr60/30; ◉fortress 24hr, guided tours & museums 10am-5pm daily 18 May-Aug) Crowning the hilltop behind Halden is the 1661 Fredriksten Fortress, which has resisted six Swedish sieges and never been captured.

To reach the fortress from the town, a half-overgrown cobbled footpath climbs from the top of Festningsgata in Sørhalden (a neighbourhood of 19th-century sea captains' cottages) up the unkempt lilaccovered slopes. The road for cars leads up from the same street.

On 28 July 1660 King Fredrik III of Denmark issued a declaration ordering a more sturdy fortification above Halden. The pentagonal citadel, as well as the adjoining Gyldenløve Fort to the east, was constructed across two parallel hills from 1661 to 1671, and augmented between 1682 and 1701. Its crowning event came on 11 December 1718, when the warmongering Swede King Karl XII was shot dead on the site (a monument now marks the spot).

The museums in the castle grounds cover various facets of the fortress' history. Downhill from the main entrance, the **War Museum** contains military artefacts and a variety of information on Halden's experiences of war from 1660 onwards, including details on the Norwegian independence movement in 1905. A tunnel leads up into **Prince Christian's Bastion** – the main vantage point for the fortress' defenders. A broader sweep of Halden's history is outlined in the **Byen Brenner Museum** ('City in Flames' Museum) exhibition about halfway down the main thoroughfare. Displays in the **Gamle Kommandantbolig** (Commandant's Residence) cover the history of trade and relations with neighbouring Sweden. The building itself was constructed between 1754 and 1758 and damaged by fire in

1826. After renovation it was used as a powder laboratory, armoury and barracks. Note the Fredrik V monogram over the doorway.

Perhaps the most interesting sites are the **brewery**, which once produced up to 3000L of beer a day, and the **bakery ovens**, which baked bread for up to 5000 soldiers. There's also a multimedia presentation and shop at the Infosenter, just inside the main entrance of the fortress.

There are many intriguing old buildings dotted around the fortress, but even better are the **views** over Halden.

Guided tours (adult/child Nkr60/30; ⊙noon, 1.30pm & 3pm Sat & Sun Jul–8 Aug) of the fortress and other buildings on the grounds are in Norwegian or English. At other times you can take an audio tour (Nkr50). There are also self-guided **ghost tours** (tour maps Nkr50; ⊙May-Aug), in which you're almost guaranteed to see the fortress' famous 'Lady in White'...

On Tuesday and Wednesday evenings in season various dance and musical shows are staged in the fortress grounds. The Wednesday night show is actually part of a national TV show, *Allsangpå Grensen* (Sing Along).

Rød Herregård　　　　HISTORIC BUILDING
(Herregårdsveien; tours adult/child Nkr60/30; ⊙tours noon, 1pm & 2pm Tue-Sat mid-Jun–mid-Aug, noon, 1pm & 2pm Sun May–mid-Jun, noon, 1pm & 3pm Sun mid-Aug–Sep) Rød Herregård manor, dating from at least 1690, has fine interiors, which include notable collections of both weapons and art and lots of the local wildlife with their heads removed from their bodies and stuck up on the wall as trophies – they look so much better like that, don't you think, old chap? The formal gardens are some of the most pleasant in Norway. It's 1.5km northwest of the town centre and is well signposted.

🛏 Sleeping

Fredriksten Camping　　　　CAMPGROUND €
(✆69 18 40 32; Fredriksten Festning; tent with car Nkr150, 4-/5-bed cabins Nkr450/700; P) A great location amid the trees and adjacent to the fortress makes this well-run place a winner. It also offers minigolf and, after the fortress closes and the crowds disappear, a quiet green spot to pitch a tent. There's an on-site restaurant selling various none-too-healthy fried things.

Park Hotel　　　　BUSINESS HOTEL €€
(✆69 21 15 00; www.park-hotel.no, in Norwegian; Marcus Thranes gate 30; s/d from Nkr890/1090; P@🛜) The smart Park Hotel, 1.5km west of the centre, represents good value thanks to its combination of attractively furnished, airy rooms and friendly staff.

Grand Hotell　　　　HISTORIC HOTEL €€
(✆69 18 72 00; www.grandhotell.net, in Norwegian; Jernbanetorget 1; s/d from Nkr900/1050; P@) The Grand Hotell, opposite the train station, has been recently renovated and has comfortable and functional rather than luxurious rooms, but the location is good, as are the buffet breakfasts, which are included in the price.

Halden Vandrerhjem　　　　HOSTEL €
(✆69 21 69 68; www.vandrerhjem.no; Brødløs; dm/ s/d/f Nkr175/300/475/625; ⊙24 Jun–8 Aug) The family-run hostel, at the suburban Tosterød school, offers standard rooms in pleasant surroundings on the edge of Halden. Take bus 102 to 104 from Busterud Park (marked Gimle).

🍴 Eating

Around Gjesthavn (Guest Harbour) you'll find several pleasant restaurants with outdoor seating.

Kongens Brygge　　　　PIZZAS €€
(✆69 17 80 60; Gjesthavn; mains Nkr96-185, pizzas Nkr100) Right on the waterfront, this place has a cruisy atmosphere and a wonderful pontoon terrace that's open in summer. The pizzas are expensive, but come in quite generous proportions and are bound to fill hungry travellers. There are several similar places nearby.

Dickens　　　　INTERNATIONAL €
(✆69 18 35 33; www.dickens.no; Storgata 9; mains from Nkr110; ⊙lunch & dinner) The very popular Dickens, with its mix of international staples such as pasta dishes and various burgers, offers a choice between outdoor seating (summer only) or the dining room in a 17th-century cellar.

Butts Bistro　　　　INTERNATIONAL €
(✆69 17 20 12; Tollbugata 3; mains from Nkr100; ⊙3pm-midnight Sun-Thu, 3pm-4am Fri & Sat) Unfortunately named, but the food is good, and it's great on weekends for a midnight curry.

🍷 Drinking & Entertainment

Dickens　　　　LIVE MUSIC
(www.dickens.no; Storgata 9) If laid-back music on a lazy summer's afternoon sounds pretty much spot-on, head to Dickens, where

MOVING ON?

For tips, recommendations and reviews, head to http://shop.lonelyplanet.com to purchase a downloadable PDF of the Sweden chapter from Lonely Planet's *Scandinavia* guide.

there's (free) jazz in the courtyard from 1.30pm to 3.30pm on Saturday during July and August.

Hannestadgården   BAR, CLUB
(Tollbugata 5; ⊙beer garden 3pm-3am Mon-Fri & 1pm-3am Sat, nightclub 10pm-3am Fri & Sat) This multipurpose nightspot has an atmospheric beer garden, a piano bar, boisterous nightclub and concerts throughout summer.

ⓘ Getting There & Away

Trains between Oslo and Halden (Nkr231, 1¾ hours) via Fredrikstad run hourly from Monday to Friday and every second hour on weekends. An average of four trains daily continue on to Göteborg and Malmö in Sweden. The long-distance bus terminal sits right on the harbour, with regular services (less on weekends) to Oslo and Fredrikstad.

Around Halden

HALDEN CANAL (HALDENKANALEN)
East and north of Halden, a canal system connects the town with Göteborg, Sweden, for all but one short dry section (1.8km). The highlight is the Brekke Locks, a system of four locks between Femsjøen and Aspern (on the Halden–Strømsfoss run), which raise and lower the boats a total of 26.6m.

Canoe hire is available from **Kirkeng Camping** (☏90 19 42 44), 5km northeast of town in Aremark, if you prefer to explore under your own steam. You can pick up a boating and recreation map from the tourist office in Halden.

Otherwise, you can take a ride on the tourist cruise boats or **M/S Turisten** (☏90 60 63 21; www.turisten.no, in Norwegian), which follows the Haldenkanalen between Tistedal (just east of Halden) and Strømsfoss (adult/child return Nkr450/free, four hours). The boat leaves Strømsfoss at 10am and begins its leisurely return from Tistedal at 3.30pm on Wednesday and Friday to Sunday from 23 June to 11 July. Yes, you read that correctly; it operates for a grand total of 18 days a year....

A shorter boat trip, and one with a slightly less work-shy crew, is the **M/S Strømsfoss** (☏90 60 63 21; www.turisten.no, in Norwegian), which follows the same route as the Turisten. The boat leaves Strømsfoss at 11am and Tistedal at 3pm on Wednesday and Friday to Sunday from 23 June to 22 August (adult/child return Nkr290/free). To reach the town of Tistedal, take bus 103 or 106 (Nkr32, 18 minutes, twice hourly except late Saturday afternoon and Sunday). You'll need to drive to Strømsfoss to do the return trip.

Southern Norway

Why Go?

Norway's southern coastline has always drawn Norwegian tourists in summer droves, and with beautiful coastal villages all dressed in white looking out across an island-studded sea it's not difficult to see why. The coast also offers a chance to see a totally different kind of Norway from that of the fjords and high plateaus of the tourist brochures.

Venture inland though and the real interest begins as the scenery turns ever more dramatic. The place we love above all others in the region's interior is Rjukan, gateway to some of Norway's most scenic high country – the Hardangervidda National Park and the spectacularly formed mountain of Gausta. Elsewhere, scattered among a landscape smothered in forest and decorated in dark lakes filled with beavers, you'll discover idyllic little villages, wooden stave churches and a rich traditional culture.

Best Places to Eat

» Blom Restaurant (p95)
» Bølgen & Moi (p101)
» Has Nabaen (p102)
» Haven Brasserie (p97)
» Restaurant Havariet (p87)

Best Places to Stay

» Rjukan Hytteby & Kro (p114)
» Buøy Camping (p112)
» Lampeland Hotell (p109)
» Lysko Gjestegaard (p91)
» Grimstad Hotell (p97)

When to Go

Kristiansand

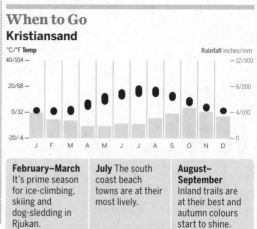

°C/°F Temp   Rainfall inches/mm

February–March
It's prime season for ice-climbing, skiing and dog-sledding in Rjukan.

July The south coast beach towns are at their most lively.

August–September
Inland trails are at their best and autumn colours start to shine.

THE COAST

You probably didn't come to Norway for the beaches, but if you did, expect to be accompanied by masses of local tourists drawn by reasonable beaches and picturesque islands. The towns along the coast are pretty, if way overpriced in summer.

Tønsberg

POP 37,500

Tønsberg is the oldest town in Norway, although so distant are its origins that few interesting remnants remain in what is now a largely modern town. There are nonetheless a few Viking-era ruins and a decrepit castle that together make Tønsberg worth a brief detour as you head along the coast.

◉ Sights

Tønsberg Castle FORTRESS
(Castrum Tunsbergis; admission free; ⊙tower noon–5pm mid-Jun–mid-Aug, shorter hr rest of yr) Tønsberg Castle, spread across the hill behind the town, was the largest fortress in Norway in the 13th century. In 1503 the Swedes destroyed the fortress and little remains of the castle itself. Nonetheless, the modern (1888), 17m-high **Slottsfjellstårnet tower** provides a good viewpoint over the ruins. Parts of the 600m-long outer wall remain intact, while the extant medieval stone foundations include **King Magnus Lagabøte's keep**, the 1191 **Church of St Michael**, the **hall of King Håkon Håkonsson** and various **guard towers**. The park is always open.

Vestfold County Museum MUSEUM
(Vestfold Fylkesmuseum; www.vfm.no, in Norwegian; Farmannsveien 30; adult/child Nkr60/10; ⊙10am-4pm Mon-Fri, noon-5pm Sat & Sun mid-May–mid-Sep, shorter hr rest of yr) At the foot of Slottsfjellet (Castle Rock) at the northern end of town is Vestfold County Museum, a five-minute walk northwest of the train station. Highlights include displays on the excavation of the impressive *Oseberg* Viking ship (now shown in Oslo's Viking Ship Museum, p57), a collection of historic period-furnished farm buildings, and a section on Tønsberg's whaling history.

⏟ Sleeping

TOP CHOICE **Tønsberg Vandrerhjem** HOSTEL €
(☑33 31 21 75; tonsberg@hihostels.no; Dronning Blancasgata 22; dm Nkr350, s/tw with shared bathroom Nkr550/650, tw with bathroom Nkr750, f Nkr950; P@) This exceptionally well-run and friendly hostel is well equipped, clean and tidy and just a five-minute walk from the train station. The cosy common areas would be the envy of many a fancy hotel. A good breakfast is served. The reception area is shut between noon and 3pm.

Thon Hotel Brygga BUSINESS HOTEL €€
(☑33 34 49 00; www.thonhotels.no; Nedre Langgate 40; r from Nkr995; @ʔ) Inside a traditional wooden warehouse, this modern waterfront hotel has pleasant (if smallish) rooms and great breakfasts, and is popular with families.

Quality Hotel Tønsberg BUSINESS HOTEL €€
(☑33 00 41 00; www.choice.no; Ollebukta 3; d from Nkr1088; P@ʔ) Another excellent option, this branch of the Quality Hotel chain has stylish (in a Nordic minimalist kind of way) rooms by the waterfront. Parking is a steep Nkr189 per day.

✗ Eating

Tønsberg has dozens of decent restaurants, with the best atmosphere along the water.

TOP CHOICE **Restaurant Havariet** INTERNATIONAL €€
(☑33 35 83 90; Nedre Langgate 30c; mains Nkr122-150; ⊙11am-1am) Arguably the most popular of the waterfront eateries, this place offers solid pub grub in a warm and inviting interior. It has good-value lunch deals and plenty of salty marine life on the menu, including a very tasty prawn, bacon and camembert salad.

Roar I Bva SEAFOOD €€
(Nedre Langgate; sandwiches Nkr70-80, mains Nkr150-180) This cute, oversized wooden shack is half-fishmongers and half-seafood cafe. However you choose to class it, the well-priced fish is so fresh it might well flop off your plate and back into the sea.

ⓘ Information

The **tourist office** (☑48 06 33 33; www.visit tonsberg.com; Storgaten 38; ⊙9am-4.30pm Mon-Fri, 10am-2pm Sat mid-Jun–early Aug, 9am-2pm Mon-Fri rest of yr) is just off the main square.

ⓘ Getting There & Around

The **Tønsberg Rutebilstasjon** (☑33 30 01 00; Jernbanegaten) is a block south of the train station. Nor-Way Bussekspress buses run to/from Kristiansand (Nkr240, 4½ hours, one to two daily) via most coastal towns en route, including

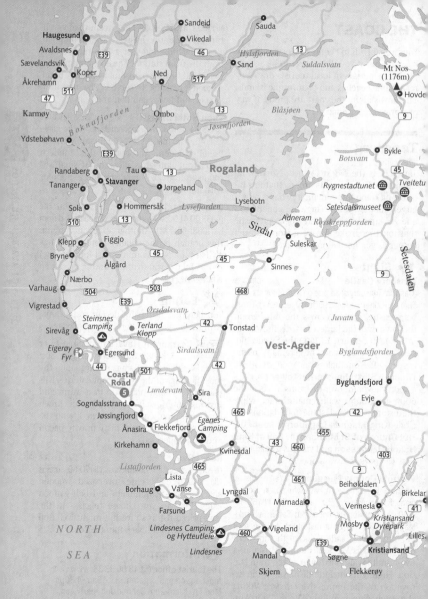

Southern Norway Highlights

❶ Strike out on foot across the reindeer haunted wilderness of the **Hardangervidda Plateau** (see the boxed text, p115)

❷ Board a slow boat down the exquisite **Telemark Canal** (p110)

❸ Busy yourself looking for beavers in the beautiful lakes and rivers around **Dalen** (p112)

❹ Climb to the summit of **Gausta** (see the boxed text, p115), Norway's most beautiful mountain

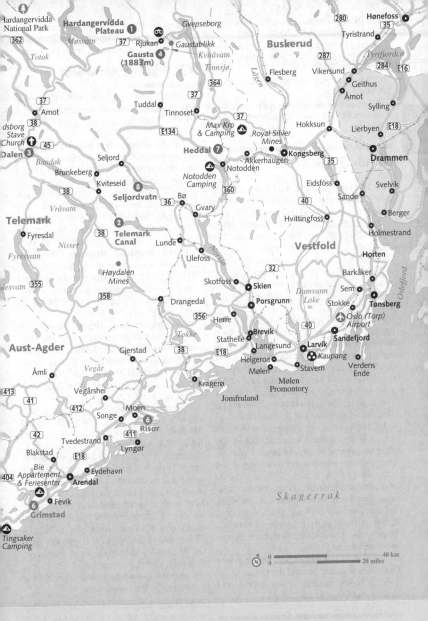

5 Take the quiet but beautiful **coastal road** (p105) between Flekkefjord and Egersund

6 Stroll through the narrow streets of the 'white towns'

of **Grimstad** (p96) and **Risør** (p93)

7 Admire the exquisite roof lines and paintings in the stave church at **Heddal** (p110)

8 Scour the surface of **Seljordvatn** (p117) in search of Selma the Serpent

Larvik (Nkr115, one hour, two daily). They also run to Oslo (Nkr149, 5 hours).

Intercity trains run hourly between Tønsberg and Oslo (Nkr201, 1½ hours) or south to Larvik (Nkr93, 34 minutes).

Bike rental is available from the tourist office for Nkr60 per day.

Drivers of their own vehicles will be stung by an automatic toll for Nkr15 on entering the town precincts.

Sandefjord

POP 41,900

This former whaling capital is worth a detour; it's home to one of only a couple of museums in the world dedicated to whaling.

The excellent Sandefjord **tourist office** (☎33 46 05 90; www.visitsandefjord.com; Thor Dahls gate 7; ☺9am-5.30pm Mon-Fri, 10am-5pm Sat, 12.30-5pm Sun Jul-Aug, 9am-4pm Mon-Fri rest of yr) is just back from the waterfront. You can use the internet in the tourist office (Nkr20 per 15 minutes) and there's free tea and coffee.

You might not agree with what it's promoting but there's no denying that Sandefjord's **Whaling Museum** (Hvalfangst-museet; www.hvalfangstmuseet.no; Museumsgaten 39; adult/child Nkr55/30; ☺10am-5pm late Jun-Aug, shorter hr rest of yr) is a well-presented exhibition of this most controversial of Norwegian activities. The museum charts the history of Norwegian whaling, with photos and equipment.

In addition to whaling-related exhibits the museum contains information and displays on general Arctic and marine wildlife. The museum offers a balanced report on both sides of the whaling debate. Exhibits here are complemented by the 1950s whaleboat **Southern Actor** (adult/child Nkr50/25; ☺9.30am-5pm late Jun-Aug), which is moored at the harbour; entry is by the same ticket. There's also the striking sculpture **monument to whalers** by the water.

There are a number of business-standard chain hotels in and around the town.

Most buses running between Oslo and Kristiansand stop in Sandefjord.

Larvik

POP 41,400

Larvik is one of the largest towns along Norway's south coast. Although it has some good museums, its main attractions are Norway's most accessible excavations from the Viking era. The town's main historical claim to fame is as the home town of Thor Heyerdahl, one of Norway's premier explorers.

◉ Sights & Activities

Larvik Museum   MUSEUM
(adult/child combined ticket Nkr50/10; ☺noon-4pm Tue-Sun late Jun–mid-Aug, shorter hr rest of yr) This four-part museum is spread across the town:

The classic baroque timber **Herregården manor house** (Herregårdsletta 6; ☺guided tours every hr) was constructed in 1677 as the home of the Norwegian Governor General, Ulrik Frederik Gyldenløve, the Duke of Larvik; as the illegitimate son of King Fredrik IV of Denmark, Gyldenløve was given a dukedom and packed off to Norwegian obscurity. It's furnished in 17th- and 18th-century style.

Larvik Maritime Museum (Kirkestredet 5), a 1730 brick structure immediately east of the harbour, is home to maritime art and a number of impressive model ships. There's also a small exhibition on the nearby Viking town of Kaupang.

Verkensgaarden (Nedre Fritzøegate 2) has tools and implements from a local 17th-century sawmill and ironworks. There's also a permanent geological exhibition documenting the evolution of blue larvikite, a beautiful, locally quarried 500-million-year-old type of granite.

Kaupang (admission free), 5km east of Larvik, was a former Viking town built around AD 800 and occupied until 960. It is believed that up to 1000 people lived here in its heyday. For us, this is the most interesting of Larvik's sights. Although most of the original artefacts are now in Oslo, the custodians of the site make the most of what they have with a small exhibition, four Viking tents and knowledgeable guides dressed as Vikings who can show you to nearby Viking graves and explain Kaupang's past. On Wednesday (family day) and weekends, they cook Viking soup and bread. The guides can also tell you where to find other Viking cemeteries in the Larvik area.

Kulturhaus Bølgen   CULTURAL CENTRE
(www.kulturhausbolgen.no, in Norwegian; Larvik Kulturhus Bølgen; ☺1-8pm) The town's swish new wave-shaped cultural centre houses a cafe and cinema (screening nondubbed films) on the ground floor and, more interestingly, a contemporary art gallery on the 2nd floor that has frequently changing exhi-

THOR HEYERDAHL

Larvik's favourite son was the intrepid and controversial Thor Heyerdahl (1914–2002), a quirky scientist, anthropologist and explorer who spent his lifetime trying to prove that the world's oceans were vast highways that were essential to understanding ancient civilisations – a novel idea in the hallowed halls of scientific research.

In 1947 he sailed 6000km in a balsa-wood raft, the *Kon-Tiki*, from Peru to Polynesia to prove that the South Pacific may have been settled by migrants from South America rather than Asia. His theories were supported by discoveries of similar fauna and cultural artefacts in Polynesia and South America, and by the fact that Pacific Ocean currents run east to west. The film of his journey won an Oscar in 1951 for best documentary and his medal-winning bravery in resisting the Nazis only added to his legend. His book describing the expedition sold an astonishing 60 million copies worldwide. The actual *Kon-Tiki* ship is on display at the Kon-Tiki Museum in Oslo (p58).

After being one of the first Europeans to excavate on the Galapagos and Easter Islands, Heyerdahl again grabbed international attention in 1970 when he crossed the Atlantic in a papyrus raft. His purpose was to prove that Columbus may not have been the first successful transatlantic navigator and that the ancient Egyptians may have made the crossing millennia before. His first raft, *Ra*, sank soon after setting out, but the dogged Heyerdahl successfully completed the crossing in *Ra II*.

In 1978, at the age of 64, the indefatigable Heyerdahl sailed the *Tigris* from the Euphrates and Tigris Rivers, down the Persian Gulf and across the Indian Ocean to Djibouti to prove how the ancient Sumerians travelled widely.

Heyerdahl died of cancer in northern Italy on 18 April 2002.

bitions highlighting the best new art coming out of Norway.

Sleeping

TOP CHOICE **Lysko Gjestegaard** GUESTHOUSE €€ (☑33 18 77 79; www.lysko-it.no; Kirkestredet 10; s/d from Nkr600/800; P☎) This quiet guesthouse occupies what is possibly Larvik's most charming location, with a lovely old timbered house opposite the Maritime Museum at the eastern end of the harbour. The rooms themselves might be small but they are crammed with character thanks to the arty owners filling them with colourful furniture and liberally splashing bright paint across the walls and ceilings. There's also a kitchen for guest use and an in-house antique shop. Prices don't include breakfast.

Hotell Greven HISTORIC HOTEL €€ (☑33 18 25 26; www.hotell-greven.no; Storgata 26; s Nkr775, d with shared bathroom Nkr775, with private bathroom Nkr900) With considerable charm, this renovated 1903 hotel represents a good choice right on the waterfront. Be warned though that the reception is often closed in the mornings.

Quality Hotel Grand Farris BUSINESS HOTEL €€ (☑33 18 78 00; www.choice.no; Storgata 38; s Nkr699-1399, d Nkr899-1599; P☎) Dated but spacious rooms fill this oversized and really

rather ugly hotel on the waterfront, but it's well run and well equipped. Parking costs Nkr50 per day.

Eating

Both the Hotell Greven and Quality Hotel have good restaurants; the former mainly does Greek and Italian dishes.

Georg Marius Larsen Fisk Delikatese SEAFOOD €€ (☑33 18 17 44; Dronningsgt 43; mains Nkr150) This newly opened fish deli/restaurant lets you pick your monster of the deep (and some of the lobsters are so big they really do qualify as monsters) from the display cabinets and then cooks it up for you to eat outside on the terrace or take away. At the time of research it was only operating as a restaurant on sunny summer days, but it hoped to have an all-weather seating area operational soon.

Information

The helpful **tourist office** (☑33 69 71 00; www.visitlarvik.no; Larvik Kulturhus Bølgen; ⊙1-8pm) is located inside the swish new Bølgen cultural centre on the waterfront.

Getting There & Away

Nor-Way Bussekspress buses pass through Larvik en route between Seljord (Nkr280, 2¼ hours, up to three times daily) and Tønsberg (Nkr115, one hour). For other destinations along the coast, you may need to change at Tønsberg or Arendal. Local trains run hourly between Oslo S (Central Station) and Larvik (Nkr199 to Nkr277, two hours). The train and bus stations are side by side on Storgata.

Around Larvik

The low-lying Brunelanes Peninsula southwest of Larvik has a few moderately interesting towns, though they are packed in summer with Norwegian holidaymakers, who flood the coastal campsites.

STAVERN
POP 5600

The pleasant little town of Stavern, just south of Larvik, is set around a stunning fold of coastline; the ocean is full of granite outcrops, creating a maze of icy waterways. The village of Stavern itself is almost as pretty as the natural beauty surrounding it. Its pedestrian streets are lined with cafes, small private galleries and creamy white houses. Highlights include the mid-18th-century fort **Fredriksvern Verft**, which is surrounded by block houses that once formed part of the fortress defences. Also worth visiting is the colourful 1756 **church** (Kommandør Herbsgata 1; admission free; ☺11am-1pm Tue-Fri), Norway's first naval house of worship.

Stavern is the start of the popular and attractive 33km-long Kyststien **coastal walk** to Ødegården on the western coast of Brunelanes. The Stavern **tourist office** (☎33 19 73 00; Kongens gate 2; ☺10am-4pm Wed-Sat, 1-4pm Sun mid-Jun–early Aug) provides route maps.

In operation since 1844, the **Hotel Wassilioff** (☎33 11 36 00; www.wassilioff.no; Havnegata 1; s Nkr1150, d Nkr1300-1400; P🐾) has learnt a thing or two about keeping guests happy and, thanks to touches such as old sepia photos of Norwegian royalty and retro dining chairs, it has character in abundance. Rooms are a little less exciting than common areas and you pay an extra Nkr200 for sea views. Its location next to the parkland surrounding the fortress and a pocket-sized beach is spot on.

To get to and from Larvik (Nkr30, 15 minutes, hourly), use bus 1.

MØLEN

The Mølen Promontory is something of a geological oddity. It forms the end of the ice-age **Ra moraine** (rock and silt pushed ahead of the glacier and deposited as a new landform), which extends from the lake Farrisvatn (which the moraine dammed) to the southwestern end of Brunelanes. The 230 stone cairns and heaps of boulders, which are laid out in parallel rows, are Iron Age burial mounds.

Damvann

Some 20km north of Larvik is the beautiful, haunting lake of Damvann, surrounded by forests. Popular legend claims it to be the home of a witch called Huldra, a woman of such exquisite beauty that it is said that any man who looked upon her was doomed. Access is difficult without a car; the nearest bus stop is at Kvelde (6km from the lake) on Numendalslågen Rd.

Kragerø
POP 10,500

One of the favourite summer retreats for Norwegians, Kragerø has narrow streets and whitewashed houses climbing up from the water's edge. Kragerø has also long served as a retreat for Norwegian artists, and Edvard Munch (see the boxed text, p413) spent a few restorative fishing holidays here and called Kragerø 'the pearl of the coastal towns'. A statue of Munch stands on the spot where he painted a winter sun over the sea.

☉ Sights & Activities

There's not much to see here; the offshore island of Jomfruland is Kragerø's most popular attraction. For a great view over the town and its skerries, climb from Kragerø Stadium to the lookout point on **Steinmann Hill**.

Seal Watching   SEAL WATCHING
(www.fjordbat.no, in Norwegian; adult/child from Nkr100/50; ☺10.45am Tue, 3.25pm Fri, 11.10am Sat, 11.45am & 7.45pm Sun Jul–mid-Aug) M/S *Kragerø*, the same boat that runs ferry services to Jomfruland, has put together a seal-watching package where you get return boat rides to Jomfruland, wildlife fact sheets and a pair of binoculars (extra fee). Seals are seen on around 50% of ferry crossings.

Berg-Kragerø Museum   MUSEUM
(Lovisenbergveien 45; adult/child Nkr50/free; ☺noon-6pm mid-Jun–mid-Aug) On the shore of Hellefjord, 3km from the centre, this museum consists of a 120-hectare estate with a country residence dating from 1803. There are gardens, walking tracks and a gallery for visiting art and history exhibits.

Sleeping & Eating

If the places listed here are full or you want to stay a while then the tourist office can put you in touch with people with apartments to rent.

For a meal you'll find a number of little cafes and restaurants almost floating in the harbour. There are also a couple of supermarkets for self-caterers.

TOP **Kragerø Sportell Apartments**
CHOICE
APARTMENTS, HOTEL €
(☑35 98 57 00; www.kragerosportell.no; Lovisenbergveien 20; r from Nkr550, apt Nkr1180; P@🛜) The former youth hostel is now privately owned but it remains an excellent deal with modern and comfortable, if plain, rooms and lovely waterfront apartments that sleep up to four and have their own kitchens. Breakfast is included in room rates but not if you're staying in an apartment. To get here leave Kragerø via the tunnel and follow the signs for 1km into the village of Kalstadkilen.

Victoria Hotel HISTORIC HOTEL €€€
(☑35 98 75 25; www.victoria-kragero.no; PA Heuchtsgata 31; s/d Nkr1175/1475; 🛜) The rooms in the grand old Victoria all differ from one another and are the best in town. Some even have little kitchenettes and others have balconies overlooking the wharf. It's well run and has a rare bit of character.

ℹ Information

The exceptionally helpful **tourist office** (☑35 98 23 88; www.visitkragero.no; Tovgaten 1; ⊙9am-7pm Mon-Fri, 9am-6pm Sat, 9am-3pm Sun Jul–mid-Aug, 9am-4pm Mon-Fri May-Jun & mid-Aug–Sep) is at the bus station. Free internet is also available at the tourist office.

ℹ Getting There & Away

Trains from Oslo or Kristiansand stop at Neslandsvatn, where most are met by a bus to Kragerø. Buses run up to five times daily to Oslo (Nkr300, 3½ hours) and Kristiansand (Nkr250, 2½ hours), although you may have to change in Tangen on the E18.

Risør

POP 6900

Snaking around the base of cliffs and hills and overlooking a moody ocean, the ice-cream-white town of Risør is one of southern Norway's prettiest. The focus of the town falls on the U-shaped harbour full of colourful fishing boats and private yachts,

and surrounded by historic white houses (dating from 1650 to 1890). This is a great place to wander and soak up the rustic charm for a few days. If you get bored by long, lazy days by the water, you probably shouldn't be here.

◉ Sights & Activities

Risør Saltwater Aquarium AQUARIUM
(Saltvannsakvariet; www.risorakvarium.no; Dampskipsbrygga; adult/child mid-Jun–mid-Aug Nkr60/40, rest of yr Nkr30/20; ⊙11am-6pm Jul, noon-4pm Jun & Aug, shorter hr rest of yr) The interesting Risør Saltwater Aquarium, on the quay in front of the Risør Hotel, is a small showcase of saltwater fish, crustaceans and shellfish common to Norway's south coast. Highlights include baby lobsters, the colourful cuckoo wrasse and the **underwater post office**. Yes, you read that correctly.

✦ Festivals

To get summer rolling, the town hosts a number of festivals, including the following.

Risør Chamber Music Festival CHAMBER MUSIC
Held in the last week of June, this festival has a growing cast of local and international performers in attendance.

Risør Wooden Boat Festival BOAT RACE
Held over the first weekend in August, this festival (known as Trebåtfestival) encompasses boat races, concerts and kids' activities. Finding accommodation at this time can be difficult.

🛏 Sleeping

Det Lille Hotell APARTMENTS €€€
(☑37 15 14 95; www.detlillehotel.no; apt per night Nkr1400-2000; P🛜) This interesting choice offers superb-value self-catering suites and apartments dotted around town. Most are in delightfully restored homes with period furnishings and are ideal if you plan to spend a week here; daily rates are cheaper outside the peak summer season, and booking for a week or more always reduces the daily cost significantly. The bigger apartments have room for several people.

Sorlandet Feriesenter CAMPGROUND €
(☑37 15 40 80; www.sorlandet-feriesenter.no; Sandnes; tent with/without car Nkr260/190, cabins Nkr500-1500) This delightful waterside campsite, on the peninsula south of Risør, has a range of very well-equipped cabins alongside lots of trees under which you can plonk a tent. Children will love all the activities

and facilities on offer (boat rides, play-grounds, 'elephant' showers, giant bouncing balloons and so on).

Risør Hotel   TRADITIONAL HOTEL €€€
(☑37 14 80 00; www.risorhotel.no; Tangengata 16; s/d from Nkr1195/1495; P☎) The only official hotel accommodation in the town centre, the Risør lacks the attention to detail you'd expect for this price. The waterfront location is, however, a winner. It's opposite the aquarium 500m west of the harbour.

✗ Eating

Around, or just back from, the harbour you'll find several moderately priced cafes and restaurants.

Kast Loss   SEAFOOD €€
(☑37 15 03 71; Strandgata 27; mains from Nkr198; ⊙4-10pm Mon-Fri, 11am-midnight Sat, 1-10pm Sun) There's a Mediterranean twang to this harbour-front restaurant. Seafood is, not surprisingly, the big deal here, and locals rate Kast Loss as about the best-value restaurant in town. If seafood isn't your thing then it also serves up good pizzas for around Nkr150.

Brasserie Krag   INTERNATIONAL €
(☑37 15 04 50; Kragsgata 12; mains Nkr75-125; ⊙11am-6pm Mon-Wed & Sat-Sun, to 8pm Thu, to 10pm Fri) This cosy restaurant has a fairly diverse selection of international staples on the menu (burgers, pasta, salads, seafood) and a laid-back ambience. The daily specials, at Nkr85, are a really good deal.

ℹ Information

The **tourist office** (☑37 15 22 70; www.risor.no; Kragsgata 3; ⊙10am-6pm mid-Jun–mid-Aug, 11am-3pm Mon-Fri, noon-2pm Sat rest of yr) is 50m west of the harbour.

ℹ Getting There & Away

The nearest train station is at Gjerstad, but you'll need your own car to get there (thus somewhat defeating the point of train travel!). NorWay Bussekspress buses between Kristiansand (Nkr250, three hours) and Oslo (Nkr340, 3¾ hours) connect at Vinterkjær with local buses to/from Risør (Nkr30, 20 minutes).

Around Risør

The skerries just offshore are a popular excursion from Risør. The southernmost island of **Stangholmen**, with a pretty lighthouse dating from 1855, is the most popular; this may be due in part to the fact that it's the only one of the islands with a restaurant, **Stangholmen Fyr Restaurant & Bar** (☑37 15 24 50; www.stangholmen.no; mains from Nkr215), which is in the lighthouse.

To get to Stangholmen take one of the twice-hourly summertime **boats** (return ticket Nkr50; ⊙10am-1am mid-Jun–mid-Aug), which run from the harbour in Risør. Note that they don't go in periods of bad weather.

Lyngør
POP 120
Tiny Lyngør, consisting of several offshore islets near the village of Gjeving, isn't shy about the fact that it won the 1991 European competition for the tidiest town on the continent. Even if it weren't for that distinction, this picturesque little settlement would be worth a visit. Part of its charm lies in the fact that visitors can't bring their vehicles across on the ferry.

The **Lyngør Båtselskap ferry** (☑41 45 41 45; adult/child Nkr32/19) between Gjeving, Holmen and Lyngør leaves every half-hour or so in July and August and about seven times daily through the rest of the year.

Arendal
POP 40,100
The main appeal of Arendal, one of the larger south coast towns, is its undeniable buzz throughout summer around the harbour (known as Pollen), with outdoor restaurants and bars next to the water and a fairly full calendar of festivals. Large enough to have an array of amenities but not too big to overwhelm, it's a nice place to spend a few days. The matchbox-sized old district of Tyholmen, which features many timbered houses, adds considerable charm, while those seeking greater communion with the sea than a harbour-side cafe can offer will find the offshore islands of Merdø, Tromøy and Hisøy to be worthwhile excursions.

◎ Sights
Tyholmen   OLD TOWN
Rising up behind the Gjestehavn (Guest Harbour) is the old harbour-side Tyholmen district, home to beautiful 17th- to 19th-century timber buildings featuring neoclassical, rococo and baroque influences. In 1992 it was deservedly awarded the prestigious Europa Nostra prize for its expert restoration. Tyhol-

men was once separated from the mainland by a canal, which was filled in after the great sailing era. Look out in particular for the **rådhus** (town hall), a striking wooden building dating from 1815.

Kulturhistoriste Senter
MUSEUM

(www.aaks.no, in Norwegian; Parkveien 16; adult/child Nkr20/10; ⊙9am-5pm Mon-Fri, noon-5pm Sat mid-Jun–mid-Aug, shorter hr rest of yr) The museum was first conceived in 1832, when the town authorities asked their globetrotting sailors to be on the lookout for items that may be of interest back home. The most interesting exhibits are those covering the ill-fated final journey of the slave ship *Fredensborg*, which went down off Tromøy in 1768.

FREE **Bomuldsfabriken Art Hall** ART GALLERY
(www.bomuldsfabriken.no, in Norwegian; Oddenveien 5; admission free; ⊙noon-4pm Tue-Fri) This new and highly regarded modern art gallery is a 10-minute walk from the town centre on the northern edge of Arendal. It's one of the largest galleries in southern Norway and its exciting content changes several times a year.

Arendal Sommerfuglpark
BUTTERFLY PARK

(www.arendalsommerfuglpark.no, in Norwegian; adult/child Nkr100/80; ⊙10am-5pm Mon-Sat mid-Jun–mid-Aug, shorter hr rest of yr; 🚼) Children will enjoy creeping through the tropical foliage looking for floppy-winged swallowtails and enormous Atlas moths at this butterfly park. As well as butterflies there are a number of slithering snakes and warty toads and frogs (we dare you to kiss one and see if it turns into a handsome prince). It's located inside the campsite on the island of Hove.

✹✹ Festivals & Events

There's always something going on in Arendal, with open-air concerts by the water quite common on weekends. Summer highlights include the following:

Sørlandet Boat Show
BOAT SHOW

(www.sorlandetsbatmesse.no, in Norwegian; ⊙late May)

Hove Festival
MUSIC FESTIVAL

(www.hovefestivalen.no; ⊙late Jun) Music festival drawing international acts to the island of Tromøy. Headliners in 2010 included the likes of Muse and Massive Attack.

Canal Street Jazz & Blues Festival
JAZZ & BLUES

(www.canalstreet.no; ⊙late Jul) World-class jazz and blues.

🛏 Sleeping

Arendal has a good sprinkling of midrange hotels, but those on a tight budget will need to head out of town.

Clarion Tyholmen Hotel
HISTORIC HOTEL €€

(☎37 07 68 00; www.choice.no; Teaterplassen 2; r from Nkr1126; 🛜) Undoubtedly Arendal's best hotel, the Clarion combines a prime waterfront position with attractive rooms in a restored old building that seeks to emulate Tyholmen's old-world ambience. The corner suites offer magnificent sea views.

Thon Hotel Arendal
CHAIN HOTEL €€

(☎37 05 21 50; www.thonhotels.no; Friergangen 1; r from Nkr1050; 🛜) It might not have the waterfront views, but this outpost of Thon Hotels is just 50m from the water's edge. Typical of the Thon chain, the rooms are modern, large and comfortable. There's a public pay carpark nearby.

Park Inn
CHAIN HOTEL €€

(☎37 00 07 20; www.parkinn.no; Vestregate 11; d from Nkr1195; 🛜) With port holes on the room doors, portraits of old ships and, in case you get really lost, shipping charts to the Philippines on the walls, there's a nautical feel to this central hotel. Rooms are merely comfortable rather than luxurious. There's public pay parking next door.

✗ Eating & Drinking

There's no need to stray too far from the harbour, and indeed you may find yourself spending much of your day and evening by the water.

TOP CHOICE **Blom Restaurant** SEAFOOD €€€
(☎37 00 14 14; Lang-brygge 5; mains Nkr299, set menus Nkr599; ⊙noon-11pm Sun-Thu, noon-3.30am Fri & Sat) Perhaps the classiest bar-restaurant by the Pollen harbour, Blom is a chic place and a cut above the beer-and-yobbo culture that sometimes afflicts other waterside bars in Arendal. Meals such as scallops and smoked mackerel will set your taste buds wobbling in excitement.

Café Victor
INTERNATIONAL €

(☎37 02 18 38; Kirkengaten 5; light meals Nkr69-129; ⊙10am-midnight Jun-Aug, to 5pm Mon-Sat Sep-May) In a prime waterfront position, Café Victor is another cool choice. Apart from the antique ceiling, the decor is sleek and modern, the service friendly and the food (sandwiches and pasta) and coffee excellent.

Madam Reiersen NORWEGIAN €€€
(☎37 02 19 00; Nedre Tyholmsvei 3; lunch mains Nkr125-159, dinner mains Nkr219-260) One of the better restaurants ringing the Pollen harbour. Considering the food quality, Madam Reiersen is good value, especially at lunchtime. And what sort of tasty morsels can you tuck into? How about mountain trout, a succulent hunk of deer leg or an Arctic char?

No.9 Kaffe & Platebar CAFE €
(☎37 02 77 92; Langbrygge 9; coffee Nkr19-34; ⊙10am-5pm Mon-Sat, noon-5pm Sun, to 7pm Jul) Another classy little cafe, No.9 is the work of Espen Larsen, a local jazz musician who sells a range of (mostly jazz) CDs and plays them while you sip your coffee or snack on a pastry – the perfect accompaniment to a lazy Arendal afternoon.

ℹ Information

Tourist office (☎37 00 55 44; www.arendal. com; Sam Eydes plass; ⊙9am-6pm Mon-Fri, 11am-6pm Sat, noon-4pm Sun Jul–mid-Aug, 8.30am-4pm Mon-Fri rest of yr) Note that outside the high season hours can be a little erratic, although even if the door is shut someone will be on hand to answer phone calls.

ℹ Getting There & Away

M/S Merdø (www.skilsoferga.no, in Norwegian) sails from Arendal (Pollen) to Merdø (adult/child Nkr50/25) twice hourly from early July to mid-August. It also runs on Saturdays year-round.

There are also ferries to Hisøy (adult/child Nkr30/20).

Nor-Way Bussekspress buses between Kristiansand (Nkr130, 1½ hours, up to nine daily) and Oslo (from Nkr350, four hours) call in at the Arendal Rutebilstasjon, a block west of Pollen harbour. Local Timekspressen buses connect Arendal with Grimstad (Nkr53, 30 minutes, half-hourly) and Risør (Nkr98, 1¼ hours, hourly).

Around Arendal

The 260-hectare island of Merdø, just off Arendal, has been inhabited since the 16th century. One peculiarity is that the island bears the remnants of vegetable species introduced in the ballast of early sailing vessels.

The favoured bathing sites are on Tromøy, Spornes, Hisøy and Hove. The nearest access to Spornes is on the bus marked 'Tromøy Vest/Øst', but you'll still have a 15-minute walk. Alternatively, take a bike on the **M/S Skilsøy ferry** (adult/child Nkr25/18, 10 min-

utes), which sails frequently between Arendal and the western end of Tromøy. Tromøy also has some enjoyable and easy-to-follow **walking trails**. Arendal tourist office can give route suggestions.

On the islets of **Store** and **Lille Torungene** rise two grand lighthouses that have guided ships into Arendal since 1844. They're visible from the coasts of both Hisøy and Tromøy.

Grimstad

POP 19,500

Unusually for a town along the coast, Grimstad is at its most beautiful in the pedestrianised streets that lie inland from the waterfront; these streets are some of the loveliest on the Skagerrak coast. Grimstad has a number of interesting calling cards: it was the home of playwright Henrik Ibsen and has a good museum; it is the sunniest spot in Norway, with an average of 266 hours of sunshine per month in June and July; and Grimstad also has an unmistakably young vibe, thanks to its large student population.

◉ Sights

Ibsenhuset Museum MUSEUM
(Grimstad By Museum; www.gbm.no, in Norwegian; Henrik Ibsens gate 14; adult/child Nkr75/free; ⊙11am-5pm Mon-Sat, noon-5pm Sun Jul–mid-Aug, shorter hr rest of yr, closed mid-Sep–late May) Norway's favourite playwright, Henrik Ibsen (see the boxed text, p409) arrived here in January 1844. The house where he worked as a pharmacist's apprentice, and where he lived and first cultivated his interest in writing, has been converted into the Ibsenhuset Museum. It contains a re-created pharmacy and many of the writer's belongings, and is one of southern Norway's more interesting museums.

Grimstad Maritime Museum MARITIME MUSEUM
(Sjøfartsmuseet; www.gbm.no, in Norwegian; Hasseldalen; adult/child Nkr50/free; ⊙11am-5pm Mon-Sat, noon-5pm Sun Jul) This important, but it has to be said rarely open, museum in the office of the 1842 Hasseldalen shipyard provides a glimpse into Grimstad's history during 'the days of the white sails' when the town was one of the ship-building capitals of Europe.

Quarry Theatre THEATRE
(☎81 53 31 33; www.fjaereheia.no, in Norwegian; tickets around Nkr250) One of the more unusual cultural experiences in Grimstad is run by Kristiansand-based Agder Teater,

which performs in an old quarry up to six days a week in summer. The tourist office (and the theatre's website) has a program of upcoming performances. The quarry, 4km north of town, became infamous during WWII when red granite blocks for Hitler's 'Victory Monument' were taken from here; the monument was, of course, never built.

🛏 Sleeping

For camping, there are at least six nearby campsites that are on the tourist office's website, while **Grimstad Hytteutleie** (☑37 25 10 65; www.grimstad-hytteutleie.no, in Norwegian; Grooseveien 103) can book holiday cabins in the area for one night or for longer stays.

TOP CHOICE **Grimstad Hotell** HISTORIC HOTEL €€ (☑37 25 25 25; www.grimstadhotell.no; Kirkegata 3; s/d from Nkr995/1195; P🐾) One of southern Norway's more memorable hotels, the stylish Grimstad Hotell, which spans a number of converted and conjoined timber houses, is the only in-town hotel and comes with loads of charm. It's the sort of quiet place where you wonder if anyone else is staying here, only to discover there's no table free at breakfast.

Bie Appartement & Feriesenter

CAMPGROUND € (☑37 04 03 96; www.bieapart.no, in Norwegian; off Arendalsveien; tent sites Nkr125, cabins from Nkr525, apt from Nkr1190; P🐾🏊) The nearest camping option to Grimstad is this friendly, well-equipped site 800m northeast of the centre along Arendalsveien. As well as big, grassy pitches it has a range of huts (the cheapest ones without running water) and some seriously dapper and kitted-out apartments that would make a great home base for a few days' exploration of the area.

Grimstad Vertshus & Kro HOTEL €€ (☑37 04 25 00; www.grimstad-vertshus.no, in Norwegian; Grimstadtunet; s/d Nkr695/850; P🐾) This friendly, cosy place is a fair hike from town. Given the shortage of other midrange places nearby, it's reasonable value, although the rooms are quite simple.

🍴 Eating & Drinking

TOP CHOICE **Haven Brasserie** SEAFOOD €€ (☑37 04 90 22; Storgata 4; lunch menus Nkr95, seafood mains Nkr200-295; ⊗noon-midnight Mon-Sat, 1pm-midnight Sun) One of the few restaurants in town that allows you to sit at a table by the water, this appealing place dishes up superb seafood such as monkfish

served in a cream sauce with saffron, or perhaps the tiger prawns or grilled salmon is more to your taste? A handful of pasta and pizza staples make it onto the menu as well.

Apotekergården SEAFOOD €€ (☑37 04 50 25; Skolegata 3; seafood mains Nkr250, pizzas Nkr119; ⊗noon-midnight) The highly recommended Apotekergården is an excellent restaurant with a breezy outdoor terrace and a cast of regulars who wouldn't eat anywhere else. It can be difficult to get a table here in summer.

Viet Thai ASIAN € (☑37 04 15 80; www.viet-thai.no, in Norwegian; Storgata 36; lunch menus Nkr65, mains Nkr75-120; ⊗1-11pm) If you're craving something a little more international, Viet Thai is cheap, extremely popular and its healthy rice meals come in large portions. It also does takeaways.

Platebaren SNACKS € (☑37 04 21 88; Storgata 15; baguettes Nkr27-35, salads Nkr49; ⊗9am-5pm Mon-Fri, to 4pm Sat Jun-Aug, shorter hr rest of yr) This highly recommended coffee bar spills out into the street in summer and is a terrific place to tuck into decent-sized snacks (baguettes, bacon and eggs etc).

Café Ibsen CAFE € (Henrik Ibsens gate 12; ⊗10am-4pm Mon-Sat, noon-4pm Sun) Come here for delicious pastries. It's opposite the Ibsenhuset Museum. The owners can also sort you out with a cheap room if required.

Café Galleri BAR € (Storgata 28; ⊗5-7pm Sun-Thu, 3pm-2am Fri & Sat) The centre of Grimstad's nightlife has DJs, jam sessions, quiz nights and a crowd that seems to spring from Grimstad's woodwork on the most unlikely of nights.

ℹ Information

Guest harbour (Gjestehavn; ☑37 25 01 69; www.grimstadgjestehavn.no, in Norwegian) Public toilets, showers and a laundry (all open to land-lubbers).

Library (Storgata 44; ⊗10am-5pm Mon-Fri, 11am-2pm Sat) Free, time-limited internet.

Tourist office (☑37 25 01 68; www.visitgrim stad.com; Sorenskrivergården, Storgata 1a; ⊗9am-6pm Mon-Fri, 10am-4pm Sat mid-Jun– mid-Aug, 8.30am-4pm Mon-Fri rest of yr) Down on the waterfront inside the big white timber building. Staff run guided tours of the town every Wednesday and Friday in July at 1pm (adult/child Nkr100/free).

ℹ Getting There & Away

The Grimstad **Rutebilstasjon** is on Storgata at the harbour. Nor-Way Bussekspress buses between Oslo (Nkr350, 4½ hours) and Kristiansand (Nkr98, one hour) call at Grimstad three to five times daily. Nettbuss buses to/from Arendal run once or twice hourly (Nkr53, 30 minutes).

Lillesand

POP 9100

Lillesand, between Kristiansand and Arendal, has a whitewashed village centre of old houses. Although nothing much happens here, this in itself can be charming. For summer boat tours through the offshore islands, contact **Brekkesto** (www.brekkesto.com, in Norwegian; per hr Nkr1000-2800).

🍴 Sleeping & Eating

Lillesand Hotel Norge   HISTORIC HOTEL **€€€**
(☎37 27 01 44; www.hotelnorge.no; Strandgata 3; s/d Nkr1490/1690; [P][⊛]) This boutique hotel has been thoughtfully renovated to reflect its original 1837 splendour and overflows with period touches, particularly in the public areas. The rooms, which aren't quite as ornate, include ones dedicated to King Alfonso XIII of Spain and author Knut Hamsun, both of whom stayed here. There's also an antiquarian library and a superb restaurant (lunch menus Nkr425, mains around Nkr285).

Tingsaker Camping   CAMPGROUND **€**
(☎37 27 04 21; fax 37 27 01 47; tent & caravan sites with car & 2 adults mid-Jun–mid-Aug Nkr305, cabins Jul Nkr1500; [P][⊛]) This crowded but well-equipped campsite, on the shore 1km east of the centre, is a typical seaside holiday resort with camping, caravans and a range of pricey cabins. No advance bookings in July.

ℹ Information

There's a **tourist office** (☎37 40 19 10; Rådhuset; ⊛9am-6pm Mon-Fri, 10am-4pm Sat, noon-4pm Sun mid-Jun–mid-Aug) in the town hall in summer.

ℹ Getting There & Away

The most pleasant way to reach Lillesand in summer is by the M/S Øya boat from Kristiansand (see p103). There's also an hourly Nettbuss to Kristiansand (Nkr66).

Kristiansand

POP 77,850

Kristiansand, Norway's fifth-largest city, calls itself 'Norway's No 1 Holiday Resort'.

That can be a bit misleading: sun-starved Norwegians do flock here in the summer, but for everyone else it serves more as a gateway to the seaside villages of Norway's southern coast and the inland region of Setesdalen (p118). The claim also reflects a newfound confidence that has seen the city clean up its environmental act (it was until a decade ago infamous for its pollution). What Kristiansand can offer though is a lively cultural and shopping scene, great restaurants and a healthy nightlife. In addition, anyone travelling with children will more than likely find themselves cajoled into visiting the town's outstanding children's park and zoo.

◉ Sights

TOP CHOICE ┐ **Kristiansand Dyrepark**   ZOO
(www.dyreparken.com; adult/child Nkr500/420; ⊛10am-7pm mid-Jun–early Aug, shorter hr rest of yr) The former Kristiansand zoo, off the E18 10km east of Kristiansand, has gradually expanded into what is probably *the* favourite holiday destination for children in Norway. The prices given here are for the high season, and including all activities.

Essentially the Dyrepark is several parks rolled into one. There's a **funfair** portion that includes rides such as the pirate ship cruise, Captain Sabretooth's Treasure Trove and enchanted houses. **Cardamom Town** (Kardamomme By), named for a key ingredient in Scandinavian waffles, is a fantasy village based on the children's stories of Thorbjørn Egner. The town has been carefully laid out exactly as it appeared in the illustrated book. There's also a **water park** (bring your swimming things) with heated pools and water slides. The biggest attraction though is the **zoo**, which offers a large variety of species, including red pandas, a crocodile house, lions and tigers and an African savannah filled with giraffe, zebra and others.

The real highlight of the zoo is the **Northern Wilderness** (Nordisk Vilmark), where visitors are transported over the habitat of moose, wolves, lynx and wolverines on elevated boardwalks.

Posebyen   OLD TOWN
The Kristiansand Posebyen (Old Town) takes in most of the 14 blocks at the northern end of the town's characteristic *kvadraturen* (square grid pattern of streets). It's worth taking a slow stroll around this pretty quarter, whose name was given by French soldiers who came to *reposer* (French for relax).

A scale model (with buildings around 1m high) of the city as it appeared when designed by Christian IV is on view at Vest-Agder Folk Museum. The annual *Kristiansand* guide, published by the tourist office, includes a good section called 'A Stroll through Posebyen' to guide your wandering. The tourist office also offers a variety of different guided tours of the Old Town, including ones that take you inside people's houses and others that will have you singing with the town's choral societies. The most well-preserved buildings include **Bentsens Hus** (Kronprinsens gate 59), which dates to 1855, the **former post office** (Kronprinsens gate 45) dating to 1695 and **Gyldenløves gate 56** (1802).

Christiansholm Fortress   FORTRESS
(Kristiansand Festning; admission free; ⊘grounds 9am-9pm mid-May–mid-Sep) The most prominent feature that sits along the Strandpromenaden is the distinctive Christiansholm Fortress. Built by royal decree between 1662 and 1672 to keep watch over the strategic Skagerrak Straits and protect the city from pirates and rambunctious Swedes, the construction featured walls up to 5m thick and an armoury buried within a concentric inner wall. It was connected to the mainland by a bridge over a moat (filled in during the 19th century) deep enough to accommodate tall ships. The fortress served its purpose – it was never taken by enemy forces.

Agder Nature Museum & Botanic Gardens   GARDENS
(www.vestagdermuseet.no; Gimleveien 23; adult/child Nkr40/15; ⊘noon-5pm mid-Jun–mid-Aug) The winding paths through the established 50-hectare park at Gimle Estate lead through a botanic garden that also contains rocks, minerals, stuffed animals and greenhouses containing the largest collection of cacti in Norway. The estate house has 19th-century period interiors and extraordinary teethlike columns at the front, and there's also a historic rose garden dating from 1850. It's just over 1km from the centre, across the Oddernes bridge.

Kristiansand Cathedral   CATHEDRAL
(Domkirke; Kirkegata; admission free, tower adult/child Nkr20/10; ⊘10am-4pm Mon-Fri, 10am-3pm Sat mid-Jun–mid-Aug, shorter hr rest of yr) Built in 1884 in late gothic style, the Kristiansand Cathedral, with seating for 1800 people, is Norway's third-largest church. Guided tours of the cathedral, including the tower, run at 11am and 2pm Monday to Saturday in summer, and there are organ recitals at 1pm Tuesday to Saturday during the same period.

Vest-Agder Folk Museum   FOLK MUSEUM
(Vest-Agder Fylkesmuseum; www.vestagdermuseet .no, in Norwegian; Vigeveien 22b; adult/child Nkr40/15; ⊘10am-5pm Tue-Fri, noon-5pm Sat-Mon mid-Jun–Aug, shorter hr rest of yr) Located 4km east of town on the E18, the open-air Vest-Agder Folk Museum houses a collection of 40 farmsteads and hamlets from the Setesdalen region and Kristiansand itself.

Baneheia & Ravnedalen   PARKS
Baneheia and Ravnedalen, both north of the city centre, offer greenery and a network of lakeside hiking and skiing tracks for those keen to escape the city for a while. Both parks were created between 1870 and 1880 by Kristiansand's city chairman, General Oscar Wergeland. Over a 30-year period, he oversaw the planting of 150,000 coniferous trees and transformed the area into a recreational green belt.

Setesdalsbanen   TRAIN RIDE
(www.setesdalsbanen.no; adult/child return Nkr100/ 50; ⊘departures 11.30am, 1.20pm & 3.10pm Sun mid-Jun–August) The 78km-long narrow-gauge railway between Kristiansand and Byglandsfjord was opened in 1896 to link Setesdalen with the coast. It was used to transport nickel from the Evje mines, and local timber and barrel staves that were used in the salting and export of herring. Although competition from the normal-gauge state railway forced its closure in 1962, the Setesdalsbanen Railway still runs steam- or diesel-powered locomotives along the last 6km between Grovane (2km north of Vennesla) and Røyknes; the journey takes 25 minutes one way. NSB trains run up to four times daily from Kristiansand to Vennesla (Nkr44, 12 minutes).

🏃 Activities

One Ocean Dive Center   DIVING
(☑91 62 85 25; www.oneocean.no; Dvergsnesveien 571, Odderhei; 1/2 dives with equipment from Nkr950/1300) A professional centre that runs dives to wrecks, which include a downed plane and even a mine sweeper. It's 8km east of Kristiansand.

🛏 Sleeping

Kristiansand can be expensive for what you get, which may be nothing unless you book early for summer, especially during the July school-holiday period when prices soar. There are a number of chain hotels (Rica and

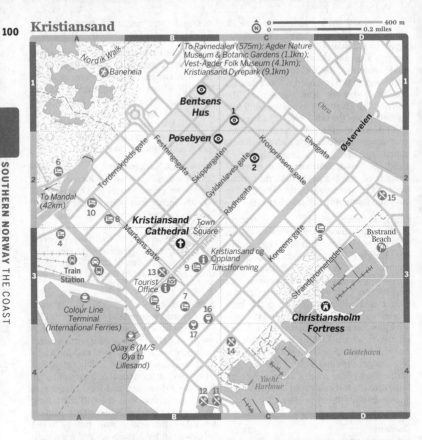

Thon being the most notable) around the entrance to Kristiansand Dyrepark 10km east of town. One unwelcome Kristiansand quirk is the 10am check-out time in some places.

Yess Hotel
HOTEL **€€**

(☑38 70 15 70; www.yesshotel.no; Tordenskjolds gate 12; s/d from Nkr695/795; ☐P☎) This is a classic example of the kind of antiseptic, but, for Norway, good value 'back to basics' hotels that seem to be slowly sprouting up in bigger towns throughout the country. The rooms at this new hotel are livened up with wall-to-wall photographs of trees. Some rooms have a double bed with a single perched, bunk-bed style, on top. Others just have a standard double bed. It has a cafe with free breakfast and parking for Nkr130 per day. All up it's a great deal.

Firmautleie B&B
B&B **€**

(☑91 12 99 06; www.gjestehus.no; Frobusdalen 2; s Nkr400-500; d Nkr600-800; ☐P) Probably the most personal place to stay in Kristiansand, this small B&B in an old timber home a 10-minute walk northwest of the centre is rustic, cosy and friendly; however, the secret's out and it's often full.

Clarion Hotel Ernst
CHAIN HOTEL **€€**

(☑38 12 86 00; www.clarionernst.com; Rådhsgata 2; s Nkr800-1490, d Nkr1000-1695; ☐P@☎) The newly renovated Clarion Hotel looks pretty dull from the outside but the inside is a whole different story with huge, pearl-string lampshades, gold and silver throne-like chairs, purple lighting and massive jet-black bedheads. It's one of the few business-class hotels in Norway with any character. Parking costs Nkr140 per day.

Budget Hotel Kristiansand
HOTEL **€**

(☑38 70 15 65; www.budgethotel.no; Vestre Strandgate 49; s/d Nkr450/550; ☎) We wouldn't normally recommend a place nestled in a car park between an overpass and the train sta-

SOUTHERN NORWAY KRISTIANSAND

tion, and even less one that from the outside resembles a bunch of cargo containers piled on top of one another, but Kristiansand's pricey accommodation scene makes this good budget value, especially if you throw in free wireless access. Rooms are small, clean and simple with bunk beds. Every day 10% of the rooms are available for just Nkr299, though you have to be quick off the mark to get one of these.

Scandic Kristiansand CHAIN HOTEL €€€
(☎21 61 42 00; www.scandic-hotels.com; Markens gate 39; s Nkr1590-1790, d Nkr1790-1990; P@🛜) If you value style as well as substance, the Scandic Kristiansand has both. The rooms and public areas are stylish, rooms have all the requisite bells and whistles, and the hotel adheres to the strictest environmental standards. It's also family friendly, with a children's play area, baby beds and family rooms. Every day it lets 10 rooms go for just Nkr530.

Hotel Norge CHAIN HOTEL €€€
(☎38 17 40 00; www.hotel-norge.no; Dronningens gate 5; s/d from Nkr1250/1450; P@🛜) It can sometimes be difficult to distinguish many of Norway's chain hotels so we welcome the effort taken here. The all-important mattresses are extremely comfortable, and there's a rooftop sun lounge, private bakery, cafe and a spa centre. Parking costs Nkr150 extra.

Thon Hotel Wergeland CHAIN HOTEL €€
(☎38 17 20 40; www.thonhotels.no; Kirkegata 15; r Sat & Sun Nkr850-1050, Mon-Fri Nkr1425-1625; 🛜) It doesn't get any more central than this attractive, modern hotel right next to the

cathedral. The high-standard rooms with hardwood floors have a touch more charm than some others in the Thon Hotels chain.

1-2-3 Hotel HOTEL €
(☎38 70 15 66; www.123-hotel.no; Østre Strandgate 25; r from Nkr595; 🛜) It's hard to know what to make of this place, which styles itself as a self-service hotel. With its electronic check-in (there's no reception except to pay), meagre breakfast and 10am check-out, we wonder if this hotel exists more for the convenience of its owners than guests. Then again, the price is good for Kristiansand and the rooms are light, airy and comfortable.

Roligheden Camping CAMPGROUND €
(☎38 09 67 22; www.roligheden.no, in Norwegian; Framnesveien; tent sites Nkr130 plus per person Nkr30, cabins from Nkr900; ⊙Jun-Aug) Tent campers are in luck at this well-run campsite situated at a popular beach 3km east of the centre. Take bus 15 from the centre.

🍴 Eating

In summer the most atmospheric places to eat are in the small, remodelled harbour around the fish market, where you'll find the freshest and best-value seafood.

TOP CHOICE **Bølgen & Moi** SEAFOOD €€€
(☎38 17 83 00; www.bolgenogmoi.no, in Norwegian; Sjølystveien 1a; light meals Nkr55-169, starters Nkr75-145, mains Nkr220-279; ⊙3pm-midnight Mon-Sat) The best restaurant around the fish-market harbour, the supercool Bølgen & Moi does a sublime fish and shellfish soup and a tasty range of fish and seafood dishes as well as set menus. In summer the outdoor

tables are packed and it's a good place for a drink after the kitchen closes.

TOP CHOICE Has Nabaen
INTERNATIONAL €€

(☎45 22 68 88; www.hosnaboen.no, in Norwegian; Markens gate 19a; mains around Nkr150; ⊙10.30am-11pm Mon-Sat) This bustling central cafe, with a warm and sociable atmosphere, pumps out great light meals (including superb meatballs stuffed with mango chutney and melted cheese), huge doorstopper wedges of cake and decent coffee.

Sjøhuset
SEAFOOD €€

(☎38 02 62 60; Markens gate; light meals & snacks Nkr75-169, mains Nkr179-269; ⊙11am-11pm) Along the waterfront next to the yacht harbour, this long-standing restaurant of quality is another fine choice for lovers of the fruits of the sea. Dishes include mussels and chips (Nkr185), shrimps (from Nkr150) or plain old fish and chips (Nkr195).

Snadderkiosken
FAST FOOD €

(Østre Strandgate 78a; dishes Nkr69-129; ⊙8.30am-11.30pm Mon-Fri, 11.30am-11.30pm Sat & Sun) We don't normally direct you to ubiquitous fast-food kiosks, but Snadderkiosken is one of the best of its kind in Norway. Near the town beach, this lovely tiled 1920s-style kiosk will sort you out with things such as hearty meatballs and mashed potatoes or grilled chicken with rice and salad.

Kjesk
CAFE €

(☎38 10 86 10; Kirkegata 15; light meals Nkr45-145; ⊙lunch & dinner Mon-Sat) Also recommended, Kjesk is a very cool coffee bar with great food.

🍷 Drinking & Entertainment

Apart from the places around the fish market where the outdoor tables are difficult to snaffle on a summer's evening, there are a couple of decent places for a drink.

TOP CHOICE Frk Larsen
BAR

(Markens gate 5; ⊙11am-midnight Mon-Wed, 11am-3am Thu-Sat, noon-midnight Sun) Our favourite drinking hole in Kristiansand, this trendy place has retro-chic fusion decor, a mellow ambience by day and late-night music for an 'in' crowd on weekend nights. The cocktail bar opens at 8pm, but if cocktails (almost) by the seashore aren't your thing then it's just as popular for a midday coffee.

Kick
BAR

(www.kickcafe.no, in Norwegian; Dronningens gate 8; ⊙3pm-late) This outdoor cafe morphs into a disco with a DJ as the night wears on. It's one of the most popular hang-outs for young people and there's occasional live music on weekends.

ℹ Information

You can change money at the **post office** (cnr Rådhus & Markens gates) or at all the major banks (there are several on Markens gate), one of which is **Nordea** (Markens gate 16).

International Internet Café (cnr Gyldenløves gate & Vestre Strandgate; per hr Nkr30; ⊙noon-10pm Mon-Sat, 2-10pm Sun) Skype-enabled internet access.

Kristiansand og Oppland Turistforening (☎38 02 52 63; www.kot.no, in Norwegian; Kirkegata 15; ⊙10am-4pm Mon-Wed & Fri, 10am-5pm Thu) Maps and information on hiking, huts and organised mountain tours in southern Norway.

Tourist office (☎38 12 13 14; www.regionkristiansand.no; Rådhsgata 6; ⊙9am-6pm Mon-Fri, 10am-6pm Sat, noon-6pm Sun mid-Jun–Aug, 9am-4pm Mon-Fri rest of yr)

ℹ Getting There & Away

Boat

For information on ferries to Denmark and Sweden, see p436.

BUSES FROM KRISTIANSAND

DESTINATION	DEPARTURES (DAILY)	COST (NKR)	DURATION (HR)
Arendal	up to 9	130	1½
Bergen	1	660	12
Evje	7-8	130	1
Flekkefjord	2-4	240	2
Oslo	up to 9	350	5½
Stavanger	2-4	380	4½

Bus

There's a bus information office and left luggage facilities inside the bus station.

Car & Motorcycle

With a vehicle, access to the E18, north of the centre, is via Vestre Strandgate; when arriving you'll most likely find yourself along Festningsgata. There's an automatic Nkr30 toll on entering the city.

Train

There are up to four trains daily to Oslo (Nkr299 to Nkr631, 4½ hours) and up to five to Stavanger (Nkr199 to Nkr427, 3¼ hours).

ⓘ Getting Around

Unlike many Norwegian towns, Kristiansand is mercifully flat and the downtown area is easily negotiable on foot. Taxis to the airport cost Nkr310 through the **Agder Taxis** (☑38 00 20 00) booth just outside the bus station.

Around Kristiansand

In summer, Kristiansand's archipelago of offshore skerries turns into one of the country's greatest sun-and-sea destinations for Norwegian holiday-makers. The most popular island, **Bragdøy**, lies close to the mainland and boasts a preservation workshop for wooden ships, nice walks and several bathing sites. In the distance, you'll see the classic lighthouse **Grønningen Fyr**.

There are various ferries to Bragdøy and other offshore islands. Ask at the tourist office for exact schedules.

M/S Øya (www.lillesand.net) sails to/from Lillesand (Nkr245/120 per adult/child one way, Nkr410/205 return, three hours) once daily except Sunday from late June to early August. The departure point in Kristiansand is from Quay 6.

Mandal

POP 14,200

Norway's southernmost town, Mandal is famous for its 800m-long beach, Sjøsanden. About 1km from the centre and backed by forests, the Copacabana it ain't, but it is Norway's finest stretch of sand, just crying out for a sunny Mediterranean climate.

◉ Sights

The moderately interesting town **Vest-Agder Bymuseum** (www.vestagdermuseet. no; Store Elvegata 5/6; adult/child Nkr40/free;

⊙11am-5pm mid-Jun–mid-Aug), which displays a host of historical maritime and fishing artefacts and works by local artists, is elevated above the mundane by impressive exhibits of works by Mandal's favourite son, Gustav Vigeland (see the boxed text, p55).

✦✦ Festivals

The second week in August, when Mandal hosts the **Shellfish Festival** (www.skalldyr festivalen.no), is a great time to be in town: there's fresh seafood everywhere and a range of musical performances.

🛏 Sleeping & Eating

Accommodation in Mandal tends to be rather expensive.

Sjøsanden Feriesenter   CAMPGROUND €
(☑38 26 10 94; www.sjosanden-feriesenter. no; Sjøsandsveien 1; tent sites without/with car Nkr110/170 plus adult/child Nkr40/20, d Nkr350-650, 2-4-person self-catering apt Nkr850-1000; P🞋🞋🞋) Being just a few metres away from the beach, this well-run place distinguishes itself from the other campsites in the vicinity. It even has its own water slide. There are also motel rooms and huts of various sizes available.

Kjøbmandsgaarden Hotel   HISTORIC HOTEL €€
(☑38 26 12 76; www.kjobmandsgaarden.no; Store Elvegate 57; s Nkr890, d Nkr995-1195; 🞋) In the heart of the icy-white Old Town streets, this pretty timber hotel has somewhat overpriced and gloomy rooms with decent bathrooms. The downstairs restaurant though is one of the most popular places in town to eat.

First Hotel Solborg   HOTEL €€
(☑38 27 21 00; www.firsthotels.no/solborg; Neseveien 1; s Nkr999-1499, d 1299-1699; P@🞋🞋) This large and none-too-pretty resort-style hotel, only a 10-minute walk west of the beach, boasts an indoor pool, restaurant, bar and Saturday disco called Soldekket. The rooms are pretty faded, though.

Provianten   ITALIAN €€
(☑48 27 88 88; Store Elvegate 43; mains Nkr185-250) In Norway's southernmost town it seems only appropriate to eat at this waterfront restaurant with its Mediterranean air. It serves genuine wood-fired pizzas, various pastas and a selection of Norwegian dishes.

ⓘ Information

The **tourist office** (☑38 27 83 00; www.region mandal.com; Bryggegaten 10; ⊙9am-7pm

Mon-Fri, 10am-4pm Sat & Sun Jun-Aug, 9am-4pm Mon-Fri Sep-May) is situated on the waterfront.

❶ Getting There & Away

The Mandal Rutebilstasjon lies north of the river, just a short walk from the historic district. The Nor-Way Bussekspress coastal route between Stavanger (Nkr360, 3½ hours) and Kristiansand (Nkr90, 45 minutes) passes through Mandal two to four times daily.

Lindesnes

Why go north when you can go south? At the almost 'polar' opposite to Nordkapp (some 2518km away) is Lindesnes, the southernmost point in Norway (latitude 57° 58' 95" N). Lindesnes (literally 'arching land peninsula') provides an occasional glimpse of the power that nature can unleash between the Skagerrak and the North Sea.

Rising above the cape is the evocative **Lindesnes Fyr** (www.lindesnesfyr.no, in Norwegian; adult/child Nkr50/free; ☺10am-8pm late Jun-early Aug, shorter hr rest of yr), a classic lighthouse. In two of the buildings you'll pass as you climb to the cape, there are exhibitions on the history of the lighthouse, while the visitors centre next to the gate has more plus an informative video about the site. The first lighthouse on the site (and the first in Norway) was fired up in 1655 using coal and tallow candles to warn ships off the rocks. The current electrical version, built in 1915, is visible up to 19.5 nautical miles out to sea.

Equally enticing are the series of intricate rocky coves that twist and turn their way around this snake-like coastline.

🛏 Sleeping

Lindesnes Camping og Hytteutleie

CAMPGROUND €

(☎38 25 88 74; www.lindesnescamping.no; Lillehavn; tent sites Nkr160, cabins Nkr390-1300; P🛜) Set beside a tiny cove and surrounded by granite outcrops, this campsite, with excellent modern facilities, is on the shore 3.5km northeast of Lindesnes Fyr. There's a small kiosk and kitchen facilities and it also organises boat hire.

Lindesnes Gjestehus

B&B €€

(☎38 25 97 00; liveueland@hotmail.com; Spangereid; s Nkr495-595, d Nkr650-750; P🛜) About 11km north of the cape lies this simple but cosy guesthouse inside a timber building.

❶ Getting There & Away

Buses from Mandal (Nkr65, one hour) travel to the lighthouse via Spangereid on Monday, Wednesday and Friday.

Flekkefjord

POP 8900

Flekkefjord is a quiet place with a pretty Old Town (the town's history dates back to 1660 when it competed for power with Kristiansand). It's also famous for having virtually no tidal variation (typically less than 10cm between high and low tides). Along with Egersund, it's one of the more enjoyable towns to base yourself on this stretch of coast.

DON'T MISS

HERE WERE VIKINGS

From the 8th to the 11th centuries, Norway's coastline was the domain of Vikings, but the cape at Lindesnes, where the waters of the Skagerrak and the North Sea collide, proved a challenge even to these formidable sea goers. Their solution? In a spirit of creative engineering that Norway's road builders would later emulate when faced with daunting geographic forms, the Vikings carved a canal across the Lindesnes Peninsula at Spangereid (once a home port of Viking chieftains) to avoid the dangerous seas of the cape. In summer 2007, a replica canal was opened to recreate the Viking detour. Close to the site, the excellent historical centre **Vikingland** (www.spangereidvikingland.no; Spangereid; adult/child Nkr80/50; ☺11am-5pm mid-Jun–mid-Aug) offers Viking exhibitions, a Viking cruise and tranquil Viking sports such as axe-throwing.

If the Vikings have caught your attention, there's another site nearby that you'll want to seek out. At Penne, west of Farsund and close to Borhaug, are some remarkable **rock paintings** dating from the Viking era, including representations, at once childlike and sophisticated, of Viking ships. For more information, contact the local tourist offices.

⊙ Sights

Before setting out to explore the town, collect the pamphlet *A Tour of Flekkefjord* from the tourist office. The richest source of old architecture is the **Hollenderbyen** (Dutch Town) district, with its narrow streets and old timber buildings. **Flekkefjord Museum** (www.vestagdermuseet.no; Dr Kraftsgata 15; adult/child Nkr40/free; ⊙10am-5pm Mon-Fri, noon-5pm Sat & Sun mid-Jun–Aug) is housed in a home from 1724, but has 19th-century interiors.

One building that stands out is the unusual octagonal log-built **Flekkefjord church** (Kirkegaten; admission free; ⊙11am-1pm Mon-Sat Jul), which was consecrated in 1833. Designed by architect H Linstow (he of the Royal Palace in Oslo), the octagonal theme continues throughout, with the columns, steeple and baptismal font all conforming to the eight-sided shape.

🛏 Sleeping & Eating

Grand Hotell   HISTORIC HOTEL €€
(☑38 32 23 55; www.grand-hotell.no, in Norwegian; Anders Beersgt 9; s/d from Nkr995/1195; 🅿🛜) For the most character and personality that you'll find in Flekkefjord, the Grand Hotell perfectly suits this old town. Housed in a delightful castlelike timber-clad building, the hotel's rooms have a certain old-world charm.

Egenes Camping   CAMPGROUND €
(☑38 32 01 48; www.egenes.no; tent sites without/with car Nkr160/240, caravan sites Nkr270, cabins per week Nkr2450-7000) This spectacularly located campsite is beside Lake Seluravatnet, 1km off the E39 and 5km east of Flekkefjord. There's boat and canoe hire, a climbing wall, minigolf, fishing and other activities on offer here, which make it a great choice for those with children to tire out.

Maritim Fjordhotell   HOTEL €€
(☑38 32 58 00; www.fjordhotellene.no; Sundegaten 9; s/d Nkr999/1199) Flekkefjord's largest hotel has a great waterfront position, stylish rooms and a decent restaurant (mains from Nkr125), although the architecture is a real eyesore.

Pizza Inn   INTERNATIONAL €€
(☑38 32 22 22; Elvegata 22; pizza/pasta from Nkr160/215, mains Nkr130-200) This pleasant harbour-side restaurant has breezy outdoor tables to pass a summer's afternoon or cosy booths for a winter's evening. The service is good, as is the food. The prawn salad

(Nkr119) seems to contain a good proportion of the Atlantic Ocean's prawns.

Fiskebrygga   INTERNATIONAL €€
(☑38 32 04 90; Elvegata 9; mains Nkr130-200; ⊙10am-4pm Mon, Tue & Sat, to 6pm Wed & Fri, to 7pm Thu) Possibly the nicest place in Flekkefjord for a light meal, this cafe-style restaurant next to the tourist office does fish and chips, marinated spare ribs, delicious cakes and ice cream. It has a certain urban sense of style, which is lovely in quiet little Flekkefjord.

ℹ Information

The small **tourist office** (☑38 32 69 95; www.regionlister.com; Elvegata 3; ⊙10am-6pm Mon-Fri, 10am-4pm Sat mid-Jun–mid-Aug, 11am-4pm Sun Jul, 9am-4pm Mon-Fri rest of yr) should be your first port of call.

ℹ Getting There & Away

The Nor-Way Bussekspress bus between Kristiansand (Nkr240, two hours) and Stavanger (Nkr240, two hours) passes through Flekkefjord.

Flekkefjord to Egersund

If your explorations of Norway are limited to the south coast, and you have your own vehicle, forsake the E39 and take the coastal Rv44 to Egersund – it's one of southern Norway's most beautiful drives and a taster of the kind of scenery you're missing elsewhere in the country. The road swerves through barren, boulder-blotched hills with a few forested sections, lakes and moorlands, before descending to **Jøssingfjord**, around 32km west of Flekkefjord; it's the site for breathtaking, perpendicular rock scenery, including a fine waterfall. Two 17th-century houses, known as **Helleren**, are nestled under an overhanging cliff and were definitely not built for the claustrophobic. Despite the danger of falling rocks, the overhang did provide protection from the harsh Norwegian climate. The houses are open year-round.

Some 30km southeast of Egersund and 2.5km south of Hauge i Dalane, **Sogndalstrand** should not be missed for its picturesque timber homes and warehouses that jut out over the river. The houses feature on the covers of tourist brochures across the region and they're well worth seeking out as it's a quiet, beautiful place. The homes date from the 17th and 18th centuries.

If this small village has won your heart, consider staying at the **Sogndalstrand Kultur Hotell** (☑51 47 72 55; www.sogndalstrand -kulturhotell.no; s/d Nkr1090/1490), a lovely place with cosy rooms and an excellent little restaurant.

For more information on scenic lighthouses, and other attractions along this route, and the entire coastal road from Kristiansand to Haugesund, visit the excellent www.nordsjovegen.no.

Egersund

POP 14,000

One of the prettiest towns along this stretch of coastline, Egersund is a serene place strewn with old timber houses that tell the story of its long history; intriguing rune stones found in nearby Møgedal are among the oldest written forms found in southern Norway. It's a quiet place to wander and to soak up the small-town ambience of the southern Norwegian coast.

⊙ Sights

Dalane Folk Museum   FOLK MUSEUM
(www.dalanefolke.museum.no, in Norwegian; Slettebø; adult/child Nkr40/20; ⊙11am-5pm mid-Jun–mid-Aug, shorter hr rest of yr) The Dalane Folk Museum is divided into two parts. The more interesting main section features eight historic timber homes at Slettebø, 3.5km north of town just off the Rv42. The other section is the **Egersund Fayance Museum** (⊙same hr), a walkable 1.5km northeast of town. It displays the history and wares of Egersund Fayance, the ceramic and porcelain firm that sustained the district from 1847 to 1979.

Historic Buildings   ARCHITECTURE
Some 92 homes, nearly two-thirds of the original town, were gutted by fire in 1843, after which Egersund was reconstructed with wide streets to thwart the spread of future fires. Most buildings in the Old Town date from this period. **Strandgaten**, a street of timber houses constructed after 1843, is well worth a stroll. **Skrivergården** (Strandgaten 58) was built in 1846 as the home of the local magistrate Christian Feyer. The small town park opposite served as his private garden. **Strandgaten 43** is arguably more beautiful and has what's known as a 'gossip mirror', which allowed the inhabitants to keep an eye on the street.

The **Bilstadhuset** (Nygaten 14) still has its original timberwork and includes a sail-

maker's loft upstairs. None of the houses are open to the public, but the tourist office hands out a leaflet, *Strolling in Egersund,* which has a map and informative commentary.

Egersund Kirke   CHURCH
(Torget; admission free; ⊙11am-4pm Mon-Sat, 12.30-3pm Sun mid-Jun–mid-Aug) There has been a church in Egersund since at least 1292. The cute, current manifestation dates back to the 1620s; the carved altarpiece, a depiction of the baptism and crucifixion of Christ by Stavanger carpenter Thomas Christophersen and painted by artist Peter Reimers, dates back to 1607, and the baptismal font is from 1583. The cross-shaped design, intimate balconies and wonderfully decorated pew doors are all worth lingering over.

🛏 Sleeping

Grand Hotell   HISTORIC HOTEL €€
(☑51 49 60 60; www.grand-egersund.no; Johan Feyersgate 3; s/d from Nkr880/1260; P🕸) The Grand Hotell is a lovely old 19th-century building with stylish, renovated rooms, although you pay more for those in the picturesque, old but refurbished wing. The corner rooms (eg 307 in the old wing and 224 in the newer section) are the best on offer. In the summer significant discounts are available with a Fjord Pass. It also has a good restaurant.

Steinsnes Camping   CAMPGROUND €
(☑51 49 41 36; www.steinsnescamping.no; Tengs; tent sites Nkr140 plus per person Nkr30, cabins Nkr300-625; P🕸) Egersund's most convenient campsite is 3km north of town alongside a rushing stream; buses heading for Hellvik will get you there. As a very Norwegian touch, it sells salmon-fishing permits.

ℹ Information

The **tourist office** (☑51 46 82 33; www. eigersund.kommune.no; Jernbaneveien 2; ⊙10am-6pm Mon-Fri, to 4pm Sat & Sun Jun-Aug) is fine for local information, but it's only open in summer. During the rest of the year the **Kulturkontonet** (Strandgaten 58; ⊙8am-3pm Mon-Fri) can help with basic tourist information. The building itself is worth checking out even if you don't need any help.

ℹ Getting There & Away

Trains to/from Kristiansand (Nkr199 to Nkr299, two hours) run four times daily, and there are eight daily services to/from Stavanger (Nkr145, one hour).

Around Egersund

If you're driving along the Rv42 west of Egersund, **Terland Klopp**, 15km northeast of town, is a lovely 60m-long bridge from 1888.

Eigerøy Fyr (Midbrødøy; adult/child Nkr20/10; ☉noon-5pm Sun Jun-Aug), the majestic 1855 lighthouse on Midbrødøy, is near the southwestern tip of Eigerøy island. Still one of the most powerful lighthouses in Europe, it has great views at any time, but especially on stormy days. From late May until the end of August a cafe and ornithological station is open here.

THE INTERIOR

Inland from Norway's southern coast, quiet mountain valleys like Setesdalen and the magnificent peak of Gausta, close to Rjukan, are wonderful places. Another highlight is the lake-studded Telemark region, connected by a canal with pretty Seljord – home to the Nessie-esque Selma the Serpent.

Kongsberg

POP 23,600

Surrounded by dark and dense forests and with cascading rapids running through the heart of town, Kongsberg is one of the more agreeable towns in southern Norway. In addition to the pretty setting there's plenty of cultural interest in the form of the fascinating Royal Silver Mines, a host of low-key museums, a pretty clapboard old quarter and one of Norway's best jazz festivals in July.

History

The history of Kongsberg begins and ends with silver, which was discovered by two children with an ox in 1623 in the nearby Numedal Valley. Their father attempted to sell the windfall, but the king's soldiers got wind of it and the family was arrested and forced to disclose the site of their discovery. Kongsberg was founded a year later and in the resulting silver rush it briefly became the second-largest town in Norway, with 8000 inhabitants including 4000 miners. Between 1623 and 1957, 1.35 million kilograms of pure threadlike 'wire' silver (one of the world's purest forms of silver) was produced for the royal coffers. Kongsberg is still home to the national mint, but the last mine closed in 1957.

☉ Sights & Activities

Royal Silver Mines   MINE TOUR

The profusion of silver mines in Kongsberg's hinterland is known collectively as Sølvgruvene. The main shaft of the largest mine plunges all of 1070m into the mountain, to a depth of 550m below sea level. The easiest way to visit the mine is the **mine tour** (adult/child Nkr150/90; ☉hourly 11am-4pm Jul–mid-Aug, shorter hr mid-May–Jun, Sep & Oct) that leaves from the signposted Kongsgruvene, 700m from Saggrenda (8km south of Kongsberg along the road to Notodden). It begins with a 2.3km **rail ride** along the *stoll,* a tunnel that was painstakingly chipped through the mountain in order to drain water from the mines. Constructed without machinery or dynamite – the rock was removed by heating it with fire, then throwing water on the rock to crack it – the tunnel moved forward at 7cm per day and took 73 years (from 1782 to 1855) to complete! Inside, visitors are guided around equipment used in the extraction of silver, including an ingenious creaking and grinding lift and work area on 65 wet and slippery ladders.

Bring warm clothing as the underground temperatures can be a chilly 6°C. The admission price includes a bus ride from outside Kongsberg's tourist office. Travellers with disabilites and children under 3 (although they don't recommend it to under 5s) are not allowed to enter the mines for safety reasons.

Other activities organised in and around the mine include learning how to mint your own coins (sadly though we're yet to find a bank willing to accept the ones we made) and a crash course in digging a mine in your own garden. With advance reservation you can join a **rope-and-torch tour** (☎91 91 32 00; per group Nkr10,000), which begins with a 1km walk through Crown Prince Fredrik's tunnel. You must then abseil by torchlight down 112m into the mine (after what is hopefully not a 'crash' course in abseiling).

Norwegian Mining Museum   MUSEUM

(Norsk Bergverks-museum; www.bvm.museum.no; Hyttegata 3; adult/child Nkr80/30; ☉10am-5pm mid-May–Aug, shorter hr rest of yr) This worthwhile mining museum, in an 1844 smelter, tells the story of mining in Kongsberg with relics, models and mineral displays; the old smelting furnaces still survive in the basement. In the same building, other sections include the **Royal Mint**, which was moved from Akershus Fortress in Oslo to the source of the silver in 1686, as well as a **skiing**

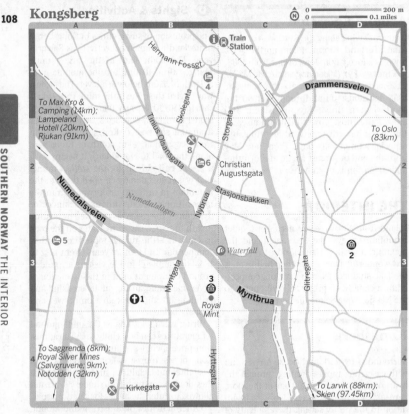

Kongsberg

museum (Kongsberg is home to one of the world's oldest ski-jumping competitions) and an **arms and industry museum**. All these are included in the same ticket.

Lågdal Folk Museum   FOLK MUSEUM
(Lågdalsmuseet; www.laagdalsmuseet.no, in Norwegian; Tillischbakken 8-10; adult/child mid-Jun–mid-Aug Nkr40/10, admission free rest of yr; ⊘11am-5pm mid-Jun–mid-Aug, shorter hr rest of yr) This folk museum, a 10-minute walk southeast

of the train station, houses a collection of 32 period farmhouses around which frolic sheep, goats and pigs. Inside the main building is a WWII resistance museum and a re-creation of 19th-century and early 20th-century Kongsberg, complete with interesting descriptions of the shop and its former owner (much of which is written in Norwegian only). In summer there are guided tours at 11am, 1.30pm and 3.30pm.

Kongsberg Kirke
CHURCH

(Kirketorget; adult/child Nkr30/10; ⊙10am-4pm Mon-Fri, 10am-1pm Sat, 2-4pm Sun mid-May–mid-Aug, shorter hr rest of yr) Norway's largest baroque church, in the Old Town west of the river, officially opened in 1761. The rococo-style interior features ornate chandeliers and an unusual altar that combines the altarpiece, high pulpit and organ pipes on a single wall. From June to August there are organ recitals held here at 8pm on Wednesday.

Hiking & Skiing

Kongsberg's best hiking and cross-country skiing is found in the green, forested Knutefjell, immediately west of the town. The Kongsberg tourist office sells the map *Kultur-og Turkart Knutefjell* (Nkr120), which details the hiking and skiing tracks.

✲ Festivals

Kongsberg Jazz Festival (www.kongsberg-jazzfestival.no), Norway's second largest (after Molde; see p237), is held over four days in early July and draws numerous avant-garde international and Norwegian performers. A percentage of profits goes towards humanitarian projects.

🛏 Sleeping

TOP CHOICE **Lampeland Hotell**   BOUTIQUE HOTEL **€€**
(☑32 76 09 00; www.lampeland.no; Rv40; s/d from Nkr995/1250; P@🛜) From the outside it might look like just a typical roadside motel but this lovely hotel, 20km north of Kongsberg on the Geilo road, has plenty of charm. The common areas are overloaded with interesting knick-knacks and cosy sofas perfect for curling up with a book on a cold day. Sadly the rooms are a bit more plain. There's a decent restaurant that has traditional Norwegian mains for around Nkr225, but it stops serving at 8pm. The Fjord Pass gives healthy discounts here.

Quality Hotel Grand   BUSINESS HOTEL **€€**
(☑32 77 28 00; www.choice.no; Christian Augustsgata 2; s/d from Nkr920/1120; P🛜❄) Swish, spacious rooms with stylish black-and-white bedspreads and memorable river views from some rooms. The attention to detail almost earns it that rare title of 'boutique business hotel'. There's a pool, sauna and on-site restaurant.

Kongsberg Vandrerhjem   HOSTEL **€**
(☑32 73 20 24; www.kongsberg-vandrerhjem.no; Vinjesgata 1; dm/s/d from Nkr350/690/770; P@🛜) Kongsberg's youth hostel bridges

the gap between budget and midrange with small but smart and comfortable rooms in a quiet but accessible part of town. There's a kitchen for guest use.

Gyldenløve Hotell   BUSINESS HOTEL **€€**
(☑32 86 58 00; www.gyldenlove.no; Hermann Foss-gata 1; s/d from Nkr950/1150; P@🛜) It's the giant black-and-white photographs of the town and its environs that first grab the eye on entering one of the rooms at this well-managed hotel. Closer inspection reveals that everything else about this modern hotel is equally appealing, although the winter prices are steep.

Max Kro & Camping   CAMPGROUND **€**
(☑090 95 025; Jondalen; tent/caravan sites Nkr150/200, 4-/6-bed cabins Nkr400/600) The nearest campsite to town is this low-key site 14km northwest of town along the Rv37. To get here use the Kongsberg–Rjukan bus.

🍴 Eating

TOP CHOICE **Fuji Sushi**   SUSHI **€**
(☑32 73 12 00; Myntgata 15; mains from Nkr49, set menus from Nkr79; ⊙noon-9pm Mon-Fri, 1-9pm Sat & Sun) The Asian dishes here are a light and healthy escape from the rigours of burgers and hotdogs. The (Vietnamese rather than Japanese) owners will also happily pack your sushi up for you to take away for a riverside picnic.

Montal Bano   ITALIAN **€€**
(☑32 72 88 00; www.montalbano.no; Nymoens torg 46; mains Nkr150; ⊙11am-11pm) This good-value Italian restaurant has realised that there's life beyond pizza and spag bog. The three-course meals (from Nkr395 to Nkr535) are good value and include, wait for it: a glass of wine!

Restaurant Opsahlgården & Christians Kjeller   TRADITIONAL NORWEGIAN **€€**
(☑32 76 45 00; Kirkegata 10; starters Nkr79-115, mains Nkr179-229; ⊙restaurant 3-10pm Mon-Fri, cafe 3-10pm Mon-Fri & 2-10pm Sat) A few doors down from Kongsberg Kirke, this fine dining restaurant is complemented by a pleasant cafe where lighter meals are available at the outdoor tables in summer. In the warmer months music in the courtyard is a regular occurrence. Note that the opening hours listed are a little 'flexible'!

ℹ Information

The **tourist office** (☑32 29 90 50; www.visit kongsberg.no; Schwabesgt 2; ⊙9am-6pm Mon-Fri, 10am-2pm Sat late-Jun–mid-Aug, shorter hr rest of yr) is excellent.

ⓘ Getting There & Around

Hourly trains connect Kongsberg with Oslo (Nkr169, 1½ hours). Several bus companies operate near-hourly buses between Kongsberg and Oslo (Nkr200, 1½ hours) as well as to Notodden (Nkr100, 35 minutes).

If you're driving your own car and park in the town's supermarket car park, make sure you take a (free) ticket otherwise you'll get nailed with a hefty fine (yes, we talk from experience – bitter experience).

The tourist office hires out bicycles for a cost of Nkr100 a day.

The Telemark Canal

The 105km-long Telemark Canal system, a series of lakes and canals that connect Skien and Dalen (with a branch from Lunde to Notodden), lifts and lowers boats a total of 72m in 18 locks. The canal was built for the timber trade from 1887 to 1892 by up to 400 workers. Today, taking a slow boat along the canals is one of the highlights of a visit to southern Norway. For some useful tourist information, check out www.visittelemark.com.

NOTODDEN
POP 12,200

Unless you're here for the hugely popular **Blues Festival** (www.bluesfest.no) in early August, drive straight past industrial Notodden and keep going until you reach the marvellous, imposing Heddal Stave Church, about 5km west of town on the E134. Otherwise, the only reason to pause in town is the Notodden **tourist office** (☏35 01 50 00; www.notodden.kommune.no; Teatergate 3; ◷8am-3pm Mon-Fri).

◉ Sights

Heddal Stave Church   CHURCH
(www.heddalstavkirke.no; Heddal; adult/child Nkr60/free, entry to grounds free; ◷9am-7pm Mon-Sat, 1-7pm Sun mid-Jun–mid-Aug, shorter hr rest of yr) This fairy-tale church is the largest and one of the most beautiful of Norway's 28 remaining stave churches.

The church possibly dates from 1242, but parts of the chancel date from as early as 1147. It was heavily restored in the 1950s. As with all stave churches, it's constructed around Norwegian pine support pillars – in this case, 12 large ones and six smaller ones, all topped by fearsome visages – and has four carved entrance portals. Of special interest are the lovely 1668 'rose' paintings

on the walls, a runic inscription in the outer passageway and the 'Bishop's chair', which was made of an old pillar in the 17th century. Its ornate carvings relate the pagan tale of the Viking Sigurd the Dragon-slayer, which has been reworked into a Christian parable involving Jesus Christ and the devil. The altarpiece originally dates from 1667 but was restored in 1908, and the exterior bell tower was added in 1850.

The displays downstairs in the adjacent building (where tickets are sold) describe the history of the church. For more information on stave churches, see p415.

From Notodden, bus 301 goes right by; otherwise take any bus heading for Seljord or Bondal. You could also walk from town in half an hour, 'admiring' the views of the busy road and slowly rusting factories on the way. Note that the church is sometimes closed for weddings.

Heddal Rural Museum   MUSEUM
(Bygdetun; www.museumaust.no; Heddal; adult/child incl church Nkr60/free; ◷10am-7pm mid-Jun–mid-Aug) This museum, 300m from the stave church, includes a collection of houses from rural Telemark.

⏢ Sleeping

Notodden Camping   CAMPGROUND €
(☏35 01 33 10; www.notoddencamping.no; Reshjemveien; tent sites without/with car Nkr50/110, caravan sites Nkr220 plus per person Nkr15, cabins Nkr450-550) Notodden Camping is an acceptable site 3km west along the E134, then 200m south on Reshjemveien. You'll be lucky to find a square inch of space at festival time. Take a bus from the centre in the direction of Seljord.

Norlandia Telemark Hotel BUSINESS HOTEL €€
(☏35 01 20 88; www.norlandia.no/telemark; Torvet 8; s/d Nkr900/1150; Ⓟ@) The member of staff who showed us around apologetically pointed out that this, the town's only hotel, 'Is not like the Sheraton'. Indeed it's not, but it's friendly enough and charges the same year-round. The hotel is closed for around 10 days at Christmas.

ⓘ Getting There & Away

Between the towns of Kongsberg and Notodden, Timekspressen buses run once or twice an hour (Nkr100, 35 minutes).

AKKERHAUGEN
POP 400

The attractive waterside village of Akkerhaugen sits on the northern fringes of the

THE HEROES OF TELEMARK

In 1933 in the USA it was discovered that 0.02% of all water molecules are 'heavy', meaning that the hydrogen atoms are actually deuterium, an isotope that contains an extra neutron. Heavy water weighs 10% more than normal water, boils at 1.4°C higher and freezes at 4°C higher than ordinary water. Why does that matter? Because such properties are sufficient to stabilise nuclear fission reactions, making heavy water invaluable in the production of an atom bomb.

During WWII in Norway the occupying Germans began building a heavy-water production plant at Vemork, near Rjukan. In response, Allied insurgents mounted Operation Grouse in October 1942 when four Norwegians parachuted into Sognadal, west of Rjukan. They were to be joined a month later by 34 specially trained British saboteurs who would arrive in two gliders at Skoland near Lake Møsvatnet, but one tow plane and its glider crashed into a mountain, and the other glider crashed on landing. All the British survivors were shot by the Germans.

Undeterred, the Norwegian group changed its mission name to Swallow and retreated to Hardangervidda, where they subsisted through the worst of the winter. On 16 February 1943 a new British-trained group called Gunnerside landed on Hardangervidda. Unfortunately a blizzard was raging and they wound up a long 30km march from their intended drop site. By the evening of 27 February the saboteurs were holed up at Fjøsbudalen, north of Vemork, waiting to strike. After descending the steep mountainside along the now-famous Sabotørruta (Saboteurs' Route, p115), they crossed the gorge to the heavy-water plant, wire-clipped the perimeter fence and planted the explosives, which largely destroyed the facility. Some of the saboteurs retreated on skis to Hardangervidda then fled into neutral Sweden, while the rest remained on the plateau, successfully avoiding capture.

The plant was rebuilt by the Germans, but on 16 November 1943, 140 US planes bombed Vemork, killing 20 Norwegians in the process. The Germans abandoned any hopes of producing heavy water in Norway and decided to shift their remaining stocks to Germany. On 19 February 1944, the night before the ferry carrying the supplies was due to sail across the lake Tinnsjø, the saboteurs placed a timed charge on the boat. The following night, the entire project was literally blown out of the water.

In 1965 this intriguing story was made into the dramatic (albeit historically inaccurate) film The Heroes of Telemark, starring Kirk Douglas.

pretty Norsjø lake, which is in itself a branch of the Telemark Canal system. The village is a popular place from which to begin or end a half-day Telemark Canal boat journey.

🛏 Sleeping

Norsjø Ferieland CAMPGROUND €
(☑35 95 84 30; www.norsjo-ferieland.no; tent sites with car Nkr320, caravan sites Nkr340, cabins Nkr1300-1900, bed linen per person Nkr100; P☏🛜🚼) This superb waterside campsite comes with an impressive array of facilities and activities, including a private beach, minigolf, wakeboarding and waterskiing, boat and canoe rental, nature trails, a restaurant and various children's activities. The setting's not bad either and the cabins are well-appointed.

Norsjø Hotell HOTEL €€
(☑35 59 50 00; www.norsjohotell.no; s/d Nkr890/1250; P☏🛜) If you prefer your accommodation to be built of brick and mortar then this is the village's only hotel, but it's dated and overpriced so we'd recommend trying a night under canvas instead.

ℹ Getting There & Away

If you're planning on taking a boat from Lunde back to Akkerhaugen, a bus leaves from the campsite at 12.15pm (Nkr45) stopping outside the hotel at 12.26pm.

SKIEN
POP 50,700

Industrial Skien has little to detain you, unless you're setting off along the Telemark Canal or you're a fan of the great Norwegian playwright Henrik Ibsen.

👁 Sights

Author, playwright and so-called 'Father of Modern Drama', Henrik Ibsen (see the boxed text, p409) was born in Skien on 20 March

DON'T MISS

A SLOW BOAT THROUGH TELEMARK

Every day from June to mid-August, a variety of different boats (mostly old-fashioned steamers) chug along the canals of Telemark. Although full-day trips are available, for most people a half-day package is sufficient. One particularly good route involves catching the boat (adult/child Nkr300/150, 3¾ hours, daily at 10am) from Akkerhaugen, 24km south of Notodden, from where you travel to Lunde, where a bus takes you back to Akkerhaugen at 1.55pm. The trip can also be done in reverse by leaving your car for free at the Norsjø Hotell in Akkerhaugen and taking the 12.26pm bus to Lunde (it stops at the hotel) from where you catch the boat at 1.45pm and sail serenely back to Akkerhaugen, arriving at 5pm.

For a full-day trip you can make the leisurely 11-hour journey between Skien and Dalen (adult/child Nkr930/465; late June to mid-August). Boats leave Skien at 8.20am and arrive in Dalen at 6.50pm, from where you can catch a special 'canalbus' back to Skien. It's also possible to jump off (or board) in Lunde, the halfway point, as well as various other combinations.

For further information, contact **Telemarkreiser** (☑35 90 00 30; www.visittelemark.com).

A great way to see the canal is by canoe, kayak or bicycle, and the ferries will transport your own boat/bicycle.

1828. In 1835 the family fell on hard times and moved out to the farm Venstøp, 5km north of Skien, where they stayed for seven years. The 1815 farmhouse has now been converted into the excellent **Henrik Ibsen-museet** (www.telemarkmuseum.no, in Norwegian; Venstøphøgda; adult/child Nkr70/30; ⊙noon-5pm Mon-Fri, 11am-5pm Sat & Sun Jun-Aug). There are some terrific audiovisual displays in the former barn, while guides (some of whom are Ibsen actors) show you around the family home. Ask also about Ibsen theatre performances here or at the tourist office, or check out the program at the **Theater Ibsen** (www.teateribsen.no, in Norwegian; Hesselbergsgt 2), which is in the town centre, a block back from the harbour.

🛏 Sleeping

Thon Hotel Høyers   BUSINESS HOTEL €€
(☑35 90 58 00; www.thonhotels.no; Kongensgate 6; d from Nkr1095) Right next to the harbour, this family-run place is set inside a grand, and very pink, building and has spacious, modern and airy rooms. As well as breakfast, a light dinner is included in the price, making it quite the bargain.

❶ Information

The **tourist office** (☑35 90 55 20; www.grenland.no; Nedre Hjellegate 18; ⊙8.30am-7pm Mon-Fri, 10am-4pm Sat, 11am-4pm Sun mid-Jun–mid-Aug, 8.30am-4pm Mon-Fri rest of yr) is moderately useful.

❶ Getting There & Away

Nor-Way Bussekspress buses run to Rjukan (Nkr273, 3¼ hours) once or twice daily. NSB trains run every hour or two to Larvik (Nkr91, 45 minutes) and Oslo (Nkr199 to Nkr300, three hours).

DALEN
POP 800

Surrounded by steep forested hills and settled comfortably beside a lazy lake busy with beavers, pretty little Dalen is a jumping-off point for ferries along the Øst Telemark Canal system. It makes for a delightfully peaceful few days' rest.

High above town on the Rv45 to Høydalsmo is the quaint, 14th-century **Eidsborg Stave Church** (guided tours Nkr40), dedicated to St Nicolas and with a single nave. The grounds are open year-round, and a caretaker can usually open the church if it's locked.

🛏 Sleeping

TOP CHOICE **Buøy Camping**   CAMPGROUND €
(☑35 07 75 87; www.dalencamping.com; tent sites Nkr240, cabins Nkr600-1150; P@🛱) Surrounded on all sides by water, this attractive and well-run campsite has plenty of activities for the children, lots of shady pitches for tents and quaint Little Red Riding Hood–style wooden cabins. Campers aren't the only ones who like this place; the waters around the campsite are home to several beaver families whom you'll almost certainly get to meet if you go on a dusk walk along the river. There's a restaurant

here and bike rental is available for Nkr150 per day.

TOP CHOICE **Dalen Bed & Breakfast** B&B €€
(☎35 07 70 80; www.dalenbb.com; s/d with shared bathroom Nkr840/890, s/d from Nkr890/970; P 📶) It might not have the history of the Dalen Hotel but in our opinion this family-run venture is the better option. Cheaper rooms match the surrounding forests with their soft pine tones, while the pricier rooms are a children's paint box of bright colours. An excellent breakfast is included, and staff dole out free maps pointing you to the area's best moose- and beaver-spotting sites.

Dalen Hotel HISTORIC HOTEL €€€
(☎35 07 90 00; www.dalenhotel.no; s/d Nkr1350/2200; P 📶) The ornate Dalen Hotel, with its faint resonance of a stave church, first opened in 1894. Although looted by the Nazis in WWII, it remains a comfortable place to soak up an old-world atmosphere. The public areas are a riot of antiques and moose heads. Room 17 is said to be haunted (by a headless moose possibly?). The restaurant serves suitably old-fashioned Norwegian countryside staples (mains around Nkr165).

Information

The **tourist office** (☎35 07 70 65; www.visitdalen.com; ⌚9am-7pm Mon-Fri, 10am-5pm Sat & Sun, closed Sep-Apr; 📶) is in the village centre and has free coffee and wi-fi access.

Getting There & Away

To get to Oslo by bus (Nkr450, 4½ hours) involves a change of bus in nearby Amot on the E134.

Rjukan

POP 6100

Sitting in the shadow of what is arguably Norway's most beautiful peak, Gausta (1883m), Rjukan is a picturesque introduction to the Norwegian high country as well as southern Norway's activities centre par excellence.

The town stretches like elastic for 6km along the floor of the steep-sided Vestfjorddalen and while the centre, which consists of a couple of blocks of pastel-painted wooden buildings, is attractive the remainder of the town stands in utter contrast to its majestic setting.

History

This hydroelectric-company town was founded in 1907 and at its peak the industry supported 10,000 residents. In the early days, the administrators' homes occupied the highest slopes, where the sun shone the longest; below them were the homes of office workers and in the valley's dark depths dwelt the labourers. The builders of the Mår Kraftverk hydroelectric plant on the eastern limits of town clearly had an eye for records: its daunting wooden stairway consists of 3975 steps (it's one of the world's longest wooden stairways and is open to very fit visitors).

Sights

Norwegian Industrial Workers' Museum MUSEUM
(Norsk Industriarbeidermuseet; www.visitvemork.com; adult/child Nkr75/45; ⌚10am-6pm mid-Jun-mid-Aug, shorter hr rest of yr) This museum, 7km west of Rjukan, is in the Vemork power station, which was the world's largest when completed in 1911. These days it honours the Socialist Workers' Party, which reached its height of Norwegian activities in the 1950s. You won't want to miss the 30-minute film *If Hitler Had the Bomb*, describing the epic events of war-time Telemark (see the boxed text, p111), nor the miniature power station in the main hall. There's also an interesting exhibition about the worldwide race in the 1930s and '40s to make an atom bomb. It consists of short films, touch-screen exhibits, photos and dioramas.

Travellers with disabilities and seniors over 65 are permitted to drive up to the entrance; everyone else must park at the swinging bridge. In summer, a **bus** (adult/child Nkr30/15; ⌚10am-4pm mid-Jun–mid-Aug) runs up from the car park to the entrance. Otherwise, it's a 15-minute, 700m climb on foot.

Krossobanen CABLE CAR
(adult one way/return Nkr50/90, child Nkr15/30, bike Nkr30/60; ⌚9am-8pm mid-Jun–Aug, shorter hr rest of yr) The Krossobanen cable car was constructed in 1928 (thus making it the oldest functioning cable car in Europe – something vertigo sufferers may prefer not to know) by Norsk Hydro to provide its employees with access to the sun. Fortunately it has since been renovated and now whisks tourists up to Gvepseborg (886m) for a view over the deep, dark recesses. The best panoramas are from the viewing platform atop the cable-car station. It also operates as the trailhead for a host of hiking and cycling trails.

Gaustabanen CABLE RAILWAY
One of Norway's most extraordinary cable railways, Gaustabanen runs 860m deep into

the core of Gausta before a different train climbs an incredible 1040m, alongside 3500 steps at a 40-degree angle, to 1800m, just below the Gaustahytte, not far from the summit. Built by NATO in 1958 at a cost of US$1 million to ensure it could access its radio tower in any weather, the railway has been closed to tourists due to safety concerns for the past couple of years but is expected to have re-opened to the public by the time this book hits the shelves. Taking the railway is an incredible experience, although it's not for the claustrophobic. The railway's base station is 10km southeast of Rjukan.

Rjukanfossen
WATERFALL

Believed to be the highest waterfall in the world in the 18th century (Angel Falls in Venezuela now has that claim), the 104m-high Rjukanfossen is still a spectacular sight, even if most of the water has been diverted to drive the Vemork power station. To get the best view, take the Rv37 heading west and park just before the tunnel 9.5km west of town; a 200m walk leads to a fine viewpoint.

Tinn Museum
FOLK MUSEUM

(www.museumaust.no; Sam Eydesgt 299; adult/child Nkr40/20; ⊙11am-7pm mid-Jun–mid-Aug, shorter hr rest of yr) This quiet little folk museum, at the eastern end of town, traces rural Norwegian architecture from the 11th century to the early 1900s.

🏃 Activities

As well as the activities listed here you can rug up against the winter cold and take a **horse-drawn sleigh ride** through a forested, magical winter wonderland or strike out across the bleak Hardangervidda Plateau on the back of a sleigh pulled by a team of **husky dogs**. The tourist office can put you in touch with local tour operators running either of these winter-only activities.

Ice-Climbing
ICE-CLIMBING

It might not appeal to all, but if the idea of hauling yourself up a giant vertical icicle that looks suspiciously as if it's going to crack and send you tumbling to an early grave sounds like your idea of fun, then Rjukan is fast gaining a reputation as *the* place for ice-climbing. There are more than 150 routes in the immediate area of the town. The **tourist office** (☑35 08 05 50; www.visitrjukan.com) can put you in touch with guides and instructors or check out **Climb Inn** (www.climb-inn.com), who can put together climbing packages

including guides, equipment rental, accommodation and food.

Bungee Jumping
BUNGEE JUMPING

(☑99 51 31 40; www.telemark-opplevelser.no; per session Nkr690; ⊙Jun-Sep, exact times vary) Described as Norway's highest land-based bungee jump, this 84m plunge into the canyon from the bridge leading to the Norwegian Industrial Workers' Museum is Rjukan's biggest adrenaline rush. We'd like to say that this author was brave enough to do it, but in fact he felt sick merely looking at the bridge. Book through the tourist office.

Skiing
SKIING

The whole area around Rjukan is pockmarked with excellent ski-runs. The **tourist office** (☑35 08 05 50; www.visitrjukan.com) has a wealth of information and its *Gaustablikk Skisenter* brochure provides the definitive guide to all things white and powdery. The main ski area is the Gaustablikk Ski Centre. One-day adult/child passes cost Nkr340/265.

Moose Safari
MOOSE SAFARI

(☑35 06 26 30; www.visitrauland.com; adult/child Nkr350/250; ⊙10pm Mon-Tue & Thu 28 Jun-23 Aug) You can get up close and personal to the largest member of the deer family in Europe on one of the moose safaris organised through the tourist office in the village of Rauland (on the RT37 southwest of Rjukan).

Rail-Biking
RAIL-BIKING

(☑35 09 05 85; Tinnsjø Kro, Miland; per 2hr incl insurance Nkr130) There's a high novelty value to taking a rail-tricycle (known as *dressin* or tricycles on bogies) for the 10km-long trip along the disused rail line between Lake Tinnsjø and Rjukan. It's only possible in summer and reservations should be made in advance.

🛏 Sleeping

Rjukan's town centre has a few places to stay, but there are more choices up in the Gaustablikk area.

RJUKAN & WEST

TOP CHOICE **Rjukan Hytteby & Kro** CABINS €€

(☑35 09 01 22; www.rjukan-hytteby.no; Brogata 9; cabins Nkr825-1050) Easily the town centre's best choice, Rjukan Hytteby & Kro sits in a pretty spot on the river bank and has carefully decorated and very well equipped huts that seek to emulate the early 20th-century hydroelectric workers'

Rjukan makes a superb base from which to strike out into the surrounding wilderness on foot or by mountain bike. To get an idea of what's possible, visit the tourist office to pick up the free *Rjukan – og Tinn,* which has a number of route suggestions.

Gausta

The most obvious goal for peak baggers is the hike to the summit of beautiful Gausta (1883m), from where you can see a remarkable one-sixth of Norway on a clear day. The popular, and easy, two- to three-hour, 4km hiking track leads from the trailhead of Stavsro (15km southeast of Rjukan) up to Den Norske Turistforening's (DNT) **Gaustahytta** (1830m), next to the rather ugly NATO radio tower. The summit is reached by walking along the rocky ridge for a further half-hour. A 13km road link, but unfortunately no public transport, runs from the far eastern end of Rjukan to Stavsro (altitude 1173m) at Lake Heddersvann. **Taxis** (☎35 09 14 00) charge around Nkr450 one-way. Allow all day for the hike, which leaves plenty of time for exploring the summit. The tourist office distributes a map of the Fv651, but the *Turkart Gausta Området* is a better option and is available for Nkr50.

More-difficult, three- to four-hour routes to the summit also run from Rjukan itself and from the Norwegian Industrial Workers' Museum.

If you can't make the hike, the soon-to-reopen Gaustabanen service takes you almost to Gaustahytta.

Hardangervidda

For something a little wilder, but bleaker, the Hardangervidda Plateau (p150), the biggest mountain plateau in Europe and home to Europe's largest herd of wild reindeer, rises up to the north of Rjukan and offers a wealth of fantastic hikes that vary from easy two- to three-hour strolls to longer day hikes and multiday challenges. From Gvepseborg, the summit of the Krossobanen cable car, the most rewarding day hike is the five-hour (without stops) round trip to the **Helberghytta DNT Hut.** The route has good way marking and although it can be very boggy in sections, it's easily achievable for any moderately fit walker (we last did it with a six-month-old baby strapped to our back). The first section winds up from the cable-car platform through a forest of stumpy, twisted trees before emerging onto the gently undulating plateau. The scenery, which takes in icy cold lakes, snow-streaked hills, barren moorland and views back over towards Mt Gausta, is supremely impressive.

For something more challenging, an eight to nine-hour route, which can also be used by cyclists, leads from the cable-car platform past the Helberghytta DNT Hut (following the route described previously) and onward to **Kalhovd Turisthytte.** From there you can either catch a bus or hike nine hours down to **Mogen Turisthytte,** where you can catch the Møsvatn ferry (Nkr255) back to Skinnarbu, west of Rjukan on Rv37; ferry timetables are available from the Rjukan tourist office. Serious hikers can also strike out north from Kalhovd, deep into the high Hardangervidda.

Alternatively, you can follow the marked route that begins above Rjukan Fjellstue, around 10km west of Rjukan and just north of the Rv37. This historic track follows the **Sabotørruta** (Saboteurs' Route), the path taken by the members of the Norwegian Resistance during WWII (see the boxed text, p111). From late June until mid-August, the tourist office organises three-hour guided hikes along this route (Nkr200; noon Tuesday, Thursday and Sunday).

The best hiking map to use for this part of the plateau is Telemark Turistforening's *Hardangervidda Sør-Øst,* at a scale of 1:60,000. It's available from the tourist office for Nkr98.

cabins. The owner is exceptionally helpful. It's a pleasant 20-minute walk along the river bank to the town centre.

Rjukan Gjestegård HOTEL €€
(☎35 08 06 50; www.rgg.no, in Norwegian; Birkelandsgata 2; dm Nkr235, s/d with shared bathroom Nkr385/580, d Nkr990; P@🤶) This central

guesthouse occupies the buildings of the old youth hostel and is something of a travellers centre. The rooms here are simple but fine enough; there's a guest kitchen; and the location is good if you want to be in town. Breakfast costs Nkr80.

Rauland Høgfjellshotell MOUNTAIN LODGE €€€
(35 06 31 00; www.rauland.no, in Norwegian; Rv37; d from Nkr1550; Jun-Apr; P) Around 45km west of Rjukan, this excellent mountain hotel promises sweeping views, hints of traditional Telemark decoration, an indoor swimming pool and an excellent spa centre. It's booked out well in advance in winter (and is nearly double the price) as it opens onto hundreds of kilometres of ski runs.

Krokan Turisthytte CABINS €
(95 18 07 02; near Rv37; cabins Nkr500) Around 10km west of Rjukan, this historic place was built in 1869 as Den Norske Turistforening's (DNT) first hut. You're housed in museum-like 16th-century log cabins and it serves traditional meals. Phone ahead as there's not always someone here.

GAUSTABLIKK

A couple of places beside the beautiful lake Kvitåvatn, off the Fv651 and 10km from town, provide a front-row view of Gausta and easy access to the Skipsfjell/Gaustablikk ski area; you'll need a car for access. For the busy winter season, contact **Gausta Booking** (45 48 51 51; www.gaustatoppenbooking.com), which can help track down a spare hut.

Gaustablikk Høyfjellshotell
MOUNTAIN LODGE €€
(35 09 14 22; www.gaustablikk.no; s/d Mon-Fri from Nkr955/1350, s/d Sat & Sun Nkr1080/1600; P) With a prime location overlooking the lake and mountain, this expansive lodge is one of Norway's better mountain hotels. The rooms are modern and many have lovely views of Gausta, while the evening buffet dinner (Nkr350) is a lavish affair. Geared towards a winter skiing crowd (prices rise considerably in winter, when advance reservations are necessary), it's also a great place in summer. Book through Fjord Pass (www.fjordpass.no) for a cheaper one-night rate.

Rjukan Vandrerhjem HOSTEL €
(35 09 20 40; www.kvitaavatn.dk; dm Nkr260, s/d with shared bathroom Nkr400/520, s/d Nkr566/686) This youth hostel offers simple accommodation in a cosy pine lodge with six bunks per room in huts. The reception is only staffed between 8.30am to 10.30am and 4pm to 7pm.

Eating

Gaustablikk Høyfjellshotell
TRADITIONAL NORWEGIAN €€€
(35 09 14 22; lunch specials from Nkr80, dinner buffet Nkr350) Even if you're not staying here, this mountain hotel's enormous buffet is worth the trip up the mountain and not just for the food – the views are stupendous.

Kinokafeen INTERNATIONAL €€
(40 85 60 48; Storstulgate 1; mains Nkr100-150) Kinokafeen, at the cinema, has a pleasing art-deco look and its outdoor tables (summer only!) and fading interior make it the most memorable place to eat in the town centre.

Roberto Gatekjokken FAST FOOD €
(off Sam Eydes St; mains from around Nkr46) A cut above most Norwegian roadside kiosks, this well-run little place offers fish and chips (Nkr53), hamburgers (Nkr46 to Nkr98), kebabs (Nkr55) and other heart-friendly delights. Eat at the shady adjacent tables.

Rjukan Hytteby & Kro INTERNATIONAL €€
(35 09 01 22; Brogata 9; mains Nkr59-159, pizzas from Nkr130) Offering simple but hearty cafeteria-style food, this place along the river does everything from pizzas to baked potatoes.

Kiwi Mini Pris SUPERMARKET €
(7am-11pm Mon-Fri, 8am-9pm Sat & Sun) Supermarket on Sam Eydes St.

Information

The **tourist office** (35 08 05 50; www.visitrjukan.com; Torget 2; 9am-7pm Mon-Fri, 10am-6pm Sat & Sun late Jun-late Aug, 8am-3.30pm Mon-Fri rest of yr) is the best of its kind in Telemark, with loads of information and knowledgeable staff. Internet is available for Nkr30 per hour.

Getting There & Around

Buses connect Rjukan to Oslo (Nkr355, 3½ hours) via Notodden (where you need to change buses) roughly every other hour between 5.30am and 3.30pm. These buses also stop in Kongsberg (Nkr240, two hours).

Rjukan's linear distances will seem intimidating, but the local Bybuss runs from Vemork to the eastern end of the valley. Bike hire from the Rjukan Gjestegård costs Nkr150 per day.

Tuddal

Lying beside a deep blue lake surrounded by snow- and forest-dappled peaks, the handful of colourful wooden houses that make up the tiny mountain village of Tuddal have a setting that is hard to top. There's nothing much to do here except relish the peace and quiet and maybe embark on a gentle ramble or two.

The village sits at the foot of a bleak and spectacular summer-only mountain road between Rjukan and the E134 Notodden–Seljord road. Halfway along this mountain road is a summer tourist office booth that has maps and route descriptions detailing a number of excellent hikes.

The village has a couple of idyllic campsites with lakeside settings.

Seljord

POP 3000

Lakeside Seljord is known mainly as the home of Selma the Serpent, the Nessie-type monster that inhabits the depths of the lake Seljordvatn. Other creatures of legend call the nearby hills home and hikers can also seek out the feuding troll women, Ljose-Signe, Glima and Tårån. Personally we haven't seen them but locals assured us that they're there. Seljord was also the inspiration for some of Norway's best-known folk legends, including Asbjørnsen and Moe's *The Three Billy Goats Gruff*, known the world over.

◉ Sights

The charming Romanesque **church** (admission free; ◷11am-5pm mid-Jun–mid-Aug) was built in the 12th century in honour of St Olav; it looks as if someone built a stave church and then changed their mind and tried to build a house around it. In the grounds, between the church and the churchyard wall, are two impressions reputedly made by two mountain trolls who were so upset by the encroachment of Christianity that they pummelled the site with boulders.

✯✯ Festivals & Events

On the second weekend of September, Seljord holds the **Dyrsku'n Festival**, which started in 1866 and is now Norway's largest traditional market and cattle show, attracting 60,000 visitors, almost as many cows and not all that many monsters.

⛏ Sleeping & Eating

Seljord Hotell　　　　　HISTORIC HOTEL **€€**
(☑35 06 40 00; www.seljordhotel.no, in Norwegian; s/d Nkr990/1250, mains Nkr210-260; 🅿@🛜) This lovely old wooden hotel, which

---

SELMA THE SERPENT

The first evidence of Selma the Serpent's existence dates back to 1750, when Gunleik Andersson-Verpe of nearby Bø was 'attacked by a sea horse' while rowing across the lake. Nearly every summer since (Selma, like Norwegians, comes out of her shell in summer), witnesses have sighted the fins and humps of this fast-moving lake creature, which reportedly measures the size of a large log, or slightly bigger. Some have described it as eel-like, while others have likened it to a snail, a lizard or a crocodile and have reported lengths of 25m, 30m and even 50m. Amateur videos filmed in 1988 and 1993 reveal a series of humps in the water, but their grainy nature renders the evidence deliciously inconclusive. Researchers have suggested that the lake is too small to support creatures more than about 7m long.

As with Scotland's famous Nessie, Selma has fuelled local folklore and drawn tourists to search the surface of the deep, pine-rimmed lake Seljordvatn (14km long, 2km wide and 157m deep) for evidence. In 1977 and again in 1988, Swedish freelance journalist Jan-Ove Sundberg scanned the lake with sonar equipment, underwater cameras and even a mini-submarine and detected several large objects moving in unison, then separating in several directions. According to Sundberg, 'The serpent does not fit any species known to humanity. It has several qualities not seen before, such as travelling on the surface at high speed and moving vertically up and down. It shows a back or a head or a neck or all three for long periods above the surface and travels very fast, maybe up to 25 knots.'

When we asked one local whether he believed in Selma's existence, he replied, 'I have never seen her, but I believe she exists and my children won't swim in the lake.' We didn't see her either, but…

dates back to 1858, started life as a ladies college, but on running out of potential 'ladies' they turned it into a hotel and now even men are welcome to stay the night! Rooms have period touches and are individually named, each with its own story. It also gets points for having the same rates all year, which is very unusual in Norway. The restaurant is Seljord's best, with gourmet local fish and game dishes, each of which is a work of art.

Seljord Camping og Badeplass
CAMPGROUND €

(☑35 05 04 71; www.seljordcamping.no; tent sites Nkr170, cabins Nkr450-1300) This pleasant campsite with soft grassy pitches beside the lake and cabins that range from the super-basic to the truly luxurious also serves as the dock for monster boats on Seljordvatn (fares vary with the number of passengers) and has a telescope to help you spot Selma. Kayaks and canoes can also be rented here for Nkr30 per hour. There are a couple of other campsites in the vicinity.

ℹ Information
The **tourist office** (☑35 06 59 88; www.seljord portalen.no; ☉10am-6pm Mon-Fri mid-Jun–mid-Aug, shorter hr rest of yr) has lots of local information and revels in good troll stories.

ℹ Getting There & Away
Nor-Way Bussekspress (Haukeliekspressen) buses connect Seljord with Notodden (Nkr140, 1¼ hours) and Oslo (Nkr350, 3¼ hours) up to four times daily.

Setesdalen
The forested hillsides and lake-filled mountain valleys of Setesdalen, one of Norway's most traditional and conservative regions, remain little frequented by travellers, although the area is becoming increasingly popular with outdoor enthusiasts.

EVJE
POP 3300

The riverside town of Evje, surrounded by forests and rolling hills, serves as the southern gateway to Setesdalen. It's famous among geologists for the variety of rocks found here – a mineral park, nickel mine and the chance to prospect for your own rocks are among Evje's primary attractions. Quiet little Evje is also a first-class base for white-water rafting and other activities.

◉ Sights & Activities

Evje Og Hornnes Museum MUSEUM
(adult/child Nkr30/free; ☉11am-5pm Jul-early Aug, shorter hr rest of yr) Budding geologists will find plenty to get excited about in Evje. First stop should be this small museum, 2km west of town and across the river in Fennefoss. Displays include more than a hundred different types of mineral found in the nearby hills, as well as exhibits on local nickel mining and rural life in Setesdalen.

Setesdal Mineral Park PARK
(www.mineralparken.no; Hornnes; adult/ child under 5yr/child 6-14yr/Nkr110/30/65; ☉10am-6pm Jul–mid-Aug, shorter hr rest of yr) For displays of local and worldwide minerals, this well-run park is every rock collector's dream come true, with a wonderful world of colour and quartz, and many items for sale. It's about 10km south of Evje.

Flåt Nikkelgruve MINE
(Flåt Nickel Mine; adult/child/family Nkr80/50/210; ☉guided tours 2pm Jul–mid-Aug) A summer visit here, once Europe's largest nickel mine with a shaft 440m deep, takes you deep into the earth on a fascinating underground tour that's not for the claustrophobic. Temperatures down there drop to 5°C so wear warm

ENERGETIC IN EVJE

TrollActiv (☑37 93 11 77; www.troll -mountain.no; ☉9am-8pm Apr-Oct), around 6km north of Evje, is the centre of most of Evje's high-energy thrills. White-water rafting (per person from Nkr440) is its forte, but it also organises all manner of other activities, including overnight kayaking trips (from Nkr1750), mountain-bike tours (Nkr400) and nightly beaver and elk safaris (adult/child Nkr300/250). Other high-thrill activities include river-boarding, rock-climbing, river kayaking, paintballing, waterskiing and fishing safaris. It puts together a range of different adult- and child-friendly activities packages that include all accommodation.

Viking Adventures Norway (☑91 17 67 09, 97 17 71 06; www.raftingsenter. no), in town, offers most of the same activities for generally slightly lower prices.

clothes. It's 3.3km off the Rv9; the turn-off is around 2km north of Evje.

Sleeping & Eating

TOP CHOICE **TrollActiv** HOSTEL €
(Evje Vandrerhjem; ☎37 93 11 77; www.troll
-mountain.no; tent sites per person Nkr60, te-
pees per person Nkr80-100, cabins from Nkr400,
d from Nkr540; P@) This energetic activities centre doubles as Evje's youth hostel,
6km north of town. It's exceptionally well
run and the place to be if you're planning
any one of the many activities on offer.
Accommodation varies from sleeping in
your own tent, kipping in a *lavvo* (tepee)
or stretching out in comfort in a cabin or
room. There are kitchen facilities as well
as a basic cafe.

Revsnes Hotell HOTEL €€
(☎37 93 46 50; www.revsneshotell.no; Byglandsfjord; s/d from Nkr895/1050; P🔊) The good-
value Revsnes is 12km north of town and set
on the banks of lush lake Byglandsfjorden.
The rooms are large and modern, and most
have wonderful big windows overlooking
the water. It's a family-run place and you'll
be made to feel welcome.

Odden Camping CAMPGROUND €
(☎37 93 06 03; www.oddencamping.setesdal.
com; tent sites without/with car Nkr130/180 plus
per adult Nkr15, caravan sites Nkr190, 2-8-bed huts
Nkr375-1225) This large, recommended campsite is extremely well run and can be found
in a postcard setting by the water just 200m
south of town. It can become crowded in
summer.

Neset Camping CAMPGROUND €
(☎37 93 42 55; www.neset.no, in Norwegian; tent
sites from Nkr200 plus adult/child Nkr10/5, 4-6-
bed cabins Nkr525-700) Also in a picturesque
lakeside spot, Neset Camping is 13km north
of Evje.

Pernille Cafeteria FAST FOOD €
(☎37 93 00 69; mains Nkr99-139; ☻8am-6pm
Mon-Fri, 8am-4.30pm Sat, 10am-6pm Sun) Right
in the heart of Evje, this upstairs place is
popular with locals although the menu is
not Norway's most inspirational. Expect
burgers, eggs and bacon alongside a few
Norwegian dishes.

Information

The **information centre** (☎37 93 14 00; www.
setesdal.com; ☻11am-6pm Mon-Thu, to 7pm
Fri, to 3pm Sat mid-Jun–mid-Aug, 10am-noon
Mon-Fri rest of yr) occupies the same old log

building as the bus terminal. Ask about permits
for mineral prospecting.

Getting There & Away

Nor-Way Bussekspress buses travel to Kristiansand (Nkr130, one hour) seven to eight times
daily. Heading north from Evje, car drivers will
be stung with a Nkr30 toll that annoys us every
time we pass.

SETESDALSMUSEET

This fine collection of **folk museums** (www.
setesdalsmuseet.no, in Norwegian; adult/child/fam-
ily Nkr20/free/40) along Rv9 is a good way to
break up your journey through Setesdalen.

Coming from the south, Rysstad's main
Setesdalsmuseet (☻11am-5pm 20 Jun–
Aug, shorter hr rest of yr) is a fine, refurbished
exhibition space displaying period interiors
and cultural artefacts, including displays of
regional dress.

Around 10km further north is **Tveitetu-
net** (in Valle), a log farm with a storehouse
dating from 1645. It was closed for renovations at the time of research, but was due to
re-open shortly.

Best of all is **Rygnestadtunet** (☻11am-
5pm Jul-8 Aug, shorter hr rest of yr), 9km northwest of Valle, where the farm has a unique
three-storey storehouse (from 1590) and
an extraordinary collection of 15th-century
painted textiles. Local legend has its owner
as Evil Åsmund, who served as a mercenary
around Europe and brought back looted
weapons and artwork from his travels, including a 14th-century painting of St George
rescuing a grateful damsel from the clutches
of a dragon and a whole set of paintings depicting the Ten Commandments. Staff may
be dressed in traditional costume.

BYKLE
POP 900

The distinctive log-built **Bykle Kirkje** (admission by donation; ☻11am-5pm Jul-8 Aug) is one of
the smallest churches in Norway and all the
more delightful because of it, with painted
stalls, altar and organ. The building and altar date from 1619; roses on the front of the
galleries and traditional rose paintings on
the wall were added in the 1820s, although
some of the paintings date back to the 15th
century. A woman in traditional dress will
magically appear to unlock the church and
show you around.

There's also a lovely signpost-guided
walk above the Otra River, 5km south of
town. The route, which takes about 30

minutes, dates from at least 1770 and was once the main route through Setesdalen.

HOVDEN
POP 450

Watching over the northern end of Setesdalen, Hovden is a winter ski resort and low-key summer hiking base.

In summer, for fine views you can reach the summit of **Mt Nos** (1176m) by taking the **chairlift** (adult/child Nkr90/60; ⊙11am-2pm Jul-Aug, 9.30am-3.30pm Dec-Apr, shorter hr rest of yr). From the summit a number of hiking trails, ranging from an hour or two's easy ramble to an overnight slog, snake out across the high moorland plateau. The tourist office can provide more information.

There's plenty of accommodation in and around the village but most of it is aimed squarely at a winter ski crowd (when prices go through the roof). **Hovden Fjellstoge & Vandrerhjem** (☏37 93 95 43; www.vandrerhjem. no/hovden, in Norwegian; dm/s/d Nkr250/750/990, cabins Nkr690-990, meals around Nkr160; Ⓟ🛜) is housed in a traditional-style wooden building with a grass roof and has something to please everyone, from rooms with fairy-tale wooden bunk beds to cute cabins. There's virtually an entire zoo of stuffed local wildlife here, including a wolf and a reindeer. It's about 3.5km north of the centre.

Hovden Høyfjellshotell (☏37 93 88 00; www.hovdenhotell.no, in Norwegian; s/d from Nkr930/1245; Ⓟ🛜🏊👨), at the top end of the town, is Hovden's finest. Highlights are the indoor pool, sauna and the children's playroom chock-full of toys.

Hovden Høyfjellsenter (☏37 93 95 01; www.rabattenskivtleie.no, in Norwegian; cabins Nkr750-1650; Ⓟ) rents out large and comfortable cabins with well-equipped kitchens.

The **tourist office** (☏37 93 93 70; www. hovden.com; ⊙9am-5pm Mon-Fri, 10am-3pm Sat & Sun) provides basic hiking-route information and plenty of skiing knowledge and can help you book various ski huts, flats, chalets and hotels.

The daily Nor-Way Bussekspress bus between Kristiansand (Nkr386, 3½ hours) and Haukeligrend passes through Hovden; from the latter there are connections to Bergen.

Sirdal

Sirdal is the access route to the scenic descent through 27 hairpin bends to Lysebotn (p197). From the well-appointed DNT hut at **Ådneram**, at the top of Sirdal, hikers can reach Lysebotn in nine hours (follow the road for the last 4km). The road is open only from mid-June to mid-September.

For tourist information and details of wilderness tours, horse riding and dogsledding, contact **Sirdalsferie** (☏38 37 78 00; www.sirdalsferie.com; Tjørhom).

Central Norway

HIGHEST ELEV: GALDHØPIGGEN 2469M

Best Places to Eat

» Fossheim Turisthotell (p146)

» Vertshuset Røros (p135)

» Røisheim Hotel (p150)

» Svare & Berg (p127)

Best Places to Stay

» Fossheim Turisthotell (p146)

» Fannaråki DNT hut (p148)

» Erzscheidergården (p135)

» Elvesæter Hotell (p149)

» Turatgrø Hotel (p150)

» Røisheim Hotel (p150)

Why Go?

National parks and dramatic mountain massifs at seemingly every turn, charming villages, stave churches, fascinating wildlife and arguably Norway's best hiking and white-water rafting – with so much going for it, Central Norway more than matches the fjords.

Here on the roof of Norway, trails snake their way past glaciers, waterfalls and snow-bound peaks. Jotunheimen National Park is king of Norway's protected areas and one of Europe's premier hiking destinations, and is bisected by one of Norway's most beautiful drives. But Rondane, Dovrefjell-Sunndalsfjella and the desolately beautiful Hardangervidda are also superb national parks. Within the parks' boundaries you may find wild reindeer, elk and the decidedly prehistoric musk ox. At the gateway to the parks, Unesco World Heritage–listed Røros, a centuries-old mining town of timber houses and turf-roofed cottages, and Lom with its gorgeous location and extremely beautiful stave church, are two of inland Norway's most attractive villages.

When to Go
Røros

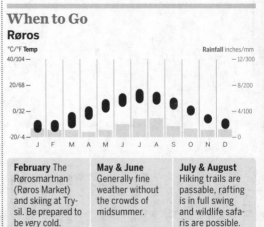

°C/°F Temp   Rainfall inches/mm

40/104 —   — 12/300

20/68 —   — 8/200

0/32 —   — 4/100

-20/-4 —   — 0

J F M A M J J A S O N D

February The Rørosmartnan (Røros Market) and skiing at Trysil. Be prepared to be *very* cold.

May & June Generally fine weather without the crowds of midsummer.

July & August Hiking trails are passable, rafting is in full swing and wildlife safaris are possible.

Central Norway Highlights

1 Return to the past in Unesco World Heritage–listed **Røros** (p132)

2 Trek along the highest trails in Norway in the endlessly beautiful **Jotunheimen National Park** (p147) or drive or maybe cycle over **Sognefjellet Road** (p147)

3 Search for the prehistoric musk ox in **Dovrefjell-Sunndalsfjella National Park** (p140)

4 Spot your first reindeer on **Hardangervidda** (p150)

5 Wet your pants while white-water rafting in **Sjoa** (p143)

6 Admire the floodlit stave church against a backdrop

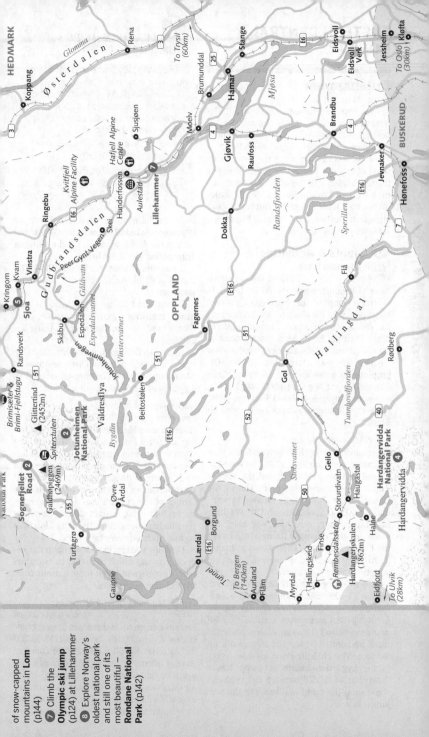

of snow-capped
mountains in **Lom**
(p144)
7 Climb the
Olympic ski jump
(p124) at Lillehammer
8 Explore Norway's
oldest national park
and still one of its
most beautiful –
**Rondane National
Park** (p142)

Lillehammer

POP 26,381

Long a popular Norwegian ski resort, Lillehammer became known to the world after hosting the 1994 Winter Olympics. These Olympics, overwhelmingly considered a great success, still provide the town with some of its most interesting sights. Lying at the northern end of the lake Mjøsa and surrounded by farms, forests and small settlements, it's a laid-back place with year-round attractions, although in winter it becomes a ski town *par excellence*.

Sights & Activities

TOP **Olympic Sites**
CHOICE

SKI JUMP, CHAIRLIFT & MUSEUM

After Lillehammer won its bid for the 1994 Winter Olympics, the Norwegian government ploughed over two billion kroner into the town's infrastructure. In an example to other Olympic host cities, most amenities remain in use and visitors can tour the main Olympic sites over a large area called the **Olympiaparken** (www.olympiaparken.no; ⊙9am-6pm mid-Jun–mid-Aug, shorter hr Oct-May).

For the Olympic Bobsled Run, see p129, while the Olympic ski slopes are covered on p129.

Lygårdsbakkene Ski Jump
The main ski jump (K120) drops 136m with a landing-slope angle of 37.5°. The speed at takeoff is a brisk 86km/h, and the longest leap at the Olympics was 104m. During the Olympics, the site was surrounded by seating for 50,000 spectators and it was here that the opening ceremony was held; the tower for the **Olympic flame** stands near the foot of the jump. There's also a smaller jump (K90) alongside, where you'll often see athletes honing their skills.

The **ski-jump chairlift** (adult or child one-way Nkr30, adult/child return Nkr50/45; ⊙9am-7pm mid-Jun–mid-Aug, shorter hr late May–mid-Jun & mid-Aug–Sep) ascends to a stunning panoramic view over the town. Alternatively, for those undaunted by the 952 steps, walk up for free. The chairlift price includes entry to the **Lygårdsbakkene ski-jump tower** (adult/child Nkr20/15; ⊙same hr). Here you can stand atop the ramp and imagine the pre-jump nerves.

LILLEHAMMER'S COMBINED TICKETS

If you plan to visit more than one of the following museums: Maihaugen Folk Museum, Norwegian Olympic Museum, Bjerkebæk and Aulestad (p129), it works out cheaper to buy one of the following combined tickets:

» Two museums: adult/child/student & senior Nkr180/90/120

» Three museums: Nkr255/125/180

» Four museums: Nkr330/165/240

At the base of the chairlift, there's an **Olympic Bobsled Simulator** (adult/child per 5 min Nkr60/50; ⊙same hr) and a **Bungee Trampoline** (per 10 min Nkr50).

A combined ticket (adult/child Nkr95/75) is also available for the chairlift, tower and simulator.

If you want to try your hand at **ski-jump training**, four/eight hours costs Nkr230/180. It's not the sort of thing for amateurs...

To reach the summit by car, take the road that leads past the Olympic Museum north out of town. The turn-off (signed as 'Lygårdsbakkene') comes after 2.8km.

Norwegian Olympic Museum
(www.ol.museum.no; Olympiaparken; adult/child/student & senior Nkr100/50/80; ⊙10am-5pm Jun-Aug, 11am-4pm Tue-Sun Sep-May) The excellent Olympic museum is at the Håkons Hall ice-hockey venue. On the ground floor there is a well-presented display covering the ancient Olympic Games as well as all of the Olympic Games of the modern era, with a focus on the exploits of Norwegian athletes as well as the Lillehammer games. The exhibition is, of course, updated every two years.

Upstairs, you can look down upon the ice-hockey arena, which is circled by corridors with displays and video presentations from the Lillehammer games.

TOP **Maihaugen Folk Museum**
CHOICE

REGIONAL FOLK MUSEUM

(www.maihaugen.no; Maihaugveien 1; adult/child/student & senior/family Jun-Aug Nkr140/70/80/350, Sep-May Nkr100/50/80/250; ⊙10am-5pm Jun-Aug, shorter hr rest of yr) Norway's finest folk museum is the expansive, open-air Maihaugen Folk Museum. Rebuilt like a small village, the collection of around 180 buildings includes the transplanted

Garmo stave church, traditional Gudbrands-dalen homes and shops, a postal museum and 27 buildings from the farm Bjørnstad. The three main sections encompass rural and town architecture, with a further section on 20th-century architecture. The life's work of local dentist Anders Sandvig, the museum also houses temporary exhibitions in the modern exhibition hall and a permanent exhibition 'We won the land', a fascinating journey through Norwegian history.

Bjerkebæk
LITERARY MUSEUM

(www.maihaugen.no/bjerkebek; Sigrid Undsets veg 1; adult/child/student & senior Nkr100/50/80; ☉10am-5pm Jun-Aug, shorter hr rest of yr) Bjerkebæk celebrates the life of Sigrid Undset, one of Norway's most celebrated authors; she won the Nobel Prize for Literature in 1928. Her home has been restored with memorabilia from her life.

Lillehammer Art Museum
ART GALLERY

(Lillehammer Kunstmuseum; www.lillehammerart museum.com; Stortorget; 2; adult/student & senior/ child Nkr90/60/free; ☉11am-5pm daily mid-Jun–mid-Aug, 11am-4pm Tue-Sun rest of yr) This art museum is not only architecturally striking, it also covers Norwegian visual arts from the early 19th century to the present. Highlights of the permanent collection include some of Norway's finest artists (including Edvard Munch) and some local painters.

Norwegian Museum of Historical Vehicles
VEHICLE MUSEUM

(Norsk Kjøretøyhistorisk Museum; Lilletorget 1; adult/child Nkr40/20; ☉10am-6pm daily mid-Jun–mid-Aug, 11am-3pm Mon-Fri, 11am-4pm Sat & Sun rest of yr) Tucked away behind the stream in central Lillehammer, the Norwegian Vehicle Museum is for car buffs, featuring everything from sleighs to vintage cars and motorcycles.

✰✰ Festivals & Events

Lillehammer Jazz Festival (☎81 53 31 33; www.dolajazz.no, in Norwegian) is held over four days in September or October; tickets go on sale from 1 July each year.

🛏 Sleeping

TOP CHOICE **Lillehammer Vandrerhjem** HOSTEL €
(☎61 26 00 24; www.815mjosa.no; 1st fl, Railway Station; dm/s/d/tr Nkr325/695/840/990, 6-bed apt Nkr1650; 🕾) If you've never stayed in a youth hostel, this one above the train station is the place to break the habit of a lifetime. The rooms are simple but come with a

bathroom, bed linen and free wireless internet. The service is arguably Lillehammer's friendliest and there's a spick-and-span communal kitchen. And if you've a train or bus to catch, it couldn't be more convenient.

First Hotel Breiseth
HOTEL €€

(☎61 24 77 77; www.firsthotels.com/breiseth; Jern-banegata 1-5; budget s/d from Nkr598/798, standard r Nkr1000-1600; P🕾) Part of the Fjord Pass network, this upmarket hotel opposite the train station has a range of attractive rooms, some of which reflect the hotel's 110-year history with original artworks in the public areas and some of the rooms. The recently renovated budget rooms are simpler but well priced.

Birkebeineren
HOTEL & APARTMENTS €€

(☎61 05 00 80; www.birkebeineren.no; Birkebei-nervegen 24; s/d Nkr740/1020, with Fjord Pass Nkr370/740, 2-/4-bed apt Nkr1170/1620; P🕾) This very good place, on the road up to the bottom of the ski jump, offers a range of accommodation to suit different budgets; prices fall the longer you stay. Rooms are light-filled and modern, and a children's playground and sauna are on-site.

Mølla Hotell
HOTEL €€

(☎61 05 70 80; www.mollahotell.no; Elvegata 12; s/d Nkr1180/1375, with Fjord Pass Nkr760/1020; P🕾) Although you wouldn't know it from the lurid yellow exterior, this hotel was built from the shell of an old mill. Fully refurbished with modern rooms, the hotel has mill memorabilia in the public areas and flat-screen TVs and comfy beds in the rooms; the straw on the pillows is a nice touch. The rooftop bar (open from 8pm to 2am Monday to Saturday) has fine views and the architecture is distinguished. Parking costs Nkr55 per day.

Gjeste Bu
GUESTHOUSE €

(☎/fax 61 25 43 21; gjestebu@lillehammer.online. no; Gamleveien 110; s/d with shared bathroom from Nkr290/390, s/d/apt with private bathroom from Nkr600/710/1200) Part-hostel, part-guesthouse and with the feel of a mountain cabin, this friendly place has a range of accommodation, shared kitchen facilities and apartments that are ideal if you'll be in town a while. Breakfast costs extra as does bed linen (Nkr60). If you understand its pricing system, let us know.

Øvergaard
B&B €

(☎61 25 99 99; http://home.c2i.net/overgaard/; Jernbanegata 24; s/d with shared bathroom Nkr290/ 490, breakfast Nkr60) Just above the centre of town, this friendly B&B has simple rooms in quiet surrounds. It's a well-run place.

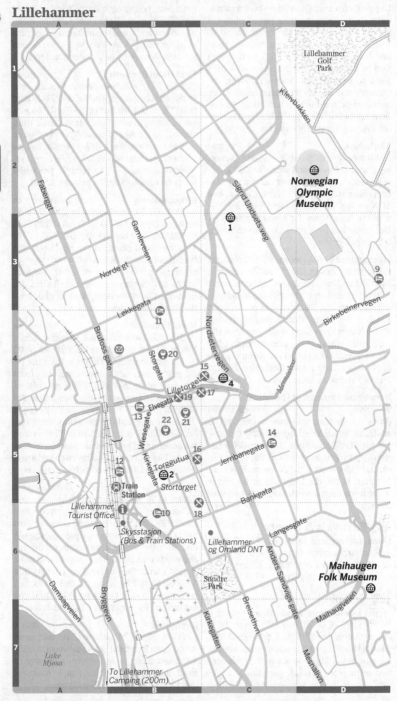

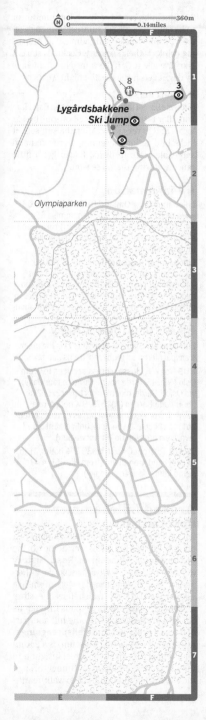

Lillehammer Camping CAMPGROUND €

(☎61 25 33 33; www.lillehammer-camping.no; Dampsagveien 47; tent/caravan sites from Nkr110/245, 2-bed cabin from Nkr510; ⊘year-round; 🛜) Camping is available here on the lakeshore. It's a typical urban site with cooking and laundry facilities, water-sports equipment, children's play areas, a Viking camp and cable TV.

✖ Eating

Svare & Berg INTERNATIONAL €€

(☎61 24 74 30; Elvegata; mains Nkr139-298; ⊘4-11pm Mon-Fri, 11am-11pm Sat) Right by Lillehammer's brook, this very cool cafe-restaurant serves tasty meals and great coffee. It's a popular spot for locals. The same people also run the neighbouring **Nikkers**, where a moose has apparently walked through the wall (look outside for the full effect); at Nikkers they do sandwiches and lighter meals (Nkr89 to Nkr149). At both places, the brook-side terrace has the best seats in the house.

Tid For Mat NORWEGIAN €€€

(☎61 24 77 77; Jernbanegata 1-5; tapas & starters Nkr45-125, mains Nkr200-295; ⊘4-10pm Tue-Sat) This stylish restaurant attached to the First Hotel Breiseth is the domain of Siegfried Sokollek, one of Norway's more celebrated chefs. The cooking is, as you'd imagine, assured.

Café Opus SNACKS €

(Storgata 63; baguettes from Nkr59; ⊘9am-5pm Mon-Wed & Fri, 9am-7pm Thu, 9am-4pm Sat) Hugely popular for its baguettes, rolls and cakes (and for its outdoor tables in summer), Café Opus gets the simple things right – tasty food, friendly service and smart-casual decor. It opens only for breakfast and lunch.

Blåmann NORWEGIAN & INTERNATIONAL €€

(☎61 26 22 03; Lilletorget 1; lunch mains Nkr59-149, dinner mains Nkr229-369, children's meals Nkr55; ⊘11am-11pm) This recommended spot has a clean-lined interior and a trendy menu that ranges from kangaroo fillet or Mexican dishes to whale and reindeer. The decor is classy, yet the atmosphere is casual.

Øverlie Café INTERNATIONAL €

(Storgata 50; mains Nkr79-149; ⊘11am-11pm) Filling, inexpensive meals (with Turkish dishes the mainstays) are the order of the day at this pleasant pavement-side cafe. It also does pizzas, salads, ice cream and good coffee.

🍷 Drinking & Entertainment

Bars are an integral part of the Lillehammer experience, especially during the ski season. **Nikkers** and **Blåmann** also double as bars.

Lillehammer

One-Hand Clapping   COFFEE BAR

(Storgata 80; ◷9.10am-5pm Mon-Wed & Fri, 9.10am-6pm Thu, 9.10am-3.30pm Sat) This very cool little coffee shop does superb coffee (from Nkr20), as well as croissants and chocolate cake (Nkr20) to die for. It's the sort of place to linger over a good book as you inhale the coffees from around the world. It also has an extensive range of teas.

Krem   COCKTAIL BAR

(Elvegata 17; ◷11am-11pm Mon & Tue, 11am-2am Wed-Fri, 11am-3am Sat, 3pm-1am Sun) Lillehammer's trendiest little bar, Krem draws a 20-something crowd to its stylish interior or to its outdoor tables in summer. Although offering some snacks, staff admit that preparing drinks is their specialty. Cocktails start at Nkr97, while a G&T goes for Nkr95. Mellow by day, it gets livelier as the night wears on.

Haakons Bar   PUB

(Storgata 93; ◷11am-3am) During the day Haakon's Bar is the preserve of elbow-on-the-bar locals and is very slow. After the sun sets, it kicks into action, becoming a crowded and agreeable place to drink. It can get a little raucous during the ski season.

❶ Information

Lillehammer og Omland DNT(✆61 25 13 06; www.turistforeningen.no/lillehammer; Storgata 34; ◷10am-3.30pm Tue, Thu & Fri) Hiking and skiing maps, mountain-hut information and mountain-hiking trips.

Lillehammer tourist office (✆61 28 98 00; www.lillehammer.com; Lillehammer Skysstasjon; ◷8am-6pm Mon-Fri, 10am-5pm Sat & Sun mid-Jun–mid-Aug, shorter hr rest of yr) Offers 15 minutes of free internet and loads of information.

❶ Getting There & Away

Lillehammer Skysstasjon (✆177) is the main transport terminal for buses, trains and taxis.

BUS Nor-Way Bussekspress services to/from Oslo (Nkr315, three hours, three to four daily) via Oslo's Gardermoen Airport (Nkr270, 2¼ hours) and Bergen (Nkr575, 9¼ hours, one daily). Lavprisekspressen buses run less often but are cheaper if you book online at https://lavprisekspressen.no (in Norwegian).

TRAIN To/from Oslo (Nkr339, 2¼ hours, 11 to 17 daily) and Trondheim (from Nkr661, 4¼ to seven hours, four to six daily).

Around Lillehammer

HUNDERFOSSEN

Some 15km north of Lillehammer, just off the E6, is Hunderfossen, home to the FREE **Norwegian Museum of Road History** (Norsk Vegmuseum; www.vegmuseum.no, in Norwegian; ◷10am-6pm mid-May–Aug, 10am-3pm Tue-Sun Sep–mid-May), which tells the story of Norway's battle to forge roads through its challenging geography. Up the hill and part of the same complex, the **Fjellsprengningsmuseet** (Rock-blasting Museum) is a 240m-long tunnel that gives you a real insight into the difficulties of building a tunnel through the Norwegian mountains. The walk, featur-

PEER GYNT VEGEN

Of all the beautiful mountain roads of Central Norway, one stands out for its combination of scenery and storytelling: **Peer Gynt Vegen** (www.peergynt vegen.no; toll Nkr70; ☺Jun-Sep). Running for 60km from Skei to Espedalen, it takes you along the trail followed by that ill-fated fictional character created by Henrik Ibsen and offers fine views of the Jotunheimen and Rondane massifs en route. Climbing up to 1053m above sea level at the Listulhøgda lookout point, it passes the Solbrå Seter farm, where Gudbrandsdal cheese was first made in 1863. An open-air arena next to Gålåvatn lake is the scene in early August for an opera concert of Edvard Grieg's *Peer Gynt*. To reach Skei, head north of Lillehammer along the E6 and at Tretten take the turn-off for the Rv254. At Svingvoll, Peer Gynt Vegen branches off to the northwest.

ing lighting, models and video commentary, takes around 30 minutes.

Nearby is the **Hunderfossen Familiepark** (www.hunderfossen.no; adult/child Nkr340/275; ☺10am-7pm mid-Jun–early Aug, closed early Sep–mid-May), one of Norway's best parks for children, with water rides, 3-D presentations, fairy-tale palaces and wandering trolls. If your child is under 90cm tall, he or she gets in free.

Also in Hunderfossen, you can career down the **Olympic Bobsled Run** (☺11am-6pm daily early Jul–early Aug, weekends only Jun & rest of August, closed rest of yr) aboard a **wheelbob** (adult/10-11yr Nkr220/150) under the guidance of a professional bobsled pilot. Wheel bobs take five passengers and hit a top speed of 100km/h. The real things, **taxibobs** (adult around Nkr1100; ☺Nov-Easter), take four passengers, reach an exhilarating 130km/h and don't give you enough time to get nervous – you're down the mountain in 70 seconds. Bookings are advisable in winter.

In summer there are up to five buses a day from the Lillehammer Skysstasjon (adult/child Nkr42/21, 30 minutes) to Hunderfossen, with less frequent departures the rest of the year. A considerable uphill walk is involved to reach the bobsled run.

OLYMPIC SKI SLOPES

Lillehammer has two Olympic ski slopes. **Hafjell Alpine Centre** (www.hafjell.no), 15km north of town, hosted the downhill events, while **Kvitfjell Alpine Facility** (www.kvitfjell. no), 50km north of town, was used for cross-country. Both offer public skiing between late November and late April and they're connected by bus with Lillehammer Skysstasjon.

AULESTAD

Bjørnstjerne Bjørnson won the Nobel Prize for Literature in 1903 and lived on a farm at **Aulestad** (www.maihaugen.no/aulestad; Follebu; adult/child/student/senior Nkr100/50/80/80; ☺10am-5pm May-Aug, shorter hours rest of yr), 18km northwest of Lillehammer. It has been lovingly restored, although you'll need your own vehicle to get here. For details on an entry ticket combined with other sights in Lillehammer, see p124.

Hamar

POP 28,344

This medium-sized town would never win a beauty contest, but it does possess a surprising number of attractions that are worth a detour on your way between Oslo and the north. The showpiece Viking Ship Sports Arena dates from the 1994 Winter Olympics in Lillehammer when Hamar hosted a number of events, but there are also some good museums.

☉ Sights

Viking Ship Sports Arena

OLYMPIC SPORTS ARENA

(Vikingskipet; ☎62 51 75 00; www.hoa.no; Åkersvikaveien 1; admission Nkr30; ☺8am-6pm Mon-Fri, 10am-4pm Sat & Sun late Jun–mid-Aug, shorter hr rest of yr) Hamar's stand-out landmark is this sports arena, a graceful structure with the lines of an upturned Viking ship. The building, which hosted the speed skating during the Winter Olympics, holds 20,000 spectators, encompasses 9600 sq metres of ice and is 94.6m long. Both in scale and aesthetics, it's an impressive place. From late July to mid-August, it's open to the public for ice-skating (Nkr70 per day).

Norwegian Railway Museum RAILWAY MUSEUM

(Norsk Jernbanemuseum; ☎62 51 31 60; www. norsk-jernbanemuseum.no, in Norwegian; Strandveien 163; adult/child Nkr75/40; ☺10am-5pm Jul–mid-Aug, shorter hr rest of yr) Established in 1896 to honour Norway's railway history, this open-air railway museum lies on the

WORLD'S OLDEST PADDLE STEAMER

Skibladner (📞61 14 40 80; www.skibladner.no; Hamar-Lillehammer return Nkr320), the world's oldest paddle steamer, is a wonderfully relaxing way to explore lake Mjøsa. First built in Sweden in 1856, the boat was refitted and lengthened to 165ft (50m) in 1888. From late June until mid-August, the *Skibladner* plies the lake between Hamar, Gjøvik and Lillehammer. Most travellers opt for the route between Hamar and Lillehammer (3½ hours) on Tuesday, Thursday and Saturday, which can be done as a return day trip (from Hamar only, Nkr320). There's also an on-board restaurant.

Mjøsa shore around 3km west of the centre. In addition to lovely historic stations, engine sheds, rail coaches and steam locomotives, you'll learn about the extraordinary engineering feats required to carve the railways through Norway's rugged terrain.

Hedmark Museum & Glass Cathedral
REGIONAL MUSEUM & CATHEDRAL RUINS

(Hedmarkmuseet; 📞62 54 27 00; www.domkirkeodden.no; Strandveien 100; adult/child/senior Nkr80/30/65; ⏱10am-5pm daily mid-Jun–mid-Aug, 10am-4pm Tue-Sun mid-May–mid-Jun & mid-Aug–mid-Sep) West of town (1.5km), the extensive open-air museum includes 18th- and 19th-century buildings, a local folk-history exhibit featuring the creepy Devil's Finger (a finger cast in pewter of unknown origin, but which is said to have caused a number of deaths when it was removed from the church), the ruins of the castle, and the extraordinary showcase 'glass cathedral' (Domkirkeodden). The cathedral and castle dominated Hamar until 1567, when they were sacked by the Swedes. Take bus 6 from the town library (Nkr35, hourly).

Norwegian Emigrant Museum
MUSEUM OF NORWEGIAN EMIGRATION

(Norsk Utvandrermuseum; 📞62 57 48 50; www.emigrantmuseum.no; Åkershagan; adult/child €50/20; ⏱9am-3.30pm Tue-Fri, 10am-4pm Sat, noon-4pm Sun Jun-Aug, 9am-3.30pm Tue-Fri Sep-May) This fine open-air museum has exhibits and archives from Norwegian emigrants to America, Australia and elsewhere. There's also a research library with around 7000 letters, 5000 photos and other resources for those trying to trace family histories. The museum is around 3km east of town; cross the bridge towards Stange and follow the signs.

🎉 Festivals & Events

Hamar Beer Festival (Hamar Ølfestival; early Jun) Beer and music.

Middle Ages Festival (www.middelalderfestival.no; 2nd weekend in Jun) Locals in period costume and Gregorian chants in the glass cathedral.

Hamar Music Festival (www.musicfest.no, in Norwegian; late Jun) Local and international acts – in 2010 Joe Cocker performed.

🛏 Sleeping & Eating

Vikingskipet Motell og Vandrerhjem
HOTEL & HOSTEL €

(📞62 52 60 60; www.815mjosa.no/hamar; Åkersvikavegen 24; dm without/with breakfast Nkr369/410; s/d Nkr695/840, 2-/3-bed apt Nkr1290/1470; 📶P) Opposite the Viking Ship Sports Arena, this is an excellent choice with a range of accommodation choices. The youth hostel wing has tidy dorms, while the simple double rooms have a cabin-style feel. There are also terrific self-contained apartments. Prices drop by 10% with a Fjord Pass.

Seiersted Pensjonat
GUESTHOUSE €€

(📞62 52 12 44; www.hamarbooking.no; Holsetgata 64; s/d with shared bathroom Nkr510/720, with private bathroom Nkr610/820; 📶P) Central Seiersted Pensjonat is a well-priced antidote to the sameness of so many Norwegian hotels. It offers a friendly family atmosphere and nicely decorated rooms. Dinner is available on request, and the operators have a B&B, **Bellevue Bed & Breakfast** (📞62 52 12 44; www.hamarbooking.no; Aluveien 65; s/d Nkr650/970; 📶), a little further up the hill.

📷 Scandic Hamar
HOTEL €€

(📞21 61 40 00; www.scandic-hotels.com; Vangsveien 121; s/d from Nkr820/1020; 📶P) With sleek-lined Scandinavian design, a gymnasium and a convenient location, Scandic Hamar could just be Hamar's best address. Rack rates are expensive but you'll find that there are always good deals happening online.

Stallgården
INTERNATIONAL CAFE €€

(cnr Bekkegata & Torggata; lunch mains Nkr89-139, dinner mains from Nkr215; ⏱11am-11pm Mon-Sat, 1-11pm Sun) Restaurants and cafes line the main pedestrianised thoroughfare, Torggata, but our pick is this cafe, which is particularly popular in summer for its outdoor tables. Dishes range from burgers to Greek salads. The upstairs restaurant here is more formal.

ℹ️ Information

Hamar Regional Tourist Office (✆62 51 75 03; www.hamarregionen.no; ☺9am-6pm Mon-Fri, 10am-4pm Sat & Sun mid-Jun–mid-Aug, 8am-4pm Mon-Fri rest of yr) At the Viking Ship Sports Arena.

ℹ️ Getting There & Away

BUS Lavprisekspressen buses go to Oslo (from Nkr149) and Trondheim (from Nkr299) once or twice a day.

TRAIN To Oslo (Nkr238, 1¼ hours, once or twice hourly), Røros (Nkr494, 3¼ hours, up to four daily), and Trondheim (Nkr722, five hours, four or five daily) via Lillehammer (Nkr120, one hour).

Elverum

POP 19,834

With a name like Elverum, you might expect a whiff of magic, but in reality this is a fairly nondescript town set amid the vast and lush green timberlands of southern Hedmark county. Its excellent forestry museum is the main reason to stop here en route elsewhere.

◉ Sights

Norsk Skog Museum FORESTRY MUSEUM
(Norwegian Forestry Museum; ✆62 40 90 00; www.skogmus.no, in Norwegian; Rv20; adult/child/student & senior Nkr90/40/60, incl Glomdal Museum Nkr120/70/90; ☺10am-5pm mid-Jun–mid-Aug, 10am-4pm rest of yr) This museum, 1km south of central Elverum, covers the multifarious uses and enjoyments of Norwegian forests. It includes a nature information centre, a children's workshop, geological and meteorological exhibits, wood carvings, an aquarium, nature dioramas with all manner of stuffed native wildlife (including a mammoth) and a 20,000-volume reference library.

Glomdal Museum REGIONAL MUSEUM
(✆62 41 91 00; www.glomdal.museum.no; adult/child/student & senior Nkr90/40/60, incl Forestry Museum Nkr120/70/90; ☺10am-5pm mid-Jun–mid-Aug, 10am-4pm rest of yr) West 2km of the town centre is this collection of 90 historic buildings from the Glomma valley.

🛏️ Sleeping & Eating

Elverum Camping CAMPGROUND €
(✆62 41 67 16; www.elverumcamping.no; Halvdans Gransvei 6; tent sites Nkr200, 2-bed cabin with/without bathroom Nkr900/500) This decent place is in a green setting just south of the Norwegian Forestry Museum.

Solvårs Bed'n Breakfast B&B €
(✆62 41 49 48; www.elverumbb.com; Barbara Ringsvei 14; s/d from Nkr450/550; 🕸) A simple but friendly guesthouse, Solvårs Bed'n Breakfast lies 2km south of the Forestry Museum; take the small turn-off marked 'Bed'n Breakfast' 1km after leaving the museum. It's a good choice for a more personal touch than most hotels offer, and there are lovely meals available upon request.

Forstmann NORWEGIAN €€
(✆62 41 69 10; mains from Nkr125; ☺lunch & dinner mid-Jun–mid-Aug) The fish-and-game restaurant at the Forestry Museum serves traditional Norwegian cooking.

ℹ️ Information

Tourist office (✆62 40 90 42; www.visit elverum.com, in Norwegian; ☺10am-5pm mid-Jun–mid-Aug, 10am-4pm rest of yr) At the Norwegian Forestry Museum.

ℹ️ Getting There & Away

The Nor-Way Bussekspress 'Trysil Ekspressen' runs between Oslo (Nkr235, 2½ hours) and Trysil (Nkr122, 1¼ hours) via Elverum seven times daily.

Trysil

POP 6763

Surrounded by forested hillsides close to the Swedish border, and overlooked by Norway's largest collection of ski slopes, little Trysil is well worth a detour with year-round activities taking you off into the wilderness.

🏃 Activities

Although Trysil lives and breathes winter **skiing**, for the rest of the year you can do just about anything to keep active, from canoeing to canyoning or the more sedate pastime of fishing. Perhaps the most rewarding activity in summer is **cycling**. There are at least six cycle routes, the shortest 6km, the longest 38km; route maps are available from the tourist office, while bike hire is available from **Trysil Hyttegrend** (1/3/6 days Nkr240/490/690). For horse-riding, contact

Trysil-stallen (☑97 41 53 94; www.trysil-stallen. no; half-/full day Nkr450/750).

🛏 Sleeping & Eating

Trysil Hyttegrend CABINS €€
(☑90 13 27 61; www.trysilhytte.com; Ørånset; 4-bed huts per day/week from Nkr800/4500; P🛜) By the water's edge, 2.5km south of town, this excellent site has many drawcards, with wireless internet, a wood-fired sauna and plenty of activities on offer.

Radisson Blu Resort HOTEL €€€
(☑62 44 90 00; www.trysil.radissonblu.com; Hotellveien 1; d from Nkr990; P🛜🏊) One of the few Trysil hotels to open year-round, this is Trysil's most luxurious accommodation. The resort also has Trysil's best restaurant, serving mostly buffet meals (from Nkr250) during the winter season and mostly à la carte choices the rest of the year.

❶ Information

Trysil Tourist Office (☑62 45 10 00; www. trysil.com; Storveien 3; ⊙9am-6pm Mon-Fri, 10am-2pm Sat & Sun mid-Jun–mid-Aug, shorter hr rest of yr)

❶ Getting There & Away

The Nor-Way Bussekspress 'Trysil Ekspressen' connects Trysil with Oslo (Nkr225, four hours) via Elverum (Nkr107, 1¼ hours) seven times daily.

NORTHERN CENTRAL NORWAY

Røros

POP 5576

Røros, a charming Unesco World Heritage–listed site set in a small hollow of stunted forests and bleak fells, is one of Norway's most beautiful villages. The Norwegian writer Johan Falkberget described Røros as 'a place of whispering history' and this historic copper-mining town (once called Bergstad, or mountain city) has wonderfully preserved and colourful wooden houses that climb the hillside, as well as fascinating relics of the town's mining past. Røros has become something of a retreat for artists, who lend even more character to this enchanted place.

Røros is one of the coldest places in Norway – in 2010, temperatures dropped below -44°C.

History

According to local legend, in 1644 Olsen Åsen shot a reindeer at Storvola (Storwartz), 13km from Røros. The enraged creature pawed at the ground, revealing a glint of copper ore. In the same year Røros Kobberverk was established, followed two years later by a royal charter that granted it exclusive rights to all minerals, forest products and waterways (and local labour) within 40km of the original discovery.

The mining company located its headquarters at Røros due to the abundant wood (fuel) and the rapids along the river Hyttelva, which provided hydroelectric power. The use of fire in breaking up the rock in the mines was a perilous business and cost Røros dearly. Røros first burnt to the ground during the Gyldenløve conflict with the Swedes between 1678 and 1679, and the smelter was damaged by fire again in 1953. In 1977, after 333 years of operation, the company went bankrupt.

⊙ Sights

TOP
CHOICE **Historic District**
FORMER MINING BUILDINGS & HOUSES

Røros' historic district, characterised by the striking log architecture of its 80 protected buildings, takes in the entire central area. The two main streets, **Bergmannsgata** (it tapers from southwest to northeast to create an optical illusion and make the town appear larger than it is) and **Kjerkgata**, are lined with historical homes and buildings, all under preservation orders. The entire area is like an architectural museum of old Norway; for one of the loveliest turf-roofed homes you'll see, head up to the top of Kjerkgata to the house signposted as **Harald Sohlbergs Plass 59**.

If Røros looks familiar, that's because several films have been made here, including Røros author Johan Falkberget's classic *An-Magrit,* starring Jane Fonda. Flanderborg gate starred in some of Astrid Lindgren's *Pippi Longstocking* classics and Røros even stood in for Siberia in *A Day in the Life of Ivan Denisovich.*

Røros Kirke CHURCH
(Kjerkgata) Closed for major renovations when we were there, Røros' Lutheran church is one of Norway's most distinctive, not to mention one of the largest, with a seating capacity of 1640. The first church on the site was constructed in 1650, but it had fallen into disrepair by the mid-18th century and

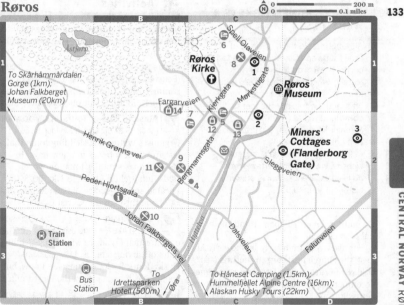

Røros

⊚ Top Sights
Miners' Cottages (Flanderborg Gate)	D2
Røros Kirke	C1
Røros Museum	C1

⊚ Sights
1	Harald Sohlsbergs Plass	C1
2	Malmplassen (Ore Place)	C2
3	Slegghaugen	D2
	Smelthytta	(see 2)

Activities, Courses & Tours
4	Røros Sport	C2

⊜ Sleeping
5	Frøyas Hus	C2
6	Erzscheidergården	C1
7	Vertshuset Røros	C2

⊗ Eating
	Frøyas Hus	(see 5)
8	Galleri Thomasgården	C1
9	Kaffestugu Cafeteria	B2
10	Lauritzen & Bruse	B3
11	Tryggstads Bakeri	B2
	Vertshuset Røros	(see 7)

⊜ Shopping
	Galleri Thomasgården	(see 8)
12	Hartzgården Sølvsmie	C2
13	Per Sverre Dahl Keramikk	C2
14	Potteriet Røros	B1

from 1780 a new baroque-style church (the one you see today) was built just behind the original at a cost of 23,000 *riksdaler* (one *riksdaler* is the equivalent of Nkr4, and at the time miners earned about 50 *riksdaler* per year).

The posh King's Gallery at the back, identified by both royal and mining company logos, has never hosted a king; visiting royals have always opted to sit among the people. Unusually, the pulpit sits over the altarpiece, while the organ (1742) is the oldest Norwegian-built organ still functioning.

Until 1865 the building was owned by the mining company and this is reflected in the church art. By the altar you'll see the grizzled Hans Olsen Åsen among other company dignitaries. There are also paintings of the author Johan Falkberget and the original 1650 church.

For five weeks from early July to early August, the church hosts **organ recitals** (adult/child Nkr100/free; ☉6pm Mon-Sat), sometimes accompanied by orchestral musicians from across Europe.

Smelthytta   MINING MUSEUM
(Malmplassen; adult/child/senior & student Nkr80/free/60; ☉10am-6pm mid-Jun–mid-Aug, shorter hr rest of yr) Housed in old smelting works, which were central to Røros' *raison d'être* until 1953, this museum is a town highlight. The building was reconstructed in 1988 according to the original 17th-century plan. Upstairs you'll find geological and conservation displays, while downstairs are a large balance used for weighing ore, some well-illustrated early mining statistics, and brilliant working models of the mines and the water- and horse-powered smelting processes. Displays of copper smelting are held at 3pm from Tuesday to Friday from early July to early August. In summer your entry ticket entitles you to a free guided tour at 11am, 12.30pm, 2pm (in English) or 3.30pm.

Outside the museum entrance spreads the large open area known as the **Malmplassen** (Ore Place), where loads of ore were dumped and weighed on the large wooden scale. Just across the stream from the museum are the protected **slegghaugan** (slag heaps), from which there are lovely views over town. Off the southwestern corner of the slag heaps, the historic smelting district with its tiny turf-roofed **miners' cottages**, particularly along Sleggveien, is one of Røros' prettiest corners.

🏃 Activities

In addition to the following activities, **canoeing**, **horse riding**, **sleigh rides** and **ice fishing** are also possible. The tourist office has a full list of operators.

Røros Sport   CYCLING
(Bergmannsgata 13; ☉9am-6pm Mon-Sat) In summer Røros Sport rents mountain bikes for Nkr175/300/385 for one/two/three days.

Alaskan Husky Tours   HUSKY EXCURSIONS
(☎62 49 87 66; www.huskytour.no; Os) Organises winter dog-sledding tours that last from a few hours to a few days. It also operates summer tours on wheel-sleds (adult/child under 16 Nkr700/350). Located some distance outside Røros; you can book through the tourist office.

Røros Husky   HUSKY EXCURSIONS
(☎72 41 41 94; www.roroshusky.no) Another operator that organises winter dog-sledding tours of varying lengths. Like Alaskan Husky Tours, it's located outside Røros, but bookings can be made via the tourist office.

Røros Rein   SAMI EXCURSIONS
(☎72 41 10 06; www.rorosrein.no; Hagaveien 17) Organises a program that includes sleigh rides, getting up close and personal with reindeer, and a traditional Sami meal in a Sami hut.

Hummelfjellet Alpine Centre   SKIING
(www.hummelfjell.no, in Norwegian) Has two lifts and six slopes. Located 16km south of Røros.

Ålen Ski Centre   SKIING
(☎41 90 65 99; www.aalenskisenter.no, in Norwegian) Boasts two lifts and four slopes. Located 34km northwest of town.

👉 Tours

Guided walking tours   WALKING TOURS
(adult/child Nkr60/free; ☉tours 10am, 11.30am, 1pm & 2.30pm Mon-Sat, 11am & 1pm Sun mid-Jun–mid-Aug, shorter hr rest of yr) Run by the tourist office, the tours take you through the historic town centre; tours at 11.30am Saturday and 1pm Sunday from mid-June to mid-August are in English and/or German.

🎉 Festivals & Events

The biggest winter event is **Rørosmartnan** (Røros Market), which began in 1644 as a rendezvous for hunters who ventured into town to sell their products to miners and buy supplies. Thanks to a royal decree issued in 1853 stipulating that a grand market be held annually from the penultimate Tuesday of February to the following Saturday, it continues today. Nowadays it's celebrated with cultural programs, street markets and live entertainment.

Other annual events include the following:

Elden
ROCK OPERA

(www.elden-roros.no, in Norwegian) In late July and early August, Røros stages a nightly three-hour rock opera that recounts the invasion of Trøndelag by Sweden in 1718, covering the occupation of Røros and the subsequent death of thousands of soldiers on their frozen trek homewards to Sweden. It's enacted on the slag heaps in the upper part of town.

Femund Race
DOG-SLED RACE

(www.femundlopet.no) One of Europe's longest dog-sled races starts and ends in Røros in the first week of February.

Winter Chamber Music Festival
CLASSICAL MUSIC FESTIVAL

(www.vinterfestspill.no) Concerts held in Røros Kirke in the first week of March.

🛏 Sleeping

The tourist office keeps a list of summer cabins and guesthouses, some within walking distance of town.

TOP CHOICE Erzscheidergården
GUESTHOUSE €€

(☎72 41 11 94; www.erzscheidergaarden. no; Spell Olaveien 6; s/d from Nkr895/1190; P🐕) This appealing 24-room guesthouse is up the hill from the town centre and behind the church. The wood-panelled rooms are loaded with personality, the atmosphere is Norwegian-family-warmth and the breakfasts were described by one reader as 'the best homemade breakfast buffet in Norway'. We're inclined to agree.

Frøyas Hus
B&B €€

(☎92 88 35 30; www.froyashus.no, in Norwegian; Mørkstugata 4; r with shared bathroom Nkr400-900) It may have only two rooms, but this gorgeous place has an intimacy you won't find elsewhere. Rooms are small, but save for a lick of paint, they've scarcely changed in over 300 years – it's rustic in the best sense of the word. Throw in friendly service, a lovely courtyard cafe and public areas strewn with local antiques and curiosities, and it's all perfectly integrated into the Røros experience.

Vertshuset Røros
HISTORIC HOTEL €€

(☎72 41 93 50; www.vertshusetroros.no, in Norwegian; Kjerkgata 34; s/d from Nkr875/1050, 2-/4-bed apt Nkr1450/2250; P🐕📶) Located in a historic 17th-century building on the main pedestrian thoroughfare, the Vertshuset Røros is another wonderful choice. The all-wood rooms are generously sized and have numerous period touches, such as wooden beds with columns – arguably the most comfortable beds in town.

Håneset Camping
CAMPGROUND €

(☎72 41 06 00; fax 72 41 06 01; Osloveien; tent or caravan sites Nkr140 plus per person Nkr30, 2-/4-bed cabins Nkr320/420) Simple but well-kept cabins are available at this excellent site, with cooking and laundry facilities, a common room and TV; it's about 2km south of town.

Idrettsparken Hotell
HOTEL €€

(☎72 41 10 89; www.idrettsparken.no, in Norwegian; Øra 25; tent/caravan sites from Nkr105/140, cabins from Nkr450, hotel s/d from Nkr750/1050; P) The family-run Idrettsparken Hotell, 500m south of the train station, has a range of options for most budgets.

Røros Hotell
HOTEL €€

(☎72 40 80 00; www.roroshotell.no; An Magrit veien 10; s/d from Nkr950/1150) This 167-room colossus at the top end of town has well-appointed rooms with a touch more character than most larger hotels (it styles itself as a mountain hotel), at least in the public areas, but far less than the smaller Røros hotels.

🍴 Eating

Opening hours for the following places are much reduced in winter.

TOP CHOICE Vertshuset Røros
TRADITIONAL NORWEGIAN €€

(☎72 41 24 11; Kjerkgata 34; lunch mains Nkr75-145, dinner mains Nkr268-345) Lunch dishes here include fairly standard soup, sandwiches and burgers, but from 4pm onwards the food is exquisite – the tenderest fillets of reindeer or elk, as well as Arctic char and desserts such as 'blue cheese and pear marinated in cinnamon, walnuts in honey and balsamico'. In short it's one of the region's finest eating experiences.

Kaffestugu Cafeteria
SNACKS & TRADITIONAL NORWEGIAN €€

(☎72 41 10 33; www.kaffestuggu.no, in Norwegian; Bergmannsgata 18; lunch specials & snacks Nkr59-115, mains Nkr125-245; ⏰10am-9pm Mon-Sat, 11am-6.30pm Sun mid-Jun–mid-Aug, shorter hr rest of yr) This historic place offers a good range of coffee, pastries, snacks and light meals, as well as some more substantial main dishes.

Its lunchtime specials are a little heavy on the potatoes, but the food in general is enduringly popular. The atmosphere wavers between old Norwegian tea room and informal cafeteria.

Lauritzen & Bruse PIZZA & INTERNATIONAL €€
(☎72 40 60 20; Bergmannsgata 1; pizza buffet Nkr99, pasta from Nkr129; ☺2-10pm Mon-Thu, 2-11pm Fri, 11am-11pm Sat, noon-10pm Sun) With old photos of Røros and traditional decor, you might be forgiven for imagining this to be a bastion of traditional cooking. But this being modern Norway, it's mostly about pizza, and we recommend it especially for its pizza buffet from 2.30pm to 6.30pm from Monday to Friday. Its outdoor tables have views up this historic street.

There are also many small coffee shops (some of which are attached to crafts and souvenir shops) that serve snacks and some light meals:

Frøyas Hus CAFE €
(Mørkstugata 4; ☺10am-5pm)

Galleri Thomasgården CAFE €
(Kjerkgata 48; ☺11am-5pm Mon-Wed, Fri & Sat, 11am-11pm Thu, noon-5pm Sun)

Tryggstads Bakeri BAKERY & CAFE €
(Kjerkgata 12; ☺8.30am-7pm Mon-Fri, 9am-5pm Sat, 11.30am-4.30pm Sun) Great coffee and baked goodies.

🔒 Shopping

Røros' two main streets are lined with small craft shops.

Galleri Thomasgården STONEWARE & PORCELAIN
(www.thomasgaarden.no, in Norwegian; Kjerkgata 48; ☺11am-5pm Mon-Wed, Fri & Sat, 11am-11pm Thu, noon-5pm Sun) At the worthwhile Galleri Thomasgården, potter Torgeir Henriksen creates rustic stoneware and porcelain. You will also find the wonderful nature-inspired wood carvings of Henry Solli. The player piano is one of only two in Norway and dates back to 1929.

Hartzgården Sølvsmie JEWELLERY
(Kjerkgata; ☺10am-6pm Mon-Fri, 10am-4pm Sat, noon-5pm Sun summer, shorter hr rest of yr) At this silversmith's shop you'll find locally handcrafted silver jewellery with an emphasis on Viking themes, as well as a small historical-jewellery exhibit.

Per Sverre Dahl Keramikk CERAMICS
(www.persverredahl.no, in Norwegian; Mørkstugata 5; ☺10am-4pm Mon-Sat summer, shorter hr rest of yr) Per Sverre creates ceramic sculptures and

wall decorations, which range across themes as diverse as trolls and modern saxophone-bearing musicians.

Potteriet Røros CERAMICS
(www.potteriet-roros.no, in Norwegian; Fargarveien 4; ☺10am-4pm Mon-Fri, 11am-5pm Sat) Here you'll find pottery based on traditional designs from all over Trøndelag, although there are some creative modern interpretations. The pottery workshop next door is open to the public and staff are always happy to explain the history behind each design.

ℹ Information

Tourist office (☎72 41 00 00; www.roros. no; Peder Hiortsgata 2; ☺9am-6pm Mon-Sat, 10am-4pm Sun mid-Jun–mid-Aug, 9am-3pm Mon-Fri, 10am-1pm Sat rest of yr)

ℹ Getting There & Away

AIR Røros has two daily **DOT LT** (www.flydot. no) flights to/from Oslo except Saturday.

BUS There are up to four daily buses to Oslo (Nkr455, six hours).

TRAIN Røros lies on the eastern railway line between Oslo (from Nkr199, five hours, six daily) and Trondheim (from Nkr199, 2½ hours).

Around Røros

OLAVSGRUVA MINE

The **Olavsgruva mine** (www.rorosmuseet.no; Kojedalen; adult/child/senior & student Nkr80/free/60; ☺guided tours 10.30am, noon, 2pm, 3.30pm & 5pm mid-Jun–mid-Aug, shorter hr rest of yr) is 13km north of Røros. The moderately interesting exhibition is made worthwhile by **mine tours** passing through the historic Nyberget mine, which dates from the 1650s. The modern Olavsgruva mine beyond it was begun in 1936. The ground can get muddy and the temperature in the mine is 5°C; bring a jacket and good footwear. To get to the mine, use your own wheels or take a taxi (Nkr550 return). For information on cheaper combined tickets with Smelthytta, see p134.

JOHAN FALKBERGET MUSEUM

The works of Røros' favourite son, author Johan Falkberget (1879–1967), have been translated into 19 languages and cover 300 years of the region's mining history. His most famous work, *An-Magrit,* which was made into a film starring Jane Fonda, tells the story of a peasant girl who transported copper ore in the Røros mining district. The **mu-**

seum (www.falkberget.no, in Norwegian; Ratvolden; adult/child Nkr60/30; ⊙ guided tours 1pm Tue-Sun Jul-early Aug, by appointment May-Jun & early Aug-Oct) is at Ratvolden, beside the lake Rugelsjø 20km north of Røros. To get there, take a local train to Rugeldalen station, where a small walking track leads to the museum.

Femundsmarka National Park

The national park (573 sq km) that surrounds Femunden, Norway's second-largest lake, was formed in 1971 to protect the lake and the birch forests stretching eastwards to Sweden. Indeed, the landscapes are more Swedish in appearance than recognisably Norwegian. The park has long been a source of falcons for use in the European and Asian sport of falconry, and several places in the park are known as Falkfangerhøgda, or 'falcon hunters' height'. If you're lucky, you may also see wild reindeer grazing in the heights and, in summer, a herd of around 30 musk oxen roams the area along the Røa and Mugga Rivers (in winter they migrate to the Funäs-dalen area). It's thought that this group split off from an older herd in the Dovrefjell area and wandered all the way here (see p140).

🛏 Sleeping

The two main sleeping options are **Johnsgård Turistsenter** (☑62 45 99 25; www.johnsgard.no; Sømådalen; tent sites Nkr155, 4-bed cabin per person from Nkr215), 9km west of Buvika; and **Langen Gjestegård** (☑72 41 37 18; www.langen-gjestegaard.com, in Norwegian; Synnervika; s/d from Nkr300/500), a cosy turf-roofed farmhouse near the lake.

❶ Getting There & Away

The historic ferry **M/S Fæmund II** (☑72 41 37 14; www.femund.no) sails daily at 9am between mid-June and late August from Synnervika (also spelt Søndervika), on the northern shore of Lake Femunden, to Elgå (adult/child one-way Nkr200/100, eight hours return). From mid-June to late August, buses leave Røros train station for Synnervika 45 minutes before the boat's departure. Buses for Røros later meet the boat at Synnervika.

Oppdal

POP 6603

Oppdal is a quintessential feeder town for the Norwegian wilderness: there's nothing much to detain you in town, but the surrounding countryside is beautiful with loads of activities on offer.

🛏 Sleeping

If you are unable to find a bed, contact Oppdal Booking or the tourist office for assistance.

Quality Oppdal Hotel   HOTEL €€
(☑72 40 08 00; www.oppdalbooking.no; Olav Skasliens vei 8; s/d from Nkr1100/1200; P⊛) This comfortable hotel next to the train station and tourist office offers pleasant rooms that are overpriced, but easily the best in Oppdal. Unlike so many larger hotels, the service has a personal touch.

Oppdal Gjestetun   HOTEL & APARTMENTS €€
(☑72 40 08 00; www.oppdalbooking.no; Olav Skasliens vei 6; s/d from Nkr690/775, apt from Nkr995; P⊛) Almost next door, this fine place has modern rooms and four- to six-bed apartments. Unusually for Norway, prices don't include breakfast.

🍴 Eating

Møllen Restaurant & Pizzeria
PIZZA & PASTA €€
(Dovreveien 2; small/large pizza from Nkr90/180, mains Nkr110-240) In the town centre alongside the E6, this is a good choice if you feel like a sit-down meal, but with a reasonable price tag.

Perrongen Steak House   STEAK €€€
(☑72 40 08 00; Olav Skasliens vei 8; mains Nkr209-339; ⊙6-11pm Mon-Sat) This place, in the Quality Oppdal Hotel, has the best food and the most sophistication of any place in town.

❶ Information

Oppdal Booking (☑72 40 08 00; www.oppdal-booking.no; Olav Skasliens vei 12; ⊙8am-4pm Mon-Fri mid-Jun–mid-Aug, shorter hr rest of yr) An efficient one-stop shop for reserving activities and accommodation; booking fees apply.

Tourist office (☑72 40 04 70; www.oppdal.com; ⊙9am-4pm Mon-Fri, 10am-2pm Sat & Sun mid-Jun–mid-Aug, 9am-4pm Mon-Fri rest of yr) In the train station.

❶ Getting There & Away

BUS Daily Nor-Way Bussekspress route between Bergen (Nkr729, 12½ hours) and Trondheim (Nkr230, two hours). Cheaper Lavprisekspressen buses (Nkr49 to Nkr299) also pass through once or twice daily en route between Oslo and Trondheim.

TRAIN Oslo (Nkr399 to Nkr725, five hours, four daily) and Trondheim (Nkr182, 1½ hours, four daily)

White-water Rafting

The nearby, wild and white Driva promises excellent rafting runs from May to October. The outdoor-adventure company **Opplev Oppdal** (☎72 40 41 80; www.opplev-oppdal. no, in Norwegian; Olav Skasliens vei 12) organises trips, from the relatively tame Class I-II family trips to full-day Class III-IV trips that provide substantial thrills. Prices range from Nkr750 to Nkr850 per person per day; the company also organises family trips (Nkr1850 for seven people).

Musk Ox & Elk Safaris

To track down the prehistoric musk ox (see p140), take one of the four- to six-hour **musk ox safaris** (adult/child Nkr310/200; ⏱9am mid-Jun–mid-Aug) organised by **Opplev Oppdal** (☎72 40 08 00; www.oppdalbooking.no; Olav Skasliens vei 12).

Oppdal Booking also organises three-hour **elk safaris** (⏱9pm Wed & Fri mid-Jun–mid-Aug), which cost Nkr300 per person.

Advance bookings are required for both safaris.

Skiing & Snowboarding

The three-part Oppdal Skisenter climbs the slopes from Hovden, Stølen and Vangslia, all within easy reach of town. The smaller Ådalen ski area nearby has two lifts. Vangslia is generally the easiest, with a couple of beginners' runs, while Stølen offers intermediate skiing and Hovden has three challenging advanced runs. The season runs from late November to late April. Ski passes for adults/children start at Nkr350/280 for one day.

Other Activities

Oppdal Booking also arranges the following activities:

» **Boat Trips** (adult/child Nkr200/160; ⏱noon Jul–mid-Aug) Four- to five-hour boat trips on Lake Gjevilvatnet with wonderful views of the Trollheimen range.

» **Cable-Car Ride** (adult/child Nkr100/70; ⏱11am-5pm Jul–mid-Aug) Gondola rides up Skjørstadhovden (1125m) to Hovden Skisenter for fine views.

» **Guided Mountain Hikes** (adult/child Nkr260/130; ⏱10am Jun-Sep) Four- to six-hour treks; advance booking required.

» **Oppdal Bike Park** (lift ticket adult/child Nkr210/185, lift ticket & equipment rental Nkr875/670; ⏱11am-5pm Fri-Sun mid-Jun–mid-Aug) A range of mountain-bike trails at Vangslia Skisenter accessible by skilift.

Trollheimen

The small Trollheimen range, with a variety of trails through gentle mountains and lake-studded upland regions, is most readily accessed from Oppdal. You can drive or hike the 15km from Oppdal up the toll road (Nkr40 by car) to **Osen**, which is the main entrance to the wilderness region. The best map to use is Statens Kartverk's *Turkart Trollheimen* (1:75,000), which costs Nkr120 at the tourist office in Oppdal.

A straightforward hiking destination in Trollheimen is the hut and historic farm at **Vassendsetra**. From Osen (the outlet of the river Gjevilvatnet), 3km north of the main road to Sunndalsøra,

you can take the boat *Trollheimen II* all the way to Vassendsetra (Nkr175 return). From July to mid-August it leaves from Osen daily at noon and from Vassendsetra at 3.30pm.

Alternatively, it is possible to drive or hike 6km along the road from Osen to the 19th-century DNT hut, **Gjevilvasshytta** (☎93 24 51 46; dm for DNT members/nonmembers Nkr125/185, breakfast Nkr95/120, dinner Nkr235/285; ⏱mid-Jun–mid-Sep), one of Norway's most beautiful DNT lodges. From there, follow the lakeshore trail for another 12km until you come to **Vassendsetra** (dm for DNT members/nonmembers Nkr125/185, breakfast Nkr95/120, dinner Nkr235/285; ⏱year-round).

The popular three-day 'Trekanten' hut tour follows the impressive Gjevilvasshytta–Trollheimshytta–Jøldalshytta–Gjevilvasshytta route; contact Oppdal Booking (p137) for details.

Dombås

POP 1116

Dombås, a popular adventure and winter-sports centre, makes a convenient break for travellers between the highland national parks and the western fjords. That said, there's more choice of activities to the north in Oppdal (p138), while Sjoa (p143) is the region's best location for rafting. The Rauma Railway (see p139) from Dombås to Åndalsnes (p223) is one of Norway's most beautiful train rides.

🏃 Activities

The following activities in the surrounding national parks can be arranged through the tourist office from mid-June through to mid-August.

🌿 **Elk Safari** This evening (8pm) tour (Nkr200) departs from the tourist office from mid-June to mid-August; advance bookings not required.

🌿 **Musk Ox Safari** This four- to five-hour tour (Nkr300) departs daily at 8.30am from the tourist office. No advance booking is necessary.

From early autumn until Easter, downhill skiing is possible at **Bjorli Skisenter** (www.bjorliskisenter.no, in Norwegian), which has 11 runs, six lifts and a dedicated children's area. Closer to town, **Dombås Skisenter** (www.trolltun.no) is also offers skiing from October to May, although with artificial snow for much of the season; day lift tickets cost Nkr250.

The **Hjerkinn Fjellstue inn** (p141) also organises these and other activities, while **Dovre Aktiv** (☎61 21 77 77; www.dovreaktiv.no) is another useful resource.

🛏 Sleeping

Bjørkhol Camping CAMPGROUND € (☎61 24 13 31; www.bjorkhol.no; Bjørkhol; tent/caravan sites Nkr100/130, 2-/4-bed cabin with shared bathroom from Nkr250/375, 2-bed cabins with bathroom from Nkr550) One of Norway's best-value and probably friendliest campsites is 6km south of Dombås. The facilities are in excellent nick and a bus runs several times daily from Dombås.

Trolltun Gjestegård & Dombås Vandrerhjem HOSTEL & GUESTHOUSE €€ (☎61 24 09 60; www.trolltun.no; hostel dm/d/f Nkr300/850/1050, hotel s/d Nkr850/1090; 🅿@📶) This excellent place is 1.5km north-east of town, up the hill from the E6. The setting is lovely, the rooms are tidy and the meals reasonably priced. You're ideally located for winter skiing and summer hiking with Dovrefjell-Sunndalsfjella National Park on your doorstep.

Dovrefjell Hotell HOTEL €€ (☎61 24 10 05; dovrefjellhotell.no, in Norwegian; s/d with Fjord Pass Nkr720/1020; 🅿📶❄) This place in the countryside 2km northwest of the centre off the E136 is in need of an overhaul. It's fine for a night, but Nkr100 per 24 hours for wireless access is a bit rich. In summer it does a good evening buffet (Nkr350).

🍴 Eating

Apart from the evening buffet for guests at the Dovrefjell Hotell, the main commercial complex in the centre of Dombås includes the following:

Frich's Cafeteria CAFETERIA € (Sentralplassen; snacks from Nkr58; ⊙breakfast, lunch & dinner) A few sandwiches but mostly pastries.

Senter-Grillen INTERNATIONAL €€ (Sentralplassen; mains Nkr75-175; ⊙breakfast, lunch & dinner) Elk burgers, pizza, and fish and chips.

ℹ Information

Tourist Office & Dovrefjell National Park Centre (Dovrefjell Nasjonalparksenter; ☎61 24 14 44; www.rondane-dovrefjell.no; Sentralplassen; ⊙9am-8pm Mon-Sat, 9am-4pm Sun mid-Jun–mid-Aug, shorter hr rest of yr) Small displays on nearby national parks and plenty of information on activities.

ℹ Getting There & Away

BUS Nor-Way Bussekspress buses between Bergen (Nkr669, 11¼ hours) and Trondheim (Nkr340, 3¼ hours) call in daily in both directions. Cheaper Lavprisekspressen buses (from Nkr49) also pass through en route between Oslo and Trondheim.

TRAIN Dombås lies on the railway line between Oslo (Nk199 to Nkr616, 4¼ hours, four daily) and Trondheim (Nkr199 to Nkr385, 2½ hours). It is also the starting point for the spectacular **Rauma Railway** (Raumabanen; www.nsb.no/raumarailway), which runs from

MUSK OX

The musk ox *(Ovibos moschatus)* is one of nature's great survivors; it has changed little in two million years. Although a member of the family Bovidae, the musk ox bears little resemblance to any other animal and its only known relative is the takin of northern Tibet.

Musk ox weigh between 225kg and 445kg, and have incredibly high shoulders and an enormous low-slung head with two broad, flat horns that cross the forehead, curving outwards and downwards before twisting upwards and forwards. Its thick and shaggy coat, with a matted fleece of soft hair underneath, covers the whole body. Only the bottom part of the legs protrude, giving the animal the appearance of a medieval horse dressed for a joust. During the rutting season, when the males gather their harems, they repeatedly charge each other, butting their heads together with a crash heard for miles around. This heated battle continues until one animal admits defeat and lumbers off. In winter, they stand perfectly still for hours to conserve energy, a position some scientists have described as 'standing hibernation'.

Traditionally, the musk ox's main predator has been the wolf; its primary defence is to form a circle with the males on the outside and females and calves inside, trusting in the force of its collective horns to rip open attackers. This defence has proven useless against human hunters, especially the Greenlandic Inuit, and numbers have been seriously depleted.

The musk ox died out in Norway almost 2000 years ago, but in 1931 ten animals were reintroduced to Dovrefjell-Sunndalsfjella from Greenland. Musk oxen all but vanished during WWII, but 23 were transplanted from Greenland between 1947 and 1953. The herd has now grown to around 80 animals and some have shifted eastwards into Femundsmarka National Park to form a new herd. Wild herds can also be found in parts of Greenland, Canada and Alaska.

In *Arctic Dreams,* Barry Lopez's account of the Arctic North, the author recalls his first encounter with a musk ox: 'In that moment I was struck by qualities of the animal that have stayed with me the longest: the movement was Oriental, and the pose one of meditation. The animal seemed to quiver with attention before he lowered his massive head and moved on, with the most deliberate step I have ever seen a large animal take.'

Your best chance of seeing the musk ox is to take a musk ox safari, either from Oppdal (see p138) or Dombås (p139). You may also see them while hiking through the Røa and Mugga Rivers section of Femundsmarka National Park (p137) in summer.

Musk oxen aren't inherently aggressive towards humans, but an animal that feels threatened can charge at speeds of up to 60km/h and woe betide anything that gets in its way.

Romsdalen to Åndalsnes (adult one-way/return Nkr216/296, child Nkr108/148, 1½ hours, two or three daily).

Dovrefjell-Sunndalsfjella National Park

This national park includes the dramatic highlands around the Snøhetta (2286m) and provides a suitably bleak habitat for Arctic foxes, reindeer, wolverines and musk oxen. The Knutshøene massif (1690m) section of the park, east of the E6, protects Europe's most diverse intact alpine ecosystem.

◉ Sights & Activities

Snøhetta can be ascended by hikers from Snøheim (allow six hours).

The **Fokstumyra marshes** are home to an astonishing array of bird life. Approximately 87 species nest in the area and 162 species in total have been observed. Among the species found here are the red-breasted merganser, long-tailed duck, black-throated diver, whimbrel, wood sandpiper and short-eared owl. For a more extensive list, pick up the brochure *Fokstumyra Nature Reserve* from the Dombås tourist office.

Many of these species can be viewed from the 7km-long marked trail near the Dombås end of the reserve; note that from May to July, visitors are restricted to this trail to prevent the disturbance of nesting birds.

Hikers will fare best with the Statens Kartverk map *Dovrefjell* (1:100,000). However, it doesn't include the Knutshøene section; for that, you need Statens Kartverk's *Einunna 1519-I* and *Folldal 1519-II* topographic sheets.

🛏 Sleeping & Eating

The original DNT **Snøheim** hut was, thankfully, judged to be too near the army's Hjerkinn firing range and was replaced by the new self-service **Reinheim** hut, 5km north and at 1341m, in Stroplsjødalen. DNT also maintains several other self-service huts in the adjacent Skrymtheimen region; keys are available from Dombås tourist office.

TOP CHOICE **Kongsvold Fjeldstue**
MOUNTAIN LODGE €€
(☎72 40 43 40; www.kongsvold.no, in Norwegian; Kongsvold; s/d with shared bathroom Nkr675/995, with private bathroom from Nkr795/1185) Park information, maps, meals and accommodation are available at this charming and historic place, 13km north of Hjerkinn on the E6. The intriguing early-18th-century timber buildings huddle deep in Drivdalen, 500m from tiny Kongsvold station (trains stop only on request). Every room is different.

Hjerkinn Fjellstue
MOUNTAIN LODGE €€
(☎61 21 51 00; www.hjerkinn.no, in Norwegian; Hjerkinn; s/d from Nkr890/1170, annexe r Nkr550) This cosy inn is about 1.5km northeast of Hjerkinn on Rv29. The rooms in the annexe are simple but fine, and cheaper than the main hotel building, although less so

once you factor in bed linen (Nkr140), towels (Nkr30) and breakfast (Nkr90). You will also find a restaurant, a campsite and horse-riding expeditions (half-/full day Nkr600/800). Camping is available.

ℹ Information

For more information, including on tours into the park, see the national park centre (p139) in Dombås.

ℹ Getting There & Away

There's no public transport into the park.
TRAIN Dombås to Hjerkinn (Nkr86, 25 minutes).

Otta

POP 1659

Set deep in Gudbrandsdalen, Otta occupies a strategic position at the confluence of the Otta and Lågen Rivers. Otta's main attraction is as the gateway to Rondane National Park.

🛏 Sleeping & Eating

Otta Camping
CAMPGROUND €
(☎61 23 03 09; www.ottacamping.no, in Norwegian; Ottadalen; tent/caravan sites for 2 people Nkr90/130 plus electricity Nkr30, 4-bed cabins Nkr350-450) The riverside Otta Camping is convenient and popular; cross the Otta

---

GURI SAVES THE DAY

During the Kalmar War between Sweden and Denmark, when Norway was united with Denmark, 550 Scottish mercenaries arrived in Norway in August 1612 to aid the Swedes. Word spread through Gudbrandsdalen and local peasants armed themselves with axes, scythes and other farming implements.

As the Scots reached a narrow section of path between the river and a steep hillside at Høgkringom, 3km south of Otta, the heroic Pillarguri (Guri) dashed up the hill to announce their arrival by sounding her shepherd's birch-bark horn. Older farmers, sent across the river as a decoy, began to fire. The Scots fired back across the river, then responded to Guri's music by waving their hats and playing their bagpipes, unaware of the trap.

As Guri sounded her horn again, more rocks were tumbled across the trail behind the column, blocking any retreat. The farmers attacked with rocks and their crude weapons, savagely defeating the trapped contingent and making the river flow red with blood.

Only six farmers were killed in the battle. The victors intended to take the 134 surviving Scots as prisoners to Akershus Fortress in Oslo. However, during the victory celebrations at Kvam, the farmers, who had to get on with their harvest and couldn't be bothered with a tiresome march, executed the prisoners one by one.

The exploits of the peasant 'army' are still remembered in Otta, where the local *bunad* (national costume) is a distinctly un-Norwegian tartan and a statue of Pillarguri is near the train station. There's also a war memorial at Kringom commemorating the victory, across the river from which rises the hill Pillarguri.

bridge from the centre, turn right and continue about 1km upstream.

Grand Gjestegård HOTEL & RESTAURANT €€

(61 23 12 00; www.grandgjestegard.com, in Norwegian; Ola Dahlsgate; s/d Nkr590/790; P) The busy hub of the little that happens in Otta, the Grand Gjestegård wins plaudits for its friendly welcome and pleasant rooms; half have been recently renovated, with the rest to follow soon. The meals (mains Nkr115 to Nkr145) here are simple, fairly standard roadside Norwegian fare, but they're filling and served with a smile.

Pillarguri Kafé CAFE-RESTAURANT €€

(Storgata 7; snacks & light meals Nkr70-145, mains Nkr115-260) Another good choice of eatery, the Pillarguri promises a varied menu, with sandwiches, pasta, salads and a handful of hearty Norwegian dishes. The outdoor tables are the place to be on a summer's afternoon.

❶ Information

Rondane National Park Centre (otta@nasjonalparker.org; Johan Nygårdgata 17a; noon-7pm Mon & Wed, 10am-4pm Tue, Thu & Fri, 10am-2pm Sat) Although focused on Rondane, there are displays on other national parks, as well as an extensive library.

Tourist office (61 23 66 78; www.visitrondane.com; Otta Skysstasjon; 8am-4pm Mon-Fri mid-Jun–mid-Aug, shorter hr rest of yr)

❶ Getting There & Away

BUS Local buses to/from Lom (Nkr120, 1½hr, six daily). Nor-Way Bussekspress has buses to/from Lillehammer (Nkr220, two hours, up to five daily) and Oslo (Nkr460, five hours). Cheaper Lavprisekspressen buses (from Nkr149) also pass through once or twice daily.

TRAIN Oslo (Nkr536, 3¾ hours), Trondheim (Nkr464, three hours, four daily) and Bergen (Nkr1011, 12 hours, four daily)

Rondane National Park

Henrik Ibsen described the landscapes that now make up the 963-sq-km **Rondane National Park** (www.rondane-dovrefjell.no) as 'palace piled upon palace'. It was created in 1962 as Norway's first national park to protect the fabulous Rondane massif, regarded by many as the finest alpine hiking country in Norway. Ancient reindeer-trapping sites and burial mounds suggest that the area has been inhabited for thousands of years. Much of the park's glaciated and lichen-coated landscape lies above 1400m and 10 rough and stony peaks rise to over 2000m,

Rodane National Park

including the highest, Rondslottet (2178m), and Storronden (2138m). Rondane's range of wildlife includes 28 mammal species and 124 bird species, and the park is now one of the last refuges of the wild reindeer.

If you're driving, the 87km-long Rv27 between Folldal and the E6 5km north of Ringebu is a stunningly beautiful route that runs along the Rondane range. This is a designated **National Tourist Route** (www.turistveg.no).

🏃 Activities

The hiking season runs only in July and August. The most accessible route into the park is from the Spranghaugen car park, about 13km uphill along a good road from Otta and via the toll road (Nkr10). From there, it's a straightforward 6km (1½ hour) hike to **Rondvassbu**, where there's a popular, staffed DNT hut. From Rondvassbu, it's a five-hour return climb to the summit of **Storronden**. Alternatively, head for the spectacular view from the more difficult summit of **Vinjeronden** (2044m), then tackle the narrow ridge leading to the neighbouring peak, **Rondslottet** (about six hours return from Rondvassbu).

The best maps to use are Statens Kartverk's *Rondane* (1:100,000; Nkr99) and *Rondane Sør* (1:50,000).

🛏 Sleeping & Eating

Camping is permitted anywhere in the national park except at Rondvassbu, where you're restricted to the designated area. There are DNT huts throughout the park.

Mysusæter Fjellstue   MOUNTAIN HUTS €
(☑61 23 39 25; www.mysuseterrondane.no; Mysusæter; dm Nkr250, d with/without bathroom Nkr650/585) A basic roof over your head. Breakfast and basic meals are available.

Rondane Spa Høyfjellshotell
                    MOUNTAIN LODGE €€
(☑61 20 90 90; www.rondane.no; Mysusæter; per person with full board from Nkr950) A comfortable upmarket option with good spa facilities, including pedicures for worn-out hikers' feet. The restaurant serves hearty Norwegian and international fare.

❶ Getting There & Around

In summer, buses run twice daily between Otta and Mysusæter (Nkr35, 45 minutes), from where it's a further 4km to the car park.

From Rondvassbu, the ferry *Rondegubben* crosses the lake Rondvatnet to Nordvika (Nkr75,

30 minutes) three times daily from early July to late August.

Other National Parks

As if the Rondane, Dovrefjell-Sunndalsfjella and Jotunheimen National Parks weren't enough, there are three further national parks in the same area.

Breheimen National Park One of Norway's newest national parks, it opened in 2009 and covers 1691 sq km. It's wedged between the Jotunheimen and Jostedalsbreen National Parks and has good hiking. For more information, visit the Lom tourist office (p146).

Dovre National Park (www.rondane -dovrefjell.no) Immediately north of Rondane National park, this 289-sq-km park was established in 2003 and is famous for having almost every Norwegian flora type within its borders. The park's highest point is Fokstuhøe (1716m). For more information, visit the Dombås tourist office (p139).

Reinheimen National Park Founded in 2006, this 1969-sq-km park stretches from Lom in the southeast to Åndalsnes in the northwest and is home to wild reindeer. For more information, visit the Lom tourist office (p146).

Sjoa

The small settlement of Sjoa, 10km south of Otta, would have little to detain you were it not for the fact that it's arguably the whitewater rafting capital of Norway.

🏃 Activities

The **white-water rafting** season runs from the middle of May until early October. Excursions range from sedate Class I runs (ideal for families) up to thrilling Class Vs. A note of warning: white-water rafting can be dangerous, with four fatalities in 2010 and another three years earlier.

Prices start from Nkr590 for a 3½-hour family trip; there are also five-hour trips (from Nkr990) through to seven-hour day trips (from Nkr1090); longer excursions are available on request.

In addition to rafting, most of the following operators also organise riverboarding (from Nkr990), low-level rock climbing (from Nkr490), canyoning (from Nkr820), caving (from Nkr690) and hiking.

Go Rafting
RAFTING

(☑61 23 50 00; www.gorafting.no, in Norwegian) About 8km west of Sjoa along Rv257.

Heidal Rafting
RAFTING

(☑61 23 60 37; www.heidalrafting.no; Sjoa) Just 1km west of E6 along Rv257.

Sjoa Rafting
RAFTING

(☑90 07 10 00; www.sjoarafting.com; Nedre Heidal) Some 7.5km upstream from Sjoa along Rv257.

Sjoa Rafting Senter NWR
RAFTING

(☑47 66 06 80; www.sjoaraftingsenter.no; Varphaugen Gård) About 3km upstream from Sjoa along Rv257.

Villmarken Kaller
RAFTING

(☑90 52 57 03; www.villmarken-kaller.no, in Norwegian) About 20km upstream from Sjoa along Rv257.

Sjoa Kajakksenter
KAYAKING

(☑90 06 62 22; www.kajakksenteret.no; Nedre Heidal) Around 8km west of Sjoa along Rv257.

🛏 Sleeping

Most of the above places also have accommodation, with huts, camping and a few doubles.

Sjoa Vandrerhjem
HOSTEL & CABINS €

(☑61 23 62 00; www.heidalrafting.no; dm Nkr175-250, 2-bed r incl breakfast Nkr350-450; ☺mid-May–Sep) This atmospheric hillside hostel is run by Heidal Rafting. Rooms are simple, while dinner costs Nkr100 and is served in the wonderful 1747 log farmhouse building.

Sæta Camping
CAMPGROUND €

(☑61 23 51 47; www.saetacamping.com, in Norwegian; tent/caravan sites Nkr130/160, 1-5-bed hut per person from Nkr325) is down by the river bank. It's a pleasant grassy site with a front-row seat for some of the minor rapids.

❶ Getting There & Away

Nor-Way Bussekspress bus routes between Oslo (Nkr370) and the western fjords pass through Sjoa twice daily.

Ringebu
POP 4540

The southernmost small community of Gudbrandsdalen, the narrow river valley that stretches for 200km between Lake Mjøsa and Dombås, Ringebu is worth a detour for its lovely stave church.

Ringebu Stave Church & Around
STAVE CHURCH & VICARAGE

(Ringebu Stavkyrkje; www.stavechurch.no; adult/child Nkr40/20; ☺8am-8pm mid-Jun–mid-Aug, 9am-5pm late May–mid-Jun & mid-end Aug) A church has existed on this site since the arrival of Christianity in the 11th century. The current version, which remains the local parish church, dates from around 1220, but was restored in the 17th century when the distinctive red tower was attached. Inside, there's a statue of St Laurence dating from around 1250 as well as some crude runic inscriptions. Entrance to the grounds is free and the gate is open year-round. The church is around 2km south of town, signposted off the E6. It hosts occasional concerts of Norwegian folk music in summer.

Some 300m beyond the church to the east is **Ringebu Samlingene** (adult/child Nkr40/20, combined ticket with Ringebu Stave Church Nkr60/30; ☺11am-5pm Tue-Sun mid-Jun–mid-Aug). It's housed in buildings dating from 1743, and served as the vicarage until 1991.

❶ Information

Tourist office (☑61 28 47 00; www.ringebu.com; ☺8am-6pm Mon-Thu, 8am-8pm Fri, 10am-1pm Sat, 5-8pm Sun mid-Jun–mid-Aug, shorter hr rest of yr)

❶ Getting There & Away

BUS Nor-Way Bussekspress bus routes between Oslo (Nkr385, 3½ hours, three daily) and the western fjords. Cheaper Lavprisekspressen buses (from Nkr149) to Oslo or Trondheim pass through one or two times a day.

TRAIN Trains go to Oslo (Nkr440, 3¾ hours, four daily) and Trondheim (Nkr560, 3¾ hours, four daily)

WESTERN CENTRAL NORWAY

Lom
POP 2410

If you were to set up a town as a travellers' gateway, you'd put it somewhere like Lom, in the heart of some of Norway's most spectacular mountain scenery. Rapids cascade through the village centre, houses in dark wood climb the steep hills and roads lead from Lom to Geiranger (74km; p227) and the staggering Sognefjellet Rd leads from here across the top of the Jotunheimen National Park. Aside from its location, Lom's main attraction is a lovely stave church.

◉ Sights

Lom Stavkyrkje
STAVE CHURCH
(adult/child Nkr50/free; ◷9am-7pm mid-Jun–mid-Aug, 10am-4pm mid-May–mid-Jun) This delightful Norman-style stave church, in the centre of town on a rise by the water, is one of Norway's finest. Still the functioning local church, it was constructed in 1170, extended in 1634 and given its current cruciform shape with the addition of two naves in 1663. Guided tours explain the interior paintings and Jakop Sæterdalen's chancel arch and pulpit (from 1793). At night, the church is lit to fairy-tale effect. Entry to the grounds, which are open year-round, is free.

In the adjacent souvenir shop, there's a small **museum** (admission Nkr10; ◷same hr as church) about the stave church.

FREE Fossheim Steinsenter
STONE & MINERAL MUSEUM
(www.fossheimsteinsenter.no, in Norwegian; ◷10am-7pm mid-Jun–mid-Aug, shorter hr rest of yr) The fascinating Fossheim Steinsenter combines Europe's largest selection of rare and beautiful rocks, minerals, fossils, gems and jewellery for sale, and it also includes a large museum of Norwegian and geological specimens from all over the world; don't miss the downstairs fossil exhibition. The knowledgeable owners of the centre are especially proud of the Norwegian national stone, thulite. It was discovered in 1820 and is now quarried in Lom; the reddish colour is derived from traces of manganese.

Norsk Fjellmuseum
NORWEGIAN MOUNTAIN MUSEUM
(www.fjell.museum.no; adult/child Nkr50/free; ◷9am-7pm Mon-Fri, 10am-7pm Sat & Sun mid-Jun–mid-Aug, shorter hr rest of yr) Acting as the visitors centre for Jotunheimen National Park, this worthwhile mountain museum contains mountaineering memorabilia, exhibits on natural history (the woolly mammoth is a highlight) and cultural and industrial activity in the Norwegian mountains. There's also an excellent 10-minute mountain slide show and, upstairs, a scale model of the park.

(Presthaugen Bygde-museum; www.gudbrandsdals musea.no; ◷11am-4pm Jul–mid-Aug) Behind the mountain museum, this museum is a collection of 19th-century farm buildings, several *stabbur* (elevated storehouses), an old hut (it's claimed that St Olav slept here) and a summer mountain dairy.

⚐ Activities
The tourist office has details of hikes, glacier walks and ice-climbing in Jotunheimen National Park.

Hiking
Although most of the serious trekking takes place in neighbouring Jotunheimen National Park, there are several **hiking trails** closer to town; ask the tourist office for maps, directions and its terrific *Walks in Lom* pamphlet, which has a map and detailed route descriptions.

The three most popular hikes:

Lomseggen (1289m) Five-hour return hike past the century-old stone cottage called Smithbue, with some excellent views of Ottadalen, Bøverdalen and Norway's highest peak, Galdhøpiggen (2469m), en route.

Tronoberget Three-hour return hike up the mountain that lies west across the river from Lom, with excellent views of the peaks of Reinheimen National Park.

Soleggen & Læshø (1204m) Five-hour return hike above Lom with views of the Rondane, Dovrefjell, Reinheimen, Breiheimen and Jotunheimen massifs.

White-Water Rafting & Other Activities
If more-famous Sjoa (see p143) is too much of a scene, white-water rafting is possible from Skjåk, 18km upstream from Lom. Both Skjåk Rafting and Lom & Skjåk Adventure also arrange climbing, kayaking, caving, canyoning, hiking and river-boarding:

Lom & Skjåk Adventure
ACTIVITIES CENTRE
(☑47 26 16 72; www.lsadventure.no)

Naturopplevingar
ACTIVITIES CENTRE
(☑61 21 11 55; www.naturopplevingar.no) No white-water rafting, but ski tours, hiking and climbing.

Skjåk Rafting
ACTIVITIES CENTRE
(☑99 77 50 88; www.skjak-rafting.no, in Norwegian)

Sleeping & Eating

TOP CHOICE Fossheim Turisthotell

HISTORIC HOTEL & RESTAURANT €€

(☑61 21 95 00; www.fossheimhotel.no; hotel s/d Nkr1100/1500, hotel annexe s/d Nkr950/1200, 4-bed apt Nkr1860; P🐾🛜☑) This historic family hotel at the eastern end of town is one of the best hotel-restaurant combinations in Norway. The all-wood rooms in the main hotel building are lovely (we especially like rooms 401 and 402 for the balconies and views), while there are also luxurious log cabins with modern interiors and simpler, cheaper rooms (some with good views) in the adjacent annexe. But this place is equally famous for formerly being the home kitchen of the renowned Norwegian chef Arne Brimi. Now under the care of Brimi's protégé, Kristoffer Hovland, the traditional Norwegian food is exquisite (lunch/dinner buffet Nkr200/375, four-/six-course dinner menu Nkr520/625; open 1pm to 3.30pm and 7pm to 10pm). Specialities include wild trout, reindeer, elk and ptarmigan.

Nordal Turistsenter

HOTEL & CAMPGROUND €€

(☑61 21 93 00; www.nordalturistsenter.no; tent sites Nkr185-315; s/d/f Nkr940/1280/1560; ⊙closed mid-Dec–late Mar) A busy, rambling place in the centre of town, the Nordal Turistsenter has something for everyone, with comfy rooms, self-catering cabins and a campsite at the water's edge. It also has a cosy pub and a casual cafeteria-style restaurant that serves simple meals (light meals from Nkr75).

Fossberg Hotell

HOTEL €€

(☑61 21 22 50; www.fossberg.no; s/d Nkr890/1340; ⊙8am-10pm Mon-Sat, 10am-10pm Sun) Although not in the same league as the Fossheim Turisthotell, this is nonetheless an appealing place in the centre of town. The pine-clad rooms are tidy and pleasant and there's a gymnasium for guests. It also has a range of cabins and apartments, and a popular cafeteria where the food is nothing to write home about, but the outdoor tables are a pleasant place to do so. Having to pay for wireless (per one/six/24 hours Nkr30/60/90), however, cheapens an otherwise reasonable package.

Kyba – Kafe Isbar

CAFE €€

(light meals & mains Nkr65-155; ⊙11am-10pm mid-Jun–mid-Aug, shorter hr rest of yr) Also in the centre of town, this informal cafe is probably the best place in Lom to eat outside the Fossheim Turisthotell. Aside from the usual snacks and fast-food choices, it does a small selection of traditional Norwegian dishes, such as sour-cream porridge and smoked roasted reindeer meat, for extremely reasonable prices (Nkr85 to Nkr155). Another big selling point is its elevated terrace with fine views.

Shopping

In addition to the gems and jewellery for sale at the Fossheim Steinsenter shop, the small **Brimi Bue** (www.brimibue.no, in Norwegian; ⊙10am-8pm mid-Jun–mid-Aug, 10am-4pm May–mid-Jun & mid-Aug–Sep), next to the Fossheim Turisthotell, has cookbooks, organic foods and kitchenware inspired by masterchef Arne Brimi.

Information

Tourist office (☑61 21 29 90; www.visitjotun heimen.com; ⊙9am-7pm mid-Jun–mid-Aug, shorter hr rest of yr) Located in the Norwegian Mountain Museum. It has free internet access available.

Getting There & Away

Three daily Nor-Way Bussekspress services between Oslo (Nkr520, 6½ hours) and Måløy (Nkr350, 4½ hours) pass through Lom, and local buses to/from Otta (Nkr120, 1½ hours, six daily). Also, two daily summer buses through the Jotunheimen National Park to Sogndal (Nkr250, 3½ hours, two daily) from late June to early September.

Around Lom

East of Lom, just off the Rv15, three sites pay homage to Arne Brimi, perhaps Norway's best-loved celebrity chef. There's also a fine rural hotel.

TOP CHOICE Vianvang

GOURMET RESTAURANT & COOKING COURSES €€€

(☑41 93 11 11; www.brimiland.no, in Norwegian; set menus Nkr395-575; ⊙by appointment ☑) Arne Brimi has retreated into the mountains, where he runs **cooking courses** (Nkr5900). If you're coming from Lom along the Rv15, take the Rv51 towards Randsverk just before you reach Vågåmo (Vågå).

Brimisæter

MOUNTAIN FARM €

(☑91 13 75 58; www.brimi-seter.no; per person around Nkr350) This former summer mountain dairy has a simple but lovely rural family ambience and plenty of animals that kids will love.

Brimi-Fjellstugu MOUNTAIN LODGE **€€**
(☑61 23 98 12; www.brimi-fjellstugu.no, in Norwegian; per person from Nkr525) This neighbouring mountain lodge, also part of the Brimi fiefdom, offers higher levels of comfort in the same stirring mountain setting, with meals cooked by the man himself.

Vågå Gardshotell FARM HOTEL **€€**
(☑61 23 06 53; www.gardshotell.no; per person from Nkr650) These converted 19th-century farm buildings just off the Rv15 between Lom and Vågå are a wonderful alternative to hotels and make a great base if you'll be in the area for more than a night.

Jotunheimen National Park

The high peaks and glaciers of the Jotunheimen National Park (1151 sq km), whose name means the 'Home of the Giants', make for Norway's best-loved and busiest wilderness destination. Hiking routes lead from ravine-like valleys and past deep lakes, plunging waterfalls and 60 glaciers to the tops of all the peaks in Norway over 2300m; these include Galdhøpiggen (the highest peak in northern Europe at 2469m), Glittertind (2465m) and Store Skagastølstind

(2403m). By one count, there are more than 275 summits above 2000m inside the park.

For park information, contact Lom tourist office (p146).

⊙ Sights & Activities

TOP/CHOICE **Sognefjellet Road** SCENIC ROAD
Snaking through the park (and providing access to most of the trailheads) is the stunningly scenic Sognefjellet Rd (Rv55),

Jotunheimen National Park

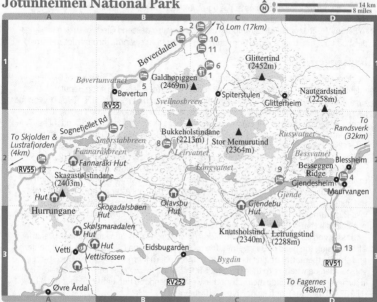

HIKING IN JOTUNHEIMEN

Jotunheimen's hiking possibilities are practically endless and all are spectacular. The best maps are Statens Kartverk's *Jotunheimen Aust* and *Jotunheimen Vest* (1:50,000; Nkr99 each). The tourist office in Lom can offer advice, route descriptions and guided hikes through the park, while **Top of Norway** (www.ton.no), which is based at the Elvesæter Hotel and Leirvassbu Lodge, organises guided hikes, as well as glacier walks, rock-climbing, ice-climbing and caving for between Nkr500 and Nkr700 per person. For more information on DNT huts, see p425. A few of Jotunheim's possible hikes:

Krossbu

Krossbu Turiststasjon, near the head of Bøverdalen, lies at the outset of a tangle of hiking routes, including a short day trip to the Smørstabbreen glacier.

Galdhøpiggen

With its dramatic cirques, arêtes and glaciers, this is a fairly tough eight-hour day hike (1470m of ascent) from Spiterstulen, where the toll road begins. Although the trail is well marked, you'll need a map and compass.

Øvre Årdal

From Øvre Årdal, head 12km northeast up the Utladalen valley to the farm Vetti, from where hiking tracks lead to Vettisfossen (275m), Norway's highest free-falling waterfall, and to the unstaffed hut at Stølsmaradalen. This is an alternative access route, via upper Utladalen, to longer hikes in Jotunheimen.

Hurrungane

The fabulous Hurrungane massif rises darkly above the westernmost end of the park. Although some of these prominent peaks are accessible to experienced mountaineers and, in some cases, skilled scramblers, most hikers head eastwards from Turtagrø Hotel. From the hotel, a four-hour hike will take you to Norway's highest DNT hut, Fannaråki, on the summit of Fannaråken (2068m). While the hut itself is your typical DNT deal (ie clean and basic), the views are some of the best from accommodation anywhere in Norway, taking in a representative sample of the Hurrungane massif and the glacier country away to the west; to reach the hut, ask for directions at the hotel. An alternative to returning to the hotel is to descend the eastern slope along the well-marked track to Keisarpasset and thence back to Ekrehytta. To launch into a multiday trip, you can also descend Gjertvassdalen to Skogadalsbøen hut and then choose from one of many routes eastwards through Jotunheimen.

Besseggen

No discussion of hiking in Jotunheimen would be complete without mention of Besseggen ridge, the most popular hike in Norway. Indeed, some travellers find it *too* popular, with at least 30,000 hikers walking it in the three months a year that it's passable. If you don't mind sacrificing solitude for one of Norway's most spectacular treks, you won't regret it. Henrik Ibsen wrote of Besseggen: 'It cuts along with an edge like a scythe for miles and miles...And scars and glaciers sheer down the precipice to the glassy lakes, 1600 feet below on either side.' One of Peer Gynt's mishaps was a plunge down to the lake on the back of a reindeer.

The day hike between Gjendesheim and Memurubu Lodge takes about six hours and climbs to a high point of 1743m. From Gjendesheim Lodge, follow the DNT-marked track towards Glitterheim for about 30 minutes, where a left fork strikes off up the Veltløyfti gorge, which leads upward onto the level Veslefjellet plateau. After a short descent from the plateau the track leads onto the Besseggen ridge, which slices between the deep-blue lake Bessvatnet and the 18km-long glacier-green lake Gjende, coloured by 20,000 tonnes of glacial silt that is dumped into it each year by the Memuru River.

Besseggen is never less than 10m wide and only from a distance does it look precarious. After passing the head of Bessvatnet, the route passes a small plateau lake, Bjørnbøltjørn, and shortly thereafter begins its descent to the modern Memurubu Lodge. Once there, you can decide whether to take the boat **M/S Gjende** (www.gjende.no; Nkr100, 30min, 5 daily in summer) back to Gjendesheim, continue west to Gjendebu hut, either on foot or by boat (Nkr67, 30 minutes), or hike north to Glitterheim.

billed as 'the road over the roof of Norway'. Put simply, it's one of Norway's most beautiful drives.

It connects Lustrafjorden with Lom and was constructed in 1939 by unemployed youths. It rises to a height of 1434m, making it the highest mountain road in northern Europe. It has been chosen as one of Norway's 18 'National Tourist Routes' (see p445); visit www.turistveg.no for more information about the road.

Access from the southwest is via the multiple hairpin bends climbing up beyond the tree line to Turtagrø, with a stirring view of the **Skagastølstindane** mountains on your right. If you're coming from Lom, the ascent is more gradual, following beautiful **Bøverdalen**, the valley of the Bøvra River, with its lakes, glacial rivers, grass-roofed huts and patches of pine forest. The road summit on **Sognefjell** offers superb views.

The snow sometimes doesn't melt until early July, although the road is usually open from May to September. The road can get very narrow and snow is often piled metres high on either side of the road. Ample camping and other accommodation options line the road.

Although this road is mainly traversed by motorised transport, the Sognefjellet Rd also has legendary status among cyclists and frequently appears on lists of the world's most spectacular cycle routes. It's a serious undertaking that requires high levels of fitness and perfect brakes.

From mid-June to late August, two daily buses run between Lom and Sogndal (Nkr255, 3½ hours) via Sognefjellet Rd.

Galdhøpiggen Summer Ski Centre

SKI CENTRE

(☑61 21 17 50; www.gpss.no; ski/snowboard rental Nkr200/250, adult/child day lift pass Nkr325/255) This ski centre, at 1850m on the icy heights of Norway's highest mountain, is a stunning spot for summer skiing. From Galdesand on the Rv55, follow the Galdhøpiggen road (Nkr85 toll) to its end at 1841m. The main season runs from June to mid-November. Apart from the skiing opportunities, this road takes you to the highest point reachable by road in Norway. Nearby, the **Klimapark 2469 & Istunnel** (www.oppland.no/klimapark2469; adult/child Nkr300/150; ⊙guided tours 10am Thu-Sun mid-Jun–mid-Aug) is a 30m-long ice tunnel with an exhibition on the region's natural history and climate change.

Buy your tickets either through the Lom tourist office or Juvasshytta.

Other Scenic Drives

SCENIC DRIVES

For other roads that connect the Sognefjellet Rd to Norway's fjord country, see p209.

Turtagrø to Øvre Årdal

The toll mountain road between Turtagrø and the industrial town of Øvre Årdal is one of Norway's most scenic short drives. Open from late May to October, it leads above the tree line through wild and lonely country. From late June to late August, the route is served by daily bus (Nkr125, one hour). The vehicle toll (Nkr75) is collected by a gatekeeper at the pass (1315m).

Randsverk to Fagernes

Between Randsverk and Fagernes, the Rv51 climbs through the hilly and forested Sjodalen country onto a vast upland with far-ranging views of peaks and glaciers; it's used by hikers heading for Jotunheimen's eastern reaches. En route it passes the DNT hut at Gjendesheim, the launching point for the popular day hike along the Besseggen ridge.

From mid-June to early September, two daily buses run between Otta and Gol, via Vågå, Randsverk, Gjendesheim, Valdresflya and Fagernes. You'll have to change at Gjendesheim. From Otta, the trip to Gjendesheim takes two hours and costs Nkr103. Valdresflya is just 15 minutes further.

Jotunheimvegen

Branching off the Rv51 at Bygdin, the 45km-long **Jotunheimvegen** (www.jotunheimvegen.no) to Skåbu is much quieter and every bit as picturesque. It's usually open from mid-June until October, depending on the weather, and you pay a Nkr100 toll; motorcycles travel for free. There's no public transport along the route but there are campsites at Beitostølen and Skåbu. The route also links up with Peer Gynt Vegen (see p129).

🛏 Sleeping & Eating

DNT maintains staffed huts along most of the routes and there's also a choice of private lodges by the main roads. The following places all lie on, or are accessible from, the Sognefjellet Rd. Most open from May to September.

Elvesæter Hotell

HOTEL **€€**

(☑61 21 99 00; www.elveseter.no; Bøverdalen; s/d from Nkr850/1150, 3-course dinner Nkr325; P) Run by the sixth generation of the Elvesæter family, this gorgeous hotel has pretty rooms and lovely architecture, and is high on novelty value, adjacent as it is to the **Sagasøyla**, a 32m-high carved wooden pillar tracing Norwegian history from unification in 872 to the 1814 constitution. A great Jotunheimen base.

Turtagrø Hotel   MOUNTAIN LODGE €€€
(☎57 68 08 00; www.turtagro.no; dm from Nkr370, s/d Nkr1440/1900, tower ste Nkr2350, full board from Nkr1835/2690; P 🖨) This historic hiking and mountaineering centre is a friendly yet laid-back base for exploring Jotunheimen and Hurrungane whatever your budget. The main building has wonderful views and supremely comfortable rooms. The hotel also conducts week-long climbing courses and guided day trips (hiking, climbing and skiing) and there's a great bar full of historic Norwegian mountaineering photos. The dining room serves hearty meals (three-course meal Nkr425; daily special Nkr89, available until late afternoon).

Røisheim Hotel
                    TRADITIONAL HOTEL & RESTAURANT €€€
(☎61 21 20 31; www.roisheim.no; Bøverdalen; s/d incl breakfast, lunch & dinner from Nkr2100/3600, with open fireplace Nkr2275/3950; P) This charming place combines architecturally stunning buildings that date back to 1858 with modern comforts, although there are no TVs. Apart from the charming accommodation, the appeal lies in the meals, which are prepared by Ingrid Hov Lunde, one of the country's best-loved chefs. Quite simply, it's a wonderful place to stay.

Bøverdalen Vandrerhjem   HOSTEL €
(☎/fax 61 21 20 64; boverdalen.hostel@hihostels.no; Bøverdalen; dm Nkr170, s/d/f with shared bathroom Nkr275/420/525; P 🖨) This fine riverside hostel has a small cafe, tidy rooms and delightful surrounds to enjoy once the day-trippers have returned home. Breakfast costs Nkr70.

Storhaugen   FARM HOTEL €€
(☎/fax 61 21 20 69; www.storhaugengard.no, in Norwegian; Bøverdalen; cabin Nkr450-2500; P) At their traditional farm, the Slettede family offers highly recommended upmarket accommodation in modern cabins and apartments with views of both the Jotunheimen heights and Bøverdalen. Children will love the farm animals. At Galdesand, turn south on the Galdhøpiggen road and continue 1.5km to the signposted turn-off for Storhaugen.

Leirvassbu Lodge   MOUNTAIN LODGE €€
(☎61 21 12 10; www.leirvassbu.no; dm incl breakfast Nkr285, s/d Nkr735/1170) Leirvassbu, a typical

mountain lodge at 1400m and beside Leirvatnet lake, is a good hiking base. Guided glacier walks on Smørstabbreen cost around Nkr700. Despite its large capacity, it can get crowded. The toll on the access road is Nkr60 per car.

Juvasshytta   MOUNTAIN LODGE €€
(☎61 21 15 50; www.juvasshytta.no; per person Nkr380-500) With a name that sounds like it came from *Star Wars*, and a location above 1800m close to Norway's summit, Juvasshytta is a fine base. It sits in the shadow of Galdhøpiggen, Norway's highest peak, and is a short walk from the Galdhøpiggen Summer Ski Centre. It can arrange guided walks, glacier hikes, and climbs to the summit. With so much else going for it, the lodge-style accommodation, which ranges from simple to more comfortable, is almost incidental.

Jotunheimen Fjellstue   MOUNTAIN LODGE €€
(☎61 21 29 18; www.jotunheimen-fjellstue.no, in Norwegian; s/d from Nkr695/1045) This modern mountain lodge has a lovely location, good rooms and decent food (three-course menu Nkr395).

Krossbu Turiststasjon   MOUNTAIN LODGE €
(☎61 21 29 22; www.krossbu.no, in Norwegian; d with/without bathroom Nkr470/310; P) At this roadside lodge, the larger rooms have attached bathroom and dinner is available. Guided glacier hikes and courses are also possible if there are enough people.

Gjendesheim Lodge   MOUNTAIN HUT €
(☎61 23 89 10; www.turistforeningen.no/gjendes heim; beds DNT members Nkr85-225, nonmembers Nkr150-290) At the trailhead to the Besseggen trek, on the eastern side of the park.

Valdresflya Vandrerhjem   YOUTH HOSTEL €
(☎90 12 23 51; www.valdresflya-vandrerhjem.com; Valdresflya; dm/s/d Nkr175/300/400) Fifteen minutes' drive south from Gjendesheim, this hostel prides itself on being the highest in northern Europe (1389m). There's no guest kitchen, but breakfast/dinner costs Nkr75/150 and there's a daytime cafe serving excellent waffles.

HARDANGERVIDDA

The desolate and beautiful Hardangervidda plateau, part of the 3430-sq-km Hardangervidda National Park, Norway's largest, ranges across an otherworldly tundra landscape that's the southernmost refuge of the Arctic fox (around eight to 10 have recently been reintroduced) and Norway's largest herd of wild reindeer (caribou). Long a trade and travel route connecting eastern and western Norway, it's now crossed by the main railway and road routes between Oslo and Bergen.

Reindeer numbers have dropped in recent years, from a high of 19,000 in 1998 to around 7000. This fall in numbers is, however, part of a program of resource management by the park's authorities, as a ban on hunting until recently meant that herd numbers became too large and reindeer body weights began to fall dangerously due to a lack of sufficient fodder.

Apart from Finse and Geilo, which are covered in this chapter, Hardangervidda National Park is accessible from Rjukan (see the boxed text, p115) and Eidfjord (p178); there's an excellent national park centre at the latter.

Geilo

POP 2265

At Geilo (pronounced Yei-lo), midway between Oslo and Bergen, you can practically step off the train onto a ski lift. In summer, there's plenty of fine hiking in the area. A popular nearby destination is the expansive plateau-like mountain called Hallingskarvet, frosted with several small glaciers. Apart from hiking across the Hardangervidda, it's possible to go glacier trekking on Hardangerjøkulen (1862m), horse-riding, white-water rafting, riverboarding and on elk safaris. For more information on these and other activities, contact the tourist office.

Sleeping & Eating

Geilo has dozens of accommodation choices, most of which are geared towards the adventure and outdoor-activity crowds. The tourist office has a full list.

Some of the more reasonable options:

Øen Turistsenter & Geilo Vandrerhjem
YOUTH HOSTEL €
(☑32 08 70 60; www.oenturist.no; Lienvegen 137; dm Nkr275, huts Nkr480-825) Breakfast Nkr60.

Ro Hotell & Kro HOTEL, RESTAURANT €€
(☑32 09 08 99; www.rohotell.no; Geilovegen 55; s/d from Nkr650/850) Dinner mains from Nkr125.

Information

Geilo tourist office (☑32 09 59 00; www.geilo.no; ⊗8.30am-6pm Mon-Fri, 9am-3pm Sat & Sun Jul–mid-Aug, shorter hr mid-Aug–Jun)

Getting There & Away

Most visitors arrive on the train between Oslo (Nkr459, 3½ hours, five daily) and Bergen (Nkr413, three hours).

HIKING THE HARDANGERVIDDA

Trekking through the western Hardangervidda is possible only in July and August – for the rest of the time, snow and the possibility of sudden changes in weather conditions make setting out hazardous; new snow is a possibility at any time of year. Before exploring the park, visit the outstanding Hardangervidda Natursenter (p179), which sells maps. This centre can offer advice on hiking routes, and has a wonderful exhibition on the park. Hikers and skiers will find the Turkart series (Nkr149 to Nkr279), at a scale of 1:100,000, to be the maps of choice for locals. You should also pick up *Hardangervidda Hytteringen* (www.hardangerviddanett.no), which gives the run-down on mountain huts. The Bergen Turlag DNT office (p171) is another good source of information.

There are numerous trailheads, among them the waterfalls at Vøringfoss (p180), Finse (p152) or Geilo (p151). Some of our favourite routes:

» **Finse to Vøringfoss** (two days) The steepest hiking country in Hardangervidda, skirting the Hardangerjøkulen glacier and overnighting in Rembesdalsseter; you could also make the four- to five-hour (one-way) detour to Kjeåsen Farm (p178).

» **Vøringfoss to Kinsarvik via Harteigen** (three days) To the picturesque mountain of Harteigen with its panoramic views of Hardangervidda, then down the monk's stairway to Kinsarvik (p181).

» **Halne to Dyranut via Rauhelleren** (two days) Trails lead south off the Rv7. There's a strong chance hikers will encounter reindeer herds.

For details of other adventure possibilities on the plateau, see the boxed text, p115.

RALLARVEGEN

The Rallarvegen, or Navvies' Rd, was constructed as a supply route for Oslo–Bergen railway workers (the railway opened on 27 November 1909). Nowadays, this 83km route of asphalt and gravel extends from Haugastøl through Finse and all the way down to Flåm, and is open only to bicycle and foot traffic; the distance from Finse to Flåm is 56km. Following this route down to Flåm means that you get the best of the stunning scenery of the Flåmsbana railway (p199), with the additional benefit of being able to stop whenever you like to enjoy the view. The popular stretch between Vatnahalsen and Flåm descends 865m in 29km. Brakes on bikes usually have to be changed after just one descent!

Cyclists and hikers will find optimum conditions between mid-July and mid-September. To rent bikes (Nkr490 to Nkr850 depending on the date and type of bike) ready for the Rallarvegen challenge, contact **Finse 1222** (✆56 52 71 00; www.finse1222.no); bikes must be booked before arriving in Finse due to high demand in summer, and prices include the return bike transportation fee on the train.

Finse

Heading west from Geilo, the railway line climbs 600m through a tundra-like landscape of lakes and snowy peaks to Finse, lying at 1222m near the Hardangerjøkulen icecap. This region offers nordic skiing in winter and hiking in summer, not to mention what could be Norway's steepest mountain-bike ride.

East of Finse station, the **Finse Navvies Museum** (Rallarmuseet Finse; adult/child Nkr75/30; ◷10am-8pm Jul-Sep) traces the history of the Oslo–Bergen railway and the 15,000 people who built this hard-won line in 2.5 million worker days.

Activities

Finse is the starting point for some exceptional treks, including the popular four-hour trek to the Blåisen glacier tip of Hardangerjøkulen; some in-the-know Norwegians claim this to be the most spectacular glacier walk in the country. Adding interest to your hike is the fact that scenes set on the planet Hof in *The Empire Strikes Back* were filmed around the glacier. **Finse 1222** (✆56 52 71 00; www.finse1222.no) offers day-long glacier hikes (per person Nkr400).

It's also possible to walk around the glacier and down to Vøringfoss (see the boxed text, p151). The wonderful three- or four-day Finse–Aurland trek follows Aurlandsdalen down to Aurlandsfjorden and has a series of DNT and private mountain huts a day's walk apart. For more on this route, see p204.

🛏 Sleeping & Eating

Most budget travellers stay at the staffed DNT hut, **Finsehytta** (✆56 52 67 32; dm Nkr130-275), while the friendly **Finse 1222** (✆56 52 71 00; www.finse1222.no; full board from Nkr1150) offers comfortable rooms within sight of the glacier, and a good three-course dinner; Finse 1222 is also the starting point and best source of information for many of the activities in the region.

ℹ Getting There & Away

Five daily trains run between Oslo (from Nkr545, 4½ hours) and Bergen (from Nkr327, 2½ hours) via Finse.

Bergen & the Southwestern Fjords

HIGHEST ELEV 1654M

Why Go?

If you could visit only one region of Norway and still capture the essence of the country's appeal, this would probably be our choice.

Two of Norway's most engaging cities serve as gateways to dramatic fjord country. Dynamic Bergen is one of the world's most beautiful cities, arrayed around harbours and hillsides, and rich in history and architecture. It's also the ideal starting point for a journey into splendid Hardangerfjord, with its gorgeous fjord-side villages, or the vast Sognefjorden network; en route to the latter, Voss is Norway's destination of choice for thrill-seekers, while the Stalheim Hotel is the ultimate room with a view.

Away to the south, agreeable Stavanger, with its brilliant museums and beguiling old quarter, is an essential staging post for Lysefjord, home to two of Norway's most recognisable images, impossibly high above the ice-blue waters of the fjord: Preikestolen (Pulpit Rock) and Kjeragbolten.

Best Places to Eat

- » Pingvinen (p166)
- » Potetkjelleren (p167)
- » Tyssedal Hotel (p183)
- » Torget Fish Market (p167)

Best Places to Stay

- » Stalheim Hotel (p175)
- » Det Hanseatiske Hotel (p164)
- » Utne Hotel (p182)
- » Skuteviken Gjestehus (p165)
- » Eidfjord Gjestegiveri (p179)

When to Go
Bergen

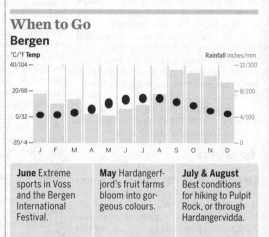

June Extreme sports in Voss and the Bergen International Festival.

May Hardangerfjord's fruit farms bloom into gorgeous colours.

July & August Best conditions for hiking to Pulpit Rock, or through Hardangervidda.

BERGEN

POP 256,600

Surrounded by seven hills and seven fjords, Bergen is a beautiful, charming city. With the Unesco World Heritage–listed Bryggen and buzzing Vågen Harbour as its centrepiece, Bergen climbs the hillsides with hundreds of timber-clad houses, while cable cars offer stunning views from above. Throw in great museums, friendly locals and a dynamic cultural life and Bergen amply rewards as much time as you can give it.

History

During the 12th and 13th centuries, Bergen was Norway's capital and easily the country's most important city. By the 13th century, the city states of Germany allied themselves into trading leagues, most significantly the Hanseatic League with its centre in Lübeck. At its zenith, the league had over 150 member cities and was northern Europe's most powerful economic entity; the sheltered harbour of Bryggen drew the Hanseatic League's traders in droves. They established their first office here around 1360, transforming Bryggen into one of the league's four major headquarters abroad, accommodating up to 2000 mostly German resident traders who imported grain and exported dried fish, among other products.

For over 400 years, Bryggen was dominated by this tight-knit community of German merchants, who weren't permitted to mix with, marry or have families with local Norwegians. By the 15th century, competition from Dutch and English shipping companies, internal disputes and, especially, the Black Death (which wiped out 70% of Bergen's population) ensured the Hanseatic League's decline.

By the early 17th century Bergen was nonetheless the trading hub of Scandinavia, and Norway's most populous city with 15,000 people. During the 17th and 18th centuries, many Hanseatic traders opted to take Norwegian nationality and join the local community. Bryggen remained an important maritime trading centre until 1899, when the Hanseatic League's Bergen offices finally closed.

◎ Sights

Bergen has lots of quaint cobblestone streets lined with timber-clad houses; apart from Bryggen, some of the most picturesque are the quiet lanes climbing the hill behind the Fløibanen funicular station, as well as in Nordnes (the peninsula that runs northwest of the centre, including along the southern shore of the main harbour) and Sandviken (the area north of Håkonshallen).

TOP CHOICE **Bryggen** HISTORIC DISTRICT
Bergen's oldest and most enchanting quarter runs along the eastern shore of Vågen Harbour in long, parallel and often leaning rows of gabled buildings with stacked-stone or wooden foundations and reconstructed rough-plank construction.

The archaeological excavations of Bryggen (Map p158), whose name means 'the wharf', suggest that the quay was once 140m further inland than its present location. The current 58 buildings (25% of the original, although some claim there are now 61) cover 13,000 sq metres and date from after the 1702 fire, although the building pattern dates back to the 12th century.

In the early 14th century, there were about 30 wooden buildings on Bryggen, each of which was usually shared by several *stuer* (trading firms). They rose two or three storeys above the wharf and combined business premises with living quarters and warehouses. Each building had a crane for loading and unloading ships, as well as a *schøtstue* (large assembly room) where employees met and ate. That atmosphere of an intimate waterfront community remains intact, and losing yourself in Bryggen is one of Bergen's great pleasures.

For an excellent summary of Bryggen's history and threats to its existence, look out for the *Bryggen Guide* (Nkr80), available from the Bryggens Museum and elsewhere, or *The Bryggen Companion* (Nkr60) by Siri Myrvoll, which is available from the Bryggen Visitors Centre.

Hanseatic Museum & Schøtstuene
(Map p158; www.museumvest.no; Finnegårdsgaten 1a & Øvregaten 50; adult/child mid-May–mid-Sep Nkr50/free, rest of yr Nkr30/free; ◎9am-5pm mid-May–mid-Sep, shorter hr rest of yr) The terrific Hanseatic Museum provides a window into the world of Hanseatic traders. Housed in a rough-timber building from 1704, it starkly reveals the contrast between the austere living and working conditions of Hanseatic merchant sailors and apprentices, and the lifestyle of the management. Highlights include the manager's office, quarters, private liquor cabinet and summer bedroom; the apprentices' quarters, where beds were shared by two men; the fish storage room, which pressed and processed over a million pounds (450,000kg) of fish a month; and

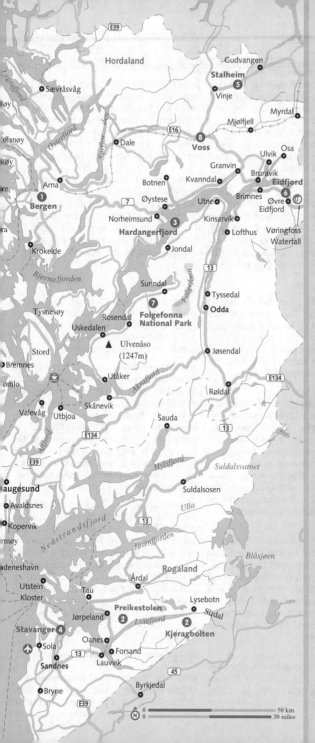

Bergen & the SW Fjords Highlights

1 Stroll through historic **Bryggen** (p154) in Bergen, a Unesco World Heritage site

2 Climb to **Preikestolen** (p195) or **Kjeragbolten** (p197) overlooking Lysefjord

3 Relax on a slow boat up **Hardangerfjord** (see the boxed text, p178) from tranquil Ulvik

4 Amble through cosmopolitan Stavanger, particularly the historic timber houses of **Gamle Stavanger** (p188)

5 Wake up to the best hotel view in Norway at the **Stalheim Hotel** (p175)

6 Climb up (or through) the mountain to **Kjeåsen Farm** (p178), high above Eidfjord

7 Go for a glacier walk atop the ice-cap in **Folgefonna National Park** (p183)

8 Parasail or para-bungee high above it all, or kayak through the fjords from **Voss** (p173)

SAVING BRYGGEN

So beautiful is Bryggen that it seems inconceivable that conservationists spent much of the 20th century fighting plans to tear it down.

Fire has destroyed Bryggen at least seven times (especially in 1702 and again in 1955, when one-third of Bryggen was destroyed). The notable tilt of the structures was caused in 1944, when a Dutch munitions ship exploded in the harbour, blowing off the roofs and shifting the pilings. The explosion and 1955 fire increased the already considerable clamour to tear down Bryggen once and for all; not only was it considered a dangerous fire hazard, but its run-down state was widely seen as an embarrassment. Plans for the redevelopment of the site included modern, eight-storey buildings, a bus station, a shopping centre and a car park.

What saved Bryggen were the archaeological excavations that took 13 years to complete after the 1955 fire and which unearthed over one million artefacts. In 1962 the **Bryggen Foundation** (www.stiftelsenbryggen.no) and Friends of Bryggen were formed; the foundation still oversees the protection and restoration of Bryggen, although the buildings are privately owned. One of the greatest challenges is the fact that Bryggen is actually sinking by an estimated 8mm each year. In 1979 Unesco inscribed Bryggen on its World Heritage list. For more information on Bryggen, visit the **Bryggen Visitors Centre** (Map p158; ⊘9am-5pm mid-May–mid-Sep).

the *fiskeskrue* (fish press), which pressed the fish into barrels. The nearby Schøtstuene is a reconstruction of one of the original assembly halls where the fraternity of Hanseatic merchants once met for their business meetings and beer guzzling. The Schøtstuene is closed in January and February.

Bryggens Museum

(Map p158; www.bymuseet.no; Dreggsallmenning 3; adult/child Nkr60/free; ⊘10am-4pm mid-May–Aug, shorter hr Sep–mid-May) This archaeological museum was built on the site of Bergen's first settlement, and the 800-year-old foundations unearthed during construction have been incorporated into the exhibits, which include medieval tools, pottery, skulls and runes. The permanent exhibition documenting Bergen in around 1300 is particularly interesting.

Theta Museum

(Map p158; Enhjørningsgården; adult/child Nkr30/10; ⊘2-4pm Tue, Sat & Sun mid-May–mid-Sep) This excellent one-room reconstruction of a clandestine Resistance headquarters, uncovered by the Nazis in 1942, is now Norway's tiniest museum. Appropriately enough, finding it is still a challenge. It's behind the Enhjørningen restaurant; pass through the alley and up the stairs to the 3rd floor.

Mariakirken
CHURCH

(Map p158; Dreggen; ⊘closed for renovations until 2015) This stone church, with its Romanesque entrance and twin towers, dates from the early 12th century and is Bergen's oldest

building. The interior features 15th-century frescos and a splendid baroque pulpit donated by Hanseatic merchants in 1676, but you'll have to wait until the restoration work is finished to catch a glimpse.

Rosenkrantz Tower
FORTRESS TOWER

(Rosenkrantztårnet; Map p158; www.bymuseet.no; Bergenhus; adult/child Nkr50/free; ⊘10am-4pm mid-May–Aug, noon-3pm Sun Sep–mid-May) Built in the 1560s by Bergen governor Erik Rosenkrantz, this tower was a residence and defence post. It also incorporates parts of the keep (1273) of King Magnus the Lawmender and the 1520s fortress of Jørgen Hansson. Spiral staircases lead past halls and sentry posts to a reasonable harbour view from the top.

Håkonshallen
HISTORIC CEREMONIAL HALL

(Map p158; www.bymuseet.no; Bergenhus; adult/child Nkr50/free; ⊘10am-4pm mid-May–Aug, shorter hr Sep–mid-May) This large ceremonial hall, adjacent to the Rosenkrantz Tower, was constructed by King Håkon Håkonsson from 1247–61 and completed for his son's wedding and coronation. The roof was blown off in 1944 thanks to the explosion of a Dutch munitions boat, but extensive restoration has been carried out. There are hourly guided tours in summer.

FREE Bergen Cathedral (Domkirken)
CHURCH

(Map p158; Domkirkeplass 1; admission free; ⊘10am-4pm Mon-Fri mid-Jun–mid-Aug, 11am-12.30pm Tue-Fri rest of yr) Bergen's cathedral,

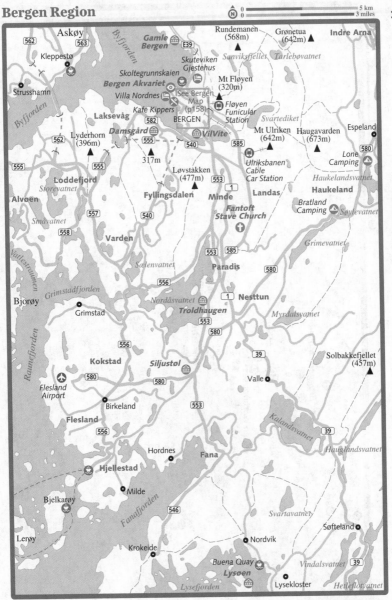

also known as St Olav's Church, is well worth a visit. The stonemasonry in the entrance hall was carved by the same stonemasons as those who adorned Westminster Abbey's chapter house in London. From mid-June until the end of August, there are free **organ recitals** (www.kirkemusikkibergen. no, in Norwegian) on Sunday and Thursday.

Bergen Kunst Museum ART GALLERY
(Map p158; www.bergenartmuseum.no; Rasmus Meyers Allé 3, 7 & 9; adult/child/student Nkr60/ free/40; ⊙11am-5pm mid-May–mid-Sep, 11am-5pm

Bergen

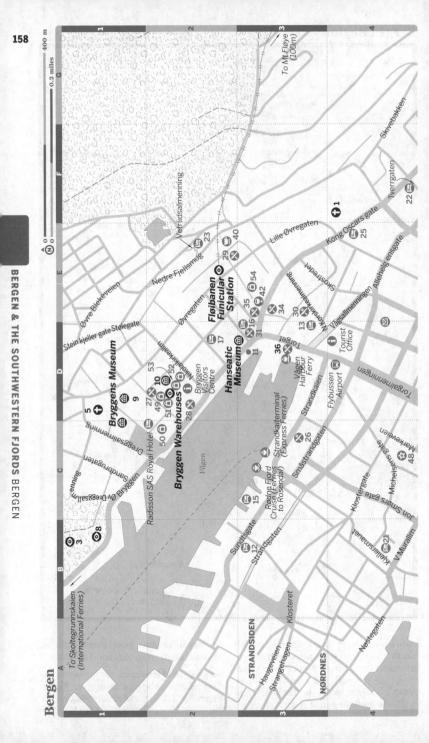

0.2 miles
400 m

To Skoltegrunnskaien
(International Ferries)

To Mt Fløye (100m)

Skivebakken

Tverrgaten
22

1

Kong Oscars gate
25

Lille Øvregaten

Altenelg ensgate

Skostredet

Vetrlidsalmenning
23
29
40

Nedre Fjellsmug

Øvregaten

Fløibanen
Funicular
Station

54
42
35
16
34
30
31
13

Vågsallmenningen

Nikolaikirkeallmenningen

Tourist
Office

Flybussen
Airport

Torget

Torgallmenningen

Øvre Blekeveien

Stein kjeller gate Stølegate

Nikolaikirkeallm

Bryggens Museum

Bryggen
Visitors
Centre

17

Hanseatic
Museum

11

36

Vågen
Harbour
Ferry

Vågskaien

Strandkaien

Snåstrandgaten

26

53
10
52
27
49
9
51
28
50

5

Bryggens Warehouses

Dreggsallmenning

Sandbrugaten
Øv Dreggsall

Radisson SAS Royal Hotel

Vågen

Rødne Fjord
Cruise (Ferries
to Rosendal)

Strandkaiterminal
(Express Ferries)

Sundtsgate
Strandgaten
15

Sundtsgate
12

Kjellersmauet
21
VI Muralln

Jon Smørs gate

Michels gate
48

Markeveien

Klostergate

STRANDSIDEN

Kloisteret

Haugeveien
Strandgehagen

NORDNES

Nøstegaten

3
8

To Skoltegrunnskaien
(International Ferries)

N

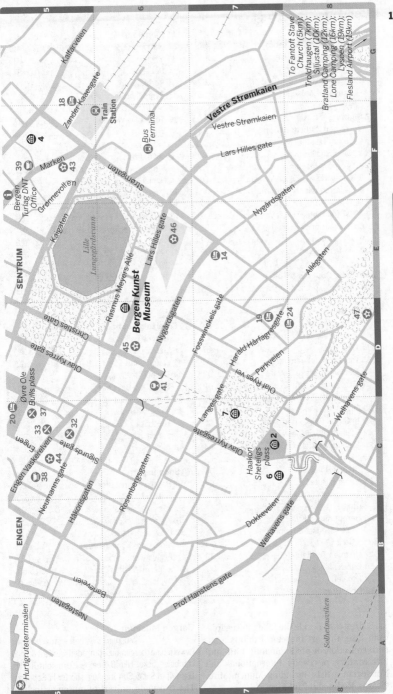

159

BERGEN

Bergen Kunst Museum

SENTRUM

ENGEN

To Fantoft Stave
Church (5km);
Troldhaugen (7km);
Siljustøl (10km);
Bratland Camping (12km);
Lone Camping (16km);
Lysøen (19km);
Flesland Airport (19km)

Vestre Strømkaien

Vestre Strømkaien

Lars Hilles gate

Nygårdsgaten

Allégaten

Welhavens gate

Olav Ryes vei

Parkveien

Harald Hårfagresgate

Fosswinckels gate

Langes gate

Olav Kyrres gate

Haakon
Sheteligs
plass

Dokkeveien

Welhavens gate

Prof Hanstens gate

Solheimsviken

Banneveien

Nøstegaten

Hurtigruteterminalen

Rosenbergsgaten

Hakonsgaten

Neumanns gate

Sigurds gate

Engen Vaskerelven

Øvre Ole
Bulls plass

Olav Kyrres gate

Christies Gate

Rasmus Meyers Allé

Nygårdsgaten

Lille
Langegårdsvann

Kaigaten

Grønnevollen

Strømgaten

Marken

Zander Kaaesgate

Kalfarveien

Train
Station

Bus
Terminal

Bergen
Turlag DNT
Office

Tue-Sun rest of yr) Beside the Lille Lungegårds-
vann lake, this art museum exhibits a superb collection of predominantly 18th- and
19th-century pieces by international and
Norwegian artists, including Munch, Miró,
Picasso, Rodín and Paul Klee.

Bergen Museum

CULTURAL & NATURAL HISTORY MUSEUMS
(www.uib.no/bergenmuseum; adult/student & child
combined ticket Nkr40/free; ⊗10am-4pm Tue-Fri,
11am-4pm Sat & Sun Jun-Aug, shorter hr Sep-May)
The two main university museums include

the **Cultural History Collection** (Kultur-Historik Samlinger; Map p158; Haakon Sheteligs plass 10), which has Viking weaponry, medieval altars, folk art, period furnishings, Inuit and Aleut culture, and displays covering everything from Henrik Ibsen to Egyptian mummies; and the **Natural History Collection** (Naturhistorisk Samlinger; Map p158; ☑55 58 29 20; Muséplass 3), which has a fine marine-mammals collection.

Sjøfartsmuseet
MARITIME MUSEUM

(Map p158; www.bsj.uib.no; Haakon Sheteligs plass 15; adult/student & child Nkr30/free; ⏱11am-3pm) Bergen's Maritime Museum is essential to understanding the history of this seafaring city. It features models of ships from Viking times to the present and exhibits that trace Norway's maritime history.

Bergen Aquarium
AQUARIUM

(Bergen Akvariet; Map p157; www.akvariet.com; Nordnesbakken 4; adult/child mid-Jun–mid-Aug Nkr200/150, cheaper rest of yr; ⏱9am-7pm May-Aug, 10am-6pm Sep-Apr) At the end of the Nordnes Peninsula, this aquarium has a big outdoor tank with seals and penguins, as well as 70 indoor tanks, snakes, crocodiles and a shark tunnel, which opened in 2010. You'll never forget the lovable steinbit, the hideous anglerfish or the school of herring, which seems to function as a single entity. There are also penguin and seal feedings throughout the day. On foot, you can get there from Torget in 20 minutes; alternatively, take the Vågen ferry (p172) or bus 11.

Leprosy Museum
LEPROSY MUSEUM

(Lepramuseet; Map p158; St George's Hospital, Kong Oscars gate 59; adult/child Nkr50/free; ⏱11am-3pm Jun-Aug, 11am-3pm Sun mid-late May) For something a bit different, visit this unusual museum. Although most of the buildings at St George's Hospital date from the 19th century, in medieval times the site served as a leprosarium. Exhibits detail Norway's contributions to leprosy research, including the work of Dr Armauer Hansen, who discovered the leprosy bacillus in Bergen in 1873 and gave his name to Hansen's disease, the modern name for leprosy.

Gamle Bergen
REGIONAL FOLK MUSEUM

(Map p157; www.bymuseet.no; Nyhavnsveien 4, Sandviken; adult/child Nkr70/free; ⏱hourly tours 10am-5pm early May-Aug) The open-air Old Bergen Museum, 4km north of the city centre, boasts a fine collection of 35 structures from the 18th and 19th centuries. A 30-minute walk from Torget will get you there, or take bus 20, 23 or

ⓘ **BERGEN CARD** 161

The **Bergen Card** (www.visitbergen.com/bergencard; adult per 24/48hr Nkr190/250, child Nkr75/100) is a worthwhile investment, although it takes careful planning, an early start and a steady pace to make sure it's economical. The card covers free travel on local buses; free entrance to some museums, with discounted entry to the rest; free or discounted return trips on the Fløibanen funicular, depending on the time of year; free guided tours of Bergen; and discounts on city and boat sightseeing tours, concerts and cultural performances. The Bergen Card is available from the tourist office, some hotels, the bus terminal and online.

24. Admission to the grounds (which are open all year) is free. In summer, the museum runs children's activities and shows.

Troldhaugen
HISTORIC HOME

(Map p157; www.troldhaugen.com; Hop; adult/child Nkr60/free; ⏱9am-6pm May-Sep, 10am-4pm Oct-Apr) This two-storey home dates from 1885 and occupies an undeniably lovely setting on a lush and scenic peninsula by the coastal Nordåsvatnet lake, south of Bergen. Composer Edvard Grieg (see p411) and his wife Nina Hagerup spent summers here from 1885 until Grieg's death in 1907. Today the house and grounds are open to the public, and there's a multimedia Grieg exhibition and a 200-seat concert hall. Of particular interest are the **Composer's Hut**, where Edvard mustered his musical inspiration; the Steinway piano, which was a gift to celebrate Edvard and Nina's 50th wedding anniversary in 1892; and the couple's **tombs**, which are embedded in a rock face that overlooks Nordåsvatnet. It's an impressive place.

In summer, **concerts** (adult/child/student & senior Nkr220/50/160) are held on Wednesday, Saturday and Sunday and during the Bergen International Festival; tickets and schedules are available at the Bergen tourist office.

There are free buses from outside the tourist office for most of the concerts. Otherwise, take any bus from platforms 19 to 21 at the bus terminal to the Hopsbroen stop. From there, follow the signs to Troldhaugen; it's a 20-minute walk.

Siljustøl Museum
HISTORIC HOME

(Map p157; www.kunstmuseene.no; Siljustøl; adult/child/student Nkr60/free/30; ⏰9am-6pm May-Sep, 10am-4pm Oct-Apr) Another well-known Norwegian composer's home lies 3km south of Troldhaugen. Harald and Marie Sæverud lived in Siljustøl, a simple timber home. It was constructed in the 1930s of natural stone and untreated wood in an attempt to create unity with the environment. Harald Sæverud's first symphony was completed in 1920 and he endeared himself to Norwegians everywhere when, during WWII, he wrote protest music against the Nazi occupation. In 1986 he was made official composer of the Bergen International Festival. When he died in March 1992, he was given a state funeral and buried at Siljustøl, as requested. To get here, take bus 30 from platform 20 at the bus terminal.

Damsgård
MANOR

(Map p157; www.bymuseet.no; Alleen 29, Laksevåg; adult/child Nkr60/free; ⏰11am-5pm Sun mid-late May, 11am-5pm daily Jun-Aug, hourly tours 11am-3pm) The 1770 Damsgård manor, 3km west of town, may well be Norway's (if not Europe's) finest example of 18th-century rococo timber architecture. The building's superb (even over-the-top) highlight is the baroque garden, which includes sculptures, ponds and plant specimens that were common 200 years ago. To get here, take bus 19 from the centre.

Lysøen
HISTORIC HOME

(Map p157; www.lysoen.no; Lysøen; adult/child incl guided tour Nkr30/10; ⏰noon-4pm Mon-Sat, 11am-5pm Sun mid-May–Aug, noon-4pm Sun Sep) This beautiful estate, on the island of the same name, was built in 1873 as the summer residence of renowned Norwegian violinist Ole Bull (see p410). After the death of his French-born wife, Felicité Villeminot, Bull purchased the 70-hectare Lysøen island, about 20km south of Bergen. Between 1872 and 1873, he and architect Conrad Fredrik von der Lippe constructed the fantasy villa 'Lysøen'. This 'Little Alhambra' took much of its extravagant inspiration from the architecture of Moorish Granada and integrated not only intricate frets and trellises, but also onion domes, romantic garden paths, Italian marble columns and a high-ceilinged music hall made of Norwegian pine.

The grounds are criss-crossed with 13km of leisurely walks and there's a small cafe. From Bergen's bus station, take the Lysefjorden bus (566 and 567, return Nkr120) from platform 19 or 20 to Buena Quay, where there's a passenger ferry (adult/child Nkr60/30; hourly noon to 3pm Monday to Saturday, 11am to 4pm Sunday) to Lysøen.

Fløibanen
FUNICULAR

(Map p158; www.floibanen.no; Vetrlidsalmenning 21; adult/child return Nkr70/35; ⏰7.30am-midnight Mon-Fri, 8am-midnight Sat, 9am-midnight Sun Apr-Aug, shorter hr rest of yr) For an unbeatable view of the city, ride the 26-degree Fløibanen funicular to the top of Mt Fløyen (320m), with departures every 15 minutes. From the top, well-marked hiking tracks lead into the forest; the possibilities are mapped out on the free *Walking Map of Mount Fløyen* or *Turløyper På Byfjellene Nord/Øst* (Nkr10), which are available from the Bergen tourist office. Track two makes a 1.6km loop near Skomakerdiket lake and track one offers a 5km loop over hills, through forests and past several lakes. For a delightful 40-minute walk back to the city from Fløyen, follow track four clockwise and connect with track six, which switchbacks down to the harbour.

Ulriken643
FUNICULAR

(Map p157; www.ulriken643.no; adult/child return Nkr145/75, with bus Nkr245/180; ⏰9am-9pm May-Sep, 9am-9pm Oct-Apr) The Ulriksbanen cable car ascends to the radio tower and cafe atop Mt Ulriken (642m), offering a fine panoramic view of the city and surrounding fjords and mountains. An antique shuttle bus to the cable-car lower station leaves every half-hour from the Torget fish market from 9am to 9pm May to September. Otherwise, it's a 45-minute walk from the centre or a few minutes' ride on bus 2 or 31 from the post office, or bus 50 from Bryggen.

A popular excursion is to ride up on the cable car and walk four to six hours north along a well-beaten track to the top of the Fløibanen funicular railway.

Fantoft Stave Church
STAVE CHURCH

(Fantoft Stavkirke; Map p157; Paradis; adult/child/student Nkr40/15/25; ⏰10.30am-6pm mid-May–mid-Sep) The Fantoft stave church, in a lovely leafy setting (which goes by the name 'Paradise') south of Bergen, was built in Sognefjord around 1150 and moved to the southern outskirts of Bergen in 1883. It was burned down by a Satanist (and recently released heavy-metal musician) in 1992, but it has since been painstakingly reconstructed. The adjacent **cross**, originally from Sola in Rogaland, dates from 1050. From Bergen take any bus leaving from platform 20 at the bus terminal, get off at the Fantoft stop on Birkelundsbakken and walk uphill through the park for about five minutes; the light rail is another alternative.

VilVite
INTERACTIVE SCIENCE CENTRE

(Map p157; www.vilvite.no; Thormøhlensgate 51; adult/child/family late Jun–mid-Aug Nkr150/110/440, rest of yr Nkr135/90/370; ☉10am-5pm Mon-Fri, 11am-5pm Sat & Sun late Jun–mid-Aug, shorter hr rest of yr) This fantastic science centre is a must if you're travelling with children. There are 3-D films, science shows and a range of exhibits that allow you to experience G-force on a loop bicycle, drill for oil, steer a ship and try your hand at weather forecasting, among other cool activities.

☞ Tours

Boat Tours

Bergen Fjord Sightseeing
HARBOUR & FJORD TOURS

(☎55 25 90 00; www.bergen-fjordsightseeing.no; harbour/fjord tour adult Nkr100/450, child & student Nkr80/250) This company operates a one-hour harbour tour, which offers good views of Bryggen and the surrounding hills; it leaves at 2.30pm daily from mid-May to the end of August. It also runs a four-hour fjord tour to Osterfjord, north of Bergen, from May to September, with an additional 3.30pm departure in July and August. Boats depart from the waterfront next to the fish market.

M/S Madammen
HARBOUR TOURS

(adult/child/family Nkr150/80/350; ☉tours 9am & 4pm mid-May–Aug) Fifty-minute harbour tours are possible on this boat, which leaves from Torget. Tickets can be bought on board or at the tourist office.

Bus Tours

Bergen Guided Tours
SIGHTSEEING TOURS

(www.tidereiser.no; 1½/3hr tours Nkr150/300; ☉Jun-Aug) These tours offer an overview of central Bergen, covering Bryggen, Håkonshallen, the fish market and other sights in a basic 90-minute Bergen Highlights tour, which leaves at 2.30pm and 4.30pm. Better value is the three-hour Bergen & Grieg Tour, which leaves daily at 11am. Both tours depart from Torget, and tickets can be purchased on board the bus, at the Strandkaiterminal and the tourist office.

City Sightseeing Bergen
HOP-ON, HOP-OFF TOUR

(www.citysightseeingbergen.com; adult/child/family Nkr150/75/400; ☉hourly 9am-4.30pm May-Sep) This daily summer sightseeing bus does

the usual hop-on, hop-off city circuit from Gamle Bergen to the aquarium, with commentary in eight languages.

Helicopter Tours

Fonnafly
HELICOPTER SIGHTSEEING

(☎55 34 60 00; www.fonnafly.no, in Norwegian) These helicopter (three passengers) and small-plane (four passengers) flights take you high above the fjords. Both cost Nkr3600 for 20 minutes, plus Nkr1000 per 10 minutes thereafter. The views are once-in-a-lifetime stuff.

Train Tours

Bergen Express Toy Train
TOY TRAIN

(Bergens-Expressen; www.bergensexpressen.no; adult/child/family Nkr120/40/240; ☉half-hourly 10am-5pm & 6pm & 7pm mid-Jun–mid-Aug, shorter hr May–mid-Jun & mid-Aug–mid-Sep) Bergen wouldn't be a tourist town if it didn't have a toy train, which trundles along the Bryggen waterfront from opposite the Hanseatic Museum and up into some of the more interesting back streets. The trip takes 55 minutes.

Walking Tours

Guided Tours of Bryggen
BRYGGEN WALKING TOURS

(☎55 58 80 10; adult/child Nkr100/free; ☉tours 10am (German), 11am & noon (English), 1pm (Norwegian) Jun-Aug) The Bryggens Museum offers excellent walking tours through the timeless alleys of Bryggen. Tours last 90 minutes, leave from the museum, and the commentary includes descriptions of life during Bergen's trading heyday. The ticket includes admission to Bryggens Museum, Schøtstuene and the Hanseatic Museum (you can revisit these museums later on the same day).

Self-Guided Tours
SELF-GUIDED TOURS

Bryggens Museum has a (free) brochure entitled *Meeting Point Bryggen*, which allows self-guided tours covering 12 stops at historic sites around (but not inside) Bryggen.

Bergen Guide Service
BERGEN WALKING TOURS

(☎55 55 20 00; www.bergenguideservice.no; adult/child Nkr95/35; ☉3pm Jun-Aug) Bergen Guide Service does 90-minute walking tours of central Bergen, which leave from the tourist office, where tickets are also sold. The tours are in English and Norwegian.

FJORD TOURS FROM BERGEN

There are dozens of tours of the fjords from Bergen; the tourist office has a full list and you can buy tickets there or purchase online in some cases. Most offer discounts if you have a Bergen Card. For a good overview, pick up the *Round Trips – Fjord Tours & Excursions* brochure from the tourist office, which includes tours offered by a range of private companies. What follows are our highlights.

Fjord Tours (☑81 56 82 22; www.fjordtours.com) has mastered the art of making the most of limited time with a series of tours into the fjords. Its popular and year-round **Norway in a Nutshell** tour is a great way to see far more than you thought possible in a single day. The day ticket (adult/child Nkr975/500) from Bergen combines a morning train to Voss, a bus to the Stalheim Hotel and then on to Gudvangen, from where a ferry takes you up the spectacular Nærøyfjord to Flåm, joining the stunning mountain railway to Myrdal, and then taking a train back to Bergen in time for a late dinner (or for Nkr1345/685 per adult/child you can continue on to Oslo to arrive at around 10pm). From May to September, Fjord Tours also runs a range of train-bus-boat round-trips from Bergen, including the 13-hour **Explore Hardangerfjord** (adult/child Nkr1320/780), which goes via Voss, Ulvik, Eidfjord and Norheimsund, and **Sognefjord in a Nutshell** (adult/child Nkr1150/575), which explores more of Sognefjord by boat. It also has four-day tours (adult/child Nkr4410/3310) that include Oslo, Sognefjorden, Geiranger and Ålesund.

Tide Reiser (☑55 23 87 00; www.tidereiser.no; ⊘May-Oct) runs 12-hour **Hardanger Fjord Adventure** tours (adult/child Nkr790/515) that include a bus to Norheimsund and a cruise that takes in Utne, Kinsarvik, Lofthus, Eidfjord and Ulvik, with a three-hour stop in Eidfjord (where additional sightseeing costs Nkr250/200 per adult/child). These tours can also be done as a one-way trip, which is ideal if you don't plan on returning to Bergen.

Rødne Fjord Cruise (☑51 89 52 70; www.rodne.no) runs a seven-hour round-trip tour (adult/child Nkr690/310) to Rosendal that leaves Bergen at 9am, spends 3½ hours in Rosendal, which includes lunch and a guided tour of Baroniet Rosendal, and returns to Bergen at 4.15pm.

✦✦ Festivals & Events

For a full list of events, see the website www.visitbergen.com.

Bergenfest   MUSIC
(www.bergenfest.no; ⊘late Apr-early May) International music festival.

Bergen International Festival   CULTURAL
(☑55 36 55 66; www.fib.no; ⊘late May-early Jun) Held over 14 days, this is the big cultural festival of the year, with dance, music and folklore presentations throughout the city.

Bergen International Guitar Festival   MUSIC
(www.bergenguitarfestival.com; ⊘late Jun)

Bergen Food Festival   FOOD
(www.matfest.no; ⊘early–mid-Sep) Showcases locally grown or caught food, which, sadly, includes whale meat.

Bergen International Film Festival   FILM
(www.biff.no; ⊘mid-late Oct)

Night Jazz Festival   MUSIC
(www.nattjazz.no; ⊘late May-early Jun) Excellent jazz festival that is popular with Bergen's large student population.

🛏 Sleeping

Bergen has outstanding accommodation, but *always* book before arriving in town, at least in the summer months or during festivals, when Bergen fills up fast.

The tourist office has an accommodation booking service (Nkr30 for walk-ins, Nkr50 for advance booking).

TOP CHOICE **Det Hanseatiske Hotel**
HISTORIC HOTEL €€€
(Map p158; ☑55 30 48 00; www.dethanseatiskehotell.no; Finnegårdsgaten 2; d/deluxe Nkr1690/1890, ste Nkr2190-2990; ☎) Now here's something special. The only hotel to be housed inside the old timber buildings that evoke Bryggen's bygone age, Det Hanseatiske Hotel is a step back into a luxurious Bergen past. Flat-screen TVs cohabit with antique bathtubs and some extraordinary architectural features from

Bryggen's days as a Hanseatic port. Spread over two buildings and connected by a wonderful walkway, this is easily Bergen's most atmospheric hotel. If you're going to splash out, do it here.

TOP CHOICE Skuteviken Gjestehus

GUESTHOUSE €€

(Map p157; ☑93 46 71 63; www.skutevikenguest house.com; Skutevikens Smalgang 11; d/attic Nkr900/1100) This authentic timber guesthouse, set on a small cobbled street in Sandviken, has traditional decoration (such as white wicker furniture and lace cushions) and a few modern touches. Painstakingly restored by two artists whose work adorns the rooms, the guesthouse is quite simply charming. The rooms are more like apartments and the atmosphere is one of quiet sophistication.

Hotel Park Pension

HISTORIC HOTEL €€

(Map p158; ☑55 54 44 00; www.parkhotel.no; Harald Hårfagresgate 35; s/d with Fjord Pass Nkr760/1020, without s Nkr840-1100, d Nkr1090-1350; ☎) Filled with character and antiques, this family-run place spreads over two beautiful 19th-century buildings. Every room is different, although those in the building across the road from reception are more subtle. In the main building expect antique writing desks. The corner rooms are gorgeous and filled with light. The location is quiet and just a 15-minute walk from the city centre.

Skansen Pensjonat

GUESTHOUSE €

(Map p158; ☑55 31 90 80; www.skansen-pensjonat. no; Vetrlidsalmenning 29; s Nkr425-475, d Nkr700-800, apt Nkr850) There are family-run guesthouses springing up all over Bergen, but this charming, seven-room place is still one of our favourites. A wonderful location up behind the lower funicular station, a real attention to detail and many personal touches from the owners, Jannicke and Svein (who add much warmth to the place), make this a terrific choice. The rooms are light and airy, none more so than the 'balcony room', one of the nicest in Bergen. They also have views instead of TVs.

Kjellersmauet Gjestehus

GUESTHOUSE, APARTMENTS €€

(Map p158; ☑55 96 26 08; www.gjestehuset.com; Kjellersmauet 22; s/d apt from Nkr700/900) This oasis of hospitality and tradition in a delightful timber-clad street southwest of the centre is outstanding. Run by the friendly Sonja, who goes the extra mile in taking care of her guests, the Kjellersmauet has a range of small, medium and large apartments in

a building dating back to the 16th century. Wooden floors, traditional decoration and modern bathrooms make for a great stay, and some recent renovations have made this place even better.

Steens Hotell

HISTORIC HOTEL €€

(Map p158; ☑55 30 88 88; www.steenshotel.no; Parkveien 22; s/d with Fjord Pass Nkr820/1020, without s Nkr760-990, d Nkr990-1340; ☎) This lovely 19th-century building oozes period charm, from the late-19th-century antiques to the gentle curve of the stairway; the bathroom facilities have recently been renovated. A welcoming place, Steens has spacious rooms and a wonderful dining room with stained-glass windows. It also boasts some of Bergen's cheapest parking (Nkr50).

Clarion Hotel Admiral

HOTEL €€€

(Map p158; ☑55 23 64 00; www.clarionadmiral. no; C Sundtsgate 9; d Nkr1280-1995, with Bryggen views extra Nkr280-380; ☎) With sweeping views across the water to Bryggen from the balconies of its harbour-facing rooms, this well-appointed hotel promises the best view to wake up to in Bergen, if you can get a waterside room.

First Hotel Marin

HOTEL €€

(Map p158; ☑53 05 15 00; www.firsthotels.no/marin; Rosenkrantz gate 8; s/d Nkr1490/1690, with Fjord Pass from Nkr880/1260; ☎) A block back from the waterfront and with elegant hardwood floors, First Hotel Marin has a maritime theme and a great location. Some rooms have harbour views and there's a touch of class here that's sometimes lacking in chain hotels. Luggage racks that actually fit a suitcase and an ironing board, and good service are some of the thoughtful touches. A good choice.

Augustin Hotel

HOTEL €€

(Map p158; ☑55 30 40 00; www.augustin.no; C Sundtsgate 22; s/d Nkr1190/1390, with Fjord Pass from Nkr820/1140; ☎) Two things make this place stand out. First, as Bergen's oldest family-run hotel, it's renowned for the friendliness of its welcome. And second, it's one of very few hotels in Bergen that has met the exacting standards of environmental sustainability set by the Norwegian government. Modern artworks; blue-dominated, spacious rooms; and Altona (p168), a funky wine bar, round out a great package. It often has cheaper last-minute room deals in summer.

City Box

HOSTEL €

(Map p158; ☑55 31 25 00; www.citybox.no; Nygårdsgaten 31; s/d Nkr700/800, with shared bathroom Nkr500/600; 🖘) The best hostel in Bergen, City Box is a place where the owners do simple things well, such as bright modern rooms with splashes of colour, free wireless access, a minimalist designer feel without the price tag and friendly young staff. For the rooms without a bathroom, there are two showers for every five rooms, most of the rooms have kitchen facilities and there's a laundry room. Let's hope the City Box idea catches on elsewhere in Norway.

Villa Nordnes
GUESTHOUSE €

(Map p157; 🖋92 44 03 80; www.villanordnes.com; Haugeveien 34; s Nkr350-420, d Nkr650-750) This lovely, rambling house out on the Nordnes Peninsula close to the aquarium is illuminated by a fine collection of antiques and by the friendly owner, Grethe Marthinussen. It's a good choice in a quiet location.

Marken Gjestehus
HOSTEL €

(Map p158; 🖋55 31 44 04; www.marken-gjestehus. com; Kong Oscars gate 45; dm Nkr185-225, s/d Nkr700/800, with shared bathroom Nkr495/570) Midway between the harbour and the train station, this fine hostel has simple but extremely well-kept rooms. The white walls and wooden floors give an attractive sense of light and space and the communal areas are clean and pleasant. It also has a washing machine and bed linen/towels cost Nkr65/15 for those in dorms.

Victoria Hotell
HOTEL €€

(Map p158; 🖋55 31 50 30; www.victoria-hotell.no; Kong Oscars gate 29; s/d Nkr795/895; ☉Jun-Aug; 🖘) This excellent modern hotel only opens for three months a year (it's used for student accommodation the rest of the year), and that's a real shame because the rooms here are terrific – light, modern and well-equipped. The location is also good.

Bergen Vandrerhjem YMCA
HOSTEL €

(Map p158; 🖋55 60 60 55; www.bergenhostel. no; Nedre Korskirkealmenning 4; dm Nkr180-300, d with private bathroom Nkr800-900; 🖘) Gone are the days when staying in a hostel meant a long hike into town; this friendly hostel could be Norway's most central. It has that unmistakable hostel feel, same-sex or mixed dorms, kitchen facilities and a terrific rooftop terrace. Bookings are essential year-round and, unusually, bed linen is included in the price. The only drawback is that single prices may not be available in summer.

Grand Hotel Terminus
HISTORIC HOTEL €€€

(Map p158; 🖋55 21 25 00; www.ght.no; Zander Kaaesgate 6; s/d Nkr1850/2050, with Fjord Pass from Nkr990/1190; 🖘) Opposite the train station, the Grand Hotel Terminus has historically been the hotel of choice for the city's well-heeled visitors. It's now in the reliable hands of the people from Augustin Hotel, and a recent overhaul has brought much-needed freshness to the place. The rooms (some a little small) are beautifully decorated. The building dates from 1928 and there's some elaborate old-world decor in the public areas.

In City Hotel & Apartments
HOTEL, APARTMENTS €€

(Map p158; 🖋53 23 16 13; www.incity.no; Øvre Ole Bulls plass 3; d Nkr890-1490, deluxe Nkr1090-1690, penthouse Nkr1690-1990, ste Nkr1990-2490; 🖘) Modern, well-equipped apartments in the heart of town are the order of the day here. The rooms don't have a lot of personality, but they're large and comfortable and there are terrific views from the more expensive rooms.

Lone Camping
CAMPGROUND €

(Map p157; 🖋55 39 29 60; www.lonecamping.no; Hardangerveien 697, Haukeland; tent sites Nkr150 plus per person Nkr30, cabins Nkr475-1200) Lakeside campsite 20km from town, between Espeland and Haukeland. It's accessible by public transport; bus 900 runs to/from town (Nkr46, 30 minutes).

Bratland Camping
CAMPGROUND €

(Map p157; 🖋55 10 13 38; www.bratlandcamping. no; Bratlandsveien 6, Haukeland; tent sites Nkr90 plus per adult/child/electricity Nkr20/10/40, cabins Nkr390-1200) Also accessible on bus 900, this well-equipped site is 4km south of Lone Camping.

🍴 Eating

Bergen is the sort of place where international trends make their mark (sushi and tapas are all the rage and have been for some years), but you'll also find bastions of Norwegian tradition.

TOP CHOICE Pingvinen
BAR, RESTAURANT €

(Map p158; 🖋55 60 46 46; www.pingvinen. no, in Norwegian; Vaskerelven 14; mains Nkr69-149; ☉1pm-3am Sun-Fri, noon-3am Sat) Devoted to small-town Norwegian cooking, and with a delightfully informal ambience, Pingvinen is one of our favourite restaurants in Bergen. It's the sort of place where Norwegians come for meals their mothers and grandparents used to cook, and although the menu changes regularly, there are usually fish-cake sandwiches, reindeer, fish pie, whale, salmon, lamb shank and, our favourite: traditional Norwegian meatballs served with mushy peas and wild-Norwegian-berry jam. The kitchen usually closes around 9pm, whereafter there are snacks until closing time, as it becomes a cool bar.

TOP CHOICE **Potetkjelleren** TRADITIONAL NORWEGIAN €€€
(Map p158; ☎55 32 00 70; Kong Oscars gate 1a; 3-/4-/5-/6-course menu from Nkr495/565/625/685; ☺4-10pm Mon-Sat) The 'Potato Cellar' is one of Bergen's finest restaurants, the sort of place that food critics rave about but that attracts more locals than tourists. The dining area has a classy wine-cellar ambience, the service is faultless, and the menu (which changes monthly) is based around the freshest ingredients, Norwegian traditions and often subtly surprising combinations of taste. The wine list is also impeccable. Save this one for a special occasion and prepare to leave with a whole new respect for Norwegian cuisine.

TOP CHOICE **Torget Fish Market** FISH MARKET €
(Map p158; www.torgetibergen.no, in Norwegian; Torget; ☺7am-7pm Jun-Aug, 7am-4pm Mon-Sat Sep-May) For price and atmosphere, it's hard to beat the fish market. Right alongside the harbour and a stone's throw from Bryggen, here you'll find everything from smoked whale meat and salmon to calamari, fish and chips, fish cakes, prawn baguettes, seafood salads, local caviar and, sometimes, nonfishy reindeer and elk. Stallholders are usually happy to make up a take-away platter or prepare a sealed bag to take home.

🌱 Bryggen Tracteursted
TRADITIONAL NORWEGIAN €€€
(Map p158; ☎55 33 69 99; Bryggen; lunch mains Nkr75-135, dinner mains Nkr285-375; ☺lunch & dinner May-Sep) This is one of the great Bryggen eating experiences. Housed in a 1708 building that ranges across the former stables, kitchen (note the stone floor, which meant that it was the only Bryggen building allowed to have a fire) and Bergen's only extant *schøtstuene* (dining hall), this fine restaurant serves traditional Norwegian dishes that change regularly; when we were there, choices included aquavit-marinated smoked salmon, and reindeer fillet with goat's cheese. It's classy and refined in the evenings, with a more informal atmosphere during the day.

Kafe Kippers INTERNATIONAL €€
(USF; Map p157; ☎55 31 00 60; Georgenes Verft 12; lunch mains Nkr65-85, dinner mains Nkr89-159; ☺lunch & dinner) Away from the hubbub of downtown Bergen, this agreeable outdoor terrace is one of the best places for a meal or just a drink when the weather's warm. Attached to a cultural centre in an old sardine-canning factory, it has an artsy vibe and serves plentiful lunch dishes, including pastas and salads.

🌱 Pygmalion Økocafé
ORGANIC CAFE-RESTAURANT €
(Map p158; ☎55 32 33 60; Nedre Korskirkealmenning 4; ciabattas Nkr69-89, pancakes Nkr79-119, salads Nkr119-149; ☺11am-11pm; 🌿) This very cool place has contemporary art adorning its walls, a casual but classy atmosphere and tasty organic food. It's a great place at any time of the day and as good for a snack as for something slightly more substantial. There are good vegetarian choices.

Enhjørningen TRADITIONAL SEAFOOD €€€
(Map p158; ☎55 30 69 50; Bryggen; mains Nkr295-330, 3-/4-course dinner Nkr530/595; ☺4-11pm) The popular, upmarket Enhjørningen offers delicious fish and seafood in a rustic Bryggen setting. Known by locals for its unimpeachable excellence, this place is all about quality food and old-style elegance. We particularly like the grilled salmon with sweet soy sauce and leeks, but everything here is good.

Escalon TAPAS €
(Map p158; ☎55 32 90 99; Vetrlidsalmenning 21; tapas Nkr38-108; ☺3pm-midnight Sun-Fri, 1pm-midnight Sat) Tapas has taken Bergen by storm, but Escalon has been doing it since 1998. The friendly young waiters are happy to make suggestions on wine selection and the tapas are tasty and the closest you'll find in Bergen to what you'll get in Spain. Choices include oven-baked king crab with olive oil, grilled mushrooms with Spanish *jamón* and, for dessert, banana crumble toffee with mint and Cointreau.

Naboen SWEDISH €€
(Map p158; ☎55 90 02 90; www.grannen.no; Neumanns gate 20; mains Nkr198-252; ☺4-11pm Mon-Sat, 4-10pm Sun) Although the cook does a range of Norwegian dishes here, Naboen is best known for its Swedish specialities, such as venison in a vanilla and port sauce. The quality is high and it has a well-earned and devoted local following.

Wesselstuen TRADITIONAL NORWEGIAN €€€
(Map p158; ☎55 55 49 49; Øvre Ole Bulls plass 6;
lunch mains Nkr119-159, dinner mains Nkr219-279;
☺lunch & dinner) The richly decorated Wesselstuen evokes the wood-panelled dining halls
of Bergen's past and is well known as the restaurant of choice for Bergen's intellectuals.
The sirloin of reindeer (Nkr279) is excellent.

Beredt Kløver Kafe CAFE, RESTAURANT €€
(Map p158; 4th fl, Strandkaien 15; lunch mains
Nkr65-125, dinner mains Nkr125-165) This quiet
cafeteria-style place has good, if fairly
predictable, Norwegian and international
food as well as a salad bar, but you come
here for the views across the water to Bryggen, which are arguably the best in Bergen.
It's upstairs in the Kløverhuset shopping
centre.

Pølse Kiosk SAUSAGE KIOSK €
(Map p158; Kong Oscars gate 1; hot dogs from
Nkr45; ☺10am-3am) If you've been travelling
around Norway for a while, you may be
heartily sick of hot dogs bought from petrol
stations, as are we. But this place has *real*
sausages (including wild game, reindeer,
lamb and chilli) and a better-than-average
range of sauces.

Godt Brød BAKERY €
(Map p158; Nedre Korskirkealmenningen 12;
☺7am-6pm Mon-Fri, 7am-4.30pm Sat)

Sol Brød BAKERY €
(Map p158; cnr Vetrlidsalmenning & Kong Oscars
gate; ☺9am-4.30pm Mon-Fri, 9am-5pm Sat,
11am-4pm Sun)

Kjøttbasarell FOOD MARKET
(Map p158; cnr Torget & Kong Oscars gate; ☺10am-
5pm Mon-Wed & Fri, 10am-6pm Thu, 9am-4pm Sat)
This lovely old food market has cheeses,
meats and all sorts of gourmet items.

🍷 Drinking

Bergen is a great place in which to go out.
Although there's no hard-and-fast rule, the
Bryggen area is where you'll find tourist-
oriented bars (with tourist-oriented prices),
while students and a discerning Bergen
crowd hang out in places southwest of Øvre
Ole Bulls plass. In the mainly student places, summer nights can be quieter than you
might think, as the main clientele is away
on holiday.

TOP CHOICE **Altona Vinbar** WINE BAR
(Map p158; C Sundtsgate 22; ☺6pm-
12.30am Mon-Thu, 6pm-1.30am Fri & Sat) Possibly our favourite wine bar in town, Altona

Vinbar is in an intimate warren of underground rooms that date from the 16th century. With a huge selection of international
wines, soft lighting and music that ranges
from jazz to rock but never drowns out
conversation, it's hard to find fault with
this place. If you've had a few glasses, take
care with the impossibly low connecting
doors!

Pingvinen CAFE, BAR
(Map p158; Vaskerelven 14; ☺1pm-3am Sun-Fri,
noon-3am Sat) As good a bar as it is a restaurant, 'Penguin' is laid-back, funky and popular with a friendly 30-something crowd. The
late-night snacks are good if you get the
munchies, and it has all the usual beers, as
well as some boutique beers from micro-
breweries around Norway.

Capello CAFE, BAR
(Map p158; Marken 16; ☺noon-5pm Mon-Wed, noon-
8pm Thu, noon-1.30am Fri & Sat, noon-7pm Sun) An
engaging little place that does smoothies,
milkshakes, beer and, on Saturdays, pancakes. While Capello is all about '50s and '60s
decor and music downstairs (the jukebox is
filled with Elvis, the Monkeys, the Beatles
and Bob Dylan), upstairs the '70s take over. It
sometimes hosts concerts and CD launches.

Sakristiet CAFE
(Map p158; Jakobsfjorden 4, Bryggen; ☺10am-6pm)
A charming little cafe in the heart of Bryggen's wooden lanes, 'Sacristy' is an oasis of
calm with comfy armchairs, good coffee,
cakes, sandwiches and cookies. It sells a
carefully selected range of local food products. The setting is marvellous.

Det Lille Kaffe Kompaniet COFFEE BAR
(Map p158; Nedre Fjellsmug 2; ☺10am-10pm Sun-
Fri, 10am-6pm Sat) In the past few years, this
place has won nationwide competitions for
the country's best coffee, and two of its waiters have been on Norway's national coffee
team (kind of like a football team but with
espresso machines). It's a lovely, quiet little
place and it overflows onto the neighbouring stairs when the sun's out.

Grand Hotel Terminus Whisky Bar WHISKY BAR
(Map p158; Zander Kaaesgate 6; ☺5pm-midnight)
Voted Norway's best whisky bar in 2008, and
one of the most prestigious such places in
northern Europe, this grand old bar (which
dates back to 1925) in the Grand Hotel Terminus is the perfect place for a quite dram. It
promises 508 different tastes, and the oldest whisky dates back to 1960.

Café Opera
ARTS CAFE, NIGHTCLUB
(Map p158; Engen 18; ⊙11am-3am Mon-Sat, noon-12.15am Sun) By day, Café Opera has a literary-cafe feel, with artworks and good coffee that attracts artists and students. On the weekends, the crowd gets dancing at around midnight to funk, soul, blues and disco (on Wednesday and Thursday), hip-hop, soul and funk (on Friday) and reggae (on Saturday).

Vågen
CAFE, BAR
(Map p158; Kong Oskars gate 10; ⊙10am-11.30pm Mon-Wed, 10am-2am Thu-Sat, 11am-midnight Sun) This quiet cafe is where old Norwegian meets Bob Marley, with traditional Norwegian decoration, rustic wooden tables and a laid-back feel helped by occasional reggae tunes. It's a cool combination and provides a great backdrop to a lazy afternoon.

Legal
STUDENT BAR
(Map p158; cnr Nygårdsgaten & Christies gate; ⊙2pm-1.30am Sun-Thu, 2pm-2.30am Fri & Sat) One of the best student bars in Bergen, this laid-back place does retro decor and music that could be rock, but is more likely to be electronica or soft funk. Upstairs is a fine place to keep the night moving.

Bocca
LOUNGE BAR
(Map p158; 1st fl, Øvre Ole Bulls plass 3; ⊙noon-2am Sun-Tue, noon-3am Wed-Sat) Upstairs from the restaurant of the same name, Bocca draws a chic 30-something crowd who flock to the open balcony, or snuggle in the dimly lit retro salon. Music is usually lounge, with a DJ from Thursday to Saturday.

Kafe Kippers
OUTDOOR TERRACE
(USF; Map p157; Georgenes Verft 12; ⊙11am-12.30am Mon-Fri, noon-12.30am Sat & Sun) This restaurant doubles as a cool bar and is great for an outdoor drink in summer.

Naboen
BASEMENT BAR
(Map p158; Neumanns gate 20; ⊙5pm-1.30am Sun-Thu, 5pm-2.30am Fri & Sat) Downstairs from the restaurant, this place is for those who love indie rock and jazz.

☆ Entertainment

Bergen has something for everyone, from high culture to late-night live-music venues. For details and schedules, contact the tourist office. For some concerts and folklore performances, the Bergen Card (p161) offers significant discounts.

Classical Music Concerts

Bergen has a busy program of concerts throughout summer, many of them classical performances focusing on Bergen's favourite son, composer Edvard Grieg (see p411). Venues include the following:

Troldhaugen
CLASSICAL MUSIC
(adult/child/student & senior Nkr220/50/160; ⊙6pm Wed & Sun, 2pm Sat mid-Jul–Sep) See p161 for details.

Bergen Cathedral
ORGAN RECITALS
(⊙Sun & Thu mid-Jun–late Aug) Free organ recitals; see p156.

Siljustøl
CLASSICAL MUSIC
(adult/child/student & senior Nkr220/50/160; ⊙3pm Sun mid-Jul–Sep) See p162.

Grieghallen
CLASSICAL MUSIC
(Map p158; ☑55 21 61 50; www.grieghallen.no; Edvard Griegs plass; ⊙Aug-Jun) Performances by the respected Bergen Philharmonic Orchestra.

Folklore

Bergen Folklore
FOLK DANCING
(Map p158; ☑55 55 20 06; adult/child Nkr100/free; ⊙9pm Tue mid-Jun–mid-Aug) This group performs traditional one-hour music and dance routines in the atmospheric Schøtstuene, behind the Bryggens Museum. Tickets are available from the tourist office or at the door.

Nightclubs & Live Music

Ask at the tourist office or check out www.bergenlive.com (in Norwegian) to see if any major acts are in town. Grieghallen is often the venue.

Garage
ROCK MUSIC, BAR
(Map p158; www.garage.no; Christies gate 14; ⊙3pm-3am Mon-Sat, 5pm-3am Sun) Garage has taken on an almost mythical quality for music lovers across Europe. It does play live jazz and acoustic, but this is a rock venue at heart, with well-known Norwegian and international acts drawn to the cavernous basement. If he's around, ask for Dennis, who's something of a local legend (he once played in the group Electric Rain), and he'll set you straight on the local music scene. Stop by to see whether the summer Sunday jam sessions are still on.

Hulen
ROCK MUSIC
(Map p158; www.hulen.no, in Norwegian; Olaf Ryes vei 48; ⊙9pm-3am Thu-Sat mid-Aug–mid-Jun) Like Garage, Hulen enjoys a legendary status. Going strong since 1968, it's the oldest rock club in northern Europe and it's one of the classic stages for indie rock. Hulen means

'cave' and the venue is actually a converted bomb shelter. Sadly, it closes during summer when many of Bergen's students head off on holidays. It hosts a heavy-metal festival in early November.

Logen
BAR, LIVE MUSIC
(Map p158; Øvre Ole Bulls plass 6; ⊙6pm-2am Mon-Thu, 6pm-3am Fri & Sat, 8pm-3am Sun) Upstairs above the Wesselstuen restaurant, Logen is Bergen's antidote to its more famous heavy-metal and rock scene. It has a loyal local following for its concerts (Nkr50 to Nkr100) at 9pm on Sunday (jazz or alternative music) and Monday (Voksne Herrers Orkester) from September to May or June. At other times, including much of summer, it's a quiet bar.

Café Sanaa
LIVE MUSIC
(Map p158; www.sanaa.no, in Norwegian; Marken 31; ⊙8pm-3am Thu-Sat) This lovely little cafe just back from the lake spills over onto the cobblestones and draws a fun, alternative crowd with live music and some of Bergen's most creative resident DJs. Music can be jazz, tango, blues or African, depending on where the mood takes them.

Calibar
CAFE, NIGHTCLUB
(Map p158; www.calibar.no, in Norwegian; Vaskerelven 1; ⊙7pm-2am Wed & Thu, 4pm-2.30am Fri, 2pm-2.30am Sat) Funky! Calibar is hip in all

the right places with stunning lighting and decor that fuses chic modern style with retro flair (it claims to have the oldest floor in Bergen). Upstairs is cafe and conversation, but downstairs is a sweaty nightclub for a 30-something crowd drawn by '80s music it can sing along to. You have to be 24 to get in.

Kafe Kippers/USF Vertfet
LIVE JAZZ
(USF; Map p157; ✆55 31 00 60; www.bergen jazzforum.com, www.usf.no; Georgenes Verft 12; admission Nkr170; ⊙10pm Fri Sep-May) Check the website for the latest concerts; see also also p167.

Café Opera
NIGHTCLUB
(Map p158; Engen 18) Great and varied DJ-spun tunes from Wednesday to Saturday from midnight to 3am. See also p169.

Felíz Club Bar Lounge
LOUNGE BAR, NIGHTCLUB
(Map p158; www.feliz.no; Øvre Ole Bulls plass 3; ⊙11pm-2.30am Thu-Sat) Slick nightclub with dancefloor and quiet corners; you must be at least 20 years old to get in on Thursday, and at least 24 on Friday and Saturday.

Rick's
BAR, NIGHTCLUB
(Map p158; Veiten 3; cover charge Nkr90; ⊙1pm-3am Sun-Thu, 1pm-3.30am Fri & Sat) Three-in-one venue with cool street-level wine bar (called Silver) and basement live music and 24-and-over disco.

SHOPPING IN BRYGGEN

The wooden alleyways of Bryggen have become a haven for artists and craftspeople, and there are stunning little shops and boutiques at every turn. Before entering the lanes, start at the waterfront with Juhls' Silver Gallery. **Per Vigeland** (www.pervigeland.no; Jacobsfjorden, Bryggen; ⊙10am-6pm mid-May–Aug, shorter hr rest of yr) is a local jewellery designer working with silver and gold-plated silver, while **Živa Jelnikar Design** (www. zj-d.com; Jacobsfjorden, Bryggen; ⊙10am-5pm Mon-Fri, 11am-4pm Sat & Sun Jun-Aug, shorter hr rest of yr), opposite the entrance to the Bryggen Visitors Centre, is the highly original work of Slovenian designer Živa Jelnikar, with mostly silver and copper pieces; both have on-site workshops. Also worth checking out is the heavier jewellery of **Svala** (Jacobsfjorden, Bryggen; ⊙11am-3pm Jun-Aug, shorter hr rest of yr).

But it's not just about jewellery. **Kvams Flisespikkeri** (Map p158; www.kvams-flisespik keri.com, in Norwegian; Bredsgården, Bryggen; ⊙9am-6pm mid-May–mid-Sep, shorter hr rest of yr) sells lovely Bryggen-centric paintings, block prints and other artworks by Ketil Kvam. **Læverkstedet** (Map p158; Jacobsfjorden, Bryggen; ⊙10am-8pm mid-May–mid-Aug, shorter hr rest of yr) is the purveyor of the softest moose leather in the form of jackets, bags and other knick-knacks.

Locally designed cushions, bags and gloves in bright colours are found at **Moe, Udd & Tollefson** (www.mut.no; Jacobsfjorden, Bryggen; ⊙noon-7pm mid-May–mid-Aug, shorter hr rest of yr), while the quirky **Bergen Steinsenter** (www.bergen-steinsenter.no; Bredsgården, Bryggen; ⊙11am-4pm Mon-Sat Jun–mid-Sep, shorter hr rest of yr) has some stunning geological specimens from around Norway and further afield. Finally, **Hetland** (Jacobsfjorden, Bryggen; ⊙10am-4pm May-Aug, shorter hr rest of yr) has reproductions of the eye-catching works of Bergen artist Audun Hetland.

Shopping

Juhls' Silver Gallery

ARCTIC JEWELLERY & HOMEWARES

(Map p158; www.juhls.no; Bryggen 39; ⊙9am-10pm Mon-Sat, noon-7pm Sun mid-Jun–Sep, 10am-5pm Mon-Fri, 10am-2pm Sat Oct–mid-Jun) This wonderful jewellery shop sells exquisite silver jewellery and other items crafted by Regine Juhls at her workshop high above the Arctic Circle (p348). Her 'Tundra' collection strongly evokes the icy wastes of the north, and Sami culture is another strong influence.

Ruben's Varme Glider

CHILDREN'S TOYS

(Map p158; www.rubens.no, in Norwegian; Vetrlidsalmenning 5; ⊙9.30am-5pm Mon-Sat) On the street climbing the hill towards the lower funicular station, this is one of the best toy shops in Norway. It's mostly modern stuff, but the selection is wide-ranging.

ⓘ Information

Dangers & Annoyances

Although Bergen is generally a safe city, pickpockets are known to operate around the fish market and Bryggen areas, so as in any tourist city, keep a close watch on your belongings.

Emergencies

Ambulance (☑113)

Police (☑112)

Tourist Information

Bergen Turlag DNT office (Map p158; ☑55 33 58 10; www.bergen-turlag.no; Tverrgaten 4; ⊙10am-4pm Mon-Wed & Fri, 10am-6pm Thu, 10am-2pm Sat) Maps and information on hiking and hut accommodation throughout western Norway.

Bryggen Visitors Centre (Map p158; Jacobsfjorden, Bryggen; ⊙9am-5pm mid-May–mid-Sep)

Tourist office (Map p158; ☑55 55 20 00; www.visitbergen.com; Vågsallmenningen 1; ⊙8.30am-10pm Jun-Aug, 9am-8pm May & Sep, 9am-4pm Mon-Sat Oct-Apr) One of the best and busiest in

the country, Bergen's tourist office distributes the free and excellent *Bergen Guide* booklet.

Websites

Lonely Planet (www.lonelyplanet.com/norway/bergen-and-the-western-fjords) Planning advice, author recommendations, traveller reviews and insider tips.

ⓘ Getting There & Away

Air

Bergen airport (Map p157; ☑67 03 15 55) is at Flesland, about 19km southwest of the centre. Apart from international airlines (see p435), there are the following domestic options:

Norwegian (www.norwegian.com) Flights to Oslo and Tromsø.

SAS (www.sas.no) Oslo and Stavanger.

Widerøe (www.wideroe.no) Tromsø, Bodø and other northern destinations.

Boat

The Hurtigruten coastal ferry leaves from the Hurtigruteterminalen (Map p158), southwest of the centre, at 8pm daily from mid-April to mid-September, and from 10.30pm the rest of the year. See p439 for details.

International ferries to/from Bergen dock at Skoltegrunnskaien (Map p157), northwest of the Rosenkrantz tower. See p436 for details on international sailings.

For more information on fjord cruises from Bergen, see the boxed text on p164. The following operators offer express boat services:

Fjord1 (☑55 90 70 70; www.fjord1.no; Strandkaiterminal) In addition to its tours, Fjord1 offers at least one daily ferry from Bergen to Sogndal (Nkr570; five hours), with some services going on to Flåm (Nkr665).

Flaggruten (☑53 40 91 20; www.flaggruten. no; Strandkaiterminal) Twice-daily services from Sunday to Friday to Haugesund (one-way/return Nkr510/625) and Stavanger (Nkr750/950), with just one on Saturdays.

Rødne Fjord Cruise (☑51 89 52 70; www.rodne.no; ⊙May-Aug) Summer express boats from Bergen to Rosendal (adult/child one-way

BUSES FROM BERGEN

DESTINATION	DEPARTURES (DAILY)	COST (NKR)	DURATION (HR)
Ålesund	1-2	619	10
Oslo	2	558-680	11
Stavanger	5	490	5½
Stryn	2	489	6½
Trondheim	1	790	14½

Nkr310/155, return Nkr470/235) twice daily from Monday to Friday and once on Saturday and Sunday. It leaves just northwest of Strandkaiterminal.

Bus

The Bergen bus terminal is located on Vestre Strømkaien.

Train

The spectacular train journey between Bergen and Oslo (Nkr299 to Nkr775, 6½ to eight hours, five daily) runs through the heart of Norway. Other destinations include Voss (Nkr169, one hour, hourly) and Myrdal (Nkr253, 2¼ hours, up to nine daily) for connections to the Flåmsbana railway.

ⓘ Getting Around

To/From The Airport

Flybussen (www.flybussen.no; adult 1-way/return Nkr90/150, child Nkr45/80; 45min) Runs up to four times hourly between the airport, the Radisson SAS Royal Hotel, the main bus terminal and opposite the tourist office on Vågsallmenningen.

Bicycle

Sykkelbutikken (www.sykkelbutikken.no; Kong Oscars gate 81; per weekend from Nkr350, mountain bike per day/week Nkr250/800, bag/helmet Nkr50/75; ⊙10am-8pm Mon-Fri, 10am-4pm Sat) Bicycle hire near the train station.

Bus

City buses (☏177) Fares (adult Nkr25) beyond the centre are based on distance. Free bus 100 runs between Bryggen and the bus terminal.

Car & Motorcycle

Metered parking limited to 30 minutes or two hours applies all over central Bergen. The largest and cheapest (Nkr100 per 24 hours) indoor car park is the 24-hour Bygarasjen at the bus terminal; elsewhere you'll pay Nkr200. The tourist office has two brochures covering where to park in Bergen.

Boat

From late May to late August, the **Vågen Harbour Ferry** (Map p158; 1-way/return adult Nkr40/60, child Nkr20/40; ⊙every 30min 10am-6pm) runs between the Torget fish market and Tollbodhopen at Nordnes (near the Bergen Aquarium); your boat ticket entitles you to a 25% discount on the aquarium admission fee.

VOSS

POP 13,902

Voss sits on a lovely lake not far from the fjords and this position has earned it a world-renowned reputation as Norway's adventure capital. It draws both beginners and veterans of the thrillseeking world for white-water rafting, bungee jumping and just about anything you can do from a parasail; many of the activities take you out into the fjords.

⊙ Sights

Vangskyrkja & St Olav's Cross
CHURCH & STONE CROSS

(Uttrågata; adult/child Nkr20/free; ⊙10am-4pm Mon-Sat, 1-4pm Sun Jun-Aug, shorter hr rest of yr) Voss' stone church occupies the site of an ancient pagan temple. A Gothic-style stone church was built here in the mid-13th century. Although the original stone altar and unique wooden spire remain, the Lutheran Reformation of 1536 saw the removal of many original features. The 1923 stained-glass window commemorates the 900th anniversary of Christianity in Voss. Miraculously, the building escaped destruction during the intense German bombing of Voss in 1940.

In a field around 150m southeast of the tourist office stands a weathered **stone cross** erected by King Olav Haraldsson den Heilige (St Olav) in 1023 to commemorate the local conversion to Christianity.

Prestegardsmoen
PUBLIC PARK

The Prestegardsmoen Recreational and Nature Reserve, which extends south from Voss Camping, is a series of hiking tracks through elm, birch and pine forests with 140 species of plants and 124 bird species.

Hangursbahnen
CABLE CAR

(www.vossresort.no; adult/child Nkr100/60; ⊙11am-5pm Jun-early Sep) This cable car whisks you to Mt Hangur (660m), high above Voss, for stunning panoramic views over the town and the surrounding mountains.

Voss Folkemuseum
REGIONAL FOLK MUSEUM

The main portion of the Voss Folk Museum is the **Mølstertunet Museum** (Mølstervegen 143; adult/child Nkr50/free; ⊙10am-5pm mid-May–mid-Sep, shorter hr rest of yr), on a hilltop at the farm Mølster, high above Voss. The collection of 16 historic farm buildings once typical of the region dates from 1600 to 1870. There are guided tours on the hour, every hour.

Dagestadmuséet
MUSEUM

(www.dagestadmuseet.no, in Norwegian; Helgavangen 52; adult/child/student & senior Nkr40/free/30; ⊙11am-2pm Tue-Sun Jun–mid-Aug) This museum, located 1.5km south of the town

If slow boats up the fjords seem like a pretty tame response to extraordinary Norwegian landscapes, Voss may be your antidote.

For booking any of the following, your best bet is to contact the operator directly. Another option is **Destinasjon Voss** (☎40 61 77 00; www.visitvoss.no; ⊙9am-5pm Mon-Fri, 9am-3pm Sat, noon-5pm Sun), a central booking service for activities and accommodation.

Paragliding, Parasailing & Bungee Jumping

Nordic Ventures (☎56 51 00 17; www.nordicventures.com; ⊙Apr–mid-Oct) is one of the most professional operators of its kind in Norway, offering tandem paragliding flights (Nkr1500), parasailing (solo/dual flights Nkr575/950) and even 180m-high, 115km/h bungee jumps (Nkr1800) from a parasail! It claims to offer the highest bungee jump in Europe. As its motto says: 'Be brave. Even if you're not, pretend to be. No one can tell the difference.'

Skydiving is also possible through **Skydive Voss** (☎56 51 10 00; www.skydivevoss.no).

Kayak Fjord Expeditions

If you do one activity in Voss (or even anywhere in the fjords), make it this one. The guided kayak tours offered by Nordic Ventures are the perfect way to experience Hardangerfjord and stunning Nærøyfjord (p203) and beyond without neither hurry nor crowds. The tours come in a range of options.

One day (nine-hour) tours cost Nkr975 (including lunch and transport to/from the fjord), while the two-day version costs Nkr2195 and allows you to camp on the shores of the fjord. But our favourite is the three-day kayaking and hiking expedition (Nkr2995), which explores the fjords in kayaks and then takes you high above them for unrivalled views.

Nordic Ventures also rents out kayaks (one/two/three days Nkr525/825/1295) if you'd rather branch out on your own.

White-Water Rafting

Voss Rafting Senter (☎56 51 05 25; www.vossrafting.no) specialises in white-water rafting (Nkr875 to Nkr1395) with some gentler, more family-friendly options (from Nkr575). Rafters (and riverboarders) can choose between three very different rivers: the Stranda (Class III to IV), Raundalen (Class III to V) and Vosso (Class II). Not to be outdone in the motto stakes, the company's motto is: 'We guarantee to wet your pants.'

Skiing

The ski season in Voss usually lasts from early December until April. The winter action focuses on the cable-car route up Mt Hangur from Voss, where there's a winter ski school. Those with vehicles can opt for Bavallen, 5km north of the centre, which is used for international downhill competitions. On the plateau and up the Raundalen Valley at Mjølfjell, you'll also find excellent cross-country skiing.

Other Activities

Voss Rafting Senter organises **canyoning** (Nkr875), **waterfall abseiling** (from Nkr850), **riverboarding** (Nkr890), **fishing** (from Nkr575) and **hiking** (from Nkr475).

For additional guided-hiking options, contact **Vossafjell** (☎99 15 15 00; www.vossafjell.no) or its partner **Heritage Adventures** (www.heritageadventures.no).

Voss tourist office can also provide details of **cycling routes** and **self-guided hikes**, and sells **fishing permits** (1-day/3-day/season Nkr50/100/300).

For **horse riding** (per hour Nkr160), contact **Mjølfjell Fjellstove** (☎56 52 31 50; www.mjolfjell.no).

centre, was opened in 1950 by renowned local woodcarver Magnus Dagestad (1865–1957) and features his lifetime of carvings, drawings and traditional wooden furniture, as well as works by his wife Helena. It's an unusual and worthwhile exhibit.

🔗 Tours

Although normally done from Oslo or Bergen, the Norway in a Nutshell tour (see the boxed text, p164) can also be done from Voss (adult/child Nkr650/340). It involves rail trips from Voss to Myrdal and from there to Flåm, then the boat to Gudvangen and the bus back to Voss. Book through the tourist office, any travel agency or directly through **NSB** (☑56 52 80 07; www.nsb.no) at the train station.

Ask also at the tourist office for details on day excursions to Ulvik and Eidfjord on Hardangerfjord.

🎊 Festivals

Extreme Sports Festival   SPORT & MUSIC
(www.ekstremsportveko.com; ☉late Jun) A week-long festival that combines all manner of extreme sports (skydiving, paragliding and base jumping) with local and international music acts.

Voss Blues & Roots Festival   MUSIC
(☉last weekend of Aug) One of Norway's better music festivals.

Vossajazz   MUSIC
(www.vossajazz.no; ☉Mar)

Sheep's Head Food Festival   FOOD
(www.smalahovesleppet.no, in Norwegian; ☉late Sep) The culinary delights of sheep heads.

🛏 Sleeping

TOP CHOICE **Fleischer's Hotel**   HISTORIC HOTEL €€
(☑56 52 05 00; www.fleischers.no; Evangervegen; s Nkr845-1195, d Nkr1195-1690; P🅿🏊) For historic character, the beautiful Fleischer's Hotel, opened in its current form in 1889, oozes antique charm and is the best place in town. Some rooms have lake views, there's a swimming pool with a child's pool and there's even a children's check-in platform – a nice touch. Edvard Grieg stayed here in 1901 if you're into celebrity hotel stays.

Park Hotel Vossevangen   HOTEL €
(☑56 53 10 00; www.parkvoss.no; Uttrågata 1; s/d from Nkr875/1250; P🅿🛜) While this place lacks the elegance of Fleischer's Hotel, the modern rooms are nonetheless very comfortable. Many overlook the lake Vossevangen.

Voss Vandrerhjem   HOSTEL €€
(☑56 51 20 17; www.vosshostel.com; Evangervegen 68; dm/s/d from Nkr195/660/880; P🅿@) This modern hostel offers decent (if a touch overpriced) rooms with en suite and fine lake views; ask for a top-floor, lakeside room. Bicycles can be hired here and there's a free sauna.

Fleischer's Appartement   APARTMENTS €€
(☑56 52 05 00; www.fleischers.no; Evangervegen 13; 2-/4-bed apt Nkr1050/1800; 🅿) This lakeside annexe of Fleischer's Hotel offers small but adequate self-catering units.

Voss Camping   CAMPGROUND €
(☑56 51 15 97; www.vosscamping.no; Prestegardsalléen 40; tent/caravan sites from Nkr150/220, cabins from Nkr600; ☉Easter-Sep; P🅿🛜) Lakeside and centrally located, Voss Camping has basic facilities and can get a bit rowdy in summer.

Tvinde Camping   CAMPGROUND €
(☑56 51 69 19; www.tvinde.no; Tvinde; tent sites per person from Nkr120, cabins from Nkr450; ☉year-round; P🅿🛜) A scenic alternative beside a waterfall about 12km north of town. Access is on the Voss–Gudvangen bus (Nkr40, 20 minutes).

🍴 Eating

TOP CHOICE **Tre Brør Café**   CAFE €
(www.vosscafe.no; Vangsgata 28; sandwiches & light meals Nkr65-135; ☉9.30am-9pm Sun-Wed, 9.30am-midnight Thu-Sat; 🛜) This lovely little cafe in one of Voss' prettiest buildings is laid-back and stylish all at once, and the food's also fantastic. It has a small selection of sandwiches, salads and pasta dishes and a changing daily menu with the odd Asian twist. It also does great coffees, teas and chai latte, and there's occasional live music.

Ringheim Kafé   TRADITIONAL CAFE €€
(Vangsgata 32; mains Nkr105-139; ☉lunch & dinner) One of numerous cafes lined up along the main Vangsgata thoroughfare, Ringheim has outdoor tables and a cafeteria-style interior. There are some real stars on the menu, including the elk burgers (Nkr139) and *hjortekoru* (Nkr125), the local smoked sausage with potato and cabbage stew. It also does children's menus (Nkr55).

Café Stasjonen   CAFE, RESTAURANT €€
(Uttrågata 1; snacks & light meals Nkr70-105, mains Nkr155-225; ☉10am-midnight Sun-Thu, 10am-1am Fri & Sat) In the Park Hotel Vossevangen, this train-themed cafe offers snacks, light meals, a small salad bar (Nkr95) and mains such as spare ribs.

ℹ Information

Tourist office (☑56 52 08 00; www.visitvoss.no; Uttrågata; ☉8am-7pm Mon-Fri, 9am-7pm Sat, noon-7pm Sun Jun-Aug, 8.30am-3.30pm Mon-Fri Sep-May)

ℹ️ Getting There & Away

BUS Buses stop at the train station, west of the centre. Frequent bus services connect Voss with Bergen (Nkr137, two hours), Flåm (Nkr126, 1¼ hours) and Sogndal (Nkr266, three hours), via Gudvangen and Aurland.

TRAIN The **NSB** (📞56 52 80 00) rail services on the *Bergensbanen* to/from Bergen (Nkr169, one hour, hourly) and Oslo (Nkr299 to Nkr686, 5½ to six hours, five daily) connect at Myrdal (Nkr103, 50 minutes) with the scenic line down to Flåm (see p199).

AROUND VOSS

Stalheim

POP 200

This gorgeous little spot high above the valley is an extraordinary place.

Between 1647 and 1909, Stalheim was a stopping-off point for travellers on the Royal Mail route between Copenhagen, Christiania (Oslo) and Bergen. A road was built for horses and carriages in 1780. The mailmen and their weary steeds rested in Stalheim and changed to fresh horses after climbing up the valley and through the Stalheimskleiva gorge, flanked by the thundering Stalheim and Sivle waterfalls. Although a modern road winds up through two tunnels from the valley floor, the **old mail road** (Stalheimskleiva) climbs up at an astonishing 18% gradient. As tour buses, improbably, use this road, it's a one-way road: you can drive down, but not up.

👁 Sights

Everyone comes here for the views from the Stalheim Hotel garden. If you're not staying at the hotel, the **terrace** (admission free; 🕘9.30am-6pm mid-May–Sep) has breathtaking views down Nærøydalen.

The **Stalheim Folkemuseum** (📞56 52 01 22; Stalheim; adult/child Nkr50/free; 🕘on request), near the hotel, includes folk exhibits and 30 log buildings laid out as a traditional farm. It only opens if there are 10 or more visitors; ask at the hotel for details.

🏃 Activities

There are at least two rewarding half-day hikes that begin at Stalheim.

Husmannsplassen Nåli   HIKE

Norwegians delight in building their homes in the most inaccessible places, but Husmannsplassen Nåli (the Cotter's Farm

of Nåli), along the ledge from Stalheim high above Nærøydalen, may just win the prize. Built in 1870 when the first cotter moved there with two cows, four sheep and 11 goats, it was occupied until 1930. Now overgrown, it's an evocative spot, although the route there (two hours return) is not for the faint-hearted. The path beneath the cliff wall is extremely narrow in parts and there is nothing between you and the valley floor far below; don't even think of walking here after rain. As long as you don't suffer from vertigo, it's one of Norway's most beautiful walks. Ask directions from the reception of the Stalheim Hotel.

Brekkedalen   HIKE

This three-hour return hike leads up into the valley above Stalheim. Locals in the know claim this is the region's prettiest walk, and the views are, as you'd expect, magnificent. It's a relatively easy way to leave behind the crowds at the hotel and have this stunning high country all to yourself. The tourist office in Voss has route descriptions, or ask at Stalheim Hotel for directions.

🛏 Sleeping

Stalheim Hotel   HISTORIC HOTEL €€€

TOP CHOICE (📞56 52 01 22; www.stalheim.com; s/d from Nkr980/1430, with Fjord Pass Nkr930/1360, half-board Nkr1380/2180; 🕘mid-May–early Oct; 🅿️📶) Arguably Norway's most spectacularly sited hotel, this stunning place has large rooms, around half of which have glorious views. Not surprisingly, the hotel (room 324 in particular) once featured in *Conde Nast's* 'best rooms with a view'. Unfortunately, rooms without a view cost the same. The buffets at lunch (Nkr250) and dinner (Nkr450) are excellent, but lighter meals are available and meals work out cheaper if you pay half-board rates. Despite the daily onslaught of tour groups, the friendly staff somehow maintain their equanimity.

Stalheim Fjord og Fjellhytter

    MOUNTAIN HUTS €

(📞56 51 28 47; www.stalheim.no; 4- to 6-person cabins per night/week from Nkr600/2400) In the village just beyond the hotel.

Stalheimsøy Gard   FARMHOUSE €€

(📞56 52 00 22; www.stalheimsoy.no; 6-bed farmhouse per night/week Nkr1200/7500) Down in the valley far below.

ℹ️ Getting There & Away

To reach Stalheim from Voss (Nkr72, one hour, four to 11 daily), take any bus towards the towns of Gudvangen and Aurland, but you may have to hike 1.3km up from the main road unless you can persuade the bus driver to make the short detour.

Myrdal

Between the towns of Voss and Finse, Myrdal is the junction of the Oslo–Bergen railway and the spectacularly steep Flåmsbana railway; it's also a famous stop on the Norway in a Nutshell tour. From here, the dramatic Flåmsbana line twists 20km down to Flåm on Aurlandsfjorden, an arm of Sognefjorden. For more information, see p199.

HARDANGERFJORD

Running from the Atlantic to the steep wall of central Norway's Hardangervidda Plateau, Hardangerfjord is classic Norwegian fjord country. There are many beautiful corners, although our pick would probably be Eidfjord, Ulvik and Utne, while Folgefonna National Park offers glacier walks and top-level hiking. For details about exploring Hardangerfjord from Bergen, see p164. Also check out www.hardangerfjord.com.

Norheimsund

POP 2132

Quiet little Norheimsund serves as the gateway to Hardangerfjord. There are more beautiful places further into the fjord network, but it's a pretty little town nonetheless and makes for a pleasant introduction to what lies ahead. Ferries from here head to Eidfjord, making it a useful staging post if you're travelling on public transport.

◉ Sights

Steinsdalsfossen   WATERFALL
Just 1km west of Norheimsund along Rv7, this 50m-high waterfall is a far cry from Norway's highest, but it does offer the chance to walk behind the water. It can get overcrowded with tour buses in summer; inexplicably, this is one of the most visited natural sites in Norway.

⚓ Hardanger Fartøyvernsenter
BOAT-BUILDING MUSEUM
(☑56 55 33 50; www.fartoyvern.no; adult/child Nkr80/30; ⊙10am-5pm early May-early Sep) This engaging museum keeps alive the local boat-building tradition and is home to old wooden boats, exhibitions on restoration procedures and rope-making, as well as temporary exhibitions. Children can also try their hand at building a boat. From late June to early August at 1pm on Wednesday and Thursday, the museum also offers two-hour cruises on the fjord in a restored cutter; prices vary depending on the number of people.

🛏 Sleeping

Sandven Hotel   HISTORIC HOTEL €€
TOP CHOICE (☑56 55 20 88; www.sandvenhotel.no; s/d from Nkr975/1250, ste Nkr1500-2000; P🅟🛜) Located right on the waterfront in the centre of Norheimsund, the atmospheric Sandven Hotel dates from 1857 and has loads of charm, expansive balconies and excellent views. You may want to try the Crown Prince suite – this is where the future king of Norway once stayed. It also has a pleasant fjord-side cafe.

Oddland Camping   CAMPGROUND €
(☑56 55 16 86; oddland.camping@kvamnet.no; tent sites Nkr140, cabins from Nkr450) This well-equipped, family-run camp by the lake has good fjord views and simple cabins. The staff can rent out rowboats.

❶ Information

Norheimsund tourist office (☑56 55 15 85; www.visitkvam.no; ⊙10am-6pm Jun–mid-Aug)

❶ Getting There & Away

Of the up to five daily buses between Bergen (Nkr120) and Norheimsund, the 7.30am bus connects with the 8.50am ferry that travels from Norheimsund to Eidfjord (one-way Nkr260). From Voss, most services require a change in Arna.

Øystese

POP 1758

Another pleasant little town, just around the shoreline from Norheimsund, Øystese has an exceptional art gallery of the kind you just don't expect to find in a small village on the shores of a Norwegian fjord. There are also some interesting excursions in the vicinity, including a visit to one of Hardangerfjord's famed fruit farms. And collectors of quirky local facts will enjoy learning that Øystese's furniture factories produce 75% of all coffee tables made in Norway. So there you go.

◉ Sights

Kunsthuset Kabuso CONTEMPORARY ART GALLERY
(www.kabuso.no; adult/child Nkr50/free; ⊙10am-5pm Tue-Sun Jun-Aug, shorter hr rest of yr) One of the best art galleries in the Norwegian fjord

country, the Kunsthuset Kabuso attracts artists of world renown – in recent years, Damien Hirst, Matthew Barney and Candice Breitz have all exhibited here. In addition to cutting-edge contemporary artists, it also showcases traditional arts. From late June until mid-August, the museum has high-quality **classical music concerts** (Nkr150) on Sundays at 1pm. The program always includes works by Edvard Grieg, as well as other well-known composers, and the museum's small theatre has fantastic acoustics. It's not usually necessary to book in advance.

Ingebrigt Vik Museum   SCULPTURE MUSEUM
(www.kabuso.no; adult/child Nkr50/free; ☺10am-5pm Tue-Sun Jun-Aug, shorter hr rest of yr) Adjacent to the Kunsthuset Kabuso and overseen by the same people, this octagonal gallery is dedicated to the renowned Norwegian sculptor of the same name (1867–1927), who was born in Øystese.

Steinstø Fruktgard   FRUIT FARM
(www.steinsto.no; Steinstø; ☺11am-6pm Sun-Fri, 11am-4pm Sat mid-Jun–mid-Oct) Hardangerfjord is renowned as a fruit-growing region, especially for its apples. Summer is a great time to visit this farm, a short distance east of Øystese, with strawberries becoming ripe in June, while July is all about raspberries, cherries, plums, apples and pears. It runs guided tours of the farm for groups, and a cafe serves great apple juice and one of the best apple pies (Nkr75) you'll ever taste.

🛏 Sleeping

Hardangerfjord Hotel   HOTEL €€€
(☑56 55 63 00; www.hardangerfjord-hotell.no; s/d from Nkr1230/1850; ⓟ🎏🏊) The best place to stay in town, this large modern hotel on the fjord has views across the water to mountains crowned by the Folgefonna ice-cap. Rooms have been attractively renovated (although the bathrooms let the side down a little). It has a restaurant, heated swimming pool and minigolf, and can arrange other activities.

ℹ Information

Øystese tourist office (☑56 55 15 85; k-reise@online.no; ☺10am-6pm mid-May–Aug) Summer-only information.

ℹ Getting There & Away

There are at least five daily buses between Øystese and Bergen (Nkr135, 1¾ hours) via Norheimsund.

Around Øystese

Hardanger Fjordreiser (☑90 71 96 40; www.hfr.no; Steinstø; adult/child return Nkr200/110; ☺late May-early Sep) runs boat tours aboard *M/S Peer Gynt* from the Steinstø pier up the lovely and narrow Fykesund to the small village of **Botnen**, which is inaccessible by road. The village is also the birthplace of the Hardanger fiddle. Services operate between two and five times weekly.

Ulvik

POP 1129
There's something special about Ulvik, which is located in the innermost reaches of Hardangerfjord and the heart of Norway's apple-growing territory. Framed by hills and mountains and with wonderful views up the fjord, Ulvik is bathed in tranquil silence once the tourist boats disappear. There's not a lot to see in Ulvik itself, but you're in the heart of stunning fjord country with plenty of cycling and hiking opportunities in the surrounding hills and with farmstead visits possible. The whole area is delightful in May, when the blossoms are out.

⊙ Sights & Activities

The tourist office can point you in the direction of hikes in the surrounding area, including a 5km trail that takes you past four **fruit farms** in the hills above town; one of these, the **Hardanger Saft og Suderfabrikk** (Hardanger Juice & Cider Factory; www.hardangersider. no, in Norwegian) also produces apple cider. Visits to the farms are possible for groups, but ask the tourist office if you can tag along to a tour that's already going.

The tourist office also has **bicycle hire** (half-/full-day Nkr100/150) and can arrange **water-skiing** (Nkr200).

🛏 Sleeping & Eating

🔺TOP CHOICE **Doktergarden**   B&B €€
(☑90 76 70 98; www.doktergarden.no; s/d from Nkr500/800; ⓟ🎏) This charming old timber farmhouse, around 2km east of the village centre and right by the fjord, dates back to the early 1920s. The lovingly kept rooms are bright and comfortable and have fjord views; four of the five rooms have shared bathrooms. As if you weren't already feeling indulged, it also offers massages (40/90 minutes Nkr400/600) and facial treatments (Nkr400). And best of all, Bjørnar

EXPLORING HARDANGERFJORD FROM ULVIK

Little Ulvik is a superb base from which to explore Hardangerfjord. The tourist office hands out a terrific brochure, *Excursions by Public Transport from Ulvik*, that outlines a range of self-guided day excursions that take in much of Hardangerfjord by boat, ferry and express boat from May to September. Options include the following:

» **Eidfjord** (adult/child return Nkr447/294, Monday to Friday except school holidays) – via Bruravik and Brimnes; allows time at Hardangervidda Nature Centre and Vøringsfossen; departs Ulvik at 8.55am and arrives back at 3.10pm.

» **Kinsarvik and Utne** (adult/child Nkr238/120, Monday to Friday) – via Bruravik, Brimnes, Kvanndal and Granvin, with a visit to the Hardanger Folk museum in Utne. It departs Ulvik at 8.55am and arrives back at 4.35pm.

» **Hardanger Grand Tour** (adult/child Nkr340/172, Monday to Friday) – the same as the previous tour but also stops in Odda.

» **Voss** (adult/child Nkr144/72, daily) – up to five departures daily.

» **Norway in a Nutshell** (adult/child Nkr767/387, daily) – Ulvik's own branch of the famous round trip leaves Ulvik at 8.55am and goes via Voss, Gudvangen, Flåm and Myrdal and returns to Ulvik at 6.40pm (5.45pm on Saturdays).

and Bjørg will make you feel like you're part of the family.

Rica Brakanes Hotel　　　FJORD HOTEL **€€**
(Strand Fjordhotel; ☎56 52 61 05; www.brakanes-hotel.no; s/d Nkr835/1210, with fjord views Nkr935/1410; P⊜🛜🛏) This huge modern hotel has a front-row seat to some of the best views in Hardangerfjord. There are no finer views in Ulvik than from the balconies in its fjord-facing rooms. Rooms are well-turned out and the restaurant serves buffet and à la carte meals (buffet dinner Nkr395, mains from Nkr185).

Ulvik Fjord Hotel　　HOTEL, CAMPGROUND **€€**
(☎56 52 61 70; www.ulvikfjord.no; tent/caravan sites Nkr150/200, 4-person cabins from Nkr500, s/d from Nkr690/950; P🛜) An excellent choice, by the fjord at the entrance to town, this well-run guesthouse offers very comfortable rooms, some of which have balconies overlooking a bubbling stream. It's across the road from the water, but the campsites and simple huts are right by the fjord. It also has a cafe serving home-cooked meals using local produce, as well as sandwiches and pizzas.

❶ Information

Ulvik tourist office (☎56 52 62 80; www.visitulvik.com; ⊙9am-5pm Mon-Fri, 11am-3pm Sat & Sun Jun-Sep, shorter hr rest of yr)

❶ Getting There & Away

Buses run three to five times daily between Voss and Ulvik (Nkr93, 1¼ hours).

Eidfjord

POP 958

In the innermost reaches of Hardangerfjord, Eidfjord is one of the most beautifully sited towns in this part of Norway. Dwarfed by sheer mountains and cascading waterfalls, only accessible via spiral tunnels and close to charming farms perched on mountain ledges with great views, Eidfjord is simply magnificent. Eidfjord's beauty does, however, come at a price: in summer, cruise ships arrive on an almost daily basis, and the town can get overwhelmed.

⊙ Sights

Viking Burial Mounds　　　VIKING GRAVES
The tourist office can point you in the direction of a number of nearby Viking burial mounds and has route maps for Nkr10. There are more than 350 burial mounds in the area dating as far back as 1600 years. Another way to reach these mounds is with **Troll Train** (adult/child Nkr90/40; ⊙hourly 10am-5.30pm Jun-Aug), a cutesy train on wheels that takes you up to the Hæreid Plateau, where the most accessible graves are. Tickets can be purchased at the tourist office.

Kjeåsen Farm　　　SCENIC FARM
Above all other sights in the region, Kjeåsen Farm, 6km northeast of Eidfjord and close to the treeline 530m above the valley floor, should not be missed. According to some accounts, there has been a farm here for 400 years, although vehicle access was only pos-

sible with the construction of the road in 1975. Now one of Norway's top scenic locations, the wonderfully remote farm buildings are still inhabited by a woman who has lived alone here for 40 years – alone, that is, apart from the busloads of tourists who visit the farm every day in summer. It's possible to climb up to the farm on foot (four hours return), but it's steep and quite perilous, involving at least one rope-bridge; ask the tourist office for directions. The vehicle road goes through a one-way tunnel, driving up on the hour, down on the half-hour; although the tunnel is open 24 hours, the latest you should drive up to the farm is 5pm, so as to respect the privacy of Kjeåsen's inhabitant. If Kjeåsen Farm has piqued your curiosity, the booklet *Kjeåsen in Eidfjord,* by Per A Holst, tells the history of the farm and its inhabitants; it's available for Nkr20 from the Eidfjord tourist office.

Skytjefossen
WATERFALLS
Plunging almost 300m off the Hardangervidda Plateau to the valley floor below, these falls, 12km north of Eidfjord in the Simadalen valley, are among the highest in Norway. To reach the trailhead, drive as far as Tveit and park just after the last house. The hike to the falls and back takes 1½ hours.

Hardangervidda Natursenter
NATURE CENTRE
(www.hardangervidda.org; Øvre Eidfjord; adult/child/family Nkr120/60/280; ⊙9am-8pm mid-Jun–mid-Aug, 10am-6pm Apr–mid-Jun & mid-Aug–Oct) The exceptional Hardangervidda Natursenter is a superlative introduction to one of Norway's most beautiful national parks. The centre shows a must-see 19-minute movie with dramatic panoramic footage of the park; if you can't visit the inner depths of the park on foot, this is the next best thing. Otherwise, there are interactive displays, informative explanations of the region's natural history, fish tanks of mountain species, and interesting geology exhibits. The centre, which is located 6.5km southeast of Eidfjord in Øvre Eidfjord, has detailed trekking maps, and staff can offer advice as to trekking and skiing in the park.

🏃 Activities
In addition to hiking up to Kjeåsen Farm and trekking in the Hardangervidda National Park (see p151), a range of other activities is available. Boat rental is also possible (half-/full-day for a medium-sized motor boat Nkr300/500); ask at the tourist office, Vik Pensjonat or Eidfjord Fjell og Fjord Hotel.

🍃 Flat Earth
ACTIVITIES CENTRE
(☑47 60 68 47; www.flatearth.no; Øvre Eidfjord; ⊙around May-Sep) One of the best activities operators in Norway's fjord country, Flat Earth arranges sea/river kayaking (Nkr420/450, three hours), abseiling (Nkr1900, full day), white-water rafting (Nkr360, two hours), climbing (Nkr250, three hours), downhill mountain-biking (Nkr280) and glacier hikes (Nkr800, full day). Its headquarters is close to the Hardangervidda Natursenter in Øvre Eidfjord, 6.5km southeast of Eidfjord. It also rents out sea kayaks (half-/full-day from Nkr150/200), canoes (Nkr200/350) and 24-gear mountain bikes (Nkr150/200).

Mini Cruises
BOAT TOURS
From mid-June to mid-August, the tourist office runs daily four-hour boat cruises that leave Eidfjord at 2.40pm and sail to Ulvik, Kinsarvik and Lofthus, from where a bus whisks you back to Eidfjord, arriving at 6.20pm. Tickets cost Nkr235/120 per adult/child.

🛏 Sleeping & Eating

TOP CHOICE Eidfjord Gjestegiveri
GUESTHOUSE €
(☑53 66 53 46; www.ovre-eidfjord.com; Øvre Eidfjord; huts Nkr360, s/d with shared bathroom & breakfast Nkr590/745; P🐾🛜) This delightful guesthouse run by Dutch owners Eric and Inge has a homely feel. The beautifully maintained building dates back to 1896. There are just five double rooms and one single; the six camping huts are only open from April to October. Breakfasts are good (the secret's in the homemade bread) and there's internet access. The other huge selling point is the **pancake café** (pancakes Nkr75-119; ⊙11am-8pm), which has around 20 varieties of fantastic and filling, sweet and salty Dutch pancakes, with toppings that range from mountain trout to Hardanger apple compote. It also has a good range of dried meals for hikers heading out into the wilds. It's 6.5km from central Eidfjord, and is close to the Hardangervidda Natursenter

TOP CHOICE Vik Pensjonat
GUESTHOUSE €€
(☑53 66 51 62; www.vikpensjonat.com; Eidfjord; s/d/f Nkr840/1050/1480, cabins Nkr750-1100; P🐾🛜) This appealing place in the centre of Eidfjord not far from the water's edge is set in a lovely, renovated old home. It offers a friendly welcome and an excellent range of cosy accommodation. The rooms with balconies (rooms 1 and 6) are our favourites, but the six-person cabin on the riverbank is also outstanding. The attached cafe is one of the

better places to eat in town, with reasonable prices (light meals Nkr65 to Nkr85, mains Nkr145 to Nkr185) and everything from soups and sandwiches to main dishes such as mountain trout.

Quality Hotel Vøringfoss FJORD HOTEL €€€

(☑53 67 41 00; www.voringfoss.no; s/d Nkr1345/1645, with fjord views Nkr1645/1845, with fjord views & balcony Nkr1745/1945; ☺May-Sep) This swish hotel opened in 2001 and offers extraordinary views from its fjord-facing rooms. This is a great place for a splurge and to wake up to an exceptional vista, unless, of course, a cruise ship has arrived blocking your view. Rooms are extremely comfortable. It also has a cafe that serves light meals and snacks, and a restaurant.

Eidfjord Fjell og Fjord Hotel HOTEL €€

(☑53 66 52 64; www.effh.no; Eidfjord; s/d Nkr965/1350, with Fjord Pass Nkr820/1140) This modern hotel on the slightly elevated ledge overlooking town has comfortable rooms, some of which have decent views of the fjord. The garden terrace with sweeping views is a fine place to chill and there are children's toys for those with young ones. The evening buffet (Nkr195) is good value.

Sæbø Camping CAMPGROUND €

(☑53 66 59 27; www.saebocamping.com; Øvre Eidfjord; tent & caravan sites Nkr130, cabins Nkr370-960; ☺mid-May–mid-Sep; ⓦ) This spacious and well-equipped lakeside campsite has a pretty location in Måbødalen, just 500m from the Hardangervidda Natursenter. The owners promise freshly baked bread in the mornings and it's worth hanging around near the kitchen simply to inhale.

ⓘ Information

Eidfjord tourist office (☑53 67 34 00; www.visiteidfjord.no; ☺9am-7pm Mon-Fri, 10am-6pm Sat, 11am-6pm Sun mid-Jun–mid-Aug, shorter hr rest of yr) Also has internet (30 minutes Nkr50) and free wireless.

ⓘ Getting There & Away

BOAT A daily ferry leaves Eidfjord at 2.40pm, bound for Norheimsund (Nkr260), where it connects with buses to Bergen.

BUS Up to five buses daily run between Eidfjord and Odda (1¾ hours) and some continue on to Geilo. In summer, a minibus service (Nkr100) operates between Tinnhølen lake/Trondsbu and the main Rv7 Eidfjord–Geilo road; it's a convenient entry/exit point for hiking on the Hardangervidda Plateau.

CAR A 1380m suspension bridge is under construction, which will replace the ferry between Bruravik and Brimnes along the Rv7/13. The project is due to be completed in June 2013.

Around Eidfjord

Eidfjord is a gateway to the **Hardangervidda Plateau** (p150), the largest mountain plateau in northern Europe and site of one of Norway's largest national parks. From Eidfjord, the Rv7 twists up through Måbødalen, including through a number of corkscrewing tunnels, before climbing up onto the plateau.

Vøringsfossen WATERFALL

At the summit after a steep 20km drive, and where Hardangervidda begins, is the stunning, 182m-high **Vøringfoss**. There are actually numerous waterfalls here, which together are called Vøringsfossen. They plunge over the plateau's rim and down into the canyon – the main section has a vertiginous drop of 145m. By some accounts, this is Norway's most-visited natural attraction, and it's hard to disagree, given the endless stream of tour buses in summer (the record is 43 buses at any one time). The best views are from the lookout next to the Fossli Hotel (parking Nkr30) or from a number of lookouts (not all of which have railings!) reached from the Vøringsfossen Cafeteria back down the valley on the Rv7. Buses between Geilo and Odda pass right by the falls.

Fossli Hotel HISTORIC HOTEL €€

(☑53 66 57 77; www.fossli-hotel.com; s/d Nkr750/1100, with Fjord Pass Nkr690/1020; ☺May-Sep; ℗) If you'd like to fall asleep to the roar of cascading water, the Fossli Hotel is set just back from the precipice. The views from the atmospheric and historic hotel are stunning and the rooms have character and modern parquet floors, but neither TV nor phones. Best of all, staying here allows you to enjoy the falls after the crowds disappear down the mountain. The hotel is run by Erik, whose great-grandfather built the hotel in the 1890s and who is a quiet but engaging host with a treasure-trove of stories from the Hardangervidda region. Edvard Grieg composed his *Opus 66* in the hotel. The hotel is well signposted 1.3km off the Rv7. The hotel's restaurant (mains Nkr160 to Nkr240) serves fine Norwegian dishes, such as lamb, baked salmon and wild deer, and there's a **waffle cafe** (☺9am-6pm May-Sep) downstairs.

Kinsarvik & Lofthus

POP 3382

The picturesque town of Kinsarvik and nearby Lofthus rest peacefully on the shore of Sørfjorden, an offshoot of Hardangerfjord in the heart of a region known as Ullensvang; there are an estimated half a million fruit trees in Ullensvang. Kinsarvik wasn't always so peaceful – it was the site of a settlement of up to 300 Vikings from the 8th to 11th centuries.

⊙ Sights & Activities

KINSARVIK

The small U-shaped patch of greenery opposite the Kinsarvik tourist office is all that remains of the former **Viking port**. Kinsarvik also boasts one of Norway's oldest **stone churches** (admission free; ☉10am-7pm late May–mid-Aug). First built in around 1180, it was restored in the 1960s and the walls still bear traces of lime-and-chalk paintings that depict the weighing of souls by Michael the Archangel with the devil trying to weigh down the scales. According to local legend, the church was built by Scottish invaders on the site of an earlier stave church.

Kinsarvik also offers an appealing access trail past the four cooling **Husedalen waterfalls**, along what's known as the **Monk's Stairway**, and onto the network of tracks through the wild forest of Hardangervidda National Park (see p151).

For children, the **Familieparken Hardangertun** (www.hardangertun.no, in Norwegian; day pass Nkr150; ☉10.30am-6.30pm daily late Jun–mid-Aug, 10.30am-6.30pm Sat & Sun mid-May–late Jun & mid-Aug–Sep) has water slides, minigolf and farm animals.

LOFTHUS

The main attraction in Lofthus is **Grieg's Hut** (☉24hr yr-round), the one-time retreat of Norwegian composer Edvard Grieg. It's in the garden of Hotel Ullensvang. Lofthus also has a **stone church** (admission free; ☉10am-7pm late May–mid-Aug) dating back to 1250 (the tower was added in the 1880s) with fine stained-glass windows; it's surrounded by a cemetery with some graves from the Middle Ages.

🛏 Sleeping & Eating

KINSARVIK

Kinsarvik Camping　　　　　CAMPGROUND €
(☎53 66 32 90; www.kinsarvikcamping.no; tent/ caravan sites Nkr130/135 plus Nkr30 electricity & per adult/child Nkr25/15, 4-bed cabins Nkr355-1450; ☒) This simple, friendly place is right by the water's edge and has a water slide for kids and the young at heart.

Dreiarstovo　　　　　TRADITIONAL HOUSE €
(Ringøy Camping; ☎53 66 39 17; www.ringoy -camping.no; 6-bed house from Nkr800; ☉May-Sep; ℗🖨) A standard fjord-side camping ground, this place is in the village of Ringøy, northeast of Kinsarvik, and it has a renovated 19th-century home a little up the hill. Furnishings are of the simple pine variety, and it has a kitchen, a washing machine and heated floors in the bathroom.

LOFTHUS

Hotel Ullensvang　　　　　HISTORIC HOTEL €€€
(☎53 67 00 00; www.hotel-ullensvang.no; d with Fjord Pass from Nkr780, s/d Nkr1300/1890, with fjord views Nkr1500/2290; ℗🖨☒) This enormous, luxurious place dates back to 1846 and has terrific views, supremely comfortable rooms and a good restaurant (lunch/ dinner Nkr245/495). There's almost nothing you can't do here: it has a sauna, swimming pool, gym, golf simulator, tennis and squash courts and boat rental – all for a price, of course.

Ullensvang Gjesteheim　　　　　GUESTHOUSE €€
(☎53 66 12 36; www.ullensvang-gjesteheim.no; s/d/ tr with shared bathroom from Nkr490/710/870; ☉Apr-Sep; ℗🖨) Kristin and Tor will make you feel right at home in this renovated 16th-century farmhouse. The rooms are simple, but there's a warm feeling about this place. The downstairs restaurant serves a few Norwegian dishes (mains Nkr125 to Nkr185) as well as dozens of (who'd have thought?) authentically Thai choices.

Lofthus Camping　　　　　CAMPGROUND €
(☎53 66 13 64; www.lofthuscamping.com; tent or caravan sites Nkr130, plus Nkr35 electricity & per adult/child Nkr30/20, 2-/4-bed cabins Nkr480/590; ☒) A well-equipped fjord-side campsite with front-row views, Lofthus Camping has a heated indoor pool and can arrange boat rental.

ⓘ Information

Kinsarvik tourist office (☎53 66 31 12; www. visitullensvang.no; ☉9am-7pm mid-Jun–mid-Aug, shorter hr rest of yr, closed Dec) Information and internet access (per minute Nkr1).

Lofthus tourist office (☎45 78 58 22; ☉11am-7pm mid-Jun–mid-Aug)

❶ Getting There & Away

BOAT Every couple of hours a ferry connects Kinsarvik with Utne (per person/vehicle Nkr32/86, 40 minutes) before continuing on to Kvanndal (Nkr39/114, one hour). There's also one daily tourist boat (passenger only) in summer to Eidfjord, Ulvik and Norheimsund, although it's more for sightseeing than getting anywhere in a hurry (it stops for three hours in Eidfjord).

BUS Buses run between Odda (one hour) and Eidfjord (one hour) around five times a day and pass through Kinsarvik and Lofthus.

Utne

One of the prettiest little villages you'll find in Hardangerfjord, Utne is famous for its fruit-growing and for the excellent open-air **Hardanger Folk Museum** (www.hardanger. museum.no; adult/child Nkr80/free; ⏱10am-5pm May-Aug, shorter hr rest of yr), which acts as a repository for the cultural heritage of the Hardanger region. It comprises a collection of historic homes, boats, shops, outhouses and a school, plus exhibitions on Hardanger women, weddings, the famed Hardanger fiddle and fiddle-making, fishing, music, dance, orchard crops and the woodcarvings of local artist Lars Kinsarvik; it also bakes delicious local cakes on Tuesdays (noon to 3pm) in July.

🛏 Sleeping & Eating

Utne Hotel   HISTORIC HOTEL €€€
(☑53 66 64 00; www.utnehotel.no; Utne; s/d annexe Nkr1190/1590, main bldg Nkr1390/1790; ⓟ🛜) The historic wooden Utne Hotel was built in 1722 after the Great Nordic War, making it Norway's oldest hotel. Restored in 2003, it overflows with period touches from the 18th and 19th centuries. The hotel's fabulous decor makes it worth a look even if you're not staying, and it also has the best restaurant in town.

Hardanger Gjestegård   GUESTHOUSE €€
(☑53 66 67 10; www.hardanger-gjestegard.no; Alsåker; d from Nkr750) This atmospheric guesthouse, 10km west of Utne on Fv550, is in a pretty 1898 building with character-filled rooms that brim with cutesy folk touches. It offers good weekly rates.

❶ Getting There & Away

Ferries run between Utne, Kinsarvik (per person/vehicle Nkr32/86, 40 minutes) and Kvanndal (Nkr15/39, 20 minutes) at least six times a day.

Odda
POP 7050

Despite the promising location at the far end of Hardangerfjord, Odda is an industrial, iron-smelting town, and pretty ugly as a result. That said, it serves as a gateway to Folgefonna National Park, home to the Folgefonn glacier, and has a host of activities on offer.

◉ Sights

Trolltunga   NATURAL ROCK FEATURE
Norway seems to make a speciality of extraordinary rock platforms offering both panoramic views and postcard-perfect photo opportunities. Up there with all the others is Trolltunga, a narrow finger of rock that hangs out over the void high above the lake Ringedalsvatnet. To reach it, drive north of Odda to Tyssedal, then northeast to Skjeggedal, from where Trolltunga is an eight- to 10-hour return hike away. En route, watch out for the **Tyssestrengene waterfall** (646m). If you continue on a little beyond Trolltunga, you reach another fine vantage point, **Preikestolen** (Pulpit Rock), a smaller version of the lookout of the same name above Lysefjord, close to Stavanger.

🏃 Activities

For hikes of up to six hours around town, pick up the helpful brochure *Hikes in Odda,* or the more detailed *Hiking and Biking – Odda, Røldal, Seljestad, Tyssedal* from the tourist office.

Glacier Hikes

Anyone in good physical condition with warm clothing and sturdy footwear can take a guided hike up the lovely Buer valley followed by a glacier walk on the Buer arm of Folgefonn (adult Nkr650, including crampons and ice axes). This is one of the best places to do a glacier walk because you're onto the ice straight away without wading first through snow. The excursions are run by the excellent **Flat Earth** (☑47 60 68 47; www.flatearth.no) and the round-trip from Odda usually lasts a full day. Transport to the starting point, at Buer, 8km west of Odda, is included in the price.

Climbing & Canyoning

Flat Earth also organises full-day canyoning (Nkr650, four hours) and climbing (Nkr250, 2½ hours) trips; the former is open to anyone 12 years old and up, while climbers can be as young as eight.

Another option is the combination of climbing up the power station's vertical 'Via Ferrata' ladders – jammed into the rock wall by power-station workers – and hiking on to Trolltunga and back with **Opplev Odda** (☑90 82 45 72; www.opplevodda.com). The eight-to nine-hour expedition costs Nkr950; you'll need to bring your own food and water.

🛏 Sleeping & Eating

TOP CHOICE **Tyssedal Hotel**   HOTEL €€
(☑53 64 00 00; www.tyssedalhotell.no, in Norwegian; Tyssedal; s/d Nkr995/1295; P🐶) The highly recommended Tyssedal Hotel has terrific rooms with parquet floors and a real sense of style. But this is above all a place for lovers of ghost stories – the hotel is reputedly haunted by the ghost of Eidfjord artist Nils Bergslien (especially on the ground and 3rd floors, we were reliably informed), whose fantastic fairy-tale and Hardangerfjord landscape paintings adorn the hotel. The restaurant (lunch mains Nkr79 to Nkr99, dinner mains Nkr229 to Nkr299) is also Odda's best, using local produce to create fusion dishes such as duck breast with raspberry sauce.

Vasstun   GUESTHOUSE €
(☑55 09 28 00; www.vasstun.no; Vasstun 1, Odda; d/tr with shared bathroom Nkr355/435, d with private bathroom Nkr435-535; P🐶) There are 27 recently refurbished rooms at this delightful guesthouse close to Odda Camping at the southern end of town. The rooms (some have lake views) are modern and comfortable, and the whole place has a more personal feel to it than many hotels in the region.

Odda Camping   CAMPGROUND €
(☑41 32 16 10; www.oddacamping.no; Odda; tent/caravan sites Nkr140/150, 4-bed cabins Nkr690-890; ◷mid-May–Aug) The most convenient camping is on the shores of the lake Sandvinvatnet, a 20-minute uphill walk south of the town centre.

ℹ Information

Odda tourist office (☑53 65 40 05; www.visitodda.com; ◷9am-7pm Mon-Fri, 10am-6pm Sat & Sun mid-Jun–mid-Aug, shorter hr rest of yr) Right on the waterfront; it also has internet access (from Nkr10).

ℹ Getting There & Away

Between Odda and Jondal (Nkr161, 2½ hours), local buses operate one to three times daily; they travel via Utne. Buses also run to/from Bergen, Geilo and Oslo.

Around Odda

RØLDAL

The pretty town of Røldal, 22km southeast of Odda, has the popular **Røldal Skisenter** (www.roldal.no; ◷Dec-Apr), a winter ski station. There's also a 13th-century **stave church** (adult/child Nkr20/15; ◷9.30am-6.30pm Jul, shorter hr mid-May–Jun & Aug–mid-Sep), where, according to local legend, the wooden cross sweats every midsummer's eve; the sweat is said to have healing powers, and this place was an important pilgrimage destination in the Middle Ages.

FOLGEFONNA NATIONAL PARK

Established in 2005, this 545-sq-km national park encompasses mainland Norway's third-largest icefield. The Folgefonn icecap covers 168 sq km and the ice is up to 400m thick in places. It's a dramatic, beautiful place, with glaciers snaking down the heights of nearby valleys.

🏃 Activities

The most popular way to explore Folgefonna is on a glacier hike, either from Odda or Jondal. Longer hikes are also possible.

For an excellent online guide to hiking on the fringes of Folgefonna, visit www.visitsunnhordland.no – click on 'Fancy a Walk?', where there are links to route descriptions and downloadable maps.

Folgefonni Breførarlag   GLACIER HIKES
(☑55 29 89 21; www.folgefonni-breforarlag.no; Jondal; ◷mid-Jun–mid-Aug) The highly professional Folgefonni Breførarlag has a range of glacier hikes that set out in summer from the Folgefonn Sommar Skisenter and hike onto the glaciers. The advantage of doing the walk here is the promise of exceptional views, although, unlike at Buer, you're required to hike across the snow to reach the glacier. Tours range from three-hour hikes across the icecap (Nkr390) to four- to six-hour 'Blue-Ice' trips to Juklavassbreen (Nkr490 to Nkr590). The minimum age for participants is 12.

Folgefonn Sommar Skisenter   SUMMER SKIING
(☑46 80 59 66; www.folgefonn.no) It's possible to do some summer skiing, snowboarding and sledding from May until October, although the season can finish earlier. Short tours to the ski centre leave from Jondal Quay at 10.30am from mid-June to mid-August and return at 3.30pm, while buses run to the ski centre during the season.

ⓘ Information

Folgefonna National Park Centre (☑53 48 42 80; www.folgefonna.net, www.visitsunnhordland.no; Rosendal; ⊙10am-7pm Jun-Aug) An excellent resource on the park, this centre in Rosendal has exhibits and a fine 20-minute film about the formation of Folgefonn and its geology.

Jondal tourist office (☑53 66 85 31; www. visitjondal.no; ⊙9.30am-4pm Jun, 9.30am-6pm Jul & Aug)

ⓘ Getting There & Away

The national park is accessible from Odda and Jondal, which are connected by semiregular buses.

Rosendal

POP 950

Separated from the rest of Hardangerfjord by high mountains and the Folgefonna National Park, Rosendal has a picturesque location by the fjord and a backdrop of high hills. Access to the national park is easier from Odda and Jondal, but Rosendal has a good national-park centre and is a worthwhile destination in its own right.

◉ Sights & Activities

The tourist office can advise on hiking, climbing, boat rental (per day/week Nkr400/1220 plus petrol) and horse riding, and it has a useful Cycling Trips in Sunnhordland brochure for longer cycling excursions around the region.

Baroniet Rosendal BARONIAL MANOR
(☑53 48 29 99; www.baroniet.no; Rosendal; adult/child Nkr75/10; ⊙10am-6pm Jul, variable hr May, Jun & Aug) Norway's only baronial mansion dates back to 1665 and features period interiors and a Renaissance rose garden in shady and extensive grounds on a gentle rise above the town. You can even sleep here in the farm annexe. It hosts excellent weekend concerts by eminent Norwegian musicians from mid-May to early September, and performances of Shakespeare by British actors, usually in late July.

🖊 Steinparken OPEN-AIR STONE PARK
Signposted off the road running to Baroniet Rosendal, this intriguing little open-air gallery has rock monoliths from the Folgefonna region, which have been sculpted and smoothed to stunning effect to show the region's geological diversity; some of it is the work of artist Bård Breivik. A path runs from an antique saw mill up through the park. Carved tables are a good choice for a picnic lunch.

Rødne Fjord Cruise SIGHTSEEING CRUISE
(☑51 89 52 70; www.rodne.no; adult/child Nkr380/200) In addition to the trips to Rosendal from Bergen (see p164), this company offers a 3½-hour sightseeing cruise of Hardangerfjord.

🎇 Festivals

Rosendal Mat & Kunstfestival (Rosendal Food & Art Festival; www.rosendalmatogkunstfestival.no, in Norwegian; ⊙early–mid-Jul)

🛏 Sleeping & Eating

The nearest campsite to Rosendal is the reasonable **Sundal Camping** (☑53 48 41 86; www.sundalcamping.no; tent sites Nkr130, cabins Nkr450-700), in Sundal, 28km northeast of Rosendal.

TOP CHOICE **Rosendal Turisthotell** GUESTHOUSE €€
(☑/fax 53 47 36 66; www.rosendalturisthotell.no, in Norwegian; Skålagato 17, Rosendal; s/d with shared bathroom Nkr680/980; Ⓟ⊙) Formerly known as Rosendal Gjestegiveri, this lovely designer guesthouse opposite the quay dates from 1887, but a recent overhaul has given it a fresh, contemporary look. The 14 rooms are filled with light, and although the bathrooms are shared, even these are stylish and a cut above your average corridor bathroom. The restaurant-cafe (lunch mains Nkr125 to Nkr186, dinner mains Nkr228 to Nkr345) is the best in town, and there's a basement wine bar that opens on Friday and Saturday until 1am (it's closed the rest of the week).

Baroniet Rosendal FARMHOUSE €€
(☑53 48 29 99; www.baroniet.no; Rosendal; s/d with shared bathroom & breakfast Nkr700/900; ⊙May-Aug; Ⓟ) Just outside the grounds of the Baroniet Rosendal, this rambling farmhouse has attractive rooms with wrought-iron bedsteads and shared bathrooms. It's as close as you'll get to feeling like royalty in Rosendal, especially if you have your dinner in the manor (three-course dinner Tuesday to Saturday in farmhouse/manor Nkr490/590).

TOP CHOICE **Snikkeriet** RESTAURANT, MUSIC BAR €€
(www.snikkeriet.no, in Norwegian; mains Nkr150-195; ⊙noon-10pm Sun-Thu, noon-1am Fri & Sat) The first time we walked into this place, we found the owner playing guitar and sing-

ing to an empty bar. We almost walked out, but we're glad we didn't because she was warming up for the hugely popular Friday night (9pm) live jam session, when musicians from all over the region come to play rock, blues and sometimes jazz. Snikkeriet does excellent and well-priced home-cooked Norwegian meals, including fjord fish and local sausages.

ℹ Information

Rosendal tourist office & Folgefonna National Park Centre (☎53 48 42 80; www.folgefonna.net, www.visitsunnhordland.no; ◷10am-7pm Jun-Aug)

ℹ Getting There & Away

BOAT Rødne Fjord Cruise (☎51 89 52 70; www.rodne.no; adult/child 1-way Nkr310/155, return Nkr470/235) has two express boats daily from Monday to Friday and one each on Saturday and Sunday.

BUS Buses run three to seven times daily between Rosendal and Odda via Sunndal.

CAR & MOTORCYCLE Rosendal can be reached via an 11km-long road tunnel (car Nkr65, free midnight to 6am) under the icefield from Odda; Rosendal is 32km along the coast from the tunnel entrance/exit. There is currently no road connection between Rosendal and Jondal, but a tunnel is due for completion in 2012. If you're heading south towards Haugesund or Stavanger, the E39 is the fastest route and includes the Rannavik–Skjersholmane ferry. However, the route via the Utåker–Skånevik ferry is cheaper.

Around Rosendal

For coverage of Folgefonna National Park, turn to p183.

SUNNDAL

At Sunndal, 4km west of the tunnel, take the road up the Sunndal valley (drivable for 1km), then walk 2km on a good track to lake Bondhusvatnet, where there's a wonderful view of the glacier **Bondhusbreen**. This is also a trail head for some fine hikes.

USKEDALEN

In Uskedalen, 14km west of Rosendal, there's an extraordinary rock-slab mountain, Ulvenåso (1247m), offering some of the best **rock climbing** in Norway; contact the tourist office in Rosendal for details.

MØSEVATNET

One of the prettiest (and quietest) roads in this part of Norway climbs up to the dam at Møsevatnet, from where there are good views to one of the glacier arms of the Folgefonn icecap. Take the Rv48 south of Rosendal and turn off to the southwest at Dimmelsvik; the road is signposted to Fjellhaugen, Matre and Åkra. From the road junction that signposts Matre and Åkra to the right, follow the signs left to Blådal and the winter-only Fjellhaugen Skisenter; later ignore the signs to the ski centre. From this road junction, the narrow but well-paved road climbs up through some glorious wooded, rocky hills, studded with lakes and dams. You pass through two tunnels, before a final climb (a 20% incline!) takes you to the water's edge.

HAUGELANDET & RYFYLKE

North and east of Stavanger lies a region of low-lying hills and relatively flat coastal inlets and islands that are reminiscent of the northern Scottish isles. Haugesund is the regional capital.

Haugesund

POP 34,100

The North Sea port of Haugesund lies well off the beaten routes. You probably wouldn't come here for its own sake, but the town has a lively waterfront restaurant strip and some excellent festivals. Ryanair flies here, so this may be your entry point into Norway. There are also some worthwhile sights on Karmøy island, south of town.

The area around Haugesund carries huge historical significance for Norwegians. It was in the nearby Hafrsfjord that the decisive battle took place in 872 and Norway was first unified. As such, the area bills itself as 'Norway's Birthplace'.

◉ Sights

Haugesund has retained many of its historical buildings, with the highlights including the **Rådhus** (town hall). About 75m south is the **Krosshaugen** mound and stone cross, erected in celebration of Christian gatherings around 1000.

Haraldshaugen, the burial site of Viking King Harald Hårfagre, who died of plague at Avaldsnes on nearby Karmøy, is 1.5km north of Haugesund. The obelisk, erected in 1872, commemorates the decisive 872 battle.

Bizarrely, Haugesund claims to be the ancestral home of Marilyn Monroe, whose father, a local baker, emigrated to the USA. A **monument** on the quay, next to the Rica Maritim Hotel, commemorates the 30th anniversary of her death.

☞ Tours
History buffs and lovers of all things Viking can sign up at the tourist office for the nine-hour **Viking Trail tour** (☏52 01 08 30; adult/child Nkr800/200). It takes in four Viking sights around Haugelandet and includes transport and a light lunch.

🎇 Festivals
Silda Jazz MUSIC
(Haugesund International Jazz Festival; www.sildajazz.no; ☉early–mid-Aug)

Norwegian International Film Festival FILM
(www.filmweb.no/filmfestivalen/; ☉mid-late Aug)

🛏 Sleeping
Scandic Haugesund HOTEL €€
(☏21 61 41 00; www.scandichotels.com; Kirkegata 166; s/d from Nkr670/870; ☎) For price-quality ratio, the Scandic Haugesund, a few blocks up from the waterfront, is the best in town. As we've come to expect from this chain, the rooms have a contemporary look with a white, black and pistachio colour scheme and terrific bathrooms. The service is also more personal than at most hotels. Rack rates are significantly higher, but no one pays these any more; the best rates are found online.

Rica Maritim Hotel HOTEL €€
(☏52 86 30 00; www.hotelmaritim.no; Åsbygaten 3; s Nkr900-1600, d Nkr1250-1800; ☎) From the aquarium in the lobby to the luxuriously appointed rooms (one suite goes for Nkr10,000!), this recently renovated hotel is high class, and its waterfront location (a two-minute walk from the main action) is the best in Haugesund.

Strandgaten Gjestgiveri GUESTHOUSE €€
(☏52 71 52 55; www.gjestgiveri.net, in Norwegian; Strandgata 81; s/d Nkr595/855; ☎) On offer at Strandgaten Gjestgiveri are tidy if unexceptional rooms that are a cosy choice in the centre of Haugesund. There are much nicer

guesthouses elsewhere in Norway, but the location is good.

🍴 Eating
Haugesund's waterfront promenade, Smedasundet, is almost entirely given over to restaurants, giving the area an agreeable hum whenever the weather's warm. Any Haugesund restaurant worth its salt morphs into a bar as the night wears on.

Café MM BAR, RESTAURANT €€
(Smedasundet; light meals & pasta Nkr89-159, dinner mains Nkr198-265; ☉11am-1.30am Mon-Sat, noon-1am Sun) As popular with families as with cool young locals looking for a quiet drink, this waterfront place has stylish decor, good international food and is almost always full with a happy crowd.

Lothes Mat & Vinhus RESTAURANT, WINE BAR €€
(☏52 71 22 01; www.lothesmat.no, in Norwegian; Skippergata 4; mains Nkr165-299; ☉11am-1.30am) With its lovely outdoor terrace overlooking the waterfront, and period wood architecture, this long-standing Haugesund landmark is always full and deservedly so.

To Glass RESTAURANT, WINE BAR €€
(☏52 70 74 00; www.toglass.no, in Norwegian; Strandgata 169; light meals Nkr149-179, mains Nkr259-299, 3-course set menus Nkr489; ☉6-11pm Mon-Thu, 6pm-midnight Fri & Sat) There aren't many reasons to drag yourself away from the waterfront, but this oh-so-cool restaurant and wine bar is one of them. It serves tapas and dishes such as mussels steamed in white wine with focaccia.

ℹ Information
Haugesund tourist office (☏52 01 08 30; www.visithaugelandet.no; Strandgata 171; ☉10am-4.30pm)

ℹ Getting There & Away
AIR SAS (www.sas.no) flies regularly to Haugesund from Bergen and Oslo, while **Norwegian** (www.norwegian.com) also flies the Haugesund–Oslo route.

BOAT Flaggruten (www.flaggruten.no) ferries between Bergen (Nkr510, 3¼ hours) and Stavanger (Nkr310, 1¾ hours) stop in Haugesund twice daily from Sunday to Friday and once on Saturday.

BUS Nor-Way Bussekspress buses connect Haugesund with Stavanger (Nkr240, 2¼ hours, up to six daily), and Bergen (Nkr320, 3½ hours) almost hourly on weekdays and every second hour on weekends.

Getting Around

Haugesund airport (☑52 85 79 00) is 13km southwest of the city. The **airport bus** (www.flybussen.no/haugesund; 1-way adult/child Nkr70/40) has services to coincide with all SAS and Norwegian flights. For Ryanair flights, the service is operated by **Kystbussen** (www.kystbussen.no), which connects with bus services to Bergen and Stavanger.

Around Haugesund

KARMØY ISLAND

Low-lying Karmøy island has some interesting historical sites and museums, and is circled by quiet and pretty wooden villages.

In early or mid-June, Karmøy island hosts a **Viking Festival** (www.vikingfestivalen.no, in Norwegian), which features Viking feasts, processions and saga evenings.

Visnes Grubeområde   MINING MUSEUM

(www.visitkarmoy.no; Visnes; adult/child Nkr60/15; ☺11am-5pm Mon-Fri, noon-5pm Sun Jun–mid-Aug) Not content with playing a role in the family history of one American icon (Marilyn Monroe; see p185), Haugesund was also essential to the founding of another. Copper from the mine at Visnes, 4km west of Avaldsnes, was used to build the Statue of Liberty in New York. Apart from the usual exhibits, there's a seaside smelting hut.

FREE St Olav's Church   CHURCH

(www.visitkarmoy.no; Avaldsnes; ☺10am-5pm Mon-Sat, noon-5pm Sun Jun-Aug) About 5km south of central Haugesund, King Håkon Håkonsson's huge stone church was dedicated to St Olav in 1250. The adjacent 7.2m spire, known as the **Virgin Mary's Needle**, leans perilously towards the church wall, and legend suggests that when it actually touches the wall the Day of Judgment is at hand – it was close but still free-standing when we were there. Local legend has it that priests of little faith have, through the centuries, climbed the needle to chip bits away.

Nordvegen Historiesenter

HISTORY CENTRE, VIKING FARM
(www.vikinggarden.no, in Norwegian; adult/child/student & senior Nkr100/50/75; ☺11am-5pm Mon-Fri, 11am-4pm Sat, noon-5pm Sun Jun-Aug, shorter hr rest of yr) Down a short path from the car park for St Olav's Church is this outstanding history centre, which recreates the history of Harald Fair-Hair and other monarchs of the newly unified Nordvegen from the 10th century onwards. Also nearby, the reconstructed **Viking farm** (Avaldsnes; adult/child Nkr60/40; ☺11am-4pm Tue-Fri, 11am-3pm Sat, noon-4pm Sun) is beyond the church and great for kids; you'll be guided by staff in period dress. A good website to check out is www.vikingkings.com.

Karmøy Fiskerimuseum   FISHERY MUSEUM

(www.visitkarmoy.no; adult/child Nkr30/10; ☺11am-5pm Mon-Fri, 2-6pm Sun Jun–mid-Aug) In Vedavågen, on the island's west coast, the Karmøy Fishery Museum will have fishing buffs enthralled with a state-of-the-art new building, fishing exhibits and a saltwater aquarium.

Skudeneshavn   HISTORIC VILLAGE

The wonderful settlement of Skudeneshavn, 37km south of Haugesund, has many traditional wooden buildings and an extensive museum, **Mælandsgården** (www.skudenes.no/museum; adult/child Nkr60/15; ☺11am-5pm Mon-Fri, 1-6pm Sun Jun–mid-Aug), which has excellent collections of household articles, rooms with period furnishings and agricultural and nautical exhibits. There's a small summer-only **tourist office** (☑52 85 80 00; www.visitskudeneshavn.no) next to the quay.

🛏 Sleeping

Norneshuset   B&B €€
(☑90 05 90 07; www.norneshuset.no, in Norwegian; Nordnes 7, Skudeneshavn; s/d Nkr700/900) This is one of the loveliest B&Bs in Norway, with character-filled rooms right by the harbour and friendly service; it's located in a former warehouse that was shipped from Riga, Latvia, in the 1830s.

Getting There & Away

To reach Avaldsnes from central Haugesund, catch bus 8, 9 or 10 (Nkr42) from next to the post office. Bus 10 continues further south to Skudeneshavn (Nkr65, 1¼ hours). There are semiregular car ferries from Skudeneshavn to Mekjarvik (for Stavanger).

STAVANGER & LYSEFJORD

Tucked away in Norway's southwest, the oil-rich city of Stavanger hums with agreeable activity. It also serves as the gateway to Lysefjord, the southernmost of Norway's signature fjords and home to one of its most recognisable vantage points – Preikestolen (Pulpit Rock).

Stavanger

POP 123,850

Stavanger has a lot going for it. Its centre is arrayed around a pretty harbour with the quiet streets of the old town climbing up from the water's edge. It's also home to almost two-dozen museums, and is said by some to be the largest wooden city in Europe. But Stavanger's appeal is as much about atmosphere as anything else. Most nights, especially in summer, the city's waterfront comes alive and can get quite rowdy in the best tradition of oil and port cities. By Sunday morning, however, it's quiet and charming once again, for this is a place that has never lost its small-town feel.

◉ Sights

TOP CHOICE **Gamle Stavanger**   HISTORIC QUARTER

Gamle (Old) Stavanger, above the western shore of the harbour, is a delight. The Old Town's cobblestone walkways pass between rows of late-18th-century white-washed wooden houses, all immaculately kept and adorned with cheerful, well-tended flowerboxes. It well rewards an hour or two's ambling.

Norwegian Emigration Center

EMIGRATION CENTRE

(www.emigrationcenter.com; Strandkaien 31; ⊙9am-5pm Mon-Fri) This centre has a small exhibition (Nkr20) dealing with, on the 1st floor, Norwegian emigration to the US. On the 2nd floor is a genealogy library for foreigners of Norwegian descent seeking to trace their roots; research costs Nkr600 for the first three hours and Nkr300 for every hour thereafter.

FREE **Stavanger Domkirke**   CATHEDRAL

(Håkon VIIs gate; admission free; ⊙11am-7pm Jun-Aug, 11am-4pm Mon-Sat Sep-May) This beautiful church is an impressive but understated medieval stone cathedral dating from approximately 1125; it was extensively renovated following a fire in 1272 and contains traces of Gothic, baroque, Romanesque and Anglo Norman influences. Despite restoration in the 1860s and 1940, and the stripping of some features during the Reformation, the cathedral is, by some accounts, Norway's oldest medieval cathedral still in its original form. Its wonderful stone columns, tapestries, elaborate baroque pulpit and stained-glass window depicting the main events of the Christian calendar are a visual feast. Watch out for organ recitals in summer.

Norsk Oljemuseum   PETROLEUM MUSEUM

(www.norskolje.museum.no; Kjerringholmen; adult/child/family Nkr80/40/200; ⊙10am-7pm daily Jun-Aug, 10am-4pm Mon-Sat, 10am-6pm Sun Sep-May) We could spend (and have spent) hours in this state-of-the-art museum, one of Norway's best. Filled with high-tech interactive displays, gigantic models and authentic reconstructions, its many highlights include the world's largest drill bit, a 12-minute documentary by former Lonely Planet TV presenter Ian Wright and another on deep-sea diving, simulators, a petrodome recreating millions of years of natural history, an escape chute that kids love and some amazing models of oil platforms.

Tracing the history of oil formation and exploration in the North Sea from discovery in 1969 until the present, the museum nicely balances the technical side of oil exploration and extraction with archive footage and newspapers of significant moments in the history of Norwegian oil. Not least among these include coverage of the *Alexander L Kielland* tragedy in 1980, when 123 oil workers were killed; the 1972 decision by Norway's parliament that Statoil should be based in Stavanger; and the 1950s declaration by a Norwegian government commission that 'the chances of finding oil on the continental shelf off the Norwegian coast can be discounted'. You'll spend longer here than you planned, especially if you have kids.

Valbergtårnet   WATCHTOWER & GUARD MUSEUM

(Valbergata 2; admission Nkr25; ⊙11am-3pm mid-Jun–mid-Aug, 11am-3pm 1st Sun of month mid-Aug–Dec & Mar–mid-Jun) This historic 26m-high tower was constructed as a guards' lookout in 1850 and served as a lookout for fire and suspicious activity until 1922. It now contains an interesting little museum, and there are reasonable views over the harbour towards the Old Town from its top; it's OK to open the windows to take photos.

Stavanger Museum   CITY MUSEUMS

(www.museumstavanger.no) The large 11-part museum, with its sites scattered around Stavanger, could easily fill a sightseeing day, but you'd have to keep up a brisk pace to fit them all in. The first museum you visit costs Nkr60/30 per adult/child, the second costs Nkr20/10 and the rest are free, provided that you visit all in the same day. The exception is the Children's

STAVANGER FOR CHILDREN

Stavanger has plenty to keep the kids occupied, with many museums including interactive exhibits. Older children will enjoy the **Norsk Oljemuseum**, while younger visitors could spend an entire day playing in the **Children's Museum** (p190). The **Arkeologisk Museum** (p190) sometimes has Viking-themed activities in summer, while children of all ages will enjoy the **playground** fashioned from oil-exploration equipment outside the Norsk Oljemuseum. The tourist office sells a booklet called *Teddy in Stavanger* (Nkr69), which is aimed at children and has routes around central Stavanger with questions for children. And the **boat trips** (p191) that take you out into the fjords always have appeal.

Museum, which has separate pricing. The three other museums we don't cover here are the **Norwegian Printing Museum**, the **Norwegian School Museum** and the **Medical Museum**.

Stavanger Bymuseum

(Muségata 16; ⊙11am-4pm mid-Jun–mid-Aug, closed Mon rest of yr) The main museum reveals nearly 900 years of Stavanger's history, 'From Ancient Landscape to Oil Town'. Features include evidence of Stone Age habitation, the medieval bishopric, the herring years and the development of the city into a modern oil capital. The Stavanger of the 1880s is described in a series of tableaux focusing on local author Alexander L Kielland. Also in the same building is the **Norwegian Natural History Museum** (⊙same hr).

Canning Museum

(Hermetikkmuseet; Øvre Strandgate 88-90; ⊙11am-4pm mid-Jun–mid-Aug, closed Mon rest of yr) Don't miss this museum; housed in an old cannery, it's one of Stavanger's most appealing museums. Before oil, there were sardines, and Stavanger was once home to more than half of Norway's canning factories; by 1922 the city's canneries provided 50% of the town's employment. Here you'll get the lowdown on canning brisling and fish balls. The exhibits take you through the whole 12-stage process from salting, through to threading, smoking, decapitat-

ing and packing. There are no labels, but there's a handy brochure available at the entrance and guides are always on hand to answer your questions or crank up some of the old machines. Upstairs, there's a fascinating display of historical sardine-can labels (more than 40,000 designs were used and have become collectors' items). An adjoining building houses a cafe and restored workers cottages furnished in 1920s and 1960s style. On the first Sunday of every month (and Tuesday and Thursday from mid-June to mid-August), the fires are lit and you can sample smoked sardines straight from the ovens.

Ledaal

(Eiganesveien 45; ⊙11am-4pm mid-Jun–mid-Aug, 11am-4pm Sun rest of yr) The empire-style Ledaal was constructed between 1799 and 1803 for wealthy merchant shipowner Gabriel Schanche Kielland. Now recently restored, it serves as the local royal residence and summer home. You'll see the king's 250-year-old four-poster bed, unusual antique furniture and a pendulum clock from 1680.

Breidablikk

(Eiganesveien 40a; ⊙11am-4pm mid-Jun–mid-Aug, 11am-4pm Sun rest of yr) The excellent Breidablikk manor was constructed for the merchant shipowner Lars Berentsen. These days, it allows you to see the opulent lifestyles of the rich and famous in late-19th-century Norway, displaying old farming implements, books and knick-knacks.

Stavanger Maritime Museum

(Sjøfartsmuseet; Nedre Strandgate 17-19; ⊙11am-4pm mid-Jun–mid-Aug, closed Mon rest of yr) This worthwhile museum covers 200 years of Stavanger's maritime history spread over two warehouses dating from around 1800. It also has a large collection of model boats, sailing vessels, a noisy wind-up foghorn, a reconstruction of a late-19th-century sailmaker's workshop, a shipowner's office and an excellent general store, as well as the merchant's living quarters. The museum also owns two historic sailing vessels: the 1848 *Anna of Sand* and the 1896 *Wyvern*, which may be visitable if they're in port.

Rogaland Art Museum

(Rogaland Kunstmuseum; Henrik Ibsensgate 55; ⊙11am-4pm Tue-Sun) This museum, 2.5km south of the town centre, displays Norwegian art from the 18th century to the present, including the haunting *Gamle*

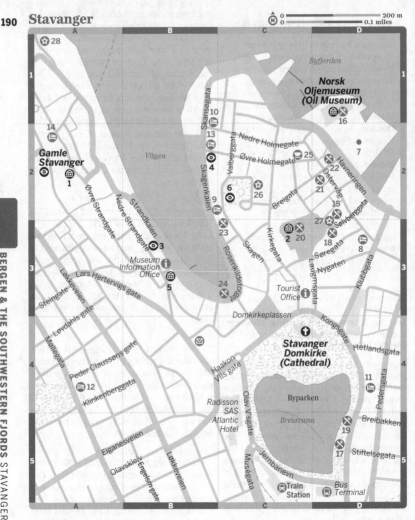

Furutrær and other landscape paintings by Stavanger's own Lars Hertervig (1830–1902). A nine-sided annexe houses the largest assemblage of mid-20th-century Norwegian art, including works by Harald Dal, Kai Fjell, Arne Ekeland and others.

Children's Museum

(Norsk Barnemuseum; www.norskbarne.museum. no, in Norwegian; off Laugmsgata; adult/child Nkr80/40; ☺11am-4pm Mon-Sat, noon-4pm Sun mid-Jun–mid-Aug, closed Monday rest of yr) A great place to take the kids is this museum, which has a range of activity-based exhibits (eg old

toys, a labyrinth) centred on the themes of landscape, labyrinth, curiosity and theatre. Part museum, part indoor playground, the kids will love you for taking them here. It's also known as the Norwegian Museum of Childhood.

Arkeologisk Museum ARCHAEOLOGICAL MUSEUM (☎51 84 60 00; www.ark.museum.no; Peder Klows gate 30a; adult/child Nkr20/10; ☺10am-5pm Mon-Fri, 11am-5pm Sat & Sun Jun-Aug, closed Mon & shorter hr rest of yr) This well-presented museum traces 11,000 years of human history, including the Viking Age. Exhibits include

Stavanger

skeletons, tools, a runestone and a description of the symbiosis between prehistoric humans and their environment. There's a full program of activities for kids (eg treasure hunts and wandering Vikings) in summer and there are a number of interactive exhibits.

Jernaldergarden — IRON-AGE FARM
(www.jernaldergarden.no; Ullandhaugvn 3, Ullandhaug; adult/child Nkr60/20; ⏰11am-4pm daily mid-Jun–mid-Aug, 11am-4pm Sun May–mid-Jun & mid-Aug–Oct) This reconstruction of a 1500-year-old Iron Age farm, 4km south of the centre, features various activities, staff in period dress and food preparation on Sunday. Take bus 5a or 5b towards Sandnes to Ullandhaug (Nkr32, 15 minutes) from next to the Radisson Hotel on Breiavannet lake.

☞ Tours

The best walking tours of downtown Stavanger are run by **Guide Companiet** (☑51 85 09 20; www.guidecompaniet.no; adult/child Nkr250/200; ⏰11am Tue, Thu & Sat mid-Jun–early Sep); tours leave from outside the tourist office and cover the cathedral, old Stavanger and Hafrsfjord.

Less ambitious in scope, the **Museum Information Office** (tour free with entrance ticket to Maritime Museum; ⏰11am in English, 1pm in Norwegian Jul–mid-Aug) has a daily tour through the Maritime Museum and the immediate vicinity. Tours focus on the city's seafaring history; they leave from outside the museum information office.

✹ Festivals & Events

Stavanger Vinfest — WINE
(www.stavangervinfest.no, in Norwegian; ⏰mid-Apr) A wine-focused celebration of food and drink.

May Jazz Festival — MUSIC
(www.maijazz.no; ⏰early May)

Gladmat — FOOD
(www.gladmat.no; ⏰late Jul) Food festival that drew Gordon Ramsay in 2010.

International Chamber Music Festival — MUSIC
(www.icmf.no; ⏰early Aug) Some concerts are held in the Stavanger Cathedral; tickets go on sale in mid-May.

Stavanger's Blomsterfest — FLOWERS
(⏰mid-Aug) The city's flower festival.

NuMusic — MUSIC
(www.numusic.no; ⏰early–mid-Sep)

🛏 Sleeping

Book well in advance for Stavanger stays. This is an oil city and prices can soar on weekdays as businesspeople arrive, but return to more reasonable levels on weekends – try to plan your visit accordingly. The tourist office website has a list of small B&Bs in and around Stavanger; some of these are listed at the end of this section.

For the Mosvangen Vandrerhjem or Mosvangen Camping, take bus 78 or 79 (Nkr32) from opposite the cathedral to Ullandhaugveien, 3km to the south.

TOP CHOICE ⟩ Skagen Brygge Hotel   HOTEL €€
(☑51 85 00 00; www.skagenbryggehotell.no; Skagenkaien 30; s/d Fri & Sat Nkr975/1275, Sun-Thu Nkr1695/1895, Jul every day Nkr1070/1370, with Fjord Pass yr-round Nkr880/1260; ☎) This large and opulent hotel (part of the Fjord Pass network) offers good weekend and summer value from its superb location right by the water. There are a range of rooms to choose from, but your best bet is to ask for a room with a harbour view and, unusually, this includes some single rooms. Guests have access to a private gym, and bills from some restaurants around town can be added to your room bill to be paid at check-out. It also serves free waffles from 2pm to 7pm.

TOP CHOICE ⟩ Myhregaarden Hotel
BOUTIQUE HOTEL €€
(☑51 86 80 00; www.myhregaardenhotel.no; Nygaten 24; s/d Fri-Sun Nkr895/995, Mon-Thu Nkr1699/1999; ☎) Opened in 2008, the Myhregaarden is Stavanger's most stylish hotel and has a far more personal touch than most chain hotels. The completely refurbished early-20th-century building, where Thor Heyerdahl once had an office, has some original features, but the contemporary rooms have soothing colour schemes and all but five have chandeliers and fireplaces; those without have original wooden beams. It's aimed at a business clientele, hence the great disparity in prices, but it's wonderful value on weekends.

Stavanger B&B   B&B €€
(☑51 56 25 00; www.stavangerbedandbreakfast.no; Vikedalsgata 1a; s/d with shared toilet Nkr690/790, with private bathroom Nkr790/890; P☎) This quiet but popular place comes highly recommended by readers and it's not hard to see why. The simple rooms are tidy and come with satellite TV, shower and a smile from the friendly owners. Packed lunches are available for a bargain Nkr40, and at 9pm nightly, free coffee, tea and waffles are served.

Skansen Hotel   HOTEL, GUESTHOUSE €€
(☑51 93 85 00; www.skansenhotel.no; Skansegata 7; guesthouse s Nkr755-1030, d Nkr970-1190, hotel s Nkr970-1130, d Nkr1110-1290; ☎) This centrally located place, opposite the old customs house, has a more personal feel to it than Stavanger's larger hotels. The hotel is divided into an older guesthouse section with simple, comfortable rooms, and newer hotel rooms that are larger and more stylish. There's also a pleasant beer garden out the back.

Mosvangen Camping   CAMPGROUND €
(☑51 53 29 71; www.stavangercamping.no; Tjensvoll 1b; tent sites without/with car Nkr120/170, with caravan or camper Nkr200, huts Nkr450-650; ☺Apr-Sep) During nesting season around Mosvangen lake, campers are treated to almost incessant birdsong amid the green and agreeable surroundings.

Thon Hotel Maritim   HOTEL €€
(☑51 85 05 00; www.thonhotels.no/maritim; Kongsgate 32; s/d Jul & Fri & Sat yr-round Nkr895/1095, Sun-Thu rest of yr Nkr1725/2025; ☎⊞) Part of the consistently comfortable Thon chain of hotels, this modern hotel just back from the lakeshore keeps up the standard with spacious, well-appointed rooms. It's really only worth it in July or on weekends. From June to August, it goes the extra mile for families, offering a family room for Nkr1190, as well as children's play areas and even a check-in ladder.

Victoria Hotel   HOTEL €€
(☑51 86 70 00; www.victoria-hotel.no; Skansegata 1; s/d from Nkr635/885; ☎) Part of the Rica Hotels network, the Victoria has a somewhat baronial air with traditionally styled rooms. Room prices can triple on weekdays outside summer, but the central waterfront location is good.

Mosvangen Vandrerhjem   HOSTEL €
(☑51 54 36 36; stavanger.hostel@vandrerhjem.no; Henrik Ibsensgate 19; dm/s/d with shared bathroom Nkr275/450/525; ☺mid-May–mid-Sep) Stavanger's pleasant and simple lakeside hostel, 3km southwest of the city centre, charges Nkr60 for breakfast. It opens only in the summer months.

Other excellent choices include the town's B&Bs and traditional homes. The more central options include the following:

Thompsons B&B   B&B €
(☑51 52 13 29; www.thompsonsbedandbreakfast. com; Muségata 79; s/d with shared bathroom

Nkr300/480; P) Housed in a 19th-century home and with a warm atmosphere generated by the English-Norwegian couple.

Tone's B&B   B&B €
(☎51 52 42 07; www.tones-bb.net; Peder Claussøns gate 22; s/d with shared bathroom Nkr350/500; P🕭) An old Stavanger home up the hill from Gamle Stavanger.

Villa Blidensol   OLD HOUSE €€
(☎51 52 53 46; www.gamlestallen.com; Øvre Strandgate 112; s/d Nkr1000/1200) Fifty sq metres all to yourself in one of Stavanger's oldest 18th-century homes with old wooden beams and underfloor heating.

✗ Eating

Stavanger has an extensive choice of restaurants, and despite the hubbub around the harbour in the evening, many places lie in the streets beyond the waterfront. We're confident about our recommendations, but for a second opinion check out www.gardkarlsen.com, which gives a local view on many of Stavanger's eateries.

Le Café Français   CAFE €
(Østervåg 30-32; sandwiches & light meals Nkr59-129; ☺9am-5pm Mon-Wed & Fri, 9am-7pm Thu, 9am-4pm Sat, 11am-5pm Sun) With the widest range of pastries and other sweet goodies in town, and outdoor tables on the pedestrian street outside, Le Café Français is a good place to wind down. It also serves sandwiches, miniquiches and good salads. A lovely spot.

NB Sørensen's Damskibsexpedition
                                           NORWEGIAN €€
(☎51 84 38 00; Skagen 26; mains Nkr125-329; ☺lunch & dinner) One of the better places along the waterfront, this restaurant serves everything from fish to pork ribs, with a seasonal lunch menu that's excellent value. The atmospheric indoor dining area is ideal when the weather turns, and locals swear that the food and service is better upstairs. When we were there, highlights on the menu included crab cakes with sweet corn salsa and chilli mayo (Nkr125), and the bargain half-kilo of prawns with dill mayo and lemon (Nkr125).

Bølgen & Moi   NORWEGIAN €€
(☎51 93 93 51; Norsk Oljemuseum, Kjerringholmen; mains Nkr95-265; ☺cafe 11am-5pm daily, bar & brasserie 6pm-1am Tue-Sat) The imaginative menus in this stylish restaurant attached to the Petroleum Museum include dishes such

as soy-and-honey-marinated salmon with potato salad (Nkr225). Lunch specials are huge. Although there are set menus in the evenings, you can also choose à la carte.

Charlottenlund   NORWEGIAN, FRENCH €€€
(☎51 91 76 00; www.charlottenlund.no; Kongsgate 45; mains from Nkr289, 3-/4-/5-course set menu Nkr445/510/565; ☺5-11pm Mon-Sat) One of Stavanger's classiest restaurants, Charlottenlund occupies an early-19th-century building and here it takes the freshest Norwegian ingredients and puts them at the service of French and Norwegian culinary traditions. The results are as impeccable as the service, and the set menus are excellent.

Emilio's Tapas Bar   SPANISH €€
(☎51 89 64 00; Sølvberggata 13; tapas Nkr50-190, lunch mains Nkr89-169; ☺lunch & dinner daily Jun-Aug, closed Sun Sep-May) Opposite the Akropolis and continuing on the Mediterranean theme, this pleasant Spanish tapas bar serves good Iberian food with friendly service that comes at no extra cost. The best order is probably the lunch-time selection of six tapas (Nkr169). It also has a small selection of Spanish wines and beers.

Kiellands   NORWEGIAN, INTERNATIONAL €€
(☎51 53 33 00; www.kiellands.restaurant.no, in Norwegian; Kongsgate 41; mains Nkr98-235; ☺lunch & dinner) With an agreeable outdoor terrace right by the lake, this casual place serves up everything from steaks, golden redfish or mussels steamed in beer to a tapas set menu (Nkr295 per person, minimum of two people). And if you can't stomach a heavy meal, it also serves salads and sandwiches.

Kult Kafeen   CAFE €
(off Laugmsgata; sandwiches & salads Nkr120-135; ☺10am-10pm Mon-Sat, noon-10pm Sun) Located in the Kulturhus in the centre of town, this cool place has won the affection of families and young professionals alike. Well-sized sandwiches and fresh salads are the high points, but many just come here for a quiet coffee.

Akropolis Greek Restaurant   GREEK €€
(☎51 89 14 54; Sølvberggata 14; specials Nkr129-179, mains Nkr219-369, Sun lunch buffet Nkr180; ☺lunch & dinner) This very popular place serves authentic Greek food at somewhat elevated prices for those in search of great salads, tzatziki, grilled meats and moussaka. It's real attraction lies in its excellent Sunday lunch buffet, served from 1pm until 6pm.

Café Sting CAFE €€

(☎51 89 32 84; Valbergata 3; light meals Nkr98-169; ☺noon-midnight Mon-Thu, noon-3.30am Fri & Sat, 3pm-midnight Sun) Pasta and sandwiches are served in this fine all-round venue.

Torget Fish Market FISH MARKET €

(Rosenkildetorget; ☺9am-4.30pm Mon-Thu, 9am-5pm Fri, 9am-4pm Sat) Not a patch on the Bergen version, but one stall sells prepared meals.

Naree Thai THAI €€

(☎51 89 05 10; Breigata 22; lunch mains from Nkr79, dinner mains from Nkr129; ☺lunch & dinner) One of the numerous Asian restaurants in town.

🍷 Drinking & Entertainment

Most of the livelier bars are right on the waterfront and cater to a younger crowd with a penchant for loud, energetic music. You'll hear them long before you see them, and as they're all similar, we think you'll be able to find them on your own.

TOP CHOICE **B.brormann B.bar** COCKTAIL BAR

(Skansegata 7; ☺4pm-2am) One of Stavanger's coolest bars, where you can actually hear the conversation, and contemporary artworks adorn the brick walls. This oddly named place draws a discerning over-30s crowd and serves great-value half-litre beers (Nkr63) and cocktails (Nkr96) prepared by Siv-Karin Helland, who won Norway's 2010 cocktail-mixing championship with her 'Monroe's Lemonade'.

Café Sting BAR, NIGHTCLUB

(☎51 89 32 84; Valbergata 3; ☺noon-midnight Mon-Thu, noon-3.30am Fri & Sat, 3pm-midnight Sun) Just up the hill but a world away, Café Sting is at once a mellow cafe and a funky cultural space with exhibitions, live jazz whenever the mood takes it, and a weekend nightclub where the DJs keep you on your toes, spinning house, hip-hop and soul.

Bøker & Brøst CAFE, BAR

(Øvre Holmegate 32; ☺10am-2am) There are dozens of engaging little cafes in the lanes climbing the hillside west of the oil museum, but our favourite is Bøker & Brøst, with its warm and eccentric decor, great coffee and laid-back feel whatever the time of day. Special mention must be made of the toilets, which have antique wallpaper and bookshelves filled to bursting – clearly staff don't mind if you linger.

Irishman IRISH BAR, LIVE MUSIC

(☎51 89 41 81; Hølebergsgata 9; ☺5pm-2am Mon-Wed, 3pm-2am Thu, Fri & Sun, 1pm-2am Sat) Stavanger's friendly Irish pub has (free) live Irish folk music at least twice a week in summer, usually on Thursday at 9.30pm and Saturday at 3pm, with an acoustic jam session at 7pm on the first Sunday of every month.

Stavanger Konserthus CLASSICAL MUSIC

(www.stavanger-konserthus.no; Nedre Strandgate 89b) If you're after something a little more sedate, Stavanger Konserthus offers free classical-music concerts in July; the tourist office has program details.

ℹ Information

Museum Information Office (Nedre Strandgate 21; ☺10am-4pm Jun-Aug) Information on most of the city's museums.

Stavanger Turistforening DNT (☎51 84 02 00; off Muségata; ☺10am-4pm Mon-Wed & Fri, 10am-6pm Thu, 10am-2pm Sat) Information on hiking and mountain huts.

Tourist office (☎51 85 92 00; www.region stavanger.com; Domkirkeplassen 3; ☺9am-5pm Jun-Aug, 9am-4pm Mon-Fri, 9am-2pm Sat Sep-May) Local information and advice on Lysefjord and Preikestolen.

ℹ Getting There & Away

Air

Stavanger airport (☎51 65 80 00) is at Sola, 14km south of the city centre. Apart from inter-

BUSES FROM STAVANGER

DESTINATION	DEPARTURES (DAILY)	COST (NKR)	DURATION (HR)
Bergen	6	490	5¾
Haugesund	6	240	2¼
Kristiansand	2-5	380	4½
Oslo	up to 5	795	9½

DESTINATION	DEPARTURES	COST (NKR)	DURATION (HR)
Egersund	hourly	145	1¼
Kristiansand	2-5 daily	427	3
Oslo	up to 5 daily	886	8

national airlines (see p435), there are the following domestic services:

Norwegian (www.norwegian.com) Flights to Oslo, Bergen and Trondheim.

SAS (www.sas.no) Oslo and Bergen.

Widerøe (www.wideroe.no) Bergen, Kristiansand and Sandefjord.

Boat

For international ferries, see p436, while boat tours of Lysefjord from Stavanger are covered on p196. Otherwise, services include the following:

Flaggruten (☑55 32 12 24; www.flaggruten. no; Fiskepirterminalen) Twice-daily services from Sunday to Friday to Haugesund (one-way/ return Nkr310/470) and Bergen (Nkr750/950), with just one on Saturday.

M/S Lysebotn (☑91 65 28 00; www.kolumbus. no) Car-and-passenger ferries from Stavanger to Lysebotn (adult/child/car Nkr173/87/356).

Tide Reiser (www.tidereiser.no; ⊙Jun-Aug) Daily summer four-hour car ferries with tourist commentary along Lysefjord to Lysebotn (adult/child/car Nkr210/120/400) from Fiskepirterminalen. There's also the fast ferry M/S *Lysefjord* that leaves Stavanger at 1.30pm (and Lysebotn at 7.20am) on Monday, Wednesday and Friday.

Bus

Note that most services to Oslo change at Kristiansand.

Car & Motorcycle

Driving between Bergen and Stavanger along the direct E39 can be expensive once you factor in ferries, road tolls and city tolls. In all, you'll end up paying around Nkr600.

Train

Note that most train services to Oslo change at Kristiansand.

❶ Getting Around
To/From the Airport

Between early morning and mid-to-late evening, **Flybussen** (☑51 52 26 00; www.flybussen.no/ stavanger) runs every half-hour between the bus

terminal and the airport at Sola (one way/return Nkr90/140).

Lysefjord

All along the 42km-long Lysefjord (Light Fjord), the granite rock glows with an ethereal, ambient light, even on dull days, all offset by almost-luminous mist. This is the favourite fjord of many visitors, and there's no doubt that it has a captivating beauty. Whether you cruise from Stavanger, hike up to Preikestolen (604m), or drive the switchback road down to Lysebotn, it's one of Norway's must-sees. For information on visiting from Stavanger, see p196.

PREIKESTOLEN (PULPIT ROCK)

The sight of people perched without fear on the edge of this extraordinary granite rock formation is one of Norway's emblematic images. Preikestolen, with astonishingly uniform cliffs on three sides plunging 604m to the fjord below, is a freak of nature, which, despite the alarming crack where it joins the mountains, is likely to be around for a few more centuries. While looking down can be a bit daunting, you won't regret the magical view directly up Lysefjord. It's quite simply a remarkable place, a vantage point unrivalled anywhere in the world.

There are no fences and those with vertigo will find themselves unable to go right to the edge (even watching the death-defying antics of people dangling limbs over the abyss can make the heart skip a beat). However, the local authorities assured us that there have been no reported cases of anyone accidentally falling off (even the French daredevil who balanced on the edge atop three chairs!). That said, take all due care even if other people seemingly don't. Rocky trails also lead up the mountains behind, offering more wonderful views.

VISITING LYSEFJORD

The most spectacular aspect of visiting Lysefjord is the two-hour hike up to Preikestolen (Pulpit Rock), although a ferry along Lysefjord is an alternative for those who can't make the hike. For general information on the region, check out www.lysefjordeninfo.no or www.visitlysefjorden.no.

Pulpit Rock by Public Transport

From May to mid-September, five to seven ferries a day run from Stavanger's Fiske-spiren Quay to Tau, where the ferries are met by a bus, which runs between the Tau pier and the Preikestolhytta Vandrerhjem. From there, the two-hour trail leads up to Preikestolen. The last bus from Preikestolhytta to Tau leaves at 7.55pm. Conveniently, two companies – **Østerhus Buss** (www.osterhusbuss) and **Tide Reiser** (www.tiderei ser.no) – offer all-inclusive round-trip tickets (adult/child Nkr200/100). Services are essentially the same and the tourist office has timetables for both. You can buy tickets for both at the tourist office, while Tide Reiser also has an office at the Fiske-spiren Quay.

Pulpit Rock by Car

If you've got your own vehicle, you can take the car ferry (adult/child/car Nkr42/21/125, 40 minutes, up to 24 departures daily) from Stavanger's Fiskespiren Quay to Tau. From the pier in Tau, a well-signed road (Rv13) leads 19km to Preikestolhytta Van-drerhjem (take the signed turn-off after 13km). It costs Nkr60/30 per car/motorcycle to park here.

An alternative route from Stavanger involves driving to Lauvik (via Sandnes along Rv13), from where a ferry crosses to Oanes (adult/child/car Nkr24/12/59, 10 minutes, departures almost every half-hour).

Either way, the trip between Stavanger and the trailhead takes around 1½ hours.

Boat Tours to Lysefjord

Two companies offer three-hour boat cruises from Stavanger to the waters below Preikestolen on Lysefjord and back:

Rødne Fjord Cruise (☎51 89 52 70; www.rodne.no; Skagenkaien 35-37; adult/child/senior & student/family Nkr380/200/280/890; ☺departures 10.30am & 2.30pm Sun-Fri & 12.30pm Sat Jul & Aug, noon daily May, Jun & Sep, noon Fri-Sun Oct-Apr)

Tide Reiser (☎51 86 87 88; www.tidereiser.no; adult/child/senior & student Nkr360/250/280; ☺departures noon late May-Aug, noon Sat Sep-late May)

Round Trips to Kjeragbolten

From mid-May to late August **Tide Reiser** (☎51 86 87 88; www.tidereiser.no; adult/child Nkr490/390; ☺departures 8am late Jun-late Aug) runs 13½-hour bus–boat–hike return trips to Kjeragbolten, which can otherwise be difficult to reach. It includes a five-hour return hike.

The two-hour, 3.8km trail up to Preikesto-len leaves from Preikestolhytta Vandrerhjem. It begins along a steep but well-marked route, then climbs past a series of alternating steep and boggy sections to the final climb across granite slabs and along some windy and exposed cliffs to Preikestolen itself. The steepest sections are at the beginning and in the middle parts of the trail and can be challenging for the unfit.

The area also offers several other fabulous walks – the **Vatnerindane ridge circuit** (two hours), **Ulvaskog** (three hours), the **Refsvatnet circuit** (three hours), and summit of **Moslifjellet** (three hours) and even a two-day hike all the way to **Lysebotn** – all of which are accessible from the Preikestol-hytta car park. For more information on possible routes and DNT huts along the trails, visit the Stavanger Turistforening DNT (p194) before setting out from Stavanger.

Sleeping & Eating

Preikestolen Fjellstue & Preikestolhytta Vandrerhjem
MOUNTAIN LODGE, YOUTH HOSTEL €

(☎51 74 20 74; www.preikestolenfjellstue.no; Jørpeland; dm Nkr245-280, s Nkr995-1295, d Nkr1295-1595) Completely overhauled in recent years, this DNT mountain lodge and hostel at the Preikestolen trailhead has a range of accommodation for all budgets. The lodge facilities are a vast improvement on what went before, which means that Preikestolen finally has accommodation worthy of its fame. This is also the place to get information and route maps about Preikestolen. The hostel closes in winter.

Preikestolen Camping
CAMPGROUND €

(☎48 19 39 50; www.preikestolencamping.com; Jørpeland; tent sites without/with car Nkr150/180 plus per adult/child Nkr30/20; ☉Apr-Oct) The closest campsite to Preikestolen (5km, or 1km off the Rv13) isn't anything to write home about, but proximity is everything. Kitchen facilities are available, but you can also eat at the attached shop-restaurant. A word of warning: the campsite is for sale, so all of this could change.

ℹ Information

Lysefjordsenteret (☎51 70 31 23; www.lysefjordsenteret.no; Oanes; adult/child Nkr50/25; ☉11am-8pm Jun-Aug, 11am-5pm Sep-May) In a fabulous setting north of the ferry terminal at Oanes, with tourist information, audiovisual displays and geological and folk-history exhibits.

LYSEBOTN

The ferry ride from Stavanger takes you to the fjord head at Lysebotn, where a narrow and much-photographed road corkscrews spectacularly 1000m up towards Sirdal in 27 hairpin bends. For details on getting to Lysebotn, see p195. From Lysebotn, the road twists up the mountain, from which you can continue on into the Setesdalen region (p118) and Oslo.

🏃 Activities

After Preikestolen, the most popular Lysefjord walk leads to **Kjeragbolten**, an enormous oval-shaped boulder, or 'chockstone', lodged between two rock faces about 2m apart – you've surely seen it on postcards around Norway. The 10km, five-hour return hike involves a strenuous 700m ascent from the Øygardsstølen Café car park (parking Nkr30), near the highest hairpin bend above Lysebotn.

The route trudges up and over three ridges and, in places, steep muddy slopes can make the going quite rough. Once you're at Kjeragbolten, actually reaching the boulder requires some tricky manoeuvring, including traversing an exposed ledge on a 1000m-high vertical cliff! From there, you can step (or crawl) directly onto the boulder for one of Norway's most astonishing views. The photo of you perched on the rock is sure to impress your friends.

If this doesn't provide sufficient thrills, then base jumping from Kjeragbolten could just be Norway's craziest sport; check out the website of the **Stavanger Base Club** (www.basekjerag.com).

Sleeping & Eating

Lysebotn Tourist Camp
CAMPGROUND & HOTEL €

(☎90 83 20 35; www.lysebotn-touristcamp.com; tent/caravan sites Nkr140/160, dm Nkr260, 4-bed cabins Nkr750-1150, d Nkr840) If you can't face the hairpin road up the mountain or, more likely, you can't bear to leave, Lysebotn Tourist Camp occupies an incredible setting at the head of the fjord. It's a lovely quiet spot to be after the ferry has left for the day.

Øygardsstølen Café
CAFE €€

(snacks & light meals Nkr59-149; ☉9.30am-8pm mid-Jun–mid-Sep) For views at this end of Lysefjord, you can't beat the 'eagle's nest', perched atop the cliff overlooking the hairpin twists down to Lysebotn. There's a viewing deck for those who don't wish to eat.

The Western Fjords

Best Places to Eat

» Maki (p233)

» Smia Fiskerestaurant
(p242)

» Restaurant Arven (p202)

» Ciderhuset (p208)

» Bryggja (p218)

Best Places to Stay

» Hotel Mundal (p213)

» Visnes Hotel (p218)

» Hotel Union (p229)

» Hotel Brosundet (p231)

Why Go?

In 2009, readers of *National Geographic Traveler* magazine elected the fjords of western Norway as the best-preserved attraction on Unesco's World Heritage list.

Scoured and gouged by glaciers, ancient and modern, these deep, sea-drowned valleys are pincered by steep, rugged terrain. They offer myriad things to see and do: in the water, up the mountains or just plain on the level.

Ferries are fun. These reliable workhorses lop off huge detours around a fjord, but they're also an enjoyable part of the journey in their own right, offering staggering and otherwise inaccessible panoramas of the coastline around you.

The western fjords are great hiking country too, whether following one of the many signed trails or lumbering along in a guided glacier-walking group. And if, after so much fresh air and wide-open space, you crave some small-town sophistication, drop into the bijou art nouveau settlement of Ålesund.

When to Go
Ålesund

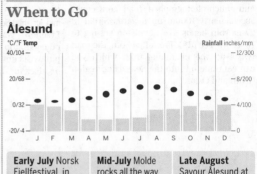

Early July Norsk Fjellfestival in Åndalsnes, a folk and outdoor jamboree.

Mid-July Molde rocks all the way from Monday to Saturday during Moldejazz.

Late August Savour Ålesund at its best during the town's Norwegian Food Festival.

SOGNEFJORDEN

Sognefjorden, the world's second-longest (203km) and Norway's deepest (1308m) fjord, cuts a deep slash across the map of western Norway. In places, sheer walls rise more than 1000m above the water, while elsewhere a gentler shoreline supports farms, orchards and villages. The broad, main waterway is impressive but by cruising into its narrower arms, such as the deep and lovely Nærøyfjord to Gudvangen, you'll see idyllic views of abrupt cliff faces and cascading waterfalls.

ℹ Getting There & Away

Fjord1 (57 75 70 00; www.fjord1.no, in Norwegian) operates a daily express boat between Bergen and both Flåm (Nkr665, 5½ hours) and Sogndal (Nkr570, 4¾ hours), stopping along the way at 10 small towns including Vik (Nkr450, 3½ hours) and Balestrand (Nkr485, 3¾ hours). Several local ferries also link Sognefjord towns, and there's an extensive, if infrequent, bus network.

Flåm

POP 550

Flåm, at the head of Aurlandsfjorden, sits in a truly spectacular setting. As a stop on the popular 'Norway in a Nutshell' tour, this tiny village receives over 500,000 visitors every year. It has its charm but its tacky side too: should you so wish, you can pick up a pair of panties decorated with the Norwegian flag or a set of plastic elk antlers.

The **tourist office** (✆57 63 33 13; www.alr.no; ⊙8.30am-4pm & 4.30-8pm Jun-Aug, shorter hr rest of yr) is within the train station, where you'll also find four internet terminals.

◉ Sights

Flåmsbana Railway　　CLASSIC RAIL JOURNEY
(www.flaamsbana.no; adult/child one-way Nkr240/115, return Nkr340/230) This 20km-long engineering wonder hauls itself up 864m of altitude gain through 20 tunnels. At a gradient of 1:18, it's the world's steepest railway that runs without cable or rack wheels. It takes a full 45 minutes to climb to Myrdal on the bleak, treeless Hardangervidda plateau, past thundering waterfalls (there's a photo stop at awesome Kjosfossen). The railway runs year-round, with up to 10 departures daily in summer.

FREE **Flåmsbana Museum**　　MUSEUM
(www.flamsbana-museet.no; ⊙9am-5pm May-Sep, 1-30-3pm rest of year) To prepare yourself for your rail journey, browse this little museum right beside the train platform. It's not just about railways; there are fascinating photos of construction gangs and life in and around Flåm before the car era.

🏃 Activities

To simply pedal along the shoreline or for something more strenuous, rent a bike from the tourist office (Nkr50/250 per hour/day). The tourist office also has six easy-to-interpret free sheets describing local walks, varying from 45 minutes to five hours, with routes superimposed upon aerial photos.

Rallarvegen　　BIKE DESCENT
(www.rallarvegen.com) Cyclists can descend the Rallarvegen, the service road originally used by the navvies who constructed the railway, for 83km from Haugastøl (1000m) or an easier 56km from Finse. You can rent bicycles in Haugastøl (two days weekday/weekend Nkr480/580, including return transport from Flåm) and the company also offers packages that include accommodation. For more information on the Rallarvegen, see the boxed text, p152.

Njord　　KAYAKING
(www.kajakk.com) Njord operates from Flåm's handkerchief of a beach. It offers a two-hour sea-kayaking induction (Nkr350), three-hour gentle fjord paddle (Nkr450) and four-hour paddle and hike trips (Nkr590), plus multiday kayaking, hiking and camping trips.

Fjord Safari　　BOAT TRIP
(www.fjordsafari.com) Bounce along in a Zodiac/RIB inflatable to see more of the fjord in less time. The team supplies full-length waterproof kit – you'll need it for this exhilarating scoot across the waters. Trips, with stops,

---

NORWAY IN A NUTSHELL

Although most visitors do the classic 'Norway in a Nutshell' tour from either Oslo or Bergen (see p445), you also can do a mini version (adult/child Nkr650/340). This circular route from Flåm – boat to Gudvangen, bus to Voss, train to Myrdal, then train again down the spectacular Flåmsbana railway to Flåm – is truly the kernel within the nutshell and takes in all the most dramatic elements. The Gudvangen boat leaves Flåm at 9am and the Flåmsbana train brings you home at 4.55pm.

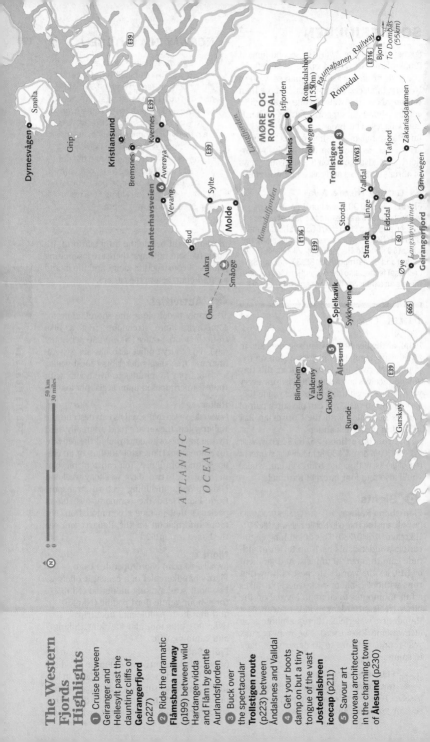

The Western Fjords Highlights

1 Cruise between Geiranger and Hellesylt past the daunting cliffs of **Geirangerfjord** (p227)

2 Ride the dramatic **Flåmsbana railway** (p199) between wild Hardangervidda and Flåm by gentle Aurlandsfjorden

3 Buck over the spectacular **Trollstigen route** (p223) between Åndalsnes and Valldal

4 Get your boots damp on but a tiny tongue of the vast **Jostedalsbreen icecap** (p211)

5 Savour art nouveau architecture in the charming town of **Ålesund** (p230)

ATLANTIC OCEAN

50 km
30 miles

Dynesvågen

Smøla

Grip

Kristiansund

Bremsnes

Averøya

Kvernes

Vevang

Atlanterhavsveien

Sylte

Bud

Molde

Aukra

Småoge

Ona

Isfjorden

Romsdalshorn (1550m)

Raumabanen Railway

Romsdal

E316

Bjorli

To Dombås (55km)

MØRE OG ROMSDAL

Åndalsnes

Trollvegen

Romsdalfjorden

Langfjorden

E136

E39

Stordal

Trollstigen Route 3

RV63

Valldal

Linge

Tafjord

Zakariasdammen

Eidsdal

Stranda

60

Øye

665

Geirangerfjord

Langtsvylvatnet

Ørnevegen

Spjelkavik

Sykkylven

Ålesund 5

Blindheim

Valderøy

Giske

Godøy

Runde

Gurskøy

6 Feel the sea
spray as you ride the
Atlantic Ocean Road,
Atlanterhavsveien
(p238)

7 Ride or cycle
the Snow Road,
SnøVegen (p204),
between Aurland and
Lærdal

last from 1½ hours (adult/child Nkr430/210) to three hours (adult/child Nkr640/320).

Flåm Marina og Apartement BOAT HIRE
If you'd rather paddle your own canoe, row or simply sit back at the tiller, Flåm Marina og Apartement, a five-minute walk from the jetty, hires out rowing boats and canoes and motorboats.

Sleeping

Fretheim Hotel HOTEL €€€
(☎57 63 63 00; www.fretheim-hotel.no; s/d Nkr1245/1690; ⏲Feb–mid-Dec; P@) A haunt of the English aristocracy in the 19th century (they came for the fishin'), the vast, 121-room – which, despite its size manages to be intimate and welcoming – Fretheim is as much sports and social centre as hotel. In the original 1870s building, 17 rooms (Nkr400 supplement) have been restored to their former condition – including replica clawfoot bathtubs – with 21st-century amenities. The hotel will arrange and advise on walking and bike trips. Exertions over, the 3rd-floor bar in the tower does a great range of beers and is a pleasant place to enjoy the view (but for the very best panorama, climb the spiral staircase to the glass-floored eyrie at the top).

TOP CHOICE **Flåm Camping & Youth Hostel** HOSTEL, CAMPGROUND €
(☎57 63 21 21; www.flaam-camping.no; car or caravan sites Nkr185-195, dm Nkr200-270, s/d from Nkr330/470, cabins from Nkr685; ⏲May-Sep) This friendly spot is only a few minutes' walk from the station. In 2010, Hostelling International judged it to be Norway's best hostel and the ninth best in the world. You can see why – there's a brand-new block with en suite facilities, amenities are impeccable and the welcome couldn't be warmer.

Heimly Pensjonat GUESTHOUSE €€
(☎57 63 23 00; www.heimly.no; s Nkr795-895, d Nkr895-1095) Overlooking the water on the fringe of the village and away from all the port hubbub, this place has straightforward rooms. The more expensive ones, plus the small patch of lawn, have a magnificent view along the fjord. From late June to early August, the guesthouse also offers **dorm beds** (Nkr255) in an adjacent building; nothing fancy and no cooking facilities but the price is right.

Flåm Marina & Apartement APARTMENTS €€
(☎57 63 35 55, www.flammarina.no; apt Nkr1150) This modern block, right at the water's edge, offers magnificent views down the length of the fjord from the terrace of its small **bar-cafe** (dishes Nkr70 to Nkr125), open to all. Its 10 self-catering apartments, comfortable for two, can sleep up to five (Nkr300 extra per bed).

Flåmsbrygga HOTEL €€€
(☎57 63 20 50; www.flamsbrygga.no; s/d Nkr1200/1600 incl breakfast) This recently established hotel has 41 attractive, identical rooms, rustic in style. All but two have a balcony, giving a superb vista down the fjord. There's original artwork on the walls, plenty of woodwork and colours of warm beige and brown.

Eating & Drinking

TOP CHOICE **Restaurant Arven** RESTAURANT €€€
(Fretheim Hotel; mains Nkr275-290) At the Fretheim Hotel, the chefs salt and smoke their own meat and there's an 'ecological and local' menu, sourced from the region's agricultural college. You can also sample local lamb, reindeer and goat kid, grilled in the barbecue hut or featuring on the coffee house menu.

Æegir Bryggeri BREW PUB
(www.flamsbrygga.no/bryggeri; ⏲noon-1am Jun-Aug, 6-10pm May & Sep, weekends only rest of year) Looking for all the world like a stave church, Æegir Brewery, all appealing woodwork and flagstones, offers six different kinds of draught beer, all brewed on the spot. It also does a tasty, creative take on burgers, pizzas and salads (around Nkr150).

WESTERN FJORDS WEBSITES

These websites will help in your planning.

www.fjordnorway.com Detailed coverage of the fjords region.

www.nordfjord.no Equally comprehensive about Nordfjord.

www.visitmr.com The Møre og Romsdal region's official website with a host of useful links.

www.fjordkysten.no Covers the region's northern coastline.

www.sognefjord.no Great for the whole of Sognefjord and its environs.

www.stavechurch.com A great introduction to stave churches, plus in-depth coverage of the major ones.

DESTINATION	PRICE (NKR)	DURATION	FREQUENCY (DAILY)
Gudvangen	47	20min	4-8
Aurland	32	15min	4-8
Sogndal	136	1¾hr	2-6
Lærdalsøyri	84	45min	2-6
Bergen	300	3hr	2-6

ℹ Getting There & Away

Boat

From Flåm, boats head out to towns around Sognefjorden. The most scenic trip from Flåm is the passenger ferry up Nærøyfjord to Gudvangen (single/return Nkr255/360). It leaves Flåm at 3.10pm year-round and up to four times daily between May and September. You can also hop aboard in Aurland. At Gudvangen, a connecting bus takes you on to Voss, where you can pick up the train for Bergen or Oslo. The tourist office sells all ferry tickets, plus the Flåm to Voss ferry-bus combination. From Flåm-Bergen, there's at least one daily express boat (Nkr665, 5½ hours) via Balestrand (Nkr225, 1½ hours).

Bus

See the boxed text for destinations reached by bus.

Train

Flåm is the only Sognefjorden village with a rail link, via the magnificent Flåmsbana railway. There are train connections to Oslo and Bergen at Myrdal.

Undredal

POP HUMANS 80, GOATS 500

Undredal, tucked midway between Flåm and Gudvangen, is a truly lovely little village, its pleasures enhanced – and its traditional quality sustained – because you need to make that bit of extra effort to get there. However, it has recently been added as a brief stop to some boat tours and its former tranquillity is at risk.

The tiny, barrel-vaulted **village church** (adult/child Nkr30/free; ⊙noon-5pm mid-May–mid-Sep), originally built as a stave church in 1147 and seating 40, is the smallest still-operational house of worship in mainland Scandinavia. Look up at the roof with its charmingly naive roof paintings of angels, Christ on the cross and other biblical figures, surrounded by stylised stars.

Undredal's other claim to fame is its cheeses. Well, not exactly fame, as you'll only find them in a few specialised cheese shops and delicatessens within Norway. Around 500 goats freely roam the surrounding grassy slopes and between them they provide the milk for around 10 tonnes of cheese per year (work it out: that's a hugely impressive yield per nipple). Farmers from the valley supply the village's two remaining dairies – once there were 10 – which still produce the firm yellow Undredal cheese and its brown, slightly sweet variant, made from the boiled and concentrated whey. You can pick up a hunk of each at the village shop; it's the light-blue building beside the shore.

Undredal is 6.5km north of the E16 down a narrow, steeply threading road (until its construction in 1988, the only access was by sea). If travelling by bus, get off at the eastern end of the 11km tunnel that leads to Gudvangen. Best of all, take the bus out, walk down the spectacular valley along the lightly trafficked road and return by boat (press the switch beside the yellow blinking lamp on the cafe wall beside the jetty to alert the next passing ferry).

Gudvangen & Nærøyfjord

Nærøyfjord, its 17km length a Unesco World Heritage Site, lies west of Flåm. Beside the deep blue fjord (only 250m across at its narrowest point) are towering 1200m-high cliffs, isolated farms, and waterfalls plummeting from the heights. It can easily be visited as a day excursion from Flåm.

Kjelsfossen waterfall tumbles from the southern wall of Nærøydalen valley, above Gudvangen village. Notice too the **avalanche protection scheme** above Gudvangen. The powerful avalanches here typically provide a force of 12 tonnes per sq metre, move at 50m/second and, local legend reckons, can bowl a herd of goats right across the fjord!

OTTERNES

Between Flåm and Aurland, high above the fjord, perches the restored hamlet of **Otternes** (www.otternes.no; adult/child Nkr50/free; ☺10am-5pm Jun–mid-Sep). This complex of 27 renovated buildings, the oldest dating from the early 17th century, was lived in until the 1990s. It's largely the initiative of one person, the ebullient Laila Kvellestad. To get full value from the visit, follow her half- to one-hour guided tour (Nkr30 extra; available in English four times daily). Plan too a rest break to lick a locally made organic ice cream, sip fresh apple juice or eat a bowl of *rømmegrøt*, a rich sour-cream porridge served with thin shavings of locally cured meat (including organic lamb from Laila's farm).

The approach by boat is wondrous but Gudvangen itself, like a mini Flåm only more constricted, is very missable. Boats belch diesel fumes at your feet, coaches back up at the rear and the cafe-restaurant plays the Viking card for all it's worth.

A pair of campgrounds flank the road, 1.3km from the ferry port. Each is well equipped and beautifully situated at the base of sheer cliffs – but oh, the noise from traffic passing on the busy E6 if you're sleeping in a tent!

Gudvangen Camping CAMPGROUND €€
(☎993 80 803; www.visitgudvangen.com; campsites Nkr120, 2-/4-person cabins with outdoor bathroom Nkr370/420, with bathroom Nkr800/1050; ☺mid-Apr–mid-Sep)

Vang Camping CAMPGROUND €€
(☎57 63 39 26; www.vang-camping.no; per person/site Nkr20/100, cabins with outdoor bathroom Nkr300-500, with bathroom Nkr800-1200; ☺mid-May–mid-Sep).

ⓘ Getting There & Away

Scenic ferries between Gudvangen and Flåm (one way/return Nkr215/294) via Aurland run up to four times daily. A car ferry runs three times daily to/from Lærdal (car and driver/passenger Nkr600/250; three hours) via Kaupanger (Nkr595/240).

Up to eight buses daily run to/from Flåm (Nkr47, 20 minutes) and Aurland (Nkr52, 30 minutes).

Aurland

POP 650

Peaceful Aurland is so much less hectic and trodden than its neighbour, Flåm, a mere 10km south along the fjord. It marks the end of the spectacular Aurlandsdalen hiking route. These days it's also renowned as one end of Lærdalstunnel (24.5km), the world's longest road tunnel. This essential link in the E16 highway that connects Oslo and Bergen (before its completion, traffic had to ferry-hop between Lærdal and Gudvangen) is a fast alternative to the beautiful but sinuous and seasonal 45km-long **Snøvegen** (☺Jun–mid-Oct). It's a choice between tunnel vision, speed and convenience, or a sometimes hair-raising ascent that offers inspirational views all the way up and down...

The Aurland **tourist office** (☎57 63 33 13; www.alr.no; ☺8.30am-6pm Mon-Fri), beside the village church, has an internet point (donation requested).

🏃 Activities

The Aurland and Lærdal tourist offices have produced six walker-friendly sheets of local **walks**, where the route is superimposed upon an aerial photo.

For consistently outstanding views and near-solitude, hike the 12km trail that mainly follows the old road between Aurland and Flåm, passing by Otternes. Until 1919 and the construction of the coast road, it was the only means of land communication between the two villages. Allow around three hours.

The classic trek down Aurlandsdalen from Geiteryggen to Aurland follows a stream from source to sea as you tramp one of the oldest trading routes between eastern and western Norway. From mid-July, you can start this four-day walk in Finse, on the Oslo–Bergen rail line, with overnight stops at Geiterygghytta, Steinbergdalen and Østerbø.

The final section, usually open between early June and late September, from Østerbø (820m) to Vassbygdi (95m) is the most scenic and makes for a hugely enjoyable day hike (allow six to seven hours). Buses run twice daily between Aurland and both Vassbygdi (15 minutes) and Østerbø (one hour).

🛏 Sleeping & Eating

Aurland Fjordhotell HOTEL €€
(☎57 63 35 05; www.aurland-fjordhotel.com; s/d from Nkr590/790; ℗) At this friendly 30-room, family-owned hotel, most of the comfortable,

well-furnished rooms have fjord views and balcony. To help you sleep, have a shot from the owner's huge collection of brandies and spirits in a couple of display cases beside reception.

Vangsgaarden   GUESTHOUSE €€
(☑57 63 35 80; www.vangsgaarden.no; d Nkr900, cabins Nkr850-1200; P⊛) The complex embraces four 18th-century buildings, six cabins down at sea level and the **Duehuset (Dovecot) Cafe & Pub** (⊙3-11pm). Most rooms are furnished in antique style; the dining room, for example, could be your grandmother's parlour.

Lunde Gard & Camping   CAMPGROUND €
(☑997 04 701; www.lunde-camping.no; campsites Nkr190, cabins with outdoor bathroom Nkr550, with bathroom Nkr950, 3-bed apt Nkr750; ⊙May-Sep) This small campground nestles agreeably beside a river, 1.2km up a side valley. Kitchen and toilet facilities are impeccable.

Aurlandskafeen   CAFE €€
(⊙10am-9pm; lunch specials Nkr90-130, fish soup Nkr70) What distinguishes this cafe from other bog-standard eateries in Norway is its neat little terrace overlooking the rippling river where it flows into Aurlandsfjord.

ⓘ Getting There & Away

Buses run up to eight times daily between Aurland and Flåm (Nkr32, 15 minutes) and one to six times daily between Aurland and Lærdal (Nkr68, 30 minutes). Express buses to/from Bergen (Nkr300, three hours) call in up to six times daily.

Watch out for the speed cameras in Lærdalstunnelen, at 24.5km they're the world's longest; they'll certainly have their eye on you...

Lærdal
LÆRDALSØYRI
POP 2200

The village of Lærdalsøyri, usually called Lærdal, is where the lovely green dale of the same name (whose fertile lower reaches produce the juiciest of cherries) meets the fjord. A quiet place nowadays, it was once a busy port, where produce from the surrounding area was loaded on Bergen-bound boats, which also bore so many rural emigrants on the first stage of their journey to a new life in the US.

If you're planning to camp anywhere within the western fjords, this place, which locals claim is Norway's second-driest village, is your spot!

⊙ Sights & Activities

The town makes for pleasant strolling beside well preserved 18th- and 19th-century timber homes, warehouses and fisherfolk's shacks. The tourist office has a free town map that describes the best of them and sets out a walking route. It will also lend you a free audio guide that takes you around the town's top 11 spots (leave your passport or ID as guarantee).

There's free **fishing** in the fjord, and the upper reaches of the Lærdal river are good for trout (day permits are normally available from the nearest campground).

For ideas about **hiking**, pick up the tourist office's free leaflet of walks in the area. It also sells a much more detailed map of the area (Nkr139) at a scale of 1:50,000.

Norsk Villaks Senter   WILD SALMON CENTRE
(www.norsk-villakssenter.no; adult/child Nkr90/55; ⊙10am-5pm, to 6pm or 7pm May-Sep) You can watch wild salmon and sea trout through viewing windows, see an excellent 20-minute film about the salmon's lifecycle, browse the interpretive panels, try to tie flies to increase the odds of you hooking one of your own and do a little virtual casting. On the top floor, 'The English Era' commemorates the time when, in the early 20th century, members of the British aristocracy fished the creeks and rivers for giant salmon.

SNØVEGEN

The 45km Snow Road, officially signed **Aurlandsvegen**, climbs from sea level, twisting precipitously to the desolate, boulder-strewn high plateau that separates Aurland and Lærdalsøyri (Lærdal). This heart-stopping drive – strictly for summertime (snow banks line the road and tarns are still deep-frozen even in late June) – has been designated as a National Tourist Route, so get there quickly before the coaches catch on. Even if you don't opt for the whole route, drive the first 8km from Aurland to the magnificent **observation point**. Projecting out over the fjord way below, pine-clad, simple and striking like the best of Norwegian design, it's almost as impressive as the stunning panorama itself.

WORTH A TRIP

BORGUND STAVE CHURCH

Some 30km southeast of Lærdalsøyri along the E16, this 12th-century **stave church** (adult/child Nkr65/45; ⊙8am-8pm mid-Jun–mid-Aug, 9.30am-5pm May–mid-Jun & mid-Aug–Sep) was raised beside one of the major trade routes between eastern and western Norway. Dedicated to St Andrew, it's one of the best known, most photographed – and certainly the best preserved – of Norway's stave churches. Beside it is the only freestanding medieval wooden bell tower still standing in Norway. Buy your ticket at the visitors centre, which has a worthwhile exhibition (included in the price of your admission) on this peculiarly Norwegian phenomenon as well as recent early Viking finds from a nearby archaeological dig. If you enjoy walking, allow time to undertake the two-hour circular hike on ancient paths and tracks that starts and ends at the church.

Lærdal Sport og Rekreasjon

OUTDOOR ACTIVITIES

(www.laerdalsport.com) Based at the campground, it rents rowing boats and canoes (Nkr75 per hour), motor boats (from Nkr150) and bikes (from Nkr50/150 per hour/day). It also arranges guided hiking and biking trips ranging from three hours (adult/child Nkr150/75) to a full day (adult/child Nkr250/100).

🛏 Sleeping & Eating

TOP
CHOICE **Lindstrøm Hotell** HOTEL €€

(⌨57 66 69 00; www.lindstroemhotel.no; s Nkr695-915, d Nkr950-1250, all incl breakfast; ⊙May-Sep; P@�🖥) The most charming house of this five-unit complex, these days a protected building, is, alas, no longer used for guest accommodation. Ask for a room in the gabled building just behind it, similarly Swiss in style and constructed at the end of the 19th century. Renovated with all modern conveniences by the family who has run this hotel for five generations, it's a great second best. Public areas in the main building (which houses reception) are attractively decorated and furnished in 'Danish contemporary' style, but for two charming, traditional little lounges, where postdinner coffee is taken.

Lærdal Ferie og Fritidspark

CAMPGROUND, HOTEL €

(⌨57 66 66 95; www.laerdalferiepark.com; campsites Nkr170, 2-/3-/4-bed cabins with bathroom Nkr875/925/975; 🖥) This campground, almost at the water's edge, has sweeping views of the fjord. Its self-styled **motel** (s/d Nkr500/595), has communal self-catering facilities, plus a common room with a terrace and broad picture window that give a magnificent panorama of the fjord.

Laksen

PUB €€

(⌨57 66 86 20; lunch dishes Nkr170, dinner mains Nkr200-245; ⊙11am-9.30pm) After the Lindstrøm Hotell, Lærdalsøyri's next best place for eating is the informal Laksen Pub & Restaurant at the Wild Salmon Centre. It dispenses tempting snacks and sandwiches during the daytime, then morphs into a restaurant from 6pm to 9pm.

ⓘ Information

The **tourist office** (⌨57 64 12 07; www.alr. no; Øyraplassen 7; ⊙10am-6pm Mon-Sat mid-Jun–mid-Aug, 9am-3pm rest of year) occupies a lovely old clapboard house, once the town's bank, that's set back from the main street. It has a neat little photo exhibition on early Lærdal and a free internet point.

ⓘ Getting There & Away

If you're driving south, you have the choice between the world's longest road tunnel linking Aurland and Lærdal (mercifully, it's toll free) or, in summer, climbing up and over the mountain, following the Snøvegen. Express buses run to/from Bergen (Nkr350, 3¾ hours) two to six times daily via the tunnel.

Three daily car ferries run to/from Gudvangen (car and driver/passenger Nkr600/250, three hours) via Kaupanger (Nkr595/240).

Vik

POP 2750

Vik has two splendid small **churches** (combined entry adult/child Nkr80/70), each owing their existence and present form to the 19th-century architect Peter Blix (who designed, among much else, many of the stations on the Oslo–Bergen railway line). The **Hopperstad Stave Church** (⊙10am-5pm May-Sep), originally built in 1140 and Norway's second oldest, escaped demolition by a whisker in the late 19th century. Blix took over the dilapidated building and largely reconstructed it. Inside, the original canopy paintings of the elaborately carved baldequin have preserved their freshness of colour. The church is on the southern outskirts of the village of Vik about 1km from the centre.

Hove Stone Church (⊙11am-4pm mid-Jun–mid-Aug), 1km to the south, was constructed in the late 12th century. The region's oldest stone building, it retains its original form. Blix's elaborate makeover includes the abstract wall painting of nave and chancel, the wooden figures from Norse legend in the roof beams and the external gables.

Balestrand
POP 1350

Balestrand sits comfortably beside the fjord, at its rear an impressive mountain backdrop. Genteel and low key, it has been a tranquil, small-scale holiday resort ever since the 19th century.

⊙ Sights

Balestrand is to be home to the **Norwegian Museum of Travel & Tourism** (Norsk Reiselivsmuseum), destined to open in 2012 and until then showing temporary exhibitions.

Church of St Olav   CHURCH
This charming wooden church (1897), in the style of a traditional stave church, was built at the instigation of English expat Margaret Green, who married a local hotel-owner. Should you find it closed, the owner of Midtnes Hotel has the key.

Viking Age Barrows   BURIAL MOUNDS
Less than 1km south along the fjord, excavation of this pair of barrows revealed remnants of a boat, two skeletons, jewellery and several weapons. One mound is topped by a statue of legendary **King Bele**, erected by Germany's Kaiser Wilhelm II. Obsessed with Nordic mythology, he regularly spent his holidays here prior to WWI (a similar monument, also funded by the Kaiser and honouring Fridtjof, the lover of King Bele's daughter, peers across the fjord from Vangsnes).

Sognefjord Aquarium   AQUARIUM
(adult/child Nkr70/35; ⊙9am-5pm or 11.30pm May–Sep) View the 15-minute audiovisual presentation then tour the 24 aquariums in which lurk saltwater creatures from Sognefjord, large, small and very small. The entry price includes an hour of canoe or rowing-boat hire.

🏃 Activities

The tourist office's free pamphlet *Outdoor Activities in Balestrand* has plenty of suggestions for **hiking**, ranging from easy to demanding. If you need more detail, it also stocks *Balestrand Turkart* (Nkr70), a good walking map at 1:50,000 with trails marked up.

Njord (☑913 26 628; www.kajakk.com) explores the fjord off Balestrand in a couple of guided sea-kayak tours, lasting either two (Nkr350) or three hours (Nkr450). Reserve at the tourist office.

🛌 Sleeping

| TOP CHOICE | **Kvikne's Hotel**   HOTEL €€ |

(☑57 69 42 00; www.kviknes.no; s/d from Nkr1080/1660; ⊙May-Sep; 🅿@🖥) The majestic pale-yellow, timber-built main building of Kvikne's Hotel, with exquisite antiques in its public areas, breathes late-19th-century luxury. Of its 190 rooms, 165 are in the newer building, erected in the 1960s. They're comfortable to a fault but the exterior is a grotesque concrete pile in comparison to the 'Swiss-style' original. **Balholm Bar og Bistro** is a reliable place for snacks and light meals. For a gastronomic delight, invest Nkr495 in the main restaurant's outstanding dinner buffet. The hotel is on a point just south of the ferry landing.

Balestrand Hotell   SUMMER HOTEL €€
(☑57 69 11 38; www.balestrand.com; s Nkr670-770, d Nkr990-1190; ⊙Jun-Aug; 🅿@🖥) This summertime-only hotel, family-run, is a friendly, jolly, intimate place that eschews the tour groups that fill so many beds elsewhere in town. It's well worth paying the more expensive rate for inspirational views over the fjord.

Midtnes Hotel   HOTEL €€
(☑57 69 11 33; www.midtnes.no; s Nkr730, d Nkr790-1150; 🅿@🖥) Beside St Olav's church, this 32-room place, also family-run, has a breakfast room with great views of the water, an attractive terrace and a lawn that extends down to a jetty, where a rowing boat, free for guests, is moored. Breakfast, with three kinds of pickled herring, hams, prawns and more, is a meal in itself. Amazingly for a hotel of this calibre, credit cards aren't accepted.

Sjøtun Camping   CAMPGROUND €
(☑950 67 261; www.sjotun.com; per person/site Nkr30/60, 4-/6-bed cabins with outdoor bathroom Nkr250/320; ⊙Jun–mid-Sep) At this green campground, a 15-minute walk south along the fjord, you can pitch a tent on soft grass amid apple trees or rent a rustic cabin at a very reasonable price.

Vandrerhjem Kringsjå HOSTEL **€€**
(☑57 69 13 03; www.kringsja.no; Laerargata 9; dm
Nkr255, s/d/tr with bathroom Nkr600/790/890,
all incl breakfast; ☺mid-Jun–mid-Aug) Uphill
from the dock, Balestrand's family-run HI-
affiliated hostel is nowadays an outdoor
activities centre during the school year. It
started life as a hotel, and this shows; it's
a fine lodge-style place with comfortable
rooms and decent self-catering facilities.

✖ Eating

TOP **Ciderhuset** RESTAURANT **€€**
CHOICE (☑908 35 673; www.ciderhuset.no, in
Norwegian; Sjøtunsvegen 32; mains Nkr100-200;
☺4-8pm mid-Jun–mid-Aug) Within a fruit farm
that produces organic juices, jams, bottled
fruits, cider and cider brandy, this delightful
restaurant fuses Nordic and Mediterranean
culinary traditions. It uses local produce
wherever possible (why, even the crockery is
fired by a local potter). Dine on the broad 1st-
floor terrace or inside the cosy glass house,
where fresh herbs and cherry tomatoes climb
the panes. Do savour one of the desserts of
organic fruit from their orchards, enhanced
by a dollop of equally organic, locally made
ice cream. Ciderhuset is signed from the road
that runs beside the campground.

Me Snakkast Café CAFE **€**
(☑915 62 842; www.detgylnehus.no, in Norwegian;
salads Nkr75-90, snacks & sandwiches Nkr65-135)
Next door but two to the tourist office, this
quaint little place is integrated into Det Gylne
Hus, the Golden House, a small, eccentric art
gallery. The food, by contrast, is simple, unpretentious and great value. Sink your teeth,
for example, into its Grizzly Burger ('No bears
were harmed in the making of this burger',
we're assured). Eat in the rather cramped
interior or on the small outside terrace, its
tables adorned with freshly cut flowers.

❶ Information

The **tourist office** (☑57 69 12 55; www.visit
balestrand.no; ☺7.30am-6pm Mon-Sat, 10am-
5pm Sun mid-Jun–mid-Aug; 10am-5.30pm
Mon-Fri May–early Jun & mid-Aug–Sep) is opposite the ferry quay. It hires out bicycles for
Nkr30/75/140 per hour/half-day/full day.

❶ Getting There & Away

Express boats run to/from Bergen (Nkr485,
3¾ hours, twice daily) and Sogndal (Nkr155, 45
minutes, once daily).

In July and August, a car ferry (Nkr215/325
one way/return, 1¼ hours, twice daily) follows the

narrow Fjærlandsfjorden to Fjærland, gateway
to the glacial wonderlands of Jostedalsbreen (in
May, June and September there's a daily passenger ferry run).

Express buses link Balestrand and Sogndal
(Nkr94, one hour, three daily).

The scenic Gaularfjellsvegen (Rv13) is an exciting drive to Førde, on Førdefjord, negotiating
hairpin bends and skirting Norway's greatest
concentration of roadside waterfalls.

Sogndal
POP 7050

Sogndal, though not the area's prettiest
place, makes a good base for a trio of magnificent day drives: Jostedalen and Nigardsbreen (p214), Urnes (p211), Lustrafjord and
the spectacular Sognefjellet circuit.

◉ Sights & Activities

TOP **Sogn Folkmuseum** FOLK MUSEUM
CHOICE (www.dhs.museum.no; adult/child Nkr70/
30; ☺10am-3pm or 5pm daily May-Sep, Mon-Fri
Oct-Apr) Extensive and open-air, it's between
Sogndal and Kaupanger, beside the Rv5.
More than 30 buildings, including farms, a
schoolhouse and a mill, have been brought
from their original sites and embedded in
the surrounding woods. Each is well documented in Norwegian and English. There
are three short, themed walking trails with
informative panels (reception has English
translation sheets). Children's can pet the
farm animals, build their own log cabin and
indulge in other backwoods activities, and
there are several gorgeous picnic spots.

FREE **Sogn Fjordmuseum** MARITIME MUSEUM
(☺10am-3pm or 5pm May-Sep) Located
in **Kaupanger**, 2km southeast along the
Rv5 and related to the much larger Folk
Museum, it has a collection of 19th- and
20th-century fishing and freight boats and
equipment and some striking old photos,
illustrating in particular the coastal trade in
wood for Bergen's expanding construction
needs.

Stave Church STAVE CHURCH
(adult/child Nkr45/35; ☺9.30am-5.30pm early Jun–
mid-Aug) Kaupanger's main claim for your attention was raised in 1184. It impresses from
within by its sheer height. Much of what you
see dates from a fundamental renovation in
the 17th century. Wall paintings in the nave
feature musical annotation, while vine and
flower motifs entwine around the chancel.
The Celtic-style chancel arch is unique.

A spectacular circular, day-long driving route, the Sognefjellet circuit runs beside one of Norway's loveliest fjords, climbs a sizeable chunk of the magnificent Sognefjellet National Tourist Route, meanders along a lonely, lightly travelled single-lane road that threads across the heights, then plunges in a knuckle-clenching descent, once more to fjord level. The trip can't be done by public transport and cyclists will need to be very fit to attempt it over a few days.

From Sogndal, head out on the Rv55 to the northeast as it hugs, for the most part, lovely Lustrafjord all the way to Skjolden at the head of the waters. About 5km beyond this tiny settlement, the road starts to seriously twist and climb. You're following an ancient highway where for centuries, when it was no more than a rough track, fish and salt would be hauled up from the coast to be exchanged for iron, butter and hides from communities deep inland.

At wind-battered Turtagrø you can continue along the Rv55, which runs through Jotunheimen National Park, up and over northern Europe's highest road pass (1434m) and on to Lom.

To return to Sogndal, turn right to leave the Rv55 and head for Årdal. The narrow road, known as Tindevegen, the Route of the Peaks, keeps climbing, just above the treeline, until the pass (1315m) and a toll booth (Nkr50 per vehicle).

Then it's a plunge down through woods of spindly birch to the emerald-green waters of Årdalsvatnet and the undistinguished village of Øvre Årdal. From here, the Rv53 takes you, via the ferry between Fodnes and Mannheller, back to Sogndal.

🛏 Sleeping

Hofslund Fjord Hotel
HOTEL €€

(☎57 62 76 00; www.hofslund-hotel.no; s/d Nkr995/1245; [P][@][?][≋]) This venerable 100-bed hotel, approaching its first century, has been run by the same family for four generations. It enjoys a wonderful location; most rooms have a balcony and view of the fjord and a neatly cropped lawn sweeps down to the water. The outdoor pool's heated and there are a couple of rowing boats and fishing gear, loaned free to guests. The **restaurant** has a nightly buffet (Nkr265) that's excellent value and open to all-comers.

TOP CHOICE Kjørnes Camping
CAMPGROUND €

(☎57 67 45 80; www.kjornes.no; per person/site Nkr30/170, 2-/5-bed cabins with outdoor bathroom Nkr380/490, 5-bed cabins with bathroom 800-950; apt Nkr850; ☉May-Sep) This large, well-maintained campground, where the young owners have expanded and improved facilities, enjoys a gorgeous fjord-side setting. Choose a large cabin with full facilities on the main site or, to be almost alone with the forest at your back and the fjord before you, take one short way along the old road to Kaupanger. Kjørnes Camping is 3km from Sogndal off the Rv5, direction Lærdal.

Loftesnes Pensjonat
GUESTHOUSE €

(☎90935171; Fjøravegen; s/d/tr Nkr450/750/850) This small place above the China House restaurant is great value. Nine of its 12 rooms have a bathroom and there are self-catering facilities and a rooftop terrace. If no one's around, take any room that has its key in the lock and sign the guest register. If no one has turned up before you leave, pay the restaurant staff downstairs (cash only).

Sogndal Vandrerhjem
HOSTEL €

(☎57 62 75 75; www.hihostels.no/sogndal; Helgheimsvegen 9-10; dm/s/d with shared bathroom Nkr210/290/500, d with bathroom Nkr680; ☉mid-Jun–mid-Aug) This well-equipped, summertime-only HI-affiliated hostel, near the bridge that carries the Rv5, functions as a boarding school during the rest of the year.

Park Hotell & Appartments
APARTMENTS, HOTEL €€

(☎57 62 84 00; www.park-sogndal.no; r Nkr1250; [@][?]) If you like a little independence, check in at Sogndal's newest accommodation choice. Rooms, each with parquet flooring and plasma TV, are particularly large and come equipped with fridge, cooker and dishwasher.

🍴 Eating

Joar's Kjøkken
RESTAURANT, PUB €€€

(☎971 53 774; www.laxen.no, in Norwegian; Allmenningen 4; lunch dishes Nkr98-198, dinner mains Nkr250-360; ☉noon-9.30pm Tue-Sat, 1-7pm

Sun) At recently established Joar's Kitchen, there's fine à la carte dining Thursday to Saturday (try, for example, grouse shot in the local mountains with mushrooms, potatoes, greens and red-currant jelly). Lunchtime is less formal but just as inventive. On other evenings there are special buffets such as taco (Tuesday) and steak (Wednesday).

Galleri Krydder Kaffe   CAFE €
(www.gallerikrydder.no, in Norwegian; Parvegen 6; salads Nkr80-90, sandwiches, Nkr60-75; ⊘11am-7pm Mon-Fri, 11am-5pm Sat & Sun) Good espresso coffee's guaranteed at this friendly cafe attached to an art gallery. Children can play on the trampoline and swings next door, parents can savour the sunshine on its ample terrace and all can indulge in its salads and well-filled sandwiches.

❶ Information

Sogndal's **tourist office** (☑976 00 443; www.sognefjord.no; Hovevegen 2; ⊘9am-6pm Mon-Fri, 10am-4pm Sat mid-Jun–mid-Aug, 10am-4pm Mon-Fri mid-May–mid-Jun & mid-Aug-Sep), a five-minute walk east of the bus station, can book accommodation for callers-in. To stretch your legs, ask for its booklet of hill walks (Nkr35). The town **library**, in the same building, has free internet access and wi-fi.

❶ Getting There & Away

Sogndal has Sognefjord's only airport, which has two daily flights to/from Bergen and three to/from Oslo.

Express passenger boats connect Sogndal with Balestrand (Nkr155, 45 minutes, daily), Bergen (Nkr570, 4½ hours, twice daily).

Bus destinations include Kaupanger (Nkr32, 20 minutes, up to 12 per day), Fjærland (Nkr73, 30 minutes, up to six per day), Balestrand (Nkr94, 1¼ hours, three per day).

Twice-daily buses (mid-June to late August) head northeast past Jotunheimen National Park to Lom (3¼ hours) and Otta (4¼ hours).

Solvorn & Around

For a delightful four hours paddling the waters of smooth-as-silk Lustrafjord and the chance to cruise among a colony of seals, sign on with one of the daily guided kayak tours of **FjordSeal** (www.fjordseal.com; adult/child Nkr500/350; ⊘tours 9.30am daily May-Sep), based at Marifjøra, just off the Rv55, 17km north of Svolvorn.

Solvorn has two splendid accommodation options.

TOP✦ **Eplet**   HOSTEL €
CHOICE (☑41 64 94 69; www.eplet.net; camping per person Nkr100, dm Nkr180, d Nkr600; ⊘May-Sep; @⊛) Eplet is run by Trond Henrik Eplet, environmental geologist, seasoned traveller, climber and seriously long-distance cyclist (just ask and he'll tell you the sexiest cycle routes and walking trails around). From its windows and terrace there are magnificent views of Lustrafjord. Below are line upon line of raspberry bushes and apple trees (you won't get scurvy here); children can feed the lambs in season and there are self-catering facilities. Not to speak of what must be the world's mini-est minigolf course on the handkerchief of a lawn. There are free bikes for guest use – ideal for slipping onto the ferry and exploring Urnes and Lustrafjord's east bank.

TOP✦ **Walaker Hotell**   HOTEL €€€
CHOICE (☑57 68 20 80; www.walaker.com; s Nkr1400-2450, d Nkr1700-2700, all incl breakfast; ⊘May-Sep; @⊛) This venerable Solvorn institution, sitting comfortably beside the fjord, is Norway's oldest family hotel, in the hands of nine generations of the Nitter family ever since 1640. Photos of the last five generations (predecessors were pre-camera) look at you from behind reception, where you'll probably be greeted by Ole Henrik, the current owner, himself. Not least of the hotel's pleasures is its lovely lawn and garden of lilac, roses, apple and cherry trees. The hotel occupies three buildings; cheaper rooms are in the new wing, constructed in 1964. Attached is Gal-

---

ⓘ **FINE TIMING IN URNES**

It's a 20-minute uphill walk from the ferry to the church. Don't dawdle – the guided tour waits for no man.

Your visit over, you won't have time to catch the very next ferry, so relax a while at **Urnes Gard** (www.urnes.no; ⊘1030am-5.30pm Jun-Sep), just below the church. Once farm stables, this cafe sells punnets of fruit fresh from the fields, and its own juices – strawberry, raspberry, gooseberry and blueberry from berries picked from the hills above. Sample too the homemade cakes, confected by the lady who lives up the road.

leri Walaker 300, its art gallery with changing exhibitions.

Urnes

Stave Church

STAVE CHURCH

(adult Nkr55, family Nkr120; ⊙10.30am-5pm late May-Sep) Norway's oldest preserved place of worship is a Unesco World Heritage Site. Directly across the fjord from Solvorn, it gazes out over Lustrafjord. The original church was built around 1070, while the majority of today's structure was constructed a century later. Highlights are elaborate wooden carvings – animals locked in struggle, stylised intertwined bodies and abstract motifs – on the north wall, all recycled from the original church, and the simple crucifixion carving, set above the chancel wall. Ticket prices include an outstanding 45-minute tour in English.

ⓘ Getting There & Away

A car and passenger ferry (adult/child/car Nkr30/15/82, 20 minutes) shuttles hourly from 10am to 4.50pm between Solvorn and Urnes; most drivers prefer to leave their vehicles on the Solvorn bank.

Skjolden

POP 500

Skjolden is at the northern limit of Lustrafjord. In Fjordstova, its main building, you'll find most that matters tucked under one roof: the **tourist office** (☑97 60 04 43; www .skjolden.com; ⊙11am-7pm or 2-7pm mid-Jun–mid-Aug; @🛜), a cafe, a swimming pool, climbing wall and even a shooting gallery. The bit of industrial-looking junk on display outside is a turbine from the Norsk hydropower station.

For land- or water-based exercise, you can hire bicycles (Nkr75/100 per half/full day) and kayaks (Nkr75/150 per half/full day) at the tourist office, which can also supply you with a brochure (Nkr20) on signed walks in the area.

East of Skjolden, the Rv55 at first runs beside the lovely turquoise glacial lake **Eidsvatnet**. **Mørkridsdalen**, the valley that runs north of the village, makes for some excellent hiking.

Further along the Rv55, 3km from Skjolden, **Vassbakken Kro & Camping** (☑57 68 61 88; www.vassbakken.com, in Norwegian; car/caravan site Nkr120/140 plus per person

WORTH A TRIP

211

DALE KYRKJE, LUSTER

Spectacular wooden stave churches get all the attention around here and this little gem of a **medieval parish church** (⊙10am-8pm), built of stone, gets overlooked. Just 13km south of Skjolden and constructed around 1250, it's mainly Gothic in style. The wooden tower and elaborately painted western entrance (the work of a typically near-anonymous ecclesiastical artist known simply as 'Nils the Painter') were added in the early 1600s. The crucifix above the chancel arch and fine multicoloured pulpit are from the church's earliest days. Opposite, one Colonel von Krogh, a local parishioner with ideas according to his station had the high, fretted pew – higher than the nave, higher than the priest in his pulpit – constructed for himself and his family in 1699. The naive 16th-century paintings in the chancel were revealed only in the 1950s, when the whitewash was removed.

Nkr25, 2-/4-bed cabins with outdoor bathroom Nkr380/480, 5-bed cabins with bathroom Nkr790, ⊙May–mid-Sep) is a smallish campsite, which is set beneath a surging waterfall. There's a popular cafe-restaurant here and all rooms in its brand-new HI-affiliated **hostel** (dm 275, s/d/Nkr545/755, all incl breakfast) come with a bathroom.

ⓘ Getting There & Away

Bus 153 connects Skjolden with Sogndal (Nkr115, 1½ hours) three to five times daily.

If you're heading north on Rv55, check your fuel gauge; Skjolden's petrol stations are the last for 77km.

JOSTEDALSBREEN

For years mighty Jostedalsbreen, mainland Europe's largest icecap, crept countercurrent, slowly advancing while most glaciers elsewhere in the world were retreating as a result, most scientists agree, of global warming. Now Jostedalsbreen herself has succumbed and is also withdrawing.

She's still a powerful player, though, eroding an estimated 400,000 tonnes of rock each year. With an area of 487 sq km and in places

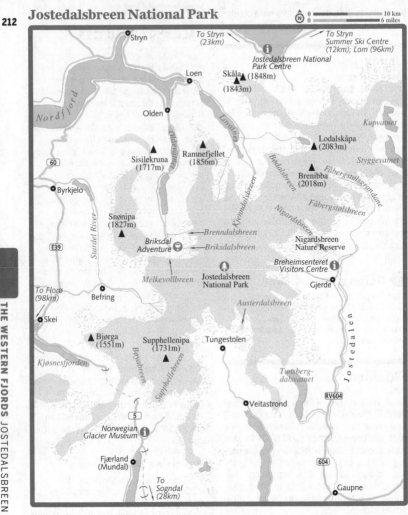

600m thick, Jostedalsbreen rules over the highlands of Sogn og Fjordane county. The main icecap and several outliers are protected as the Jostedalsbreen National Park.

The best hiking map for the region is Statens Kartverk's *Jostedalsbreen Turkart* at 1:100,000. The free *Jostedalsbreen Glacier Walks* brochure, available at tourist offices and many other venues, gives a comprehensive list of glacier walks, their levels and guiding companies.

For more details on the gateway towns of Stryn, Olden and Loen, see p217.

Fjærland

POP 300

The village of Fjærland (also called Mundal), at the head of scenic Fjærlandsfjorden, pulls in as many as 300,000 visitors each year. Most come to experience its pair of particularly accessible glacial tongues, Supphellebreen and Bøyabreen. Others come to be bookworms. This tiny place, known as the Book Town of Norway (www.bokbyen.no), is a bibliophile's nirvana, with a dozen shops selling a wide range of used books, mostly in Norwegian but with lots in English and other European languages.

The village virtually hibernates from October onwards, then leaps to life in early May, when the ferry runs again.

◉ Sights

Supphellebreen & Bøyabreen · GLACIERS

You can drive to within 300m of the Supphellebreen glacier, then walk right up and touch the ice. Ice blocks from here were used as podiums at the 1994 Winter Olympics in Lillehammer.

At blue, creaking Bøyabreen, more spectacular than Supphellebreen, its brother over the hill, you might happen upon glacial calving as a hunk tumbles into the meltwater lagoon beneath the glacier tongue.

TOP CHOICE Norwegian Glacier Museum · GLACIER MUSEUM

(Norsk Bremuseum; ☑57 69 32 88; www.bre museum.no; adult/child Nkr110/50; ☺9am-7pm Jun-Aug, 10am-4pm Apr, May, Sep & Oct) For the story on flowing ice and how it has sculpted the Norwegian landscape, visit this superbly executed museum, 3km inland from the ferry jetty.

The hands-on exhibits will delight children. You can learn how fjords are formed, see an excellent 20-minute multiscreen audiovisual presentation on Jostedalsbreen (so impressive that audiences often break into spontaneous applause at the end), touch 1000-year-old ice, wind your way through a tunnel that penetrates the mock ice and even see the tusk of a Siberian woolly mammoth, which met an icy demise 30,000 years ago. There's also an exhibit on the 5000-year-old 'Ice Man' corpse, which was found on the Austrian–Italian border in 1991.

Our Fragile Planet is a multimedia exhibition with sounds, smoke, rumblings underfoot, a 2040 TV newscast and more that leads you from the earth's creation to the present – and the consequences of our generation's overuse of the world's resources. After a doomsday visual hypothesis, it ends on a note of qualified optimism expressed by the breathy voice of Sir David Attenborough. In synopsis, it sounds preachy. On the spot, it's stimulating and thought-provoking.

🏃 Activities

Book Browsing

As you saunter through this one-street village, pause to browse a selection of its dozen secondhand bookshops. Tusand og Ei Natt (Thousand and One Nights), the large – unsigned – bookshop nearest to the ferry jetty, has a 15m-long row, stacked seven shelves high, of novels in English. Gamle Posten too carries plenty of titles in English. If thrillers are your bedtime frisson, call by Bok & Bilde, at the tourist office.

Kayaking

At the small fjord-side shack belonging to Fjærland Kayak & Glacier (☑928 54 674; www.kayakglacier.no), you can hire a kayak, canoe, motor or rowing boat or join one of its daily guided kayaking trips (May to August), ranging from 2½ hours (Nkr400) to a full day (Nkr870).

Walking

The tourist office's free sheet, *Escape the Asphalt*, lists 12 marked walking routes, varying from 30 minutes to three hours. For greater detail, supplement this with *Turkart Fjærland* (Nkr70) at 1:50,000, which comes complete with route descriptions and trails indicated; pull on your boots and you're away. Most walks follow routes the local shepherds would have used until quite recently to lead their flocks to higher summer pastures. Stamp a card at the end of each and, after you've completed four, the tourist office will grant you a diploma (Nkr25).

Fjærland Kayak & Glacier offers more demanding guided glacier treks (Nkr600 to Nkr750), leaving at 8.30am each morning.

☞ Tours

Between June and August, a bus meets the twice-daily ferry from Balestrand, leaving the quayside at 9.55am (adult/child Nkr150/75) and 1.20pm (adult/child Nkr115/60). Both tours stop en route to allow visits to the interactive Glacier Museum and Bøyabreen glacier. The earlier tour also takes in the Supphellebreen glacier and leaves plenty of bookshop-browsing time before you catch the ferry back to Balestrand.

Alternatively, a taxi from the Fjærland dock to Bøyabreen, with waiting time, costs about Nkr800 return.

🛏 Sleeping & Eating

TOP CHOICE Hotel Mundal · HOTEL €€€

(☑57 69 31 01; www.hotelmundal.no; s/d from Nkr1120/1700; ☺May-Sep; ℗@🤶) Retaining much of its period furniture and run by the same family ever since it was built in 1891, it features a welcoming lounge and a lovely round tower. Invest Nkr24000 and

ⓘ MISSING THE BOAT

Should you be unfortunate enough to miss the last ferry shuttle back over Nigardsvatnet, there's always a rowing boat left at the landing point for the use of the unwary.

you can sleep the night in the tower's one room with wraparound views – as did US ex-president Walter Mondale, whose family came from Mundal, and the present Queen of Norway (not, as the charming receptionist explains, on the same occasion). The **restaurant** serves truly wonderful traditional four-course Norwegian dinners (Nkr360). Because the food comes fresh, nonguests need to book by 6pm at the latest. On one wall of its **Mikkel Kaffe**, a cafe with a mountaineering theme, there's a giant evocative 1898 map of Sognefjorden.

Mrs Haugen's Rooms   GUESTHOUSE € (✆57 69 32 43; d Nkr400-500; ⊙May–mid-Oct) In the white building behind the village church, Mrs Alma Haugen rents just a couple of rooms with shared kitchen and bathroom that represent outstanding value. The welcome's particularly warm, just like stepping into a friendly home and a special delight if you've spent night after night in clone hotels or cabins.

Bøyum Camping   CAMPGROUND € (✆57 69 32 52; www.fjaerland.org/boyumcamping; campsites Nkr150, dm Nkr160, d Nkr270-340 with shared bathroom, 4-/8-bed cabins Nkr710/1010; ⊙May-Sep) Beside the Glacier Museum and 3km from the ferry landing, Bøyum Camping has something for all pockets and sleeping preferences, including a great view of the Bøyabreen glacier at the head of the valley.

Brævasshytta Cafeteria   CAFE € (⊙8am-8pm May-Sep) Do visit the Brævasshytta, built into the moraine of Bøyabreen's latest major advance, even if it's only for a cup of coffee. With the glacier right there and in your face, it's like eating in an IMAX cinema, but for real. There's also a good cafeteria at the glacier museum.

ⓘ Information

Fjærland's exceptionally friendly **tourist office** (✆57 69 32 33; www.fjaerland.org; ⊙10am-6pm May-Sep) is within the Bok & Bilde bookshop on the main street, 300m from the ferry point. It displays a full list of accommodation options, together with prices, on the main door.

ⓘ Getting There & Away

A car ferry (Nkr215/325 one way/return, 1¼ hours) runs twice daily between Balestrand and Fjærland in July and August (in May, June and September there's a daily passenger-ferry run).

Buses bypass the village and stop on the Rv5 near the glacier museum. Three to six run daily to/from Sogndal (Nkr73, 30 minutes) and Stryn (Nkr200, two hours).

ⓘ Getting Around

Both the tourist office (Nkr30/140 per hour/day) and Bøyum Camping (Nkr25/125 per hour/day) rent bikes.

Jostedalen & Nigardsbreen

The Jostedalen valley pokes due north from Gaupne, on the shores of Lustrafjord. This slim finger sits between two national parks: long established Jostedalsbreen on the west side and, to its east, Breheimen national park, Norway's newest, recognised in 2009. It's a spectacular drive as the road runs beside the milky turquoise river, tumbling beneath the eastern flank of the Nigardsbreen glacier.

Of the Jostedalsbreen glacier tongues visible from below, Nigardsbreen is the most dramatic and easy to approach. There are several walks in its vicinity that families can undertake. If you're an experienced walker and fancy communing alone with (but not on) the ice, nip further up the road past the braided glacial streams at Fåbergstølsgrandane to the dam that creates the big glacial lake, Styggevatnet. Along the way you'll find several scenic glacial tongues and valleys offering excellent wild hiking.

⊙ Sights

Breheimsenteret Visitors Centre

VISITORS CENTRE

(✆57 68 32 50; www.jostedal.com; ⊙9am-7pm mid-Jun–mid-Aug, 10am-5pm May–mid-Jun & mid-Aug–Sep; 🛜) Jostedal's visitor centre sadly burnt to the ground in 2011. Until the new centre opens in 2013, you'll find tourist services operating out of temporary buildings; check the website for details.

✴ Activities

You can book directly or at the visitors centre for each of these outfits.

Ice Troll KAYAKING, GLACIER WALKING
(📞970 14 370; www.icetroll.com) Andy – from New Zealand and with a decade of guiding experience on Nigardsbreen – and his team offer a couple of truly original glacier visits. After a kayak trip, enjoy an ice walk where those without paddles never get. Both, lasting eight to 10 hours (Nkr890), are suitable for first-timers as well as the more experienced. They also do longer overnight and two-day sorties.

Riverpig RAFTING
(📞970 14 370; www.icetroll.com) Run by the same outfit, Riverpig does white water rafting on the Jostedalen river (Nkr650) and, for the truly hardy, riverboarding (Nkr800).

Jostedalen Breførarlag GLACIER WALKS
(📞57 68 31 11; www.bfl.no) Leads several guided glacier walks on Nigardsbreen. The easiest is the family walk to the glacier snout and briefly along its tongue (around one hour on the ice, adult/child Nkr200/100). Fees for the two-hour (Nkr430), three-hour (Nkr525) and five-hour (Nkr740) walks on the ice include the brief boat trip across Nigardsvatnet lake.

Leirdalen Bre og Juv
CANYON CLAMBERING, GLACIER HIKING
(Leirdal Glacier & Canyon; 📞470 27 878; www.breogjuv.no) Offers canyon clambering (Nkr500) and six- to eight-hour glacier hikes (Nkr650) on Tunsbergsdalsbreen, Norway's longest glacier arm.

Raudskarvfjellet Turriding PONY TREKKING
(📞57 68 32 50; www.jostedal-horseguiding.no) Less strenuously, take a five-hour pony trip (Nkr700) with these stables.

🛏 Sleeping & Eating

Two sisters run the valley's most tempting sleeping options.

TOP CHOICE 🌿 **Jostedal Camping** CAMPGROUND €
(📞57 68 39 14; www.jostedalcamping.no; car/caravan sites Nkr90/110 plus Nkr25 per person, 4-bed cabins with outdoor bathroom Nkr350-470, fully equipped bungalows, up to 6 persons Nkr1050; ☺May–mid-Oct) Astrid, after travelling and working around the world, has returned to her home village and with her partner runs this trim, well kept campground, right beside the Jostedal river. Both keen hikers, they've researched a range of local walks, described with photos on the camp bulletin board. Facilities are impeccable and there's a lovely riverside terrace. All in all, fit for royalty – as indeed it was briefly, when Britain's Prince William stayed here on a university field trip.

🌿 **Jostedal Hotel** HOTEL €€
(📞57 68 31 19; www.jostedalhotel.no; s/d incl breakfast Nkr720/1020; @🛜) Just 2.5km south of the visitors centre, this friendly place has been run by the same family for three generations. Meat, milk and vegetables for the restaurant come from their farm. There are also family rooms (Nkr1120) with self-catering facilities that can accommodate up to five guests. For a great view, enjoy a coffee or snack in the visitors centre cafe.

❶ Getting There & Around

If you're driving, leave the Rv55 Sognefjellet Rd at Gaupne and head north up Jostedal along the Rv604.

From mid-June to mid-September, **Jostedals-brebussen** (No 160; the Glacier Bus; www.jostedal.com/brebussen) runs from Sogndal (with connections from Flåm, Balestrand and Lærdal) via Solvorn to the foot of the Nigardsbreen glacier, leaving at 8.45am and setting out on the return journey at 4.50pm.

From the visitors centre, a 3.5km-long toll road (Nkr30 per vehicle), or a pleasant walk with interpretive panels, leads to the car park at Nigardsvatnet, the lagoon at the glacial snout. From mid-June to August, a ferry (Nkr40 return; 10am-6pm) shuttles over the lagoon. From the landing, it's a sturdy walk over rocks to the glacier face itself.

Briksdalsbreen

From the small town of **Olden** at the eastern end of Nordfjord, a scenic road leads 23km up Oldedalen past Brenndalsbreen, and from there on to the twin glacial tongues of Melkevollbreen and Briksdalsbreen. More easily accessible, Briksdalsbreen attracts hordes of tour buses. It's a temperamental glacier; in 1997 the tongue licked to its furthest point for around 70 years, then retreated by around 500m. In 2005, the reaches where glacier walkers would clamber and stride cracked and splintered. So for the moment, there are no guided hikes on Briks-dalsbreen, but she's a fickle creature and this may change.

It's about a 5km-return walk to the Briks-dal glacier face, either up the steepish path or along the longer, gentler cart track. Alas, the traditional pony-carts that plied the route for over 100 years no longer transport visitors but **Oldedalen Skyss** (☏57 87 68 05) has 'troll cars', vehicles like giant golfing carts (Nkr180 per person). From their turn-around point, there's still a 15-minute hike on a rough path to see the ice. To breathe up close in the glacier's face, take a guided trip in an inflatable dinghy. Dinghies (adult/child Nkr250/125), operated by **Briksdal Adventure** (☏57 87 68 00), depart approximately hourly in summer. We strongly recommend advance reservation for both troll cars and dinghies as places are often snapped up by tour groups.

🛏 Sleeping & Eating

TOP CHOICE **Melkevoll Bretun** CAMPGROUND € (☏57 87 38 64; www.melkevoll.no; per person/site Nkr20/100, dm Nkr110, cabins with outdoor bathroom Nkr350 plus Nkr50 per person, with bathroom Nkr650-750 plus Nkr50 per person; ⊗May-Sep) You'll find accommodation for all pockets and gorgeous views whichever way you turn. Look south and the Melkevollbreen glacier is sticking its tongue out towards you, spin west and the long, slim Volefossen waterfall cascades, turn north and the long reach of Oldevatnet lake shimmers, while eastwards, the Briksdalsbreen glacier blocks the horizon. There's a gorgeous green campsite with stacks of space between pitches.

THE LOVATNET DISASTERS

Ascending Lodalen, you'll see what appear to be islands that nearly split the lake into two. These giant rocks were dislodged from Ramnefjell and crashed down into the lake in three separate calamities. In 1905, the resulting giant wave swept away 63 people, only nine of whom were ever found, and deposited *Lodalen*, the lake steamer, 400m inland. In 1936, an estimated 1 million cu metres of rock crashed down, its wave killing 72 and lifting the steamer even higher. The third, in 1950, just left a bigger scar on the mountain. Collectively, they're known as the Lovatnet disasters.

The larger cabins are particularly well furnished. For budget sleeping with attitude, spread your sleeping bag in the 'stone-age cave' (Nkr110).

Briksdalsbre Fjellstove LODGE, CAFE €€ (☏57 87 68 00; www.briksdalsbre.no; s/d Nkr700/1090, 4-bed cabins Nkr850) This cosy mountain lodge has six comfortable rooms and a cafe-restaurant serving delicacies such as trout and reindeer.

❶ Getting There & Away

Between June and August, buses leave Stryn for Briksdal(Nkr70, one hour) once or twice daily, calling by Loen and Olden.

Kjenndalsbreen & Bødalsbreen

The **Kjenndalsbreen** glacier is a delightful 21km run up Lodalen, a parallel valley to Oldendalen, from the Nordfjord village of Loen. The least visited of the four best-known glacial tongues, it vies with Nigardsbreen for the most beautiful approach as you run parallel to the turquoise glacial lake of Lovatnet. You won't be completely alone but you'll be in far less company than at Briksdal, just over the mountain.

Bødalsbreen, up a short side valley to the east, provides a couple of good hiking possibilities. Between May and September, **Briksdal Adventure** (☏57 87 68 00; www. briksdal-adventure.com) leads daily five- to six-hour guided glacier hikes (Nkr600). Walks leave at 10am from Sande Camping and your crampons crunch the ice for about half the total time. Reserve directly or via the Stryn tourist office.

After paying a road toll (Nkr40), call by **Kjenndalstova Cafe** (www.kjenndalstova.no, in Norwegian), a lovely little spot where you can snack and hire a bike, canoe or rowing boat, before undertaking the final 5km to the glacier viewing point.

🛏 Sleeping

TOP CHOICE **Sande Camping** CAMPGROUND € (☏57 87 45 90; www.sande-camping.no; Loen; per person/site Nkr20/130, 2-4-bed cabins Nkr315-495, 4-6-bed apt Nkr495-895) You could spend an active day or two in the lovely environs of Sande Camping, near the northern end of Lovatnet. There's also a free sauna and, for hire, rowing boats, canoes and bikes. Its small **cafe-restaurant**, open to

LOVATNET CROSS

Around 100m before a panel indicating the toll road to Kjenndalsbreen, drop down a steepish path, signed Pilgrimssti (Pilgrim's Path), indicated by blue markers. It descends through birchwood to a simple wooden cross that marks the site of a memorial to the victims of the 1905 disaster – itself swept away in the 1936 cataclysm. On the way, which is punctuated by a series of edifying biblical tracts, notice the rusting remains of **Lodalen**, the lake steamer beached this far inland after being carried on the waves of disasters one and two. Allow 35 to 45 minutes for this out-and-back walk.

all, serves fresh fish from the lake or you can try your luck and dangle your own line (rods per day Nkr70). Add in bags of walking possibilities and you might never move on.

NORDFJORD TO THE COAST

For most travellers the 100km-long Nordfjord is but a stepping stone between Sognefjorden and Geirangerfjorden. These two popular fjords are linked by a road that winds around the head of Nordfjord past the villages of Byrkjelo, Olden and Loen to the larger town of Stryn.

Stryn, Olden and Loen make good bases for visiting the spectacular Briksdalsbreen and Kjenndalsbreen glaciers.

Olden

POP 550

Olden serves as a gateway to Briksdalsbreen. It has a seasonal **tourist office** (☑57 87 31 26; ☺11am-5pm mid-Jun–mid-Aug) in the fjord-side shopping complex.

If you fancy a little fishing, the **Isabella** (☑91 35 10 42; www.skarstein-fjordcruise.com, in Norwegian) does two- to three-hour trips (per person including gear Nkr220), leaving Olden marina at 4pm and 7.30pm, Monday to Friday. Reserve directly or via the Olden or Stryn Tourist Office.

For walks in and around the valley, pick up the map *Olden og Oldendalen* (Nkr50;

🛏 Sleeping & Eating

There are around 10 campsites in the area, most of them along the route to Briksdalsbreen and several in stunningly pretty sites.

Olden Fjordhotel HOTEL €€
(☑57 87 04 00; www.olden-hotel.no; s Nkr930-1170, d Nkr1260-1670, all incl breakfast; ☺May–mid-Sep) The automatic swing doors that purr open when you're still a couple of metres away are symptomatic of the warm welcome beyond the threshold. Most of the comfortable rooms have fjord views, nearly all have balconies and its **restaurant** does a fine Norwegian buffet or three-course dinner (both Nkr425).

Loen

POP 400

Loen, at the mouth of dramatic Lodalen, is, like Olden, a gateway to the glaciers. From this tiny village, a road leads to the spectacular Bødalen and Kjenndalen glacial tongues.

Like Olden, it makes a good base for hikers. Arm yourself with *Walking in Loen & Lodalen* (Nkr50; 1:50,000), which describes 20 day walks. One great though strenuous hike leads to the Skålatårnet tower, atop the 1848m-high summit of Skåla. The route begins at a signed car park 2.5km east of Loen. Allow seven to eight hours – considerably more than the course record of under one hour 10 minutes for La Sportiva Skaala annual uphill race.

🛏 Sleeping & Eating

Hotel Alexandra HOTEL €€€
(☑57 87 50 00; www.alexandra.no; s/d incl breakfast from Nkr1280/1960; P@🛜) Loen's undisputed centre of action is as much holiday centre as hotel and dominates tourism in the valley. It offers two restaurants, two cafes, bars, a nightclub, swimming pools (both indoor and open), a spa and fitness centre, a tennis court and marina. Run as a family hotel since 1884, it's managed nowadays by the fifth generation. Pleasant enough inside, its external architecture approaches eyesore level.

Hotel Loenfjord HOTEL €€€
(☑57 87 50 00; www.loenfjord.no; s/d incl breakfast from Nkr1020/1540; ☺Jun-Sep, Fri-Sun only Oct-May; P@🛜) The Loenfjord offers waterside accommodation that's a little less expensive than the Alexandra, to which it belongs. It's

altogether gentler on the eye, less crowded and offers bicycle and rowing-boat hire.

Lo-Vik Camping CAMPGROUND €

(☎57 87 76 19; www.lo-vik.no; per person/site Nkr25/140, 4-bed cabins with outdoor bathroom Nkr485, with bathroom Nkr675-1100; ☺May-Sep) Install yourself at the furthest, northern end beside the fjord, where there's a peaceful green area, well away from the road and its traffic.

Stryn

POP 2200

The small town of Stryn, de facto capital of upper Nordfjord, is something of a sprawl. The helpful **tourist office** (☎57 87 40 40; www.nordfjord.no; ☺8.30am-5pm or 8pm daily Jun-Aug, 8.30am-3.30pm Mon-Fri rest of year; @☎) is two blocks south of Tonningsgata, the main drag. It can arrange accommodation and rents mountain bikes (Nkr50/200 per hour/day). Its booklet, *Guide for Stryn,* (Nkr10) includes local hikes. For greater detail, invest Nkr30 in *Kart over Fjallturar I Stryn,* a map of mountain walks in the Stryn region at a scale of 1:50,000 that features a whole holiday's worth of hiking trails.

🛏 Sleeping

TOP CHOICE Visnes Hotel HOTEL €€

(☎57 87 10 87; www.visnes.no; Prestestegen 1; s Nkr750-900, d Nkr1000-1495; ☺mid-May–Sep; P☎) The Visnes, tautly run by the same family for six generations, occupies two magnificent listed properties, each with its own character. Most rooms are in the larger building, constructed in 1850. Higher room rates are for stunning fjord views and there are also a couple of large family rooms (Nkr1750). To feel like royalty, request a room in the smaller 1890 'dragon style' building that was occupied by King Rama V of Siam during his 1908 tour, or the one where King Oscar of Sweden and Norway rested his head in 1913. The Visnes' **restaurant** (3-course dinner Nkr395; ☺Jul–mid-Aug), in the hotel's larger building, serves exquisite gourmet food.

Stryn Hotel HOTEL €€

(☎57 87 07 00; www.strynhotel.no; Visnesvegen 1; s/d Nkr995/1295; P@☎) The Stryn, right beside the river, has 70 well furnished rooms, each with plenty of attractive woodwork. Those overlooking the water come at no extra cost. There's a good restaurant that also has river views.

Stryn Camping CAMPGROUND €

(☎57 87 11 36; www.stryn-camping.no; Bøavegen 6; car/caravan sites Nkr150/240, 4-bed cabins with outdoor bathroom Nkr350, 3-/6-bed cabins with bathroom Nkr650/950; ☺year-round) The facilities are well maintained and the welcome friendly at trim Stryn Camping. It's at the eastern end of town, just two blocks uphill from the main street.

🍴 Eating & Drinking

Bryggja FISH RESTAURANT €€

(☎90 16 81 34; www.bryggja.info, in Norwegian; Perhusvegen 11; mains Nkr135-285, 3-course meals Nkr398; ☺4pm-midnight mid-Jun–mid-Aug) Dine on the tiny outside terrace and savour its gorgeous riverside location. If it rains, the staff simply pulls over the sail-shaped cover. Decorated in nautical style, the interior too is an intimate place (there are only 30 seats) so it's wise to reserve a table.

Stryn Vertshus CAFE, RESTAURANT €€

(☎57 87 05 30; www.strynvertshus.no, in Norwegian; Tonningsgata 19; mains Nkr225-250; ☺10am-4.30pm Mon-Sat; @☎) Both inside and on its flower-bedecked terrace, the Stryn Tavern serves tasty lunch snacks (Nkr80 to Nkr95). In the evening, there's a varied tapas platter (Nkr200) and a good selection of mains.

Coop Supermarket Cafe CAFE €

(cnr Tonningsgata & Tinggata; ☺10am-5pm) For wholesome food at very reasonable prices, go up to the 1st-floor cafeteria of the Coop, where half the population of Stryn, especially its senior citizens, seems to eat at lunchtime.

Base Camp BAR

(1st fl Tonningsgata 31) Also on the main street, Stryn's most popular bar sometimes operates as a disco too.

ℹ Getting There & Away

Express bus destinations include the following:

Måløy (Nkr200, two hours, three daily)

Ålesund (Nkr250, 3¾ hours, one to four daily) via Hellesylt (Nkr105, one hour) – from where the ferry runs to Geiranger

Bergen (Nkr460, 6¾ hours, three daily) via Loen (Nkr32, 10 minutes) and Olden (Nkr42, 15 minutes)

Florø

POP 8450

Florø, Norway's westernmost town, is a pleasant if unexciting little place whose coat

GAMLE STRYNEFJELLSVEGEN: A DRIVING TOUR FROM STRYN

This spectacular 130km route takes a comfortable four hours. Head eastwards from Stryn along the **Rv15** as it runs alongside the river that descends from Lake Strynevat-net, then follows the lake shore itself. It's an inspirational ride with mountain views as impressive as anywhere in the country.

After 20km, stop to visit the **Jostedalsbreen National Park Centre** (Jostedalsbreen Nasjonalparksenter; www.jostedalsbre.no; adult/child Nkr80/40; ☺10am-4pm or 6pm May–mid-Sep) in the village of **Oppstryn**. There's a worthwhile and informative 10-minute film about the glacier plus exhibits illustrating avalanches and rock falls and a variety of stuffed wildlife. Outside, enjoy its unique garden with more than 300 species of endemic vegetation, each labelled in Norwegian, English and French. A cluster of picnic tables offers a spectacular vista over the lake.

At an interpretive panel and sign 17km beyond the National Park Centre, turn right to take the **Rv258**. It took a team of local and immigrant Swedish navvies more than 10 years to lay the **Gamle Strynefjellsvegen** (old Stryn mountain road) over the mountain. The road, considered a masterpiece of civil engineering at the time, opened to traffic in 1894. For more than 80 years, it was the principal east-to-west route in this part of the country. Until well into the 1950s, a team of some 200 workers, armed only with spades, would keep it clear in winter, digging through several miles of metres-high snow.

The climb to the high plateau is spectacular, enhanced by thin threads of water tumbling from the heights and a trio of roaring roadside torrents carrying glacial melt. There are several stopping points as you ascend this narrow strip. Savour, in particular, the viewing platform above Videfossen, where the water churns beneath you.

Some 9km along the Gamle Strynefjellsvegen, you reach **Stryn Summer Ski Centre** (Stryn Sommerskisenter), a bleak place outside the short season. But from late May until some time in July, it offers Norway's most extensive summer skiing; most of those photos of bikini-clad skiers you see around were snapped right here.

The steep ascent behind you, continue along a good-quality unsurfaced single-track road that runs above a necklace of milky turquoise tarns overlooked by bare, boulder-strewn rock. Here on this upland plateau, the sparse vegetation hugs the ground close.

After crossing the watershed 10km beyond the ski centre, there begins a much more gentle descent to rejoin the Rv15 beside the **Grotli Høyfiellshotel** (☺cafe 10am-7pm), a fine stop for lunch or a drink. Turn left for a fast, smooth, two-lane run beside **Lake Brei-dalsvatn** before diving into the first of three long tunnels that will bring you back to the National Park Centre and onward, retracing your steps back to Stryn.

After the completion of these three linked tunnels in 1978, the old road was overshadowed by its younger alternative: 12 speedy kilometres along a wide road against 27km of winding single track – there was no comparison. But the Gamle Strynefjellsvegen always drew travellers with time on their hands and lovers of wild scenery. Now, freshly designated a National Tourist Route, it again enjoys a share of a different, softer limelight.

The Gamle Strynefjellsvegen is normally free of snow from June to October. Electronic signs along the Rv15 indicate if the 'Strynfjellet' (its official name) is indeed open.

---

of arms features, appropriately, three her-rings rampant.

Nowadays, wealth comes from the black gold of the oil industry. The large Fjord Base, just northeast of town, serves the giant Snorreankeret offshore oil field. Florø is also enriched by fish farming and shipbuilding – while the herring, the town's original raison d'être, plays a some-what diminished role.

For a scenic overview, it's an easy 10-minute climb up the Storåsen hill from the Florø Ungdomsskule on Havrenesveien.

◉ Sights

Sogn og Fjordane Kystmuseet

COASTAL MUSEUM

(www.kystmuseum.no, in Norwegian; Brendøyve-gen; adult/child Nkr50/free; ☺11am-6pm Mon-Fri, noon-4pm Sat & Sun Jun-Aug, 10am-3pm Mon-Fri

& Sun Sep-May) The main building of the Kystmuseet is chock-full of fishing exhibits, including a model 1900 fishing family's home. There's also a section on the history of Florø from its foundation as a small herring trading post barely 150 years ago. A second building houses a collection of typical coastal boats. The **Snorreankeret** display – in a building that has the shape of the original oil platform that first pumped the country's oil – illustrates with plenty of hardware and equipment the history, exploration and exploitation of the North Sea oil and gas fields.

The Old Quarter   HISTORIC QUARTER
On and around Strandgata, the main street, the most significant 19th-century timbered houses are well signed and documented in both Norwegian and English.

Offshore Islands   ISLANDS
Local ferries leaving from Fugleskjærskaia Quay connect the mainland to several small islands, each making for a stimulating off-the-beaten-track day trip. The tourist office can reserve ferries and also advise on island accommodation.

Askrova has a prehistoric Troll Cave, whose deepest depths have never been explored. On the island of **Batalden**, check out the gallery and small museum at **Batalden Havbu fishing cottages** (☑57 74 54 22; www.bataldenhavbu.no). You can overnight in their sensitively restored **cottages** (d from Nkr920; ☺Apr-Sep).

Kinn has a beautifully restored 12th-century **church**, believed to have been built by British Celts sheltering from religious persecution. On the second or third weekend in June, it's the site of the **Kinnespelet pageant**, which celebrates the history of the church on the island. Climbers and hikers will savour the dramatic landscapes, particularly the **Kinnaklova cleft**.

On **Svanøy**, enjoy the hiking and pass by the small **deer centre** (☑57 75 21 80; www.svanoy.com, in Norwegian).

At 233m, the highest point on **Tansøy** offers great panoramic views over the surrounding archipelago.

🏃 Activities

Boating

Florø Rorbu (☑57 74 81 00; www.florbu.com; Krokane Kai) hires motor boats (Nkr200 to Nkr400 per day) and sea kayaks (Nkr200 per day), while **Krokane Camping** (☑57 75 22 50; www.krocamp.no) rents out rowing boats

THE WORLD'S LONGEST HERRING TABLE

OK, so the competition may not be all that extensive but a herring table 400m long is an impressive achievement in its own right. Each year, Florø and Haugesund, further down the coast, used to vie with each other for the year's largest and longest spread but, now that Haugesund has retired, there's no longer the same north–south rivalry and Florø has the field to itself.

On the third Friday in June, the table is erected in the heart of Florø. Just imagine a standard 400m running track, straightened out and laden with plates of herring, potatoes, bread and drinks, all free of charge, and you've got the scene. Then, once the table's cleared away, the festivities continue all weekend.

(Nkr100 per day) and motor boats (from Nkr200/300 per three hours/day).

Hiking & Cycling

The tourist office sells a useful booklet, *Cycling in Flora* (Nkr10), and has map sheets on local hikes.

Swimming

If the fjord's too chilly for a dip, visit **Havhesten** (adult/child Nkr110/65; ☺10am-5pm or 8pm). Work up a sweat in the gym or get all aglow in the sauna. Then plunge into one of its three indoor heated pools and savour the fantastic view of the fjord as you bob up. Everything, even the view, is included in your admission.

👉 Tours

Between June and August, the tourist office runs a number of tempting guided tours. Pick up its leaflet of summer venues.

🛏 Sleeping

TOP CHOICE **Quality Hotel Florø**   HOTEL €€
(☑57 75 75 75; www.choicehotels.no; Hamnegata 11; s/d from Nkr950/1150; ▣@🛜) On the quayside, right beside the marina and constructed in the style of a dockside warehouse (the present banqueting area is a former fish store), this is Florø's best option. Rooms with sea views cost no extra and a couple have 'boat beds', made of recycled rowing boats.

Bryggekanten, its restaurant, sources most of its food locally and warrants a visit in its own right.

Florø Rorbu
CABINS €

(☎57 74 81 00; www.florbu.com; Krokane Kai; apts Nkr600-900) These excellent, family-owned, fully furnished flats are right beside a tiny inlet and have their own moorings (you can hire a boat or kayak and putter around the fjord to celebrate sunset).

Krokane Camping
CAMPGROUND €

(☎57 75 22 50; www.krocamp.no; campsites Nkr130, 2-/4-bed cabins Nkr450/550, 5-/6-bed cabins Nkr650-850, all with bathroom; 🛜) Krokane Camping occupies a wooded site on a peninsula 2.5km east of town. The shoreside meadow, though a trek to the toilets, is a tent camper's delight.

✖ Eating & Drinking

Hjørnevikbua
PUB, RESTAURANT €€€

(☎57 74 01 22; www.tokokker.as, in Norwegian; Strandgata 23; lunch dishes Nkr65-125, dinner mains Nkr255-285) The 2nd floor of Hjørnevikbua, with its shiplike interior, serves lunch that includes some mean fish soups, then gourmet evening meals. You can also eat outdoors on its barge that's moored to the quay.

Bistro To Kokker
CAFE €

(☎57 75 22 33; Strandgata 33; dishes Nkr106-130; ⊙9am-10pm) This gloomy place where ageing bachelors stare into their cocoa does well-priced fare and portions are large. There's squid, salmon, monkfish and other seafood on the menu or, for more pedestrian palates, it has fish and chips, burgers, good salads, pizzas and a changing dish of the day (Nkr82).

Hjørnevikhagen
CAFE, RESTAURANT

(☎57 74 42 33; Strandgata 28; lunch mains Nkr70-135, dinner mains Nkr135-190; ⊙Mon-Sat) The menu is short, unexceptional but reliable. You can eat outside on the split-level terrace or within, with good views of the marina. Just behind the tourist office, it's also a good spot for a quiet drink.

🍷 Drinking & Entertainment

Shamrock
PUB

(Strandgata 58) There's little that is identifiably Irish at the Shamrock, apart from its green-bordered bar menu, though they do keep bottled Guinness under the counter. Even so, it's where the young folk of Florø head to sip a cocktail, down a beer, nibble on a snack or let their hair down at the Saturday-night disco. It also shows all major football matches.

Churchill
PUB

(Markegata 43) Just up the hill from the Shamrock, Churchill, which was undergoing an elaborate facelift at the time of writing, is another Florø favourite.

❶ Information

Florø's **tourist office** (☎57 74 30 30; www .fjordkysten.no; Strandgata 30; ⊙9am-6pm Mon-Fri, 10am-4pm Sat, 11am-3pm Sun Jun-Aug) has a computer terminal and wi-fi.

❶ Getting There & Away

DAT (www.dat.dk) offers four budget flights daily to/from both Oslo and Bergen.

Florø is the first stop on the Hurtigruten coastal ferry as it heads north from Bergen.

Express boats call in twice daily on the run between Bergen (Nkr580, 3½ hours) and Måløy (Nkr205, one hour).

If you're driving, the most scenic way north to Måløy by road is via Bremanger island.

WORTH A TRIP

KALVÅG

If you're travelling between Florø and Måløy via Bremanger island, do make the 5km detour from the ferry landing point at Smørhamn to the small, sensitively preserved fishing village of Kalvåg. Nowadays it's picture-postcard pretty and there's just one giant fish-processing factory on its outskirts that operates when the herring and mackerel shoals come near. But at its peak Kalvåg had over 50 herring salt houses that employed a seasonal workforce of around 10,000. You can still visit a couple of them; ask at the quayside **tourist office** (☎481 40 488; www.fordkysten.no; ⊙10am-6pm Mon-Fri, 10am-4pm Sat, noon-4pm Sun Jul–mid-Aug, 10am-4pm Mon-Fri rest of year). To while away the time between ferries, scoff a plate of shrimps, split some crab claws or down a beer, brewed specially for the restaurant, on the dockside terrace of **Knutholmen** (☎57 79 69 00; www.knutholmen.no, in Norwegian; ⊙8am-midnight) with the fishing boats right before you.

THE ROLLING ROAD TO KRÅKENES LIGHTHOUSE

This 42km round trip can be comfortably driven in a couple of hours, including stops. Take the Rv617 from Måløy, then follow signs for Kråkenes Fyr (Kråkenes Lighthouse). On the way there or back, it's worth the short, signed detour to visit **Refviksanden**, a 1.4km reach of white sand, voted Norway's finest beach in a 2010 online poll.

The road rolls over treeless, windswept grassland, runs past a long line of twirling windmills (step outside your car and you'll understand why they're sited right here) and offers staggering views of steep cliffs.

Kråkenes Lighthouse, at the very end of the road, perches precariously on a rock shoulder. Sunny or stormy, it's a romantic spot with stunning views of the cliffs and pounding ocean where it's also possible to overnight (see www.krakenesfyr.no).

A couple of kilometres before the lighthouse, **Nilsestova Feriehaus** (57 85 41 55; www.nilsestova.no; 4-/8-person cabins with bathroom Nkr500/700) has two beautifully situated cabins, the larger one formerly the family home of landlord Norvall Kråkenes.

Måløy

POP 3500

The little fishing town of Måløy, at the mouth of Nordfjord, lies on Vågsøy island. Nestling beneath a pair of rounded hills, for all the world like a pair of giant breasts, it's linked to the mainland by the graceful S-curve Måløybrua bridge.

Though there are no monuments or sights to make you gasp, commercial boats ply up and down and it's a refreshingly real, alive place when compared to the tourist toy-towns to its south.

Vågsøy island and neighbouring Selje are laced with sea-view hiking routes (pick up the 1:50,000 walking map *Outdoor Pursuits: Selje & Vågsøy Communes*).

A short drive for about 10km west of town brings you to the bizarre rock **Kannesteinen**, rising from the sea like the tail of a whale.

🛏 Sleeping

Måløy Hotell   HOTEL €€
(57 84 94 00; www.maloyhotell.no; Gate 1 No 25; s/d from Nkr835/1070) This large glass-fronted hotel is the centre of most tourist activity in town. Recently affiliated to the Best Western group, it has 40 comfortable rooms and offers guests a free light evening meal.

Steinvik Camping   CAMPGROUND €
(57 85 10 70; www.steinvik-camping.no; per person/site Nkr25/150, cabins Nkr450-800, 4-bed self-catering apt Nkr550-800; year-round) The nearest campsite to Måløy has spectacular views over the busy sea lane and a particularly cosy common room with sofas and armchairs. To get there, cross the bridge to the east bank, turn right after 2km beside a school and follow the track downhill for 1.2km. No credit cards.

🍴 Eating

You'll find a cluster of three good places to eat and drink very near the express boat jetty.

Kraftstasjonen   FISH RESTAURANT €€
(57 85 12 60; Gate 1; dinner mains Nkr235-285; 11am-10pm Mon-Thu, 11am-1am Fri & Sat) In their recently opened restaurant, Rita and Arne Andal offer the freshest of fish. Lunch dishes are simple and inexpensive while the dinner menu features cod, halibut and monkfish, prepared a variety of ways. For dessert, there's an irresistible crème brûlée with mango and strawberry coulis. For something simpler, try the tapas – and wangle a table on the bath-towel-sized terrace overlooking the harbour.

Havfruen Fiskeutsalg   FISH CAFE €
(57 85 23 36; 10am-4.30pm Mon-Fri, 10am-2pm Sat) The Mermaid is both a wet fish shop ('Born to fish, forced to work' says the plaque on the wall) and small cafe, serving rich fish soups (Nkr85), salmon and shrimp sandwiches (Nkr35) and other piscatorial products.

Din & Min   CAFE, BAR €
(57 85 18 75; Gate 1 44) Yours and Mine is a hip little cafe and drinking hole. And small's the word; sip a coffee or something stronger or nibble a snack within the confines of its agreeably woody interior, or climb to its upstairs terrace, where you'll have the harbour at your feet.

ℹ Information

Måløy's seasonal **tourist office** (57 84 50 77; 9am-5pm Mon-Fri, 10am-4pm Sat & Sun

Jul, 10am-4pm Mon-Sat mid-end Jun & early Aug) didn't know where it would be the summer after we last visited, having been driven from its previous location by rising damp.

ℹ Getting There & Away

The express boat from Bergen (Nkr705, 4½ hours) to Selje (Nkr73, 25 minutes) puts in at Måløy. The Hurtigruten coastal ferry also calls in.

Nor-Way Bussekspress runs three times daily to/from Oslo (Nkr720, 11 hours) via Stryn (Nkr200, two hours).

Selje & Selja Island

POP 700

Few visitors make it to **Selje** and therein lies the charm of this pleasant village on the western edge of Norway, with its strand of pristine, white beach. **Vestkapp**, 32km by road from Selje, isn't Norway's westernmost point despite the name but it still provides superb sea views.

The haunting ruins of **Selja monastery** and the **church of St Sunniva** on Selja Island date from the 11th and 12th centuries respectively. You can climb the 40m-high tower for a splendid panorama. From mid-June to the end of August, the tourist office arranges guided tours.

The **Selje Hotel** (✆57 85 88 80; www.selje hotel.no; r Nkr975-1200), a delightful wood and shaped-stone pile right beside the beach, is the village's only hotel. Within it is Spa Thalasso, a health centre with pool, jacuzzi and a range of relaxing activities and treatments.

ℹ Information

Selje's **tourist office** (✆57 85 66 06; www. nordfjord.no; ⊗9am-7pm Jul, shorter hr rest of yr; @), at the harbour, keeps a list of cabins and apartments in the area.

ℹ Getting There & Away

From Måløy, you have two stunningly attractive ways of reaching Selje – the splendid fjord-side drive along the Rv618, or aboard the twice-daily Nordfjord express boat (Nkr73, 25 minutes).

Local buses run between Måløy and Selje (Nkr94, one hour) six times daily on weekdays and once on Sunday.

THE NORTHERN FJORDS

It's yet more crinkly coastline and more deeply incised fjords as you push further northwards into the region of Møre og

Romsdal. Geirangerfjord, a Unesco World Heritage Site, a must on most tours and a favourite anchorage for cruise ships, staggers beneath its summer influx. Stray from this tour operators' mecca and you'll find the waterways and roads less crowded and the scenery almost as spectacular as further south. The coastal towns of Ålesund and Kristiansund each deserve an overnight stop – and the spectacular drive over the Trollstigen pass will have you checking your safety belt.

Åndalsnes

POP 2650

There are two dramatic ways to approach Åndalsnes: by road through the Trollstigen pass or along Romsdalen as you ride the spectacularly scenic Raumabanen. The rail route down from Dombås, it ploughs through a deeply cut glacial valley flanked by sheer walls and plummeting waterfalls. Badly bombed during WWII, the modern town, nestled beside Romsdalfjord, is nondescript, but the surrounding landscapes are magnificent.

◉ Sights

Trollveggen   SHEER CLIFF

From Dombås to the southeast, the E136 and rail line drop in parallel down Romsdalen (you might have a sense of déjà vu if you've seen *Harry Potter & the Half-Blood Prince*, where the valley features). Near Åndalsnes, dramatic Trollveggen (Troll Wall), first conquered in 1958 by a joint Norwegian and English team, rears skywards. The highest vertical mountain wall in Europe, its ragged and often cloud-shrouded summit, 1800m from the valley floor, is considered the ultimate challenge among mountaineers.

Trollstigen   MOUNTAIN ROAD

(www.trollstigen.net) South of Åndalsnes, the Troll's Ladder is a thriller of a climb or descent. Recently declared a National Tourist Route, it was completed in 1936 after eight years of labour. To add an extra daredevil element to its 11 hairpin bends and a 1:12 gradient, much of it is effectively single lane. Several dramatic waterfalls, including the thundering 180m-high Stigfossen, slice down its flanks.

More energetically, you can also take it at a slower pace and puff your way up and over the old horse trail, narrow and blazed with white spots, that was previously the only communication between the two valleys.

ⓘ CAR WALKS

No, not an oxymoron but a most useful little brochure for walkers. Invest Nkr35 in *Car Walks*, available from Åndalsnes, Valldal, Geiranger and Hellesylt tourist offices. It has suggestions for more than 20 waymarked walks, lasting from 15 minutes to six hours. Ranging from Geiranger to south of Åndalsnes, each walk sets out from a public car park.

The route is also being upgraded in order to make it more cyclist-friendly, separating bicycles from the motorhomes and caravans that wheeze their way up.

The pass is usually cleared and open from late May to mid-October; early in the season it's an impressive trip through a popular cross-country ski field, between high walls of snow. At the top, a brand-new visitors centre was being constructed when we last crossed. Of the two new viewpoints, walk just that bit further to the far one, from where the panorama of the snaking road and wide valley far below is much more impressive.

Around you as you descend are the open reaches of Reinheimen National Park, established in 2006 and Norway's third largest, where wild reindeer still crop the mosses and soft grass.

Raumabanen   CLASSIC TRAIN JOURNEY
Trains run daily year-round along this spectacular route, meeting the main line, after 114km, at Dombås. There's also a **tourist train** (adult/child return Nkr296/148; one child per adult travels free) with on-board commentary that runs twice daily from June to August from Åndalsnes' lakeside station up to Bjorli, at 600m. Book at the station or tourist office.

🏃 Activities

Hiking

The pamphlet *Geiranger Trollstigen* (Nkr30) describes seven signed hiking trails in the Trollstigen area. You'll need to supplement this with the map *Romsdals-Fjella* at 1:80,000. The tourist office carries both.

An excellent day hike, signed by red markers, begins in town, 50m north of the roundabout before the Esso petrol station, and climbs to the summit of Nesaksla (715m), the prominent peak that rises above Åndalsnes. At the top, the payoff for a steep ascent is a magnificent panorama. In fine weather,

the view extends up and down Romsdalen and into Isterdalen, rivalling any in Norway.

From the shelter at the top, you can retrace your steps (2½-hour return journey) or undertake the straightforward ascent to the summit of Høgnosa (991m) and trek on to Åkesfjellet (1215m). Alternatively, traverse along the marked route 5km eastward and descend to Isfjorden village, at the head of Isfjord.

The tourist office can arrange mountain walks of four to six hours with a qualified guide.

Climbing

The best local climbs are the less extreme sections of the 1500m-high rock route on Trollveggen and the 1550m-high Romsdalshorn, but there are a wealth of others. Serious climbers should buy *Klatring i Romsdal* (Nkr300), which includes rock- and ice-climbing information in both Norwegian and English.

Fishing

John Kofoed (📞971 79 442; www.rauma-jakt -fiskesafari.no) runs three-hour fishing tours (adult/child Nkr350/175 plus Nkr75 per rod) on Romsdalsfjorden three times daily in summer. Reserve directly or through the tourist office.

✹ Festivals & Events

Norsk Fjellfestival   OUTDOOR ACTIVITIES
(Norway Mountain Festival; www.norsk-fjellfestival. no, in Norwegian) A week-long jamboree for lovers of the great outdoors with plenty of folk events thrown in. Early July.

Rauma Rock   ROCK MUSIC
(www.raumarock.com, in Norwegian) Central Norway's largest outdoor rock gathering. Two days in early August.

World Base Race   BASE JUMPING
(www.worldbaserace.com) Organised base jumping – if that's not a paradox – as contestants leap into the void in a head to head contest. Invented in Åndalsnes, it's now spreading to other countries, and is held in mid-August.

🛏 Sleeping

[TOP CHOICE] **Hotel Aak**   HOTEL €€
(📞71 22 71 71; www.hotelaak.no, in Norwegian; s/d Nkr850/1100; ⊙mid-Jun–Aug; P 🛜) This charming place, the oldest tourist hotel in Norway, lies beside the E136, direction Dombås, 4km from town. Most of the 16 comfortable bedrooms are named after a mountain

that you can see from the bedroom window (though in one or two you may have to poke your head out a little). Its **restaurant** (mains Nkr150-190; ⊙4-10pm) is equally impressive and offers excellent traditional cuisine. As it's so small, do reserve in advance.

Grand Hotel Bellevue   HOTEL €€
(☑71 22 75 00; www.grandhotel.no; Åndalgata 5; s/d 1030/1240; ℗@≋) This large white-washed structure caps a hillock in the centre of town. Most of its 86 rooms have fine views, particularly those facing the rear. There's a public swimming pool barely 100m away. Its **restaurant** (mains Nkr135-275; ⊙dinner only) offers the town's most formal dining, but you can always nibble on a lighter dish for around Nkr100. Take a look at the vintage black-and-white photos in the corridor, including one of a very young and sprightly Cliff Richard. From the hotel, you can walk straight into the interconnecting town library, cinema and auditorium.

Åndalsnes Vandrerhjem Setnes   HOSTEL €
(☑71 22 13 82; www.aandalsnesvandrerhjem.no; dm/s/d Nkr275/480/690; ⊙Mar-Nov) This welcoming, HI-affiliated, sod-roofed hostel is 1.5km from the train station on the E136, direction Ålesund. It's worth staying here for the bumper pancakes-and-pickled-herring breakfast alone. The Ålesund bus that meets the train passes right by. Rise early and you can be first aboard the bus that runs to Valldal and on to Geiranger via Trollstigen; the bus driver parks his bus right beside the hostel.

Trollstigen Resort   CAMPGROUND €
(☑71 22 68 99; www.trollstigenresort.com; car/caravan sites Nkr100/140, 4-/5-bed cabins from Nkr500/800; ≋) Recognisable by the strapping wooden troll at its entrance, this well-kept campground is 2km along the Rv63 highway, direction Geiranger. The welcome's warm and the location, overlooking the River Rauma, is scenic and altogether quieter than the riverside alternatives. There are plans to construct a small hotel and restaurant.

Åndalsnes Camping   CAMPGROUND €
(☑71 22 16 29; www.andalsnes-camping.com; car/caravan sites Nkr125/140, 4-bed cabins with outdoor bathroom Nkr450, 6-7-bed cabins with bathroom Nkr880; ⊙May-mid-Sep; @≋) Less than 2km from town, it enjoys a dramatic setting beside the River Rauma. There's internet access (Nkr60 per hour) and you can hire canoes (Nkr50/200 per hour/day) and bikes (Nkr50/110 per hour/day).

✗ Eating & Drinking

Kaikanten   CAFE, RESTAURANT €
(daily specials Nkr98, snacks Nkr35-78, dishes Nkr60-195; ⊙10am-11pm Mon-Sat, noon-9pm Sun mid-May–Aug) Sit back and relax here at the jetty's edge and enjoy a drink, a snack and one of Norway's prettiest panoramas in this welcoming place, run by the Grand Hotel.

Måndalen Bakeri   CAKE SHOP €
(Havnegate 5; ⊙8.30am-5pm Mon-Fri, 8.30am-2pm Sat) For sandwiches, sweet treats and all things delicious, call by Måndalen Bakeri, on the waterfront near the train station.

Kjellar'n   PUB
(⊙Fri & Sat) What a contrast with the sober, slightly dated decor of the Grand Hotel Bellevue! The hotel's cellar bar, backlit in pink and lime green, is where the town meets at weekends to drink, chat and dance until late.

ⓘ Information

The **tourist office** (☑71 22 16 22; www.visit andalsnes.com; ⊙9am-7pm mid-Jun–mid-Aug, rest of year 9am-3pm Mon-Fri) is at the train station. It rents bikes (Nkr50/180 per hour/day) and has internet and wi-fi.

Romsdal Libris, the bookshop over the road from the tourist office, also has wi-fi, which extends to the quayside in front of it.

ⓘ Getting There & Away

Bus
Buses along the spectacular National Tourist Route to Geiranger (Nkr222, three hours), via Trollstigen, the Linge–Eidsdal ferry and the steep Ørnevegen (Eagle's Way), run twice daily between mid-June and mid-August.

There are also services to Molde (Nkr127, 1½ hours, up to eight daily) and Ålesund (Nkr255, 2¼ hours, four times daily).

Train
Trains to/from Dombås (Nkr217, 1½ hours) run twice daily in synchronisation with Oslo–Trondheim trains. Trains connect in Åndalsnes twice daily with the express bus service to Ålesund via Molde.

Valldal & Around
VALLDAL
Valldal is a place that travellers tend to pass through, having driven over the famous Trollstigen pass from Åndalsnes or savoured the exquisitely beautiful ferry journey from Geiranger. Perched in a nick of Norddalsfjord, its agricultural surrounds

lay claim to being Europe's northernmost orchards. Here apples, pears and even cherries thrive – and you'll also find strawberries in profusion, commemorated in an annual **Strawberry Festival**, usually on the last weekend in July.

Syltetøysbutikken (Syltegata) is the place to sample the fruits, whatever the season. On the road behind and east of the church, it has a healthy selection of jams and juices, pressed and simmered in the small factory behind the shop and sourced in the main from local farmers.

From Valldal you can experience a four-hour white-water rush (Nkr690) down the Valldøla River or a shorter two-hour trip (Nkr490). Contact **Valldal Naturopplevingar** (www.valldal.no; ☉May-Sep), whose headquarters is 200m from the tourist office. It also offers kayak hire and a variety of other outdoor activities such as wilderness camping and, in winter, moonlight ski trips.

🛏 Sleeping & Eating

There's no shortage of campgrounds, many overpopulated with caravans parked semi-permanently.

Fjellro Turisthotell HOTEL €€
(☎70 25 75 13; www.fjellro.no; Syltegata; s/d incl breakfast Nkr785/1020; ☉May-Sep) At charming 'Mountain Peace', just behind (northeast of) Valldal's church, the welcome is warm and rooms are well appointed. There's a **cafe-restaurant** (☉7-10pm) that specialises in fish, and a pub on the ground floor, open at weekends. At the rear is a tranquil garden with a small playground for children.

Jordbærstova CAFE €
(☉May-Sep) About 6km up the Åndalsnes road, Jordbærstova honours the valley's mighty strawberry. Stop in for a fat slice of its gooey, creamy *svele,* the local pancake speciality served with strawberries and cream. It also offers light meals.

Lupinen Café CAFE €
(mains Nkr55-95) This waterside cafe serves pizza, beef and fish dishes and puts on an inexpensive buffet (Nkr170).

❶ Information

Valldal's **tourist office** (☎70 25 77 67; www.visitalesund-geiranger.com; ☉10am-6pm mid-Jun–mid-Aug, rest of year 10am-5pm Mon-Fri) rents bikes (Nkr25/100 per hour/day) and can also arrange motor-boat hire (Nkr85/400 per hour/day).

WORTH A TRIP

STORDAL

If you're travelling between Valldal and Ålesund on the Rv650, do make a short stop at Stordal's **Rose Church** (Rosekyrka; adult/child Nkr30/15; ☉11am-4pm mid-Jun–mid-Aug). Unassuming from the outside, it was constructed in 1789 on the site of an earlier stave church, elements of which were retained. Inside comes the surprise: the roof, walls and every last pillar are sumptuously painted with scenes from the Bible and portraits of saints in an engagingly naive interpretation of high baroque.

❶ Getting There & Away

Valldal lies on the 'Golden Route' bus service that runs twice daily from mid-June to August between Åndalsnes (Nkr105, 1¾ hours) and Geiranger (Nkr65, 1¼ hours), up and over the spectacular Trollstigen pass. If you're driving, pause at **Gudbrandsjuvet**, 15km up the valley from Valldal, where the river sluices and thrashes through a 5m-wide, 20m-deep canyon.

Equally scenic is the spectacular ferry cruise (adult/child single Nkr206/103, return Nkr327/157, 2¼ hours) that runs twice daily between Valldal and Geiranger from mid-June to mid-August.

TAFJORD

In 1934 an enormous chunk of rock 400m high and 22m long – in all, a whopping 8 million cu metres – broke loose from the hillside. It crashed into Korsnæsfjord and created a 64m-high tidal wave that washed up to 700m inland and claimed 40 lives in Fjørra and Tafjord.

FREE **Tafjord Power Station Museum**
MUSEUM
(Kraftverkmuseum; ☎70 17 56 00; www.tafjord.net/museum; ☉noon-5pm mid-Jun–early Aug) Within the now-defunct power station, this museum shows how the advent of hydroelectric power changed the valley. The road that climbs from the village up to the Zakarias reservoir passes through a bizarre corkscrew tunnel and, a couple of kilometres higher up, a short walking route drops to the crumbling bridge at the dam's narrow base, where you feel at close range the stresses this 96m-high structure has to tolerate.

Geiranger

POP 250

Scattered cliffside farms, most long abandoned, still cling to the towering, near-sheer walls of twisting, 20km-long emerald-green Geirangerfjord, a Unesco World Heritage Site. Waterfalls – the Seven Sisters, the Suitor, the Bridal Veil and more – sluice and tumble. The one-hour scenic ferry trip along its length between Geiranger and Hellesylt is as much minicruise as means of transport – take it even if you've no particular reason to get to the other end.

If you arrive from Hellesylt, Geiranger village, despite its fabulous location at the head of the fjord, comes as a shock to the system as you mingle with the hordes of visitors brought in by bus and ship. Every year Geiranger wilts under the presence of over 600,000 visitors and more than 150 cruise ships (two were moored offshore last time we visited, each polluting the pure air with dark fumes from its smokestack, while their bumboats belched diesel vapours at the jetty).

You'll gasp for another reason if you drop from the north down the Ørnevegen, the Eagle's Way, as the final, superspectacular 7km of the Rv63 from Åndalsnes is called. As it twists down the almost sheer slope in 11 hairpin bends, each one gives a yet more impressive glimpse along the narrow fjord.

And whichever way you're coming or going, once the last cruise ship and tour bus of the day has pulled out, serenity returns to this tiny port.

◎ Sights

Norsk Fjordsenter FOLK MUSEUM
(www.verdsarvfjord.no, in Norwegian; adult/child Nkr100/50; ⊙9am-6pm or 9pm mid-Jun–mid-Aug, 10am-3pm Mon-Sat rest of year) The Norwegian Fjord Centre has tools, artefacts and even whole buildings that have been uprooted and brought here, illustrating the essential themes – the mail packet, avalanches, the building of early roads and the rise of tourism – that have shaped the land and its people. Take in too its evocative audiovisual presentation.

Flydalsjuvet VIEWPOINT
Somewhere you've seen that classic photo, beloved of brochures, of the overhanging rock Flydalsjuvet, usually with a figure gazing down at a cruise ship in Geirangerfjord. The car park, signposted Flydalsjuvet, about 5km uphill from Geiranger on the Stryn

road, offers a great view of the fjord and the green river valley, but doesn't provide the postcard view down to the last detail. For that, you'll have to drop about 150m down the hill, then descend a slippery and rather indistinct track to the edge. Your intrepid photo subject will have to scramble down gingerly and with the utmost care to the overhang about 50m further along...

Dalsnibba MOUNTAIN VIEWPOINT
For the highest and perhaps most stunning of the many stunning views of the Geiranger valley and fjord, take the 5km toll road (Nkr85 per car) that climbs from the Rv63 to the **Dalsnibba lookout** (1500m). A **bus** (adult/child Nkr180/90 return) runs three times daily from Geiranger between mid-June and mid-August.

🏃 Activities

Sea Kayaking
Coastal Odyssey (☑911 18 062; www.coastalodyssey.com), based at Geiranger Camping, is run by Jonathan Bendiksen, a Canadian from the Northwest Territories who learnt to kayak almost before he could walk. He rents sea-kayaks (Nkr150/400/750 per hour/half-day/day). He also does daily kayaking-with-gentle-hiking trips (adult/child 800/640), lasting five to six hours, to a trio of the finest destinations around the fjord. As his publicity flyer says with pride, these are 'the only trips available in Geiranger that have no environmental impact'.

Boat Tours
Geiranger Fjordservice (☑70 26 30 07; www.geirangerfjord.no) does 1½-hour sightseeing **boat tours** (adult/child Nkr155/80, up to 4 sailings daily mid-May–mid-Sep). Its kiosk is within the tourist office. From mid-June to August, it also operates a smaller, 15-seater boat (Nkr395/195) that scuds deeper and faster into the fjord.

Hiking
Get away from the seething ferry terminal and life's altogether quieter. All around Geiranger there are great signed hiking routes to abandoned farmsteads, waterfalls and vista points. The tourist office's aerial-photographed *Hiking Routes* map (Nkr10) gives ideas for 18 signed walks of between 1.5 and 5km.

A popular longer trek begins with a ride on the Geiranger Fjordservice sightseeing boat. A steep 45-minute ascent from the landing at Skagehola brings you to Skageflå, a precariously perched hillside farm. You can retrace your steps to the landing, where the boat stops (on request; tell the crew on the way out or just wave). To stretch your legs more, continue over the mountain and return to Geiranger via Preikestolen and Homlung.

Cycling

Geiranger Adventure (☑47 37 97 71; www.geiranger-adventure.com) will drive you up to Djupvasshytta (1038m), from where you can coast for 17 gentle, scenically splendid kilometres by bike down to the fjord; allow a couple of hours. It also rents bikes (Nkr50/200 per hour/day).

🛌 Sleeping & Eating

Hotels are often booked out by package tours.

TOP CHOICE **Villa Utsikten**　　　HOTEL €€

(☑70 26 96 60; www.villautsikten.no; s Nkr940, d Nkr1340-1600; ⊙May-Sep; P@) 'A temple to lift your spirits' – so observed King Rama V of Siam when he stayed here in 1898 during his grand Norwegian tour. Over a century later, there's no reason to gainsay his judgement. High on the hill above Geiranger (take Rv63, direction Grotli) the venerable family-owned Utsikten, constructed in 1893, has stunning views over town and fjord.

Grande Fjord Hotel　　　HOTEL €€

(☑70 26 94 90; www.grandefjordhotel.com; d Nkr980-1150; P) This warmly recommended 48-room hotel does great buffet breakfasts and dinners. It's well worth paying the higher rate for a room with a balcony and magnificent view over the fjord. Take the shoreside Rv63, direction Åndalsnes, for 2km to find yourself half a world away from the ferry terminal bustle. Ask to see its magnificent 1931 Buick, once used to shuttle guests around.

Union Hotel　　　HOTEL €€€

(☑70 26 83 00; www.union-hotel.no; r per person Nkr780; ⊙Feb–mid-Dec; P@�☀) The large, spectacularly situated Union Hotel is high on the hill above town. It's a healthy place with a couple of pools (one indoor and heated), sauna and spa. Even if you're not staying here, head up the hill, then roll back down after tucking into their gargantuan dinner buffet (Nkr475), which has a minimum of 65 dishes. The restaurant also offers à la carte (mains Nkr310 to Nkr325) and 'Taste the Coast', its four-course set menu (Nkr490).

Geiranger Camping　　　CAMPGROUND €

(☑70 26 31 20; www.geirangercamping.no; per person/site Nkr25/125; ⊙mid-May–mid-Sep; @☀) A short walk from the ferry terminal, Geiranger Camping is sliced through by a fast-flowing torrent. Though short on shade it's pleasant and handy for an early morning ferry getaway.

Below the Grande Fjord Hotel are a couple of friendly, tranquil campsites in unbeatable locations. Even if you're carrying a weighty pack, it's well worth the 2km walk northwestwards to get there. Both rent rowing and motor boats.

Grande Hytteutleige og Camping

CAMPGROUND €

(☑70 26 30 68; www.grande-hytteutleige.no; per person/site Nkr30/135, 4-bed cabins with outdoor bathroom Nkr350, with bathroom from Nkr890; ⊙Apr-Oct; @☀) Take the smaller, northernmost of its two fields for the best views up the fjord. It also hires out sea kayaks and fishing gear and can arrange a boat taxi to the fjord farms, accessible only by sea or on foot.

Geirangerfjorden Feriesenter CAMPGROUND €

(☑95 10 75 27; www.geirangerfjorden.net; car/caravan sites Nkr135/155, cabins from Nkr850; ⊙late Apr–mid-Sep; @☀) Right next door to Grand Hytteutleige Og Camping, this is another excellent camping option with similarly well-maintained facilities.

Laizas　　　CAFE €

(⊙10am-10pm mid-Apr–Sep; @☀) At the ferry terminal, just beside the tourist office, the young team at this airy, welcoming place puts on a handful of tasty hot dishes, good salads and snackier items such as focaccia, wraps and sandwiches.

🛍 Shopping

Geiranger Sjokolade　　　CHOCOLATE SHOP

(⊙10am-10pm) You may get a whiff of Geiranger Chocolate – 'Chocolate With a View', as it announces itself – before you reach this shop of sweet delights. Hand-made chocolates are fashioned in the workshop below Geiranger's newest enterprise and you can also mix taste sensations with its so-lickable ice cream and rich hot chocolate.

ℹ Information

Geiranger's **tourist office** (☑70 26 30 99; www.visitalesund-geiranger.com; ⊙9am-6pm mid-May–mid-Sep) is beside the pier.

❶ Getting There & Away

Boat

The popular, hugely recommended run between Geiranger and Hellesylt (passenger/car with driver Nkr133/278, adult/child return Nkr169/85; one hour) is quite the most spectacular scheduled ferry route in Norway. It has four to eight sailings daily between May and mid-October (every 90 minutes until 6.30pm, June to August).

Almost as scenic is the ferry that runs twice daily between Geiranger and Valldal (adult/child single Nkr206/103, return Nkr327/157, 2¼ hours). A mini-cruise in itself, it runs from mid-June to mid-August.

From mid-April to mid-October, the Hurtigruten coastal ferry makes a detour from Ålesund (departs 9.30am) to Geiranger (departs 1.30pm) on its northbound run only.

Bus

From mid-June to mid-August two buses daily make the spectacular run over Trollstigen to Åndalsnes (Nkr222, three hours) via Valldal (Nkr65, 1½ hours). For Molde, change buses in Åndalsnes; for Ålesund, change at Linge.

Hellesylt

POP 250

The old Viking port of Hellesylt, through which a roaring waterfall cascades, is altogether calmer, if less breathtaking, than Geiranger.

The **Peer Gynt Galleriet** (adult/child Nkr50/free; ⊙11am-7pm Jun-Aug) is a collection of fairly kitsch bas-relief wood carvings illustrating the Peer Gynt legend and fashioned by local chippy Oddvin Parr. You may find the food at the complex's cafeteria more to your taste.

The **tourist office** (☑94 81 13 32; ⊙10am-5pm mid-Jun–Aug) is in the Peer Gynt Gallery. For hikers, it carries *Tafjardfjella*, a walking map at 1:50,000, and for cyclists, *Hellesylt Mountain Biking Map*.

🛏 Sleeping & Eating

Hellesylt Vandrerhjem HOSTEL €
(☑70 26 51 28; www.hihostels.no/hellesylt; dm Nkr245, s/d with shared bathroom Nkr430/650, d with bathroom Nkr730; ⊙year round; @🛜) This HI-affiliated hostel perches on the hillside overlooking Hellesylt. Bedrooms in the main block, once a school, are decidedly run-down. Ask for one in the new buildings, architecturally as exciting as rows of pigeonholes. On the plus side, breakfast is good and varied. If you're arriving by bus,

ask the driver to drop you off to save a long slog back up the hill.

Hellesylt Camping CAMPGROUND €
(☑90 20 68 85; car/caravan sites Nkr130/150 plus per person Nkr20; 🛜) The absence of shade is more than compensated for by its fjord-side location and proximity to the ferry pier.

❶ Getting There & Away

For details of the spectacular ferry ride to/from Geiranger, see p229.

In summer, some ferries from Geiranger connect with buses to/from Stryn (Nkr100, one hour) and Ålesund (Nkr160, 2¾ hours).

Norangsdalen

Norangsdalen is one of the most inspiring yet little-visited crannies of the northern fjords. This glorious hidden valley connects Hellesylt with the Leknes–Sæbø ferry on the scenic Hjørundfjorden, via the village of Øye.

The boulder-strewn scenery unfolds among towering snowy peaks, ruined farmsteads and haunting mountain lakes. In the upper part of the valley at Urasætra, beside a dark mountain lake, are the ruins of several stone crofters' huts. Further on, you can still see the foundations of one-time farmhouses beneath the surface of the pea-green lake Langstøylvatnet, created in 1908 when a rock slide crashed down the slopes of Keipen.

Hikers and climbers will find plenty of scope in the dramatic peaks of the adjacent Sunnmørsalpane, including the lung-searingly steep scrambling ascent of Slogen (1564m) from Øye and the superb Råna (1586m), a long, tough haul from Urke.

Beside the road about 2km south of Øye, there's a monument to one CW Patchell, an English mountaineer who lost his heart to the valley.

TOP CHOICE **Hotel Union** HOTEL €€€
(☑70 06 21 00; www.unionoye.no; Øye; s/d from Nkr920/1840; ⊙May-Sep) Constructed in 1891, the Union has attracted mountaineers, writers, artists and royalty for over a century. With period artwork and furnishings, panelled in wood and speaking old-world charm, it's a delight. Rooms are named after celebrities who have slept in them: Sir Arthur Conan Doyle, Karen Blixen, Kaiser Wilhelm, Edvard Grieg, Roald Amundsen, Henrik Ibsen, a host of kings and queens – even Coco Chanel. The restaurant serves

one-/three-course lunches (Nkr195/Nkr350) and a three-/five-course dinner will cost Nkr475/595.

Runde

POP 100

The squat island of Runde, 67km southwest of Ålesund and connected to the mainland by a bridge, plays host to half a million sea birds of around 230 species, including 100,000 pairs of migrating puffins that arrive in April to breed and stay around until late July. There are also colonies of kittiwakes, gannets, fulmars, storm petrels, razor-billed auks, shags and guillemots, plus about 70 other species that nest here.

You'll see the best bird sites – as well as an offshore seal colony – on a **boat tour** (adult/child Nkr180/90). Three boats – the *Aquila*, the *Casablanca* and the *Rundø* – put out from Runde's small harbour, each two or three times daily.

Within the **Runde Miljøsenter** (Runde Environmental Centre; www.rundecentre.no; s/d Nkr1000/1500; 5-bed apt Nkr2250), there's a **tourist office** (⊘10am-6pm May-Aug) and cafe.

With a range of cabins and rooms around the campground itself, **Goksøyr Camping** (☏70 08 59 05; www.goksoyr.no, in Norwegian; per person/site Nkr20/110; 2-/4-bed cabins with outdoor bathroom Nkr250/440, 4-bed cabins with bathroom Nkr520; ⊘May-Sep) is a fairly basic, waterside place. The owners, long-term residents on the island, readily dispense information on birdwatching and walking trails.

Ålesund

POP 23,000

The coastal town of Ålesund is, for many, just as beautiful as Bergen, if on a much smaller scale, and it's certainly far less touristy. The home base for Norway's largest cod-fishing fleet, it sits on a narrow, fishhook-shaped sea-bound peninsula. So tightly packed is the town centre that expansion would be impossible; today most of the townspeople live scattered across nearby islands and peninsulas.

⊙ Sights & Activities

Sunnmøre Museum   OPEN-AIR MUSEUM
(www.sunnmore.museum.no, in Norwegian; Borgundgavlen; adult/child Nkr70/20; ⊘11am-5pm late Jun-Aug, 11am-3pm Mon-Fri rest of year) Ålesund's celebrated Sunnmøre Museum is 4km east of the centre. Here, at the site of the old Borgundkaupangen trading centre, active from the 11th to 16th centuries, over 50 traditional buildings have been relocated. Ship-lovers will savour the collection of around 40 historic boats, including replicas of Viking-era ships and a commercial trading vessel from around AD 1000. Take bus 613, 618 or 624.

Should you coincide with its restricted opening hours, don't overlook – as many visitors often do – its **Medieval Age Museum** (Middelaldermuseet; ⊘noon-3pm Tue-Fri & Sun mid-Jun–mid-Aug). Displayed around excavations of the old trading centre are well documented artefacts discovered on-site and reproductions of medieval illustrations depicting the way of life of the west Norwegian coastal folk who inhabited this thriving community. A pity that entry hours are so reduced...

Jugendstil Art Nouveau Centre   ART CENTRE
(Jugendstil Senteret; ☏70 10 49 70; www.jugendstilsenteret.no; Apotekergata 16; adult/child Nkr60/30; ⊘10am-5pm Jun-Aug, 11am-4pm Tue-Sun Sep-May) Everyone from serious aesthetes to kids out for fun will get pleasure from this art centre. The introductory Time Machine capsule presents 'From Ashes to Art Nouveau', a 14-minute high-tech, very visual story of the rebuilding of Ålesund after the great fire, while the displays offer carefully selected textiles, ceramics and furniture of the genre. It's in and above a renovated chemist's shop that has retained its magnificent corkscrew staircase and 1st-floor dining room.

A tunnel connects you to **Kube**, in the one-time Bank of Norway building next door. Here, Ålesund's most recent cultural asset mounts quality temporary exhibitions of architecture, art and design.

Atlanterhavsparken   AQUARIUM
(www.atlanterhavsparken.no; Tueneset; adult/child Nkr130/65; ⊘10am-7pm Sun-Fri, 10am-4pm Sat Jun-Aug, 11am-4pm Tue-Sun Sep-May) At the peninsula's western extreme, 3km from the town centre, the Atlantic Ocean Park can merit a whole day of your life. It introduces visitors to the North Atlantic's undersea world, with glimpses of the astonishing richness of coastal and fjord submarine life. Children can

> **i** **COMBINATION TICKET**
>
> A combined ticket (adult/child Nkr50/20) gives entry to the Sunnmøre Museum, Aalesunds Museum and Fisheries Museum.

dangle a line for crabs or feed the fish in the touch pool while the whole family will gasp at the enormous 4-million-litre aquarium. Be there at 1pm (also 3.30pm, June to August) when the largest ocean fish thrash and swirl as they're fed by human divers.

The grounds offer superb coastal scenery and walking trails (look out for WWII bunkers and gun batteries).

In summer, a special bus (adult/child Nkr35/18) leaves from beside the town hall hourly from 9.55am to 3.55pm, Monday to Saturday.

Aalesunds Museum   MUSEUM
(www.aalesunds.museum.no, in Norwegian; Rasmus Rønnebergs Gate 16; adult/child Nkr50/20; ⊙9am or 11am-4pm mid-Jun–mid-Aug, rest of year 11am-3pm Mon-Fri) The town museum illustrates the history of sealing, fishing, shipping and industry in the Sunnmøre region, the fire of 1904, the Nazi WWII occupation and the town's distinctive art nouveau architecture. There's also a collection of boats and ships, including the *Uræd* lifeboat (piloted across the Atlantic in 1904 by an intrepid Ole Brude), and an 1812 barn, converted into an old-time grocery.

Fiskerimuseet   FISHERIES MUSEUM
(Molovegen 10; adult/child Nkr40/10; ⊙11am-4pm mid-May–mid-Sep) In the 1861 Holmbua warehouse (one of the very few buildings to survive the 1904 fire), there are exhibits on the development of fishing across the centuries and special sections on klipfish and the processing of cod-liver oil.

Aksla   HILLTOP VIEWPOINT
The 418 steps up Aksla hill lead to the splendid **Kniven viewpoint** over Ålesund and the surrounding mountains and islands. Follow Lihauggata from the pedestrian shopping street Kongensgata, pass the **Rollon statue**, and begin the 15-minute puff to the top of the hill. There's also a road to the crest; take Røysegata east from the centre, then follow the Fjellstua signposts up the hill.

Up top, **Fjellstua Kafé** (⊙mid-May–late Aug) is a good place to recover your breath while enjoying a drink with a view.

Ålesund Church   CHURCH
(⊙10am-4pm Tue-Sun) Built of solid stone in 1909, Ålesund's parish church has a strikingly wide chancel, every square inch covered in frescos over the wide sweep of its tunnel arch. Notable too are the stained glass windows, especially those in the north aisle with their appropriately nautical theme.

⌖ Tours

To really delve into Ålesund's art nouveau heritage, sign on for the tourist office's excellent 1½- to two-hour **guided town walk** (adult/child Nkr90/free; ⊙daily mid-Jun–mid-Aug), which leaves the office at noon.

⭐ Festivals & Events

Midsummer Jazz   JAZZ
(www.midtsommerjazz.no, in Norwegian) Takes place on a weekend in late June.

Ålesund Boat Festival   BOATS
(www.batfestivalen.no, in Norwegian) A week of watery pleasures in the first half of July.

Jugendfest   MUSIC
(www.jugendfest.no, in Norwegian) Norwegian and international bands all over town on one weekend in the second half of August.

Norwegian Food Festival   FOOD
(www.matfestivalen.no, in Norwegian) A treat for all gourmands in the last week of August.

🛏 Sleeping

TOP CHOICE **Hotel Brosundet**   HOTEL €€
(☎70 11 45 00; www.brosundet.no; Apotekergata 5; s/d from Nkr1190/1390 incl breakfast; 🅿@🛜) This boutique hotel, right on the waterfront, has oodles of charm. An ex-warehouse and protected building – just look at the wonderful old beams they've preserved – it combines tradition with strictly contemporary comfort and style. Bedroom furnishings are of light pine, contrasting with the warm-brown draperies and whitest of white sheets, while bathrooms, behind their smoked-glass walls, have the latest fittings. Rooms overlooking the harbour carry a Nkr200 supplement. For extra character take room 47, once the Molja lighthouse, or 502, a junior suite at roof level with the original winch support above you. Breakfast is taken in its Maki restaurant, whose broad picture windows give onto the port.

Clarion Collection Hotel Bryggen   HOTEL €€
(☎70 10 33 00; www.choice.no; Apotekergata 1-3; s/d from Nkr1080/1280; @) This wonderful waterfront option occupies a converted fish warehouse, artfully decorated with former tools and equipment. Rates include a light evening meal and free waffles throughout the day. There's a sauna, free to guests, too.

Rica Scandinavie Hotel   HOTEL €€
(☎70 15 78 00; www.rica.no; Løvenvoldgata 8; s/d from Nkr795/1045 🅿@🛜) This fine place, Ålesund's oldest hotel, was the first to be

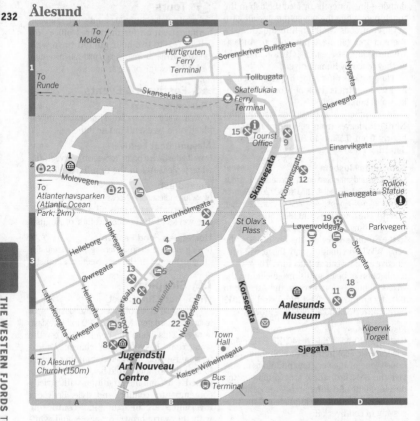

constructed after the 1904 fire. With touches and flourishes of art nouveau – the furniture is original and in keeping with this theme, and even the lobby flatscreen TV seems to blend in – it exudes style and confidence.

Scandic Hotel Ålesund
HOTEL €€

(☎21 61 45 00; www.scandichotels.com; Molovegen 6; s/d from Nkr890/990; @ 🛜) The Scandic has a lot going for it. Around 30% of its 150 rooms, all of which have parquet flooring, overlook the harbour, there's a free sauna and three rooms are equipped for the disabled. Guests – and those dropping in – also eat well; choices at the buffet breakfast are truly substantial and the summer dinner buffet (Nkr245) at its restaurant, the **Molja**, is a bargain.

Ålesund Vandrerhjem
HOSTEL €

(☎70 11 58 30; www.hihostels.no; Parkgata 14; dm/s/d incl breakfast Nkr255/570/790; @ 🛜) This central, HI-affiliated hostel is in an at-tractive building (see the murals in the vast common room) that recently celebrated its first century. There are self-catering facilities and a heavy-duty washing machine. Most doubles come with bathroom and, for those with a head for heights, bunk beds in the women's dorm are three tiers tall.

Volsdalen Camping
CAMPGROUND €

(☎70 12 58 90; www.volsdalencamping.no; Vols-dalsberga; sites Nkr150, r Nkr550, 2-/4-bed cabins with outdoor bathroom Nkr300/450, with bathroom Nkr800; ☺year-round) Above the shore about 2km east of the centre, this particularly friendly campsite is the nearest to town. Mainly for caravans and motorhomes, it has a secluded grassy area for campers at its far end. Take bus 613, 614, 618 or 624.

Annecy Sommerpensjonat
HOSTEL €

(☎70 12 96 30; Kirkegata 1b; s/d with shared bath-room Nkr420/570, s/d with bathroom Nkr490/640; ☺July–mid-Aug) This simple place is a good

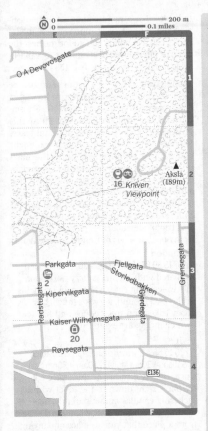

budget choice, letting out self-contained student rooms in summer.

✗ Eating

At the top end of the spectrum, you can dine very well indeed in Ålesund. For a simple snack from a bag, buy a scoop of fresh shrimps directly from the fishing boats that moor along the harbour front beside Skansegata.

Maki FISH RESTAURANT €€€

TOP CHOICE (☎70 11 45 00; www.maki.no; Apotekergata 5; mains Nkr285-315) The menu changes regularly at this ultracool restaurant at Hotel Brosundet. Sip a cocktail in its suave bar, then enjoy new takes on mussels, cod and other finny delights, presented to perfection.

Sjøbua FISH RESTAURANT €€

(☎70 12 71 00; www.sjoebua.no, in Norwegian; Brunholmgata 1a; mains Nkr250-360; ⊙4pm-1am Mon-Fri) In yet another converted wharfside building with thick masonry walls skewered by stout beams and posts, stylish Sjøbua is one of northern Norway's finest fish restaurants. Choose your crustacean, wriggling and fresh, from the lobster tank.

Lyst CAFE, RESTAURANT €

(☎991 00 560; Kongensgata 12; lunch dishes Nkr75-85, dinner mains Nkr165-295; ⊙10am-11pm) This new arrival on Ålesund's gastronomic scene offers good dining within a classic converted art nouveau building (you'll spot it from a distance by the stucco Mediterranean flowers trailing down the elegant grey-and-green facade). Separate lunch and

FRIENDLY FIRE?

Ålesund owes her appearance to a devastating fire. On 23 January 1904, it swept through the wooden buildings (only the jail and now-demolished church were made of stone), leaving 10,000 residents homeless out of an estimated population of 12,000. Help came swiftly from across the North Sea as the German emperor Kaiser Wilhelm II sent shiploads of provisions and building materials. Skilled workmen arrived from all over Norway, many trekking for days, and Ålesund was rebuilt in record time. Teams of young, committed Norwegian architects, trained for the most part in Germany, designed the town in the characteristic art nouveau (Jugendstil) style of the time, while bringing to the movement traditional Viking, Celtic and other local motifs and ornamentation as they designed buildings graced with turrets, spires, gargoyles and other fanciful features. The best examples are along Apotekergata, Kirkegata, Øwregata, Løvenvoldgata and, especially, Kongensgata.

dinner menus (with enticing items such as fillet of lamb gratiné in a red wine sauce) are, in fact, served throughout the day.

XL Diner FISH RESTAURANT €€€
(70 12 42 53; Skaregata 1; mains around Nkr250; 5pm-midnight Mon-Sat) Nothing could be further from your traditional greasy diner than this 1st-floor fish restaurant overlooking the harbour. Bacalao is the house speciality. This quintessentially Norwegian dish is offered with a variety of sauces – Italian, Spanish, Portuguese, even Louisiana. Vegetables, still firm and crunchy, are cooked to perfection. It's better not to request one of the tropical display fish that eye you apprehensively from their heated aquarium.

Hummer & Kanari BAR, RESTAURANT €
(70 12 80 08; www.hummerkanari.no, in Norwegian; Kongensgata 19; mains Nkr145-260; from 4pm Mon-Fri, from 2pm Sat & Sun) Behind the bar sit row upon row of liqueur and spirit bottles for mixers and shakers. At the downstairs bistro, you order at the counter. Upstairs, it's waiter service. But both call upon the same kitchen, which turns out ample portions of pasta (around Nkr150) and pizza

(Nkr100). For a main course, save the decision making, sit back, put yourself in the cook's capable hands and go for the best the sea can offer that day, 'Hummer & Kanari's selection of fish and shellfish' (Nkr280).

Lyspunktet CAFE, RESTAURANT €€
(70 12 53 00; www.lyspunktet.as, in Norwegian; Kipervikgata 1; mains around Nkr200; 10am-10pm Tue-Fri, noon-10pm Sat & Sun;) At this great-value, great-ambience, youthful place, loll back in its deep sofa (though you might not want to sit directly beneath the magnificent swirls and pipes of the giant glass chandelier). There are free refills for coffee and soft drinks, and dishes, such as the garlic turkey marinated in coconut, lime and chilli, are creative and great value.

A trio of alluring cafes gaze at each other from opposite sides of trendy Apotekergata.

Nomaden CAFE €
(97 15 89 85; Apotekergata 10; 11am-5pm) Affiliated with the art gallery next door, this welcoming cafe, where cool jazz trills in the background, serves sandwiches, gooey cakes and fresh coffee and has its own changing art exhibition.

Invit CAFE €
(70 15 66 44; www.invit.no; Apotekergata 9; 8.15am-4.30pm Mon-Fri, 10am-4.30pm Sat) Gosh, the style shows at this suave coffee bar – right down to the toilet with its flickering candles and apparently free-floating washbasin. Just what you'd expect from a place that runs the accompanying interior-design boutique. You can also sip your espresso and enjoy a tasty snack outside on the floating pontoon, where they considerately supply blankets if the wind whips up.

Apoteker'n CAFE €
(70 10 49 70; Apotekergata 16; sandwiches around Nkr50) Within the Jugendstil Art Nouveau Centre and completing the trio of tempting choices on the same street, this stylish, friendly little place rustles up good snacks, tempting cakes and sandwiches, and great coffee.

Drinking & Entertainment
Ta Det Piano BAR
(Kipervikgata 1b; from 11am) 'Take it Easy' is just that – a laid-back bar with a steep rear garden (live bands sometimes use its flat roof as a stage). Now in its second decade, it's the place to meet the town's younger movers and shakers.

Lille Løvenvold
CAFE, BAR

(Løvenvoldgata 2; ⊙11am-midnight Sun-Thu, 11am-3am Fri & Sat; 🛜) Here's a Jekyll and Hyde of a place. By day an intimate spot for a coffee in relaxing surroundings, it morphs each evening into a bar where canned music of all genres is the accompaniment to your beer. There's a DJ, Thursday to Saturday, and the small rear yard is strewn with cushions and soft sofas.

Løvenvold Kino
CINEMA

(Løvenvoldgata 11) Take in a film at this wonderful, little-changed neobaroque cinema, constructed in 1922 and still carrying its original wall paintings.

🛍 Shopping

Ålesund offers a couple of quality glass-blowing workshops.

Ingrids Glassverksted
GLASSWARE

(www.ingridsglassverksted.no, in Norwegian; Molovegen 15; ⊙10am-5pm Mon-Fri, 10am-3pm Sat) You'll find everything from practical glasses and bowls and ornaments with attitude to quirky, multicoloured chickens with spiky cockscombs. Should you pass by out of hours, you can watch Ingrid at work on the DVD that plays in her window.

Celsius
GLASSWARE

(www.celsius-glass.com, in Norwegian; Kaiser Wilhelmsgata 52; ⊙Tue-Sat) 'Luxury for everyday use' is the motto of this small glass studio, where each piece is designed to be stylish yet functional. The kiln is at the front, the shop at the rear.

Trankokeriet Antikk
ANTIQUES

(☎70 12 01 00; www.trankokeriet.no; Moloveien 6b; ⊙10am-5pm Mon-Sat) This wonderful hotchpotch antique gallery has something of everything, both nautical and landlubber. There's an art gallery and small coffee bar too.

Invit Interior
INTERIOR DESIGN

(☎70 15 66 44; Apotekergata 9) Appropriate for such a stylish town, this shop-cum-gallery displays the very best of creative modern furniture and Scandinavian kitchenware and home appliances.

ℹ Information

Library (10am-4pm or 6pm Mon-Sat) Free internet access; within the town hall.

Tourist office (☎70 15 76 00; www.visitalesund-geiranger.com; Skaregata 1; ⊙9am-6pm or 7pm Jun-Aug, 9am-4pm Mon-Fri Sep-May) Its free booklet *On Foot in Ålesund* details the town's architectural highlights in a walking tour. Internet access costs Nkr60 per hour.

ℹ Getting There & Away

Air

Norwegian has direct summertime flights to Edinburgh and London (Gatwick). Internal destinations include Bergen (three times daily), Trondheim (twice daily) and Oslo (up to 10 times daily).

Boat

An express boat speeds down the coast daily to Måloy (3¾ hours).

On its northbound run, the Hurtigruten makes a popular detour, mid-April to mid-October, to Geiranger, departing at 9.30am.

Bus

Local buses run to/from Åndalsnes (Nkr255, 2¼ hours, four times daily).

Express buses run to/from Bergen (Nkr610, 9¼ hours, one to three times daily), Hellesylt (Nkr160, 2¾ hours, up to five daily), Molde (Nkr130, 1½ hours, hourly), Oslo (Nkr840, 12½ hours, twice daily), Trondheim (Nkr535, 7½ hours, one to three daily) via Molde (Nkr146, 2¼ hours), and Stryn (Nkr250, 3¾ hours, one to four daily).

ℹ Getting Around

Ålesund's airport is on Vigra island, connected to the town by an undersea tunnel. **Flybussen** (Nkr100, 20 minutes) airport buses depart from Skateflukaia and the bus station approximately one hour before the departure of domestic flights.

Sykkel Spesialisten (☎70 12 28 20; Notenesgata 3) rents bicycles (Nkr140 per day). For a taxi, call ☎70 10 30 00.

Around Ålesund

OFFSHORE ISLANDS

With wheels, you can take in the four offshore islands of Valderøy, Vigra, Giske and Godøy in a pleasant day trip from Ålesund. All offer excellent short hill or coastal walks.

GODØY

At the furthest, northern extremity of the furthest island, Godøy, is the picturesque 1876 **lighthouse** (adult/child Nkr20/10; ⊙noon-6pm Jun-Aug) in the fishing station of **Alnes**. For that end-of-the-world feeling, climb to the circular balcony via the five floors of this all-wood structure. Each displays the canvases of Norwegian artist and Godøy resident Ørnulf Opdahl. Don't leave without sampling one of the delightful cakes, baked on the spot by Eva, the lighthouse custodian.

Giske was the home of Gange-Rolv (known as Rollon in France; he's also claimed by Vigra), the Viking warrior who besieged Paris. He subsequently founded the Duchy of Normandy in 911 and was an ancestor of England's William the Conqueror. Highlight of the island is its ornate 12th-century **church** (adult/child incl guided tour Nkr20/10; ⊙10am-5pm Mon-Sat, 1-7pm Sun mid-Jun–mid-Aug). Built largely of marble, its real jewels are the elaborately carved polychrome altarpiece and pulpit. The island's Makkevika marshes are a prime spot for birdwatching. Nowadays, it's renowned for its annual **free music festival** (www.verdensbestefestival .no), with music of all genres, on the last Saturday in July.

VALDERØY

On Valderøy, the **Skjonghellaren caves** have revealed bones of Arctic fox, sea otter and ringed seal, plus evidence of human occupation at least 2000 years ago. In the northwest of the island, they're reached by a breezy 500m walk from the parking spot between cliff and shoreline, then a steep five-minute boulder scramble.

VIGRA

Vigra has Ålesund's airport as well as **Blindheimssanden** (also called Blimsand), a long white-sand beach.

Molde

POP 19,900

Molde, hugging the shoreline at the wide mouth of Romsdalsfjorden, is known as the 'Town of Roses' for its fertile soil, rich vegetation and mild climate. But the town's chief claim to fame is its annual jazz festival, held in July.

Modern Molde, though architecturally unexciting, is a pleasantly compact little place whose coastal landscapes recall New Zealand or Seattle's Puget Sound. To test the comparison, drive or take the one-hour signed walking trail up to the **Varden overlook**, 400m above the town.

◉ Sights

FREE **Romsdalmuseet** FOLK MUSEUM

(Per Amdamsveg 4; ⊙8am-10pm) Within this open-air museum are nearly 50 old buildings, shifted here from around the Romsdal region. Among the barns, farms and storehouses, there's a short street of typical town houses and a small reconstructed

chapel with adornments rescued from abandoned churches. After rambling around the ample grounds, take a break in **Bygata**, a town house that functions as a summertime cafe. In summer, there are very worthwhile **guided tours** (adult/child Nkr70/free; ⊙11am-3pm or 6pm Jun–mid-Aug).

Fiskerimuseet FISHERIES MUSEUM

(Hertøya; adult/child Nkr60/free; ⊙noon-5pm mid-Jun–early Aug) This museum, on the small island of Hertøya, is a 10-minute boat ride from the Torget terminal, beside the tourist office. Also open-air, its cod-liver oil factory, cottages and fishermen's shacks, tiny schoolroom and collection of boats bring to life the coastal fishing cultures around the mouth of Romsdalsfjorden from the mid-19th century onwards. During opening hours, a **boat** (adult/child Nkr70/free) runs hourly from Molde between 11am and 5pm.

🛏 Sleeping & Eating

The tourist office has a number of private homes on its books, most with self-catering facilities and costing from Nkr350 per person. During the Molde International Jazz Festival, there's a large temporary campsite, Jazzcampen, 3km west of the centre.

Our three hotel choices are just south of Torgat, the main square. Their most coveted rooms overlook the fjord, where sleek, lowslung, brand-new ferries glide slowly by.

TOP CHOICE **Molde Fjordstuer** BOUTIQUE HOTEL €€

(☎71 20 10 60; www.havstuene.no; Julsundvegen 6; s/d from Nkr790/990; 🐾) Architecturally exciting, the welcoming Fjordstuer replicates the squat, solid forms of typical fisherfolk cottages. Half of its 18 rooms have fjord views and balconies (Nkr200 supplement). Enjoy the vista from its quality restaurant **Fjordstua** (mains Nkr240-305; ⊙6-11pm Mon-Sat) with its broad picture windows. Or snack on shrimps, fish soup and other delicacies from the sea at the equally stylish **Løkta** (⊙11am-6pm Mon-Sat) on the quayside below.

Rica Seilet Hotel HOTEL €€

(☎71 11 40 00; www.rica.no; Gideonvegen 2; s/d from Nkr1120/1220; 🅿@🐾) This soaring hotel contrasts with its near-neighbour, the Fjordstuer, designed by the same architect, as it juts out into the sound like a huge silver sail. Within, the artwork in public areas is particularly striking. There are bedrooms up to the 14th floor, each with large picture windows and magnificent views. For a dreamier

MOLDEJAZZ

Every year, Moldejazz pulls in up to 100,000 fans and a host of stars, mainly Scandinavian plus a sprinkling of international top liners (such as, in 2010, Sonny Rollins and Herbie Hancock).

The town rocks all the way from Monday to Saturday in the middle of July. Of over 100 concerts, a good one-third are free, while big events are very reasonably priced at Nkr100 to Nkr330.

Trad jazz sweats it out in Perspiration Hall, while the big draws perform outdoors near the Romsdalsmuseet and there are plenty of free supporting events (including a daily street parade) from noon onwards in front of the Rådhus.

For the low-down on this year's events, log onto www.moldejazz.no. You can book by credit card for a Nkr10 surcharge through **BillettService** (✆81 53 31 33).

vista, relax in the Lobby Bar at water level; for a bird's-eye perspective, shoot up to the Sky Bar on the 15th floor.

Quality Hotel Alexandra　　　HOTEL €€
(✆71 20 37 50; www.choice.no; Storgata 1-7; s/d from Nkr720/790; P@🅿️) Most rooms have a balcony and offer great views. Its gothic ground-floor **Bar Alex**, where the vermilions, blues and maroons of the upholstery contrast with the dark hues of the walls, has great cocktails and plenty of long drinks too. You may be lucky to catch some live music. Its restaurant, **Vertshuset** (✆71 20 37 75, dinner mains Nkr195-258), all attractive panelled wood and bare brickwork, has a bistro menu of pastas, salads and sandwiches (dishes around Nkr160) and tempting dinner choices such as fillet of lamb in a red-wine sauce with ginger-glazed vegetables.

Kviltorp Camping　　　CAMPGROUND €
(✆71 21 17 42; www.kviltorpcamping.no; Fannestrandveien 142; car/caravan sites Nkr120/140 plus per person Nkr10, 2-bed cabins Nkr400, 4-bed cabins with shower Nkr650-750) This fjord-side campsite occupies a potentially noisy spot at the end of the airport runway but fortunately there's very little air traffic. Cabins are available year-round. Bus 214 and the Flybussen pass right by.

Drinking
Syd　　　WINE BAR
(www.motsyd.no; Fjordgata 3; ⏱from 11.30am Mon-Sat) No, not the name of your host for the night but Norwegian for 'south', the way this recently opened wine bar faces. Looking out over the fjord, its terrace offers an inspirational panorama. Wines – reds mainly from Italy, whites from France – have their perfect accompaniment in one of landlord Jan Erik Nyland's cheese or cold-cut platters (Nkr165) or, if you're a hungry couple, his *affettati misti* for two (Nkr245) – 'with everything I have', says Erik.

Dockside Pub　　　CAFE, PUB
(Torget; mains Nkr100-135, salads Nkr115; ⏱noon-midnight; 🛜) This popular place is just off the main square. Depending on the air temperature, you can snack on pizzas, salads and burgers or simply sip a drink either inside or on the attractive jetty that extends above the water. There's live music at least weekly.

ℹ️ Information
Tourist office (✆71 20 10 00; www.visitmolde. com; Torget 4; ⏱9am-6pm Mon-Fri, 9am-3pm Sat, noon-5pm Sun mid-Jun–mid-Aug, rest of year 8.30am-4pm Mon-Fri; @) In the main square near the express ferry terminal, it sells *Molde Fraena* (1:50,000), the best hiking map of the area.

ℹ️ Getting There & Away
Air
Molde's shoreside **Årø airport** (✆71 21 47 80) is 5km east of the city centre. Local bus 701 (Nkr25, 10 minutes) from Molde's bus terminal passes by the airport at least hourly. There are up to six planes daily to/from Oslo and Bergen and two daily to/from Trondheim.

Boat
Northbound, the Hurtigruten coastal ferry leaves at 10pm (6.30pm mid-September to mid-April); southbound, at 9.30pm. Express ferries also operate from Molde.

Bus
Inland buses run hourly to and from Kristiansund (Nkr156, 1½ hours). Much more attractive and scarcely longer is the coastal run that rolls along the Atlanterhavsveien (see the boxed text, p238).

Regular buses run to/from Ålesund (Nkr130, 2¼ hours, hourly) and Åndalsnes (Nkr127, 1½ hours, up to eight daily).

Car & Motorcycle

Travelling northwards on the Rv64, the Tussen-tunnelen shortcut (Nkr20) avoids a dog's leg and lops off a good 15 minutes off travel time.

Around Molde

ONA

The beautiful outer islet of Ona, with its bare rocky landscapes and picturesque lighthouse, is still home to an offshore fishing community. It makes a popular day trip from Molde. En route, WWII buffs may want to stop off at **Gossen Krigsminnesamling** (adult/child Nkr40/20; ⊘noon-5pm Tue-Sun late Jun-early Aug), a former Nazi wartime airstrip built by Russian POWs on the low island of Gossen. The abandoned summer-house village of Bjørnsund also warrants a brief stop.

From Molde, you can visit Ona by public transport in a day. Take the 8am bus 561 to the ferry point at Småge. From here, it's a gorgeous trip by the 9.35am ferry, which stops at three islands en route and docks at Ona at 11.10am. You *could* scurry around and leave by the noon ferry. Better to take the 3.35pm boat from Ona, then the 5.10pm linking bus in Småge to reach Molde at 6.35pm. If you have wheels, leave your vehicle in Småge (it's an encumbrance on the island) and hop on the ferry there.

From Ålesund, **62° Nord** (www.62nord. net) does a four-hour evening cruise (adult/child Nkr495/250) to Ona three times weekly from late June to mid-August. It allows more than an hour – ample time – to explore the island.

WORTH A TRIP

THE ATLANTIC OCEAN ROAD

The eight storm-lashed bridges of Atlanterhavsveien, the Atlantic Ocean Road, recently designated a National Tourist Route, buck and twist like sea serpents, connecting 17 islets between Vevang and the island of Averøya. The UK's *Guardian* newspaper once crowned it the 'world's best road trip'. That's going it a bit for a stretch of highway barely 8km long but it's certainly hugely scenic and in a storm you'll experience nature's wrath at its most dramatic. In season, look out for whales and seals offshore.

From **Molde**, hit the coast at Bud; from **Kristiansund** and the north, take the new sub-sea road tunnel that connects with Bremsnes. Whichever your direction, rather than driving the Rv64, which cuts across inland Averøya, choose the quieter, prettier road, signed for Kvernes, that loops around the island's southern coast and takes no longer.

Kvernes Stave Church (adult/child Nkr40/free; ⊘10am-5pm mid-Jun–mid-Aug) dates from the early 14th century and was rebuilt in the 17th. Inside are a large 300-year-old votive ship and a 15th-century hybrid altarpiece, Catholic at its heart, with the Virgin Mary figuring prominently. While many such altarpieces were discarded at the time of the Reformation, this one survived, and a stylised Lutheran surround was added in 1695. The church narrowly escaped demolition when the larger one beside it was erected in 1893.

There are two attractive sleeping options along the route.

Skjerneset Bryggecamping (✆71 51 18 94; www.skjerneset.no; per person/site Nkr30/90, cabins Nkr600-850, d with shared bathroom Nkr390, tr with bathroom Nkr550) is a hyperfriendly place, right beside the sea at Sveggevika, west of Bremsnes. The owners, themselves former commercial fisherfolk, organise deep-sea trips in their own boat, or you can hire a motor boat and sling your own line. Rooms are in a former fish warehouse, which houses a fascinating family museum on the top floor.

Håholmen Havstuer (✆71 51 72 50; www.haholmen.no; s/d Nkr910/1330) is a former fishing station on an offshore islet north of the middle of the archipelago. Its 49 rooms, scattered around the renovated complex, are simply and tastefully furnished in rustic style. **Ytterbrugga**, its restaurant, serves the freshest of fish. To transport you there, a motor boat (Nkr50 return) makes the five-minute sea journey, leaving the roadside car park on the hour, between 11am and 9pm, late June to mid-August.

If you're travelling under your own steam, **Eide Auto** (90 77 30 63) buses (Nkr130, 2¼ hours, two to six daily) link Molde and Kristiansund year-round, via the coastal route and Atlanterhavsveien.

BUD

The Rv664 coastal route between Molde and Kristiansund is a pleasant alternative to the faster E89. En route lies the little fishing village of Bud, huddled around its compact harbour. It's difficult to believe, but in the 16th and 17th centuries Bud was the greatest trading centre between Bergen and Trondheim.

In late 2011, a new visitors centre will illustrate the resources of the sea – oil, fish, seaweed – and gas from the giant offshore Ormen Lange field, destined to provide 20% of the UK's requirement. On a more human scale, you'll learn about the mysterious wreck from 1750 that lies on the seabed, too deep for human divers.

Serving as a WWII museum and memorial, **Ergan Coastal Fort** (Ergan Kystfort; adult/child Nkr70/30; ⊗10am-6pm Jun-late Aug) was erected by Nazi forces in 1940. Various armaments and a network of bunkers and soldiers' quarters are dispersed around the hill with the sick bay and store sunk deep inside the mountain.

Bryggjen i Bud (☑71 26 11 11; www.bryggjen. no, in Norwegian; buffet lunch Nkr210; ⊗noon-7pm May-Sep, Fri-Sun only Oct-Apr), perched beside the small harbour, is a simple, unpretentious place. 'People weep if they arrive and find it closed,' said the lady in the visitors centre up the hill with perhaps a touch of exaggeration. But we know what she meant. It indeed attracts folk from miles around for its gargantuan lunch buffets: fish soup, two varieties of fish ball, salted coalfish, a couple of meat dishes and, of course klipfish (Norway's largest klipfish-drying sheds are just up the road). Spoon on the vegies in moderation, though – they might remind you of school dinners at their mushiest.

Bus 352 travels regularly between Molde and Bud (one hour; four to seven times daily, except Sunday).

Kristiansund

POP 21,100

The historic cod-fishing and drying town of Kristiansund ranges over three islands. Its restaurants serve dishes from the deep; fishing boats, large and small, still moor alongside its quays. Mellemværftet, unkempt and chaotic, hangs on as a working boatyard.

These days, Kristiansund still looks below the sea for its wealth. Even though the waters are no longer so bountiful – the huge hauls of yesteryear are now the source of tales as tall as any angler's – cod-processing

remains important. A significant amount of the world's klipfish is cured in and around the town. And, as the most significant place between Trondheim and Stavanger for servicing Norway's North Sea oilfields, Kristiansund takes its share of black gold.

⊙ Sights & Activities

Gamle Byen   HISTORIC QUARTER

Kristiansund's old town lives on in a part of Innlandet Island, a few of whose clapboard buildings date back to the 17th century. The grandiose **Lossiusgården**, at its eastern end, was the distinguished home of an 18th-century merchant. The venerable 300-year-old **Dødeladen Café** – where you can still get a decent meal and a drink – hosts cultural and musical events. The most convenient and enjoyable way of getting there from the centre is on the stubby Sundbåt ferry from Piren ferry port.

Mellemværftet   SHIPYARD

Something of a nautical junkyard, Mellemværftet, free and accessible any time, is best approached on foot along the quayside from the Smia Fiskerestaurant. It's difficult to make out what's what amid the clutter but it includes the remnants of Kristiansund's 19th-century shipyard, a forge, workshop, and workers' quarters. There are some illustrative photographs, captioned in Norwegian.

Nordmøre Museum   MUSEUMS

Nordmøre Museum is responsible for several museums in Kristiansund and Møre og Romsdal county. They're housed, for the most part, in historic buildings whose exteriors alone warrant a visit. Happily so, since most have severely reduced opening hours – or none at all except by appointment. Kristiansund's helpful tourist office will be au fait. Otherwise, try your luck on ☑71 58 70 00 or www.nordmore.museum.no.

FREE Handelshuset   CLASSIC CAFE

(Freiveien; ⊗11am-4pm daily mid-Jun–Aug, Sun only rest of year) Handelshuset, formerly a lively place serving traditional food, seems to have been overcome by the general cultural languor. Its magnificent vintage jukebox, with old 45rpm hits by Elvis Presley, the Stones, the Beach Boys and other distant icons, may have played its last platter unless someone gets around to repairing it. But you can still browse among Handelshuset's old posters and signs, learn something of Kristiansund's commercial history and drink the

Kristiansund

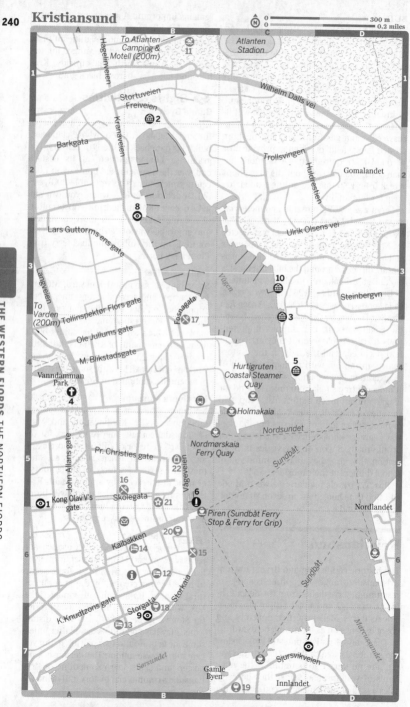

Kristiansund

freshest coffee, toasted on Norway's oldest operational coffee roaster.

FREE **Norsk Klippfiskmuseum** FISH MUSEUM (Gomalandet; adult/child incl guided tour Nkr50/free; ☺noon-5pm late Jun-early Aug) The Norwegian Klipfish museum, in the 1749 **Milnbrygga warehouse** on Gomalandet peninsula, presents the 300-year history of the dried-cod export industry in Kristiansund. It continues to produce modest quantities of klipfish in the traditional way. From the town centre, take the Sundbåt ferry and ask to be dropped off.

Just north of this museum are two other classic buildings, both normally closed to the public: **Hjelkrembrygga**, a former klip-

fish warehouse dating from 1835, and **Woldbrygga**, a barrel factory constructed in 1875.

Kirkelandet Church CHURCH
(Langveien; ☺9am-3pm Sun-Fri) Architect Odd Østby's inspirational church was built in 1964 to replace the one destroyed by Nazi bombs. The angular exterior, where copper and concrete alternate, is sober and measured. Inside, all lines direct the eye to the 320 panes of stained glass at the rear of the chancel. Moving upward from the earthy colours at the base, they become paler and, at the top, replicate the 'celestial light of heaven'.

Behind the church lies **Vanndamman Park**, with plenty of greenery, walking tracks and the eagle's-eyrie Varden watchtower viewpoint.

Petrosenteret INTERPRETIVE CENTRE
(www.petrosenteret.no, in Norwegian; Storkaia 9; adult/child incl guided tour Nkr75/50; ☺11am-4pm Mon-Fri late Jun-early Aug) Presenting the modern face of Kristiansund in terms that are accessible to lay folk, this centre portrays through film, models, an exhaustive guided tour and mind-numbing megastatistics, the impact of oil and gas upon contemporary Norway.

Atlanterhavsbadet SWIMMING BATHS
(www.atlanterhavsbadet.no, in Norwegian; Dalaveien 16; adult/child Nkr120/80; ☺10am-6pm or 9pm) With a couple of pools, a bubbling jacuzzi, well-being area, wave pool and 77m of curling waterslide, the Atlantic Ocean Baths are liquid fun for serious swimmers and families alike.

Festiviteten THEATRE
(Kong Olav V's gate 1) Constructed in 1914, Kristiansund's monumental theatre, although plain enough from the outside, has an attractive art nouveau interior.

Klippfiskkjerringa statue MONUMENT
In front of the Piren landing stage, it's a graphic representation of a fishwife bearing cod for drying.

🛏 Sleeping

Rica Hotel HOTEL €€
(☎71 57 12 00; www.rica.no; Storgata 41; s/d from Nkr895/995; P@☎) Recently overhauled, the fjord-side Rica still has that almost-new feel to it. All rooms have a bathtub and most overlook the water. The view gets better – and best of all from its top-floor bar, open to all – the higher you rise. There's a free sauna and minigym for guest use.

Quality Hotel Grand
HOTEL €€

(☑71 57 13 00; www.choice.no; Bernstorffstredet 1; r from Nkr1120; [P][@][⌂]) With its 158 rooms, the Hotel Grand is significantly Kristiansund's largest. Six rooms are equipped for the handicapped and around 40 take into account guests with allergies. Rooms are comfortable and attractively furnished and the hotel's **Edward Restaurant** has an à la carte menu that's as good as anywhere in town.

Atlanten Camping & Motell
CAMPGROUND, MOTEL €

(☑71 67 11 04; www.atlanten.no, in Norwegian; Dalaveien 22; car/caravan sites Nkr130/150 plus per person Nkr10, 4-bed cabins with outdoor bathroom Nkr395-495, with bathroom Nkr595, motel s/d Nkr595/695) This hostel and campground is an easy 20-minute walk from the centre. It's a friendly place and the well-equipped motel kitchen boasts 13 fridges. Camping facilities have recently been fully renovated and the furnished apartments are a great deal for small groups.

Utsyn Pensjonat
GUESTHOUSE €

(☑71 56 69 70; Kongens Plass 4; r with shared bathroom Nkr580) With only eight rooms, the Utsyn is a quiet, uncomplicated, bog-standard boarding house whose chief virtue is its price. Under Asian ownership, its **cafe** offers both Norwegian and Chinese cooking.

✗ Eating

For a cafe that's rich in atmosphere, go out of your way to visit Handelshuset.

TOP CHOICE Smia Fiskerestaurant
FISH RESTAURANT €€

(☑71 67 11 70; www.smia.no; Fosnagata 30b; mains Nkr220-275; ⊙1pm-midnight) The much-garlanded Smia fish restaurant is in an old forge, adorned from wall to ceiling with bellows and blacksmith's tools – plus a couple of whale vertebrae and a hanging split cod. The fish soup (Nkr95) makes a great starter, or you can also have it as a main (Nkr165).

Sjøstjerna
FISH RESTAURANT €€

(☑71 67 87 78; www.sjostjerna.no, in Norwegian; Skolegata 8; mains Nkr195-255; ⊙noon-midnight Mon-Sat) Here's another recommended fish restaurant, which offers a similar menu and marine-themed interior. Eat inside or on its pleasant street-side terrace, beside pedestrianised Skolegata.

Bryggekanten
RESTAURANT, BAR €€

(☑71 67 61 60; www.fireb.no, in Norwegian; Storkaia 1; pizza Nkr115, mains Nkr235-295; ⊙1.30pm-midnight Mon-Sat) This cheerful brasserie and bar sits right beside the harbour. It's a great choice, even if only for a drink. Even better, tuck into a pizza, bruschetta or sandwich on its broad terrace. Inside, where full dinners are served, is more intimate. Here, too, the menu is imaginative, taking traditional ingredients and giving them a new twist in creative dishes, such as klipfish with chorizo and creamed cabbage.

🍺 Drinking & Entertainment

Onkel og Vennene
BAR, CAFE

(☑71 67 58 10; Kaibakken 1; [@][⌂]) At 1st-floor level this is a popular place for an evening beer or snack (Nkr85 to Nkr150). It has great harbour views, whether inside or from the small veranda, where smokers can puff away.

Christian's Bar
BAR

(☑71 57 03 00; Storgata 17) On the 1st floor of Hotell Kristiansund, Christian's Bar is an attractive pub where the over-25s congregate.

Mocca
CLUB

(☑71 67 74 04; Hauggata 16; ⊙from 8pm Fri & Sat) The town's younger crowd tends to hang out at this cool weekends-only venue.

JP Clausens
BAR

(☑71 57 12 00; Storgata 41-43; ⊙8pm-2am Fri & Sat) The piano and wine bar of the Rica Hotel is more for slow waltzers.

🛍 Shopping

Klippfiskbutikken
FOOD

(Våogeveien) Genial Knut Garshol, a member of the international slow-food ecogastronomy movement, will buttonhole you and enthusiastically proclaim the virtues of klipfish at this splendid temple to the mighty cod. Try too his grandmother's recipe for bacalao, to eat in or take away.

❶ Information

Tourist office (☑71 58 54 54; www.visitkristiansund.com; Kongens plass 1; ⊙9am-6pm Mon-Fri, 10am-3pm Sat, 11am-4pm Sun mid-Jun–mid-Aug, 9am-4pm Mon-Fri rest of year) Free internet access.

❶ Getting There & Away

Air

The town's Kvernberget **airport** (☑71 68 30 50) is on Nordlandet island. There are frequent flights daily to/from both Oslo and Bergen.

Buses travel regularly to/from the airport (Nkr60, 15 minutes, up to eight daily) to meet incoming flights.

Boat

Express boats connect Kristiansund with Trondheim (3½ hours, up to three daily from Nordmørskaia). The Hurtigruten coastal ferry also calls in daily at Holmakaia.

Bus

Inland buses run hourly to Molde (Nkr156, 1½ hours) and on to Ålesund (3¾ hours). The coastal run that rolls along the Atlanterhavsveien (see the boxed text, p238) is much more impressive and scarcely longer. Northwards, there are up to three buses daily to Trondheim (Nkr400, 4¾ hours).

ⓘ Getting Around

The **Sundbåt ferry** (adult/child Nkr25/13, day ticket Nkr50) claims to be 'the world's oldest public transport system in uninterrupted use'. That's a heavy reputation for these small, squat boats to bear. Whatever the history, it's well worth the ride for its own sake and for the special perspective it gives of the harbour. Boats link the town centre and the islands of Innlandet, Nordlandet and Gomelandet, running every half hour, Monday to Saturday. The full circuit takes 20 minutes.

Around Kristiansund

GRIP

Huddled together on a tiny rocky island as though for protection against Atlantic gales, the village of Grip with its pastel-painted houses sits amid an archipelago of 80 islets and skerries. The only elevation is the 47m-tall Bratthårskollen lighthouse on a nearby skerry, built in 1888 and prodding skywards.

In the early 19th century, after a drop in cod hauls and two powerful storms, the village was practically abandoned. But it bounced back, its population swelling during the cod-fishing season when basing yourself on the island saved three hours of hard rowing each way from the mainland. Imagine, as you wander among today's sprinkle of houses, spring fishing seasons, when more than 1000 fisherfolk hunkered down here.

The last permanent inhabitants gave up the fight in 1974. There's a small photographic display with an accompanying sheet in English in one of the storehouses. A summertime cafe serves snacks in what was once the village school (only three pupils were left when its bell rang for the last time in 1972).

The island's **stave church**, much restored, dates from the late 15th century. Its altarpiece, discarded at the time of the Reformation, was found in a boathouse and restored to its rightful place in the 1930s. The lively frescos in the nave were revealed when later whitewash was stripped off.

From late May to late August, the **M/S Gripexpressen** (www.gripexpressen.no, in Norwegian) plies the 14km between Kristiansund's Piren terminal and Grip (40 minutes; adult/child Nkr275/135 return) once or twice daily. Total journey time is 3½ hours, including time ashore. In principle, there's a guided tour included within the fare.

Trøndelag

Best Places to Eat

» Vertshuset Tavern (p253)

» Brod & Cirkus (p259)

» Baklandet Skydsstasjon (p254)

» Havfruen (p253)

Best Places to Stay

» Britannia Hotel (p252)

» Tingvold Park Hotel (p258)

» Chesterfield Hotel (p252)

» Trondheim InterRail Centre (p253)

Why Go?

Trondheim, the most northerly place in Norway that merits the title 'city', is the major draw. You'll find fulfilment wandering its medieval streets and quays, savouring its buzzing student life and sampling its pretty wharfside restaurants and bars. Dig into its history too as you visit Nidaros Cathedral, Scandinavia's largest medieval structure, and prowl around the vast, open-air Sverresborg Trøndelag Folkemuseum.

Trøndelag is a region of rumpled hills, stippled with ox-blood-coloured farmsteads and ruffled green with wheat and barley. Hay stands out to dry on distinctive long, low trellises like a line of shaggy yaks in procession, and always there's water near at hand, whether sea, lake or incised fjord. Amid such rural splendour, atmospheric Stiklestad, famous as the site of the martyrdom of King Olav (St Olav) and an easy detour from the Arctic Highway, is at the heart of every Norwegian's sense of national identity.

When to Go

Trondheim

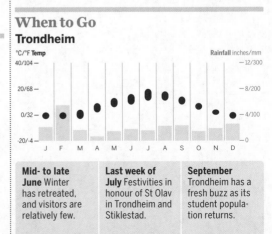

Mid- to late June Winter has retreated, and visitors are relatively few.	**Last week of July** Festivities in honour of St Olav in Trondheim and Stiklestad.	**September** Trondheim has a fresh buzz as its student population returns.

TRONDHEIM

POP 170,000

Trondheim, Norway's original capital, is nowadays the country's third-largest city after Oslo and Bergen. With its wide streets and partly pedestrianised heart, it's a simply lovely city with a long history. Fuelled by a large student population, it buzzes with life. Cycles zip everywhere, it has some good cafes and restaurants, and it's rich in museums. You *can* absorb it in one busy day, but it merits more if you're to slip into its lifestyle.

History

In 997, King Olav Tryggvason moored his longboat alongside a broad sandbank at Nidaros (meaning 'mouth of the River Nid') and established his farm. One plausible theory has it that Leifur Eiríksson (or Leif Ericson as he's usually transcribed in English) visited the king there before setting sail for Iceland and Greenland and possibly becoming the first European to set foot in North America. (If you're from the USA, the Viking staring out to sea near the Hurtigruten quay

Trøndelag Highlights

❶ Browse **Nidaros Cathedral** (p246), Trondheim, Norway's most sacred building

❷ Trundle a **trolley** (p259) along the no-longer-active Namsos–Skage railway line

❸ Explore the cultural centre and grounds of **Stiklestad** (p258), where St Olav was martyred

❹ Learn about coastal life at multimedia **Norveg** (p260) in Rørvik

❺ Tuck into Norwegian specialities in Trondheim's historical **Vertshuset Tavern** (p253)

❻ Hike in the wilderness of **Bymarka** (p251), right in Trondheim's backyard

THE PILGRIMS' WAY

Nidaros Cathedral was built on the site of the grave of St Olav, who was canonised and declared a martyr after his death at the Battle of Stiklestad on 29 July 1030. The cult of St Olav quickly grew in popularity and as many as 340 churches were dedicated to the saint in Scandinavia, Britain, Russia, the Baltic states, Poland, Germany and the Netherlands. Pilgrims from all over Europe journeyed to his grave at Nidaros, making it the most popular pilgrimage site in northern Europe. Historically, both rich and poor journeyed from Oslo for up to 25 days, while others braved longer sea voyages from Iceland, Greenland, Orkney and the Faroe Islands. St Olav's grave became the northern compass point for European pilgrims; the other spiritual compass points were Rome in the south, Jerusalem in the east and Santiago de Compostela in the west.

As pilgrims travelled from village to village, their routes became arteries for the spread of the cult of St Olav. The pilgrims' way, with wild mountains, forests and rivers to cross, certainly gave plenty of opportunity to reflect upon the hardships of life's journey towards eternity. Most pilgrims travelled on foot, while the better off journeyed on horseback. Those without means relied on local hospitality; pilgrims were held in high esteem and openly welcomed.

In 1997 the Pilgrims' Way – 926km in all, counting alternative sections – was inaugurated, reviving the ancient pilgrimage route between Oslo and Trondheim. The rugged route, mainly mountain tracks and gravelled roads, has been blazed (look for the logo: the cross of St Olav intertwined with the quatrefoil knot indicating a tourist attraction, which you see everywhere). It follows, wherever practicable, ancient documented trails. Along the trail are signs indicating place names and monuments linked to the life and works of St Olav, as well as ancient burial mounds and other historic monuments.

For more information, call up www.pilgrim.info/en.

The Pilgrim Road to Nidaros – a Trekker's Guidebook by Alison Raju, published by Cicerone Press, is an indispensable, well-written guide if, whether pilgrim or hiker, you're thinking of taking on a stretch.

---

may seem familiar. That's because he's an exact replica of the Ericson statue in Seattle that commemorates the tens of thousands of Norwegian emigrants to the New World.)

In 1030 another, subsequently more famous, King Olav (Haraldsson) was martyred in battle at Stiklestad, about 90km to the northeast, and canonised. Nidaros became a centre for pilgrims from all over Europe, its bishopric embracing Norway, Orkney, the Isle of Man, the Faroe Islands, Iceland and Greenland. It served as the capital of Norway until 1217, ruling an empire that extended from what is now western Russia to, possibly, the shores of Newfoundland. The cult of St Olav continued until the Reformation in 1537, when Norway was placed under the Lutheran bishopric of Denmark.

After a fire razed most of the city in 1681, Trondheim was redesigned with wide streets, enjoying its golden age in the 18th century, when merchants outbid each other in the grandeur of their dwellings. The city's location became key once again in WWII, when German naval forces made it their base for northern Norway, although fortunately the city avoided major damage. Nowadays, Trondheim, with its Norwegian University of Science & Technology and a research institute that employs more than 2000 staff, is the recognised technological capital of Norway.

The epicentre of town is Torvet, the central square (also spelt 'Torget') with its statue of King Olav Tryggvason atop a column that acts as a huge sundial.

⊙ Sights

Nidaros Cathedral   CATHEDRAL
(Nidaros Domkirke; www.nidarosdomen.no; Kongsgårdsgata; adult/child Nkr50/25; ⊙9am-3pm or 5.30pm Mon-Fri, 9am-2pm Sat, 1-4pm Sun May–mid-Sep, shorter hr rest of yr) Nidaros Cathedral is Scandinavia's largest medieval building. Outside, the ornately embellished west wall has top-to-bottom statues of biblical characters and Norwegian bishops and kings, sculpted in the early 20th century. Several are copies of medieval originals, housed nowadays in the museum. Within, the cathedral is subtly lit (just see how the vibrantly coloured, modern stained-glass glows, es-

pecially in the rose window at the west end), so let your eyes attune to the gloom.

The altar sits over the original grave of St Olav, the Viking king who replaced the Nordic pagan religion with Christianity. The original stone cathedral was built in 1153, when Norway became a separate archbishopric. The current transept and chapter house were constructed between 1130 and 1180 and reveal Anglo-Norman influences (many of the craftsmen were brought in from England), while the Gothic choir and ambulatory were completed in the early 14th century. The nave, repeatedly ravaged by fire across the centuries, is mostly a faithful 19th-century reconstruction.

Down in the crypt is a display of medieval carved tombstones (the majority restored from fragments since many headstones were broken up and carted away to be recycled in domestic buildings). Look for one inscribed in English and dedicated to William Miller, Shipmaster, of Dundee, Scotland, who met his end near Trondheim in the 18th century.

You can wander around freely but, between early June and early August, it's worth joining a tour (a 15-minute canter or a more detailed 45-minute visit). Times vary but there are up to four daily in English. Music-lovers may want to time their visit to take in a **recital** (admission free; ⊙1pm Mon-Sat early Jun-early Aug) on the church's magnificent organ.

From early June to early August, you can climb the cathedral's **tower** for a great view over the city. There are ascents every half hour from its base in the south transept.

Archbishop's Palace   MUSEUM

The 12th-century archbishop's residence (Erkebispegården), commissioned around 1160 and Scandinavia's oldest secular building, is beside the cathedral. In its west wing, Norway's **crown jewels** (adult/child Nkr70/25) shimmer. Its **museum** (adult/child Nkr50/25; ⊙10am-3pm or 5pm Mon-Sat, noon-4pm Sun May–mid-Sep, shorter hr rest of yr) is in the same compound. After visiting the well-displayed

statues, gargoyles and carvings from the cathedral, drop to the lower level, where only a selection of the myriad artefacts revealed during the museum's construction in the late 1990s are on show. Take in too its enjoyable 15-minute audiovisual program.

Stiftsgården   ROYAL PALACE

(Munkegata 23; adult/child Nkr60/30; ⊙10am-4pm Mon-Sat, noon-4pm Sun Jun-late Aug) Scandinavia's largest wooden palace, the late-baroque Stiftsgården, was constructed as a private residence in the late 18th century, at the height of Trondheim's golden age. It is now the official royal residence in Trondheim. Admission is by tour only, every hour on the hour.

Sverresborg Trøndelag Folkemuseum
FOLK MUSEUM

(Sverresborg Allé 13; www.sverresborg.no; adult/child incl guided tour Nkr85/35; ⊙11am-6pm Jun-Aug, to 3pm rest of yr) West of the centre, this folk museum is one of the best of its kind in Norway. The indoor exhibition, Livs-bilder (Images of Life), displays artefacts in use over the last 150 years – from clothing to school supplies to bicycles – and has a short multimedia presentation.

The rest of the museum, with over 60 period buildings, is open-air, adjoining the ruins of King Sverre's castle and giving fine hilltop views of the city. Houses, the post office, the dentist's and other shops splay around the central market square in the urban section. There are farm buildings from rural Trøndelag, the tiny 12th-century Haltdalen stave church and a couple of small museums devoted to telecommunications (some great old phones) and skiing (with elaborately carved wooden skis). There are guided tours in Norwegian and English four times daily.

The museum's restaurant, **Vertshuset Tavern**, itself in a wonderfully preserved old building, is a great place to try Norwegian specialities.

Take bus 8 (direction Stavset) from Dronningens gate.

National Museum of Decorative Arts
APPLIED ARTS GALLERY

(Nordenfjeldske Kunstindustrimuseum; Munkegata 5; adult/child Nkr60/30; ⊙10am-5pm Mon-Sat, noon-5pm Sun Jun–mid-Aug, 10am-3pm Tue-Sun rest of yr) The permanent collection of this splendid museum exhibits the best of Scandinavian design, including a couple of bijou art nouveau rooms. A whole floor is devoted to the pioneering works of three acclaimed women artists: the tapestry creations of

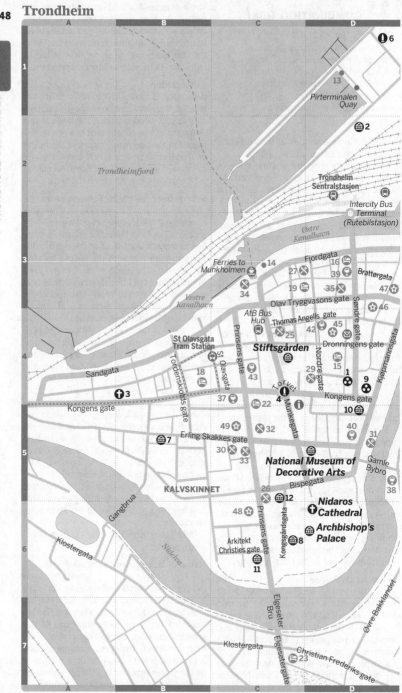

Trondheimfjord

Pirterminalen Quay

13

2

Trondheim Sentralstasjon

Intercity Bus Terminal (Rutebilstasjon)

Østre Kanalhavn

Fjordgata

Ferries to Munkholmen

14

16

27 39 Brattørgata

47

19 35

Vestre Kanalhavn

34

Olav Tryggvasons gate

46

AtB Bus Hub

Thomas Angells gate

42 45

Søndre gate

25

St Olavsgata Tram Station

Prinsens gate

Stiftsgården

Dronningens gate

15 1

Sandgata

St Olavsgata

Nordre gate

29

9

18

43

Kjøpmannsgata

Tordenskiolds gate

3

Kongens gate

37

Torvet

4

Kongens gate

10

22

40

31

49 32

National Museum of Decorative Arts

Gamle Bybro

7

Erling Skakkes gate

30 33

38

KALVSKINNET

Bispegata

26 12

Nidaros Cathedral

Gangbrua

48

Prinsens gate

Kongsgårdsgata

Archbishop's Palace

8

Klostergata

Nidelva

Arkitekt Christies gate

11

Elgeseter Bru

Øvre Bakklandet

Klostergata

Elgesetergate

Christian Frederiks gate

23

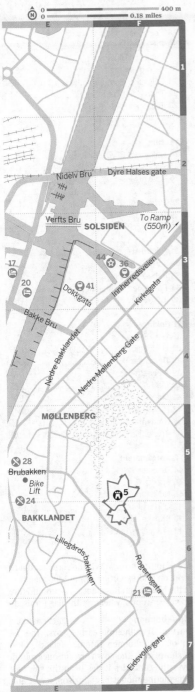

Hannah Ryggen and Synnøve Anker Aurdal, and the innovative glasswork of Benny Motzfeldt.

FREE National Military Museum
MILITARY MUSEUM

(Ruskammeret; ☉10am-4pm Mon-Sat, noon-4pm Sun mid-May–mid-Sep) In the same courtyard as the Archbishop's Palace, it's full of antique swords, armour and cannons, and recounts the days from 1700 to 1900, when the palace served as a Danish military installation. On the top floor is the **Hjemmefront** (Home Front) museum, devoted to Trondheim's role in the WWII resistance.

Ringve Museum
MUSIC MUSEUM

(www.ringve.no; Lade Allé 60; adult/child Nkr80/30; ☉11am-4pm or 5pm mid-Apr–mid-Sep, 11am-4pm Sun only rest of yr) The Ringve Museum is Norway's national museum for music and musical instruments. The Russian-born owner was a devoted collector of rare and antique musical instruments, which music students demonstrate. You can also browse the old barn with its rich collection of instruments from around the world. The botanic gardens, set within the surrounding 18th-century estate, are a quiet green setting for a stroll. Take bus 3 or 4 and walk up the hill.

Home of Rock
ROCK & POP MUSEUM

(www.rockheim.no, in Norwegian; Brattørkaia 14; adult/child Nkr90/50; ☉11am-6pm) Trondheim has its share of national museums. This one's devoted to pop and rock, mainly Norwegian, from the 1950s until yesterday. It's a dockside temple to R&B, where a huge projecting roof, featuring Norwegian record covers, extends above an equally vast converted warehouse. Within, there's plenty of action and interaction (mix your own hip-hop tape, for example). Home of Rock is on the quayside, very near Pirbadet and the fast-ferry landing stage.

Historic Neighbourhoods
OLD QUARTER

From **Gamle Bybro** (Old Town Bridge), there's a superb view of the **Bryggen**, colourful 18th- and 19th-century riverfront warehouses similar to their better-known counterparts in Bergen. To the east, the one-time working-class neighbourhoods of **Møllenberg** and **Bakklandet** are now gentrified latte-land, all cobbles, car-free alleys, trim houses in pastel shades and gardens scarcely bigger than a towel that burst with flowers. Here, within old warehouses and renovated workers housing, are some of the city's most colourful places to eat and drink.

The cobblestone streets immediately west of the centre are also lined with mid-19th-century wooden buildings, notably the octagonal 1705 timber church, **Hospitalkirken** (Hospitalsløkka 2-4), in the hospital grounds.

FREE **Kristiansten Fort** FORT
(Festning; Festningsgata; ⊙10am-4pm Jun-Aug) For a bird's-eye view of the city, climb 10 minutes from the Gamle Bybro to Kristiansten Fort, built after Trondheim's great

fire of 1681. During WWII the Nazis used it as a prison and execution ground for members of the Norwegian Resistance. The grounds are open year-round, whenever the flag is raised.

Munkholmen OFFSHORE ISLAND
During Trondheim's early years, the islet of Munkholmen (Monks' Island), 2km offshore, was the town execution ground. Over the centuries it has been the site of a Benedictine monastery, a prison, a fort and

finally a customs house. Today, it's a popular picnic venue and has the city's best beach. From mid-May to early September, **ferries** (adult/child Nkr60/30 round trip) leave at least hourly between 10am and 4pm or 6pm from beside the Ravnkloa Fish Market.

FREE **Museum of Natural History & Archaeology** NATURAL HISTORY MUSEUM
(Vitenskapsmuseet; www.vitenskapsmuseet.no; Erling Skakkes gate 47; ☺9am-4pm Mon-Fri, 11am-5pm Sat & Sun Jul-Aug, 10am-4pm Tue-Sun Sep-Jun) This museum belongs to the Norwegian University of Science & Technology (NTNU). There's a hotchpotch of exhibits on the natural and human history of the Trondheim area: streetscapes and homes, ecclesiastical history, archaeological excavations and southern Sami culture. More ordered is the small, alluring display in a side building devoted to church history and the fascinating everyday artefacts of the medieval section, covering Trondheim's history up to the great fire of 1681.

Trondheim Kunstmuseum FINE ARTS MUSEUM
(Bispegata 7b; adult/child Nkr50/30; ☺10am-5pm mid-Jun-mid-Aug, 11am-4pm Tue-Sun rest of yr) Trondheim's Art Museum houses a permanent collection of modern Norwegian and Danish art from 1800 onwards, including a hallway of Munch lithographs. It also runs temporary exhibitions.

Medieval Church Ruins ARCHAEOLOGICAL REMAINS
During excavations for the library on Kongens gate, archaeologists found the ruins of a 12th-century church, thought to be **Olavskirken**, now visible beneath the courtyard, together with the skeletons of two adults and a child. In the basement of nearby Søndre gate 4 (which was being gutted when we last passed by) are the ruins of the medieval **Gregorius Kirke** (Sparebanken), discovered during earlier excavations. There's normally free access to both during regular business hours.

Synagogue SYNAGOGUE
(Arkitekt Christies gate 1b; ☺10am-4pm Mon-Thu, noon-3pm Sun) Trondheim's synagogue claims to be the world's northernmost. It has a small **museum** (admission Nkr25) of the history of the local Jewish community, which was decimated by the Holocaust.

Vitensenteret SCIENCE CENTRE
(Kongens gate 1; adult/child Nkr75/45; ☺10am or 11am-5pm) Children especially will enjoy the hands-on experiments at this practi-cal, active centre with over 150 models to choose from.

🏃 Activities

The free map, *Friluftsliv i Trondheimsregionen* (Outdoor Life in the Trondheim Region; text in Norwegian), available at the tourist office, shows nearby outdoor recreation areas and walking trails. *Hike and Bike* (www.hikebike.no) has a host of suggestions for walks and rides in and around Trondheim and the whole of Trøndelag, complete with online maps.

Hiking

Two easy strolls within town are the steep but short ascent through the traffic-free lanes of Bakklandet to Kristiansten Fort and the riverbank footpaths beside the Nidelva between Bakke Bru and Gangbrua bridges.

West of town spreads the Bymarka, a gorgeous green woodland area laced with wilderness footpaths and ski trails. Take the Gråkallbanen tram, in itself a lovely scenic ride through the leafy suburbs, from the St Olavsgata stop to **Lian**. There you can enjoy excellent views over the city and a good swimming lake, **Lianvannet**.

To the east of Trondheim, **Ladestien** (The Lade Trail) follows the shoreline of the Lade peninsula, beginning only 1km from the town centre.

Skiing

The Vassfjellet mountains, south of town, offer both downhill and cross-country skiing. In season, a daily ski bus runs directly from Munkegata to the Vassfjellet Skisenter, only 8km beyond the city limits. The Bymarka also offers good cross-country skiing, as does the Trondheim Skisenter Granåsen, where the brave or foolhardy can launch themselves from the world's largest plastic-surfaced ski jump.

Boat Trips

Tripps (☎950 82 144; www.trippsbatservice.no; adult/child Nkr150/60; ☺Tue-Sun Jul–mid-Aug) runs a 1½-hour cruise along the estuary of the River Nid and out into the fjord, sailing at noon and 2.30pm from July to mid-August. Departures are from beside the Ravnkloa Fish Market and you buy your ticket on the boat.

Pirbadet Water Park

On the Pirterminalen quay, **Pirbadet** (adult/child Nkr145/125) is Norway's largest indoor water park with a wealth of liquid pleasures,

TROND-WHAT?

Listen to Trondheimers talk about their city, and you may wonder whether they're all referring to the same place.

Since the late Middle Ages, the city has been called Trondhjem, pronounced 'Trond-yem' and meaning, roughly, 'home of the good life'. But in the early 20th century the fledgling national government was bent on making Norwegian city names more historically Norwegian; just as Christiania reverted to its ancient name of Oslo, on 1 January 1930 Trondhjem was changed back to Nidaros.

Some 20,000 locals took to the streets in protest and by 6 March the government relented – sort of. The compromise was 'Trondheim', the etymologically Danish '*hj*' having been duly exorcised.

Nowadays the official pronunciation is 'Trond-haym', but many locals still say 'Trond-yem'. Thanks to the vagaries of the local dialect, still others call it 'Trond-yahm'. Typical of this tolerant city, any of these pronunciations is acceptable, as is the 'Trond-hime' that most English speakers hazard.

including a wave pool, sauna and 100m water slide.

☞ Tours

The tourist office arranges a couple of worthwhile daily tours, each leaving from Torget, in front of its premises.

Bus tours (adult/child Nkr235/free; ⊘tours late May–mid-Sep) Two-hour multilingual city bus tours, departing at noon.

Walking tours (Nkr150; ⊘tours early Jul–late Aug) Two-hour guided tours in English and Norwegian, departing at 2pm.

✹ Festivals & Events

ISFIT   STUDENTS

(www.isfit.org) A student-mounted international youth gathering with participants from over 100 countries. Altogether more serious in tone and intent than UKA but has plenty of concerts and events to occupy the leisure hours. In February or March every second year. The next moot is scheduled for 2011.

Kosmorama   FILM

(www.kosmorama.no) Trondheim's international film festival occupies an intensive week in late April.

Nidaros Blues Festival   MUSIC

(www.nidarosbluesfestival.com, in Norwegian) The Fabulous Thunderbirds topped the bill in 2010. Also in late April.

Olavsfestdagene   HISTORICAL

(www.olavsfestdagene.no) In honour of St Olav and held during the week around his saint's day, 29 July. There's a medieval market and a rich program of classical music, folk, pop and jazz (Esperanza Spalding, Barack Obama's favourite artiste, and Noora Noor, Grammy Award winner, topped the bill in 2010).

Trondelag Food Festival   FOOD

Coincides with Olavsfestdagene. Stalls selling local fare pack Kongens gate, east of Torvet.

Pstereo   MUSIC

(http://pstereo.net) Major pop and rock festival over a weekend in late August.

UKA   STUDENTS

(www.uka.no, in Norwegian) Trondheim's 25,000 university students stage this three-week celebration, Norway's largest cultural festival. Every other year in October and November, it's a continuous party with concerts, plays and other festivities based at the round, red Studentersamfundet (Student Centre). It's next due to take the city by storm in 2011.

⌟ Sleeping

TOP CHOICE **Britannia Hotel**   HOTEL €€

(☎73 80 08 00; www.britannia.no; Dronningens gate 5; s/d from Nkr1095/1295; ▣@⊛⊠) This mastodon of a hotel with nearly 250 rooms was constructed in 1897. It exudes old-world grace from the mellow, wooden panelling of public areas to the magnificent oval Moorish-revival **Palmehaven restaurant** – but one of three places to eat – with its Corinthian pillars and central fountain. The hotel's the perfect place to relax or, should you so wish, to exert yourself in the brand new sauna and minigym.

Chesterfield Hotel   HOTEL €€

(☎73 50 37 50; www.bestwestern.no; Søndre gate 26; s/d from Nkr790/990; @⊛) All 43 rooms at this venerable hotel are spacious. They were decorated and fundamentally renovated, with fresh beds and furniture, in 2006 following a major fire in the adjacent building. Those on the 7th (top) floor have huge skylights giving broad city views.

Clarion Collection Hotel Grand Olav
HOTEL €€

(☎73 80 80 80; www.choice.no; Kjøpmannsgata 48; s/d from Nkr880/980; @⊚) Two of Trondheim's finest hotels stare across the street at each other in perpetual competition. The Clarion offers sleek luxurious living above an airy shopping complex and the Olavshallen concert hall. It has 27 different styles among more than 100 rooms, so no guest can complain of lack of choice.

Radisson Blu Royal Garden Hotel
HOTEL €€

(☎73 80 30 00; www.radissonblu.com; Kjøpmannsgata 73; s/d from Nkr1095/1195; P@⊚≋) Opposite the Clarion, this first-class, contemporary riverside hotel (you can fish from your window in some rooms) is open and airy from the moment you step into the atrium, where the light streams in through its all-glass walls.

Singsaker Sommerhotel
SUMMER HOTEL €

(☎73 89 31 00; http://sommerhotell.singsaker .no; Rogertsgata 1; dm/s/d with shared bathroom Nkr230/445/685, s/d with bathroom Nkr560/810; ⊙mid-Jun–mid-Aug; P) On a grassy knoll in a quiet residential neighbourhood, this imposing building, usually a student hostel, was originally built as a club for occupying German officers. It represents great value. Bus 63 from the train station passes by. If driving, take Klostergata eastwards from the Studentersamfundet and follow the signs.

P-Hotel
HOTEL €€

(☎73 80 23 50; www.p-hotels.no; Nordre gate 24; s/d from Nkr795/995; @⊚) This slick, modern hotel, part of an expanding Norwegian minichain, has 49 spruce rooms, each with beverage-making kit, that speak of good Scandinavian style. Someone pads by in the early morning and hangs your breakfast bag on the door. There's a washing machine for guest use.

Pensjonat Jarlen
GUESTHOUSE €

(☎73 51 32 18; www.jarlen.no; Kongens gate 40; s/d Nkr520/650) There's nothing fancy about this central spot but it does have price, convenience and value for money on its side. All 25 rooms have full bathroom and all except the sole single have a fridge and self-catering facilities.

Thon Hotel Trondheim
HOTEL €€

(☎73 88 47 88; www.thonhotels.com; Kongens gate 15; s/d from Nkr710/975; @⊚) This central hotel offers pleasant, nothing-fancy accommodation at a reasonable price year-round. Inside is more appealing than the plain, boxy exterior might suggest and rooms have a simple, trim design.

Trondheim InterRail Centre
SUMMER HOSTEL €

(☎73 89 95 38; www.tirc.no; Elgesetergate 1; dm Nkr180; ⊙Jul–mid-Aug; @⊚) OK, so you're on a cot bed in a mixed dorm with between 15 and 35 sweating, snoring others but the advantages outweigh the downside at this convivial, excellent-value place, run by the Studentersamfundet. There's free internet access, wi-fi and luggage storage, frequent live music and curfew is an ugly word. Its **Edgar Café** serves inexpensive meals, chocolate cake that more than one reader swears by and beer (especially cheap during bi-weekly backpacker evenings). Should you hear strange shufflings, it's just the ghost of one S Møller, a student who mysteriously disappeared in the 1930s.

Flakk Camping
CAMPGROUND €

(☎72 84 39 00; www.flakk-camping.no; car/caravan sites Nkr170/200, cabins with outdoor bathroom Nkr400-550; ⊙May-Aug) Sitting right beside Trondheimfjord (there's minimal disturbance from the nearby ferry point), this welcoming campground is about 10km from the city centre. Take Rv715 from Trondheim.

✖ Eating

Trondheim has plenty of lovely cafes for a light meal, coffee and cakes. Some stay open at night and turn into lively pubs. For self-caterers, there's a grand little open-air fruit and veg market on Torvet each morning.

[TOP CHOICE] Vertshuset Tavern
TRADITIONAL NORWEGIAN €€€

(☎73 87 80 70; Sverresborg Allé 11; mains Nkr195-295) Once in the heart of Trondheim, this historic (1739) tavern was lifted and transported, every last plank of it, to the Sverresborg Trøndelag Folkemuseum on the outskirts of town. Tuck into its rotating specials of traditional Norwegian fare or just peck at waffles with coffee in one of its 16 tiny rooms, each low-beamed, with sloping floors, candlesticks, cast-iron stoves and lacy tablecloths.

Havfruen
FISH RESTAURANT €€€

(☎73 87 40 70; www.havfruen.no, in Norwegian; Kjøpmannsgata 7; specials Nkr195, mains around Nkr300, 3-course menu Nkr525; ⊙5pm-midnight

Mon-Sat) This characterful riverside restaurant, all odd-angled pillars and rustic beams, specialises in the freshest of fish. The quality, reflected in the prices, is excellent, as are the accompanying wines, selected by the resident sommelier. The short menu changes regularly according to what's hauled from the seas.

To Rom og Kjøkken
CONTEMPORARY NORWEGIAN €€€

(☎73 56 89 00; www.toromogkjokken.no; Carl Johansgate 5; mains Nkr265-285; ☺4pm-2am Mon-Sat) At Two Rooms & a Kitchen, service is friendly. The ambience, with original, changing artwork on the walls, is bright and brisk, and prices are reasonable. Vegetables and meat are sourced locally, wherever feasible. For a sample of its subtle cuisine, savour its daily bar special (Nkr150).

TOP CHOICE Baklandet Skydsstasjon
TRADITIONAL NORWEGIAN €€

(☎73 92 10 44; www.skydsstation.no, in Norwegian; Øvre Bakklandet 33; mains Nkr130-245; ☺noon-1am) Within what began life as an 18th-century coaching inn are several cosy rooms with poky angles and listing floors. It's a hyperfriendly place where you can tuck into tasty dishes, such as its renowned fish soup ('the best in all Norway', a couple of diners assured us), while always leaving a cranny for a gooey homemade cake (around Nkr50).

Ramp
BAR, RESTAURANT €

(cnr Strandveien & Gregusgate; mains Nkr85-140; ☺noon-midnight) Well off the tourist route and patronised by in-the-know locals, friendly, alternative Ramp gets its raw materials, organic where possible, from local sources (its veg man, for example, calls by each morning). It's renowned for its juicy house burgers filled with lamb, beef, fish or chickpeas.

Credo
INTERNATIONAL €€€

(☎73 53 03 88; Ørjaveita 4; 5-course menu Nkr660; ☺6-11pm Mon-Sat) There's no need for a formal à la carte menu at this adventurous Spanish-influenced world-cuisine spot – the chef chooses the day's best items and serves them up in fine style. Upstairs, there's a trendy bistro and bar, which serves an excellent-value three-course meal (Nkr150), prepared in the shared kitchen. At weekends, there's often live music.

Emilies
RESTAURANT €€€

(☎73 92 96 41; www.emilies.no, in Norwegian; Erling Skakkes gate 45; 3-5 courses Nkr400-500;

☺4pm-midnight Mon-Sat) The menu, carefully selected and constantly changing to reflect what's available locally, couldn't be shorter or sweeter at this sophisticated restaurant, its table linen and furniture an essay in contrasting blacks and whites.

Persilleriet
VEGETARIAN €

(☎73 60 60 14; Erling Skakkes gate 39; lunch Nkr99; ☺11am-6pm Mon-Fri; ☑) This tiny lunchtime-only box of a place does tasty vegetarian fare, to eat in or take away. The menu changes regularly and the cuisine is eclectic. On any day it may include, for example, elements of Thai, Middle Eastern or Mexican dishes.

Bari
ITALIAN CAFE, BAR €€

(☎73 60 60 24; www.bari.no, in Norwegian; Munkegata 25; dishes around Nkr130) Eat in the stylish, modern, jazzy interior or choose the small streetside terrace. Bari has a reputation for good Italian fare (pasta and bruschettas), as well as superior burgers.

Frati
MEDITERRANEAN €€

(☎73 52 57 33; www.frati.no, in Norwegian; 1st fl, Munkegata 25; mains Nkr195-260) Upstairs from Bari and under the same ownership, Frati complements its ground-floor brother. More formal and conventional, its decor is all varnished wood, browns and darker hues. There are plenty of pasta choices (around Nkr150) here, too. Although dishes are labelled in Italian, the cuisine is as much mainstream Europe as peculiar to Italy.

Jordbær Pikene
CAFE €

(☎73 92 91 80; www.jordbarpikene.no, in Norwegian; cnr Erling Skakkes gate & Prinsens gate; dishes around Nkr120; ☺9am-8pm Mon-Sat) 'Strawberry Girls' serves up pasta, frondy salads and sandwiches in an informal, congenial setting. It's good for juices, too. You won't find anything particularly original but you will enjoy decent, reliable, well-priced cooking.

Ravnkloa Fish Market
FISH RESTAURANT €

(Munkegata; ☺10am-5pm Mon-Sat) You can munch on inexpensive fish cakes and other finny fare at this excellent, informal place, which also sells an impressive range of cheeses and other gourmet goods.

Dromedar
CAFE €

(Nedre Bakklandet 3) This longstanding local self-service favourite serves light dishes and very good coffee indeed, in all sizes, squeezes and strengths. Inside is cramped so, if the weather permits, relax on the exterior terrace bordering the cobbled street. There's a second **branch** (Nørdre gate 2), similar in style, also with a street-side terrace, that serves equally aromatic coffee.

Café ni Muser
CAFE €

(Bispegata 9; dishes around Nkr125) For inexpensive light meals and an arty crowd, go to the cafe at the Trondheim Kunstmuseum. On sunny afternoons, the outdoor terrace turns into a beer garden.

🍷 Drinking

As a student town, Trondheim offers lots of through-the-night life. The free papers, *Natt & Dag* and *Plan B,* have listings, mostly in Norwegian. Solsiden (Sunnyside) is Trondheim's trendiest leisure zone. A whole wharf-side of bars and restaurants nestles beneath smart new apartment blocks, converted warehouses and long-idle cranes.

TOP CHOICE Den Gode Nabo
PUB

(www.dengodenabo.com, in Norwegian; Øvre Bakklandet 66; ☉1pm-1am) The Good Neighbour, dark and cavernous within and nominated more than once as Norway's best pub, enjoys a prime riverside location. Indeed, part of it is on the water; reserve a table on the floating pontoon. There's a reproduction Wurlitzer jukebox; US visitors will find Sam Adams on tap while UK ale connoisseurs can savour Shepherd Neame's Bishop's Finger in the bottle.

Trondheim Microbryggeri
BREW PUB

(Prinsens gate 39) This splendid home-brew pub deserves a pilgrimage as reverential as anything accorded to St Olav from all committed *øl* (beer) quaffers. With up to eight of its own brews on tap and good light meals (around Nkr150) coming from the kitchen, it's a place to linger, nibble and tipple. It's down a short lane, just off Prinsens gate.

Bare Blåbær
BAR, CAFE

(Innherredsveien 16) Join the throng that packs both the interior and dockside terrace of this popular place. It's renowned for its cocktails, shorts and juleps – and for preparing the finest pizzas (around Nkr125) in town, including the intriguing *chili bollocks* (presumably a wintertime special).

Bruk Bar
MUSIC BAR

(Prinsens gate 19; ☉11am-1.30am) Inside, a stuffed elk head gazes benignly down, candles flicker and designer lamps shed light onto the 30-or-so-year-olds who patronise

ℹ️ **WI-FI IN DOWNTOWN TRONDHEIM**

Trondheim is one of Europe's first wireless cities. If you're carrying your laptop, you can wi-fi (Nkr10/30 per three/24 hours) at multiple spots within the city centre. For details and to log on, go to http://tradlos etrondheim.no.

this welcoming joint. The music is eclectic, varying at the whim of bar staff, but guaranteed loud.

Rick's Café
MUSIC BAR

(Nordre gate 11; ☉from 11am) The original Rick's burnt down (at least one major conflagration over the years is almost a rite of passage in Norway) and this slick reconstruction opened in 2007. The ground floor is all edgy stainless steel while upstairs, more for quiet cocktails and lingering wines, has sink-down-deep leatherette sofas and armchairs. The weekend nightclub in the basement has two zones – one for rock, the other playing house.

Løkka
BAR, CAFE

(Dokkgata 8) Long before its latest makeover, Løkka was a boat repair workshop. Part of its large external terrace straddles a former slipway, its rusting pulleys and hawsers still taut below. It carries a good range of beers, on draught and in bottle.

Macbeth
BAR

(Søndre gate 22b; ☉3pm-midnight) Homesick Scots will feel at home, Geordies with nostalgia can weep into their draught Newcastle Brown, and the rest of us can watch big-screen football or car racing (don't get yourself into the corner where the committed racegoers sit, though, or you'll be persona-really-non-grata). Absolutely everyone can enjoy a dram or two of its more than a dozen single malt whiskies...

Studentersamfundet
STUDENT CENTRE

(Student Centre; Elgesetergate 1) During the academic year, it has 10 lively bars, a cinema and frequent live music, while in summer it's mostly a travellers' crash pad.

Metro
GAY CLUB

(Kjøpmannsgata 12; cover charge Nkr50-70; ☉10.30pm-2am Thu-Sat) Trondheim's only gay bar is also a pub, lounge, disco and friendly meeting place for both boys and girls.

TRONDHEIM: CYCLE CITY

You have to admire the Kommune of Trondheim for its tenacity. Some years ago, it laid on around 200 green bicycles, available free of charge for use on the central peninsula. But they were soon stolen, wrecked or simply not returned. Undeterred, the municipality tightened up on security and tried again.

This time the distinctive bikes are red and widely used for short hops around town. You borrow one for a maximum of three hours before returning it to any of 12 racks around central Trondheim (including one at the train station). To join in, get a bike card (Nkr70 per 24 hours plus a refundable deposit of Nkr200) from the tourist office, pick up a cycle from the nearest rack and jump into the saddle.

Other cycle-friendly measures include clear signing of cycle routes, often traffic-free and shared with pedestrians, a lane of smooth flagstones along cobbled streets that would otherwise uncomfortably judder your and the bike's moving parts – and Trampe, the world's only bike lift, a low-tech piece of engineering to which cyclists heading from the Gamle Bybro up the Brubakken hill to Kristiansten Fort can hitch themselves.

☆ Entertainment

There's a cluster of clubs, including Clash, Gossip and Juba Juber, at the northern end of Nordre gate.

Dokkhuset   CAFE, CULTURAL CENTRE
(☺11am-1am Mon-Thu, 11am-3am Fri & Sat, 1pm-1am Sun) In an artistically converted former pumping station (look through the glass beneath your feet at the old engines), the Dock House is at once auditorium (where if it's the right night you'll hear experimental jazz or chamber music), restaurant and cafe-bar. Sip a drink on the jetty or survey the Trondheim scene from its roof terrace.

Frakken   NIGHTCLUB
(Dronningens gate 12; ☺6pm-3am) This multistorey nightclub and piano bar features both Norwegian and foreign musicians and has live music nightly.

Olavshallen   CONCERT HALL
(☎73 99 40 50; Kjøpmannsgata 44) Trondheim's main concert hall is within the Olavskvartalet cultural centre. The home base of the Trondheim Symphony Orchestra, it also features international rock and jazz concerts, mostly between September and May.

Trøndelag Teater   THEATRE
(☎73 80 50 00; Prinsens gate 18-20) Constructed in 1816 and handsomely refurbished, it stages large-scale dance and musical performances and also more intimate theatre.

Trondheim has two main cinemas.
Nova Kinosenter (Olav Tryggvasons gate 5)
Prinsen Kino (Prinsens gate 2b)

ⓘ Information

Library (Kongens gate; ☺9am-7pm Mon-Thu, 9am-4pm Fri, 10am-3pm Sat) Free internet access. Carries international press.

Tourist office (☎73 80 76 60; www.trondheim.no; Torvet; ☺8.30am-8pm Mon-Fri, 10am-6pm Sat & Sun late Jun–mid-Aug, 8.30am-6pm Mon-Fri, 10am-4pm Sat & Sun late May-late Jun & mid-late Aug, 9am-4pm Mon-Fri, 10am-2pm Sat rest of yr)

ⓘ Getting There & Away

Air

Værnes airport is 32km east of Trondheim. There are flights to all major Norwegian cities, as well as Copenhagen and Stockholm. Norwegian flies to/from London (Gatwick) and KLM covers Amsterdam.

Boat

Trondheim is a major stop on the Hurtigruten coastal ferry route. Express passenger boats between Trondheim and Kristiansund (3½ hours) depart from the Pirterminalen quay up to three times daily.

Bus

The intercity bus terminal (Rutebilstasjon) adjoins Trondheim Sentralstasjon (train station, also known as Trondheim S).

As the main link between southern and northern Norway, Trondheim is a bus transport crossroads. Nor-Way Bussekspress services run up to three times daily to/from the following:

Ålesund (Nkr596, seven hours, two to three daily)

Bergen (Nkr790, 14½ hours) One overnight bus.

PARKING IN CENTRAL TRONDHEIM

At Nkr20 per hour, parking in the centre of town can quickly gobble up your holiday money. However, during school summer vacation, Trondheim Katedralskole lets both cars and campervans park in its playground for Nkr60 per day (7.30am to 9pm). Check with the tourist office in case a different school takes it over.

Namsos (Nkr350, 3½ hours) Via Steinkjer it's Nkr295, 2¼ hours.

If you're travelling by public transport to Narvik and points north, it's quicker – all is relative – to take the train to Fauske or Bodø (the end of the line), then continue by bus.

Car & Motorcycle

There's an E6 bypass that avoids Trondheim – but why would you want to take it? The main route ploughs through the heart of the city.

Train

There are two to four trains daily to/from Oslo (Nkr810, 6½ hours). Two head north to Bodø (Nkr982, 9¾ hours) via the following:

Fauske (Nkr947, 9¼ hours)
Mo i Rana (Nkr795, 7½ hours)
Mosjøen (Nkr700, 5½ hours)

A *minipris* ticket (see the boxed text, p446) will considerably undercut these standard prices.

You can also train it to Steinkjer (Nkr186, two hours, hourly).

Getting Around

To/From the Airport

Flybussen (tickets Nkr90, 45 minutes) runs every 15 minutes from 4am to 9pm (less frequently at weekends), stopping at major landmarks such as the train station, Studentersamfundet and Britannia Hotel.

Trains run between Trondheim Sentralstasjon and the Værnes airport station (Nkr64, 35 minutes, hourly).

Bicycle

As befits such a cycle-friendly city, Trondheim has its bike-hire scheme (Nkr70 per 24 hours). Pick up a card at the tourist office in return for a refundable deposit of Nkr200, then borrow a bike from any of 12 cycle stations around town.

Car & Motorcycle

There's a toll of Nkr60 every time you enter or leave central Trondheim. Pay up or you risk a steep fine.

Public Transport

The city bus service, run by **AtB** (www.atb.no, in Norwegian), has its central transit point (all lines stop at or near it) on the corner of Munkegata and Dronningens gate. Buses and trams cost Nkr30 per ride (Nkr70 for a day card). You'll need the exact change.

Trondheim's tram line, the Gråkalbanen, runs west from St Olavsgata to Lian, in the heart of the Bymarka. Antique trolleys trundle along this route on Saturdays in summer. Transfers are available from city buses.

Taxi

To call a cab, ring **Trønder Taxi** (☎07373) or **Norgestaxi** (☎08000).

THE ROUTE NORTH

If you're heading north, from Steinkjer you have a choice of routes: the more frequented, inland Arctic Highway (E6) or the slower E17 Kystriksveien (Coastal Route). The railway line north to Bodø via Hell and Steinkjer more or less follows the Arctic Highway to Fauske.

Hell

Hell has little to offer but its name, meaning 'prosperity' in Norwegian. All the same, some travellers stop here for a cheap chuckle or at least to snap a photo of the sign at the train station. Forever after, whenever someone suggests you go here, you can honestly say you've been to Hell and back and it wasn't all that bad.

Stiklestad

The site of Stiklestad lies 5km east of the E6 on Rv757. It commemorates what in terms of numbers was a small skirmish but which, in its impact, is at the heart of Norwegians' sense of national identity. They flock here by the thousands, some as pilgrims visiting the church associated with St Olav but most simply to picnic and enjoy the fresh air, open space and associated exhibitions.

Here in Stiklestad on 29 July 1030 the larger and better-equipped forces of local feudal, pagan chieftains defeated a force of barely 100 men led by the Christian King Olav Haraldsson, who had been forced from the Norwegian throne by King Knut (Canute) of Denmark and England.

The Battle of Stiklestad marks Norway's passage between the Viking and medieval eras. Although Olav was killed, the battle is generally lauded as a victory for Christianity in Norway and the slain hero recalled as a martyr and saint. St Olav developed a following all over northern Europe and his grave in Trondheim's Nidaros Cathedral became a destination of pilgrims from across the continent.

The site, around most of which you can wander for free, is laid out rather like a sprawling theme park, with exhibits on the Battle of Stiklestad, an outdoor folk museum and, predating all, the 12th-century Stiklestad church.

◉ Sights

The **Stiklestad National Cultural Centre** (Stiklestad Nasjonale Kultursenter; www.stiklestad .no, in Norwegian; adult/child Nkr120/50; ⏰11am-5pm) is a grandiose wooden structure. Entry entitles you to visit **Stiklestad 1030**, an evocative exhibition about the battle, with dioramas and plenty of shrieks and gurgles on the soundtrack; a 15-minute film on St Olav; a guided tour that includes a visit to the church; and a small WWII resistance museum. Within the complex too is a **restaurant** specialising in locally sourced food and a smart **hotel** (s/d Nkr750/1000).

In the grounds there's a collection of over 30 historical buildings (admission free), ranging from humble crofts and artisans workshops to the **Molåna**, a much grander farmhouse and, within it, a small, summertime cafe. In summer, actors in period costume bring several of the buildings to life.

Across the road is lovely Stiklestad **church** (⏰11am-6pm Mon-Sat, 12.30-6pm Sun mid-Jun–mid-Aug), built between 1150 and 1180 above the stone on which the dying St Olav reputedly leaned. The original stone was believed to have healing powers but it was removed during the Reformation and hasn't been seen since.

There's an excellent free booklet *Stiklestad – Meeting Place for Almost 2000 Years*.

✨ Festivals & Events

Every year during the week leading up to St Olav's Day (29 July) Stiklestad hosts the **St Olav Festival** with a medieval market, lots of wannabe Vikings in costume and a host of other folksy activities. The high point of the festival is an outdoor pageant (held over the last five days) dramatising the conflicts between the king and local farmers and chieftains. Some of Norway's top actors and actresses traditionally take the major roles while locals play minor parts and swell the crowd scenes.

Steinkjer & North

Medieval sagas speak of Steinkjer (population 11,000) as a major trading centre and indeed it continues to be a crossroads, requiring a decision from northbound travellers: to opt for the more scenic Kystriksveien coastal route (Rv17) to Bodø or to continue northwards on the E6 (Arctic Highway).

◉ Sights & Activities

Steinkjer's main attraction is its **Egge Museum** (www.eggemuseum.no, in Norwegian; Fylkesmannsgården; adult/child Nkr60/free; ⏰11am-4pm mid-Jun–mid-Aug), an open-air farm complex 2.5km north of town. On the same hilltop site are several Viking burial mounds and stone circles.

Leaving Steinkjer, the E6 follows the north shore of the 45km-long, needle-thin lake **Snåsavatnet**, bordered by majestic evergreen forests. You may prefer to take the Rv763 along the quieter southern shore to see the **Bølarein**, a 5000- to 6000-year-old rock carving of a reindeer and several other incised carvings. Pass by the **Bølabua restaurant & gift shop** (⏰late Jun-early Aug), a short walk from the carving, for information.

🛏 Sleeping & Eating

Tingvold Park Hotel   HOTEL **€€**
(☎74 14 11 00; www.tingvoldhotel.no; Gamle Kongeveien 47; s/d from Nkr850/1050; P@🖥) Beside an old Viking burial site, this secluded, good-value option is a member of the Best Western group. Overlooking Steinkjer, it has a pleasant lawn and garden.

Føllingstua   CAMPGROUND **€**
(☎74 14 71 90; www.follingstua.com; E6, Følling; car/ caravan sites Nkr180/190, cabins Nkr580-1200, d with shared bathroom Nkr500-600) Beside the E6 14km north of Steinkjer, near the lake's southwestern end, this lovely, welcoming camping ground may tempt you to linger for a day or two, fish in the lake or rent one of its boats and canoes (Nkr200 per day).

Guldbergaunet Sommerhotel
& Camping
HOTEL, CAMPGROUND €

(☑74 16 20 45; g-book@online.no; Elvenget 34; car/caravan sites Nkr160/190, r from Nkr450, cabins Nkr395-490; ⊙hotel mid-Jun–mid-Aug, cabins yr-round) Normally student accommodation, this campground and summer hotel is 2.3km from town amid a grassy area. A small river, ideal for paddling and bathing, flows right by.

Brod & Cirkus
RESTAURANT €€€

(☑74 16 21 00; www.brodogcirkus.no, in Norwegian; Sannagata 8; mains Nkr250, 3-course meals Nkr435; ⊙from 6pm Wed-Sat) Chef Lars Knutsen creates his menu day-by-day, based upon what's best at the moment. Meat, fish and shellfish are all sourced locally and bread and desserts are all confected on the premises. It's one block east of main Kongens gate, behind the Statens Hus.

Breidablikk
NORWEGIAN €

(☑934 06 047; Kongens gate 22-24; mains Nkr110-145; ⊙9am-6pm Mon-Sat, noon-6pm Sun) Breidablikk serves up honest, reliable Norwegian fare. Choose from its short à la carte selection, which includes several Sami dishes, or go for the dish of the day. Fish balls in white sauce, dessert and coffee for just Nkr105? You won't find better value in all Norway.

ℹ Information

Steinkjer's **tourist office** (☑74 40 17 16; www.visitinnherred.com; Namdalsvegen 11; ⊙9am-8pm Mon-Fri, 10am-7pm Sat, noon-7pm Sun Mid-Jun–mid-Aug, 9am-4pm Mon-Fri rest of yr; @) is beside the E6, opposite the Amfi shopping centre. From the train station take the foot tunnel. Doubling as the Kystriksveien Info-Center, it can book accommodation in town and along the coastal route. It also rents bikes (per hour/day Nkr40/160).

Namsos
POP 9000

Namsos is the first port town of consequence on the northbound coastal route between Trondheim and Bodø; it makes a pleasant overnight stop and has a few interesting diversions.

⊙ Sights

Lysstøperiet
CANDLE FACTORY

(www.lysstoperiet.no, in Norwegian; Finn Christiansens Vei 14; ⊙10am-6pm Mon-Fri, 10am-3pm Sat) Geir Arne Opdahl and Mona Nordfjellmark have converted a former train shed into an artisan-scale candle factory where they fashion around 15 tonnes of prime-quality paraffin wax each year into pumpkins, peppers, boots, cats, flowers, and candles all colours of the rainbow.

Rock City
ROCK & ROLL MUSEUM

(www.rockcity.no, in Norwegian) The large white cube under construction when we last visited is a temple to rock and roll – and homage to the disproportionately large numbers of artists from Namsos who have made it big on the Scandinavian popular-music scene.

Norsk Sagbruksmuseum
FORESTRY MUSEUM

(Spillumsvika; adult/child Nkr40/free; ⊙9am-4pm Sun-Fri mid-Jun–mid-Aug, 9am-3pm Mon-Fri rest of yr) If you're interested in wood chopping and chipping, take a guided tour around this tribute to an important local industry. Over the bridge 4km east of town, it commemorates Norway's first steam-powered sawmill (1853).

Namdalsmuseet
FOLK MUSEUM

(☑74 27 40 72; Kjærlighetstien 1; adult/child Nkr40/free; ⊙noon-4pm Tue-Sun mid-Jun–mid-Aug) Namdal Museum has displays on local history, including the typical wooden sailing boats of the area, and is – hold on to your hat – 'Norway's only museum featuring exhibits of hospital equipment presented in chronological order'.

🏃 Activities

Bjørumsklumpen
VIEWPOINT

An easy scenic 20-minute walk up Kirkegata from the centre will take you to the lookout atop the prominent loaf-shaped rock (114m) with good views over Namsfjorden, the town and its environs. About a third of the way up, a sign identifies a track leading to some impressive WWII Nazi bunkers hewn from solid rock.

Trolley Ride
TROLLEY RIDE

For exercise and for the sake of nostalgia, you can hire a **trolley** (single Nkr250, up to 4 riders Nkr350) from Namsos Camping and trundle it for 17km along the disused railway line between Namsos and Skage as it follows the gentle River Nansen.

Oasen
SWIMMING

(www.oasen-namsos.no, in Norwegian; Jarle Hildrums veg; adult/child Nkr100/60; ⊙9am-8pm Mon-Fri, 10am-4pm Sat & Sun) About 1km east of town and built deep inside the mountain, this swimming hall has three heated pools and a 37m water slide.

☕ Sleeping & Eating

Børstad Hotel   HOTEL €€

(☎74 21 80 90; www.borstadhotel.no, in Norwegian; Carl Gulbransons gate 19; s/d Nkr950/1190; ☎) Bright and friendly, this 19-room hotel has large sunny rooms and a pleasant outdoor garden. There's a cosy lounge, and the huge oak dining table (over a century old and at which breakfast is served) was once used for company board meetings.

Tino's Hotell   HOTEL, RESTAURANT €€

(☎74 21 80 00; www.tinoshotell.no, in Norwegian; Verftsgata 5; s/d Sun-Thu from Nkr1000/1300, Fri & Sat Nkr800/1100) Rooms are large and comfortable at this hotel, just a stone's throw from the waterside. Tino, the owner and Italian as they come despite many years in Norway, runs a great **restaurant** (pizzas Nkr180-200, mains Nkr235-260; ☺noon-11pm) that serves both international food and fine Italian cuisine (such as 24 varieties of pizza), a continent away from Norway's usual pizza and pasta joints.

Namsos Camping   CAMPGROUND €

(☎74 27 53 44; www.namsos-camping.no; tents/ caravans Nkr200/250, 4-bed cabins with outdoor bathroom Nkr400-450, with bathroom Nkr850-950) This superior campground has a large kitchen and dining room, playground and minigolf. Basic cabins are a bargain and the more expensive ones are well equipped. Alongside is a shallow lake that's ideal for children, who'll also enjoy the go-karts, communing with the romping squirrels and two tame goat kids. Take Rv17, direction Grong, then follow the airport signs.

🛍 Shopping

Aakervik   DELICATESSEN

(cnr Havnegata & Herlaugs gate 16; ☺9am-4.30pm Mon-Sat) This gourmet food shop is a great place for wild salmon and other fish, reindeer, roe deer and elk. The interior is a mini-menagerie of stuffed animals and birds eyeing you glassily from all angles; pay your respects to the amiable brown bear.

ⓘ Information

The seasonal **tourist office** (☎74 22 66 04; www.namsosinfo.no; Havnegata 9; ☺9am-5pm Mon-Fri, 10am-4pm Sat mid-Jun–mid-Aug) rents cycles (Nkr40/100 per hour/day) and also provides information about the Kystriksveien.

ⓘ Getting There & Away

Nor-Way Bussekspress runs twice daily between Namsos and Trondheim (Nkr350, 3½ hours). There are up to eight local buses daily to/from Steinkjer (Nkr132, 1½ hours).

Rørvik

Tiny Rørvik buzzes when the northbound and southbound Hurtigruten coastal ferries meet each other here every day around 9.30pm. What gets passengers up early from the dinner table is the splendid **Norveg** (☎74 36 07 70; adult/child incl audio guide Nkr70/35; ☺10am-10pm mid-Jun–Jul, 10am-5pm rest of yr & when the Hurtigruten's in port). Architecturally exciting and resembling a sailing ship, it recounts 10,000 years of coastal history through a variety of media, including an accompanying audio guide, available in English. It also runs a well-regarded gourmet restaurant.

A combined ticket (adult/child Nkr120/ 60), valid for two days, gives admission to Norveg, Berggården (an old trading house once typical of coastal communities) and several other historical buildings. Whether or not you go for the package, pick up from Norveg *Coastal Town Rørvik*, a useful free brochure that guides you around this small community's principal sites.

The swiftest way to travel between Rørvik and Namsos is by express passenger boat (Nkr178, 1½ hours, one to three times daily).

Leka

POP 600

You won't regret taking a short side-trip to the wild and beautiful island of Leka; for hikers, the desertlike Wild West landscape is particularly enchanting. This prime habitat for the white-tailed sea eagle (hold on to your little ones; in 1932, a three-year-old girl was snatched away by a particularly cheeky specimen) also has several Viking-age burial mounds and Stone Age rock paintings.

Bed down at **Leka Motell og Camping** (☎74 39 98 23; www.leka-camp.no; tent/ caravan sites Nkr120/190, d/q with bathroom & kitchen Nkr680/840). For comfort, reserve one of its well-equipped, reasonably priced motel rooms. For something different and more spartan, hire a sod-roofed stone hut (Nkr400), sleeping up to four in bunk beds.

Leka is accessed by hourly ferry from Gutvik, a 20-minute drive from the Rv17 coastal road.

Spectacular
Norway

Fjords »
Activities »
Lofoten »
Svalbard »

lime snowscape: the village of Reine, on the island of Moskenesøy (p300), Lofoten Islands

Fjords

The fjords of Norway rank among the most dramatic landforms on earth. To travel to Norway and not draw near to one of its signature fjords is to miss an essential element in Norway's enduring appeal.

If Norway's fjords were an art collection, Unesco World Heritage–listed Geirangerfjord would be its masterpiece. Yes, it gets overwhelmed by tour buses and cruise ships in summer, but they're there for a very good reason and their presence only slightly diminishes the experience. Also inscribed on the World Heritage list, Nærøyfjord is similarly popular yet unrelentingly breathtaking. It's merely one of many tributary arms of Sognefjorden which, at 203km long and 1308m deep, is the world's second-longest and Norway's deepest fjord.

Hardangerfjord is another extensive fjord network sheltering charming villages that promise front-row seats from which to contemplate the beauty at every turn, while away to the south, Lysefjord is long and boasts some of Norway's best views. And that's just the beginning...

TOP MAINLAND FJORDS

» **Geirangerfjord** (p227) – the king of Norwegian fjords

» **Sognefjorden** (p199) – a vast fjord network

» **Hardangerfjord** (p176) – rolling hills and lovely villages

» **Lysefjord** (p195) – plunging cliffs, cruises and death-defying lookout points

» **Nærøyfjord** (p203) – one of Norway's narrowest and prettiest fjords

» **Eidfjord** (p178) – the most spectacular branch of Hardangerfjord

» **Trollfjord** (p292) – an astonishingly steep fjord on Lofoten

» **Vestfjorden** (p291) – sheltered bays and pretty villages separate Lofoten from the mainland

ANDERS BLOMQVIST

ANDERS BLOMQVIST

Clockwise from top left

1. The view of Eidfjord from Kjeåsen Farm (p178)
2. Waterside Balestrand (p207), Sognefjorden
3. Smooth sailing on Geirangerfjord (p227)

Activities

Norwegians are experts at combining an appreciation of the country's wild beauty with a true sense of adventure. There's a seemingly endless list of summer activities, but winter is a wonderful time for heading out into the snow.

Hiking (Summer)

1 The right to wander at will in Norway has been inscribed in law for centuries and there's world-class hiking (p30) throughout the country. The best trails traverse glaciers or climb through the high country that, by some estimates, covers 90% of Norway.

Extreme Sports (Summer)

2 Voss (see the boxed text, p173) and its mountainous, fjord-strewn hinterland is Norway's thrill-seeking capital. It's the perfect place to take to the air strapped into a parasail or hurtle towards the earth on a bungee-rope.

Snow Sports (Winter)

3 Slip through the snow on a sled pulled by huskies. Speed across the ice astride a snowmobile. Or join the Norwegians in their national pastime of skiing downhill or cross-country. Whichever you choose, winter (p33) is a terrific time to visit.

White-Water Rafting (Summer)

4 Norway's steep slopes and icy, scenic rivers create an ideal environment for veteran and beginner rafters alike. Central Norway is rafting's true Norwegian home, but the cascading waters around Sjoa offer the widest range of experiences (p32).

Cycling (Summer)

5 Cyclists in search of seriously challenging but seriously beautiful routes will find their spiritual home in Norway (see p28). Longer routes abound, but there isn't a more exhilarating descent than the one from Finse down to Flåm.

Clockwise from top left
1. Hikers, Jostedalsbreen National Park (p211) 2. Base jumping at Gudvangen (p203) 3. Ski-jump thrills in Stryn (p218) 4. White-water rafters on Sjoa River (p143)

ANDERS BLOMQVIST

ANDERS BLOMQVIST

CHRISTIAN ASLUND

Lofoten

It is the fjords that have forever marked Norway as a land of singular natural splendour, but the surreal beauty of the Lofoten Islands is a worthy rival. For sheer drama, this magical archipelago (which in summer is bathed in the crystal-clear light of the north) could well be Norway's most beautiful corner.

Moskenesøy

1 Tolkienesque landscapes and glacier-carved landforms lend Moskenesøy (p300) a supernatural beauty that is truly special. The village of Å is the island's soul, while Reinefjord is particularly scenic.

Flakstadøy

2 Isolated, wind-blown crags along the southern shore are the most eye-catching feature of Flakstadøy (p299), but the old-world beauty of Nusfjord and the utter improbability of white-sand beaches at Ramberg and Flakstad also deserve attention.

Austvågøy

3 Most people's entry point into the Lofoten, Austvågøy (p292) is a gentle introduction to the islands' charm. The Raftsund strait and the dizzyingly narrow Trollfjord provide the backdrop, while the villages of Kabelvåg and Henningsvær offer perfect bases.

Vestvågøy

4 Many travellers rush across Vestvågøy (p297) on their way deeper into the Lofoten, but the Lofotr Viking Museum captures the spirit of more epic times and the walk from Unstad to Eggum is magnificent.

Værøy

5 Intimate little Værøy (p303), occupying Lofoten's southern reaches, is Moskenesøy's rival for the title of Lofoten's most picturesque island. The combination of vast colonies of seabirds, soaring ridgelines and remote, tiny villages is glorious.

Clockwise from top left
1. Picture-perfect Moskenesøy (p300) 2. Beach solitude on Flakstadøy (p299) 3. Boats moored at Henningsvær (p296) on Austvågøy

Svalbard

The Svalbard archipelago – as close to the North Pole as it is to mainland Norway, and the world's most accessible slice of the polar north – is one of the natural world's grand epics.

Arguably Europe's last and most extensive great wilderness area, Svalbard has all the elements for an Arctic idyll. Here you'll find more polar bears than people, as well as a roll-call of Arctic wildlife that includes walruses, reindeer, Arctic foxes and a stunning collection of bird species. They roam a landscape that, for the most part, remains ice-bound throughout the year – an astonishing 60% of Svalbard is covered by glaciers. Splendidly uninhabited fjords, formidable peaks never traversed by a human and the echoes of the great sagas of polar exploration are all part of the mix. Whether experienced in the strange blue half-light of the Arctic night (late October to mid-February) or the midnight sun (mid-April to mid-August), Svalbard is quite simply unforgettable.

GRAEME CORNWALLIS

JOHN FREEMAN

STAND-OUT SVALBARD

» **Midnight-sun hiking** (p357) – trek deep into the interior or close to Longyearbyen

» **Pyramiden** (p362) – take a summer boat trip or winter snowmobile expedition past the Nordenskjöldbreen glacier to this former Russian mining settlement

» **Dog-sledding** (p358) – the perfect way to experience the silence of Spitsbergen

» **Polar bears** (see the boxed text, p354) – spot the Arctic's most soulful presence, but hopefully from afar

» **Magdalenefjord** (p364) – a serious contender for the title of Norway's most beautiful fjord

Right
1. A cruise ship amid the icebergs of Magdalenefjord (p364) 2. Polar bear and her cub on Svalbard (p354)

Nordland

Best Places to Eat

» Søilen (p275)

» Isqueen (p305)

» Sjøstua restaurant, Sjøhus Senteret (306)

» Maren Anna (p302)

Best Places to Stay

» Fru Haugans Hotel (p270)

» Norumgården Bed & Breakfast (p281)

» Henningsvær Bryggehotel (p297)

» Vega Havhotell (p284)

Why Go?

Heading northwards through long, slim Nordland, lush fields give way to lakes and forests, vistas open up, summits sharpen and the treeline descends ever lower on the mountainsides. Above the imaginary curve of the Arctic Circle, travellers get their first taste of the midnight sun in summer, while in winter, the northern lights slash the night sky.

Linger along the spectacular Kystriksveien coastal route, ferry hopping and perhaps detouring to take in a glacier and offshore island or two. Or travel the almost-as-stunning inland Arctic Highway, more direct, almost as lovely, yet still lightly trafficked.

Offshore the razor-sharp peaks of Lofoten prod the sky. Here, cod is still king and motive for small fishing museums, *rorbuer* (fishing huts) and rickety drying frames. Connected by bridges, the islands are easy to hop around, cycling is for softies and hiking is as gentle or as tough as you care to make it.

When to Go

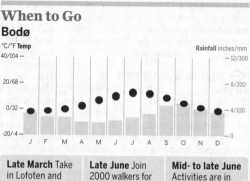

Bodø

Late March Take in Lofoten and then Svolvær's World Cod Fishing Championship.

Late June Join 2000 walkers for Narvik's mass hike on the last Saturday in June.

Mid- to late June Activities are in gear and southern European visitors are yet to arrive.

USEFUL NORDLAND WEBSITES

www.visit nordland.no Official tourist site for the region.

www.177nordland.no Comprehensive listings, together with links, of Nordland bus, boat, ferry, train and plane time-tables. Alternatively, phone ☑177 within Nordland or ☑75 77 24 10 beyond.

www.torghatten-nord.no Nord-land passenger express and car ferries.

In addition to Nordland, this chapter also includes the Harstad region, which technically belongs to the county of Troms.

ARCTIC HIGHWAY

Mosjøen

POP 9850

When arriving in Mosjøen (pronounced moo-sher-en), along the E6, you may be put off by the industrial face of this aluminium-producing town. Don't be. About 1km south, along lake-like Vefsnfjorden, historic Sjøgata and a street or two nearby are among the most charming in northern Norway and well merit a browse.

The town has a strong historical connection with the UK; in the mid-19th century, five Englishmen imported technically advanced steam engines and sawmill machinery and established the North of Europe Land & Mining Company Ltd to provide timber for constructing Britain's burgeoning industrial towns and cities. What was a tiny coastal settlement quickly became the region's first registered town.

⊙ Sights & Activities

Sjøgata HISTORIC STREET

A stroll around the Sjøgata area, with over 100 listed buildings, takes you past galleries, coffee shops, restaurants and private homes in attractively renovated former warehouses, workshops and boat sheds. *The History of a Town* (Nkr20), on sale at the museum and tourist office, is an excellent small booklet that brings Mosjøen's history to life.

Vefsn Museum FOLK MUSEUM

A **combined ticket** (adult/child Nkr30/free) gives entry to both branches of Mosjøen's museum.

In Sjøgata, the **Jakobsensbrygga warehouse** (Sjøgata 31b; ⊙10am-3pm or 8pm Mon-Fri, 10am-3pm Sat) is an excellent small museum that portrays, via some particularly evocative photo blow-ups, the history of Mosjøen from the early 19th century onwards. There's an English guide-pamphlet for each section.

Northeast of the centre, the **rural building collection** (Bygdesamlinga; ⊙10am-3pm Tue-Fri & Sun Jul only) features 12 farmhouses, shops and the like from the 18th and 19th centuries, which you can view from the exterior. It too has a pamphlet in English. Adjacent is the **Dolstad Kirke** (1735), built on the site of a medieval church dedicated to St Michael.

Laksforsen WATERFALL

About 30km south of Mosjøen and a 600m detour from the E6, the roaring 17m-high Laksforsen waterfall has leaping salmon in season and makes a pleasant picnic spot, although it's a bit of a struggle to reach the shore below the torrent. The cafe here, with its 'no photo' and 'guests only beyond this point' notices, is a place to avoid.

🛏 Sleeping

TOP CHOICE **Fru Haugans Hotel** HOTEL €€

(☑75 11 41 00; www.fruhaugans.no; Strandgata 39; s/d from Nkr775/975; @🛜) Don't be deterred by the bland main facade that somehow slipped past the planning authorities. Fru Haugans (she was the original owner; see her stare from her portrait in the lounge beside the hotel's Ellenstuen restaurant) is northern Norway's oldest hotel. Dating in part from 1794, it occupies several buildings and has grown organically over the years. Drop by its little museum, which recounts the hotel's long history. The lovely green garden gives panoramic views directly onto the fjord. The hotel has two magnificent restaurants. **Ellenstuen** (mains Nkr235-260) is an intimate place that preserves many of the hotel's original fittings. It offers a particularly creative menu (if you're in luck, you'll find roasted stag fillet and lightly smoked grouse breast in a raspberry sauce on the menu). **Hagestuen** (mains Nkr190-220), tapestry-bedecked and altogether larger, offers both à la carte dining and a copious evening buffet (Nkr235).

Aspnes Camping CAMPGROUND €

☑75 18 68 77; Fustvatn; sveinaage@nax.no; campsite Nkr150, cabin Nkr400-550; ⊙Jun-Sep) For a

Nordland Highlights

1 Ferry hop and hug the splendid **Kystriksveien coastal route** (p283)

2 Feel eider duck down float from your fingers at Vega's **E-Huset museum** (p284)

3 Be a wide-eyed kid again at the **Norwegian Aviation Museum** (p286) in Bodø

4 Linger in the tiny, preserved fishing village of **Å** (p301) in Lofoten

5 Hike the coastal **Queen's Route** (p307) to Stø in Vesterålen

6 Get cold feet on one of the glaciers in **Saltfjellet-Svartisen National Park** (p276)

DECISION TIME

At Steinkjer, to the south in Trøndelag (p258), those with wheels have a binary choice. The swifter, more direct yet lightly trafficked Arctic Highway to Narvik? Or the slower, even less-frequented, more expensive but more beautiful Kystriksveien (coastal route)? If you can spare the extra time and cash, take the 650km-long Kystriksveien (known more prosaically as the E17) as far as Bodø, ferry hopping your way northwards and perhaps detouring to take in a glacier and offshore island or two.

Unfortunately, If you're reliant upon public transport, going along the Arctic Highway, by either bus or train, is the only practical choice.

touch of tranquillity, push on to this relatively small lakeside campground, 13km north of Mosjøen. Sandwiched between the lake and E6, it's particularly well equipped and cared for.

Mosjøen Hotell
HOTEL €€

(✆75 17 11 55; www.mosjoencamping.no; Vollanveien 35; s/d with shared bathroom Nkr400/600, with bathroom from Nkr590/920; 🅿@🛜) Under the same ownership as Mosjøen Camping and about 100m north of the train station, this run-of-the-mill roadhouse offers cosy, good-value but unexceptional rooms and serves an ample buffet breakfast.

Mosjøen Camping
CAMPGROUND €

(✆75 17 79 00; www.mosjoencamping.no; Mathias Bruuns gata 24; tent/caravan site Nkr120/170, 4-person cabin from Nkr400; ☀year-round; 🏊) Beside the E6 about 500m southeast of the town centre, this campground tends to be overcrowded with travellers doing the North Cape rush. There's a pool with waterslide, snack bar, children's playground – and even tenpin bowling. In this land of superlatives, the sole urinal in the men's toilet must rank as Norway's, if not the world's, highest.

🍴 Eating & Drinking

Lille Torget
BAR-CAFE €

(✆75 17 04 14; Strandgate 24; ☀Mon-Sat) With its decorative interior (admire the gorgeous reproduction art nouveau maiden bearing a lamp at her heart) and a terrace opening onto the main square, this one-time bank,

then clothing store, now pub has seen lots of action over the years. You're guaranteed an excellent brew; Rune, its owner, was the 2008 winner of Coffee in Good Spirits, the key event in Norway's annual coffee-making championship (he'll fashion subtle shapes in your foam too).

Café Kulturverkstedet
CAFE €

(Sjøgata 22-24; ☀8am-4pm Mon-Sat) Run by the local heritage society, this delightful cafe enjoys, appropriately, one of Sjøgata's largest and most appealing renovated buildings. There are books to leaf through and you can sip and nibble in its interconnecting art gallery.

Oksen Ferdinand
CAFE-RESTAURANT €€€

(✆75 11 99 91; Sjøgata 23; snacks around Nkr100, mains Nkr195-270) You can also eat well, inside or overlooking the street, on the terrace of this historic building, which does tasty daytime sandwiches and snacks and meaty dinner mains.

ℹ Information

The **tourist office** (✆75 01 80 00; www.visithelgeland.com; ☀9am or 10am-6pm or 8pm Mon-Fri, 11am-6pm Sat & Sun) is beside the E6, which bypasses central Mosjøen.

ℹ Getting There & Away

There are flights to Bodø (via Mo i Rana) and Trondheim.

Buses run from Mosjøen to Brønnøysund (three hours, once or twice daily except Saturday) and Sandnessjøen (1¾ hours, three to five daily) There's also at least one service daily to/from Mo i Rana (1¾ hours) but the train takes less time.

Mosjøen lies on the rail line between Trondheim (Nkr700, 5½ hours, three daily), Fauske (Nkr486, 3½ hours, three daily) and Bodø (Nkr581; 4¼ hours, three daily).

WORTH A TRIP

A DETOUR VIA HATTEN

For drivers, a lovely detour follows the wild, scenic Villmarksveien route, which runs parallel to the E6 east of Mosjøen and approaches the bizarre 1128m peak of Hatten (or Hattfjell). From the end of the nearest road, the hike to the top takes about two hours. However, taking this route cuts out Mosjøen itself.

Mo i Rana

POP 25,300

Mo i Rana (just plain Mo to those who know her) is the third-largest city in the north and gateway to the spruce forests, caves and glaciers of the Arctic Circle region. Its friendly reputation is often attributed to its rapid expansion due to the construction of the now-closed steel plant, which in its time employed more than 1000 workers; nearly everyone here once knew how it felt to be a stranger in town.

Although Mo's predominant architectural style is boxy, the town is becoming lighter in tone now that heavy industry has given way to a tech-based economy.

◉ Sights & Activities

A **combined ticket** (adult/child Nkr30/free) gives entry to Mo's two small **museums** (◔10am-3.30pm Mon-Fri, 11am-3pm Sat mid-Jun–mid-Aug), which merit a brief glance.

The **Rana Museum of Natural History** (Moholmen) illustrates the geology, ecology, flora and wildlife of the Arctic Circle region, and features several hands-on exhibits that will engage children. The highlight of its sister museum, the **Rana Museum of Cultural History** (Fridtjof Nansensgata 22), is a giant model of old Mo before the steelworks altered its complexion for ever.

At the **indoor water park** (Moheia Fritidspark; ☎75 14 60 60; Øvre Idrettsveien 1; adult/child Nkr95/65; ◔noon-8pm Mon-Fri, noon-6pm Sat & Sun), also called Badeland, you can dip into four pools and three saunas – and zoom down the 42m-long waterslide.

The oldest building in town, Mo's original **church** was constructed in 1724. With its steeply pitched roof and onion dome, it deserves to be open to visitors during more than the current brief hours. In the graveyard is a monument to Russian prisoners who died in captivity and the gravestones of eight British soldiers, killed in commando raids in May 1940.

Havmannen (Man of the Sea), a sculpture forever up to his knees in water, turns his back on the town and gazes resolutely out over the fjord. His clean lines and rounded profile are the work of iconic British sculptor Antony Gormley.

AROUND MO I RANA

Grønligrotta   CAVE

(www.gronligrotta.no; adult/child Nkr120/60; ◔tours hourly 10am-6pm mid-Jun–Aug) The most accessible and most visited of the caves around Mo is 22km north of town. There's electric lighting (it's the only illuminated tourist cave in Scandinavia). The 30-minute tour takes you along an underground river, through a rock maze, then past a granite block torn off by a glacier and deposited in the cave by the brute force of moving water.

Setergrotta   CAVE

(www.setergrotta.no; Røvassdalen; adult/child Nkr275/240; ◔tours twice daily early Jun-late Aug) Setergrotta is altogether less dragooned and considerably more adventurous than Grønligrotta. Highlights of the two-hour trip include a couple of tight squeezes and a thrilling shuffle between rock walls while straddling a 15m gorge. The operators provide headlamps, hard hats, gumboots and overalls. No credit cards.

⛏ Tours

For tours to the **Svartisen glacier**, see p276.

There's no public transport from Mo but you can hire a bike from the tourist office (Nkr150) and pedal the 32km each way to the ferry point beside Svartisen lake to explore **Østisen**.

🛏 Sleeping

Meyergården Hotell   HOTEL €€

(☎75 13 40 00; www.rica.no; 28 Fridtjof Nansens gate; s/d from Nkr890/1040; 🅿@🛜) An affiliate of the Rica chain, Mo's longest-established hotel is full of character, with fine rooms, most of them recently refurbished. If price is a factor, go for one of the six economical rooms with shared facilities (s/d Nkr470/680) in the original – and much more atmospheric – late-19th-century wing.

Mo Hotell og Gjestegaard   GUESTHOUSE €€

(☎75 15 22 11; www.mo-gjestegaard.no; Elias Blix gate 5; s/d incl breakfast from Nkr600/800) Up the hill, this pleasant 15-room guesthouse is welcoming and impeccably kept. On the top floor is a pair of large family rooms (Nkr1400), accommodating up to four. It's in a quiet location and has a small garden where you are welcome to sit and relax. It's often fully booked so do reserve in advance.

Svartisen Hotell   HOTEL €€

(☎75 15 19 99; www.hotelsvartisen.no, in Norwegian; Ole Tobias Olsens gate 4; s/d Nkr1095/1195; @🛜) Belonging to the Comfort Hotel owners, the Svartisen with its mini-apartments is a bright, cheerful choice that offers free beverages and waffles. All rooms have mini-kitchens. Those on the ground floor are

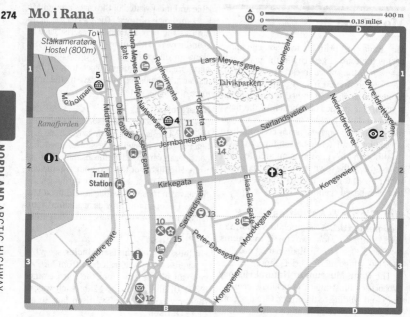

Mo i Rana

◉ Sights

🛏 Sleeping

✖ Eating

🍷 Drinking

🎭 Entertainment

particularly large and split-level, with the sleeping area upstairs.

Comfort Hotel Ole Tobias HOTEL **€€**
(☏75 12 05 00; www.ole-tobias.no; Thora Meyersgate 2; s/d from Nkr1095/1295 incl breakfast; @ 🛜) This railway-themed hotel – the corridor carpets simulate a railway track and each of its thirty rooms has the name of a station – commemorates the local teacher and priest who convinced the government to build the Nordlandsbanen railway connecting

Trondheim with Fauske and Bodø. As well as breakfast year-round and free beverages, summer tariffs include a light evening meal.

Stålkameratøne HOSTEL **€**
(☏41 92 62 15; Stålbrakka, Søderlundmyra; dm Nkr200, s/d with shared bathroom Nkr350/500; ⏱mid-Jun–mid-Aug; P @) Mo's biggest bargain is just off the first left bend of the E6, heading northwards. This hostel has four plainly furnished single rooms, occupied by stu-

ARCTIC MENU

To guarantee yourself a good meal in northern Norway, visit a restaurant affiliated to the Arctic Menu scheme. Members, who range from small, family-owned concerns to the restaurants of chain hotels, undertake to use the region's natural ingredients. It may be a sauce simmered with local berries; an Arctic char pulled from the icy waters; reindeer, seal, whale or, of course, cod – every last bit of it from the rich flesh to local delicacies such as the cheek, roe, liver, stomach or tongue.

You'll find such restaurants indicated within each town's Eating section. The scheme's website (www.arktiskmeny.no) has a full list of its 40 or so participants and most tourist offices carry its booklet. This comes complete with a few recipes so you can try a dish or two out back home – if, that is, you can get those fresh, northern Norway ingredients...

dents during the school year, an eight-bed dorm and a couple of doubles.

✗ Eating

For liquid picnics, both Bunnpris supermarket and Vinmonopolet are just south of the tourist office.

Søilen   RESTAURANT €€€
(☎75 13 40 00; mains Nkr225-295, menu Nkr725). The highly regarded Arctic Menu restaurant of Meyergården Hotell gets its meat, dairy products and even honey from local sources. Save a corner for its signature caramel pudding with whipped cream. If you aren't in the mood for a full meal, indulge in its dish of the day (around Nkr150).

Abelone   RESTAURANT €€
(☎75 15 38 88; Ole Tobias Olsens gate 6; mains Nkr175-225) Abelone is your best dining option outside the hotels. It looks unprepossessing from the street but inside the cosy simulated log cabin makes for a congenial dining environment. Opt for one of its quality meat dishes.

Babette's   CAFE-RESTAURANT €€
(☎75 15 44 33; Ranheimgata 2) Large and set back in a pedestrianised square, Babette's, a popular pizza, grills and kebab place, is

essentially three venues in one with something for everybody. There's a long bar, a cafe with a large, open terrace and a more formal restaurant area.

Bimbo Veikro   CAFE-RESTAURANT €
(☎75 15 10 01; Saltfjelletveien 34; mains Nkr68-125) Just 2km north of town beside the E6, this roadhouse, popular with locals, serves up the usual sandwiches, pizzas and grills. 'Bimbo' alludes to a nearby elephant-shaped rock formation, not the classy waitresses. It also has a few rooms (singles/doubles Nkr620/850).

🍷 Drinking & Entertainment

As Norsk Jernverk   BAR
(☎75 14 32 02; TV Westens gate 2; ⊙6pm-2am) This local watering hole carries, not without irony, the name of Mo's long defunct steelworks. On the same premises as Big Horn Steakhouse, its narrow door is easy to miss. Not so for locals in the know, who congregate here to drink, chat and, if the mood takes them, dance.

Ramona   NIGHTCLUB
(Fridtjof Nansens gata 28; ⊙Thu-Sat) Within the Meyergården Hotell, this spot – and here comes another superlative – claims to be the largest nightclub in northern Norway.

Kinoteatret   CINEMA
(Rådhusplassen 1) Mo i Rana's cinema is at the top of Jernbanegata.

TP Bowlingsenter   BOWLING
(Fridtjof Nansens gata 1; ⊙1-10pm) You can knock down a few pins here for Nkr50 per set.

ℹ Information

The **tourist office** (☎75 13 92 00; www.arctic-circle.no; Ole Tobias Olsens gate 3; ⊙8am-8pm Mon-Fri, 10am-6pm Sat, noon-6pm Sun) has free internet access.

ℹ Getting There & Away

Mo i Rana's Røssvoll airport, 14km northeast of town, has flights to/from Bodø and Trondheim. You'll enjoy an excellent panorama of the Svartisen icecaps unless it's misty down below.

By bus, options are fairly limited. There are one to three daily services to/from both Sandnessjøen (2¾ hours) and Mosjøen (1¾ hours). At least one bus of **Länstrafiken** (www.tabussen.nu) runs daily between Mo i Rana and Umeå (eight hours) in Sweden.

Most visitors arrive at Mo i Rana's attractive octagonal **train station** (☎75 15 01 77), from where trains run to the following destinations:

DESTINATION	DURATION (HR)	FREQUENCY (DAILY)
Bodø	3	4
Fauske	2¼	4
Mosjøen	1½	5
Trondheim	7½	3

ℹ️ Getting Around

If you're driving, pick up a free visitors' parking permit from the tourist office, which also hires bicycles.

Call ☎7550 for a taxi.

Saltfjellet-Svartisen National Park

The 2102-sq-km Saltfjellet-Svartisen National Park is an area of contrast. In the west, it embraces the rugged peaks of the Svartisen icecap, Norway's second-largest glacier. To the east, the bleak, high moorlands of the Saltfjellet massif roll to the Swedish border.

The best map for trekking is Statens Kartverk's *Saltfjellet* at 1:100,000.

Northbound travellers on the Hurtigruten coastal ferry can visit the Svartisen glacier as an optional add-on to their journey.

SVARTISEN

The two Svartisen icecaps, separated by the valley Vesterdalen, straddle the Arctic Circle between Mo i Rana and the Meløy peninsula. At its thickest, the ice is around 600m deep. The average height is about 1500m but some tongues lick down into the valleys and are the lowest-lying glaciers in mainland Europe. You can experience Svartisen from either its eastern or more spectacular western side. Most visitors to either just make a quick hop by boat, but hikers will find more joy approaching from the east.

Østisen, the eastern glacier, is more accessible from Mo. From the end of the Svartisdalen road, 20km up the valley from Mo i Rana's airport, **ferries** (adult/child return Nkr90/45; ☺mid-Jun–Aug) cross Svartisen lake (Svartisvatnet) four times daily. From the ferry landing, it's a 3km hike to the beginning of the Austerdalsisen glacier tongue. There's a kiosk and campground at the lake.

From the end of the road you can also trek up to the hut on the shore of the mountain lake Pikhaugsvatnet, which is surrounded by peaks and ice. This is an excellent base

for day hikes up the Glomdal valley or to the Flatisen glacier.

For the western and more dramatic Svartisen icecap, see p285.

SALTFJELLET

The broad upland plateaus of the Saltfjellet massif transcend the Arctic Circle, connecting the peaks surrounding the Svartisen icecap and the Swedish border. Within this relatively inhospitable wilderness are traces of several ancient Sami fences and sacrificial sites, some dating from as early as the 9th century.

A 15km walk to the east leads to Graddis, near the Swedish border, and the venerable **Graddis Fjellstue og Camping** (☎75 69 43 41; graddis@c2i.net; s/d from Nkr480/620; ☺mid-Jun–mid-Aug). This cosy little guesthouse has been run by the same family since its establishment in 1867. It makes an excellent base to launch yourself into one of Norway's least-tramped hiking areas. Camping is also available, and Methuselah, a 1000-year-old pine tree, is a nearby attraction.

By car, access to Saltfjellet is either along the E6 or the Rv77, which follows the southern slope of the Junkerdalen valley. Rail travellers can disembark at Lønsdal en route between Fauske and Trondheim. Check whether you need to request a stop.

Arctic Circle Centre

Latitude 66°33' N marks the southernmost extent of the midnight sun on the summer solstice and the ragged edge of the polar night on the winter solstice. As the Arctic Highway between Mo i Rana and Fauske cuts across this imaginary line, it should be a magical moment.

But the **Polarsirkelsenteret** (www.polarsirkelsenteret.no; optional exhibition adult/child Nkr50/20; ☺May–mid-Sep), beside the E6 and surrounded by the bleak moors that roll in from Saltfjellet-Svartisen National Park, is something of a tourist trap. There's an exhibition of stuffed wildlife and an audiovisual presentation on the Arctic regions. However, the place exists mostly to stamp postcards with a special Arctic Circle postmark and sell certificates (Nkr99) for visitors to authenticate their crossing the line. Boreal kitsch is flogged here by the basketload – leering trolls, woolly reindeer, fluffy polar bears and briefs emblazoned with 'Arctic Circle' to show off to your more intimate friends back home. On the plus side, as its website choos-

ARTSCAPE NORDLAND

You'll spot them on lonely promontories and windswept moorland, tucked beneath crags, in urban parks or lapped by the sea. As you travel through Nordland, follow the sign *Skulpturlandskap* to discover a work of creative modern sculpture, enhancing and in harmony with the landscape around it. In all, 33 works were commissioned from prominent sculptors in Norway, other Scandinavian countries and the wider international community. Representatives of 18 nations, including artists such as Antony Gormley, Anish Kapoor and Tony Cragg, have each left their individual mark upon the Nordland countryside. For more on this ambitious project, see www. artscape.no.

es to highlight, it has 'very good lavatory facilities'. Outside and altogether more sober and serious are the memorials to Slav forced labourers who, during WWII, constructed the Arctic Highway for the occupying Nazi forces and died far from home.

Northbound travellers will feel spirits rising again as they leave these bleak uplands and descend into a relatively lush, green environment that's much more typical of northern Norway.

Fauske

POP 9500

Fauske is known mainly for fine marble. Its 'Norwegian Rose' stone features in many a monumental building, including the Oslo Rådhus, the UN headquarters in New York and the Emperor's palace in Tokyo. The town is also the jumping-off point for Sulitjelma and the Rago National Park.

The seasonal **tourist office** (☎75 50 35 15; Sjøgata; ⏰9am-4pm Mon-Sat, 11am-4pm Sun mid-Jun–mid-Aug) shares its premises with the main building of Salten museum.

Sights include the marble-themed **town square**, and the parklike collection of historic buildings of the Fauske branch of **Salten museum** (www.saltenmuseum.no; Sjøgata; adult/child Nkr35/10; ⏰11am-5pm mid-Jun–mid-Aug), whose grounds are a lovely spot for a picnic.

🍴 Sleeping & Eating

Fauske Hotell HOTEL **€€**
(☎75 60 20 00; www.rica.no; Storgata 82; s/d from Nkr750/1000) Fauske's only year-round upmarket choice has cheerful rooms although common areas feel decidedly dated. Its **restaurant** (mains Nkr68-130) does an Arctic Menu. **Brygga Hotell** (⏰mid-Jun–end Jul), its less monolithic 30-room annexe right beside the fjord, is an attractive alternative should you pass through town during the brief window when it's open.

Lundhøgda Camp & Café CAMPGROUND **€**
(☎75 64 39 66; www.lundhogdacamping.no; Lundveien; car/caravan site Nkr160/190, 2-/4-bed cabin Nkr375/475 with bathroom 675/775; ⏰May-Sep) This complex, 3km west of town, has superb views of the fjord and surrounding peaks.

ℹ Getting There & Away

Bus

There are three to six buses daily running to/from Bodø (Nkr114; 1½ hours). The express bus from Bodø to Narvik (Nkr438; five hours) passes through Fauske twice daily.

Train

Trains ply the Nordlandsbanen between Trondheim (Nkr947, 9¼ hours) and Bodø (Nkr115, 45 minutes), via Fauske, twice daily and there are additional trains (up to four daily) between Fauske and Bodø. To continue further northwards, you've no option but to hop on a bus.

Around Fauske

SALTDAL & MUSEUMS

Just off the E6 near Saltnes, **Saltdal Historical Village** (adult/child Nkr35/10; ⏰11am-5pm mid-Jun–mid-Aug) is a collection of typical rural and fishing-related buildings. Reception and cafe (try the local speciality, *møsbromlefse*, a sweetish light pancake laced with cream and cheese) are in the Skippergården building.

The moving **Blodveimuseet** (Blood Road Museum; adult/child Nkr35/10; ⏰11am-5pm mid-Jun–mid-Aug), in a former German barracks within the museum grounds, is visited by a 30-minute guided tour. It reveals conditions for Slav and Russian forced labourers who forged the road and railway northwards. The prisoners' cemetery, with the remains of some 7000 men, and the nearby graveyard for German soldiers are in **Botn**, about 3km north.

SULITJELMA

As an interpretive panel just north of Fauske will confirm, you're exactly halfway along the E6. By now, you're probably eager to strangle every slow-moving motorhome driver on its two-lane highway, so it's an appropriate moment to break free from the Arctic Highway for a short while.

It's a gorgeous 40km run along the Rv830, up scenic Langvassdalen to the tiny community of Sulitjelma. It wasn't always such a backwater; in 1860 a Sami herder discovered copper ore in the forested country north of Langvatnet and suddenly the Sulitjelma region was attracting all sorts of opportunists from southern Norway. Large ore deposits were revealed and the Sulitjelma Gruber mining company was founded in 1891. By 1928 the wood-fuelled smelter had taken its toll on the surrounding birch forests, as did high concentrations of carbon dioxide, a byproduct of the smelting process. Nowadays, with the furnaces long since cold, the environment is well on its way to recovery.

◉ Sights & Activities

Gruvemuseum MINING MUSEUM
(adult/child Nkr30/10; ⊙11am-5pm daily mid-Jun–mid-Aug, 9am-3pm Mon-Fri rest of yr) Alongside the fjord, the Sulitjelma Mining Museum records the area's 100 years of mining history and displays some awesome rusting equipment.

Besøksgruve SHOW MINE
(adult/child Nkr200/50) A one-hour guided tour of the Sulitjelma Show Mine includes a 1.5km rail ride deep into the mountain. In 2010 it was closed for maintenance.

RAGO NATIONAL PARK

The small (171 sq km), scarcely visited Rago National Park is a rugged chunk of forested granite mountain and moorland, riven with deep glacial cracks and capped by great icefields. Rago, together with the large adjoining Swedish parks, Pakjelanta, Sarek and Stora Sjöfjallet, belongs to a wider protected area of 5500 sq km. Wildlife includes not only beavers in the deep Laksåga (aka Nordfjord) river valley, but also wolverines in the higher areas. Along the relatively lush Storskogdalen valley, a series of foaming cascades and spectacular waterfalls tumble.

From the main trailhead at Lakshol, it's a three-hour, 7km walk up the valley to the free Storskogvasshytta and Ragohytta huts, then a stiff climb up and over the ridge into

Sweden to connect with the well-established trail system over the border.

Maps to use are *Sisovatnet*, at 1:50,000, or *Sørfold*, at 1:75,000. To reach Lakshol, turn east off the E6 at the Trengsel bridge and continue about 6km to the end of the road.

Narvik
POP 18,450

Narvik is pincered by islands to the west and mountains in every other direction, while spectacular fjords stretch north and south. The town is a relative youngster, established in 1902 as an ice-free port for the rich Kiruna iron mines in Swedish Lapland. Recently it has begun to capitalise on the unique sporting and sightseeing activities offered by its majestic surroundings and the spectacular Ofotbanen railway to Sweden.

◉ Sights

Ofoten Museum FOLK MUSEUM
(Administrasjonsveien 3; adult/child Nkr50/free; ⊙10am-3pm or 4pm daily mid-Jun–mid-Aug, Mon-Fri rest of yr) The museum tells of Narvik's farming, fishing, railway-building and ore transshipment heritage. There's a rolling film about the Ofotbanen Railway and children will enjoy pressing the button that activates the model train. Linger too over the display case of Sami costumes and artefacts and the collection of historic photos, contrasted with modern shots taken from the same angles. To reach the museum, take the minor road beside the restored building that served as Narvik's post office from 1888 to 1898.

Red Cross War Museum WAR MUSEUM
(Kongens gate; adult/child Nkr50/25; ⊙10am-4pm or 9pm Mon-Sat, noon-4pm or 6pm Sun) This small but revealing museum illustrates the military campaigns fought hereabouts in the early years of WWII. The presentation may not be flash but it will still move you. Pick up a folder that explains each of the museum's sections.

Water Spout WATER JET
No, Narvik can't claim geothermal activity. But locals reckon that its water is the purest in the land. Each day at 1pm and 9pm from May to September, a valve is released and a mighty 75m-high plume of water spurts skywards. Clearly visible from town, it's even more impressive up close at the viewpoint beside Norvik's hydropower station. The fine spray is a source of huge fun for kids in rain gear and you might see a magic rainbow

During WWII control of this strategic port was essential to the Nazi war machine, intent upon halting iron supplies to the Allies and usurping the bounty. In April 1940, 10 German destroyers ploughed through a blizzard to enter the port and sink two Norwegian battleships. Next day five British destroyers arrived and a fierce naval battle resulted in the loss of two ships on each side. In May, British, Norwegian, French and Polish troops disembarked and took back the town.

The Nazis, however, didn't retreat and the town was decimated, as evidenced by the remains of soldiers in the cemeteries and 34 ships of five nations (Norway, Britain, France, the Netherlands and Germany) in the harbour. On 8 June 1940 the Allies surrendered Narvik, which remained under German control until 8 May 1945.

Although the town was admirably rebuilt, downtown Narvik is less than prepossessing (some would say it's ugly). Still, the surrounding fjord, forest and mountain country borders on the spectacular in all directions, and the trans-shipment facility bisecting the city still loads several million tonnes of ore annually from train wagons onto ships.

through the droplets. To get there, take the road that rises eastwards opposite the Best Western Narvik Hotel.

Main Cemetery WAR GRAVES
In this cemetery, beside the E6 on the north side of town, are monuments to the French and Polish troops who fought alongside the Norwegians on land, and the graves of German defenders and British sailors who died at sea.

🏃 Activities

Narvik og Omegns Turistforening (NOT; www.turistforeningen.no/narvik) is an excellent source of information about hiking. It maintains more than 20 cabins, mostly between Narvik and the Swedish border. Collect keys from the tourist office against a deposit of Nkr100.

Narvikfjellet CABLE CAR
(Mårveien; www.narvikfjellet.no; adult/child return Nkr100/free; ⊘1-9pm or 1am Jun-Aug, shorter hr Feb-Apr) Climbing 656m above town, this cable car offers breathtaking views over the surrounding peaks and fjords – even as far as Lofoten on a clear day. Several marked walking trails radiate from its top station or you can bounce down a signed mountain-bike route. From February to April, it will whisk you up high for trail, off-piste and cross-country skiing with outstanding views.

Rallarveien HIKING TRAIL
This popular hike parallels the Ofotbanen railway, following the Rallarveien, an old navvy (railway worker) trail. Few walkers attempt the entire way between Sweden's Abisko National Park and the sea, opting

instead to begin at Riksgränsen, the small ski station just across the Swedish border, or Bjørnfell, the next station west. It's an undemanding descent as far as Katterat, from where you can take the evening train to Narvik. For more exertion, drop down to Rombaksbotn at the head of the fjord and site of the main camp when the railway was being built (it's since returned to nature). From here, a **boat** (adult/child Nkr280/100) runs erratically to Narvik in summer. Check with the tourist office to avoid an unwelcome supplementary 10km at the end of the day.

Narvik Golfklubb SCENIC GOLF COURSE
(www.narvikgolf.no, in Norwegian) The fjord-side journey to this unique golf course at Skjomendalen is wondrous (follow the signs to Skjomdal just before the Skjomen bridge on the E6, about 18km south of town). Sheer, treacherous faces will leave you guessing how there could possibly be a golf course here. Yet nature works wonders, and there's a valley hidden amid the peaks. Find golf a bore? There's also worthwhile hiking nearby.

Fjord Cruise Narvik OUTDOOR ADVENTURE
(📞91 39 06 18; www.fcn.no) This outfit mounts summer fishing and sea-eagle viewing trips. From November to mid-January, when the orcas (killer whales) gather to gorge themselves on the winter herring run, it runs trips to their feeding grounds in search of the action.

🎉 Festivals & Events
Each year during March, Narvik holds its **Vinterfestuka**, an action-packed winter week of events, partly in commemoration of the navvies who built the railway.

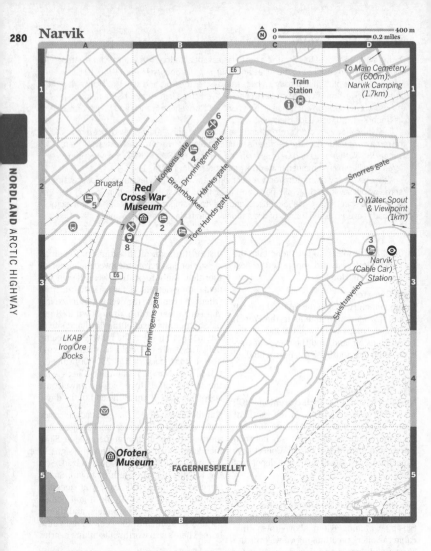

Narvik

◉ Top Sights
Ofoten Museum	A5
Red Cross War Museum	B2

🛏 Sleeping
1 Breidablikk Gjestehus	B2
2 Narvik Vandrerhjem	B2
3 Best Western Narvik Hotell	D3
4 Quality Hotel Grand Royal	B2
5 Spor 1 Gjestegård	A2

🍴 Eating
6 Baguetten	B1
7 Fiskehallen	A2
Rallar'n	(see 4)
Victoria Café	(see 2)

🍷 Drinking
8 Litt Større Plass	A3

No one knows for sure whether there actually was a comely cook nicknamed Svarta Bjørn (Black Bear) who dished up meals for the navvies (railway workers) who built the railway of the Ofoten line. But her name certainly lives on in legend and in fiction. In his Malm trilogy, published in 1914, novelist Ernst Didring recounts some of the stories the navvies passed on to him.

It's said that this dark, beautiful girl, although still too young to be away from home, got on well with the rail workers and was a great little cook into the bargain. But she fell in love with the same man that another woman coveted and was beaten to death with a laundry paddle.

It's said that the navvies arranged for her burial at the Tornehamn cemetery. Today, the grave site bears the name of Anna Norge, but the date of death has been changed at least three times to fit different women who at different times have been assumed to be the genuine Svarta Bjørn.

On the last Saturday in June, some 2000 walkers take the train to various stops along the Rallarveien, then hike back to party at Rombaksbotn.

Tours

The tourist office puts on a **bus tour** (adult/child Nkr160/free; ⊙11am Fri mid-Jun–mid-Aug) of Narvik and its environs, including a visit to the massive LKAB iron ore trans-shipment complex, an impressive tangle of machinery, conveyors, ovens and hillocks of iron pellets, where an average tanker-load of ore, weighing in at 125,000 to 175,000 tonnes, takes an entire day to fill.

It also mounts an equivalent **walking tour** each Monday, leaving at 11am.

Sleeping

TOP CHOICE Norumgården Bed & Breakfast

B&B €

(☏76 94 48 57; http://norumgaarden.narviknett.no; Framnesveien 127; s/d Nkr450/600, d with kitchen Nkr600; ⊙late Jan-Nov) This little treasure of a place (it has only four rooms so reservations are essential) is very special and offers excellent value. Used as a German officer's mess in WWII (the owner will proudly show you a 1940 bottle of Coca Cola, made under licence in Hamburg), nowadays it brims with antiques and character. Choose the Heidi room (it's the only one without a shower but the little balcony more than compensates) and you'll be sleeping in the bed once occupied by King Olav. Cross the bridge beside the bus station and head west for about 1km.

TOP CHOICE Spor 1 Gjestegård HOSTEL, GUESTHOUSE €

(☏76 94 60 20; www.spor1.no; Brugata 2a; dm Nkr230, s/d with shared bathroom Nkr500/600; ☎) Welcoming 'Track 1' is indeed right beside the railway track but don't worry, the sound insulation's good. Britt Larsen and her partner, both Narvik born and bred and seasoned world travellers, run this delightful place. It has the facilities of the best of hostels (especially the gleaming, well-equipped guest kitchen) and the comfort and taste of a guesthouse (bright, cheerful fabrics and decor and soft duvets). Next door, and run by the same family, is a great **pub** (⊙Tue-Sat) with outdoor terrace.

Breidablikk Gjestehus GUESTHOUSE €€

(☏76 94 14 18; www.breidablikk.no, in Norwegian; Tore Hunds gate 41; dm/s/d from Nkr250/995/1195; P@☎) It's a steep but worthwhile walk from the centre to this pleasant hillside guesthouse with rooms for all budgets and sweeping views over town and fjord. There's a cosy communal lounge and it serves a delicious buffet breakfast (Nkr50). Dorms have four or six beds.

Narvik Vandrerhjem HOSTEL €€

(☏76 94 66 15; www.hihostels.no/narvik; Dronningens gate 58; dm Nkr350, s/d Nkr750/950; P@☎) Narvik's smart but overpriced HI hostel is a friendly place with a good on-site cafe and ample self-catering facilities. Its 48 beds are quickly snapped up in summer so do reserve.

Best Western Narvik Hotell HOTEL €€

(☏76 96 48 00; www.narvikhotell.no; Skistuaveien 8; s/d from Nkr850/1050; P@☎) This 90-room tour-group favourite, stretching long and low at the base of the cable car, offers great vistas. Accommodation is in comfortable chalet-type buildings.

Quality Hotel Grand Royal HOTEL €€€

(☏76 97 70 00; www.choice.no; Kongens gate 64; s/d from Nkr1090/1290; P@☎) Narvik's top hotel, although something of a monolith from the exterior, makes an attractive stop-over. It has a beauty salon and a few rooms equipped for travellers with disabilities.

Narvik Camping
CAMPGROUND €

(☎76 94 58 10; www.narvikcamping.com; Rombaksveien 75; tent/caravan site Nkr120/200; 2-bed cabin Nkr300, 4-/6-bed cabin with bathroom Nkr650/800) Sound sleep's not guaranteed for those under canvas at what's otherwise a perfectly adequate campground, overlooking the fjord and E6, 2km northeast of the centre and Narvik's only choice. Trucks rumble along the highway and long wagon trains clank by on the railway, just above.

✖ Eating

Victoria Café
CAFE €

(☎76 96 28 00; Dronningens gate 58; ⊙11am-5pm Mon-Fri) On the ground floor of Narvik's youth hostel and open to all-comers, this light, pleasant, self-service cafe serves snacks and a range of main dishes.

Fiskehallen
FISH CAFE €

(☎76 94 36 60; Kongens gate 42; mains Nkr80-150; ⊙11am-4.30pm Mon-Fri) This tiny cafe, offshoot of the adjacent fish shop, offers tasty ready-to-eat dishes, such as fish cakes, bacalao and whale stew, to eat in or take away.

Rallar'n
BAR, RESTAURANT €€€

(☎76 97 70 77; Kongens gate 64; daily special Nkr145, mains Nkr200-295; ⊙1pm-1am) The pub/restaurant of Quality Hotel Grand Royal is all atmospheric low ceilings, bare brick and dark woodwork. Divided into intimate compartments, it offers pizza, pasta and creative mains.

Baguetten
CAFE €

(Kongens gate 66; ⊙Mon-Sat) Opposite Vinmonopolet on the top floor of the Narvik Storsenter, the Baguette will serve you rich cakes and Narvik's best coffee.

🍷 Drinking & Entertainment

Litt Større Plass (Dronningensgate 45) is a rough and ready, take-us-as-you-find-us bar run by a group of ski fanatics. It's popular with a young crowd and guaranteed to impart human warmth on even the coldest night.

In winter you can tumble out of the cable car into the bar at the **Best Western Narvik Hotell**, Narvik's leading après-ski venue.

ℹ Information

The **tourist office** (☎76 96 56 00; www.destinationnarvik.com; ⊙9am-6pm Mon-Fri, 10am-5.30pm Sat & Sun mid-Jun–mid-Aug, variable rest of yr) is at the train station. It has internet access (Nkr10 per 15 min) and rents bikes (Nkr200 per day). Allow time to view its 25-minute film about the Ofotbanen railway and browse its small display of arts and crafts in northern Norway.

ℹ Getting There & Away

Air

Nearly all flights leave from Harstad/Narvik Evenes airport, 1¼ hours away by road. Narvik's tiny Framneslia airport, about 3km west of the centre, serves only Bodø, Tromsø and Andenes.

Bus

Express buses run northwards to Tromsø (Nkr360, 4¼ hours, three daily) and south to Bodø (Nkr534, 6½ hours, two daily) via Fauske (Nkr407, five hours). For Lofoten, two Lofotekspressen buses run daily between Narvik and Svolvær (Nkr225 or Nkr425, 4¼ hours) and continue to Å.

Between late June and early September, bus 91 runs twice a day up the E10 to Riksgränsen (45 minutes) in Sweden and on to Abisko and Kiruna (three hours).

Train

Heading for Sweden, there are two daily services between Narvik and Riksgränsen (one hour), on the border, and Kiruna (three hours). Trains continue to Lulea (7¼ hours) via Boden, from where you can pick up connections to Stockholm. The route takes you up the spectacular Ofotbanen Railway and, in Sweden, past Abisko National Park, which offers excellent hiking and lovely Arctic scenery.

ℹ Getting Around

Narvik's Framneslia airport is 3km from the centre. Flybuss runs four to eight times daily between Narvik and Harstad/Narvik Evenes airport (Nkr210, 1¼ hours), 79km away.

For a taxi, phone **Narvik Taxi** (☎07 550).

Ofotbanen Railway & Rallarveien

The spectacular mountain-hugging **Ofotbanen railway** (☎76 92 31 21) trundles beside fjord-side cliffs, birch forests and rocky plateaus as it climbs to the Swedish border. The railway, which opened in 1903, was constructed by migrant labourers at the end of the 19th century to connect Narvik with the iron-ore mines at Kiruna, in Sweden's far north. Currently it transports around 15 million tonnes of iron ore annually and is also a major magnet for visitors.

The train route from Narvik to Riksgränsen, the ski resort just inside Sweden (one way adult/child Nkr100/free, one hour), features some 50 tunnels and snowsheds. Towards the Narvik end of the rail line, you might make out the wreck of the German ship *Georg Thiele* at the edge of the fjord.

You can run the line as a day or half-day trip, leaving Narvik at 10.26am. The 11.39pm return train from Riksgränsen allows time for coffee and a quick browse or you can walk a trail in this stunning alpine country and catch the 4.02pm back to Narvik. For the best views, sit on the left side heading from Narvik.

Meteorologen Ski Lodge (☑46-7350 324 17 in Sweden; www.meteorologen.se; s/d from Nkr1000/1490; P@) Occupying what was originally a weather station, this is a very attractive option should you wish to overnight up high. Rooms all have large windows giving vistas of either lake or mountains and there's a pleasant dining room and restaurant, primarily for guests. It also manages self-catering apartments year-round (three-/six-person Nkr800/1000) in the vast adjacent winter hotel.

In Sweden, several long-distance trails radiate out from the railway, including the world-renowned Kungsleden, which heads south from Abisko into the heart of Sweden.

KYSTRIKSVEIEN – THE COASTAL ROUTE

Longer, yes, more expensive, yes (gosh, those ferry tolls mount up). But if you've even a day or two to spare, divert from the Arctic Highway lemming-run and enjoy the empty roads and solitary splendours of Kystriksveien, the coastal alternative. If the whole route seems daunting, it's quite possible to cut in or out from Steinkjer, Bodø or, midway, Mosjøen and Mo i Rana. It's one to drive; don't even attempt it by bus or you'll still be waiting when the first snows fall.

Off the coast are around 14,000 islands, some little more than rocks with a few tufts of grass, others, such as Vega, supporting whole communities that for centuries have survived on coastal fishing and subsistence agriculture. The sea was the only highway and the living was harsh year-round – especially between mid-January and Easter, when the menfolk would be absent, working the fishing grounds off Lofoten for cod.

ℹ Information

The splendid free *Kystriksveien* (Coastal Route) booklet, distributed by tourist offices and many lodgings along the way, is a mini-Bible. Its website, www.rv17.no, gives even more detail. For greater depth, invest in *The Coastal Road: A Travel Guide to Kystriksveien* (Nkr298) by Olav Breen.

Click on www.rv17.no/sykkel for a recommended 12-day bike-and-ferry journey along the full length of the Kystriksveien. The free brochure *Cycling from Steinkjer to Leka* has detailed maps, and lists highlights and bicycle-friendly accommodation.

For information on the southern part of Kystriksveien, see p258.

Brønnøysund
POP 7650

Brønnøysund is flanked on one side by an archipelago of islets and on the other by rolling farm country.

⦿ Sights & Activities
Hildurs Urterarium   GARDENS, RESTAURANT
(www.urterariet.com, in Norwegian; Tilrem; adult/child Nkr40/free; ⊙10am-5pm mid-Jun–mid-Aug). Around 400 types of herb, 100 varieties of rose and 1000 species of cactus flourish at Hilde's Herb Garden. At Tilrem, about 6km north of Brønnøysund, the team also produce their own wine. There are some rustic old farm buildings, a small art gallery and a shop carries locally grown products. The garden also makes a lovely stop for lunch, where dishes are seasoned with locally grown herbs, of course.

Torghatten   PEAK
A significant local landmark rears up from Torget island, some 15km south of Brønnøysund. The peak, pierced by a hole 160m long, 35m high and 20m wide, is accessed from its base by a good 20-minute walking track. The best perspective of the gap is from the southbound Hurtigruten coastal ferry as it rounds the island. For the lowdown on the legend of Torghatten, see p408.

☞ Tours
This one's a real winner. The tourist office sells tickets for a spectacular **minicruise** (adult/child Nkr363/182) on the Hurtigruten. Leaving at 5pm, the coastal ferry passes Torghatten on its way south to Rørvik in Trøndelag – allowing an hour to explore the town and visit its splendid Norveg Centre for Coastal Culture and Industries before you hop aboard the northbound ferry to reach Brønnøysund again at 1am.

🛏 Sleeping & Eating

The Brønnøysund tourist office can book private farm cabins and *rorbuer* (Nkr600 to Nkr900) accommodating four to eight people.

Torghatten Camping CAMPGROUND €
(☑75 02 54 95; www.visittorghatten.no; tent/caravan site Nkr100/140, 4-6-bed cabin with bathroom Nkr900, 6-bed apt from Nkr1000) This lovely option with its small beach beside a constructed lake is great for children. Around 10km southwest of Brønnøysund, it's handy for an ascent of the Torghatten peak.

Galeasen Hotell HOTEL €€
(☑75 00 88 50; www.galeasen.com, in Norwegian; Havnegata 32-36; s/d from Nkr880/1180) The 22-room Galeasen sits right beside the quay and runs a small restaurant. Ask for a room in the more recent main building, not the less-attractive annexe, which occupies a converted fish-processing plant.

ℹ Information

Brønnøysund's **tourist office** (☑75 01 80 00; www.visithelgeland.com; ⊙9am-6pm Mon-Fri, 10am-6pm Sat & Sun mid-Jun–mid-Aug, 10am-3pm Mon-Fri rest of yr) is one block from the Hurtigruten quay. It rents bicycles (Nkr150 per day).

ℹ Getting There & Away

There are at least five daily flights to/from Trondheim; the approach route passes right over Torghatten and the azure seas that lap around it.

Up to three buses run between Brønnøysund and Sandnessjøen (Nkr200, 3½ hours, daily except Sunday) and to/from Mosjøen (three hours, once or twice daily except Saturday).

Brønnøysund is also a port for the Hurtigruten coastal ferry.

Vega

POP 1300

The island of Vega remains a very Norwegian destination (we were the only non-nationals on our ferry journeys to and from the island). It and the more than 6000 skerries, islets and simply large rocks that form the Vega archipelago are a Unesco World Heritage Site. This distinction comes not for any grand building or monument, nor for the scenery (which is stunning, nevertheless). It's for human endeavour, recognising that the archipelago reflects the way generations of fisherfolk and farmers have, over the past 1500 years, maintained a sustainable living in an inhospitable seascape. This lifestyle is based on the now unique practice of eider-down harvesting, undertaken mostly by women. For more on these very special ducks and their down, visit the splendid little E-huset (E-house) museum or click on www.verdensarvvega.no or www.lanan.no.

◉ Sights

TOP CHOICE **E-huset** MUSEUM
(☑415 07 364; adult/child Nkr35/free; ⊙noon-4pm daily mid-Jun–mid-Aug) In the tiny fishing hamlet of Nes, this delightful, engagingly informative small museum celebrates the eider duck and the way the birds were nurtured as domestic pets, when they returned – each one to its very same nesting box – after their winter migration. The E-house occupies a former trading post, which still retains its original counter and row upon row of goods that your great-grandparents used to buy.

🛏 Sleeping & Eating

TOP CHOICE **Vega Havhotell** HOTEL €€
(☑75 03 64 00; www.havhotellene.no, in Norwegian; Viksås; s/d Nk1090/1390; ⊙closed Oct & Mon Nov-Mar) This isolated getaway, down a dirt track at Vega's secluded northern limit, is tranquillity itself (you won't find a radio or TV in any of its 21 rooms). It's a place to unwind, go for breezy coastal strolls or simply watch the mother eider duck and her chicks pottering in the pool below. Even if you don't stay overnight, call by to enjoy the fine fare, sourced locally for the most part, of its gourmet **restaurant** (lunch Nkr295, 5-course dinner Nkr650), where reservations are essential.

Vega Camping CAMPGROUND €
(☑943 50 080; http://hjem.monet.no/camping, in Norwegian; Floa; car/caravan site Nkr150/165, 4-bed cabin Nkr550, apartment Nkr550-680; ⊙year round) The close-cropped green grass extending to the still water's edge make this simple campground one of the prettiest in Norway. You can rent a boat or bike (Nkr250/100 per day) or go for a trot at the adjacent horse-riding school.

ℹ Information

Vega's **tourist office** (☑75 03 53 88; www.vega.kommune.no; ⊙9am-7pm Mon-Fri, 9.30am-3.30pm Sat & Sun mid-Jun–mid-Aug, 8.30am-3.30pm rest of yr) is in Gladstad, the island's largest hamlet.

ℹ Getting There & Away

Express boats make the trip to/from both Brønnøysund and Sandnessjøen, while car ferries cross to Vega from the mainland at Horn and Tjøtta.

Sandnessjøen

POP 5800

Watching over Sandnessjøen, the main commercial centre of Nordland's southern coast, is the imposing Syv Søstre (Seven Sisters) range, just to its south. Hardy hikers can reach all seven summits (ranging from 910m to 1072m) in a day. Every several years there's a competition that takes in all the peaks, but don't bust a gut trying to crack the record of three hours, 54 minutes.

Central Sandnessjøen's backbone is pedestrianised Torolv Kveldulvsons gate, one block from the harbour.

🏃 Activities

The tourist office can suggest **walks** in the Syv Søstre range, reached most conveniently via the Rv17 at Breimo or Sørra, about 4km south of town. From there it's a couple of kilometres' walk to its foot. Trails are blazed with red dots but pack *Alstahaug*, a reliable map at 1:50,000. Sign your name in the book at each summit, fill in a control card and leave it at the tourist office and be proud of the diploma that will be sent to you.

🛏 Sleeping

Rica Hotel Sandnessjøen HOTEL €€
(☑75 06 50 00; www.rica.no; Torolv Kveldulvsons gate 16; s/d from Nkr850/1050) Sandnessjøen's top-end choice, this large hotel with 69 trim rooms offers all the comfort you'd expect from a member of the Rica chain.

ℹ Information

The **tourist office** (☑75 04 45 00; www.helge landskysten.com; ⊘9am-7pm Mon-Fri, 10am-3pm Sat, noon-3pm Sun mid-Jun–mid-Aug, 10am-3pm Mon-Fri rest of yr) is by the docks. It hires bicycles (Nkr50/175 per hour/day) and has internet access (Nkr1 per minute).

ℹ Getting There & Away

There are direct flights to Bodø, Trondheim, Mo i Rana and Mosjøen.

Bus destinations from Sandnessjøen include Brønnøysund (3½ hours, daily except Sunday), Mosjøen (1¾ hours, three to five daily except Saturday), Mo i Rana (2¾ hours, one to three services daily).

Sandnessjøen is also a stop for the Hurtigruten coastal ferry.

Træna & Lovund

Træna is an archipelago of over 1000 small, flat skerries, five of which are inhabited.

Ferries from the mainland dock on the island of Husøy, which has most of Træna's population and lodgings, but the main sights are on the adjacent island of Sanna. This drop in the ocean is just over 1km long with a miniature mountain range running the length of its spine and culminating at the northern end in the 318m spire, Trænstaven.

Near Sanna's southern end, archaeologists discovered a cemetery and artefacts (now at the Tromsø Museum) a good 9000 years old inside the cathedral-like **Kirkehelleren Cave**.

Prolific bird colonies roost on the steep-sided island of **Lovund**, which rises 623m above the sea. Every 14 April the island (home to barely 250 people) celebrates Lundkommardag, the day 200,000 puffins return to the island to nest until mid-August.

Express passenger boats connecting Sandnessjøen and Træna run daily.

Stokkvågen to Storvik

If you do only one segment of the coastal highway, make it the length between Stokkvågen, west of Mo i Rana, and the broad sandy beach at Storvik, 100km south of Bodø. This stretch is a National Tourist Route, a designation awarded only to the most scenic of scenic roads.

From Mo i Rana to the coast, it's a dramatic run in its own right alongside pretty **Ranafjord**, where you can roam around the Nazi coastal fort of **Grønsvik**, one of more than 350 defences built along Norway's coastline.

The vistas will drain you of superlatives as you follow the coast northwards, cross the Arctic Circle and run within sight of islands, islets and skerries too numerous to count, while sea eagles wheel and peer for prey above you. Wildflowers show off their best in the relatively mild climate, warmed by the very last of the Gulf Stream's flow and for long stretches the highway rolls right beside the water. You catch enticing glimpses of the Svartisen glacier from the Kilboghamn-Jektvik and Ågskardet-Forøy ferries, supplemented by magnificent views from the road alongside Holandsfjorden.

From Holand, a **ferry** (☑47 99 40 30; adult/child return Nkr90/50) makes the 10-minute trip across Holandsfjorden roughly hourly. You can hire a bike (three/six hours Nkr40/60) to travel the 3km gravel track between the jetty and the tip of the Engebreen glacial tongue.

A 15-minute walk from the ferry landing takes you to the **Svartisen Turistsenter** (☑75 75 10 00; http://svartisen.com/; ⊘Jun–mid-Aug) with its cafe, shop and restaurant. It does guided one- to two-hour glacier walks (Nkr400) and longer four- to five-hour treks (Nkr800) from the end of Engabrevatnet lake. Reserve in advance. You can also slog independently up the steep route along the glacier's edge to the Tåkeheimen hut (1171m), near the summit of Helgelandsbukken (1454m). Follow the 'T' markers and allow eight hours out and back.

Holand Hytter (☑415 76 528; walterjoh@combitel.no; cabin Nkr600-900) has two attractive cabins, each with bathroom and kitchen. Both are a short walk from the Svartisen ferry jetty and the larger one can accommodate up to eight.

Furøy Camping (☑75 75 05 25; www.furoy camp.no; Forøy; tent/caravan site Nkr150/180, cabin Nkr500-900, room from Nkr600) Keep the children quiet as you work your way along the Kystriksveien with the promise of the five-star playground, complete with trampoline and minicabins, at this campground, barely 1km from the Ågskardet-Førøy ferry terminal. Adults can soak in the hot tub (Nkr100 for up to six people) and everyone can savour the magnificent views of the Startisen glacier across the fjord. Do reserve your cabin in advance; a trail of vehicles heads from the ferry towards reception.

Bodø

POP 47,300

Bodø, Nordland's largest town, was founded in 1816 as a trade centre, then turned to fishing in 1860 during an especially lucrative herring boom. The town centre, rebuilt after being almost completely levelled by WWII bombing, is unexciting architecturally – and in summer it can reek of the fish that sustain it – but it's open, tidy and has a pleasant marina. The city's main charm lies in its backdrop of distant rugged peaks and vast skies. Dramatic islands that support the world's densest concentration of white-tailed sea eagles – not for nothing is Bodø known as the Sea Eagle Capital – dot the seas to the north.

Many holidaymakers bypass Bodø in their rush to reach the far north or simply leap on a ferry to Lofoten. However, it's a great place to spend a day or two and acts as the gateway to Norway's true north; only 63km west of Fauske on the Arctic Highway, it's the northern terminus of Norway's railway system and marks the northernmost point of the staggeringly beautiful Kystriksveien coastal route.

◉ Sights

Norwegian Aviation Museum MUSEUM
(Norsk Luftfartsmuseum; www.luftfart.museum.no; Olav V gata; adult/child Nkr95/50; ⊘10am-6pm) Norway's aviation museum is huge fun to ramble around if you have even a passing interest in flight and aviation history. Allow at least half a day to roam its 10,000 sq metres. If you're flying into Bodø for real, you'll see that, from above, the striking modern grey and smoked-glass main museum building has the shape of an aeroplane propeller.

Exhibits include a complete control tower and hands-on demonstrations. The affiliated Norwegian Air Force Museum has plenty of examples of historic military and civilian aircraft from the Tiger Moth to the U2 spy plane (the ill-fated US plane that was shot down over the Soviet Union in 1960, creating a major diplomatic incident, was en route from Peshawar in Pakistan to Bodø). Children and kids-at-heart will thrill and shudder at the small simulator, which, for an extra charge, takes you on some pretty harrowing virtual flights, including piloting a fighter jet. Head south along Bankgata, then 750m eastwards along Olav V gata.

Nordland Museum FOLK MUSEUM
(Nordlandmuseet; Prinsens gate 116; adult/child Nkr35/10; ⊘9am-4pm Mon-Fri, 11am-4pm Sat & Sun) Recounting the short history of Bodø, this little gem of a museum has a cheerily entertaining and informative 25-minute film with English subtitles on the town's development. Museum highlights include a mock-up of a fisherman's *rorbu*, a section on Sami culture complete with sod hut, realia relating to the town's fishing heritage and a small hoard of 9th-century Viking treasure.

Bodøsjøen Friluftsmuseum OPEN-AIR MUSEUM
This open-air museum is 3km from town, near Bodøsjøen Camping. Here you'll find 4 hectares of historic homes, farm buildings, boat sheds, WWII German bunkers and the square-rigged sloop, the *Anna Karoline*. You can wander the grounds for free but admission to the buildings is by appointment. Here too is the start of a **walking track** up the river Bodøgårdselva, which eventually leads to the wild, scenic Bodømarka woods.

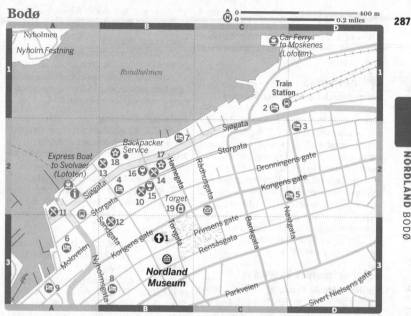

Bodø

Cathedral
CATHEDRAL

(Kongens gate; admission free; ☉noon-3pm mid-Jun–Aug) This striking structure, completed in 1956, has a soaring, freestanding tower and spire. Shaped like an inverted ship's hull, the walls of its nave are clad with tufty, multicoloured tapestries and there's a fine stained-glass window.

Bodin Kirke
CHURCH

(Gamle Riksvei 68; ☉10am-3pm late Jun–mid-Aug) The charming little onion-domed stone church, around 3km from downtown, dates from around 1240. The Lutheran

Reformation brought about substantial changes to the exterior, including the addition of a tower. A host of lively baroque elements – especially the elaborately carved altar – grace the interior.

☆ Activities

Norlandsbadet & Spektrum Velvære

AQUATIC COMPLEX

(www.bodospektrum.no, in Norwegian; Plassmyrveien; adult/child Nkr140/95; ⊙11am-6pm) Here's a very superior place to relax, tone up and warm yourself if it's freezing outside. Exhaust yourself in its six swimming pools (you can zoom down an 85m waterslide and splosh into one of them) then head upstairs to unwind in its six saunas (the one with therapy music and scents perhaps? Or does eucalyptus vapour tempt?). Soak yourself to the skin in the tropical rainforest shower or shiver in the ice grotto.

☆☆ Festivals & Events

Nordland Music Festival

MUSIC

(www.musikkfestuka.no) Ten days of classical music, jazz and opera in the first half of August.

Parken Festival

MUSIC

(www.parkenfestivalen.no, in Norwegian) An action-packed, twin-staged fiesta of rock, R&B and pop over a weekend in late August.

🛏 Sleeping

Skagen Hotel

HOTEL €€

(⌨75 51 91 00; www.skagen-hotel.no; Nyholmsgata 11; s/d from Nkr725/925; @⚏) The Skagen occupies two buildings (one originally a butcher's, though you'd never guess it). Facing each other, they're connected by a passage that burrows beneath the street. Rooms are attractively decorated and a continent away from chain-hotel clones. There's a bar and free afternoon waffles and coffee. Staff can also give advice on a whole raft of vigorous outdoor activities.

Clarion Collection Hotel Grand

HOTEL €€

(⌨75 54 61 00; www.choice.no; Storgata 3; s/d incl breakfast from Nkr795/980; P@⚏) With the resources of the Glasshuset shopping centre right beside it and the shortest of strolls from the quayside, the Grand is well positioned. All rooms were radically overhauled in 2009 and have parquet flooring, new bed linen and duvets and freshly tiled bathrooms with large sinks. Rates include both breakfast and light-buffet dinner, and there's a sauna with steam bath (free to guests).

Thon Hotel Nordlys

HOTEL €€

(⌨75 53 19 00; www.thonhotels.no; Moloveien 14; s/d from Nkr850/1050) Bodø's most stylish hotel, with touches of subtle Scandinavian design throughout, overlooks the marina and runs a reasonable restaurant.

Bodøsjøen Camping

CAMPGROUND €

(⌨75 56 36 80; www.bodocamp.no, in Norwegian; Kvernhusveien 1; tent/caravan site Nkr150/200 plus per person Nkr30, cabin Nkr250-430, with bathroom Nkr690-840) At this waterside campground, 3km from the centre, cabins are particularly well equipped. There's an attractive grassy area with picnic tables exclusively for tent campers. Buses 12 and 23 stop 250m away.

City Hotell

HOTEL €

(⌨75 52 04 02; www.cityhotellbodo.no, in Norwegian; Storgata 39; dm bed Nkr200, s/d Nkr600/700; @⚏) Bodø's newest hotel has 19 smallish but well-priced standard rooms and plenty of flexibility. Three dorms sleeping three to six cater for backpackers – a rarity in a town through which so many hikers and budget travellers pass. Beneath the eaves are a couple of very large family rooms and two rooms have a kitchenette.

Radisson Blu Hotel Bodø

HOTEL €€

(⌨75 51 90 00; www.radissonblu.com; Storgata 2; from s/d Nkr750/995; P⚏@⚏) This contemporary hotel has bright rooms and a top-floor bar to better view the harbour and mountains. Breakfast is served in the Sjøsiden restaurant with its picture windows.

Rica Hotel Bodø

HOTEL €€

(⌨75 54 70 00; www.rica.no; Sjøgata 23; s/d Nkr795/995; ⚏) This is a welcoming, well-managed recent addition to the Rica chain. Its 114 rooms are especially large and the hotel enjoys a prime quayside position.

Opsahl Gjestegård

B&B €€

(⌨75 52 07 04; www.opsahlgjestegaard.no; Prinsens gate 131; s/d Nkr800/1040) On a quiet residential street, this guesthouse has 18 comfortable rooms with decor ranging from flowery to the less florid, and a small bar for guests. New owners have jacked up the prices considerably but it still remains an attractive alternative to hotel life. There are also four apartments with minikitchens.

Bodø Vandrerhjem

HOSTEL €€

(⌨75 50 80 48; www.hihostels.no/bodo; Sjøgata 57; dm Nkr325, d with bathroom Nkr840; @) At last

Bodø has a youth hostel to cater for travellers waiting for the next day's ferry to Lofoten! Brand new and right beside the station, it couldn't be better positioned.

✗ Eating

You can buy inexpensive fresh shrimp at the docks. Inside the Glasshuset shopping centre you'll find a supermarket and several quick-service choices.

Bjørk   CAFE-RESTAURANT €€€
(☑75 52 40 40; www.restaurantbjork.no, in Norwegian; 1st fl, Glasshuset; lunch special Nkr150, mains around Nkr275) This pleasant, relatively new place has quickly become a popular haunt, especially of Bodø's younger movers and shakers. It serves a variety of creative snacks, wood-fired pizzas and sushi and partly occupies the sealed bridge above the shopping mall's main alley so you can snoop upon the shoppers below – one of the reasons why it's also a popular spot for a drink.

Bryggeri Kaia   RESTAURANT-BAR €€€
(☑75 52 58 08; Sjøgata 1; snacks around Nkr160, mains Nkr195-295) Bryggeri Kaia is another firm favourite. You can dine well, snack, enjoy its weekday lunch buffet (Nkr168) or quaff one of its several beers (no longer brewed on the premises, alas). Enjoy your choice in its large pub-decor interior, on the street-side terrace or, best of all should you find a seat spare, on the veranda overlooking the harbour.

Paviljongen   CAFE-RESTAURANT €
(☑75 52 01 11; Torget; mains around Nkr120) This great outdoor spot in the main square is the place to down a coffee or one of its three choices of draught beer; and perhaps nibble on an inexpensive lunch while watching the world pass (see how people adapt their pace to the rhythm of the buskers who strum and play nearby).

Løvolds   CAFE €
(☑75 52 02 61; Tollbugata 9; dishes Nkr105-135, daily special Nkr90-115; ☉9am-6pm Mon-Fri, 9am-3pm Sat) This popular historic quayside cafeteria, Bodø's oldest eating choice, offers sandwiches, grills and hearty Norwegian fare with quality quayside views at no extra charge.

Kafé Kafka   CAFE €
(☑93 40 60 03; Sandgata 5b; daily special with coffee Nkr125, sandwiches Nkr115; ☉11am-1am Mon-Sat, 3pm-midnight Sun; ☎) You couldn't ask for a wider choice at this stylish contemporary cafe. It brews great coffee 12 different ways (you'll smell the aroma before you enter) and

swirls 18 distinct kinds of milkshake. Some weekends, it turns into a club with DJs.

Kaffe Lars   CAFE €
(☑75 52 04 02; Storgata 39; daily special Nkr95; mains Nkr120-135; ☉7.15am-6pm Mon-Fri) Below and belonging to City Hotell, this little place is well priced. The daily special has a choice of fish or meat and mains are rooted in local cuisine.

▼ Drinking & Entertainment

Nordlænningen   MUSIC BAR
(Torvgata; ☉noon-3.30am) This low-key basement pub beside the main square has occasional live music – see the signed posters of bands who've played here as you descend into the depths.

Public   BAR
(Sjøgata 12; ☉8pm-3.30am) Supersized stills from punk-rock shows line the walls of this minimalist bar with its black leather stools.

Rock Café & Nightclub   CLUB
(☑75 50 46 33; Tollbugata 13b; cover charge Nkr50; ☉10pm-3am Fri & Sat) This, the town's largest disco, can cram in more than 500 punters. It puts on live bands about twice a month.

G   CLUB
(☑75 56 17 00; Sjøgata; ☉9pm-3am Fri & Sat) With its cave-like entrance on Sjøgata, below the main square, G is a *discoteka* that packs in the over-25s.

Fram Kino   CINEMA
(Storgata 8) Bodø's cinema is situated near the entrance to the Glasshuset.

Royal Bowling   BOWLING
(☑75 52 28 80; Storgata 2) You can knock some pins down at Royal Bowling, on the ground floor of the Radisson Blu Hotel.

🔒 Shopping

Ludvig's Bruktbokhandel   BOOKSHOP
(Dronningens gate 42) This is the place to stack up on reading material for the long onward drive or ferry journey. Ludvig has a good selection of used books in English (German, Dutch and Russian too) and will accept yours in part-exchange. With old LPs, comics and videos too, his shop is a treasure trove for all addicted browsers.

❶ Information

Backpacker Service (☑75 65 02 89; backpacker@nfk.no; Sjøgata 15-17; ☉10am-6pm late Jun–mid-August; @☎) An excellent service that provides luggage storage, travel information, document printing, a couple of internet points, wi-fi, toilets and use of a tandem bicycle – every last one absolutely free.

Tourist office (☑75 54 80 00; www.visit bodo.com; Sjøgata 3; ⊙9am-8pm Mon-Fri, 10am-6pm Sat, noon-8pm Sun mid-May–Aug, 9am-3.30pm Mon-Fri rest of yr) Publishes the excellent free *Bodø Guide* brochure and has two internet terminals (Nkr60 per hour). Also wi-fi (NKr15). There's a bank of left-luggage lockers (Nkr20 to Nkr50) just outside.

ℹ Getting There & Away

Air

From Bodø's airport, southwest of the city centre, there are at least 10 daily flights to Oslo, Trondheim and Tromsø. Other destinations in northern Norway include Leknes, Narvik, Harstad and Mo i Rana.

Boat

Bodø is a stop on the Hurtigruten coastal ferry.

Car ferries sail five to six times daily in summer (less frequently during the rest of the year) between Bodø and Moskenes on Lofoten (car including driver/passenger Nkr568/158, three to 3½ hours). At least one calls in daily at the tiny southern Lofoten islands of Røst and Værøy. If you're taking a car in summer avoid a potential long wait in line by booking in advance (an additional Nkr100; online reservation at www.torghatten-nord.no).

Most days, at least one ferry calls in at the southern Lofoten islands of Røst and Værøy.

There's also an express passenger ferry between Bodø and Svolvær (adult/child Nkr324/165, 3¾ hours) once daily.

Bus

The Nor-Way Bussekspress bus runs to/from Narvik (Nkr534, 6½ hours) via Fauske (Nkr114, 1½ hours) twice daily.

Train

Main destinations from Bodø:

Fauske Nkr115, 45 minutes, up to five daily

Mosjøen Nkr581; 4¼ hours, two to four daily

Mo i Rana Nkr421, three hours, two to four daily

Trondheim Nkr982, 9¾ hours, two daily

ℹ Getting Around

Local buses cost Nkr30 per ride. The tourist office rents bikes from Nkr100 per day.

Around Bodø

KJERRINGØY

It's easy to see why this sleepy peninsula, washed by turquoise seas and with a back-

drop of soaring granite peaks, is a regular location for Norwegian film-makers.

Bus 10 connects Bodø and Kjerringøy twice daily. In summer it's possible to squeeze in on the same day a return trip that allows a good 2½ hours browsing time. Check the current timetable at Bodø's tourist office.

Whether by bus or car, the trip includes the 10-minute ferry crossing between Festvåg and Misten. Along the way, you pass the distinctive profile of **Landegode Island** (see p408), the white sandy beaches at **Mjelle** (whose car park is some 20 minutes' walk away) and the dramatic peak **Steigtind**, which rises a few kilometres south of Festvåg.

SALTSTRAUMEN MAELSTROM

You need to plan your day to take in this natural phenomenon, guaranteed to occur four times every 24 hours. At the 3km-long, 150m-wide Saltstraumen Strait, the tides cause one fjord to drain into another, creating the equivalent of a waterfall at sea. The result is a churning, 20-knot watery chaos that shifts over 400 million cubic metres of water one way, then the other, every six hours. It's an ideal environment for plankton, which in turn attract an abundance of fish and therefore anglers. In spring, you can also see the squawking colonies of gulls that nest on the midstream island of Storholmen.

This maelstrom, claimed to be the world's largest, is actually a kinetic series of smaller whirlpools that form, surge, coalesce, then disperse.

At its best – which is most of the time – it's an exhilarating spectacle. Should you be unlucky enough to hit an off day, it may recall little more than the water swirling around your bath plug.

Saltstraumen is 32km south of Bodø by road (and much nearer by boat). There are seven buses daily (two on Saturday and Sunday; one hour) between Bodø and Saltstraumen bridge.

LOFOTEN

The pure air in your lungs (except for the strong reek of fish in some of the small ports), daylight around the clock and summer's infinite shades of green and yellow: Lofoten comes as a tonic. You'll never forget your first approach by ferry, especially if you've sailed from Bodø. The islands spread their tall, craggy physique against the sky like some spiky sea dragon and you wonder how humans eked a living in such inhospitable surroundings.

The main islands, Austvågøy, Vestvågøy, Flakstadøy and Moskenesøy, are separated from the mainland by Vestfjorden. On each are sheltered bays, sheep pastures and picturesque villages. The vistas (the whole of the E10 from tip to toe of Lofoten is designated a National Tourist Route, a title bestowed only upon the most scenic roads) and the special quality of the Arctic light have long attracted artists, represented in galleries throughout the islands.

But Lofoten is still very much commercially alive. Each winter the meeting of the Gulf Stream and the icy Arctic Ocean draws

WORTH A TRIP

KJERRINGØY TRADING POST

Here, some 40km north of Bodø, the entrepreneurial – some would say exploitative – Zahl family established an important **trading station** (adult/child Nkr70/35; ⏱11am-5pm late May-Aug). The station provided local fishing families with supplies in exchange for their catches, and after making its fortune, expanded into mining, banking and steam-transport concerns.

Most of the timber-built structures of this self-contained community have been preserved. The spartan quarters and kitchens of the fishing families contrast with the sumptuous decor of the merchants' housing. There's a 20-minute audiovisual presentation included in the entry price. Admission to the main building is by guided tour.

spawning Arctic cod from the Barents Sea. For centuries, this in turn drew farmer-fishermen from the mainland's north coast. Although cod stocks have dwindled dramatically in recent years, fishing still vies with tourism as Lofoten's largest industry, as

Lofoten

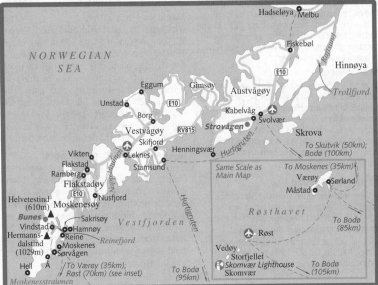

evidenced by the wooden drying racks that lattice nearly every village on the islands.

History

The history of Lofoten is essentially that of its fishing industry. Numerous battles have been fought over these seas, exceptionally rich in spawning cod ever since the glaciers retreated about 10,000 years ago. In 1120 King Øystein set up the first church and built a number of *rorbuer*, basic 4m by 4m wooden cabins for the fisherfolk with a fireplace, earthen floor and small porch area. It wasn't entirely philanthropy: in so doing, he took control of the local economy and ensured rich tax pickings for himself.

In the early 19th century power over the trade fell to local *nessekonger* (merchant squires) who'd bought up property. These new landlords forced the tenants of their *rorbuer* to deliver their entire catch at a price set by the landlords themselves. The Lofoten Act of 1857 greatly diminished the power of the *nessekonger* but not until the Raw Fish Sales Act of 1936 did they lose the power to set prices.

❶ Information

The official www.lofoten.info website is rich in information about the whole archipelago.

❶ Getting There & Away

FROM THE SOUTH

The shortest option is the car ferry between Svolvær and Skutvik, on the mainland (1¾ hours). The most popular and frequent service runs between Bodø and Moskenes (three to 3½ hours) and also takes cars. There's also a Norlandsekspressen passenger ferry (3¾ hours) that runs between Bodø and Svolvær.

FROM THE NORTH

A car ferry (25 minutes) runs between Hadseløya and Melbu Fiskebøl. The completion of a couple of tunnels on neighbouring Hinnøya now allows ferry-free access from the mainland. Known as Lofast in Norwegian, this stretch of fast highway has almost halved driving time to Harstad-Narvik airport and on to Narvik itself and the Arctic Highway.

❶ Getting Around

Getting around is easy. The main islands are linked by bridge or tunnel, and buses run the entire E10 from the Fiskebøl-Melbu ferry in the north to Å at road's end in the southwest.

Tourist offices sell an excellent Lofoten cycling guide (Nkr298), full of information for cyclists and including handy pull-out maps.

Austvågøy

POP 8960

Many visitors make their acquaintance with Lofoten on Austvågøy, the northernmost island in the archipelago.

SVOLVÆR

POP 4400

The port town of Svolvær is as busy as it gets on Lofoten. The town once sprawled across a series of skerries, but the in-between spaces are being filled in to create a reclaimed peninsula.

◉ Sights & Activities

Trollfjord BOAT CRUISE

(Nkr450/200 per adult/child) From the port, several competing companies offer sailings into the constricted confines of nearby Trollfjord, spectacularly steep and narrowing to only 100m. Take the three-hour cruise or sign on for a four-hour trip that includes the chance to dangle a line and bring home supper; the price is the same. Buy your ticket at the quayside.

Lofoten Krigsminnemuseum WWII MUSEUM

(Fiskergata 12; adult/child Nkr60/30; ☺10am-4pm & 6.15-10pm Jun-Sep, 6.15-10pm May & early Oct) Lofoten War Memorial Museum, privately and passionately run, is a fascinating place. Models in original military uniforms gaze down and there are plenty of artefacts and evocative, largely unpublished WWII-era photos.

Magic Ice ICE BAR

(Fiskergata 36; adult/child Nkr95/65; ☺noon-10.30pm mid-Jun–mid-Aug, 6-10pm rest of yr) Housed, appropriately, in what was once a fish-freezing plant, this is the ultimate place to chill out, perhaps with something to warm the spirit, served in an ice glass. The 500-sq-metre space is filled with huge ice sculptures, illustrating Lofoten life. If you can't come back to northern Norway in winter, here's a great, if brief, approximation.

FREE **Nordnorsk Kunstnersenter**

ART GALLERY

(Torget; ☺10am-6pm mid-Jun–mid-Aug, 10am-4pm rest of yr) On the main square and beside the tourist office, the North Norwegian Artist's Centre hosts changing exhibitions of paintings, sculpture, ceramics and more by artists from northern Norway. Its shop is a good source for a tasteful souvenir of Norway's north.

FREE **Lofoten Temagalleri**

FOLK MUSEUM, GALLERY

(Lofoten Temagalleri; ⊗8am-10pm Jun-Aug) The Lofoten Theme Gallery is very much the creation of one man, Geir Nøtnes, a keen photographer from a fishing background. It's devoted in the main to cod fishing and whaling, with plenty of photos and equipment. Ask to see the splendid 20-minute DVD about Lofoten through the seasons.

Festivals & Events

The town's annual **World Cod Fishing Championship**, a celebration of all things piscatorial, takes place over the last weekend of March.

Sleeping

TOP CHOICE **Svolvær Sjøhuscamp** SEA HOUSE €

(☑76 07 03 36; www.svolver-sjohuscamp. no; Parkgata 12; d/q Nkr540/800, d with kitchen Nkr690, all with shared bathroom; ☎) This friendly *sjøhus* (sea house) straddling the water is a convivial, excellent-value place to fetch up and meet fellow travellers. There's also a gem of an apartment with balcony and full facilities (Nkr1900) that sleeps up to six.

Svinøya Rorbuer CABINS €€

(☑76 06 99 30; www.svinoya.no; Gunnar Bergs vei 2; 2-/4-bed cabin from Nkr1200/1600) Across a bridge on the islet of Svinøya, site of Svolvær's first settlement, are several cabins, some historic, most contemporary, and all cosy and comfortable. Reception is a veritable museum, a restored and restocked *krambua* (general store), constructed in 1828, which was Svolvær's first shop.

Rica Hotel Svolvær HOTEL €€

(☑76 07 22 22; www.rica.no; Lamholmen; s/d Nkr1195/1445; @☎) The Rica too is built on a tiny island, above the water and supported by piles. Some rooms have balconies, while room 121 has a hole in the floor so guests in the adjacent room can drop a fishing line directly into the briny. The restaurant (for great harbour views reserve a table in its bow window, shaped like a boat) has attractive lightweight wooden furnishings and does a gargantuan dinner buffet (Nkr295).

Best Western Svolvær Hotell HOTEL €€

(☑76 07 19 99; www.svolvar-hotell.no; Austnesfjordgata 12; s/d Nkr1100/1500; ℗@☎) Intimate (there are only 22 rooms) and in a residential neighbourhood away from the portside bustle, this is a comfortable, if unexceptional place. Some rooms have balconies, others come with kitchens. Public areas are decorated with prints of Edvard Munch – happily not at his most sombre – who was the owner's grand-uncle.

Eating

TOP CHOICE **Børsen** RESTAURANT €€€

(☑76 06 99 31; Svinøya; mains Nkr265-290; ⊗5-11pm daily) This Arctic Menu restaurant brims with character. A former fish house, it was called the 'stock exchange' after the harbour-front bench outside, where the older men of the town would ruminate endlessly over the state of the world. In its dining room, with its cracked and bowed flooring, you'll still catch the scent of tar and cod-liver oil.

Bacalao BAR, CAFE €€

(☑76 07 94 00) With its upbeat interior, Bacalao offers leafy, innovative salads (Nkr135 to Nkr155), sandwiches and some equally creative pasta dishes; the *hot rekepasta* (hot shrimp pasta; Nkr165) will set your taste buds tingling. Bacalao also expresses what must be about the best coffee anywhere in

NORDLAND AUSTVÅGØY

LODGING LOFOTEN STYLE

King Øystein's legacy lives on today, as Lofoten's lodging of choice remains the *rorbu*, along with its cousin the *sjøhus*. Whereas *rorbu* (plural *rorbuer*) once meant a dingy, tiny red-painted fishing hut, nowadays the name is applied increasingly loosely to just about any wooden ox-blood or ochre-coloured structure, from historic cabins to simple holiday homes to plush, two-storey, multiroom, fully equipped self-catering units.

A *sjøhus* (literally 'sea house') was traditionally a bunkhouse-style building on the docks where fishery workers processed the catch and, for convenience, also ate and slept. While some *sjøhus* retain this style, others have been converted into summer tourist lodges and apartments, usually of the simpler, less-expensive kind.

Lofoten also has a few higher-end hotels and some wonderfully situated campgrounds.

While summer prices tend to be lower in the rest of Norway, the opposite obtains in Lofoten; in hotels you can expect to pay more than Nkr250 per room above the rest-of-the-year prices, although the difference is less pronounced in *rorbuer* and *sjøhus*.

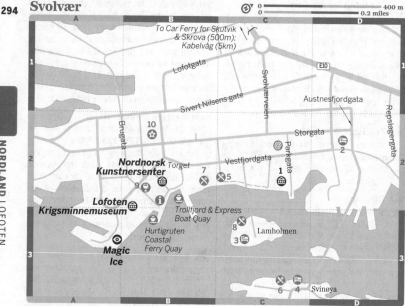

Svolvær

◎ Top Sights
Lofoten Krigsminnemuseum	B2
Magic Ice	A3
Nordnorsk Kunstnersenter	B2

◎ Sights
1 Lofoten Temagalleri (Lofoten Theme Gallery)	C2

🛏 Sleeping
2 Best Western Svolvær Hotell	D2
3 Rica Hotel Svolvær	C3
4 Svinøya Rorbuer	C3
Svolvær Sjøhuscamp	(see 1)

🍴 Eating
5 Bacalao	C2
6 Børsen	C3
7 Du Verden	B2
8 Kjøkkenet	C3
Norden	(see 7)

🍷 Drinking
Bryggabaren	(see 8)
9 Styrhuset	B2

🎭 Entertainment
10 Svolvær Filmteater	B2

Norway, a country that so often settles for watery black brews.

Norden & Du Verden RESTAURANT-CAFE €€
(☎76 07 70 99; www.duverden.net) Sharing premises and kitchen, these two eateries complement each other. **Norden**, open daily, has an airy, modern interior and waterfront terrace. It's a very congenial cafe-restaurant serving lunches of salads and sandwiches (around Nkr150) and dinner (mains Nkr265 to Nkr290), where the house speciality is sushi. To the rear, **Du Verden**, open only for

dinner, offers fine gourmet dining in a more intimate ambience with a set menu (from Nkr435) of between three and 10 courses. They share a pretty but singularly uninformative website.

Kjøkkenet TRADITIONAL NORWEGIAN €€€
(☎76 06 64 80; Lamholmen; mains Nkr300-325) Kjøkkenet, originally a shack for salting fish and nowadays furnished like an old-time kitchen, is a wonderfully cosy place to dine. The cuisine is just as traditional and the recommended menu choice is of

course fish – try the kitchen's signature dish, *boknafisk*, semidried cod with salted fat and vegetables.

🍷 Drinking & Entertainment

Styrhuset   PUB
(OJ Kaarsbøs gate 5) Svolvær's oldest pub is all dark crannies that speak of sailors long gone.

Bryggabaren   PUB
(Lamholmen) In the same complex as Kjøkennet, this low-beamed, cosy watering hole is bedecked with tools of all kinds. The bar is a lifeboat from a WWII Polish troop ship that washed up in Svolvær in 1946.

Svolvær Filmtheater   CINEMA
(Storgata 28) Screens recent films and Hollywood blockbusters.

ℹ️ Information
Library (Vestfjordgata; ⊙11am-3pm Mon-Sat) Free internet and wi-fi.
Tourist office (☎76 06 98 07; www.lofoten.info; Torget; ⊙9am-8pm or 10pm mid-Jun–Jul, shorter hr rest of yr) Provides information on the entire archipelago.

ℹ️ Getting There & Around
From Svolvær's small airport there are up to six flights daily to Bodø.

Svolvær is a stop on the Hurtigruten coastal ferry. Two other sea routes connect Svolvær to the mainland.

To/from Skutvik (car/driver Nkr104/36, 1¾ hours, up to 10 daily) The shortest, most popular crossing (from Skutvik you can connect by bus with Narvik).

To/from Bodø (Nkr324, 3½ hours) Daily express passenger boat calling by Skutvik (one hour).

Useful bus routes include the following:

Bus 8 To/from Sortland on Vesterålen (2¼ hours, three to five times daily), via Stokmarknes (1¾ hours).

Bus 9 To/from Leknes (Nkr134, 1½ hours, four to six times daily), with connections to Å (Nkr242, 3½ hours).

Lofotekspressen To/from Narvik (Nkr225 or Nkr425, 4¼ hours, twice daily).

For a taxi, call ☎76 07 06 00.

KABELVÅG
Kabelvåg, 5km southwest of Svolvær, is an altogether more intimate and cosy place. At its heart is a small square and tiny harbour while its **Storvågen** district, 2km off the E10 to the south, has an enticing trio of museums and galleries.

◉ Sights & Activities
Behind the old prison in Storvågen, a trail climbs to the statue honouring King Øystein. In 1120 he ordered the first *rorbuer* to be built to house fishermen, who previously had been sleeping beneath their overturned rowing boats. This wasn't just an act of kindness; His Majesty needed to keep his fisherfolk warm, dry and content since the tax on exported dried fish was the main source of his revenue.

Lofotmuseet   FOLK MUSEUM
(www.lofotmuseet.no; adult/child Nkr60/25; ⊙9am-6pm Jun-Aug, 9am-3pm Mon-Fri rest of yr) The islands' major folk museum is on the site of what can be considered to be the first town in the polar region, where traces of the original *rorbu* have been excavated. The museum's main gallery was once the merchant's mansion. Here, typically, lived the man who hired out the *rorbuer* and sea houses to the fishermen and bought their catch. An easy, undulating, scenic 2km **Heritage Path** leads from the museum to the centre of Kabelvåg.

Lofotakvariet   AQUARIUM
(www.lofotakvariet.no; adult/child Nkr110/55; ⊙10am-6pm Jun-Aug, 11am-3pm Sun-Fri Feb-May & Sep-Nov) Fish and sea animals of the cold Arctic waters swim and flap. Children will particularly enjoy the seal and sea otter feeding frenzies (noon and 4pm) and there's a multimedia show five times daily on the hour.

Galleri Espolin   ART GALLERY
(www.galleri-espolin.no, in Norwegian; adult/child Nkr65/30; ⊙10am-6pm Jun–mid-Aug, 11am-3pm rest of yr) The gallery features the haunting etchings and lithographs of one of Norway's great artists, Kaare Espolin-Johnson (1907–94). Espolin – his work all the more astounding as he was nearly blind for much of his life – loved Lofoten and often featured its fisherfolk, together with other Arctic themes.

Vågan Kirke   CHURCH
(admission Nkr30; ⊙10am-6pm Mon-Sat, noon-6pm Sun late Jun–mid-Aug) Built in 1898 and

---

ℹ️ COMBINATION TICKET

A combination ticket (adult/child Nkr160/70) gives entry to Lofoten Museum, Lofoten Aquarium and Galleri Espolin, all in Storvågan. They're an easy walk from each other.

Norway's second-largest wooden church, Vågan rises above the E10 just north of Kabelvåg. Built to minister to the influx of seasonal fisherfolk, its seating capacity of 1200 far surpasses Kabelvåg's current population.

Sleeping & Eating

A couple of inlets and 3km west of Kabelvåg, there are a pair of great campgrounds, right beside each other.

Ørsvågvær Camping CAMPGROUND €

(☎76 07 81 80; www.orsvag.no; car/caravan site Nkr150/190, 4-bed cabin Nkr850, 7-bed sea house apt Nkr1150; ☺May-Sep) Most *rorbuer* and the sea house are right beside the fjord and offer splendid views. You can rent a motorboat (per hour/day Nkr200/600).

Sandvika Fjord og Sjøhuscamp

CAMPGROUND €

(☎76 07 81 45; www.lofotferie.no; car/caravan site Nkr145/180, 4-bed cabin Nkr650, with bathroom from Nkr850, sea house apt Nkr800) This shoreside campground has its own small beach. It rents motorboats (from Nkr200 per hour) and is a base for sea-kayak trips. The camping area is significantly larger than its neighbour's.

Kabelvåg Vandrerhjem & Sommerhotell

HOSTEL €

(☎76 06 98 80; www.hihostels.no/Kabelvag; Finnesveien 24; dm/s/d with shared bathroom Nkr260/450/600, d with bathroom Nkr900; ☺Jun-early Aug; @) Less than 1km north of the centre, the Lofoten Folkehøgskole school becomes a hostel and hotel outside the teaching year. There's a kitchen for guest use. Hostel rooms have one, two or four beds.

Kabelvåg Hotell HOTEL €€

(☎76 07 88 00; www.kabelvaghotell.no, in Norwegian; Kong Øysteinsgate 4; summer s/d Nkr990/1410, winter full board Nkr1195; ☺Jun–mid-Aug & late Feb-Apr) On a small rise close to the centre of Kabelvåg, this imposing seasonal hotel has been tastefully rebuilt in its original art deco style. Rooms overlook either the port or mountains. It also functions as a centre for skiing and a host of other winter activities.

Nyvågar Rorbuhotell CABINS €€€

(☎76 06 97 00; www.nyvagar.no, in Norwegian; Storvåganveien 22; 4-bed rorbuer 2000) At Storvågan, below the museum complex, this snazzy, modern seaside place owes nothing to history, but its strictly contemporary *rorbuer* are attractive and fully equipped. Guests can also rent bikes (Nkr55/200 per hour/day) and motorboats (Nkr200/590 per hour/day). Its acclaimed **Lorchstua restaurant** (mains Nkr175-300, 3-course menu Nkr395) serves primarily local specialities with a subtle twist, such as baked fillet of halibut in a cod brandade.

Præstengbrygga PUB €€

(☎76 07 80 60; Torget; mains around Nkr150) In central Kabelvåg, this friendly pub with its all-wood interior and dockside terracing, front and rear, serves sandwiches, pizzas and tasty mains, including a rich combination platter of marinated salmon, smoked whale, shrimps and salad. There's often live music and, for Nkr25, you can drink coffee all day with free refills.

HENNINGSVÆR

A delightful 8km shore-side drive southwards from the E10 brings you to the still-active fishing village of Henningsvær, perched at the end of a thin promontory. Its nickname, 'the Venice of Lofoten', may be a tad overblown but it's certainly the lightest, brightest and trendiest place in the archipelago. It's also the region's largest and most active fishing port.

◉ Sights & Activities

Ocean Sounds WHALE CENTRE

(☎918 42012; www.ocean-sounds.com; Hjellskjæret; adult/child Nkr200/free; ☺2-6pm Jul–mid-Aug, May, on request Jun & mid-Aug–Sep) Beside the Henningsvær Bryggehotel, this not-for-profit research centre is the initiative of one committed, hugely determined young biologist, Heike Vester. Enjoy a 45-minute multimedia presentation about cod, whales and other Arctic marine mammals, supplemented by an evocative 30-minute slide show featuring whales and other marine animals in the waters around Henningsvær. Or get out and about on a three- to four-hour marine safari in the Zodiac research boat (adult/child Nkr800/600, daily departures, weather permitting).

FREE **Engelskmannsbrygga** CRAFT GALLERY

(Dreyersgate 1; ☺10am-8pm mid-Jun–mid-Aug, noon-4pm Tue-Sun rest of yr) Here at 'Englishman's Wharf' is the open studio and gallery of three talented local artists: potter Cecilie Haaland, wildlife photographer and guide John Stenersen and glass-blower Kari Malmberg, with whom you can try your hand at blowing your own glass (Nkr150; 5pm to 7pm Monday to Thursday).

Lofotens Hus Gallery
ART GALLERY

(www.galleri-lofoten.no; Hjellskjæret; adult/child/concession Nkr80/30; ⊙9am-7pm or 10am-6pm late May–early Sep) In a former fish-processing house, this gallery displays a fine collection of paintings from what is known as the golden age of Norwegian painting, between 1870 and 1930, plus canvases by contemporary Norwegian artist Karl Erik Harr. Admission includes an 18-minute slide show of photos by Frank Jenssen, shown on the hour. Revealing the people and landscapes of Lofoten throughout the seasons, it's marred only by the trite, syrupy background music.

North Norwegian Climbing School
CLIMBING SCHOOL

(Nord Norsk Klatreskole; ☑90 57 42 08; www.nordnorskklatreskole.no, in Norwegian; Misværveien 10; ⊙Mar–Oct) This outfit offers a wide range of technical climbing and skiing courses all around northern Norway. Climbing the peaks with an experienced guide costs Nkr2000, including equipment, for one to four people. For a multitude of ideas, check out the thick *Lofoten Rock* by Chris Craggs and Thorbjørn Enevold, the school's director. The last word on climbing in Lofoten, it's on sale at the school's mountaineering shop.

Lofoten Adventure
OUTDOOR TOURS

(☑905 81 475; www.lofoten-opplevelser.no) Based in Henningsvær, it offers a cluster of maritime tours and activities between mid-June and mid-August. Advance booking is essential. Tours include **sea-eagle safaris** (2.30pm, adult/child Nkr430/330, 1½ hours), **Midnight safaris** (10pm, adult/child Nkr650/500, 2½ hours) and **snorkelling** sorties with equipment provided (11am, Nkr650, two hours). **Whale safaris** (Nkr850, 3 hours, Nov–mid-Jan) are available on demand.

🛏 Sleeping & Eating

TOP CHOICE Henningsvær Bryggehotel HOTEL €€€
(☑76 07 47 50; www.henningsvaer.no; Hjellskjæret; s/d from Nkr1070/1500) Overlooking the harbour, this attractive hotel is Henningsvær's finest choice. It's modern, with comfortable rooms furnished in contemporary design, yet constructed in a traditional style that blends harmoniously with its neighbours. Bluefish, its award-winning restaurant, is just as stylish; it serves Arctic Menu dishes and succulent sorbets, using fresh berries in season.

Johs H Giæver Sjøhus og Rorbuer
SEA HOUSE €

(☑76 07 47 19; www.giaever-rorbuer.no; Hellandsgata 79; rorbuer from Nkr650, sea house s/d Nkr450/500) From mid-June to mid-August, workers' accommodation in a modern sea house belonging to the local fish plant is hired out to visitors. Spruce rooms (some with space for four) have shared facilities, including a large kitchen and dining area, and are good value. The company also has 10 *rorbuer* with bathrooms in the heart of town.

Fiskekrogen
RESTAURANT €€€

(☑76 07 46 52; Dreyersgate 29; mains Nkr235-275, lunch dishes Nkr95-160) At the end of a slipway overlooking the harbour, this dockside restaurant, a favourite of the Norwegian royal family, is Henningsvær's other culinary claim to fame. Try, in particular, the outstanding fish soup (Nkr175).

Klatrekafeen Café
CAFE €

(Misværveien; dishes Nkr115-195) The North Norwegian Climbing School and its cafe (which also has limited accommodation (doubles Nkr550, four-bed apartments Nkr1200) face each other down an alley. Friendly and informal, the cafe crosses a *rorbu* with a British hikers' pub and serves up snacks and a small selection of good-value homemade dishes.

❶ Information

Tourist Office (☑912 45702; www.henningsvar.com; turistinfo@henningsvar.com; ⊙10am-6pm Mon-Fri, 11am-4pm Sat & Sun mid-Jun–mid-Nov) Henningsvær's brand-new tourist office is beside the main car park.

❶ Getting There & Away

In summer, bus 510 shuttles between Svolvær (40 minutes), Kabelvåg (35 minutes) and Henningsvær 10 times on weekdays (three services Saturday and Sunday).

Vestvågøy

POP 10,700

⊙ Sights & Activities

Lofotr Viking Museum
OPEN-AIR FOLK MUSEUM

(☑76 08 49 00; www.lofotr.no; adult/child incl guided tour Nkr120/60; ⊙10am-4pm or 7pm May–mid-Sep) In 1981 at Borg, near the centre of Vestvågøy, a farmer's plough hit the ruins of the 83m-long dwelling of a powerful Viking chieftain, the largest building of its era ever discovered in Scandinavia.

The Lofotr Viking Museum, 14km north of Leknes, offers a glimpse of life in Viking

GLORY BE TO COD

For centuries, catching and drying cod has been a way of life in Lofoten and by far its biggest industry.

Although cod populations have been depleted by overfishing, the overall catch is still substantial: an estimated 50,000 tonnes annually (30,000 tonnes without the heads). The fishing season peaks between January and April when the fish swim round from the Barents Sea to Vestfjorden to spawn. Around the end of March each year the unofficial World Cod Fishing Championship is held in Svolvær, attracting up to 300 entrants.

There are two ways to preserve cod. For saltfish, it's filleted, salted and dried for about three weeks. For klipfish, the saltfish is cleaned, resalted and dried, originally on cliffs (*klipp* in Norwegian) and nowadays in large heated plants.

However, Lofoten is all about stockfish. In this ancient method, 15,000 tonnes of fish are decapitated each year, paired by size, then tied together and, dangling in pairs like sleeping bats, hung to dry over the huge wooden A-frames you see everywhere on the islands. The fish lose about 80% of their weight, and most are exported to Italy, with some to Spain and Portugal.

Stockfish stays edible for years, and it's often eaten raw (a trifle chewy but goes well with beer), salted or reconstituted with water. It's concentrated goodness; with a protein content of 80%, 1kg of stockfish has the same nutritional value as 5kg of fresh fish.

Even before drying, very little of a cod goes to waste: cod tongue is a local delicacy – children extract the tongues and are paid by the piece – and the roe is salted in enormous German wine vats. The heads are sent to Nigeria to form the basis of a popular spicy dish.

Then there's the liver, which produces oil rich in vitamin D that has long been known to prevent rickets and assuage the depression brought on by the long, dark Arctic winters. In 1854 Lofoten pharmacist Peter Møller decided to introduce this magic-in-a-bottle to the world and constructed a cauldron for steam-boiling the livers. The oil he skimmed received honours at trade fairs in Europe and abroad. After skimming, the livers were steamed in large oak barrels and then pressed to yield every last, profitable drop. Every summer, thousands of barrels of it were shipped to Europe, and the smell pervaded the village of Å, whose inhabitants liked to comment that it was the scent of money.

And what of cod-liver oil's notorious taste? Locals will tell you that it tastes bad only when it becomes rancid. Fresh cod-liver oil can be quite flavoursome, like salad oil with a slightly fishy bouquet.

Modern Norwegian fishing folk are vociferously protective of this asset – in certain northern districts as many as 90% of votes were against EU membership. For if Norway joined the EU, the Spanish fishing fleet and others would have access to Norway's in-shore waters – a potential modern-day Armada that Norway's fisherfolk are determined to repel. There have also been skirmishes with Icelandic trawlers over territorial fishing rights.

Fun cod fact: one in 20,000 cod is a king cod; the distinctive lump on its forehead is said to indicate intelligence and bring good luck to the fishing family that catches it. King cod are often dried and hung on a string from the ceiling; as the string expands and contracts with humidity, the fish rotates like a barometer, hence the nickname 'weather cod'.

The latest news from the world of cod involves the fishes' mating calls; it seems that the grunts they use to attract mates can be loud enough to block a submarine's sonar devices, impeding its underwater navigation!

Mark Kurlansky's book *Cod* (1999) is an excellent, thoroughly entertaining study of this piscatorial powerhouse.

times. You can walk 1.5km of trails over open hilltops from the replica of the chieftain's longhouse (the main building, shaped like an upside-down boat) to the Viking-ship replica on the water. Costumed guides conduct multilingual tours and, inside the chieftain's hall, artisans explain their trades.

The Svolvær–Leknes bus passes the museum's entrance.

Galleri 2

CONTEMPORARY ART GALLERY

(www.galleri2.no; admission Nkr20; ⏰11am-8pm Jun-Aug) The gallery of Lofoten painter and long-term resident Scott Thoe is barely 175m from the Hurtigruten quay in Stamsund, a short detour from the Rv185. It displays the works of a number of contemporary Norwegian artists, including scale models of his own grand open-air projects.

Unstad to Eggum Hike

HIKE

A popular hike connects these two tiny villages on the island's west coast. A 9km coastal track winds past several headlands, a solitary lighthouse, superb seascapes and the ruins of a fortress by the ocean.

Take care after rain as the trail, particularly around Unstad, can be slick with mud. Eggum and Unstad are both about 9km from the main road and are served infrequently by buses.

🛏 Sleeping & Eating

TOP CHOICE Justad Rorbuer og Vandrerhjem

HOSTEL €

(☎76 08 93 34; www.hihostels.no/stamsund; dm/ s/d with shared bathroom Nkr135/335/445, 4-bed cabin Nkr550-850; ⏰Mar–mid-Oct) The island's HI-affiliated youth hostel is a 1.2km walk from the Hurtigruten quay and has its regular clientele who come back year after year – one particularly loyal guest has stayed here over 50 times – so be sure to reserve. It's right beside the water in an old fishing complex. Roar Justad, the friendly owner, dispenses information about local hiking routes, rents bicycles (Nkr80 to Nkr100 per day) and lends rowing boats and fishing lines for free.

Brustranda Sjøcamping

CAMPGROUND €

(☎916 28682; www.brustranda.no; Rolvsfjord; car/caravan site Nkr140/160, 4-bed cabin Nkr450, with bathroom Nkr750-1200; ⏰mid-May–Aug) This well-tended, beautifully situated seaside campground (with a new reception and cafe, the old one having burnt to the ground) stretches around a tiny harbour. It's beside the Rv815, 14km northeast of Stamsund.

Skjærbrygga Sjøhus

CAFE-RESTAURANT €€€

(☎76 05 46 00; dinner mains Nkr225-310; ⏰pub food from 11.30am, dinner 5-10pm) Low-beamed, large yet cosy, this place is right at the water's edge. It has a limited dinner menu (three starters, three fish dishes and two meat mains) that includes all the local favourites such as a starter of smoked whale (Nkr100) and tender Lofoten lamb (Nkr310).

WORTH A TRIP

BREAKING FREE FROM THE E10

Instead of continuing to roll along the E10 as it snakes its way through the heart of Vestvågøy island, take the even more attractive, much less travelled and only slightly longer Rv815. It starts just beyond the bridge that links Austvågøy, runs southwestwards for 28km and rejoins the E10 at Leknes. For the most part it hugs the shoreline with sheer mountains rearing to landward.

ⓘ Information

Vestvågøy's **tourist office** (☎76 08 75 53; Storgata 31; ⏰9am-7pm Mon-Fri, 10am-2pm Sat & Sun mid-Jun–early Aug, 9am-4pm Mon-Fri rest of yr) is tucked into the ground floor of Lofotsenteret, a large shopping centre in the lacklustre town of Leknes.

ⓘ Getting There & Away

Up to eight flights daily connect Leknes airport with Bodø. Leknes has bus connections to Å (1¾ hours, four to five daily), Stamsund (25 minutes, three to seven daily) and Svolvær (1½ hours, four to six daily). Stamsund is the island's port for the Hurtigruten coastal ferry.

Flakstadøy

POP 1450

Most of Flakstadøy's residents live along its flat north shore, around the town of Ramberg, but, as with Vestvågøy, it's the craggy south side that has the most dramatic scenery. Many visitors just zip through but it's worth stopping to sun yourself (sandy beaches are the exception in Lofoten) and perhaps to build in a detour to the arty village of Nusfjord.

NUSFJORD

A spectacular 6km diversion southwards from the E10 beneath towering bare crags brings you to the cutesy village of Nusfjord (www.nusfjord.no), sprawled around its tiny, tucked-away harbour. Many artists consider it to be the essence of Lofoten but be warned: so do tour operators. And the locals are smart: it costs Nkr30 just to walk around plus a further Nkr30 to see *The People & The Fish*, a 12-minute video about Nusfjord, past and present. In the country store that recently celebrated its centenary, upper shelves are crammed with vintage cans, bottles and boxes while the lower ones are stocked with contemporary fare. There's the old cod-liver oil factory, boat house, sawmill and a cluster of *rorbuer,* most of them modern. The most original feature that relates to other than a sanitised past is **Krismar** (☑76 09 33 99), the workshop of Italian Michele Sarno and his intricate creations in silver.

RAMBERG & FLAKSTAD

Imagine an arch of tropical white sand fronting a sparkling blue-green bay against a backdrop of snowcapped Arctic peaks. That's pretty much **Ramberg** and **Flakstad** beaches, on the north coast Flakstadøy, when the sun shines kindly on them. Should you hit such a day, no one back home will believe that your holiday snaps of this place were taken north of the Arctic Circle, but you'll know it if you stick a toe in the water.

Set back from Flakstad beach and by-passed these days by the E10, the red onion-domed **Flakstad Kirke** (guided tours adult/child Nkr30/free; ⊙11am-3pm, late Jun-late Jul) was built in 1780 but has been extensively restored over the years. Most of the original wood was ripped out of the ground by the Arctic-bound rivers of Siberia and washed up here as driftwood.

◉ Sights

Sund Fiskerimuseum　　　　　　MUSEUM
(www.sundfiskerimuseum.no, in Norwegian; adult/child Nkr60/10; ⊙10am-4pm or 6pm mid-May–Aug) This fishery museum lies 3km off the E10. In one dim shack, there's an astounding clutter of boats, ropes and floats while within another is an unlabelled yet fascinating jumble of pots and pans, skis, old valve radios and the like. All this is set amid the throb and curling fumes from the collection of permanently beached ship diesel engines. Tor-Vegard Mørkved, the young resident blacksmith, bashes out cormorants in iron (the cheapest around Nkr300, but Nkr1700 for something you'd be proud to have on your mantelpiece).

Glasshytta　　　　　　CRAFT WORKSHOP
(⊙10am-7pm May-Aug) A 4km side trip from the E10 brings you to Vikten and the gallery of glassblower Åsvar Tangrand. Tangrand is the designer of the Lofoten Rune, the region's seven-pronged logo evoking a longboat, which you'll see all around the islands.

🛏 Sleeping & Eating

TOP CHOICE **Ramberg Gjestegård**　　CAMPGROUND €
(☑76 09 35 00; www.ramberg-gjestegard.no; E10; car/caravan site Nkr150/190, 2-/4-bed cabin Nkr850/1050) At this welcoming campground, right on the beach, you can rent a kayak or rowing boat (per hour/day Nkr25/100), upgrade to a motorboat (Nkr100/450) or explore the island by bike (Nkr40/150). There's a justifiably popular Arctic Menu **restaurant** (mains Nkr210 to Nkr260) that does mainly fish dishes and its own splendid Flakstad Menu (cod, cured roast lamb and rhubarb compote for dessert). It also offers cheaper but still very tasty lunch specials (Nkr90 to Nkr178).

ℹ Information

The island's seasonal **tourist office** (☑76 09 31 10; henkirk@online.no; ⊙9am-7pm mid-May–Aug) is in Ramberg's Galleri Steinbiten.

Moskenesøy

POP 1150

The 34km-long island of Moskenesøy is the southernmost and perhaps the most interesting of the Lofoten islands. Its spiky, pinnacled igneous ridge, rising directly from the sea and split by deep lakes and fjords, could almost have been conceived by Tolkien. A paradise for mountaineers, some of the tight gullies and fretted peaks of this tortured island – including its highest point, Hermannsdalstind (1029m) – are accessible to ordinary mortals as well.

🏃 Activities

The comprehensive *Moskenes Guide* has 14 suggestions for hikes of between one and 10 hours. You'll need to supplement this with Staten Kartverk's *Lofoten* at 1:100,000.

From June to mid-August, you can **deep-sea fish** (Nkr500 to Nkr600) for three to four hours using traditional long lines and hand lines. From the *Hellvåg* in Å and the *Carina* in Reine, both working cod-fishing vessels in winter, you're all but guaranteed a fat catch. Other options include fishing the Reinefjord, off Nusfjord, or near the maelstrom off Å.

At sea, there's excellent **birdwatching** and the possibility of **whale sightings** in season.

ℹ Information

The island's **tourist office** (☑76 09 15 99; www.lofoten-info.no; ⊙9am-7pm or 10am-5pm) is at

NORDLAND BOATS

You're bound to come across the uniquely shaped, stubby Nordland boat, which has served local fishing communities from the earliest days of settlement. These informal symbols of the tough, self-sufficient lifestyle of the hardy coastal folk here up north are still in use from Namsos, in Trøndelag, right up to the Kola Peninsula in Arctic Russia, but the greatest concentrations are found in Lofoten.

The smallest versions are known as *færing*, measuring up to 5m, while larger ones are called *hundromsfæring* (6m), *seksring* (7m), *halvfjerderømming* (7.5m), *firroing* (8m), *halvfemterømming* (9m), *åttring* (10m to 11m) and *fembøring* (11m to 13m).

Traditionally, the larger the boat, the greater the status of its *høvedmann* (captain). Whatever the size, Nordland boats are excellent for both rowing and sailing, even in rough northern seas. Until quite recently, sailing competitions, pitting fishing communities against each other, were one of the great social events of the year.

A good place to see museum-quality examples is in the harbour at Å in Lofoten.

Moskenes harbour. It publishes the free, informative *Moskenes Guide*, has an internet terminal (per hour Nkr60) and makes reservations for a variety of tours and activities.

❶ Getting There & Away

Car ferries sail five to six times daily in summer (less frequently during the rest of the year) between Moskenes and Bodø (car including driver/passenger Nkr568/158, 3½ hours). At least one calls in daily at the tiny southern Lofoten islands of Røst and Værøy.

Four to five buses daily connect Leknes and Å (1¾ hours) in summer, stopping in all major villages along the E10.

Å

At the southern tip of Moskenesøy and the Lofoten islands, the bijou village of Å (appropriately, the last letter of the Norwegian alphabet), sometimes referred to as Å i Lofoten, is truly a living museum – a preserved fishing village with a shoreline of red *rorbuer*, cod-drying racks and picture-postcard scenes at almost every turn. It's an almost feudal place, carved up between two families, now living very much from tourism but in its time a significant fishing port (more than 700,000 cod would be hung out to dry right up to WWII).

Do the village a favour and leave your vehicle at the car park beyond a short tunnel and walk in.

◉ Sights

Norsk Fiskeværsmuseum FOLK MUSEUM
(adult/child Nkr50/25; ☺10am-6pm mid-Jun–mid-Aug, 11am-3.30pm Mon-Fri rest of yr) What's called collectively the Norwegian Fishing Village Museum is in fact a fair proportion of this hamlet: 14 of Å's 19th-century

boathouses, storehouses, fishing cottages, farmhouses and commercial buildings. Highlights (pick up a pamphlet in English at reception) include Europe's oldest cod-liver oil factory, where you'll be treated to a taste of the wares and can pick up a bottle to stave off those winter sniffles; the smithy, who still makes cod-liver oil lamps; the still-functioning bakery, established in 1844; the old *rorbu* with period furnishings; and a couple of traditional Lofoten fishing boats.

Lofoten Tørrfiskmuseum FOLK MUSEUM
(adult/child Nkr50/30; ☺11am-4pm or 5pm Jun-Aug) The Lofoten Stockfish Museum is housed in a former fish warehouse. You'll be bowled over by Steinar Larsen, its enthusiastic, polyglot owner, who meets and greets every visitor. This personal collection, a passionate hobby of his, illustrates well Lofoten's traditional mainstay: the catching and drying of cod for export, particularly to Italy. Displays, artefacts and a DVD take you through the process, from hauling the fish out of the sea through drying, grading and sorting to despatch.

Moskenesstraumen Strait SEASCAPE
Beyond the campground at the southern limit of Å, there's an excellent hillside view of Værøy island, across the waters. The mighty **maelstroms** created by tidal flows between the two islands were first described 2000 years ago by Pytheas and later appeared as fearsome adversaries on fanciful early sea charts. They also inspired tales of maritime peril by Jules Verne and Edgar Allan Poe (seas 'lashed into ungovernable fury' was how he qualified them). They're still said to be among the world's most dangerous waters. This formidable

expanse is exceptionally rich in fish and attracts large numbers of sea birds and marine mammals.

🛏 Sleeping & Eating

Å-Hamna Rorbuer & Vandrerhjem
HOSTEL, CABINS €

(☑76 09 12 11; www.lofotenferie.com; hostel s/d/t/q Nkr300/400/540/720; 4-8-bed rorbuer with bathroom Nkr800-1200) Sleep simple or sleep in more comfort; either way, this is an attractive choice. Newly affiliated to Hostelling International, it has dorms above the Stockfish Museum and in a quiet villa, set in its garden. For more space and privacy, choose one of the restored fishing huts, where prices drop significantly outside high summer.

Å Rorbuer
FISHERMAN'S HUT €€

(☑76 09 11 21; www.lofoten-rorbu.com, in Norwegian; old sea house d/tr/q per person Nkr250, new sea house d Nkr780; 2-6 person rorbuer Nkr1350-2300) *Rorbu* accommodation is dispersed throughout Å's historic buildings, the more expensive ones fully equipped and furnished with antiques. The newer sea house, above Brygga restaurant and with trim but plain rooms, has shared bathrooms, despite the hefty price.

Moskenesstraumen Camping
CAMPGROUND €

(☑76 09 11 48; camping for 1/2/3 persons Nkr90/140/180, caravans Nkr200, 2-/4-bed cabin from Nkr450/650, with bathroom Nkr650/750; ☉Jun-Aug) This wonderful cliff-top campground, just south of the village, has flat, grassy pitches between the rocks, just big enough for your bivouac. Cabins too have great views, as far as the mainland on clear days.

Brygga Restaurant
FISH RESTAURANT €€€

(☑76 09 15 72; mains Nkr200-315, set menu Nkr425, bar lunch special Nkr125; ☉Jun-Sep) Hovering above the water, this is Å's one decent dining choice. The menu, as is right and proper in a village with such a strong fishing tradition, includes mainly things with fins.

SØRVÅGEN

Norsk Telemuseum
MUSEUM

(adult/child Nkr40/20; ☉11am-5pm mid-Jun–mid-Aug) The Norwegian Telecommunications Museum presents itself as a study in 'cod and communications'. Granted, it's not an immediately winning combination but in fact this small museum commemorates a huge advance in fishing techniques. In 1906,

what was Norway's second wireless telephone station was established in this tiny hamlet. From that day on, weather warnings could be speedily passed on and fishing vessels could communicate with each other, pass on news about where the shoals were moving and call up the bait boats.

TOP CHOICE Maren Anna
FISH RESTAURANT €€€

(☑76 09 20 50; mains Nkr220-235, lunch dishes Nkr110-195) Maren Anna is at once pub, restaurant and cafe. Serving its mainstay of fish, bought daily, fresh from the quayside, portions are generous. For a table with views over the fishing boats below and what's claimed, tongue in cheek, to be Norway's smallest beach, reserve ahead. It also has a selection of rooms (singles/doubles Nkr400/600) in a nearby building and a couple of *rorbuer* sleeping five to nine (Nkr1200).

MOSKENES

Moskenes Camping
CAMPGROUND

(☑99 48 94 05; tent/caravan site Nkr120/200; ☉May-Aug) In a bleak location yet with great waterside views, Moskenes' only campground is gravel surfaced yet also has a sheltered grassy area for tent campers. Facilities are continually being upgraded (the owner's a carpenter) and it couldn't be more convenient for an early getaway from the ferry terminal, only 400m away.

REINE

Reine is a characterless place but gosh, it looks splendid from above, beside its placid lagoon and backed by the sheer rock face of Reinebringen. You get a great view from the head of the road that drops to the village from the E10.

From June to mid-August, three-hour boat trips are run by **Aqua Lofoten** (www.aqualofoten.com; adult/child Nkr550/400) to the bird- and fish-rich Moskstraumen maelstrom.

AROUND REINE

In summer, the **M/S Fjordskyss** (www.reinefjorden.no, in Norwegian; adult/child return Nkr120/60; 25min; 3 daily) runs between Reine and Vindstad through scenic Reinefjord. From Vindstad, it's a one-hour hike across the ridge to the abandoned beachside settlement of **Bunes**, in the shadow of the brooding 610m Helvetestind rock slab.

SAKRISØY

In Sakrisøy, Dagmar Gylseth has collected more than 2500 dolls, antique teddy bears and historic toys over 25 years for her **Museum of Dolls & Toys** (Dagmars Dukke og Leketøy Museum; adult/child Nkr50/25; ⊙10am-6pm or 8pm late May-Aug). There's also an affiliated antique shop upstairs.

Reserve at the Doll Museum for **Sakrisøy Rorbuer** (☑76 09 21 43; www.lofoten.ws; cabin Nkr745-1640), a relatively authentic complex of ochre-coloured cottages hovering above the water. You can also hire motorboats (Nkr450 to Nkr550 per day).

For self-catering, the fish shop and cafe **Sjømat**, across the street from the Doll Museum, is famous for its fish cakes, salmon burgers, smoked salmon, prawns, whale steaks and – go on, be adventurous – seagulls' eggs.

HAMNØY

TOP CHOICE **Hamnøy Mat og Vinbu** FISH RESTAURANT (☑76 09 21 45; mains Nkr175-225; ⊙May-early Sep) This welcoming restaurant is run by three generations of the same family (the teenage boys are co-opted for washing-up duties). It's well regarded for local specialities, including whale, bacalao and cod tongues. Grandmother takes care of the traditional dishes – just try her fish cakes – while her son is the main chef. Its fish is of the freshest, bought daily from the harbour barely 100m away.

Southern Islands

This remote pair of islands is superb for birdwatching. Værøy, mainly high and rugged, and Røst, flat as a pancake, both offer good walking and relative solitude in well-touristed Lofoten.

VÆRØY
POP 550

Craggy Værøy, its handful of residents hugely outnumbered by over 100,000 nesting sea birds – fulmars, gannets, Arctic terns, guillemots, gulls, sea eagles, puffins, kittiwakes, cormorants, eiders, petrels and a host of others – is a mere 8km long with white-sand beaches, soaring ridges, tiny, isolated villages, granite-gneiss bird cliffs and sparkling seas.

The **tourist office** (☑75 42 06 00; ⊙9am-3pm Mon-Fri mid-Jun–mid-Aug) is in the town hall at Sørland, the main village.

⊙ Sights & Activities

Walking routes approach some of the major **sea-bird rookeries**. The most scenic and popular trail begins at the end of the road around the north of the island, about 6km from Sørland and 300m beyond the former airstrip. It heads southward along the west coast, over the Eidet isthmus to the mostly abandoned fishing village of **Måstad**, on the east coast, where meat and eggs from the puffin colonies once supported 150 people.

Fit hikers who relish a challenge may also want to attempt the steep climb from Måstad to the peak of Måhornet (431m), which takes about an hour each way. Alternatively, from the quay at Sørland you can follow the road (or perhaps the more interesting ridge scramble) up to the NATO installation at Håen (438m).

FISHY MEDICINE

Remember the breakfast tantrums, the spoon being forced into your mouth and that strong fishy flavour overcoming the nutty taste of cornflakes, as your parents forced the fluid down your throat to stave off winter colds?

It wasn't always so. *Tran*, cod-liver oil, was originally used as fuel for lamps or in the tanning process for skins and nobody would have dreamed of imbibing it. But gradually its medicinal properties were understood and, in an early example of deliberate – and highly successful – marketing, cod-liver oil became the preventative of choice throughout Europe. It's a bit like olive oil; the first pressing, the virgin oil, is considered the purest while steam cooking – a technological advance that reduced production costs and enhanced yield – enables much more of the oil to be used.

Early hunch is nowadays backed up by objective medical evidence. Cod-liver oil, rich in vitamins A and D, plus omega-3 fatty acids, is good for your heart and blood circulation, eyesight, skin, bone development and brain.

So take a breath, pinch your nostrils, join one in three of all Norwegians and take your medicine like a man/woman...

Sleeping

Gamle Prestegård   GUESTHOUSE €

(Old Vicarage; ☎76 09 54 11; www.prestegaarden.
no, in Norwegian; s/d Nkr395/690, with bathroom
Nkr495/790) Værøy's smartest lodging and
dining is on the island's north side. It's the
large house with a flagpole in the garden beside the church, just where you'd expect the
vicar to have lived.

ⓘ Getting There & Away

Lufttransport (☎75 43 18 00; www.lufttrans
port.no, in Norwegian) runs helicopter flights
between Bodø and Værøy once or twice daily,
February to October. The rest of us take the
car ferry that runs most days to/from Bodø
(passenger/car Nkr147/525), directly or via
Moskenes. The ferry also links Værøy with Røst
(passenger/car Nkr82/282).

RØST
POP 600

The 365 islands and skerries of Røst (one for
each day of the year) form Lofoten's ragged
southern edge. Røst stands in sharp contrast
to its rugged neighbours to the north, and
were it not for a small pimple in the middle,
the main pond-studded island of Røstlandet
would be dead flat. Thanks to its location in
the heart of the Gulf Stream, this cluster of
islets basks in one of the mildest climates in
Norway and attracts 2.5 million nesting sea
birds to some serious rookeries on the cliffs
of the outer islands.

An unusual view of medieval life on the
island is provided in the accounts of a shipwrecked merchant of Venice, one Pietro
Querini, who washed up on Sandøy in 1432
and reputedly introduced stockfish to Italy.
Røst's **tourist office** (☎454 92 186; ⊙mid-
Jun–mid-Aug), a short walk from the ferry
dock, has a sheet outlining the tale.

ⓖ Tours

From June to mid-August the M/S *Inger
Helen*, belonging to Kårøy Rorbucamping, does five-hour **boat tours** (adult/child
Nkr300/125) that cruise past several bird
cliffs, including the Vedøy kittiwake colony.
Weather permitting, the boat makes a stop
for a short walk to the 1887 Skomvær lighthouse or, if you prefer, you can try a little
fishing (lines provided).

Sleeping & Eating

Kårøy Rorbucamping   CAMPGROUND €

(☎76 09 62 38; www.karoy.no; per person Nkr180;
⊙May–mid-Sep; @�🛜) Rooms sleep two, four
or six at this authentic *rorbu*. Bathrooms are
communal and there are self-catering facilities. You can borrow a rowing boat for free or
rent a motor boat. This great budget choice is
on the minuscule island of Kårøy; phone from
the ferry and a boat will be sent to collect you.

Røst Bryggehotel   HOTEL €€

(☎76 05 08 00; www.rostbryggehotell.no; d Nkr750
Jul–mid-Aug, Nkr900 rest of yr) This modern development in traditional style is right on the
quayside. It has 16 comfortable doubles, and
hires out both bikes, boats and fishing tackle.

Querini Pub og Restaurant   PUB €

(☎76 09 64 80) Named after the shipwrecked
merchant from Venice, this is a reliable
choice among Røst's few eating options.

ⓘ Getting There & Away

There are flights to/from both Bodø and Leknes.
Røst, like Værøy, is served by the car ferry that
runs between Bodø (passenger/car Nkr178/647)
and Moskenes (passenger/car Nkr125/446).

VESTERÅLEN

Administratively, the Harstad region falls
within the county of Troms but, for the sake
of convenience, we cover it in this chapter.
Although the landscapes here aren't as dramatic as those in Lofoten, they tend to be
much wilder and the forested mountainous regions of the island of Hinnøya are a
unique corner of Norway's largely treeless
northern coast.

*An Encounter with Vesterålen – Culture,
Nature & History* (Nkr170), sold at tourist
offices, gives a good introduction to the region, its sights and walking routes.

Hadseløya
POP 7800

Vesterålen's link to Lofoten is the southernmost island of Hadseløya, connected by
ferry from the port of Melbu to Fiskebøl
on Austvågøy. The other main town, Stokmarknes, is best known as the birthplace of
the Hurtigruten coastal ferry.

ⓘ Information

Hadseløya's **tourist office** (☎76 16 46 60;
⊙10am-5pm Mon-Sat, 11am-4pm Sat & Sun
mid-Jun–mid-Aug only) is on the waterfront in
Stokmarknes.

ⓘ Getting There & Around

The Hurtigruten coastal ferry still makes a detour stop in its home port of Stokmarknes.

Buses between Melbu and Stokmarknes run several times daily on weekdays and twice daily at weekends.

STOKMARKNES

The Hurtigruten coastal ferry was founded in Stokmarknes in 1893 by Richard With. Originally a single ship, the S/S *Vesterålen,* it sailed into nine ports between Trondheim and Hammerfest, carrying post, passengers and vital supplies. Now the line boasts 11 ships, carries half a million passengers annually, serves 35 towns and villages and is a vital link for Norway, providing transport for locals and a scenic cruise experience for tourists.

◉ Sights

Hurtigrutemuseet   MUSEUM
(www.hurtigrutemuseet.no; Markedsgata 1; adult/child Nkr90/35; ⊙10am-6pm mid-Jun–mid-Aug, core hr 2-4pm rest of yr) The Hurtigruten Museum portrays the history of the coastal-ferry line in text and image. Hitched to the quayside is the retired ship M/S *Finnmarken,* claimed to be the world's largest museum piece, which plied the coastal route between 1956 and 1993.

⊨ Sleeping & Eating

Hurtigrutens Hus   HOTEL €€
(☑76 15 06 00; www.hurtigrutenshus.com; Markedsgata 1; s/d Nkr1075/1380; ⊙Jun–mid-Aug) Hurtigruten House is a luxurious hotel, conference and arts venue, where rooms represent good value for your krone. Located in the same complex as the museum, this is one of the few places where it's more fun to be alone than accompanied; single rooms are furnished to resemble ships' cabins.

Hurtigrutens Hus Turistsenter   HOTEL €€
(☑76 15 29 99; s/d Nkr1075/1380) This friendly extension to the Hurtigruten complex is over the bridge that spans the fjord and has more conventional cabins and rooms.

TOP CHOICE **Isqueen**   RESTAURANT €€€
(☑76 15 29 99; mains Nkr245-315; ⊙6-11pm) Within the Turistcenter grounds, this one-time whaler, forever beached, is now an excellent Arctic Menu restaurant. You can dine within its hull, in the grafted-on restaurant with its wraparound windows, or up top on the outdoor terrace with fine views over the sound.

Rødbrygga Pub   PUB €€
(Markedsgata 6a; mains Nkr70-200; ⊙11am-3am) Just across from the Hurtigruten Museum,

this all-wood place does good grills, seafood, pizzas at more modest prices and a mean fish soup (Nkr80).

MELBU

In an abandoned herring oil factory (romantically named Neptune despite its stark functionality), the **Norwegian Fishing Industry Museum** (Norsk Fiskerindustrimuseum; Neptunveien; adult/child Nkr50/free; ⊙9am-3pm Mon-Fri) traces the life of a fish from the deep sea to the kitchen table. There's also a children's exhibition about the goings-on on the sea floor. Across the harbour from the ferry pier, it's 750m from the E10. In summer there are guided visits, included in the admission fee.

The **Sommer-Melbu festival** (www.sommermelbu.no), held each July, is one of northern Norway's liveliest cultural festivals with seminars, lectures, music of all genres, theatre and art exhibitions.

Langøya

POP 14,650

The high points, both literally and figuratively, of Langøya, Vesterålen's central island, are the historic, little-visited fishing villages at its northern tip. Should you be passing through Sortland around bedtime, you'll find a pair of decent lodging options that also offer good dining.

The annual **Arctic Sea Kayak Race** (www.askr.no), held over six days in July, is one of the ultimate challenges in competitive sea-kayaking. Normal beings can opt for less intensive kayak touring or an introductory course in sea-kayaking.

SORTLAND

POP 9800

Sortland, Vesterålen's commercial centre and transit hub, occupies a nick in the island's east coast. Its mostly chunky, rectangular buildings are painted a soothing sea-blue.

In September the town hosts **Sortland Jazz,** a festival that takes place over a couple of weeks.

⊨ Sleeping

TOP CHOICE **Sjøhus Senteret**   GUESTHOUSE, CABINS €€
(☑76123740; www.lofoten-info.no/sjohussenteret; Ånstadsjøen; d/tr Nkr770/870, 3-/5-bed cabin Nkr1345/2000) Precisely 1.4km north of the bridge, this appealing spot has both comfortable rooms and waterside cabins with

views. Its **Sjøstua restaurant** (mains Nkr200-235; ⊙3-9.30pm Mon-Sat, 1-8.30pm Sun), where owner and chef Marit Asbjørnsen produces a delightful range of à la carte dishes, is worth a visit in its own right. Intimate and all-wood, it has superb views over the fjord in three directions. Try the cod baked with herbs and garnished with prawns, or the reindeer stew with mushrooms and juniper berries.

Sortland Camping og Motell CAMPGROUND €
(☑76 11 03 00; www.sortland-camping.no; Vestervegen 51; car/caravan site Nkr200/225, cabin Nkr350-450, for 5-7 persons with bathroom Nkr950-1500) Around 1.3km from the centre, this place offers home cooking, strong on northern Norway cuisine. Occupying an extensive, semiwooded area, it produces a useful information sheet about the area.

❶ Information
The **tourist office** (☑76 11 14 80; www.visitvesteralen.com; Kjøpmannsgata 2; ⊙9am-5.30pm Mon-Fri, 10am-3.45pm Sat, noon-3.45pm Sun mid-Jun–mid-Aug, rest of yr 9am-2.30pm Mon-Fri) covers the whole of the Vesterålen region.

❶ Getting There & Away
Sortland is a stop on the Hurtigruten coastal ferry.
Bus services include:
Andenes Two hours, two to four daily, via Risøyhamn (one hour)
Harstad 2¼ hours, one to three daily
Narvik 3½ hours, three to five daily
Svolvær 2¼ hours, two to four daily

NYKSUND
A dramatic drive along a narrow ribbon of road that hugs the shoreline brings you to this long-abandoned fishing village that's been reborn as an artists' colony. From the crumbling old structures to the faithfully renovated commercial buildings, it's picture-perfect. It's hard to imagine that, until recently, Nyksund was a ghost town.

The bakery and post office, heart of any community, shut up shop in the 1960s and nearly everyone else left in 1975 after a storm destroyed the mole. The last inhabitant, blacksmith Olav Larsen, packed his bags in 1977.

Sheep and vandals took over but slowly, over the decades, life has been breathed back into this charming, remote settlement. Nowadays, modern Nyksund boasts a summer population of around 60 and some half-dozen hardy souls hack it throughout the harsh winters.

This tiny community manages to support an active summer cultural program and a small **museum** (www.nyksund.as; ⊙11am-5pm mid-Jun–mid-Aug).

TOP CHOICE **Holmvik Brygge** CAFE-GUESTHOUSE
(☑76 13 47 96; www.nyksund.com; s/d Nkr450/800; lunch Nkr95-220, dinner Nkr165-365; ⊙year-round) This cosy, hugely welcoming guesthouse and cafe in itself justifies the detour. You can either cater for yourself or eat at its Holmvik Stua, where the food's locally sourced and the fish smoked on the premises.

STØ
The small, distinctive fishing village of Stø clings to Langøya's northernmost tip. From late May to mid-September, **Arctic Whale Tours** (☑76 13 43 00; www.arcticwhaletours.com) mount one (two in high season) six-hour whale-watching cruises (adult/child Nkr795/500) daily. On the way to the sperm whales' feeding grounds, boats pause to view sea-bird and seal colonies.

The walk over the headland between Nyksund and Stø, waymarked with red letter T's, merits a short day of your life. Most hikers sweat a little on the outward leg of this five-hour circular trek via the 517m Sørkulen, then breathe easy, returning via the simpler

RECLAIMED & RECYCLED
Ssemjon Gerlitz, the sparky German owner of Holmvik Brygge, has lived year-round in Nyksund for a decade and more. Over the years, he and his team of helpers have gleaned, picked and scavenged what could be salvaged from Nyksund's crumbling buildings and incorporated them into higgledy-piggledy Holmvik Brygge, where every room's different, each with its own personality.

Two things in particular keep him here, at road's end. Modulating his rat-a-tat delivery for just a millisecond, he slows to speak of the lure of silence, nothing but the rhythm of wind and waves for most of the year. Then, changing a gear, of his sense of communion with long-gone fisherfolk ('Every rusty nail I pull out was hammered in by someone who lived and worked here') and, once again in overdrive, of the sheer energy of this splendid place where mountains tumble to the sea.

sea-level route. Called the **Queen's Route**, its name derives from a hike taken by Norway's Queen Sonja in 1994. The Sortland tourist office carries a free guide leaflet.

Small, waterside **Stø Bobilcamp** (☎76 13 25 30; www.stobobilcamp.com; campsite Nkr150, cabin Nkr1200; ☻mid-May–mid-Aug) is stark indeed and a windy spot to pitch your tent but it does run an unpretentious little restaurant, serving primarily fish.

Two weekday buses run between Sortland and Stø (1¼ hours).

Andøya

POP 5000

Andøya, long, narrow and flat except for the mountains on its western flank, is atypical of Vesterålen. The 1000m-deep, dark, cold waters of its northwestern shore attract abundant stocks of squid, including some very large specimens indeed, and these in turn attract the squid-loving sperm whales. The result is fairly reliable whale-watching, centred on the town of Andenes at the island's northern end.

Andenes is the only place of any size but other nature safaris depart from the tiny ports of Bleik and Stave, about 10km and 25km southwest of the town.

ANDENES

POP 2700

The straggling village of Andenes with its rich fishing history is northern Norway's main base for whale-watching. Its harbour front is a charming jumble of wooden boat sheds and general nautical detritus.

◉ Sights & Activities

Whale Safari   WHALE VIEWING
(☎76 11 56 00; www.whalesafari.no) Far and away the island's biggest outfit, Whale Safari runs popular whale-watching cruises (adult/child Nkr830/500) between late May and mid-September. It also operates the Whale Centre. Tours begin with a guided visit to the Centre, followed by a two- to four-hour boat trip. If you fail to spot at least one sperm whale, your money is refunded or you can take another trip for free. There's a good chance of spotting minke, pilot, humpback and orca (killer whale). Trips depart at least once daily with up to six sailings in high summer. Your fee includes a snack, if you can face it – staff pass around the seasickness pills, just like airline boiled sweets, before takeoff. Bad weather and/or

The tourist office sells a combined ticket (adult/child Nkr100/50) that gives access to its Hisnakul Natural History Centre and nature slide show, the adjacent Northern Lights Centre and the Whale Centre, just across the wharf. If you've signed on for a whale safari, both venues are free.

high seas only rarely prevent a Whale Safari sailing. All the same, try to build in an extra day on the island, just in case you're unlucky.

Hvalsenteret   WHALE CENTRE
(Havnegate 1; adult/child Nkr40/20; ☻8.30am-4pm or 8pm late May–mid-Sep) The Whale Centre provides a perspective for whale-watchers, with displays on whale research, hunting and the life cycle of these gentle giants. Most people visit the centre in conjunction with a whale safari.

Hisnakul   ARCTIC NATURE CENTRE
(Hamnegata 1; ☻9am-6pm mid-Jun–Aug, 8am-3pm Mon-Fri rest of yr) This nature centre shares a restored wooden warehouse with the tourist office. It showcases the natural history of northern Norway, including sea birds, marine mammals, topography, farming, fisheries and local cultures. There's also a 23-minute slide show with spectacular shots of the natural life of northern Norway.

Northern Lights Centre   EXHIBITION
(☻10am-6pm late Jun–late Aug) Next door to Hisnakul, this impressive high-tech aurora borealis exhibition first featured at the 1994 Winter Olympics in Lillehammer.

Polarmuseet   POLAR MUSEUM
(Havnegate; adult/child Nkr30/free; ☻10am-5pm mid-Jun–mid-Aug) The quaint, Arctic-themed Polar Museum has displays on local hunting and fishing traditions. There's extensive coverage of the 38 winter hunting expeditions in Svalbard undertaken by local explorer Hilmar Nøis, who also collected most of the exhibits.

Andenes Fyr   LIGHTHOUSE
(adult/child Nkr40/20; ☻late Jun-Aug) The town's landmark red lighthouse, automated for many years, opened in 1859 and still shines on. To climb up 40m and 148 steps, ask for the key at the tourist office.

THE ROAD LESS TRAVELLED

Unless you leave Andøya by the seasonal ferry from Andenes to Gryllefjord (in itself a lovely way to go), there's no way of avoiding the 100km drive the length of the island's slim northern finger, poking up from Sortland. To avoid repetition, but all the more so because it's a simply spectacular drive, take the minor, lightly trafficked west coast road from Risøyhamn as you head northwards. Designated a National Tourist Route, it offers magnificent coastal panoramas as it threads along the shoreline. Returning by the Rv82, notice the giant hillocks of peat, extracted, dried and ready to be transported to garden centres around the world.

To experience the route at the pace it deserves, hire a bike from Fargeklatten and ride the coast as far as Sortland, where you can sling your bike on the bus for delivery back to Andenes.

🛏 Sleeping & Eating

Hotell Marena TOP CHOICE   BOUTIQUE HOTEL €€
(☑915 83 517; www.hotellmarena.no; Storgata 15; s/d Nkr860/1090; 🛜) Hotell Marena is an exciting and particularly tasteful recent addition to Andenes' accommodation choices. Public areas feature nature photographs by local photographer Espen Tollefsen, as do each of the 12 bedrooms, individually designed with colours that match the tones of the blown-up photographs. There's free coffee around the clock, together with scrummy homemade cakes.

Den Gamle Fyrmesterbolig GUESTHOUSE €
(☑76 14 10 27; Richard Withs gate 11; r with shared bathroom Nkr500) In the shadow of Andenes' resplendent lighthouse, this charming, well-equipped option with self-catering facilities occupies the first floor of what was once the lighthouse-keepers' cottage. There are only two rooms and it doesn't take advance reservations, but if you ring up on the day they'll hold one for you.

Fargeklatten ROOMS, APARTMENTS €€
(☑977 60 020; www.fargeklatten.no; Sjøgata 38a; r Nkr800, 5-bed apt Nkr1500) Rooms in 'Veita', a restored 18th-century home, are attractively furnished in antique style, while apartments are spacious and well equipped at these re-

cently renovated properties at the eastern end of the village.

Andenes Camping CAMPGROUND €
(☑76 11 56 00; car/caravan site Nkr100/140; ⊙late May-Sep) This basic campground, located 3.5km from town, is on a gorgeous seaside meadow, green and smooth as a golf course. It has a well-equipped kitchen and large common room.

Hisnakul ROOMS €
(☑76 14 12 03; s/d with shared bathroom Nkr300/450) Hisnakul nature centre has well-priced budget rooms above its gallery and there are facilities for self-caterers. It has only 14 beds so phone to reserve.

Norlandia Andrikken Hotell HOTEL €€
(☑76 14 12 22; www.norlandia.no/andrikken; Storgata 53; s/d Nkr850/1150; 🛜) Norlandia's housebrand lodging, although dull and boxy from the outside, has rooms that, once you penetrate, are comfortable and well equipped. It also runs a decent restaurant (mains around Nkr200).

Lysthuset RESTAURANT €€
(☑76 14 14 99; Storgata 51; pizzas Nkr130-200, mains Nkr155-250) The Lysthuset is the best of Andenes' limited dining options. In front, it's your typical takeaway burgers, pizzas and other speedy stuff. Behind, the restaurant proper offers altogether more subtle fare. For dessert, indulge in a little 'Sex on the Mountain' – an orgasmic confection of ice cream, cream, blackberries and cloudberries, all doused in eggnog.

FARGEKLATTEN

Fargeklatten, meaning the splash of colour, is a very special place, the creation of Grethe Kvalvik. For years, Grethe was the receptionist at Andrikken Hotell until she lost her sight. After two long years of blindness, partial vision returned and she could again perceive shapes and, above all, colours.

Determined to live a full life anew, she rescued Fargeklatten, at the time earmarked for demolition to make way for a car park. This complex of historical buildings now includes a couple of small **galleries** (⊙11am-4pm) displaying the art and crafts of northern Norway and a small **turf museum** (adult/child Nkr50/free) – plus some attractive accommodation options.

ⓘ Information

Andenes's **tourist office** (☎76 14 12 03; www. andoyturist.no; Hamnegata 1; ⊙9am-6pm mid-Jun–Aug, 8am-3pm Mon-Fri rest of yr; @⊋) covers the whole island and shares premises with the Hisnak Nature Centre. Its leaflet in English, *Andanes Vær* (Nkr35), outlines a walking tour of the old quarter. There's internet access (Nkr20 per 15 minutes) and free wi-fi.

Yanthi (☎75 91 75 75; Storgata 2) has three internet terminals (Nkr25 per 30 minutes) and brews good coffee.

ⓘ Getting There & Around

AIR The flight between Andenes and Tromsø, via Narvik or Bodø, is a contender for the world's most scenic flight with spectacular aerial views of the landscapes, seas and agricultural patterns.

BICYCLE Fargeklatten rents bicycles (per hr/day/week Nkr50/150/750) and also cycle trailers (per day/week Nkr100/500) and child seats.

BUS Two to four daily buses run south to Sortland (two hours) via Risøyhamn, where a bus to/from Andenes meets and greets the Hurtigruten.

FERRY From late May to the end of August, a car ferry (www.senjafergene.no) connects Andenes with the port of Gryllefjord (1¾ hours, two to three daily) on the island of Senja, passing magnificent coastal scenery.

AROUND ANDENES

Nordtun Gård   FARM

(☎926 44 906; www.nordtungard.no; admission Nkr75; ⊙noon-6pm Tue-Sun late Jun-late Aug) In the hamlet of Bø, on Andøya's west coast, Nordtun Gård is a working farm and dairy where children can play with the animals while adults sample its range of cheeses.

ⓣ Kvalnesbrygga   CAMPGROUND €
TOP CHOICE (☎76 14 63 78; www.kvalnesbrygga.no, in Norwegian; tent/caravan site Nkr110/130, d Nkr450; ⊙year round) This small campground, 22km south of Andenes on the Rv82, is right beside the fjord. The tent area, of soft, springy grass, is tiny. The main building, much modified, was built by the present owner's grandfather over a century ago and functioned in its time as home, post office and village store. There are well-equipped guest kitchens for both campers and those in rooms. The six rooms, each named after a local bird, are simply yet tastefully furnished. You can rent a small fishing boat with reel and catch your dinner.

BLEIK

A long, ash-white beach, one of several claimants to be Norway's longest, extends for almost 3km from the hamlet of Bleik.

Puffin Safari (☎908 38 594; www.puffinsa fari.no), based in Bleik, does warmly recommended, well-presented and informative daily 1½-hour **birdwatching boat trips** (adult/child Nkr350/200; ⊙1pm & 3pm Jun–mid-August) off Bleiksøya, with sighting of sea eagles guaranteed. You can also bring home dinner from their four-hour **deep-sea fishing trips** (adult/child Nkr500/200; ⊙5pm Jun–mid-Aug).

Stave Camping   CAMPGROUND €

(☎926 01 257; www.stavecamping.no; camping Nkr75 per person, caravans Nkr180, 2-bed cabin with outside bathroom Nkr430, apt 450-850; ⊙late May-August) Camp at the water's edge overlooking the fjord or take one of the more sheltered set-back sites. The day's exertions over, steep yourself in an ocean hot pool or sweat in the sauna.

Hinnøya

Administratively, Hinnøya, the largest island off mainland Norway, splits between the two counties of Troms and Nordland. Contrasting with the islands to the south, it's mostly forested green upland punctuated by snowcaps and deeply indented by stunning fjords. Off Hinnøya's west coast, Vesterålen is divided from Lofoten by the narrow Raftsund strait and even narrower, hugely scenic Trollfjorden, whose sheer walls plunge down to the water, dwarfing all below.

HARSTAD
POP 23,250

On a hillside close to the northern end of Hinnøya, Harstad, the area's largest town, technically tumbles within Troms county. It's a small industrial and defence-oriented place, full of docks, tanks and warehouses. Contrasting with so many tourism-'n'-fishing towns to the south, it has a certain purposeful bustle.

◉ Sights & Activities

Most sights are on the **Trondenes Peninsula**, some 2.5km north of town.

Trondenes Kirke   CHURCH
(⊙variable) Trondenes Church was built by King Øystein around 1150. For ages it was the northernmost church in Christendom – and still lays claim to being Norway's northernmost mediaeval *stone* church. Originally of wood, the current stone structure replaced it around 1250 and quickly came to double as a fortification against Russian aggression.

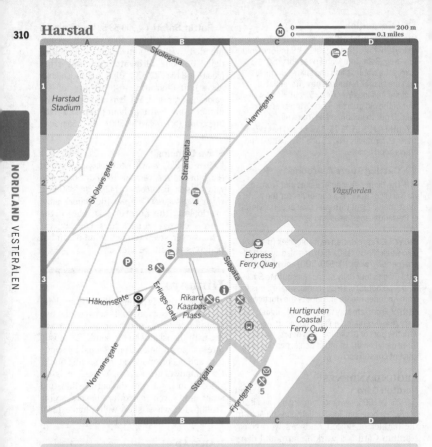

Harstad

◎ Sights

🛏 Sleeping

⊗ Eating

Its jewels are the three finely wrought altars at the east end, all venerating Mary. Most interesting is the central one of the Virgin surrounded by her extended family with infants in arms and children tugging at skirts on all sides. Glance up too at the pair of trumpet-wielding cherubs, precariously perched atop the main pillars of the rood screen. Entry is free – if, that is, you can get in; absurdly for one of northern Norway's major cultural sights, it's often locked so do check with the tourist office.

Trondenes Historiske Senter　MUSEUM
(Trondenesveien 122; adult/child Nkr70/50; ☉10am-5pm mid-Jun–mid-Aug, Sun only rest of yr) Trondenes Historical Centre, just south of the church, has well-mounted and equally well-documented displays and artefacts illustrating the social history of the area from Viking days to the present.

Adolfkanonen
GIANT GUN

(guided tours adult/child Nkr60/30; ☺mid-Jun–mid-Aug) Here's another biggest/furthest claim for Harstad: This formidable WWII weapon is the world's largest land-based big gun, with a calibre of more than 40cm and a recoil force of 635 tonnes. Because it lies in a military area, you're obliged to take a guided tour of the site and to have your own vehicle. Just turn up 10 minutes before departure. The bunker also contains a collection of artillery, military equipment and instruments used by Nazi coastal batteries during WWII.

Grottebadet
SWIMMING BATHS

(☎77 04 17 70; www.grottebadet.no, in Norwegian; Håkonsgate 7; adult/child Nkr135/100; ☺noon-8pm Mon-Fri, 11am-6pm Sat & Sun) This heated indoor complex, tunnelled a full 150m into the hillside, has pools, rapids, slides, flume rides, steam rooms and other watery activities. Huge fun for all the family.

☆ Festivals & Events

Harstad's **Festival of North Norway** (www.festspillnn.no), approaching its 50th incarnation, is a full week of music, theatre and dance in the second half of June.

🛏 Sleeping

Clarion Collection Hotel Arcticus
HOTEL €€

(☎77 04 08 00; www.choice.no; Havnegata 3; s/d from Nkr850/1050 incl breakfast & light evening meal; @�) This hotel shares a harmonious modern building with Harstad's cultural centre. A short, pleasant jetty walk from the centre, it has 75 particularly large rooms. It's Nkr200 extra for a superior standard, waterside room with splendid views over the fjord to the mountains beyond.

Grand Nordic Hotel
HOTEL €€

(☎77 00 30 00; www.rica.no; Strandgata 9; s/d from Nkr790/990; P@�) This is the grand dame of Harstad hotels. Request one of the larger, more pleasantly decorated rooms in the newer section.

Thon Hotel Harstad
HOTEL €€

(☎77 00 08 00; www.thonhotels.com/harstad; Sjøgata 11; s/d from Nkr850/1050; @�) All 141 rooms at this decent chain hotel have attractive parquet flooring and most have views over the port and fjord. Buffet breakfast, taken in the hotel's Egon restaurant, is copious.

Harstad Camping
CAMPGROUND €

(☎77 07 36 62; www.harstad-camping.no; Nesseveien 55; car/caravan site Nkr175/200, 4-bed cabin Nkr400, with bathroom Nkr900-1100) Follow the Rv83 to-

wards Narvik for 4km, then take a side road to reach this small waterside site, where you can rent rowing boats (per hour/day Nkr80/290) and motorboats (Nkr150/570).

✕ Eating

Café & Restaurant De 4 Roser
CAFE-RESTAURANT €€€

(☎77 01 27 50; www.de4roser.no, in Norwegian; Torvat 7; mains Nkr160-320; ☺cafe 10am-10pm, restaurant 6-10pm Mon-Sat) Two quite separate dining experiences with a single name occupy the same building. On one floor, the Four Roses is a buzzing cafe that offers sandwiches, pasta, burgers and salads and a trio of daily specials (around Nkr150). Portions are large and salads, such as the variant with fried trout, mushrooms and feta cheese, are innovative. Above the cafe, in more intimate surroundings, the restaurant offers fine gourmet cuisine and a short, tempting menu, from which you can pick between four courses (Nkr625) and 10 (Nkr1150). The restaurant entrance is at street level.

Hoelstuen
RESTAURANT €€€

(☎77 06 55 00; www.hoelstuen.com, in Norwegian; Rikard Kaarbøs plass 4; mains Nkr300-345; ☺5-11pm Mon-Sat) This trim place rivals the 4 Roser restaurant for the title of best dining experience in a town of limited eating opportunities. Its cuisine has flair. Dig your fork, for example, into the garlic fried fillet of stag with mushrooms and port glaze. It also does a particularly rich and creamy fish soup (Nkr105).

Kaffistova
CAFE €

(☎77 06 12 57; Rikard Kaarbøsgata 6; dishes Nkr30-166; ☺8am-6pm Mon-Fri, 9am-3.30pm Sat, noon-5pm Sun) This agreeable spot, established in 1913, does sandwiches, a choice of meat and fish mains as long as your arm and as many as 16 kinds of cake. Split-level and smelling of coffee and cakes, it's a good, informal place for lunch or a snack despite the dull decor.

Lyst
CAFE-BAR €

(☎77 00 30 30; Hakons gate; mains around Nkr120; ☺3pm-midnight Mon-Fri, noon-1.30am Sat) Lyst (Pleasure) is a cheerful place with a pub atmosphere, popular with locals of all ages. You can munch on a good pizza, made on the spot. To help it down, select from the ample range of beers or Harstad's widest selection of whiskies and spirits.

❶ Information

The **tourist office** (☎77 01 89 89; www.destinationharstad.no; ☺10am-6pm mid-Jun–mid-Aug,

8am-3.30pm rest of yr) is located beside the bus station.

ⓘ Getting There & Away

AIR From the Harstad-Narvik airport at Evenes there are direct flights to Oslo, Bodø, Tromsø and Trondheim.

BOAT If you're heading for Tromsø, the easiest and most scenic option is by boat. There are two to four express passenger ferries daily between Harstad and Tromsø (three hours), via Finnsnes (1¾ hours).

There's also a seasonal express passenger ferry (www.senjafergene.no) between Stornes, just north of Harstad and Skrolsvik (Nkr134; 1¼ hours; two to three daily mid-May to August), at the southern end of Senja island. There, you'll find bus connections to Finnsnes and then on to Tromsø. Harstad is also a stop on the Hurtigruten coastal ferry.

BUS Buses to/from Sortland (2½ hours) run one to three times daily. There's one bus to/from Narvik via Harstad-Narvik airport (2½ hours; daily except Saturday) and a daily service between Harstad and Fauske (5¾ hours).

ⓘ Getting Around

Flybussen (Nkr150, 50 minutes) shuttles between the town centre and Evenes airport several times daily.

Buses connect Trondenes with the central bus station approximately hourly, Monday to Saturday.

Parking may not be easy to find but – God bless the good burghers of Harstad – it's free in public car parks for vehicles with non-Norwegian licence plates.

For a taxi, call ☏77 04 10 00.

The Far North

Why Go?

Norway's northernmost counties of Troms and Finnmark arc across the very top of Europe, where broad horizons share the land with dense forest. Like most of the relatively few visitors who make it this far north, come in summer to enjoy Tromsø, the region's only town of any size. The museums of this sparky, self-confident place will orient you for the Arctic lands beyond. You'll probably respond to the call of Nordkapp (North Cape), the European mainland's most northerly point. But to really feel the pull of the north, you need to push beyond to explore the sparsely populated plateaus of Inner Finnmark and its wild northeastern coast, the Norwegian heartland of the Sami people. For alternative adventure (say, scudding aboard a snowmobile or behind a team of yapping huskies), plan to return in winter, when soft blue light envelops the snowy lands, outsiders are even fewer and the northern lights streak the sky.

Best Places to Eat

» Arctandria (p322)
» Gapahuken (p344)
» Aunegården (p321)
» Emma's Drømekjøkken (p321)

Best Places to Stay

» Engholm Husky Design Lodge (p348)
» Park Hotell (p326)
» Arran (p335)
» Thon Hotel Vica (p327)
» Bungalåven Vertshus (p335)

When to Go

Tromsø

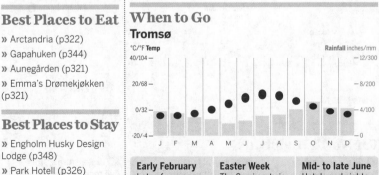

	Early February	Easter Week	Mid- to late June
	Lots of snowy activities and, with luck, the northern lights on tap.	The Sami party in Kautokeino before dispersing to their summer pastures.	Hotels and sights reopen, and the crowds have yet to come.

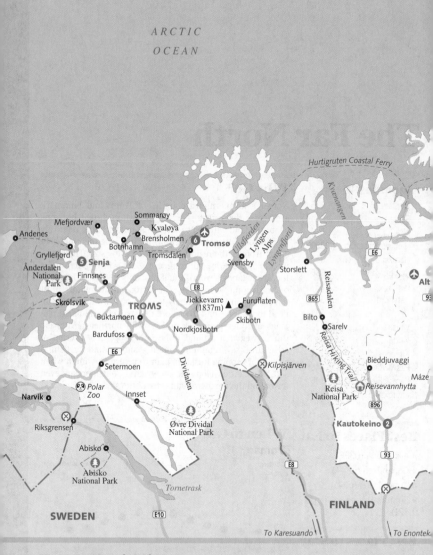

ARCTIC
OCEAN

Hurtigruten Coastal Ferry

Kvænangen

Andenes

Mefjordvær ○
Sommarøy ○
Kvaløya ○
Brensholmen ○
Botnhamn ○
Tromsdalen ○
6 **Tromsø**

Gryllefjord ○
5 Senja
Ånderdalen National Park ○
Finnsnes ○

Skrolsvik

TROMS

Buktamoen ○

Bardufoss ○

E6

Setermoen ○

Narvik ○

Riksgrensen ○

Abiskø ○

Abisko National Park

SWEDEN   E10

Ullsfjorden

Lyngen Alps

Lyngenfjord

Svensby ○
Storslett ○

E8

Jiekkevarre (1837m) ▲   Furuflaten ○

Skibotn ○

Nordkjosbotn ○

Dividalen

Reisadalen

865

Bilto ○
Sarelv ○

Reisa Hiking Trail

⊗ Kilpisjärven

Reisa National Park

896

Bieddjuvaggi

Reisevannhytta   Máze

Kautokeino **2**

E6

93

E8

93

E6

⊗

Polar Zoo

Innset ○

Øvre Dividal National Park

⊗

Torneträsk

FINLAND

To Karesuando   To Enontek

Alt

93

Far North Highlights

1 Reach dramatic **Nordkapp** (p332) after the long haul northwards, then leave the crowds behind to hike to **Knivskjelodden** (p332), continental Europe's northernmost point

2 Learn about the unique culture of the Sami in **Karasjok** (p346) and **Kautokeino** (p348)

3 Explore **Alta's Stone Age rock carvings** (p326), a Unesco World Heritage Site, and learn more at its award-winning museum

4 Dog-*mush* through the snow and bruise-blue winter light near **Karasjok** (p347)

5 Cycle the spectacular, lightly trafficked northern coast of the island of **Senja** (p324)

6 Listen to an organ recital as the midnight sun peeks through the windows of Tromsø's **Arctic Cathedral** (p316)

TROMS

Troms, where the Gulf Stream peters out, mitigating the harshness of winter, boasts a couple of near-superlative places: Tromsø, the only place large enough to merit the name 'city' in northern Norway, and Senja, Norway's second-largest island, a less trodden rival to the Lofotens for spectacular scenery. This section covers the northern two-thirds of Troms county; the Troms portion of the island of Hinnøya features in the Nordland chapter.

Tromsø

POP 67,300

Simply put, Tromsø parties. By far the largest town in northern Norway and administrative centre of Troms county, it's lively with cultural bashes, buskers, an animated street scene, a midnight-sun marathon, a respected university, the hallowed Mack Brewery – and more pubs per capita than any other Norwegian town. Its corona of snow-topped peaks provides arresting scenery, excellent hiking in summer and great skiing and dog-sledding in winter.

Many Tromsø landmarks claim northernmost titles, including the university, cathedral, brewery, botanic garden and even the most boreal Burger King. Although the city lies almost 400km north of the Arctic Circle, its climate is pleasantly moderated by the Gulf Stream. The long winter darkness is offset by round-the-clock activity during the perpetually bright days of summer.

Tromsø received its municipal charter in 1794, when the city was developing as a trading centre, but its history goes way back to the 13th century, when the first local church was built. In more recent times, the city became a launching point for polar expeditions, and thanks to that distinction, it's nicknamed 'Gateway to the Arctic' (more appropriate than 'Paris of the North', a soubriquet ironically touted on T-shirts).

The main part of town stretches along the east shore of the island of Tromsøya, linked to the mainland by a gracefully arched bridge.

◉ Sights & Activities

The tourist office's *Summer Activities in Tromsø* and its winter equivalent both give a comprehensive checklist of tours and activities.

Polaria   ARCTIC INTERPRETIVE CENTRE
(Hjalmar Johansens gate 12; www.polaria.no; adult/child Nkr100/50; ◷10am-7pm) Daringly designed Polaria is an entertaining multimedia introduction to northern Norway and Svalbard. After a 14-minute film about the latter (screened every 30 minutes), an Arctic walk leads to a northern lights display, aquariums of cold-water fish and – the big draw – a trio of energetic bearded seals. Beside it is **Polstjerna** (adult/child Nkr25/10; ◷noon-5pm mid-Jun–mid-Aug), a historic seal-hunting ship. Between 1949 and 1981, it killed (or 'brought home,' as the literature euphemistically expresses it) nearly 100,000 seals.

Tromsø University Museum   ARCTIC MUSEUM
(Lars Thøringsvei 10; adult/child Nkr30/15; ◷9am-4.30pm or 6pm) Near the southern end of Tromsøya, it has well-presented and documented displays on traditional and modern Sami life (in the garden, a *gammen*, or traditional Sami sod house, offers free coffee in summer) and ecclesiastical art and accoutrements (look for the set of hourglasses, turned to warn the vicar that his sermon time was running out). There's also a small section on the Vikings, who were of lesser importance in the history of northern Norway.

Downstairs, learn about rocks of the north. The newest section presents a number of thought-provoking themes (such as the role of fire, the consequences of global warming and loss of wilderness – until recently as much as 45% of Norway's area) with plenty of illustration and touch-screen involvement. See too the replica 'northern lights machine', or terrella, an early invention that gives you in miniature a sense of the splendour of the aurora borealis. Take bus 37.

Ishavskatedralen   CHURCH
(www.ishavskatedralen.no; Hans Nilsensvei 41; adult/child Nkr30/free; ◷9am-7pm Mon-Sat, 1-7pm Sun) The 11 arching triangles of the **Arctic Cathedral** (1965), as the Tromsdalen Church is more usually called, suggest glacial crevasses and auroral curtains. The magnificent glowing stained-glass window that occupies almost the whole of the east end depicts Christ redescending to earth. Look back toward the west end and the contemporary organ, a work of steely art in itself, then up high to take in the lamps of Czech crystal, hanging in space like icicles. Take bus 20 or 24.

Polar Museum   MUSEUM
(Polarmuseet; www.polarmuseum.no; Søndre Tollbugata 11; adult/child Nkr60/10; ◷10am-7pm

mid-Jun–mid-Aug, 11am-3pm or 5pm rest of year) The 1st floor of this harbourside museum illustrates early polar research, especially the ventures of Nansen and Amundsen. Downstairs there's a well-mounted exhibition about the hunting and trapping of fuzzy Arctic creatures on Svalbard before coal became king there. Note the nasty exploding harpoons outside; the whale didn't stand much of a chance.

Fjellheisen CABLE CAR
(www.fjellheisen.no; adult/child return Nkr100/50; ☺10am-1am late May–mid-Aug, 10am-5pm rest of year) For a fine view of the city and midnight sun, take the cable car to the top of Mt Storsteinen (421m). There's a restaurant at the top, from where a network of hiking routes radiates. Take bus 26 and buy a combined bus and cable-car ticket (adult/child Nkr135/80).

Mack Brewery BREWERY
(Mack Ølbryggeri; ☎77 62 45 80; www.olhallen.no; Storgata 5) This venerable institution merits a pilgrimage. Established in 1877, it produces 18 kinds of beer, including the very quaffable Macks Pilsner, Isbjørn, Haakon and several dark beers. At 1pm year-round (plus 3pm, June to August) tours (Nkr150, including a beer mug, pin and pint) leave from the brewery's own Ølhallen Pub, Monday to Thursday. It's wise to reserve in advance.

Tromsø War Museum MUSEUM
(www.tromsoforsvarsmuseum.no; Solstrandveien; adult/child Nkr50/25; ☺noon-5pm Wed-Sun Jun–mid-Aug, Sun only May & late Aug-Sep) The cannons of a Nazi coastal artillery battery and a restored command bunker form the basis of the Tromsø Forsvarsmuseum. It also tells of the giant German battleship *Tirpitz*, sunk near the town on 12 November 1944, and the Nazi army's retreat from Leningrad, when many of its 120,000 troops were evacuated by ship from Tromsø. The museum's on the mainland, beside the E6 4.5km south of Tromsø bridge. Take bus 12 or 28.

TOP CHOICE **Botanic Gardens** BOTANIC GARDENS
(Breivika; admission free) Within the Arctic, Antarctic and alpine areas of Tromsø's carefullly maintained and cared for Botanisk Hage grows flora from all over the world's colder regions. And yes, it's the world's northernmost. Take bus 20.

Other Churches CHURCHES
Domkirke (Storgata), the Lutheran Church of Norway's cathedral, is one of Norway's largest wooden churches. Its opening hours

» www.finnmark.no
» www.visittroms.no
» www.visittromso.no

are erratic. Up the hill is the town's **Catholic Church** (Storgata 94; ☺9am-7.30pm). Both were built in 1861 and each lays claim to be – here comes yet another superlative – 'the world's northernmost bishopric' of its sect.

Andreas Aagaard House HISTORIC BUILDING
(Søndre Tollbugate 1) Constructed in 1838, it was the first building in town to be electrically lit.

Perspektivet HISTORIC BUILDING
(Storgata 95; www.perspektivet.no; ☺11am-5pm Tue-Sun) Dating from 1831, it houses a permanent photo exhibition illustrating Tromsø's history and mounts quality temporary displays too. You'll find more early-19th-century timber buildings around the centre, including a stretch of 1830s shops and merchants' homes along Sjøgata.

Bibliotek LIBRARY
(Grønnegata 94; ☺10am-4pm Mon-Fri) Tromsø's recently constructed library is a wonderful example of contemporary Norwegian architecture, streaming with light and airiness. Free internet access.

FREE **Blåst** GLASS BLOWING
(www.blaast.no, in Norwegian; Peder Hansens Gate 4). Pass by the world's most northerly glass-blowing workshop to see the young team puffing their cheeks and perhaps to pick up an item or two.

FREE **Art Museum of Northern Norway** ART GALLERY
(www.nnkm.no; Sjøgata 1; ☺noon-5pm Tue-Sun) The Nordnorsk Kunstmuseum shows mainly 19th-century to present-day sculpture, photography, painting and handicrafts by artists from northern Norway.

FREE **Tromsø Kunstforening** ART GALLERY
(Muségata 2; ☺noon-5pm Tue-Sun) The Tromsø branch of this national contemporary art foundation makes the most of its late-19th-century premises and promotes rotating exhibitions of contemporary art.

Winter Activities

In and around Tromsø (operators will normally collect you from your hotel) there's a

FRIDTJOF NANSEN

Fridtjof Nansen (1861–1930), the Norwegian all-rounder, explorer and diplomat, pushed the frontiers of human endurance and human compassion.

Growing up in rural Store Frøen outside Oslo (then known as Christiania), he enjoyed a privileged childhood. An excellent athlete, he won a dozen or so national nordic-skiing championships and broke the world 1-mile skating record. Studies in zoology at the University of Christiania led to a voyage aboard the sealing ship *Viking* to observe ocean currents, ice movements and wildlife. His first tantalising glimpses of Greenland planted the dream of travelling across its central icecap.

He didn't hang around. In 1888 Nansen, still only 27, headed a six-man expedition. He overwintered in Greenland and his detailed observations of the Inuit (Eskimo) people formed the backbone of his 1891 book, *Eskimo Life*.

In June 1893, aboard the 400-tonne, oak-hulled, steel-reinforced ship *Fram*, Nansen's next expedition left Christiania for the Arctic with provisions for six whole years. Nansen left behind his wife Eva and six-month-old daughter Liv, not knowing when, if ever, he'd return.

On 14 March 1895, he and Hjalmar Johansen set out in the *Fram* for the North Pole. They journeyed for five months, including 550km on foot over the ice, before holing up for nine winter months in a tiny stone hut they'd built on an island. On heading south, they encountered lone British explorer Frederick Jackson (for whom Nansen later, magnanimously, named the island where they'd spent the winter). Having given up on reaching the Pole, all three headed back to Vardø.

In 1905 a political crisis arose as Norway sought independence from Sweden. Nansen, by then a national hero, was dispatched to Copenhagen and Britain to represent the Norwegian cause.

Upon independence, Nansen was offered the job of prime minister but declined in order to keep exploring (he's also rumoured to have turned down offers to be king or president). He did, however, accept King Håkon's offer to serve as ambassador to Britain. In 1907, after the sudden death of his wife, he abandoned his dreams of conquering the South Pole and – again with a generosity untypical of the competitive world of polar exploration at the time – allowed fellow Norwegian explorer Roald Amundsen to take over the *Fram* for an expedition north of Siberia.

After WWI Nansen threw himself into large-scale humanitarian efforts: the new League of Nations, repatriating half a million German soldiers imprisoned in the Soviet Union, and an International Red Cross program against famine and pestilence in Russia. When some two million Russians and Ukrainians became stateless after fleeing the 1917 Bolshevik revolution, 'Nansen Passports' enabled thousands of them to settle elsewhere. Perhaps Nansen's greatest diplomatic achievement was the resettlement of several hundred thousand Greeks and Turks after the massive population shifts in the eastern Mediterranean following WWI.

In 1922 Nansen received the Nobel Peace Prize – then gave it all away to international relief efforts. After 1925 he concentrated on disarmament and lobbying for a non-Soviet homeland for Armenian refugees. Although this didn't happen in his time, he is still revered among Armenians worldwide.

On 13 May 1930, Nansen died quietly at his home in Polhøgda, near Oslo, and was buried in a garden nearby.

The standard biography of this extraordinary man is *Nansen* by Roland Huntford.

whole range of robust activities in the winter twilight.

» Experiencing the northern lights
» Cross-country skiing and snowshoeing
» Reindeer- and dog-sledding
» Snowshoe safaris
» Ice fishing
» Snowmobiling

To whet your winter appetite, check the tourist office website and these outfits too:

» **Arctic Adventure Tours** (www.arcticadventuretours.no)
» **Arctic Pathfinder** (www.arcticpathfinder.no)
» **Natur i Nord** (www.naturinord.no)
» **Tromsø Friluftsenter** (www.tromso-friluftsenter.no)

» **Tromsø Villmarkssenter** (www. villmarkssenter.no)

Tours

Tromso Townwalk (http://tromsotownwalk. weebly.com; ⊙tours noon-1.30pm Tue, Thu & Sat), a team of enthusiastic local guides, leads walking tours (Nkr150) that leave from the Domkirke.

You can fish from the *Signe I,* then have your catch sizzled on board. Built in 1908, she sails on three-hour evening **fishing trips** (adult/child Nkr400/250; ⊙trips 6pm Mon-Sat late Jun–mid-Aug).

For both outings, reserve at the tourist office.

Festivals & Events

Tromsø's two biggest annual bashes take place in deepest winter.

Northern Lights Festival   MUSIC (www.nordlysfestivalen.no) Six days of music of all genres. Late January.

Sami Week   SAMI CELEBRATIONS Includes the national reindeer sledge championship, where skilled Sami whoop and crack the whip along the main street. Early February.

Midnight Sun Marathon   MARATHON (www.msm.no) The world's most northerly marathon. In addition to the full-monty 42km, there's also a half-marathon and a children's race. A Saturday in June.

Insomnia Festival   ELECTRONIC MUSIC (www.insomniafestival.no) A long, loud weekend of electronic music in October.

Musical Recitals

In summer at the **Arctic Cathedral**, there are half-hour Midnight Sun Concerts (Nkr120; ⊙11.30pm mid-May–mid-August) and organ recitals (Nkr70; ⊙2pm June and July). The swelling organ and the light of the midnight sun streaming through the huge west window can be one of the great sensory moments of your trip.

Also, the **Domkirke** holds half-hour organ recitals (Nkr60; ⊙5pm June, 3pm July) of classical music and folk tunes.

Sleeping

Tromsø's peak tourist time is June, when the university's still in full throe, summer tourism has begun and reservations are essential. Check out too the home-stay section of the tourist office website (www.visittromso.no) for apartments and rooms in private homes.

Ami Hotel   HOTEL €€
(☎77 62 10 00; www.amihotel.no; Skolegata 24; s/d with shared bathroom Nkr560/820, with bathroom Nkr660/870; P@☎) Located beside a traffic-free road and park, this is a quiet, friendly, family-owned choice. There's a well-equipped kitchen for self-caterers and a couple of communal lounges, each with TV, internet access and free tea and coffee (nibble on something more substantial and simply sign the list).

Clarion Hotel Bryggen   HOTEL €€
(☎77 78 11 00; www.choice.no; Sjøgata 19/21; s/d from Nkr895/1095; P@☎) This stylish 121-room waterside hotel, poking towards the sea like the prow of a ship, is architecturally stunning with its odd angles, aluminium trim, pictures on bedroom ceilings, sauna – and a top-floor jacuzzi where you can savour the picturesque harbour and mountain views as you bubble and boil in the hot tub. Its restaurant too has great fjord views.

TOP CHOICE **Rica Ishavshotel**   HOTEL €€
(☎77 66 64 00; www.rica.no/ishavshotel; Fredrik Langes gate 2; s/d from Nkr995/1195; @☎) Occupying a prime quayside position, it's immediately recognisable by its tall spire resembling a ship's mast. It sometimes swallows as many as five tour groups per day so summer reservations are advisable. Of its 180 attractive rooms, 74, including many singles, have superb views of the sound. Both guests and nonguests will enjoy its **Brasseriet** restaurant and **Skibsbroen** bar.

Radisson Blu Hotel Tromsø   HOTEL €€
(☎77600000;www.radissonblu.com/hotel-tromso; Sjøgata 7; s/d from Nkr895/1095; P@☎) Bedrooms have recently been comprehensively renovated and an attractive new wing has been grafted onto the solid, rectangular block of the original building. Of its 269 rooms (it's worth the Nkr100 extra for one in the new wing), around half have harbour views. Reception, with two staff and two desks to receive arrivals, is swift, smart and friendly. It runs a decent pub, the **Rorbua**, and a fine Arctic Menu restaurant, the **Aurora** (⊙3-10pm).

Quality Hotel Saga   HOTEL €€
(☎77 60 70 00; www.sagahotel.no/international/; Richard Withs plass 2; s/d from Nkr795/995; P@☎) This comfortable option offers free afternoon waffles and 103 modern rooms, each with tea- and coffee-making facilities plus – when did you last come across this

Tromsø

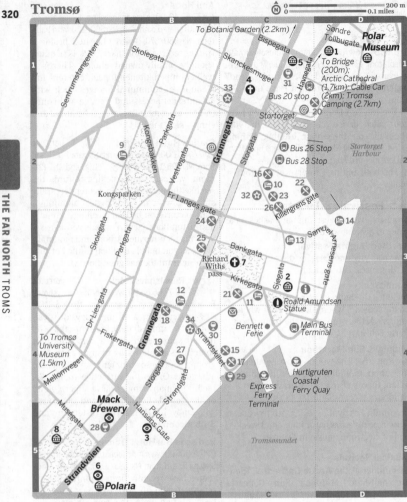

particular feature? – a trouser press. Opt for a room in its brand-new wing, its facade the colour of burnished copper.

Grand Nordic Hotel
HOTEL €€
(☎77 75 37 77; www.rica.no/nordic; Storgata 44; s/d Nkr790/1040; P@☎) The Grand Nordic is Tromsø's oldest hotel. There's little that's antique inside, however, since the place has twice burnt to the ground. Ask for a room on one of the brand-new top two floors. Rates include a particularly ample breakfast with fresh fruit and hot dishes.

Tromsø Camping
CAMPGROUND €
(☎77 63 80 37; www.tromsocamping.no; Troms-dalen; car/caravan sites Nkr205/230, 2-/4-bed cabins Nkr465/570, 4-bed cabins with bathroom Nkr1470; P@☎) Tent campers enjoy leafy green campsites beside a slow-moving stream. However, bathroom and cooking facilities at this veritable village of cabins are stretched to the limit. Take bus 20 or 24.

Eating

In Tromsø, the line is blurry between restaurants, cafes and pubs and many places function in all three modes, simultaneously or at different times of the day.

TOP CHOICE Aunegården   CAFE, RESTAURANT €€
(☎77 65 12 34; Sjøgata 29; mains Nkr125-260, cakes around Nkr70) You can almost lose yourself in this wonderful cafe-cum-restaurant that's all intimate crannies and cubbyholes. In a 19th-century building that functioned as a butcher's shop until 1996, it's rich in character and serves excellent salads (from Nkr140), sandwiches (from Nkr105) and mains. If you don't fancy a full meal, drop by just to enjoy a coffee and one of its melt-in-the-mouth cakes.

Emma's Under   RESTAURANT €€
(☎77 63 77 30; www.emmas.as, in Norwegian; Kirkegata 8; mains Nkr135-165; ☺11am-10pm Mon-Sat) Intimate and sophisticated, this is one of Tromsø's most popular lunch spots, where mains include northern Norwegian staples such as reindeer fillet, lamb and stockfish. Upstairs is the more formal **Emma's Drømekjøkken** (mains Nkr285-345; ☺dinner Mon-Sat), a highly regarded gourmet restaurant where advance booking is essential.

Brasseriet   RESTAURANT €€€
(☎77 66 64 00; Fredrik Langes gate 2; mains Nkr210-325) Rica Ishavshotel's excellent restaurant serves creative dishes, such as the fried fillet of reindeer with forest-mushroom sauce and lingen berries or the saffron poached cod.

Pastafabrikken   BAR, ITALIAN RESTAURANT €€
(☎77 67 27 82; Sjøgata 17; mains Nkr125-155; ☺11am-11pm) Drop by for a coffee, a Mack or a filling slice of Italy at this fresh Tromsø choice with its high stools, cosy armchairs and wood everywhere, even up to the slatted ceiling. Pasta (which comes with 17 kinds of sauce) and pizza dough are confected on the spot, before your eyes.

Fiskekompaniet   FISH RESTAURANT €€
(☎77 68 76 00; www.fiskekompani.no; Killengrens gate; lunch mains Nkr125-165; dinner mains around Nkr250; ☺4-11pm) This longstanding Tromsø fish and seafood favourite has recently moved to a prime portside site, interlocking – and sharing toilets with – Pastafabrikken. Apart from a token roast-chicken dish, all starters and mains, subtly prepared and

SKIBSBROEN: A BAR WITH A VIEW

For quite the most exceptional view of the harbour, fjord and mountains beyond, take the lift/elevator of the Rica Ishavshotel to the 4th floor. Skibsbroen (Ship's Bridge), its intimate crow's-nest bar (☺8pm-2am Mon-Thu, 6pm-3.30am Fri & Sat) has friendly staff, great cocktails – and a superb panoramic view of all below.

enhanced, are from the ocean. Enjoy too its delightful range of dinner desserts and savour the pleasingly contemporary design.

Driv
BAR, CAFE €

(☎77 60 07 63; www.driv.no; Tollbugata 3; www.driv.no, in Norwegian; mains around Nkr120; ☺noon-6pm mid-Jun–mid-Aug, 2pm-2am rest of year) This student-run converted warehouse serves meaty burgers (try its renowned Driv burger, made on the spot) and great salads. It organises musical and cultural events and has a disco every Saturday. In winter you can steep yourself in good company within its open-air hot tub.

Flyt
CAFE, BAR €€

(www.cafeflyt.no, in Norwegian; Sjøgata 25; mains Nkr100-170; ☺3-11pm) Build your own burger at this friendly restaurant and bar, picking the size of your meat, fish or vegie filling and selecting its extras and trimmings. Flyt's theme is outdoor activities, its beer is ice-cold and the music's heavy metal and rock. The intimate upstairs cocktail bar fills to capacity after midnight on Fridays and Saturdays.

Circa
CAFE, BAR €€

(☎77 68 10 20; Storgata 36; mains Nkr174-194; ☎) Circa (Approximately) and its upstairs neighbour Presis (Precisely), under the same ownership, complement each other. Circa, downstairs, is cavernous, both bar and light-meal venue. It serves tasty pasta, salads and sandwiches (around Nkr115) until 5pm. Thereafter, its cool jazz and electronic music attracts a 25- to 35-year-old crowd. There's a great range of quality international beers (homesick Geordies will cry into their Newcastle Brown Ale on draught). Circa puts on occasional live music plus, at weekends, a live DJ. Wednesday, wine night, is normally packed.

Presis
TAPAS €€

(☎77 68 10 20; Storgata 36; tapas Nkr70-90; ☺kitchen 4-11pm Tue-Sat, bar until very late Fri & Sat) Step upstairs, above Circa, to snack on Presis' great range of Spanish and Nordic tapas. The air's calmer here, the atmosphere more rarefied, and frequently changing artwork decorates the walls.

Arctandria
FISH RESTAURANT €€€

(☎77 60 07 25; Strandtorget 1; mains Nkr255-315; ☺4pm-midnight Mon-Sat) Upstairs and upscale, Arctandria serves filling and supremely fresh ocean catches, including a sample starter of whale steak and seal. Save a cranny for its crème brûlée with cloudberries dessert.

Biffhuset
GRILL €€€

(☎77 60 07 28; Strandtorget 1; mains Nkr235-355; ☺3.30pm-midnight) On two floors, wood-panelled and low-beamed, the Beef House is a seriously meaty place, strictly for ardent carnivores. Just tick/check your menu card, indicating size, cut and accompanying sauce, hand it to the server and sit back.

There's one common entrance to Arctandria and Biffhuset as well as the much more pub-style Skarven (see Drinking).

Café Opera
RESTAURANT, BAR €€

(☎77 61 36 39; Grønnegata 37-39; mains €185-240) Here's another brand-new, multifunctional place, long and low with candles flickering and chandeliers glowing. It does a good range of snacks, grills and fish dishes and makes a pleasant, laid-back drinks stop.

Helmersen Delikatesser
DELICATESSEN €

(Storgata 66) This grand little delicatessen carries a good range of cheeses, cold meats and salady items to fill your sandwich. It does great coffee too.

Knoll og Tott
SANDWICHES, SALADS €

(Storgata 62; ☺10am-6pm Mon-Fri, 10am-4pm Sat) Run by a cheerful young team, this popular upstairs-downstairs place with its fresh salads, crisp baguettes and house quiches is ideal for a filling midday snack, to eat in or take away.

Drinking

Ølhallen Pub
PUB

(☺9am-6pm Mon-Sat) At Mack Brewery's Ølhallen Pub you can sample its fine ales right where they're brewed. Perhaps the world's only, never mind most northerly, watering hole to be closed in the evening, it carries eight varieties on draught.

HARD DRINKING, TROMSØ STYLE

It takes stamina to stay the course. With work over, friends will meet for *Fredagpils;* Friday drinks to plan the campaign ahead. Then it's time for *Vorspiel,* or foreplay, a preliminary oiling at a friend's house before setting off around midnight for a club or bar. At the statutory throwing-out time of 3.30am, it's *Fyllemat,* fill-up time, when you pick up a burger, kebab or hot dog from one of the street stalls that lurk outside major venues before heading once more to a friend's pad for a few hours' *Nachspiel,* or afterplay.

By now it's bed for middle-distance runners while the marathon crowd stamps its feet outside Ølhallen's, waiting for the sliding of bolts that marks its 9am opening. 'If you can stand, we'll serve you', is the bar staff's rule of thumb.

TOP CHOICE **Verdensteatret** CAFE
(Storgata 93b; ☏) Norway's oldest film house will satisfy both cinephiles and thirsters after great cafes. The bar is a hip place with free wi-fi and weekend DJs. At other times, the bartender spins from its huge collection of vinyl records, so expect anything from classical music to deepest underground. Ask staff to let you peek into the magnificent cinema, its walls painted roof-to-ceiling with early 20th-century murals. It shows art-house and independent films on an ad hoc basis.

Blå Rock Café MUSIC BAR
(Strandgata 14/16; ☏11.30am-2am) The loudest, most raving place in town has theme evenings, almost 50 brands of beer, occasional live bands and weekend DJs. The music's rock, naturally. Every Monday hour is a happy hour.

Skarven BAR, RESTAURANT
(www.skarven.no; Strandtorget 1; ☏from 11am) Companion to Arctandria and Biffhuset (and sharing its website with both), Skarven has an extensive waterfront terrace and offers fine bar meals and well-priced fish dishes – unsurprisingly since it includes selections from these two choice restaurants.

Tromsø Jernbanestasjon BAR
(Strandgata 33; ☏3pm-2am) This engaging railway-themed pub with its ex-train-carriage seating is typical local humour – Tromsø has never, ever had a railway station.

☆ Entertainment

This university town has plenty of thriving nightspots, many of which also serve light meals.

TOP CHOICE **Bastard** MUSIC, SPORTS BAR
(Strandgata 22; ☏8pm-2am Mon-Sat, 3-11pm Sun) Bastard (with the stress on the second syllable; let's not get unwittingly confrontational) is a cool basement hang-out with low beams and white, furry walls (no polar bears killed during construction). It engages art-house and underground DJs (Friday and Saturday) and bands (up to three times weekly). Carrying UK and Norwegian football, it also has a faithful following of armchair-sporting regulars. The house sausages, stuffed specially for Bastard, go well with beer or to stave off those wee-hours clubbing hunger pangs. These juicy bangers are so popular, they even have their own Facebook page.

Fokus Kino CINEMA
(Grønnegata 94) Tromsø's six-screen cinema shares premises with the town hall.

Compagniet BAR, NIGHTCLUB
(Sjøgata 12; ☏9pm-3.30am Fri & Sat) Above the restaurant of the same name, this is another lively weekend venue.

❶ Information

Bennett Ferie (☏77 62 15 00; Roald Amundsensplass 1; 8am-4pm Mon-Fri) Can book Svalbard flights and accommodation.

Dark Light (Stortorget 1, 1st fl; per hr Nkr60; ☏3-10pm Mon-Sat, 6-10pm Sun) Internet access. Take the entrance to the Coop supermarket and go up the stairs.

Tourist office (☏77 61 00 00; www.visit tromso.no; Kirkegata 2; ☏9am-7pm Mon-Fri, 10am-6pm Sat & Sun) Produces the comprehensive *Tromsø Guide.* Has two free internet points.

❶ Getting There & Away
Air

Destinations with direct SAS flights to/from Tromso Airport (☏77 64 84 00), the main airport for the far north, include Oslo, Narvik/Harstad, Bodø, Trondheim, Alta, Hammerfest, Kirkenes and Longyearbyen.

Norwegian (www.norwegian.no) flies to and from London (Gatwick), Edinburgh, Dublin and Oslo.

Boat

Express boats connect Tromsø and Harstad (2½ hours), via Finnsnes (1¼ hours), two to four times daily. Tromsø is also a major stop on the Hurtigruten coastal ferry route.

Bus

The main bus terminal (sometimes called Prostneset) is on Kaigata, beside the Hurtigruten quay. There are at least two daily express buses to/from Narvik (Nkr390, 4¼ hours) and one to/from Alta (Nkr494, 6½ hours), where you can pick up a bus for Honningsvåg, and from there, on to the Nordkapp.

Car & Motorcycle

A two- or four-wheeled vehicle is the best way to negotiate Norway's far-northern reaches.

Car-hire companies include the following:

Avis (☎90 74 90 00; Strandskillet 5)

Budget (☎77 65 19 00)

Europcar (☎77 67 56 00; Alkeveien 5)

Hertz (☎40 43 64 81; Fridtjof Nansenplass 3C)

All have desks at the airport. Contrasting with steep rates in summer (when it's essential to reserve in advance), car rental can be very reasonable in winter.

ⓘ Getting Around

To/From the Airport

Tromsø's airport is about 5km from the centre, on the western side of Tromsøya island. **Flybuss** (Nkr55, 15 minutes) runs between the airport and Rica Ishavshotel, connecting with arriving and departing flights and stopping by other major hotels along the way. Alternatively, take city bus 40 or 42 (Nkr26); when you arrive, wait for it on the road opposite the airport entrance.

Metered taxis between the airport and centre cost around Nkr160.

Bicycle

You can hire town bikes from **Intersport** (Storgata 89; per day/weekend/week Nkr175/400/1000).

Car & Motorcycle

Tromsø has ample paying parking in the centre. There's also the huge Trygg underground car park tunnelled into the hill, its entrance on Vestregata (closed to trailers and caravans).

Public Transport

Local buses cost Nkr26 per ride – purchase your ticket on board. For a **taxi**, call ☎77 60 30 00.

Around Tromsø

SOMMARØY & KVALØYA

From Tromsø, this half-day trip is more for the drive than the destination. It's an extraordinarily pretty, lightly trafficked run across Kvaløya, much of it down at wet-your-feet shore level as far as the small island of Sommarøy. Here you can grab a drink or a snack and even overnight at **Sommarøy Kurs & Feriesenter** (☎77 66 40 00; www.sommaroy.no; s/d from Nkr975/1195, 6-8-person cabins Nkr1690-2000; ℗@☎) with its restaurant, bar, small children's playground, hot tub and sauna.

If you're arriving from Senja by the **Botnhamn-Brensholmen ferry** (www.senjafergene.no), the vistas as you cross Kvaløya island, heading westwards for Tromsø, are equally stunning.

LYNGEN ALPS

Some of the most rugged alpine heights in all Norway ruck up to form the spine of the heavily glaciated Lyngen Peninsula, east of Tromsø; you get the best views of them from the eastern shore of 150km-long Lyngenfjord. The peaks, the highest of which is Jiekkevarre (1837m), offer plenty of opportunities for climbers but this challenging glacial terrain is strictly for the experienced.

The Lyngsdalen Valley, above the industrial village of Furuflaten, is an altogether more accessible and popular hiking area. The usual route begins at the football pitch south of the bridge over the Lyngdalselva and climbs up the valley to the tip of the glacier Sydbreen, 500m above sea level.

The best map for hiking is Statens Kartverk's *Lyngenhalvøya* at 1:50,000.

Senja

Senja, Norway's second-largest island, rivals Lofoten for natural beauty yet attracts a fraction of its visitors (we meandered the length of its northern coastline and saw only two non-Norwegian vehicles).

A broad agricultural plain laps at Innersida, the island's eastern coast facing the mainland. By contrast, birchwoods, moorland and sweetwater lakes extend beneath the bare craggy uplands of the interior. Along the northwestern coast, Yttersida, knife-ridged peaks rise directly from the Arctic Ocean. Here, the Rv86 and Rv862, declared a National Tourist Route, link isolated, still-active fishing villages such as Hamn and Mefjordvær and traffic is minimal. The now flat, mildly bucking road, almost always within sight of the shore, is a cyclist's dream. On the way, pause at the **Tungeneset viewing point** and scramble over broad slabs of weathered rock to savour the spiky peaks to the west and, eastwards, more gently sculpted crests.

Hamn i Senja
TOURIST VILLAGE €€

(☎77 85 98 80; www.hamnisenja.no; s/d Nkr890/1100, 1/2-bed apt Nkr1390/1440; ⬜) On the site of a former fishing hamlet, Hamn i Senja is a delightful, self-contained, get-away-from-it-all place that sits in its own little cove. Everything's smart and new, rebuilt after fire ripped through the former premises. Nearby is the small dam that held back the waters for what is claimed to be the world's first hydro-electric plant, established in 1882.

Senjatrollet
TROLL THEME PARK

(www.senjatrollet.no; ⊙9am-9pm Jun-Aug) True, there can't be much competition outside Scandinavia. But the Senja Troll, 18m high and weighing in at 125,000kg, is the world's biggest, attested by the *Guinness Book of Records*. There's a tractor and railway carriage for kids to clamber on and a cafe (some fine pewterwork on display for mum and dad to look at) with shelf upon shelf of warty, bucktoothed trolls. Parents (Nkr100) and children (Nkr70) can enter the bowels of the grinning giant and explore his intestines.

❶ Getting There & Away

Two to three daily buses run from Finnsnes to Tromsø (2¾ hours) and Narvik (three hours) with a connection in Buktamoen.

Express ferries connect Finnsnes with Tromsø (1¼ hours) and Harstad (1¾ hours) two to three times a day.

It's possible to drive the whole of the northwest coast from Gryllefjord (linked by car ferry with Andenes) to Botnhamn, with its car-ferry link to Brensholmen on Kvaløy, then onwards to Tromsø.

Westbound, a summertime car ferry connects Skrolsvik, on Senja's south coast, to Harstad (1½ hours, two to four daily).

Finnsnes is also a stop for the Hurtigruten coastal ferry.

Setermoen & Around

The wooded town of Setermoen is best known to Norwegians as a military training centre and venue for NATO exercises.

Polar Zoo
ARCTIC ANIMAL PARK

(www.polarzoo.no; adult/child Nkr215/125; ⊙9am-4pm or 6pm) This large open-air zoo is 23km south of Setermoen and 3.3km east of the E6. It features wildlife of the boreal taiga in spacious enclosures that, but for the metal fencing, are scarcely distinguishable from the surrounding birch forests. Here you can watch and photograph animals such as brown bears, deer, musk oxen, reindeer, wolves, lynx, wolverines, badgers and both red and polar fox. Follow the keeper around at feeding time (normally 1pm; check at reception). For a supplement, children can take part in a Bear Party, making toys to hide for Salt and Pepper, the zoo's pair of brown bears, to hunt. Meet the Wolves, by contrast, is an hour of close encounters of the vulpine kind, strictly for over-15s.

Setermoen Church
CHURCH

(⊙10am-5pm Mon-Sat late Jun-early Aug) A bell in the porch of this early-19th-century octagonal church dates from 1698. The ingenious heating system, with wood stoves and hot-water pipes beneath the pews, must encourage attendance – or perhaps somnolence – during even the longest sermons.

Forsvarsmuseum
MILITARY MUSEUM

(adult/child Nkr50/free; ⊙10am-3pm Mon-Fri) Those who are aroused by war games will have fun at the **Troms Defence Museum** with its evocative interior dioramas and over 20 military vehicles to explore outside.

🛏 Sleeping

Bardu Hotell
HOTEL €€

(☎77 18 59 40; www.barduhotell.no; Toftakerlia 1; s/d from Nkr900/1050; ⓟ@🛜🏊) The lobby, with pelts splayed across its walls, has a hunting-lodge feel while rooms are decorated in a variety of themes such as the four seasons and Adam and Eve. With plenty of character, it's popular with adventure-tour groups and visiting military, not least for the comfortable bar and its restaurant, **Trollstua**. There's a sauna, jacuzzi and year-round heated pool, all free to guests.

WESTERN FINNMARK

Norway's northernmost mainland county, Finnmark has been inhabited for around 12,000 years, first by the Komsa hunters of the coastal region and later by Sami fishing cultures and reindeer pastoralists, who

MIND THAT REINDEER

Do keep an eye out for reindeer on the road. They're not dangerous and they're decidedly more charming than annoying. But they might slow your progress and bring you to a very abrupt halt if you hit one at speed. Sometimes wandering alone, now and again in herds, they might not be fazed by your inanimate car. If they refuse to budge, just get out, walk towards them and they'll amble away.

settled on the coast and in the vast interior, respectively.

Finnmark's wild northern coast, dotted with fishing villages, is deeply indented by grand fjords, while the vast interior is dominated by the broad Finnmarksvidda plateau, a stark wilderness with only two major settlements, Karasjok and Kautokeino.

Virtually every Finnmark town was decimated at the end of WWII by retreating Nazi troops, whose scorched-earth policy aimed to delay the advancing Soviets. Towns were soon reconstructed in the most efficient, yet boxy, building style. So, in contrast to the spectacular natural surroundings, present-day Finnmark towns are architecturally uninspiring.

Alta

POP 18,700

Although the fishing and slate-quarrying town of Alta lies at latitude 70°N, it enjoys a relatively mild climate. The Alta Museum, with its ancient petroglyphs, is a must-see and the lush green Sautso-Alta canyon, a quick hop away, is simply breathtaking.

The river Altaelva, which runs east of town, was once a Sami fishery and a popular haunt of sporting 19th-century English aristocrats. In the late 1970s, it became an environmental cause célèbre when, despite fierce local and national opposition, a 100m-high dam, the Altadammen, was built to exploit this rich salmon-spawning stream for hydroelectric power.

Alta, stretching along some 15km of coastline, has a large footprint. Its two main centres are about 2km apart: hilly Bossekop to the west, and Sentrum in – well, just that, with its uninspiring blocks and parking lots and a pleasant enough traffic-free central square.

◎ Sights

Alta Museum   PETROGLYPHS, MUSEUM
(www.alta.museum.no; Altaveien 19; adult/child Nkr85/20; ⊙8am-5pm or 8pm) This superb award-winning museum is in Hjemmeluft, at the western end of town. It features exhibits and displays on Sami culture, Finnmark military history, the Alta hydroelectric project and the aurora borealis (northern lights). The cliffs around it, a Unesco World Heritage Site, are incised with around 6000 late–Stone Age carvings, dating from 6000 to 2000 years ago. As the sea level decreased after the last ice age, carvings were made at progressively lower heights. Themes include hunting scenes, fertility symbols, bear, moose, reindeer and crowded boats. The works have been highlighted with red-ochre paint (thought to have been the original colour) and are connected by 3km of boardwalks that start at the main building.

✿ Festivals & Events

Borealis Alta   SPRING
(www.borealisalta.no) Five days of concerts and culture in March, designed to dispel winter's gloom.

Finnmarksløpet 1000km dog-sled endurance race   DOG-SLED RACE
(www.finnmarkslopet.no) Europe's longest dog-sled race coincides with Borealis Alta.

Alta blues and soul festival   MUSIC
(www.altasoulogblues.no, in Norwegian) Brings in top Norwegian bands and stars from afar in late May or early June.

⌯ Sleeping

TOP CHOICE **Park Hotell**   HOTEL €€
(☎78 45 74 00; www.parkhotell.no; Markedsgata 6; s/d from Nkr895/1195; @ ⚛) Owned by a consortium of three women, the Park could scarcely be more environmentally sensitive and minimal impact. Its 34 rooms are spacious, each with a sofa

WHICH LOOP?

The short walking loop (1.2km; allow around 45 minutes, including viewing time) is the most visited. A longer one (2.1km, taking around 1¼ hours) begins with a steepish descent, followed by a pleasant seaside walk that takes in more sites.

Alta

Alta

🛏 Sleeping
1 Park Hotell	B1
2 Rica Hotel Alta	A2

🍴 Eating
3 Alfa-Omega	B2
4 Han Steike	A1

🍸 Drinking
5 Barila	B1

🛍 Shopping
6 Studentbokhandelen	B1

or pair of armchairs, and bathrooms are white-tiled and sparkling. Although just off the main square, it's a tranquil spot with a roof terrace that's ideal for summer sunbathing and northern-lights observing in winter. Guests have free use of the sauna; skis and kick-sledges are loaned at no charge; and you can rent a bike (Nkr150 per day).

Thon Hotel Vica　　　　　HOTEL **€€**
(☑78 48 22 22; www.thonhotels.no/Vica; Fogdebakken 6; s/d from Nkr900/1100; P@🖰) In a timber-built former farmhouse, the Vica, right from the stuffed brown bear that greets you at the door and the birds and furry mammals winking from above reception, beckons you in. Until recently a family-run concern but now assimilated by the Thon chain, it has, at least for the moment, preserved its originality. There's a sauna (Nkr100), steaming outdoor hot tub (wonderful in winter when all around

is snowcapped) and **Haldde**, Alta's finest restaurant.

Bårstua Gjestehus　　　　GUESTHOUSE **€€**
(☑78 43 33 33; www.baarstua.no; Kongleveien 2a; s/d from Nkr630/830) This friendly B&B is set back from the E6. Its eight rooms, decorated with striking photographs, are spruce and well furnished. Each has self-catering facilities.

Rica Hotel Alta　　　　　HOTEL **€€**
(☑78 48 27 00; www.rica.no; Løkkeveien 61; s/d from Nkr850/1050; @🖰) The already vast Rica has recently grafted on a whole new wing, adding a few curves to what was a boring cube with parking-lot views, and renovated its existing rooms. Its Arctic Menu **restaurant** (mains Nkr150 to Nkr312) merits a visit in its own right. The hotel's **Pernille** nightclub generally has live music on Fridays and a DJ most Saturdays.

Alta Vandrerhjem　　　　　HOSTEL **€€**
(☑91 00 30 03; www.hihostels.no/alta; dm/s/d Nkr350/700/950; ☺May-Aug) Alta's youth hostel has recently changed premises. It's now at Kvenvik, off the E6, around 5km west of town, and part of Kvenvik Hotell & Golf.

Wisløff Camping　　　　CAMPGROUND **€**
(☑78 43 43 03; www.wisloeff.no, in Norwegian; per person/site Nkr20/150, 2-bed cabins with outside bathroom Nkr400, 4-bed cabins with bathroom Nkr850) One of three excellent riverside campsites in Ovre Alta, 3.5km south of the E6 along the RV93 to Kautokeino, Wisløff Camping was declared Campground of the Year in 2000, and it still deserves the accolade. Readers too sing its praises.

Alta Strand Camping　　CAMPGROUND **€**
(☑78 43 40 22; www.altacamping.no; site for 2/4 persons Nkr190/250, 2-/4-bed cabins with outdoor bathroom Nkr390/460, with bathroom Nkr750-850; self-catering apt s/d Nkr700/850) This spacious campsite has mountain views, table football (a cultural rarity east of Tromsø), a small children's playground, trampoline and crazy golf.

Alta River Camping　　CAMPGROUND **€**
(☑78 43 43 53; www.alta-river-camping.no; car/caravan sites Nkr170/180, d/q with shared bathroom 400/600; cabins with outside bathroom Nkr600-700, 6-bed cabins with bathroom Nkr1200) Special features are its sauna, from which you can plunge straight into the river, and a couple of cute little barbecue huts, furnished with skins.

✕ Eating & Drinking

Pickings are slim indeed.

🌿 Restaurant Haldde   RESTAURANT €€€

(lunch dishes Nkr100-200, dinner mains Nkr250-360) This quality restaurant within Thon Hotel Vica relies almost entirely upon local ingredients in the preparation of choice dishes such as a smoked half leg of reindeer in red wine sauce and its *Flavour of Finnmark* dessert of cloudberries and cowberry-blueberry sorbet.

Han Steike   STEAKHOUSE €€

(⌨78 44 08 88; www.hansteike.no, in Norwegian; Løkkeveien 2; mains Nkr215-280; ☺3pm-midnight Tue-Sun) This steakhouse, all dark wood and grey flagstones, is the place if you're after something red and raw.

Alfa-Omega   CAFE, BAR €€

(⌨78 44 54 00; Markedsgata 14-16; mains Nkr120-280; ☺Mon-Sat) As its name suggests, this place has two parts: Omega, its contemporary cafe, open 11am to midnight, serves salads, sandwiches, pastas and cakes. Sink your teeth into its hugely popular Ole Mattis reindeer steak sandwich. Alfa, a pleasant, casual bar, comes into its own from 8pm. There's also a terrace, ideal for taking a little summer sunshine, overlooking Alta's bleak central square.

Barila   BAR

(Parksentret Bldg, Sentrum; ☺11am-1am) This chic, sassy little place serves great coffee, good beer and exotic cocktails. You may be tempted by a 'Blow Job' (Nkr79).

ℹ Information

Tourist office (⌨78 44 50 50; www.altatours. no; Parksentret Bldg, Sentrum; ☺9am-6pm or 8pm Jun-Aug, 9am-3.30pm Mon-Sat rest of year)

Seasonal tourist office (Sorekskriverveien, Bossekop; ☺10am-6pm Mon-Fri mid-Jun–mid-Aug)

ℹ Getting There & Away

Alta's **airport** (⌨78 44 95 55) is 4km northeast of Sentrum at Elvebakken. **SAS** has direct flights to/from Oslo, Tromsø, Hammerfest, Lakselv and Vadsø. **Norwegian** connects Alta with Oslo.

Buses leave from the terminal in Sentrum.

Tromsø (Nkr494, 6½ hours, one daily)

Hammerfest (Nkr260, 2¼ hours, two daily)

Honningsvåg (Nkr405, four hours, one daily)

Karasjok (Nkr405, 4¾ hours, two daily except Saturday)

Kautokeino (Nkr235, 2¼ hours, one daily except Saturday).

ℹ Getting Around

Fortunately, this sprawling town has a local bus to connect its dispersed ends. On weekdays, buses run more or less hourly between the major districts and to the airport. Services are less frequent on Saturday and don't run at all on Sunday.

You can park for free in the square beside the central tourist office.

Taxis (⌨78 43 53 53) cost about Nkr120 from airport to town.

Around Alta

SAUTSO-ALTA CANYON

The Altaelva hydroelectric project has had very little effect on the most scenic stretch of river, which slides through 400m-deep Sautso, northern Europe's grandest canyon. The easiest way to see this impressive forested gorge is to take the 3½-hour tour (adult/child Nkr545/275) that the tourist office organises each Monday, Wednesday and Friday in July, leaving at 4pm, numbers permitting (minimum six people). In addition to spectacular views of the Sauto-Alta Canyon, the tour also includes a pass through the Alta Power Station dam and a snack.

KÅFJORD

Kåfjord's **Tirpitz Museum** (⌨92 09 23 70; www.tirpitz-museum.no; adult/child/concession Nkr60/30/50; ☺10am-6pm Jun-Aug), commemorating the *Tirpitz*, once the world's largest battleship, is the achievement of local resident Even Blomkvist, who has single-handedly collected, bought, begged and borrowed the artefacts, uniforms, memorabilia and nearly 3000 evocative photographs relating to the battleship. It hid away deep in Kåfjord from March 1943 to October 1944, then sneaked out and was sunk in waters near Tromso.

At its peak in the 1840s, this tiny settlement 18km west of Alta was a prosperous town of over 1000 inhabitants thanks to the copper works (Kåfjord Kobberverk), which were then Norway's largest. You can follow an easy 1.3km signed trail around the little that remains (you'll find plenty more information in Alta Museum). Half hidden in the grass opposite the explanatory panel is a plaque in memory of three British midget submarines that entered the fjord and severely damaged the *Tirpitz* in 1943.

To the right of the E6, a 9km cart track begins 250m north of the parish church and leads past copper-mine tailings up to the observatory at the summit of **Mt Haldde** (904m), a mountain venerated by the Sami.

🏃 Activities

Boat Trips

Sorrisniva (☑78 43 33 78; www.sorrisniva.no) runs several riverboat rides along the Altaelva river, lasting from 20 minutes to three hours and costing between Nkr195 and Nkr495 per person. Boats set out at noon daily from June to mid-September. To reach Sorrisniva, head 16km south of town along the Rv93, then a further 6.5km along a marked road.

Winter Activities

Sorrisniva has 80 snowmobiles, the largest such herd in northern Norway. It offers guided outings, and, your exertions over, you can relax in its steaming hot tub. You can also scud over the snow with **Gargia Fjellstue** (☑78 43 33 51; www.gargia-fjellstue.no, in Norwegian), then replenish your energy with a hot Sami meal. **Holmen Hundesenter** (www.holmenhundesenter.no) specialises in dogsledding, with outings ranging from three hours to five days. For all trips, reserve directly or through the tourist office.

Two other local outfits offer a raft of outdoor activities in both summer and winter.

Alta Adventure   OUTDOOR ADVENTURE
(☑78 43 40 50; www.alta-adventure.no, in Norwegian) Trekking canoeing, fishing. Also, on request and not something you'll do around home, ptarmigan hunting.

Glød   OUTDOOR ADVENTURE
(☑997 94 256; www.glod.as) Both a summer and wintertime player (its name means 'Glow'), Glød can lay on ice fishing, dogsledding, snowshoe trekking and other icy fun.

Hiking

For experienced hikers, Alta makes a good launching pad for long-distance hiking trails that follow historic routes across the Finnmarksvidda plateau to the south. Alta's tourist office can advise and you can pick up hiking maps at **Studentbokhandelen** (Sentrumsparken 2), which carries a comprehensive selection for western Finnmark.

🛏 Sleeping

Sorrisnava Igloo Hotel   ICE HOTEL €€€
(☑78 43 33 78; www.sorrisnava.no; per person Nkr2000; ⊙mid-Jan–mid-Apr) Its 30 bedrooms – and beds too – are made entirely of ice, as are the chapel, bridal suite (no complaints of wedding night frigidity so far) and stunning ice bar with its weird-and-wonderful sculptures lit by fibre-optics. Then again, you might just want to drop by and visit (adult/child Nkr100/50).

Gargia Fjellstue   LODGE, CABINS €€
(☑78 43 33 51; www.gargia-fjellstue.no, in Norwegian; s/d Nkr775/990, cabins with outdoor bathroom Nkr600, with bathroom Nkr875) Around 25km south of Alta, direction Kautokeino, this mountain lodge offers a forest getaway and a range of summer and winter outdoor activities, including the best foot access to the Sautso-Alta canyon.

Hammerfest

POP 9700

Because of its strategic location and excellent harbour, Hammerfest has long been an important way station for shipping, fishing and Arctic hunting. In its heyday, ladies wore the finest Paris fashions and in 1890 Europe's first electric street lighting was installed. Nowadays it proudly claims to be the world's northernmost town (other Norwegian communities, while further north, are, Hammerfest vigorously argues, too small to qualify as towns!).

Neither man nor nature has been kind to the town: it was set alight by the British in 1809, decimated by a gale in 1856, burned severely in 1890, then torched again by the Nazis in 1944. Its parish church has gone up in flames five times over the centuries. All the same, God may at last be smiling on the town in a way that is having a huge impact.

A 143km-long undersea pipeline starts beneath the Barents Sea, fed from the huge natural gas fields of Snøhvit (Snowhite: one great friendly, evocative name for such a giant industrial project). It runs to the small island of Melkøya out in the bay, where the gas is liquefied and transported by tanker to Europe and the US. With estimated reserves of 193 billion (yes, *billion*) cu metres, the pumps, which came on tap in 2007, are expected to pound for at least 25 years.

If you're arriving on the Hurtigruten coastal ferry, you'll have only 1½ hours to pace around, pick up an Arctic souvenir and scoff some fresh shrimp at the harbour. For most visitors that will be ample.

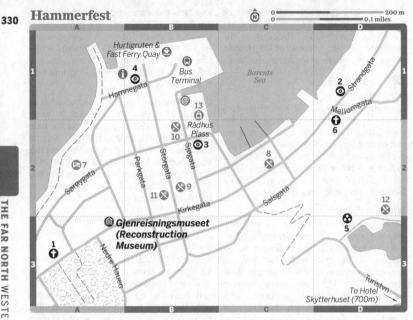

Hammerfest

⊙ Sights

Gjenreisningsmuseet   FOLK MUSEUM
(Kirkegata 21; www.gjenreisningsmuseet.no; adult/
child Nkr50/free; ⊙9am-4pm mid-Jun–mid-Aug,
11am-2pm rest of year) Hammerfest's Reconstruction Museum is a great little museum
with particularly thoughtful and sensitive
panels and captions (each section has a
synopsis in English). It recounts the forced
evacuation and decimation of the town during the Nazi retreat in 1944; the hardships
that its citizens endured through the fol-

lowing winter; and Hammerfest's postwar
reconstruction and regeneration.

FREE **Kulturhuset**   CULTURAL CENTRE
(Strandgata 30) Hammerfest's recently
completed Kulturhuset is worth a brief visit,
simply to savour its striking architecture.
Within, there's a theatre, a couple of cinemas
and a small cafe that does a decent cup of
coffee.

Salen Hill   VIEWPOINT
For panoramic views over the town, coast
and mountains (there's a free pair of binocu-

lars for you to sweep the bay), climb Salen Hill (86m), topped by the Turistua restaurant, a couple of Sami turf huts and a lookout point. The 15-minute uphill walking trail begins at the small park behind the Rådhus.

Galleri Syvstjerna
ART GALLERY

(www.syvstjerna.no; Fjordaveien 27; ◎10am-5pm Mon-Thu, 10am-3pm Fri) Local artist Eva Arnesen designed the Nobel Peace Prize diploma that was awarded to Jody Williams and the campaign to ban landmines. Her gallery is about 4km south of town, opposite the Statoil petrol station. Arnesen's paintings evoke the colours of the region from the northern lights to the bright palette of summer. The handsome pair of carved and silvered polar bears on Rådhus Plass was fashioned by her husband, woodcarver Knut Arnesen.

FREE Fuglenes
HISTORICAL SITE

On this peninsula, just across the harbour, are the foundations of the **Skansen Fortress**, which dates from the Napoleonic Wars, when the British briefly held and plundered the town; and the **Meridianstøtta**, a marble column commemorating the first survey (1816–52) to determine the arc of the global meridian and thereby calculate the size and shape of the earth.

FREE Royal & Ancient Polar Bear Society
MUSEUM

(Hamnegata 3; ◎as tourist office) Dedicated to preserving Hammerfest culture, the Royal & Ancient Polar Bear Society features exhibits on Arctic hunting and local history and shares premises with the tourist office. The place is, it must be said, a bit of a come-on (the Norwegian name, Isbjørklubben, simply Polar Bear Club, lacks the portentousness of the English but is nearer the mark). For Nkr180, you can become a life member and get a certificate, ID card, sticker and pin. For a little more, you also receive a schnapps glass and, as the demure young receptionist will explain without blanching, get dubbed with the bone from a walrus's penis. It's well worth the extra for the conversation this unique honour will generate down the pub, once you're home.

Hammerfest Kirke
CHURCH

(Kirkegata 33; ◎7.15am-3pm Mon-Fri, 11am-3pm Sat, noon-1pm Sun mid-Jun–mid-Aug) Behind the altar of Hammerfest's contemporary church, consecrated in 1961, the glorious stained-glass window positively glows in the summer sun. The wooden frieze along the organ gallery depicts highlights of the town's history. The chapel in the cemetery across the street is the only building in town to have survived WWII.

St Michaels Catholic Church
CHURCH

(cnr Strandgata & Mellomgata) With a strong claim to be the world's most northerly Catholic church, St Michaels, serving a congregation of barely 90 souls, is immediately recognisable by the striking mosaic of the eponymous saint that extends the length of its facade.

🛏 Sleeping

Rica Hotel Hammerfest
HOTEL €€

(✆78 42 57 00; www.rica.no; Sørøygata 15; s/d from Nkr950/1200; P@🤶) Constructed in agreeable mellow brick, this hotel has an attractive bar and lounge and well-furnished rooms, most with harbour views. Its Arctic Menu restaurant, Skansen Mat og Vinstue, serves excellent local fare.

Hotel Skytterhuset
HOTEL €€

(✆78 42 20 10; www.skytterhuset.no; Skytterveien 24; s/d Nkr850/1050; P@🤶) The three spurs of this secluded hotel, overlooking the town, look decidedly barrackslike from the outside and with good reason; it was originally built as living quarters for summertime fishwives from Finland who worked in the large Findus processing factory. Long ago converted to a friendly, cosy hotel, it's a good option with solarium and free sauna.

Camping Storvannet
CAMPGROUND €

(✆78 41 10 10; storvannet@yahoo.no; Storvannsveien; car/caravan sites Nkr155/215, 2-/4-bed cabins Nkr400/460; ◎late May-late Sep) Beside a lake and overlooked by a giant apartment complex, this pleasant site, Hammerfest's only decent camping option, is small so do book your cabin in advance.

🍴 Eating & Drinking

Vinmonopolet, for wine and hooch, is within the Nissen Senter shopping complex.

Qa Spiseri
CAFE €

(✆78 41 26 12; Sjøgata 8; mains Nkr120-160; ◎10am-5pm Mon-Sat) Just off Sjøgata and run by a young team, this popular place offers reliable cuisine with a great price-to-quality ratio with a choice of Norwegian, Italian and Thai dishes.

Kaikanten
PUB €

(www.kaikanten.no, in Norwegian; Sjøgata 19) The Quayside is a popular pub that serves pizzas and other snacks. Nautically themed (the backdrop to the bar represents old Hammerfest's dockside, and sail canvases billow beneath the ceiling), it has comfy sofas into which you sink deep.

Redrum CAFE, BAR €
(www.redrum.no, in Norwegian; Storgata 23; snacks Nkr80-160; ⏲11am-5pm Mon-Thu, 11am-3am Fri & Sat) Just around the corner, Redrum, with its attractive contemporary decor and flickering candles, saves its energy for weekend wildness, when there's regularly live music. To the rear, there's a deep, more relaxed wooden patio.

Turistua CAFE, RESTAURANT €€
(☎78 42 96 00; Salen; mains Nkr150-190) From atop Salen Hill, Turistua offers great views over the town and sound. The off-putting name is for a lady named Turi, though 'turist' buses often stop here too.

Ellens Café CAFE €
(Strandgata 14-18; mains around Nkr80; ⏲9am-5pm Mon-Fri, 10am-3pm Sat) Upstairs from the Coop Supermarket, this is an unpretentious, inexpensive cafeteria.

ℹ Information

Library (Bibliotek; Sjøgata; ⏲10am-4pm Mon-Fri) Has free internet access.

Tourist office (☎78 41 31 00; www.hammerfest-turist.no; Hamnegata 3; ⏲9am-5pm Mon-Fri & 10.30am-1.30pm Sat-Sun mid-Jun–mid-Aug, 9am-3pm Mon-Fri & 10.30am-1.30pm Sat-Sun rest of year) Has free internet access.

ℹ Getting There & Around

Buses run to/from Alta (Nkr260, 2¼ hours, two daily), Honningsvåg (Nkr390, 3½ hours, one to two daily) and Karasjok (Nkr370, 4¼ hours, twice daily except Saturday), with one service extending to Kirkenes (Nkr941, 10¼ hours) via Tana Bru (Nkr665, eight hours) four times weekly.

The Hurtigruten coastal ferry stops in Hammerfest for 1½ hours in each direction. A Hurigruten hop to Tromsø (11 hours) or Honningsvåg (five hours) makes a comfortable alternative to a long bus journey.

To call a taxi, ring ☎78 41 12 34.

Nordkapp & Magerøya

POP 3200

Nordkapp is the one attraction in northern Norway that everybody seems to visit even if it is a tourist trap. Billing itself as the northernmost point in continental Europe, it sucks in visitors by the busload, some 200,000 every year.

> WORTH A TRIP
>
> **KNIVSKJELODDEN**
>
> The continent's real northernmost point, Knivskjelodden, is mercifully inaccessible to vehicles and devoid of tat. Lying about 3km west of Nordkapp, it sticks its finger a full 1457m further northwards. You can hike to the tip of this promontory from a marked car park 6km south of the Nordkapp toll booth. The 9km track, waymarked with giant cairns, isn't difficult despite some ups and downs, but it's best to wear hiking boots since it can be squelchy. When you get to the tall beehive-shaped obelisk at latitude 71° 11' 08"N, down at sea level, sign the guest book. Should you wish, note down your reference number from the book and you can buy – nothing but the hike comes free on this island – a certificate (Nkr50) authenticating your achievement from Nordkapp Camping or the tourist office. Allow five to six hours round trip.

Nearer to the North Pole than to Oslo, Nordkapp sits at latitude 71° 10' 21"N, where the sun never drops below the horizon from mid-May to the end of July. Long before other Europeans took an interest, it was a sacrificial site for the Sami, who believed it had special powers.

Richard Chancellor, the English explorer who drifted here in 1553 in search of the Northeast Passage, first gave it the name North Cape. Much later, after a highly publicised visit by King Oscar II in 1873, Nordkapp became a pilgrimage spot for Norwegians. It's also, bizarrely, one for Thais, of all people, thanks to a visit by King Chulalongkorn in 1907.

Now here's a secret: Nordkapp isn't continental Europe's northernmost point. That award belongs to Knivskjelodden, an 18km-round-trip hike away, less dramatic, inaccessible by vehicle – and to be treasured all the more for that.

ℹ Getting There & Away

There are a few options for getting to and from Nordkapp and Magerøya.

The Hurtigruten coastal ferry calls by Honningsvåg. Its 3½-hour northbound stop allows passengers a quick buzz up to Nordkapp.

An express bus connects Honningsvåg with Alta (Nkr405, four hours, one to two daily) and there's also a run to/from Hammerfest (Nkr390, 3½ hours, one to two daily).

The road approach from the E6 is via Olderfjord, where the E69 branches north. The one-way toll for the 6.8km-long Nordkapptunnelen is a heavy Nkr145 for a saloon car and driver plus Nkr47/24 per adult/child passenger – nothing compared to the Nkr460 exacted for a motor home.

ⓘ Getting Around

Car & Motorcycle

Until the blacktop road to Nordkapp was constructed in the mid-1950s, all access was by boat. Nowadays, the route winds across a rocky plateau past herds of grazing reindeer. Depending upon snow conditions, it's open to private traffic from April to mid-October. In fringe months, ring the tourist office if the weather looks dicey.

A taxi to/from Nordkapp from Honningsvåg costs Nkr1300, including an hour of waiting at the cape – plus that Nkr235 admission charge per passenger.

In Honningsvåg, **Avis** (🕿78 47 62 22) has a special five-hour deal on car hire for Nkr870, including petrol and insurance. The **Shell petrol station** (🕿78 47 60 60) offers a similar four-hour deal for Nkr950.

Public Transport

Between mid-May and late August, a local bus (adult/child Nkr100/50, 45 minutes) runs daily at 11am and 9.30pm between Honningsvåg and Nordkapp. It sets off back from the cape at 1.15pm and 12.45am (so that you can take in the midnight sun at precisely midnight). From 1 June to 15 August, there's a supplementary run at 5pm, though this returns at 6.15pm, giving you barely half an hour at Nordkapp unless you want to hang around for the service that returns at 12.45am.

If you're on a budget, scan carefully the terms of any inclusive tours, which probably charge considerably more for similar services. And bear in mind that even if you arrive by bus, you still get dunned for that Nkr235 entry fee.

NORDKAPP & AROUND

So you've finally made it to Europe's northernmost rip-off – an opinion shared by the regular emails we receive from readers who've felt exploited. To reach the tip of the continent, by car, by bike, on a bus or walking in, you have to pay a toll (adult/child Nkr235/80). This allows unlimited entry over two days but it's small compensation for the majority who simply roll in, look around, take a snap or two and roll out.

This vast bunker of a place, topped by a giant, intrusive golf ball, is a love/hate kind

ⓘ **A FREE RIDE?**   333

The fee for taking the tunnel from the mainland to Magerøya will, as with all toll tunnels in Norway, be dropped, once construction costs are recovered. This happy moment should occur in 2013, or maybe earlier – scarcely surprisingly given the savage rates imposed since it was opened.

of place. Within are a tediously detailed account of WWII naval actions off the cape, a cafeteria and restaurant, the striking Grotten bar with views of Europe's end through its vast glass wall, a one-room Thai museum, the St Johannes chapel ('the world's northernmost ecumenical chapel'), a post office (for that all-important Nordkapp postmark) and an appropriately vast souvenir shop. A five-screen, 120-degree theatre runs an enjoyable 17-minute panoramic film.

But it's the view that thrills the most. In reasonable weather – which is a lot of the time – you can gaze down at the wild surf 307m below, watch the mists roll in and simply enjoy the moment.

🛏 Sleeping

Astoundingly, you can spend the night in your motor home or caravan at Nordkapp itself (fill up on water and electricity though, because you won't find any there for the taking).

Kirkeporten Camping   CAMPGROUND €
(🕿78 47 52 33; www.kirkeporten.no; Storvannsveien 2, Skarsvåg; per person/site Nkr20/150, r with shared bathroom Nkr350-550, cabins with outdoor bathroom Nkr500-575, 2-/4-bed cabins with bathroom Nkr850/950; ☉mid-May–Aug) Just outside the hamlet of **Skarsvåg**, this is another welcoming campsite, a favourite of British adventure tour groups. Its claim to be the 'world's northernmost camping' stands up; there's a rival on Svalbard but it's without cabins. The cosy cafe does reindeer, a fresh-fish dish daily special (both Nkr160), a bubbling tureen of soup (Nkr75) and pizzas (Nkr115).

HONNINGSVÅG
POP 2400

Honningsvåg is by far the island's largest settlement.

👁 Sights & Activities

Honningsvåg's **Nordkapp Museum** (🕿78 47 72 00; www.nordkappmuseet.no; Fiskeriveien 4;

ⓘ GUARANTEEING A BUS SEAT

Should you see a cruise ship heading for port, rush to the tourist office to reserve your bus journey to the North Cape. The Nkr25 extra that you pay is well worthwhile; readers tell horror tales of scrimmages, arguments and bus drivers simply riding on by, once these monsters of the waves disgorge their masses.

adult/child Nkr50/10; ⊙10am-7pm Jun–mid-Aug, noon-4pm Mon-Fri rest of year), upstairs and in the same block as the tourist office, illustrates the impact of early visitors to the cape, the hard days in the immediate aftermath of WWII and the daily life of a town that, until the advent of tourism, lived primarily from the sea.

The 19th-century **church** (Kirkegata; ⊙8am-10pm mid-May–mid-Sep) was the only building in town to survive the Nazis' scorched-earth retreat in 1944. For a time it was a communal dwelling until the first new houses were hastily erected.

🛏 **Sleeping**

Northcape Guesthouse   GUESTHOUSE €
(☑47 25 50 63; www.northcapeguesthouse.com; Elvebakken 5a; dm Nkr250, d with shared bathroom Nkr600; ⊙May-Aug) A 15- to 20-minute walk from the Hurtigruten quay, this bright, modern hostel is an excellent budget choice. There's a cosy lounge, washing machine, well-equipped kitchen for self-caterers – and great views over the town below. It's often full so do reserve well in advance.

Nordkapp Vandrerhjem   HOSTEL €
(☑918 24 156; www.hihostels.no/nordkapp; dm Nkr330, s/d Nkr450/760; @🛜) About 400m south of the turn-off for Honningsvåg from the E69, this 156-bed HI hostel, constructed for workers from the nearby fish factory, is a welcome and welcoming new budget addition to Magerøya's sleeping options. There's a free washing machine and dryer for guest use and a large common room with a commensurately big-screen TV and dangling chandeliers. Sleep in room 407, reputed to house the hostel ghost, if you dare...

Rica Hotel Honningsvåg   HOTEL €€€
(☑78 47 72 20; www.rica.no; s/d from 1380/1630) The big plus of this hotel, reliable as all others in this Norway-wide chain, is its posi-

tion, right beside the docks. **Grillen**, its à la carte restaurant, is well worth a visit, whether you're staying at the hotel or elsewhere, whereas its sister **Caroline** serves a copious, varied evening buffet.

Nordkapp Camping   CAMPGROUND €
(☑78 47 33 77; www.nordkappcamping.no; E69, Skipsfjorden; per person/site Nkr35/110, d Nkr590, 2-/4-bed cabins with outdoor bathroom Nkr570/625, cabins with bathroom Nkr990-1150; ⊙May–mid-Sep; 🛜) The well-equipped communal kitchen, friendly service and variety of lodging options more than compensate for the stark location of this campground, the nearest to Honningsvåg.

🍴 **Eating & Drinking**

Corner   CAFE €€
(☑78 47 63 40; www.cnr.no, in Norwegian; Fiskerveien 1; mains Nkr175-245; ⊙10am-11pm) Corner serves the usual pizzas and snacks but also great seafood such as crispy cod tongues, whale or, more conventionally, fried fillet of cod. It also offers plenty of meaty mains and has a bar with an inviting outdoor terrace overlooking the water.

Artico   ICE BAR
(www.articoicebar.com; Sjøgata 1a; adult/child Nkr125/30; ⊙10am-9pm Apr-Sep) For a shiver in summer and sense of how Nordkapp must hit the senses in winter, visit this ice bar. Owner José Milares, himself a polar photographer and adventurer, talks with passion of the shapes, bubbles and inadvertent abstract art in the pure ice that he garners freshly each season. The kids can crawl into an igloo that he constructs each year and, if they're lucky, meet Lonchas, his particularly furry and charming Alaskan malamute hound.

Nøden Pub   PUB
(☑78 47 27 11; Larsjorda 1; ⊙8pm-2am Tue-Sun) This local favourite near the Rica Hotel often has live music.

ⓘ **Information**

Magerøya's **tourist office** (☑78 47 70 30; www.nordkapp.no; Fiskeriveien 4b; ⊙8.30am-10pm Mon-Fri, noon-8pm Sat & Sun mid-Jun–mid-Aug, 8.30am-4pm Mon-Fri rest of year), beside the harbour, has one internet point (per session up to one hour Nkr25).

GJESVÆR
POP 150

It's a stunning drive to the remote fishing village of **Gjesvær**, 34km northwest of Honningsvåg, where you'll find two excellent birdwatching outfits. Rolling tundra, punctuated by dark pools and cropped by reindeer, gives way to a stark, rocky landscape, and then a sudden view of low skerries and the Gjesværstappan islands.

Bird Safari
BIRDWATCHING

(📞41 61 39 83; www.birdsafari.com; adult/youth/child Nkr495/250/free) sails two to three times daily between June and late August to the bird colony on the Gjesværstappan islands. There are an estimated three *million* nesting birds, including colonies of puffins, skuas, razorbills, kittiwakes, gannets and white-tailed eagles. Bird Safari also has seafront **accommodation** (s/d with shared bathroom & kitchen Nkr450/550, apt Nkr895; ⊙Jun-Aug).

Stappan Sjøprodukter
BIRDWATCHING, FISHING

(📞95 03 77 22; www.stappan.com; ⊙Jun-Aug, rest of year by reservation) is an altogether smaller concern. Fisherman Roald Berg, who built the complex with his own hands, will take you birdwatching (adult/child Nkr500/250) in *Aurora*, his small boat (two departures daily). Or join him for a fishing expedition (Nkr2000 per hour, maximum four passengers). He and his photographer partner also run a splendid waterside summer **cafe-restaurant** (⊙11am-10pm; mains around Nkr240) offering delights such as smoked wild salmon sandwiches (Nkr85), cloudberries and cream (Nkr85) and waffles with homemade blueberry jam (Nkr45). He also has a well-furnished **apartment** (d/tr/q Nkr900/1200/1350) and will probably have finished building a trio of waterfront cabins by the time you read this.

KAMØYVÆR

A short detour from the E69 brings you to this tiny, sheltered fishing hamlet, its pastel-shaded cottages and cabins encircling the small harbour.

Arran (📞78 47 51 29; www.arran.as; s Nkr750-850, d Nkr950-1050; ⊙mid-May–Aug; P🐾) has 44 rooms spread over three quayside buildings. The Sami family who run it bake their own bread and the menu is always the freshest of fish, hauled from the seas off Magerøya. To vary the cuisine it also offers a reindeer special.

If you find it full, several other houses in the village advertise rooms. And should you fancy a cultural diet, call by the **Gallery East of the Sun** (⊙noon-9pm mid-May–mid-Aug), featuring the sinuous shapes and bright canvases of artist Eva Schmutterer.

Lakselv & Around
POP 3000

The plain fishing village of Lakselv, at the head of long, slim Porsangerfjord, has little to detain you. The name means 'salmon stream', which reflects its main appeal for Norwegian holidaymakers.

The **tourist office** (📞78 46 07 00; www.arctic-active.no, in Norwegian; ⊙9am-5pm Mon-Fri, 10am-5pm Sat & Sun mid-Jun–mid-Aug, 8.30am-4pm Mon-Fri rest of year) is in the lugubrious Porsanger Vesthus hotel.

🛏 Sleeping

TOP CHOICE **Bungalåven Vertshus**
CABINS €

(📞95 77 82 11; www.bungalaaven.com; Børselv; d with shared bathroom Nkr650, 2-bed cabins Nkr450; ⊙Jun-Sep) Some 40km up the Rv98 northeast of Lakselv, take a signed turning to reach this convivial converted farmhouse after 2km. It serves dinner in summer with traditional food for a bargain Nkr200. The lounge is a cosy haven and the owner plays a mean squeezebox so you may find yourself up and dancing. There's also a small camping space too (site Nkr230).

Lakselv Vandrerhjem
HOSTEL €

(📞78 46 14 76; www.hihostels.no/lakselv; dm Nkr300, s/d with shared bathroom Nkr450/550, cabins with bathroom & kitchen Nkr700-800; ⊙mid-Jun–mid-Aug) This HI-affiliated hostel is in a secluded site amid the trees and surrounded by small lakes. It makes a great base for gentle strolls and has self-catering facilities. Follow the E6 southwards from Lakselv for 6km, then take a dirt road to the left for 2km.

Lakselv Hotell
HOTEL €€

(📞78 46 54 00; www.lakselvhotell.no; Karasjokveien; s/d Nkr960/1220; P@) Just 2km south of town beside the E6, it has cosy rooms, hilltop fjord views, a sauna that's free for guests and a restaurant that does a good summertime dinner buffet (Nkr280). Guests can rent bikes (per day Nkr80).

🍴 Eating

Åstedet Café & Bistro
CAFE, RESTAURANT €€

(📞78 46 13 77; mains around Nkr150) Don't expect anything fancy to eat in Lakselv itself. Your best of few options is Åstedet, beside Porsanger Versthus and the tourist office. Both pub and cafe-restaurant, it serves a range of decent meaty mains plus the usual burgers, pizzas and salads.

❶ Getting There & Away

Lakselv's North Cape Airport, an important link for central Finnmark, has up to three daily flights to/from Tromsø.

In summer, a daily bus running between Nordkapp and Rovaniemi via Ivalo (both in Finland) calls by.

Within Finnmark, services running Sunday to Friday include the following:

Alta (Nkr300, 3¼ hours, four daily)

Karasjok (Nkr138, 1¼ hours, three daily)

Honningsvåg (Nkr285, 3hours, three daily)

Stabbursnes

At Stabbursnes, 16km north of Lakselv and beside one of the most attractive sectors of Porsangerfjord, there are a couple of important protected areas.

STABBURSNES NATURE RESERVE

The Stabbursnes Nature Reserve extends over the wetlands and mudflats at the estuary of the River Stabburselva. Birdwatchers come to observe the many species of ducks, geese, divers and sandpipers that rest in the area while migrating between the Arctic and more temperate zones. Among the more exotic species are the bar-tailed godwit, dunlin, knot and the increasingly rare lesser white-fronted goose. Coastal marshes are closed to visitors during the nesting season (May and June) and also from mid-August to mid-September.

A signed nature trail (2.8km one-way) leads along the estuary and beside the shore of Porsangerfjord. Ask at the visitors centre for its useful trail description in English.

The **Stabbursnes Naturhus og Museum** (⊘9am-8pm Jun-Aug, noon-3pm Tue-Thu rest of year) serves both the nature reserve and national park. It sells field guides, maps and fishing permits and has a well-mounted **exhibition** (adult/child incl a 20min DVD Nkr60/10) about the birds, animals and geology of the interior high plateau, river valleys and coast.

STABBURSDALEN NATIONAL PARK

No roads cross through the 747 sq km of Stabbursdalen National Park, which offers a spectacular glacial canyon and excellent hiking in the world's most northerly pine forest. For hikers, there are two mountain huts, Rørkulphytta and Ivarstua, as well as a turf hut. For longer treks, consult the Stabbursnes visitors centre, which carries the relevant walking maps: Statens Kartverk's *Stabbursdalen* and *Laksdal*, both at 1:50,000. Less arduously, there are three signed trails, the longest requiring around four hours.

🛏 Sleeping

Stabbursdalen Feriesenter CAMPGROUND €
(☎78 46 47 60; www.stabbursdalen.no; car/caravan sites Nkr120/160 plus per person Nkr20, 2-bed cabins with outdoor bathroom Nkr450, 2-6 bed cabins with bathroom Nkr650-850; ⊘mid-May–mid-Sep)
Beside the salmon-rich River Stabburselva and packed with gumbooted fisherfolk in quest of The Big One (the cafe's TV relays live, real-time images from the riverbed), this extensive campsite enjoys a beautiful position. Facilities, however, are stretched in high season.

EASTERN FINNMARK

Relatively little visited, Eastern Finnmark, heartland of the Eastern Sami culture, has some charming coastal villages and a unique frontier history that embraces Finns, explorers and wartime destruction.

Nordkyn Peninsula

The church-shaped rock formation known as the **Finnkirka** marks the entrance to the village of **Kjøllefjord** and provides a majestic introduction to this remote corner of Finnmark, a treasure trove for collectors of 'northernmosts'.

Across the peninsula, the tiny coastal village of Gamvik claims the world's northernmost **museum** (Strandveien 94; adult/child Nkr50/10; ⊘9.30am-4.30pm daily mid-Jun–Aug, 10am-4pm Mon-Fri rest of year; @). In a former fish-drying shed, it reveals the fishing cultures of these far-flung environs. Nearby, a birdwatchers' trail runs through the **Slettnes Nature Reserve**, frequented by nesting and migrating ducks and wading birds (accessible only on foot or by private vehicle), and **Slettnes Fyr** is the world's northernmost mainland lighthouse.

In the centre are **Kinnarodden**, the northernmost point of mainland Europe (Nordkapp is, technically, on an island) and the town of **Mehamn**, unremarkable except as the site of one of Norway's earliest environmental movements. In 1903 troops were brought in to subdue local fishermen, who protested that whaling was exterminating the whales that had historically made fishing easy by driving cod towards the shore.

Kjøllefjord and Mehamn are both brief stops on the Hurtigruten coastal ferry.

Berlevåg

POP 1050

◉ Sights & Activities

The **Harbour Museum** (Havnemuseum; ☑78 78 20 55; Havnegate; adult/child Nkr40/10; ◷10am-6pm Mon-Fri, 1-6pm Sat & Sun mid-Jun–mid-Aug, 10am-3pm Mon-Fri rest of year) has the usual maritime displays as well as an unusual old expedition dory, the *Berlevåg II*.

About 12km away is a **Sami sacrificial site** atop the 269m Tanahorn, with a wonderful view over the Arctic Ocean. The 8km return walk begins 9km west of town, along the gravel road towards the evocative abandoned fishing village of Store Malvik (20km west of Berlevåg).

⌂ Sleeping

Berlevåg Pensjonat og Camping

GUESTHOUSE, CAMPGROUND €

(☑78 98 16 10; www.berlevag-pensjonat.no; Havnegate 8b; person/site Nkr20/140, s/d Nkr600/700) This friendly, well-kept complex has facilities for self-caterers and can arrange a visit to a fish farm, as well as birdwatching, scuba-diving and fishing excursions.

❶ Getting There & Away

Buses run from Tana Bru (Nkr215, 2½ hours) and Båtsfjord (Nkr151, 1¾ hours) at least once a day except Saturday. The run takes you by the spectacular, polychrome folded sedimentary layers in the Gamasfjellet cliffs, along the eastern shore

---

BERLEVÅG: THE SINGING VILLAGE

This pint-sized fishing village of scarcely 1000 souls has produced one big thing, the **Berlevåg Mannsangforening**, a male-voice choir that was the subject of Knut Erik Jensen's 2001 documentary *Heftig og Begeistret* (Cool and Crazy). Something of a Nordic *Buena Vista Social Club*, the film caused a national sensation when it was released and earned international respect.

---

of Tanafjord. Berlevåg is also a stop on the Hurtigruten coastal ferry route.

Båtsfjord

POP 2100

If Berlevåg is rustic, its neighbour, the small port of Båtsfjord, has a much more bustling, industrial feel to it.

The main site in town is the **Båtsfjord church** (◷mid-Jun–mid-Aug). Constructed in 1971, its mundane exterior contrasts sharply with the view from within of its glowing 85 sq metres of stained glass.

A 25km hike eastward along the fjord's southern shore leads to Makkaur, an **abandoned fishing village** that dates from medieval times and escaped burning during WWII. There are all sorts of interesting junk to poke around, including the remains of a German POW camp.

Båtsfjord's best accommodation choice is **Polar Hotell** (☑78 98 31 00; www.polarhotel.no, in Norwegian; s/d from Nkr1000/1250; ◷Apr-Oct), trim and tidy with a bar and restaurant. Beside it there's limited **camping** (sites Nkr150) with access to the hotel's facilities.

❶ Getting There & Away

Flights run from the airport, 5km from town, to Tromsø and Kirkenes, offering excellent views of the Arctic landscape, complete with grazing reindeer.

Buses connect Båtsfjord with Tana Bru (Nkr174, two hours) once or twice daily except Saturday. Båtsfjord is also a stop on the Hurtigruten coastal ferry.

Tana Bru

POP 600

Tiny Tana Bru takes its name from the picturesque bridge over the great Tana River, the only one for miles up- and downstream. Here, on one of Europe's best salmon reaches, locals use the technique of constructing barrages to obstruct the upstream progress of the fish; the natural barrage at Storfossen falls, about 30km upstream, is one of the finest fishing spots in all Norway. Test its waters, though you'll need singular good luck to pull out anything to compare with the record 36kg specimen that was once played ashore.

Tana Gull og Sølvsmie (www.tanagullog solv.com; ◷10am-6pm Mon-Sat) was established over 30 years ago as eastern Finnmark's first

OPORINIA AUTUMNATA

Throughout Finnmark and over the border in Finland too, you'll come across desolate forests of birch, leafless, their trunks blackened as though fire had swept through. But the culprit is something smaller, slower, more insidious and just as destructive.

The *Oporinia autumnata* moth is dowdy and looks harmless; the caterpillars come bright green, up to 2cm long and hungry as hell, devouring the leaves and swinging on gossamer threads to their next chlorophyll meal.

Eventually, they'll eat themselves out of house and home and numbers will drop but until that time, their impact can be devastating for fragile *taiga* forest. What's needed for them to be eradicated is at least two consecutive days of temperatures below -35°C. But, while winters are harsh up here, years can go by before it gets *that* bitter.

gold- and silversmith. Andreas Lautz creates some very fine gold, silver and bronze jewellery, inspired by traditional Sami designs. The shop also displays quality textiles, ceramics and glassware.

You'll find a campground, comfortable – though overpriced – rooms, a restaurant and bar at **Hotel Tana** (☎78 92 81 98; www.hoteltana .no; campsites Nkr150; s/d Nkr1258/1645; ☺mid-Jun–mid-Aug; **P**), a convenient staging post in a classic wooden building at the junction of the Rv98 and E6/E75. Hotel rates include a light evening meal.

There are daily **buses** to/from Kirkenes (2½ hours) and Vadsø (1¼ hours). Local buses run to/from Berlevåg (2½ hours) and Båtsfjord (two hours) daily except Saturday. Westbound, the Kirkenes to Alta bus passes through four times weekly.

Sami Museums

Between Tana Bru and Vadsø are two Sami treasures, each worth a brief visit.

Varanger Sami Museum   MUSEUM
(Várjjat Sámi Musea; adult/child Nkr50/30; ☺10am-6pm mid-Jun–mid-Aug, 10am-3pm Mon-Fri rest of year) Within, there's a fun, informative and high-tech display about Sami life and culture. The museum also mounts Sami-related temporary exhibitions and artwork by contemporary Sami artists. Outside is a small permanent open-air display of Sami turf huts, fishing equipment and domestic life. The museum's at **Varangerbotn**, where the E6 meets the E75 17km east of Tana Bru.

FREE **Ceavccageadge**   HISTORIC SAMI SITE
(Fish Oil Stone; ☺11am-4pm mid-Jun–late Aug) At **Mortensnes**, on the E75, about 15km east of Verangerbotn, you can stroll towards the shore amid traces of early Sami culture. At the western end, past burial sites, the remains of homesteads and a reconstructed turf hut, is the namesake *ceavccageadge*, a pillar standing near the water, which was smeared with cod-liver oil to ensure luck while fishing. On a hill to the east the Bjørnstein, a rock resembling a bear, was revered by early Sami inhabitants.

Vadsø

POP 6100

The administrative centre of Finnmark, Vadsø experienced large-scale immigration from Finland; in the mid-19th century the town's population was 50% Kven, as the Fins were known. A monument at the north end of Tollbugata commemorates this cultural heritage. Vadsø is also renowned as a site for polar exploration, with several expeditions having started or ended here. Like other Finnmark towns, it was badly mauled in WWII, by both Russian bombers and retreating Nazi troops.

In the cemetery on Vadsø island, across a short bridge from the mainland, rest the remains of several Pomors, Russian traders and fisherfolk from the White Sea area, who prospered here in the 17th century. There are also traces of several protected prehistoric turf huts. If visiting in early summer, watch for the rare Steller's eider, a duck that nests hereabouts.

⊙ Sights

Vadsø Museum   MUSEUM
(www.varangermuseum.no, in Norwegian; ☺10am-5pm Mon-Fri, 10am-4pm Sat & Sun mid-Jun–mid-Aug, 10am-3pm Mon-Fri rest of year) This museum has three sites: Tuomainengården, Esbensengården and Kjeldsen Fish Factory (each adult/child Nkr50/free).

Tuomainengården   HISTORIC FARMHOUSE
(Slettengate 21) This Finnish farmhouse, built in 1840, in its time had its own bakery, sauna and blacksmith.

Esbensengården
HISTORIC FARMHOUSE

(Hvistendalsgata) Just around the corner and als constructed in the mid-19th century, this is an altogether more opulent merchant's dwelling, complete with stable and servants' quarters.

Kjeldsen Fish Factory
FORMER FISH FACTORY

(⊙noon-6pm mid-Jun–mid-Aug) The third museum site is at **Ekkerøy**, 15km east of town. The complex retains its old stores and lodgings, a mass of arcane fishing equipment, the former shrimp processing and bottling room and – to make you wince at childhood memories – a vast black vat and boiler for extracting cod-liver oil. Plan to arrive when hunger is beginning to bite and you can enjoy an excellent fish meal in the **Havhesten Restaurant** (☑90 50 60 80; mains Nkr120-180; ⊙2-10pm Tue-Sun), housed in one of the outbuildings. Its maritime artefacts could be an extension of the museum and, if the wind isn't whipping, you can dine on the jetty with the sea sloshing beneath you.

Luftskipsmasta
HISTORIC AIRSHIP SITE

This oil-rig-shaped airship mast on Vadsø island was built in the mid-1920s as an anchor and launch site for airborne expeditions to the polar regions. The expedition of Roald Amundsen, Umberto Nobile and Lincoln Ellsworth, which floated via the North Pole to Alaska in the airship *Norge N-1,* first used it in April 1926. Two years later it was the launch site for Nobile's airship, *Italia,* which attempted to repeat the journey but crashed on Svalbard. Amundsen – together with 12 steamships, 13 planes and 1500 men – joined the rescue expedition and disappeared in the attempt, becoming a national martyr as well as a hero. It's well worth the breezy 600m stroll across the grass flats to savour the rich variety of aquatic birds that quack and croak in the small lake just beyond.

Vadsø Church
CHURCH

(Amtmannsgate 1b; ⊙8.30am-3pm Mon-Fri mid-Jun–mid-Aug) As so often in these small Finnmark communities, the church is the most interesting structure architecturally – and all too often the only building to have survived the devastation wreaked by retreating Nazi forces. Vadsø's didn't. Built anew in 1958, it's simple enough yet rich in symbolism. The twin peaks are intended to recall an iceberg, the Orthodox-inspired altarpiece looks metaphorically over the frontier and the rich stained glass depicts the seasons.

🍴 Sleeping & Eating

Rica Hotel Vadsø
HOTEL €€

(☑78 95 25 50; www.rica.no; Oscarsgate 4; s/d from Nkr700/1000; ℗@🛜) Plumb in the centre, the friendly Rica has spruce rooms with parquet flooring. Complete with free sauna and minigym, it represents Vadsø's best choice. **Oscar Mat og Vinhus**, its restaurant, is the town's finest, offering a great buffet breakfast and a daily fish or meat special.

Vadsø Apartments
APARTMENTS €

(☑78 95 44 00, 92 06 86 03; Tibergveien 2; s/d Nkr500/750; @) The town's only midrange choice is three blocks from the harbour. It's an excellent deal. The five singles and three doubles are furnished in homely style and have both bathroom and minikitchen. Capacity is limited, so book in advance.

Vestre Jakobselv Camping
CAMPGROUND €

(☑78 95 60 64; www.vj-camping.no; Lilledalsveien; per person/site Nkr10/150, cabins/r from Nkr425/400; ⊙May-Sep) Rooms and cabins are very reasonably priced at Vadsø's nearest campsite, 17km west of town. Only 200m from a fast-flowing salmon river, it's a popular venue for fisherfolk.

Påls Matopplevelser
CAFE €

(Hvistendalsgata 6b; ⊙9am-5pm Mon-Fri, 10am-3pm Sat) Pål dishes up tasty, well-priced baguettes and salads and does a fresh-fish daily special (Nkr100 to Nkr150), all to eat in or take away.

Indigo
INDIAN RESTAURANT €€

(☑78 95 39 99; Tollbugata 12; mains Nkr150-255; ⊙Tue-Sat) It makes no such claim but surely the long-established Indigo must rank as Europe's, if not the world's, northernmost Indian restaurant. Its related takeaway adjunct is something of a culinary UN, dishing up kebabs, burgers, pizzas and Tex-Mex as well as curries.

Hildonen
CAFE €

(Kirkegata 20) The aroma of warm bread and sweet cakes draws you into this bakery and cafe, hugely popular with locals and bang opposite the tourist office.

ℹ Information

Vadsø's seasonal **tourist office** (☑78 94 04 44; www.varanger.com; ⊙10am-6pm Mon-Fri, 10am-4pm Sat & Sun mid-Jun–mid-Aug) is at Tollbugata 16.

THE FAR NORTH VADSØ

❶ Getting There & Away

Vadsø is a stop only on the northbound Hurtigruten coastal ferry, which heads for Kirkenes at 8am. There are at least two buses daily to/from Tana Bru (1¼ hours) and Vardø (1½ hours).

Vardø

POP 2100

It's a pancake-flat 75km drive between Vadsø and Vardø, well off the beaten track for all but the most die-hard travellers. But the ribbon of road has a lonely charm as it threads its way between the shoreline, hardy grasses and tough, low shrubs.

Vardø qualifies as Norway's easternmost town. Also, although this butterfly-shaped island is connected to the mainland by the 2.9km-long Ishavstunnelen (Arctic Ocean tunnel), locals maintain that theirs is the only 'mainland' Norwegian town lying within the Arctic climatic zone (its average temperature is below 10°C). Once a stronghold of trade with the Russian Pomors, it's now a major fishing port and home to many Russian and Sri Lankan immigrants.

◉ Sights & Activities

Vardøhus Festning COASTAL FORT
(Festningsgate 20; admission Nkr30; ⊗8am-9pm mid-Apr–mid-Sep, 10am-6pm rest of year) The star-shaped Vardøhus Fortress – yes, of course it's the world's most northerly – was constructed in 1737 by King Christian VI. For a fortress, it's painted in gentle fairy-tale colours. On a nice, sunny day it's pleasant to stroll around the flower-festooned bastions, past turf-roofed buildings and Russian cannons. You pay the admission fee either at the guard office or by dropping it into the WWII sea mine that guards the entrance.

Pomor Museum MUSEUM
(✆40 48 03 32; Kaigata; adult/child Nkr40/20; ⊗11am-5pm mid-Jun–mid-Aug) This small museum recalls the historic trade between Russia and Norway. Based principally upon the bartering of fish against corn, it lasted until the Bolshevik Revolution in 1917.

Hornøya BIRDWATCHING
In summer there are regular **boat trips** (Nkr200 return) from the port to the island of Hornøya with its picturesque lighthouse and teeming bird cliffs. To be all alone after the last shuttle pulls out, reserve one of the only three beds at the **lighthouse** (✆78 98 72 75; Nkr350).

⌔ Sleeping

Kiberg Bed & Boat SEA HOUSE €
(✆413 28 679; Havnegata 37, Kiberg; s/d with shared bathroom Nkr380/520) In Kiberg, 13km south of Vardø, genial owner Ronny Larsen runs these renovated fisherfolk's sleeping quarters with their lounge and well-equipped guest kitchen. Rooms are trim and tidy and there's no better place in all of Norway to suck on the limbs of a giant king crab (around Nkr350). Ronny can organise four-hour fishing trips and birdwatching walks. Reception is open between 6pm and midnight.

Vardø Hotell HOTEL €€
(✆78 98 77 61; www.vardohotel.no; Kaigata 8; s/d from Nkr860/960) The staff are willing and cheerful at Vardø's only hotel. However, rooms and corridors are decidedly threadbare and passé. On the plus side, summer prices are very reasonable, many rooms overlook the harbour and a couple are equipped for travellers with disabilities.

✖ Eating & Drinking

Asia Burger Café CAFE €€
(Kristian IV gate 3; mains Nkr130; ⊗Tue-Sun Feb-Nov) Disregard the off-putting name, shun the burgers and order a dish of tasty, authentic Thai cooking in – you've guessed it – mainland Europe's most northerly Thai restaurant. Accompany this with one of the 36 kinds of bottled beer on offer, including equally authentic Thai Singha beer.

Nordpol Kro PUB
(Kaigata 21; ⊗10am-midnight) No, despite the name, the Northpole Pub isn't another 'northernmost'. But, dating from 1858 with wooden boards and antique bric-a-brac, each telling a story about the island, it does lay good claim to being northern Norway's oldest. Your friendly landlord, Bjørn Bredesen, has what must be just about anywhere's

---

WITCHCRAFT IN VARDØ

Between 1621 and 1692, around 90 Vardø women were accused of witchcraft and burned; a sign and flag at Kristian IV gate 24 commemorate the site. On **Domen**, a hill about 2km south of town on the mainland, is the cave where they were supposed to have held their satanic rites and secret rendezvous with the devil.

A warmly recommended 88km round trip northwards from Vardø along the coast brings you to the tiny, semi-abandoned, timber-built settlement of Hamningberg.

The wisp of a single-lane road runs through some of northern Norway's most fascinating geology: inky tarns, copses of scrubby bushes clinging to the meagre topsoil for dear life, flecks of snow even in late July and looming, lichen-covered eroded stone pillars, the remnants of sedimentary layers turned on end. En route, you'll pass reindeer herds and several sandy beaches. Save the bucket-and-spading, though, until the return journey when, 7.3km south of Hamningberg, you can walk to the broadest beach through the small nature reserve of **Sandfjordneset**, with its protected sand dunes set back from the shoreline.

What makes the village special is that, being so remote, it was saved from the general destruction of the Nazi retreat in WWII. Only one house was destroyed – and that by a Russian bomber. The rest, abandoned in the 1960s except for summer visitors, still stand as living reminders of what was once one of eastern Finnmark's largest fishing villages. Here where the road ends, there's a small summertime **cafe**.

most comprehensive collection of beer mats. Pick the right night and you can enjoy live music too.

ℹ Information

Vardø has a seasonal **tourist office** (☎78 98 69 07; www.varanger.com; Havnepromenaden; ⊙9am-5pm Mon-Fri, 2-5pm Sat & Sun mid-May–Sep).

ℹ Getting There & Away

Vardø is a stop on the Hurtigruten coastal ferry route. Buses follow the scenic seaside route between Vadsø and Vardø (1½ hours) at least twice daily and two services run to Kirkenes (3½ hours) daily except Saturday.

Kirkenes

POP 3500

This is it: you're as far east as Cairo, further east than most of Finland, a mere 15km from the border with Russia – and at the end of the line for the Hurtigruten coastal ferry. It's also road's end for the E6, the highway that persistent travellers will have been following along the Arctic Highway ever since southern Norway.

This tiny, nondescript place, anticlimactic for many, has a distinct frontier feel. You'll see street signs in Norwegian and Cyrillic script and hear Russian spoken by trans-border visitors and fishermen, who enjoy better prices for their catch here than in their home ports further to the east.

The town reels with around 100,000 visitors every year, most stepping off the Hurtigruten to spend a couple of hours in the town before travelling onward. But you should linger a while here, not primarily for the town's sake but to take one of the many excursions and activities on offer.

History

The district of Sør-Varanger, with Kirkenes as its main town, was jointly occupied by Norway and Russia until 1926, when the Russian, Finnish and Norwegian borders were set.

In 1906 iron ore was discovered nearby and Kirkenes became a major supplier of raw materials for artillery during WWI. Early in WWII the Nazis coveted its resources and strategic position not far from the Russian port of Murmansk. They occupied the town and posted 100,000 troops there. As a result, tiny Kirkenes was, after Malta, the most bombed place during WWII, with at least 320 devastating Soviet raids. The town was also an internment site for Norwegians from all over the country who did not cooperate with the Nazi occupiers.

The retreating forces burned to the ground the little left of Kirkenes before advancing Soviet troops liberated its ruins in October 1944. Subsequently rebuilt, it continued to supply iron ore to much of Europe, became economically unviable in 1996 – and reopened in 2009, this time run by Northern Iron Ltd, an Australian company.

◉ Sights & Activities

For such a small place, Kirkenes offers a wealth of tours and activities in and around town. For an overview according to season, pick up one of the tourist office's comprehensive brochures, *Summer Activities* and *Winter Activities*.

Kirkenes

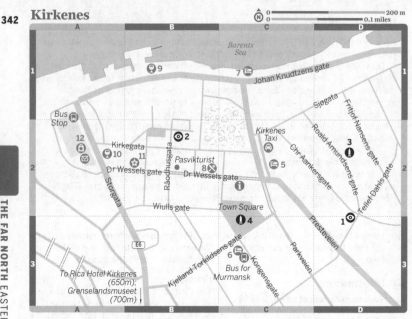

Kirkenes

There's a summertime **reservation point** (☑ 48 18 97 97; www.incomingkirkenes.no; ☉ 10am-3pm Jun-Aug) in the lobby of the Rica Hotel.

Principal Tour Agencies

Arctic Adventure (www.arctic-adventure.no; Jarfjordbotn)

Barents Safari (www.barentssafari.no)

Pasvikturist (www.pasvikturist.no; Dr Wessels gate 9)

Radius (www.radius-kirkenes.com; Kongens-gate 1-2)

Summer Activities

The following activities are popular from late June to mid-August.

King crab safari (adult/child Nkr1290/645)

Half-day tours of the Pasvik Valley (adult/child Nkr800/400)

Visiting the Russian border and iron-ore mines (adult/child Nkr480/240)

Boat trips along the Pasvik river, which demarcates the Norway–Russia border (adult/child from Nkr840/400)

Winter Activities

Activities to try between December and mid-April:

Snowmobile safaris (from Nkr1150)

Ice fishing (Nkr790)

Snowshoe walks (Nkr750)

Dog-sledding (from Nkr1250)

King crab safari (adult/child Nkr1290/645)

Book through the tourist office, at most hotels or directly with tour operators.

Grenselandsmuseet FOLK MUSEUM

(Førstevannslia; adult/child Nkr50/free; ⌚10am-6pm Jul–mid-Aug, 10am-2pm rest of year) This well-presented frontier museum, 1km from the centre, illustrates the geography and culture of the border region with special displays on WWII and mining. Within it, the **Savio collection** displays the distinctive woodblock prints of local Sami artist John A Savio (1902–38), whose works evoke the tension between indigenous life and the forces of nature.

Andersgrotta WWII AIR-RAID SHELTER

(Tellef Dahls gate; admission Nkr100; ⌚visits 10.30am & 11am) Drop down the steep stairs of Andersgrotta into this cave that once served as an air-raid shelter and bunker as wave upon wave of Russian bombers sought to knock out the Nazi ore shipping facility. There's a multilingual presentation, and a nine-minute video also tells the tale. Wrap up warmly since the temperature is 3°C, even in summer.

Gabba Reindeer & Husky Park REINDEER PARK

(adult/child Nkr275/50; ⌚10am-3pm Jun-Sep) This may not be so much of a treat for the children if you've been driving in Eastern Finnmark and stopped to relate to communing roadside reindeer. But it's worth the visit if you've just rolled in on the Hurtigruten and they'll enjoy petting the huskies too.

Russian Monument WAR MEMORIAL

Located up a short hill, it's dedicated to the Red Army troops who liberated the town in 1944.

A FORBIDDING FRONTIER

Don't even think about stepping across the Russian border for a photo. Nowadays, in addition to vestiges of old Cold War neuroses on both sides, Norway, as a Schengen Agreement country, is vigilant in keeping illegal immigrants from entering. Both Norwegian and Russian sentries are equipped with surveillance equipment and the fine for illegal crossing, even momentarily, starts at a whopping Nkr5000. Using telephoto or zoom lenses or even a tripod all qualify as violations. As the guidance document sternly warns: 'It is prohibited to intentionally make contact with, or act in an insulting manner towards persons on the other side of the border and to throw items across the borderline. Any attempts at violations will be punished as if they had been carried out'. You have been warned!

War Mothers Monument WAR MEMORIAL

In the town square, it commemorates women's efforts during the war.

Bear Sculpture SCULPTURE

Outside the Russian consulate, there's an engaging little sculpture of a bear mounting – in every sense of the word, it would appear – a lamppost.

Sleeping

TOP CHOICE **Sollia Gjestegård** HOTEL €€

(☎78 99 08 20; www.storskog.no; 2-/6-bed cabins Nkr750-1050, d from Nkr750) The Sollia, 13km southeast of Kirkenes, was originally constructed as a tuberculosis sanatorium and you can see why. The air could scarcely be purer or the atmosphere more relaxed at this wonderful getaway haven. The whole family can sweat it out in the sauna and outdoor tub, while children will enjoy communing with the resident huskies. Just below, beside the lake, its Gapahuken restaurant is just as enticing.

TOP CHOICE **Thon Hotel Kirkenes** HOTEL €€

(☎78 97 10 50; www.thonhotels.no/kirkenes; Johan Knudtzens gate 11; s/d from Nkr990/1190; @☜) This brand-new waterside hotel is Thon-boxy from the exterior. Within, though, it's open, vast and exciting, offering

On the last Thursday of most months, Russian merchants set up shop around the town centre, selling everything from craftwork to binoculars. Prices aren't as cheap as in Russia, but they're still a bargain for Norway.

great views of the sound and a cluster of laid-up Russian trawlers to starboard. The restaurant is just as architecturally stimulating, while you could easily dangle a line from the open-air terrace.

Rica Arctic Hotel
HOTEL €€

(☑78 99 11 59; www.rica.no/arctic; Kongensgate 1-3; s/d from Nkr875/1125; 🅿@🛜🏊) The Rica Arctic, a pleasing modern block, boasts Norway's most easterly swimming pool, heated and open year-round. The other special attribute, its Arctic Menu restaurant (summer buffet Nkr295), is the best of the town's hotel dining options.

Kirkenes Snow Hotel
SNOW HOTEL €€€

(☑78 97 05 40; www.kirkenessnowhotel.com; incl transfer from Kirkenes, half-board & sauna Nkr2250; ☺20 Dec–mid-April) Yes, the price is steep but you'll remember the occasion for life. And bear in mind that 25 tonnes of ice and 15,000 cu metres of snow are shifted each winter to build this ephemeral structure. For dinner, guests cook reindeer sausages over an open fire, then enjoy a warming main course of baked salmon.

Barents Frokosthotell
HOTEL €

(☑78 99 32 99; www.kbhotel.no; Presteveien 3; s/d Nkr650/875, without bathroom Nkr600/700; 🛜) Reception staff and most of your fellow guests will probably be Russian at this unpretentious place. Overlooking the main square, it has 14 fresh, comfortable, bog-standard rooms and there's a guest kitchen.

Kirkenes Camping
CAMPGROUND €

(☑78 99 80 28; Maggadalen, Hesseng; tent/caravan sites Nkr100/150 plus per person Nkr30, 4-bed cabins with outside bathroom Nkr390-500, with bathroom Nkr950-1500; ☺Jun-Aug) Beside the E6 and 8km west of Kirkenes, this is the sole option for campers. Reception opens only between 9am and 7pm (no way to run a campsite in high season) so reserve in advance if you're after a cabin.

✗ Eating

TOP CHOICE **Gapahuken**
RESTAURANT €€€

(☑78 99 08 20; mains Nkr240-290; ☺3-10pm Tue-Sun) From the broad picture windows of Gapahuken, restaurant of the Sollia Gjestegård hotel, there's a grand panorama of the lake at its feet and the Russian frontier post beyond. Discriminating diners drive out from Kirkenes to enjoy gourmet Norwegian cuisine based upon fresh local ingredients such as reindeer, king crab, salmon and halibut.

Ritz
PIZZA €€

(☑78 99 34 81; www.ritzkirkenes.no, in Norwegian; Dr Wessels gate 17; pizzas Nkr160-186; ☺3-11.30pm) Has an all-you-can-eat dinnertime taco buffet (Nkr120) on Wednesday and pizza buffet (Nkr115) each Friday.

Amundsen
CAFE €

(☑78 99 34 80; ☺2-11.30pm) This neat cafe attached to Ritz has a good selection of sandwiches, salads and cakes. It's equally pleasant inside or, the wind willing, outdoors on the terrace flanking Dr Wessels gate.

🍷 Drinking & Entertainment

Havna Pub
PUB

(Johan Knudtzens gate 1; ☺6pm-1am Wed-Sun) An earthy sailors' hangout overlooking the harbour and a rusting Russian hulk. A great place to play pool or darts.

Rallar'n
PUB

(Storgata 1) While by no means snooty, less rough-and-ready than Havna.

Ritz
PUB, DISCO

(www.ritzkirkenes.no, in Norwegian; Dr Wessels gate 17; ☺Fri & Sat night) A disco and pub attracting a mainly younger crowd.

Ofelas
PUB, DISCO

(Dr Wessels gate 3; ☺Fri & Sat night) Pulls in a slightly older clientele.

❶ Information

Library (Bibliotek; Sjøgata; ☺10am-4pm Mon-Fri) Has free internet access. Shares premises with the tourist office.

Tourist office (☑78 97 17 77; www.kirkenesinfo. no; Town Sq; ☺10am-5pm Mon-Fri, 10am-2pm Sat & Sun) Has two free internet terminals.

❶ Getting There & Away

From **Kirkenes airport** (☑78 97 35 20), there are direct flights to Oslo (SAS and Norwegian) and Tromsø (Widerøe).

Kirkenes is the terminus of the Hurtigruten coastal ferry, which heads southwards again at 12.45pm daily. A bus (Nkr85) meets the boat and runs into town and on to the airport.

Buses run four times weekly to Karasjok (five hours), Hammerfest (10¼ hours), Alta (10½ hours) and many points in between.

Independent travellers armed with a Russian visa (which you'll need to get in your home country) can hop aboard one of the two daily buses to Murmansk (one way/return Nkr350/Nkr600, five hours).

ⓘ Getting Around

The airport, 13km southwest of town, is served by the Flybuss (Nkr85, 20 minutes), which connects the bus terminal and Rica Arctic Hotel with all arriving and departing flights. **Kirkenes Taxi** (☏78 99 13 97) charges Nkr270/310 for a day/ evening run between town and airport.

Hourly buses (less frequent at weekends) run between the centre and Hesseng (Nkr25, 15 minutes).

Car-rental agencies in Kirkenes itself include **Rent a Wreck** (☏78 99 32 80) and **Europcar** (☏78 97 01 00), which also has a kiosk at the airport.

Grense Jakobselv

The first settlement at Grense Jakobselv, 60km northeast of Kirkenes, probably appeared around 8000 years ago, when the sea level was 60m lower than it is today. Only a small stream separates Norway and Russia here, and along the road you can see the border obelisks on both sides. The only real attraction – apart from the chance to gaze over the magic line – is the isolated 1869 stone church. It was constructed within sight of the sea to cement Norway's territorial claims after local people complained to the authorities that Russian fishing boats were illegally trespassing into Norwegian waters; it was thought that the intruders would respect a church and change their ways. During school holidays, you can make a day trip between Kirkenes

and Grense Jakobselv (1½ hours) on Monday, Wednesday and Friday. The bus leaves at 9am and returns at 11.30am, allowing an hour to explore.

Pasvik River Valley

Even when diabolical mosquito swarms make life hell for warm-blooded creatures, the remote lakes, wet tundra bogs and, to their south, Norway's largest stand of virgin *taiga* forest lend appeal to little Øvre Pasvik National Park, in the far reaches of the Pasvik River valley.

Some 100km south of Kirkenes and 200 sq km in area, this last corner of Norway seems more like Finland, Siberia or even Alaska. Here, wolves, wolverines and brown bears still roam freely. The park is also home to elk and a host of relatively rare birds such as the Siberian jay, pine grosbeak, redpoll and smew.

The Stone Age Komsa hunting culture left its mark here in the form of hunters' pitfall traps around lake Ødevann and elsewhere in the region; some date from as early as 4000 BC. Nearer to our own times in the mid-19th century, farmers from southern Norway established homesteads here with government support, opening up these near-virgin lands and helping to assert this ill-defined frontier territory as Norwegian.

⊙ Sights & Activities

It's worth a stop at the Strand branch of the **Sør-Varanger Museum** (☉Jul–mid-Aug), which preserves Norway's oldest public boarding school and illustrates the region's ethnic mix. Visit, too, the timber-built **Svanvik chapel** dating from 1934, and a couple of 19th-century farms, **Bjørklund** and **Nordre Namdalen**.

The Cold War lookout tower **Høyde 96** offers a view eastward to the bleak Russian mining town of Nikel.

Douse yourself liberally in mosquito repellent before heading off into the wilds. The most accessible route is the poor road that turns southwest 1.5km south of Vaggatem and ends 9km later at a car park near the northeastern end of Lake Sortbrysttjørna. There, a marked track leads southwestward for 5km, passing several scenic lakes, marshes and bogs to end at the Ellenvannskoia hikers' hut, beside the large lake, Ellenvatn.

Also from the Ødevasskoia car park, it's about an 8km walk due south to Krokfjell

CROSSING THE BORDER?

Head to shop.lonelyplanet.com to purchase a downloadable PDF of the Finland chapter from Lonely Planet's *Scandinavian Europe* guide, or the Russia chapter from Lonely Planet's *Eastern Europe* guide.

(145m) and the **Treriksrøysa**, the monument marking the spot where Norway, Finland and Russia meet. Although you can approach it and take photos, you may not walk around the monument, which would amount to an illicit border crossing!

The topographic sheet to use is Statens Kartverk's *Krokfjellet*, which conveniently covers the entire park at 1:25,000.

🛌 Sleeping & Eating

Pasvik Taiga Restaurant
RESTAURANT, GUESTHOUSE €€
(☑78 99 54 44; www.pasvik-taiga.no; Skogfoss; 3-4 course dinner Nkr550) This highly acclaimed former farmhouse presents a range of gourmet fish and game dishes prepared using local herbs and berries. There are only eight rooms (per person including breakfast Nkr600) so it's essential to book ahead – for the restaurant, too, since all food is freshly prepared on the day.

Øvre Pasvik Café & Camping CAMPGROUND €
(☑78 99 55 30; www.pasvik-cafe.no, in Norwegian; Vaggetem; cabins Nkr350-620) This place rents canoes and bicycles, and provides information on local wilderness and attractions.

❶ Information

The **Øvre Pasvik National Park Centre** (☑46 41 36 00; www.nasjonalparksenter.no/pas viknps; ⊙8am-8pm daily mid-Jun–mid-Sep, 9am-3pm Mon-Fri rest of year) is set in lovely gardens near Svanvik, about 40km south of Kirkenes.

❶ Getting There & Away

Two weekday buses leave Kirkenes for Skogfoss (1½ hours) via Svanvik and one continues to Vaggetem (2¼ hours).

INNER FINNMARK

Nestled against the Finnish border, Norway's 'big sky country' is a place of lush greenery and epicentre of the Sápmi, the 'land of the Sami'. Kautokeino, a one-street town if ever there was one, is the traditional heart of the region, although Karasjok is altogether livelier and has more Sami institutions.

Karasjok

POP 2800

It's a lovely forested drive between Karasjok and Kautokeino, following, for the most spectacular stretch, the River Jiešjokka.

Kautokeino may have more Sami residents, but Karasjok (Kárášjohka in Sami) is Sami Norway's indisputable capital. It's home to the Sami Parliament and library, NRK Sami Radio, a wonderful Sami museum and an impressive Sami theme park. Only 18km from the border with Finland, the town pulls in coaches, caravans and cars by the hundred, all heading for Nordkapp.

◉ Sights & Activities

Sápmi Park
THEME PARK
(www.sapmi.no; Porsangerveien; adult/child Nkr160/70; ⊙9am-4pm or 7pm Jun-Aug, 10am-2pm Mon-Fri rest of year) Sami culture is big business here, and it was only a matter of time before it was consolidated into a **theme park**. There's a wistful, high-tech multimedia introduction to the Sami in the 'Magic Theatre', plus Sami winter and summer camps and other dwellings to explore in the grounds. There's also, of course, a gift shop and cafe – and **Boble Glasshytte**, Finnmark's only glassblowing workshop and gallery and the park's most recent accretion. The whole is actually very good and presents the Sami as the normal fellow human beings they are rather than as exotic anachronisms. If you want more substance, the smaller Sami museums in Karasjok and Kautokeino are less flash and more academic.

Sami National Museum
FOLK MUSEUM
(Sámiid Vuorká Dávvirat; Museumsgata 17; adult/child Nkr75/free; ⊙9am-3pm or 6pm) The Sami National Museum is also called the Sami Collection. Smaller and more serious, it's been rather upstaged by the genial razzmatazz down the road. Devoted to Sami history and culture, it has displays of colourful, traditional Sami clothing, a bewildering array of tools and artefacts and works by contemporary Sami artists. Outdoors, you can roam among a cluster of traditional Sami constructions and follow a short trail,

Sami life was for centuries based on hunting and fishing, then sometime during the 16th century reindeer were domesticated and the hunting economy transformed into a nomadic herding economy. While reindeer still figure prominently in Sami life, only about 15% of Sami people are still directly involved in reindeer herding. These days, a mere handful of traditionalists continue to lead a truly nomadic lifestyle. The majority these days fish or are engaged in tourist-related activities.

A major identifying element of Sami culture is the *joik* (or *yoik*), a rhythmic poem composed for a specific person to describe their innate nature and considered to be owned by the person it describes (p405). Other traditional elements include the use of folk medicine, artistic pursuits such as woodcarving and silversmithing, and striving for ecological harmony.

The Sami national dress is the only genuine folk dress that's still in casual use in Norway, and you might see it on the streets of Kautokeino and Karasjok. Each district has its own distinct features, but all include a highly decorated and embroidered combination of red-and-blue felt shirts or frocks, trousers or skirts, and boots and hats. On special occasions, the women's dress is topped off with a crown of pearls and a garland of silk hair ribbons.

To learn more, look out for *The Sami People* published by Davvi Girji (1990) or *The Sami: Indigenous People of the Arctic* by Odd Mathis Hælta, both available in English translation. *The Magic of Sami Yoik* by Dejoda is one of several CDs devoted to this special genre, while the tracks on *Eight Seasons* by Mari Boine, a Karasjok singer, offer a greater variety of Sami music.

signed in English, that leads past and explains ancient Sami reindeer trapping pits and hunting technique. In summer, guiding is included within the ticket price.

FREE **Sami Parliament**   NOTABLE BUILDING
(Sámediggi; Kautokeinoveien 50) The Sami Parliament was established in 1989 and meets four times annually. In 2000 it moved into a glorious new building, encased in mellow Siberian wood, with a birch, pine and oak interior. The main assembly hall is shaped like a Sami tent, and the **Sami library**, lit with tiny lights like stars, houses over 35,000 volumes, plus other media. From late June to mid-August, there are 30-minute tours leaving hourly, on the half hour, between 8.30am and 2.30pm (except 11.30am). The rest of the year, tours are at 1pm, Monday to Friday. There are similar Sami parliaments in Finland and Sweden.

Ássebákti Cultural & Nature Trail
WALKING TRAIL
On the Rv92, 12km south of Karasjok heading for Kautokeino, this 3.5km trail (signed 'Kulturminner' on the highway) is well worth undertaking for a taste of the forest even though, despite its name, it doesn't actually have much that's cultural. This said, around 25 minutes out (allow two hours for the full out-and-back route), there are traces of trappers' pits, store mounds and, across the river, turf huts.

Gamlekirke   CHURCH
Finnmark's oldest timber church, constructed in 1807, was the only building in town to survive WWII destruction.

Tours

Engholm's Husky (www.engholm.no) offers winter dog-sled and cross-country skiing tours, as well as summer walking tours with a dog to carry most of your pack. All-inclusive expeditions range from five days of dog-sledding (Nkr5700), radiating out each day, to an 11-day expedition to the Arctic sea (Nkr27,000). Consult the website for the full range of activities.

Sleeping & Eating

Karasjok Camping   CAMPGROUND €
(☑78 46 61 35; halonen@online.no; Kautokeinoveien; per person/site Nkr10/110, dm Nkr150, cabins with outdoor bathroom Nkr275-450, with bathroom Nkr650-990) Friendly Karasjok Camping occupies a hillside site with river views and a range of cabins. Campers can pitch their tents on its particularly lush, springy grass. Everyone can lie back on reindeer skins to the crackle of the nightly birch-wood fire in the cosy *lavvo* (Sami tent).

TOP CHOICE Engholm Husky Design Lodge

CABINS €€

(☑91 58 66 25; www.engholm.no; cabins Nkr400-500 plus per person Nkr300) About 6km from Karasjok along the Rv92, Sven Engholm, the owner of Engholm's Husky, has built this wonderful haven in the forest with his own hands. Each rustic cabin is individually furnished with great flair, all have kitchen facilities and two have bathrooms. You sink into sleep to the odd bark and yelp from the sled dogs. A plentiful dinner costs Nkr280. Signed trails lead through the forest and barely a five-minute stroll away there's a salmon stream with a fine beach, where you can rent a double canoe (Nkr400 per day). You can also join the team on their daily puppy walk or, for Nkr500, enjoy a boat ride on a nearby lake as the adult huskies run, yap and swim alongside. Sven's place is also Karasjok's HI-affiliated youth hostel. However, there are no self-catering facilities and HI card carriers merely receive a 10% discount on normal rates.

Rica Hotel Karasjok

HOTEL €€

(☑78 46 88 60; www.rica.no; Porsangerveien; s/d from Nkr995/1195; P@�) Adjacent to Sápmi Park, this is Karasjok's premier lodging, with handsome rooms and Sami motifs throughout, plus, outside summertime, an impressive Arctic Menu restaurant. The internet terminal for guests – run, staff are at pains to point out, by an external company – may, at Nkr3 per minute, rank as the world's most expensive. Older rooms in the hotel's more traditional Gjestehus (s/d Nkr795/895) are substantially cheaper. In the park grounds, it also has some recently renovated modern rooms, priced as for the main building.

Gammen

TRADITIONAL SAMI DINING €€€

(☑78 46 88 60; mains Nkr235-295; ⊙11am-10.30pm mid-Jun–mid-Aug) It's very much reindeer or reindeer plus a couple of fish options at this rustic complex of four large interconnected Sami huts run by the Rica Hotel. Although it may be busy with bus tour groups, it's an atmospheric place to sample traditional Sami dishes from reindeer stew to fillet of reindeer or simply to drop in for a coffee or beer. And hey, although cigarettes are banned from all Norwegian eateries, tenacious puffers may derive more than cold comfort from this dark, smoky environment where a fire constantly burns.

🛍 Shopping

Knivsmed Strømeng

SAMI KNIFE MAKER

(☑78 46 71 05; Badjenjárga; ⊙Mon-Fri) This shop calls on five generations of local experience to create original handmade Sami knives for everything from outdoor to kitchen use.

ℹ Information

The **tourist office** (☑78 46 88 00; www.sapmi. no; ⊙9am-7pm Jun–mid-Aug, 9am-4pm Mon-Fri rest of year) is in Sápmi Park, near the junction of the E6 and the Rv92. It will change money if you're stuck with euros after crossing the border from Finland.

ℹ Getting There & Away

Twice-daily buses (except Saturday) connect Karasjok with Alta (Nkr405, 4¾ hours) and Hammerfest (Nkr370, 4¼ hours). There's a service to Kirkenes (Nkr529, 5 hours) four times weekly.

A daily Finnish Lapin Linjat bus runs to Rovaniemi (Nkr610, eight hours) via Ivalo (Nkr240, 3½ hours), in Finland.

Kautokeino

POP 2950

While Karasjok has made concessions to Norwegian culture, Kautokeino, the traditional winter base of the reindeer Sami (as opposed to their coastal kin), remains more emphatically Sami; some 85% of the townspeople have Sami as their first language and you may see a few nontourist-industry locals in traditional costume. The *kommune,* or municipality, is Norway's largest, covering nearly 10,000 sq km. That's an awful lot of forest and lake. The town is, frankly, dull in summer since so many of its people are up and away with the reindeer in their warm-weather pastures (in winter, by contrast, around 100,000 reindeer live hereabouts). What makes a visit well worthwhile is Juhls' Silver Gallery, just out of town and a magnificent example of the best of Scandinavian jewellery design.

From as early as 1553, during the gradual transition between nomadic and sedentary lifestyles, records reveal evidence of permanent settlement. Christianity took hold early and the first church was built in 1641.

◉ Sights & Activities

TOP CHOICE Juhls' Sølvsmie

SILVER WORKSHOP, GALLERY

(www.juhls.no; Galaniitoluodda; admission free; ⊙9am-8pm mid-Jun–mid-Aug, 9am-6pm rest of year) Juhls' Silver Gallery is on a hill above the town and clearly signed. This wonderful building, all slopes and soft angles, was designed and built by owners Regine and Frank Juhls, who first began working with the Sami over half a century ago. Their acclaimed gallery creates traditional-style and modern silver jewellery and handicrafts. One wing of the gallery has a fine collection of oriental carpets and artefacts, reminders of their work in support of Afghan refugees during that blighted country's Soviet occupation. Staff happily show you around and you're welcome to buy items.

Kautokeino Museum FOLK MUSEUM
(Boaronjárga 23; adult/child Nkr40/free; ☺9am-6pm Mon-Sat, noon-6pm Sun mid-Jun–mid-Aug, 9am-3pm Mon-Fri rest of year) Outside, this little museum has a fully-fledged traditional Sami settlement, complete with an early home, temporary dwellings and outbuildings such as the kitchen, sauna, and huts for storing fish, potatoes and lichen (also called 'reindeer moss' and prime reindeer fodder). Pick up a sheet with plan and description on the reverse at reception since nothing's signed. Inside is a fascinating if cluttered display of Sami handicrafts, farming and reindeer-herding implements, religious icons and winter transport gear. Items are simply numbered; a good, comprehensive pamphlet in English, loaned at reception, will guide you around.

Kautokeino Kirke CHURCH
(Suomalvodda; ☺9am-9pm Jun–mid-Aug) The timbered Kautokeino church, which dates from 1958, is one of Norway's most frequented, particularly at Easter. Its cheery interior, alive with bright Sami colours, has some fixtures salvaged from the earlier 1701 church that was torched in WWII.

FREE Samekniv SAMI KNIVES
(Galaniitoluodda; ☺9am-8pm Jun-Aug, 9am-4pm rest of year) Samekniv, beside the road that leads to Juhls' Silver Gallery, is the workshop and gallery of Sami knifesmith Josef Per Buljo, who crafts a wide range of traditional and modern knives.

⚜ Festivals & Events
Easter week is a time for weddings and an excuse for a big gathering to mark the end of the dark season, before folk and flocks disperse to the summer grazing. It's celebrated with panache: the reindeer-racing world championships, the Sami Grand Prix – no, not a souped-up snowmobile race but the

premier *yoik* and Sami pop contest – and other traditional Sami and religious events.

🛏 Sleeping & Eating

TOP CHOICE **Thon Hotel Kautokeino** HOTEL €€
(☑78 48 70 00; www.thonhotels.no/kautokeino; Biedjovaggeluodda 2; s/d Nkr895/1095; @📶) This brand-new hotel is built on the site of its predecessor, which burnt to the ground a few years ago. It's a lovely structure with an exterior of mellow wood, built low to blend with its few neighbours. Within, rooms are cheerful and cosy. **Duottar** (lunch mains Nkr165-175, dinner mains Nkr220-335), its gourmet restaurant, serves fine cuisine. Main item on the menu, as you'd expect in such a town, is reindeer in several guises – smoked, fillet, minced in a cream sauce or (very Sami, this one) salted and smoked in a *lavvo* (tepee). For dessert, enjoy the delightful fusion of cloudberry *panna cotta* soused in a brandy syrup.

Arctic Motell & Camping CAMPGROUND €
(☑78 48 54 00; www.kauto.no in Norwegian; Suomaluodda 16; car/caravan sites Nkr160/200, cabins with outdoor bathroom Nkr300, with bathroom Nkr750-1800, motel s/d Nkr500/600) At the southern end of town, this is a hyperfriendly place, where campers and cabin dwellers have access to a communal kitchen. Its *lavvo* is a warm and cosy spot to relax by a wood fire and sip steaming coffee, laid on nightly at 8pm. If you ask, the small cafe will also rustle up *bidos*, the traditional reindeer-meat stew served at Sami weddings and other rites of passage.

Kautokeino Villmarksenter HOSTEL €€
(☑78 48 76 02; isakmathis@hotmail.com; Hannoluohkka 2; s/d Nkr750/900, 4-bed cabins Nkr500) Set above the main road, this is a functional, cheerless sort of place whose main asset is its cafe-restaurant (mains Nkr155 to Nkr195) with an attractive open-air deck.

🍷 Drinking
Caffé Galleriat CAFE
With its principal entrance on the main drag, this is a convivial little place for a relaxing coffee.

Maras Pub PUB
(☺8pm-midnight or 2am Thu-Sun) Just off the main road. An animated dive that sometimes has live music, both pop and traditional. Once the ale starts flowing, patrons are quite likely to spontaneously break into a *yoik* or two.

ℹ Information

The **tourist office** (☎78 48 65 00, 957 55 199; www.kautokeino.nu; ☺10am-6pm Mon-Fri, 10am-5pm Sun mid-Jun–mid-Aug only) has occupied three different venues on our last three visits. You might still find it on the ground floor of the Thon hotel.

ℹ Getting There & Away

Public transport is slim. Buses run between Kautokeino and Alta (Nkr235, 2¼ hours) daily except Saturday. In July and early to mid-August, the Finnish Lapin Linjat bus connects Kautokeino with Alta (1¾ hours) and Rovaniemi (eight hours), in Finland once daily.

Reisa National Park

Although technically in Troms county, Reisa National Park is most readily accessible by road from Kautokeino. For hikers, the 50km route through this remote Finnmarksvidda country is one of Norway's wildest and most physically demanding challenges. The northern trailhead at Sarelv is accessible on the Rv865, 47km south of Storslett, and the southern end is reached on the gravel route to Reisevannhytta, 4km west of Bieddjuvaggi on the Rv896, heading northwest from Kautokeino.

Most people walk from north to south. From Bilto or Sarelv, you can either walk the track up the western side of the cleft that channels the Reisaelva river or hire a riverboat for the three-hour 27km trip upstream to Nedrefoss, where there's a DNT hut. En route, notice the 269m Mollesfossen waterfall, east of the track on the tributary stream Molleselva. From Nedrefoss, the walking route continues for 35km south to the Reisavannhytta hut on lake Reisajävri, near the southern trailhead.

Svalbard

POP 2481 / HIGHEST ELEV 1713M

Includes »

Best Places to Eat

» Huset (p351)

» Kroa (p352)

» Mary-Ann's Polarrigg (p352)

» Brasseri Nansen (p352)

Best Places to Stay

» Basecamp Spitsbergen (p350)

» Spitsbergen Guesthouse (p351)

» Mary-Ann's Polarrigg (p351)

» Radisson SAS Polar Hotel (p351)

Why Go?

Svalbard is the Arctic North as you always dreamed it existed. This wondrous archipelago is a land of dramatic snow-drowned peaks and glaciers, of vast icefields and forbidding icebergs, an elemental place where the seemingly endless Arctic night and the perpetual sunlight of summer carry a deeper kind of magic. One of Europe's last great wildernesses, this is also the domain of more polar bears than people, a terrain rich in epic legends of polar exploration.

Svalbard's main settlement and entry point, Longyearbyen, is merely a taste of what lies beyond and the possibilities for exploring further are endless: boat trips, glacier hikes and expeditions by snowmobile or led by a team of huskies. Whichever you choose, coming here is like crossing some remote frontier of the mind: Svalbard is as close as most mortals can get to the North Pole and still capture its spirit.

When to Go
Longyearbyen

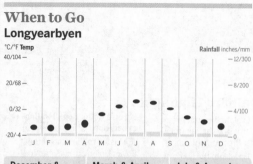

December & January A jazz festival and deep immersion in the polar night.

March & April The light returns with week-long festivities.

July & August Days without end and an array of activities in the summer light.

Svalbard Highlights

1 Explore the Arctic wilderness by **hiking** (p350) under the midnight sun

2 Travel into the fjords of inner Svalbard with a boat trip to **Pyramiden** (p355) and the Nordenskjöldbreen glacier

3 Experience the polar silence like the explorers of old on a winter **dog-sledding expedition** (p350)

4 Listen to the echo of the Soviet Union on a day trip to the Russian settlement of **Barentsburg** (p354)

5 Feel the exhilaration of racing through the icy wastes on a winter **snowmobiling expedition** (p350)

6 Spend a sunny morning surrounded by the brilliant glaciers and turquoise waters of **Magdalenefjord** (p356)

7 Immerse yourself in the natural and human history of Svalbard at the **Svalbard Museum** (p347) and **Spitsbergen Airship Museum** (p348)

History

The first mention of Svalbard occurs in an Icelandic saga from 1194. Officially, however, the Dutch voyager Willem Barents, in search of a northeast passage to China, is regarded as the first visitor from the European mainland (1596). He named the islands Spitsbergen, or 'sharp mountains'. The Norwegian name, Svalbard, comes from the Old Norse for 'cold coast'. Today, Spitsbergen is the name of Svalbard's largest island. In 1920 the Svalbard Treaty granted Norway sovereignty over the islands and restricted military activities. Initially signed by nine nations, it now has over 40 adherents, whose citizens enjoy the same rights and obligations on the islands as Norwegians themselves.

WHALING & HUNTING

At the time of Barents' discovery, the archipelago was uninhabited. From 1612 to 1720 English, Dutch, French, Norwegian and Danish ships engaged in whaling off the western coast of Spitsbergen island; it's estimated that the Dutch alone slaughtered 60,000 whales.

An English group undertook the first known overwintering at Bellsund in 1630, followed by a Dutch group at Smeerenburg three years later; the following winter, however, scurvy took its toll and the settlement was abandoned for winter, leaving behind a small caretaker team, who all perished. From the early 18th century, Russian Pomor (coast-dwelling) hunters and traders focused their attentions on Svalbard, hunting walruses, moose, seals and belugas. From around 1795 Norwegians exploited the islands' wildlife resources and began hunting both polar bears and Arctic foxes.

POLAR EXPLORATION

Longyearbyen is precisely 1338km from the North Pole, and in the late 19th and early 20th centuries a series of explorers used Svalbard to launch attempts on the North Pole using airships and balloons; most met with failure. Roald Amundsen and Umberto Nobile were successful in 1926, but two years later Amundsen and his crew died while on a rescue mission to find Nobile, who had disappeared on a similar expedition and was later rescued.

COAL MINING

Perhaps as early as 1612 whalers had discovered coal at Ny Ålesund, but the first modern mine wasn't opened until 1906, when the Arctic Coal Company (ACC) began extracting coal from a rich seam. The settlement that grew up around this mine was named for the ACC's US owner, John Munroe Longyear. In 1916 ACC sold out to the Store Norske Spitsbergen Kull Compani (SNSK). Over the next few years, two other Norwegian companies set up operations on the archipelago's southernmost island, Bjørnøya, and the Kings Bay Kull Compani opened a mine at Ny Ålesund.

Mining was halted during WWII and on 3 September 1941 the islands were evacuated. Even so, the Nazis bombed Longyearbyen and the settlements of Barentsburg and Sveagruva (Mine No 2, just east of Longyearbyen, was shelled and set alight and continued to burn for 14 years). When the Nazis surrendered in 1945, Norwegian civilians returned, Longyearbyen was rebuilt and the Russians resettled and again mined in Pyramiden and Barentsburg.

Mine No 7 has been in operation for nearly 40 years and nowadays is the only one around Longyearbyen still producing; it yields around 70,000 tonnes per year. The big one these days is the Svea Nord coalfield, 44km southeast of Longyearbyen. It produces around 3 million tonnes annually, extracting more in two days than Mine No 7 does in a year. There are estimated reserves of over 30 million tonnes and the project will extend until at least 2013.

OTHER NATURAL RESOURCES

The most optimistic predictions of Svalbard's gold reserves beneath the Arctic soil put them on a level with South Africa's. There are also indications of rich oil and gas deposits, which will become more easily and economically accessible if global warming continues.

Geography & Climate

Svalbard's vital statistics are suitably impressive: 13% vegetation, 27% barren stone and an astonishing 60% glacier. Svalbard's latitude ranges from 74°N at Bjørnøya in the south to over 80°N on northern Spitsbergen and Nordaustlandet.

The archipelago is about the size of Ireland and consists mainly of glaciated and eroded sedimentary layers that were deposited beneath the sea up to 1.2 billion years ago. It's difficult to imagine but between 300 million and 60 million years ago, Svalbard was lush and tropical. Rich layers of organic matter built up on the surface, then metamorphosed under great heat and pressure into coal. Continental drift shifted it to its present polar location, and most present-day landforms were created during the ice ages of the past two million years. Its highest

POLAR BEARS UNDER THREAT

Polar bears are one of the most enduring symbols of the Arctic wilderness – loners, immensely strong and survivors in one of the world's most extreme environments. But for all the bears' raw power, some scientists predict that they could be extinct by the end of this century if the world continues to heat up.

Polar bear numbers had been in decline since the late 19th century, when intensive hunting began. But ever since the 1973 treaty for the Conservation of Polar Bears and their Habitat, signed by all the countries whose lands impinge upon the Arctic, polar bear numbers have been gradually increasing again and latest estimates suggest that there are between 20,000 and 25,000 left in the wild; Svalbard has a population of between 3000 and 3500.

But as is the case throughout the Arctic, Svalbard's glaciers are retreating and the ice sheet, their natural habitat and prime hunting ground for seals, the mainstay of their diet (an adult bear needs to eat between 50 and 75 seals every year), is shrinking. Although polar bears are classified as marine mammals and are powerful swimmers, many risk drowning as they attempt to reach fresh ice floes. Less sea ice also means that some populations will become isolated and inbred, their genetic stock weakened. The birth rate may fall since females need plenty of deep snow to dig the dens in which they will whelp. And hungry bears, on the prowl and desperate for food, could lead to increasing confrontations with humans.

Your chances of seeing one, unless you're on a cruise and observing from the safety of a ship, are minimal, especially in summer. In any event, on Svalbard contact is actively discouraged, both for your and the bear's sake (if a snowmobiler gives chase, for example, he or she will be in for a stiff fine). Bears under pressure quickly become stressed and overheat under their shaggy coats and may even die of heat exhaustion if pursued.

Should you be unlucky enough to come within sight of one on land, don't even think of approaching it. An altogether safer way to track polar bears is to log onto www.panda.org/polarbears, managed by the World Wildlife Fund. Here, you can track the movements of bears that scientists have equipped with a collar and satellite transmitter.

points are Newtontoppen (1713m) and Perriertoppen (1712m).

Most of Svalbard's glaciers are retreating: Austre Brøggerbreen has lost almost 16m since 1977, while Midre Lovenbreen (12.3m) isn't far behind.

The archipelago enjoys a brisk polar-desert climate, with only 200mm to 300mm of precipitation annually. Although the west coast remains ice-free for most of the summer, pack ice hovers just north of the main island year-round. Snow and frost are possible at any time of year; the mean annual temperature is -4°C, and in July it's only 6°C. On occasion, however, you may experience temperatures of up to 20°C. In January the mean temperature is -16°C, but temperatures of -30°C aren't uncommon.

In Longyearbyen the midnight sun lasts from 19 April to 23 August, while it never even peeks above the horizon between 28 October and 14 February.

Wildlife

In addition to polar bears, Svalbard is home to other emblematic Arctic species. The species you're most likely to see are the Arctic fox (also known as the polar fox) and Svalbard's unusually squat reindeer. Svalbard's reindeer are genetically akin to their distant Canadian cousins and some have been found bearing Russian tags, proving that they walked in over the ice. Unlike their cousins on the mainland, they don't live in herds but in family groups of two to six animals. Since they have no predators other than humans they thrive and the estimated population of around 10,000 is kept constant by an annual cull. Most Svalbard reindeer starve slowly to death when they're about eight years old, their teeth having been ground to stumps by the stones and pebbles they mouth along with sprigs of edible matter.

Despite having been hunted to the brink of extinction in centuries past, whales can still be seen on occasion in Svalbard's waters, while seals are also common. Walruses, too, suffered from relentless hunting, although a population of between 500 and 2000 still inhabits Svalbard.

For more on Svalbard's fascinating bird life, see p349.

Dangers & Annoyances

Don't let your desire to see Svalbard's symbol, the polar bear, blind you to the fact that a close encounter with these iconic creatures rarely ends well. As the signs on the outskirts of Longyearbyen attest, polar bears are real danger almost everywhere in Svalbard. If you're straying beyond Longyearbyen's confines, you're strongly advised to go with an organised tour. Walk leaders carry a gun and know how to use it. Standard equipment too, especially if you're camping, are trip wires with flares and distress flares too – to fire at the ground in front of the bear, not to summon help, which could be hours away. The last bear fatality was in 1995, but it happened only 2km from Longyearbyen...

Tours

For reasons of security and sheer logistics, it's difficult to arrange independent trips on Svalbard and we endorse the governor's advice that you should book organised tours through recognised operators. Fortunately, there's a huge range of options. The official tourist information website (www.svalbard. net) lists dozens of tours and we detail but a sample of the most popular ones.

Longyearbyen

POP 2000

Svalbard's only town – indeed, only centre with more than a handful of inhabitants – Longyearbyen enjoys a superb backdrop including two glacier tongues, Longyearbreen and Lars Hjertabreen. The town itself is fringed by abandoned mining detritus and the waterfront is anything but beautiful, with shipping containers and industrial buildings. The further you head up the valley towards the glaciers, the more you'll appreciate being here. Even so, Longyearbyen is a place to base yourself for trips out into the wilderness rather than somewhere to linger for its own sake.

History

Although whalers had been present here in previous centuries, the town of Longyearbyen was founded in the early 20th century

---

SVALBARD TOUR COMPANIES

The following are the main companies offering tours around Svalbard, starting with day excursions from Longyearbyen to longer boat cruises and multiday expeditions out into the wilderness. All of the following operate in both summer and winter.

Arctic Adventures (☏79 02 16 24; www.arctic-adventures.no) Small company offering the full range of activities.

Basecamp Spitsbergen (☏79 02 46 00; www.basecampexplorer.com) Basecamp Spitsbergen mainly offers winter activities, including a stay aboard the *Noorderlicht*, a Dutch sailing vessel that's set into the fjord ice as the long freeze begins each autumn. It also offers winter and summer stays at Isfjord Radio, the ultimate remote getaway on an upgraded, one-time radio station at the western tip of Spitsbergen.

Poli Arctici (☏79 02 17 05; www.poliartici.com) Poli Arctici is the trading name of Stefano Poli, originally from Milan and with 13 years of experience as a Svalbard wilderness guide.

Spitsbergen Tours (☏79 02 10 68; www.terrapolaris.com) The owner of Spitsbergen Tours, Andreas Umbreit, is one of the longest-standing operators on the archipelago.

Spitsbergen Travel (☏79 02 61 00; www.spitsbergentravel.no) One of the giants of the Svalbard travel scene, with a staggering array of options.

Svalbard Hestesenter (☏91 77 65 95) Kayaking, horse riding and hiking.

Svalbard Husky (☏98 40 40 89) Year-round dog-sledding.

Svalbard Snøscooterutleie (☏79 02 46 61; www.scooterutleie.svalbard.no) Winter snowmobile safaris as well as a handful of summer activities.

Svalbard Villmarkssenter (☏79 02 17 00; www.svalbardvillmarkssenter.no) Experts in dog *mushing*, whether by sledge over the snow or on wheels during summer.

Svalbard Wildlife Expeditions (☏79 02 56 60; www.wildlife.no) Offering many of the usual and several unusual trips.

as a base for Svalbard's coal-mining activities; the town's gritty coal-mining roots still show through, commemorated in the statue of a grizzled miner and his pick near the Lompensenteret. For decades, Store Norsk, owner of the pits, possessed the communal mess, company shop, transport in and out, and almost the miners' souls. Then in 1976 the Norwegian state stepped in to bale the company out from bankruptcy. Today, most of the few people who live here year-round enjoy one-year tax-free contracts. There are at least seven mines dotted around Longyearbyen and the surrounding area, although only one, Mine No 7, 15km east of town, is still operational.

Reflecting the days when miners would remove their coal-dust-encrusted boots at the threshold, local decorum still dictates that people take off their shoes upon entering most buildings in town. Exceptions include the majority of shops and places to eat.

⊙ Sights

In addition to the following sights, keep an eye out for wild reindeer and even the Arctic fox in and around the town.

TOP CHOICE Svalbard Museum

MINING & NATURAL HISTORY MUSEUM

(adult/child Nkr75/40, combined ticket with Spitsbergen Airship Museum Nkr130/60; ⊙10am-5pm May-Sep, shorter hr rest of yr) Museum is the wrong word for this impressive exhibition space. Themes include the life on the edge formerly led by whalers, trappers, seal and walrus hunters and, more recently, miners. It's an attractive mix of text, artefacts and birds and mammals, stuffed and staring. There's a cosy book-browsing area, too, where you can lounge on sealskin cushions and rugs.

TOP CHOICE Spitsbergen Airship Museum

EXPLORERS' MUSEUM

(www.spitsbergenairshipmuseum.com; adult/child Nkr75/40, combined ticket with Svalbard Museum Nkr130/60; ⊙10am-5pm mid-Jun–Aug, shorter hr rest of yr) This recently opened museum is a fascinating complement to the main museum, with a stunning collection of artefacts, original newspapers and other documents relating to the history of polar exploration. With labels in English and intriguing archive footage, you could easily spend a couple of hours here reliving some of the Arctic's most stirring tales.

Galleri Svalbard

ART GALLERY

(adult/child/concession Nkr60/20/40; ⊙11am-5pm Jun-Aug, shorter hr rest of yr) Galleri Svalbard features the Svalbard-themed works of renowned Norwegian artist Kåre Tveter, so pure and cold they make you shiver. It also has interesting reproductions of antique maps of Svalbard, historical drawings with a Svalbard focus, temporary exhibitions, and a marvellous 10-minute film, *The Arctic Nature of Svalbard*. The gallery has a small cafe and an excellent shop.

Atelier Aino

GALLERY, WORKSHOP

(admission free; ⊙11am-5pm Jun-Aug, shorter hr rest of yr) One floor above Galleri Svalbard is the gallery and workshop of Danish artist Aino Grib. A resident of Svalbard, she captures in her canvases the hues and tones of the Arctic seasons and most of her works are available for sale.

Historic Sites

HISTORIC SITES

The original site for Longyearbyen was on the rise above the west bank of the stream that runs down to the fjord from the two glaciers. Today the rise is dominated by the wooden **Svalbard Kirke**, which was first built in the 1920s but later rebuilt after being destroyed in the German invasion during WWII; it's usually left open. Some 50m south of the church stand five weathered **wooden steps**, all alone, and a sign, 'Sykhustrappa' (Hospital Stairs). They're all that remain of Longyearbyen's first hospital and they have a special significance for the town's residents. Traditionally, a week of celebrations to dispel the weeks of winter darkness begins once the first of the spring sun's rays touched the forehead of someone standing on the top step.

South of the church and the steps, **wooden pillars** emerging from the permafrost are all that remains of the original settlement; again, the houses that once stood here were burned to the ground during WWII.

Further into the valley to the south lies a haunting little **graveyard** with its simple white, wooden crosses with dates. It dates from the early 20th century and includes the bodies of seven young men in Longyearbyen who were struck down by the Spanish flu in October 1918, a virus that killed 40 million people in Europe, Asia and North America.

From here there's a fine view across the valley to the evocative remains of former **Mine No 2**.

🏃 Activities

You'll be disappointed if you restrict yourself to scruffy Longyearbyen and you'll leave with little sense of the sheer majesty of Svalbard's wilderness. Fortunately, there's a

Deep inside the mountain, down beneath the permafrost, a vast man-made cavern, already dubbed the Doomsday Vault or a vegetarian Noah's Ark, was opened in 2008. It's a repository with a capacity for up to four million different seed types (and up to 2.25 billion seeds in all), representing the botanical diversity of the planet. Samples from seed banks and collections all over the world are kept here at a constant temperature of -18°C so that, should a species become extinct in its native habitat, it can be revived and won't be lost for eternity. The vault is built into the mountain above the airport, 130m above sea level to ensure the vault survives any future rise in sea levels; Svalbard was chosen due to its lack of tectonic activity and the preservative powers of its permafrost. As of mid-2010, the vault was home to over 500,000 different seed varieties, with approximately 250 million individual seeds in all.

dizzying array of short trips and day tours that vary with the season. The tourist office's weekly activities list details of many more. All outings can be booked through individual operators (directly or via their websites; see the boxed text, p347) or online at the **tourist office** (www.svalbard.net).

In the section that follows, we only cover half- or full-day excursions; for multiday expeditions, contact the operator directly.

Summer
BIRDWATCHING
More than 160 bird species have been reported in Svalbard, with the overwhelming number of these present during the summer months; apart from a few stray individuals, the only species to overwinter in the archipelago is the Svalbard ptarmigan. If you're in Longyearbyen in summer, among the common species you're likely to see are the barnacle goose, king eider, common eider, Arctic tern, purple sandpiper, glaucous gull and snow bunting; the best chance for sighting these species is in the Adventdalen delta southeast of the centre on the road to Mine No 7. A little further afield, especially on the boat trips to Barentsburg or Pyramiden, the little auk, black guillemot, puffin and fulmar are among the most commonly sighted species. Some tour operators run short boat trips to the 'bird cliffs' close to Longyearbyen, while birders should buy the booklet *Bird Life in Longyearbyen and surrounding area* (Nkr50), which is available from the tourist office.

BOAT TRIPS
Polar Charter (☎97 52 32 50) sends out the *MS Polargirl* to Barentsburg and the Esmark Glacier (p354; adult/child Nkr1250/990, eight to 10 hours) four times a week, and to Pyramiden and Nordenskjöldbreen (p355; adult/child Nkr1250/990, eight to 10 hours);

prices include a lunch cooked on board. On Fridays, it also organises five-hour trips to the Borebreen glacier (adult/child Nkr950/850). **Henningsen Transport & Guiding** (☎79 02 13 11; www.htg.svalbard.no) runs a near-identical service aboard the *Langøysund* to Barentsburg and Pyramiden, although it's more expensive (adult Nkr1340). It also runs six-hour Friday-evening trips to Tempelfjorden and the Van Post glacier (Nkr1040).

Spitsbergen Travel (3/6hr trips Nkr640/990) also arranges up to 13 weekly boat cruises around Isfjord, which take in **birdwatching, fossil-hunting** and **glacier views**.

DOG-SLEDDING
It may not be quite the same as winter dog-sledding, but **Svalbard Villmarkssenter** (3hr trips Nkr590), **Arctic Adventures** (4hr trips Nkr690), **Basecamp Spitsbergen** (3½hr trips Nkr690) and **Svalbard Husky** (4hr trips Nkr550) offer half-day excursions with wheeled sleds pulled by pack dogs. There are up to 38 weekly departures in summer.

HIKING & FOSSIL-HUNTING
Summer hiking possibilities are endless and any Svalbard tour company worth its salt can organise half-, full- and multiday hikes.

The easiest options are three-hour fossil-hunting hikes (from Nkr330), some of which take you up onto the moraine at the base of the Longyearbreen glacier.

Popular destinations for other hikes, many of which include glacier hikes, include Platåberget (p353; three/four hours Nkr300/490), up onto the Longyearbreen glacier itself (p353; five hours Nkr590), Sarkofagen (525m above sea level; five hours Nkr590), Hiorthfjellet (900m above sea level; eight hours Nkr1050), Nordenskjöldtoppen (1050m above sea level; seven hours

Nkr950) and the Foxfonna ice field (six hours Nkr590).

HORSE RIDING

Svalbard Hestesenter (3hr trips Nkr650) organises short horse-riding expeditions in the country beyond Longyearbyen.

KAYAKING

Svalbard Wildlife Expeditions runs seven-hour kayaking expeditions to Hiorthamn (Nkr890) with an additional 10-hour hiking and kayaking challenge to Hiortfjellet (Nkr1100). Another option is the excursion along Adventdalen offered by **Svalbard Hestesenter** (6hr trips Nkr590).

Winter
DOG-SLEDDING

The environmentally friendly rival to snowmobiling, dog-sledding is in many ways the iconic Svalbard winter activity – the soundtrack of huskies barking and the scrape of the sled across the ice are a far more agreeable accompaniment in the wilderness than the drone of a snowmobile engine. Dedicated dog-sledding operators include Svalbard Husky and Svalbard Villmarkssenter and the standard four-hour expedition (adult/child Nkr990/690) will give you a taste. For longer excursions (including some wonderful multiday trips), it's worth checking what **Basecamp Spitsbergen** (7hr trips adult/child Nkr1990/995) has on offer.

SNOWMOBILING

Spitsbergen Travel has numerous single- and multiday snowmobile expeditions. Among its single-day options are the East Coast Snowmobile Safari (eight to 10 hours driver/passenger Nkr2350/1200), Barentsburg (seven to nine hours Nkr1950/1200), Pyramiden (eight to 10 hours Nkr2350/1200), Coles Bay (four hours Nkr1250/700), Elveneset (four hours Nkr1250/700) and the Polar Night Safari (three hours, Nkr1290/590).

Svalbard Snøscooterutleie offers many of the same routes for similar prices, as well as offering snowmobile rental. To drive a snowmobile scoot, you'll need to flash your home driving licence. Check with the tourist office; many areas are off-limits for snowmobiles. Daily rates start from Nkr900 to Nkr1100 for the basic model.

☞ Tours

Svalbard Maxi Taxi   MINIBUS TOURS
(☎79 02 13 05; per person Nkr250; ⊙10am & 4pm Jun–Aug) This local taxi company offers two-hour minibus tours that take you fur-

ther than you might think possible around Longyearbyen. The route is flexible, but generally takes you up to the southern end of the Longyearbyen valley with good views over the town, as well as west of the town and up past the Svalbard Global Seed Vault above the airport, and east along Adventdalen to the satellite station above Mine No 7. From each of these spots there are stunning views when the weather's fine and these last two spots are much further than you can get on foot and without a gun and guide.

★ Festivals & Events

Polar Jazz   MUSIC
(www.polarjazz.no, in Norwegian; ⊙Jan or Feb) A long winter weekend of jazz.

Sunfest   END-OF-WINTER CELEBRATION
(⊙early Mar) Week-long celebrations to dispel the polar night.

Blues Festival   MUSIC
(http://blues.svalbard.com; ⊙late Oct) Five-day jam session to mark the onset of winter.

⌂ Sleeping

Most accommodation consists of miners' accommodation with corridor bathrooms, a kitchen for self-caterers and small lounge.

In addition to the following places, the new Svalbard Hotel was due to open in the town centre in March 2011.

TOP **Basecamp Spitsbergen**   LODGE €€€
CHOICE (☎79 02 46 00; www.basecampexplorer. com; s Nkr990-1990, d Nkr1450-2390, tr Nkr1680-3150; ☎) Imagine a recreated sealing hut, built in part from recycled driftwood and local slate. Add artefacts and decorations culled from the local refuse dump and mining castoffs. Graft on 21st-century plumbing and design flair and you've got this place, also known as Trapper's Lodge. Its 16 cabin-like rooms are cosiness and comfort defined and the breakfasts are splendid. It's a special place and easily the most atmospheric choice in Longyearbyen.

Spitsbergen Guesthouse   GUESTHOUSE €€
(☎79 02 63 00; www.spitsbergentravel.no; dm Nkr300-365, s Nkr495-690, d Nkr795-990; ⊙mid-Mar–mid-Sep; ☎) This guesthouse is a subsidiary of Spitsbergen Travel spread over four buildings, one of which houses a large breakfast room (once the miners' mess hall), and can accommodate up to 136. The rooms are simple, but terrific value for money.

Mary-Ann's Polarrigg
HOTEL, GUESTHOUSE €€€

(☎79 02 37 02; www.polarriggen.com; Skjæringa; s/d with shared bathroom Nkr850/995, d/f with private bathroom Nkr2200/2800) Run by the ebullient Mary-Ann and adorned with mining and hunting memorabilia, the Polarrigg brims with character, although most of this is in the public areas and rooms are quite simple. In the main wing, rooms have corridor bathrooms and doubles come with bunk beds. There are two large, comfortably furnished lounges, while in the smart if somewhat overpriced annexe, rooms have every comfort.

Radisson SAS Polar Hotel
HOTEL €€€

(☎79 02 34 50; www.radissonsas.com; s Nkr1270-2690; d Nkr1570-2990; 🐾) This 95-room chain hotel ('the world's northernmost full-service hotel') is the town's most luxurious. Rooms are stylishly furnished and it costs Nkr200 extra for a 'superior room' with reasonable views of the fjord and Hiorthfjellet mountain beyond. Its annexe was originally accommodation for the Lillehammer Winter Olympic Games, then transported here. Unusually, children under 17 stay free of charge.

Haugen Pensjonat
PENSION €€

(☎79 02 17 05; www.haugenpensjonat.no; s/d with shared bathroom Nkr600/900; 🐾) Run by the people at Poli Arctici, Haugen Pensjonat, close to the Spitsbergen Hotel, has nine well-sized rooms with a double bed and sofa. Shared bathroom facilities work out at roughly one bathroom per two rooms. Wireless access costs Nkr50/200 per day/week.

Spitsbergen Hotel
HOTEL €€

(☎79 02 62 00; www.spitsbergentravel.no; s Nkr790-2480, d Nkr990-2780; ⏱mid-Feb–mid-Oct; 🐾) This comfortable place (sink yourself low into the leather armchairs of its salon), where the mine bosses once lived, contrasts to this day with the two Nybyen guesthouses up the hill that were previously the miners' more spartan quarters. Rooms are comfortable with a vaguely old-world air.

Gjestehuset 102
GUESTHOUSE €

(☎79 02 57 16; www.gjestehuset102.no; dm/s/d with shared bathroom Nkr320/550/890; ⏱Mar-Nov; 🐾) Friendly Guesthouse 102 (which, to confuse things, occupies building 7) belongs to Svalbard Wildlife Expeditions and was once sardonically nicknamed 'Millionaire's Residence'. As the former accommodation for mine workers, the rooms are simplicity itself. They come with washbasins and there's

a kitchen for self-caterers. Wireless internet access costs Nkr20/100 per hour/day.

Longyearbyen Camping
CAMPGROUND €

(☎79 02 10 68; www.longyearbyen-camping.com; per person Nkr100-150; ⏱Apr & mid-Jun–mid-Sep) Near the airport on a flat stretch of turf, this particularly friendly campsite overlooks Isfjorden and the glaciers beyond and has a kitchen and showers. It's about an hour's walk from town or you can rent a bicycle (per day for campers Nkr100). You can also hire a tent (per night Nkr100), mattress (Nkr10) and sleeping bag (first/subsequent nights Nkr50/20). There are no cabins, but it does issue certificates for those who bathe naked in the fjord...

Svalbard Lodge
APARTMENTS €€

(☎79 02 16 66; www.scooterutleie.svalbard.no; per person Nkr395-365) Located right in the heart of Longyearbyen, these two- and three-room modern apartments run by Svalbard Snøscooterutleie are a good Longyearbyen base. There's a two-night, two-person minimum-stay requirement.

✖ Eating

Locals will tell you that the two best places to eat and drink are the pub and the house. But not just any old pub or house...In addition to the places listed below, the Funktionærmessen Restaurant in the Spitsbergen Hotel is also good.

┌TOP┐ Huset
└CHOICE┘ NORWEGIAN, INTERNATIONAL €€

(The House; ☎79 02 25 00; cafe mains Nkr88-175, restaurant mains Nkr295-349, restaurant 3-/4-course Arctic Menu Nkr465/560; ⏱cafe 4-11pm Mon-Sat, 2-11pm Sun, restaurant 7-10pm Tue-Sun) It's something of a walk up here but it's worth it. Dining in the cafe-bar is casual, and well-priced pasta, pizza and reindeer stew are on the menu, while its signature dish is *hamburger med alt* (Nkr105) – a meaty burger with all the trimmings, so juicy, a researcher told us, that lonely scientists in their tents dream of it. The daily specials are wonderful. In the same building, the highly regarded restaurant serves up dishes like terrine of Svalbard reindeer, fillet of reindeer and quail. A curiosity for a place so far from the nearest vineyard: its wine cellar has over 20,000 bottles.

┌TOP┐ Kroa
└CHOICE┘ NORWEGIAN, INTERNATIONAL €€

(The Pub; ☎79 02 13 00; lunch mains Nkr76-139, dinner mains Nkr219-235; ⏱11.30am-2am) This pub and restaurant was reconstructed from the elements of a building brought in from Russian Barentsburg (the giant white bust of Lenin peeking from behind the bar gives a clue), and it feels like a supremely comfortable and spacious trapper's cabin. Service is friendly and mains verge on the gargantuan. Delicious soups, hearty mains (such as perfectly cooked venison) and starters such as smoked minke whale and carpacio of monkfish were on the menu when we last passed through. In high season, it's worth booking a table if you don't want to wait. The kitchen closes at 11pm.

Mary-Ann's Polarrigg   THAI €€€
(☑79 02 37 02; Skjæringa; mains Nkr189-245; ☺noon-midnight) The world's most northerly Thai restaurant offers up spicy rice dishes in a wonderful glasshouse setting, festooned with living plants that, unlike their native Svalbard counterparts, entwine and climb much more than 2cm high.

Brasseri Nansen   HOTEL RESTAURANT €€€
(☑79 02 37 02; mains from Nkr215, dinner buffet Nkr325; ☺11am-11pm) The hotel at the Radisson SAS Polar Hotel serves up an outstanding dinner buffet in summer, with seal, whale, reindeer and other local specialities making a regular appearance.

Fruene Kaffe og Vinbar   CAFE €
(☑79 02 76 40; Lompensenteret; lunch mains from Nkr59; ☺10am-6pm) 'The Missus', run by three sprightly young women, is a welcoming and popular cafe, serving decent coffee, baguettes, pizza and snacks.

Classic Pizza   PIZZA, KEBABS €
(Lompensenteret; kebabs & pizzas from Nkr79; ☺4pm-3am Sun-Thu, 4pm-5am Fri & Sat) Another tick in your list of 'world's most northerlies', this kebab place is good if you're feeling like a snack rather than a sit-down meal.

🍷 Drinking & Entertainment

Although alcohol is duty-free in Svalbard, it's rationed for locals and visitors must present a valid onward airline ticket in order to buy beer and spirits (but not wine...). The Nordpolet booze outlet is at the back of the Coop Supermarket.

In addition to the following places, three hotel bars – the Radisson's **Barents Pub & Spiseri** (☺4pm-2am Mon-Thu, 2pm-2am Fri-Sun), the Spitsbergen Hotel's **Funken Bar** (☺11am-2am) and **Mary-Ann's Polarrigg** (☺11am-2am) – can also get lively in season.

Kroa   BAR
(The Pub; ☺11.30am-2am) Bustling Kroa, its metal bar stools fashioned from old mine stanchions and with sealskin rugs, is enduringly popular, especially with younger locals.

Huset   BAR, NIGHTCLUB
(The House; ☺bar 4-11pm Mon-Sat, 2-11pm Sun, nightclub 11pm-4am Fri & Sat) Huset is your all-purpose night spot, with a bar and weekend nightclub (cover charge Nkr80) where live acts take to the stage on weekends. It also houses the town cinema, which screens feature films a couple of nights a week.

Karls-Berger Pub Café   BAR
(Lompensenteret; ☺5pm-2am Sun-Fri, 3pm-2am Sat) Enter this place, put on your shades and prepare to be dazzled at the sight of over 1000 bottles of whiskies, brandies and sundry spirits shimmering behind the bar of this snug pub.

Svalbar   BAR
(☺11am-2am Mon-Fri, 1pm-2am Fri & Sat) A newcomer to the Longyearbyen bar scene, Svalbar is your fairly standard Norwegian bar with a dartboard and billiard table and a small menu of food until 11pm. It's popular with a younger crowd.

ℹ Information

Sysselmannen På Svalbard (☑79 02 43 00; www.sysselmannen.no; ☺8.30am-3.30pm Mon-Fri) The place to go for independent hiking and gun permits.

Tourist office (☑79 02 55 50; www.svalbard. net; ☺10am-5pm May-Sep, noon-5pm Oct-Apr) Produces the comprehensive *Guide Longyearbyen* and a helpful weekly activities list.

ℹ Getting There & Away

SAS (www.flysas.com) flies to/from Oslo directly in summer (three flights weekly) or via Tromsø (once or twice daily) year-round. There are as many as 11 different tariffs; book early to avoid paying the 11th least expensive.

ℹ Getting Around

AIRPORT BUS The SAS Flybussen (Nkr50) connects with flights and runs between the airport and all of the hotels.

BICYCLE Bicycles can be rented for between Nkr150 and Nkr300 from **Poli Arctici** (☑79 02 17 05) or **Basecamp Spitsbergen** (☑79 02 46 00).

TAXI Svalbard Maxi Taxi (☑79 02 13 05) and **Longyearbyen Taxi** (☑79 02 13 75) charge Nkr100 to Nkr150 for the journey between town and airport.

To really get a taste for the inner and outer reaches of Svalbard in a short space of time, there's no alternative than a coastal boat cruise. All prices do not include airfares.

Spitsbergen Travel (☎79 02 61 00; www.spitsbergentravel.no) has at least three summer cruises. Its five-day Spitsbergen Adventure Cruise (from Nkr7930) sails the length of Spitsbergen's west coast, including Magdalenefjord, with just one sailing in early July. Its eight-day Spitsbergen Expedition Cruise (from Nkr23,950) goes as far as northeastern Svalbard, weather permitting, and is the ultimate Svalbard cruise. Its nine-day Spitsbergen Explorer Cruise (from Nkr18,400) runs from Bjørnøya in the south to Magdalenefjord in the northwest.

Basecamp Spitsbergen (☎79 02 46 00; www.basecampexplorer.com) also has a small range of boat trips with three-/five-/10-day cruises starting from Nkr8790/13,500/22,900, while **Svalbard Wildlife Expeditions** (☎79 02 56 60; www .wildlife.no) has three-day, twice-weekly summer cruises to a wildlife camp at Ymer Bay. **Hurtigruten** (www.hurtigruten.com) has at least six coastal summer cruises.

A handful of international companies also offer guided cruises around the archipelago. These include **Discover the World** (www.discovertheworld.co.uk), **GAP Adventures** (www .gapadventures.com), **Naturetrek** (www.naturetrek.co.uk) and **Exodus** (www.exodus.co.uk).

Around Longyearbyen

Although on the cusp of Longyearbyen, even these short hikes carry the risk of a polar bear encounter. For that reason, you'll either need to seek permission (to hike *and* carry a gun) from the governor's office (see p352) or, more likely, join an organised group with an armed guide.

PLATÅBERGET & BJØRNDALEN

The extensive upland region that overlooks Longyearbyen to the west is known as Platå-berget (commonly called The Plateau) and makes for a popular day hike. Either ascend a steep, scree-covered route from near the governor's office or sneak up Blomster-dalen, not far from Mine No 3. You can also get onto Platåberget via Bjørndalen (yes, it means 'bear valley'), south of the airport. Once on the plateau it's possible to continue to the summit of Nordenskiöldsfjellet (1050m), where a Swedish observatory is said to have once operated.

LONGYEARBREEN

The prominent glacier tongues licking at the upper, southwestern outskirts of Long-yearbyen have scoured and gouged through many layers of sedimentary material, including fossil layers, created when Svalbard enjoyed a more tropical climate. The terminal moraine churns up plant fossils – leaves and twigs that left their marks 40 to 60 million years ago. Several guided walks build in time for a little foraging.

The trail leads up past the Huset and up the river's true left bank, past the abandoned mine buildings, and onto a rough track. After the remains of a bridge (on your left), you'll approach the terminal moraine and cross a stream that flows down from your left. The track then traverses some steep slopes, crosses the river and continues upstream to its end at the fossil fields. The 5km return hike from Huset takes about 1½ hours, not counting fossicking time.

ADVENTDALEN

Stark, wide-open Adventdalen beckons visitors with wild Arctic landscapes. After leaving town, you'll pass the pungent husky kennels; Isdammen, a freshwater lake that provides drinking water for Longyearbyen and an important habitat for the barnacle goose; then a northern lights station. With a car or bike, you can also cruise out to the defunct **coal mine Nos 5 and 6** and pass **No 7** (the only one that still functions). Above Mine No 7 is a satellite station.

Barentsburg

POP 400

Visiting the Russian mining settlement of Barentsburg is like stumbling upon a forgotten outpost of the Soviet Union somewhere close to the end of the earth. The first thing you see is its power-station chimney, belching dark black smoke into the blue sky. This isolated village continues to mine coal against all odds and still produces up to 350,000 tonnes per year, though selling it on the open market is a constant problem and stockpiles are huge. With its signing in Cyrillic script, a still-standing bust of Lenin, murals of muscly workers in heroic pose and a run-down and dishevelled air, the overwhelming feeling is of a settlement whose time has past.

History

Barentsburg, on Grønfjorden, was first identified as a coal-producing area around 1900, when the Kullkompaniet Isefjord Spitsbergen started operations. Several other companies also sank shafts and in 1920 the town was founded by the Dutch company Nespico. Twelve years later it passed to the Soviet Trust Arktikugol.

Like Longyearbyen, Barentsburg was partially destroyed by the British Royal Navy in 1941 to prevent it falling into Nazi hands (ironically, the German navy itself finished the job later). In 1948 it was rebuilt by Trust Arktikugol and embarked on a period of growth, development and scientific research that lasted until the fall of the Soviet Union.

Barentsburg, like every other pit on Svalbard, has known tragedy. In 1996 many of those who perished in a plane crash during a blizzard near Adventdalen were miners' families from the Ukraine. Then, a year later, 23 miners died in a mine explosion and fire.

These days, most of Trust Arktikugol's coal shipments go directly to the west, notably to power stations in the Netherlands. Pay cheques are now being eaten up by Russian inflation and obsolete mining equipment is breaking down. The scientific community is reduced, though a small team of geophysicists, meteorologists and glaciologists still researches, and the town's population continues to dwindle.

◉ Sights

You'll almost certainly be visiting Barentsburg as part of an organised tour. Once the guiding is over, do rush around in the short time left before the boat weighs anchor and fit in a visit to the following sights.

Pomor Museum   MUSEUM

(admission Nkr40; ⊙when tour boats are in port) This simple, appealing little museum outlines (in Russian only) the historic Pomor trade with mainland Russia, plus Russian mining and history on Svalbard. Especially worthwhile are the excellent geological exhibits and the collection of artefacts suggesting Russian activity in Svalbard prior to the archipelago's accepted European 'discovery' by Willem Barents.

Chapel   CHAPEL

The small wooden Orthodox chapel above the football pitch commemorates the twin disasters of 1996 and 1997.

🛏 Sleeping & Eating

Barentsburg Hotel   HOTEL, RESTAURANT €

(☎79 02 10 80, 79 02 18 14; d Nkr650) The Barentsburg Hotel (the settlement's only accommodation for visitors) has reasonable rooms that are, like Barentsburg itself, in need of an overhaul although they're fine for a night. The restaurant serves traditional Russian meals, featuring such specialities as boiled pork with potatoes and Arctic sorrel, parsley and sour cream. If you're one of very few visitors who overnight, sign on for the gourmet dinner, offering both Russian and Ukrainian cuisine, lubricated with Russian champagne and vodka. In the bar, you can enjoy a deliciously affordable and generous slug of vodka or a Russian beer. It also sells large tins of the Real McCoy caviar at prices you'll never find elsewhere in the West, let alone Norway.

🔒 Shopping

The Polar Star Souvenire Shop sells babushka dolls, Lenin lapel badges and some Soviet army surplus.

ⓘ Getting There & Away

Two companies (see p349) offer summertime nine- to 10-hour **boat trips** (from Nkr1250) to Barentsburg from Longyearbyen. The boats head across the fjord to the vast Esmark glacier on the homeward journey. The price includes 1½ hours in Barentsburg, mostly occupied by a guided tour.

In winter, it's possible to travel between Longyearbyen and Barentsburg as part of a snowmobile safari (see p350).

Pyramiden

Formerly Russia's second settlement in Svalbard, Pyramiden, named for the pyramid-shaped mountain that rises nearby, is a rewarding day trip from Longyearbyen.

In the mid-1910s coal was discovered here and operations were set up by the same Swedish concern that exploited Sveagruva. In 1926 it was taken over by a Soviet firm, Russkiy Grumant, which sold out to the Soviet Trust Arktikugol, exploiters of Barentsburg, in 1931. In the 1950s there were as many as 2500 Russian residents, well exceeding the population of Longyearbyen today. During its productive heyday in the early 1990s it had 60km of shafts, 130 homes, agricultural enterprises similar to those in Barentsburg and the world's most northerly hotel and swimming pool. But with the mine no longer yielding enough coal to be profitable and with Russia no longer willing or able to subsidise the mine, Pyramiden was abandoned in 1998. A skeleton staff of (at last count) eight Russians still live at Pyramiden to keep the flag flying, but the sense of abandonment in this remote corner of Svalbard is poignantly evocative.

◉ Sights

As with other sights around Svalbard, there are startling juxtapositions between the near-pristine surroundings and the apparent meltdown of industrial infrastructure all across Pyramiden. Focal points for your walk around town are the 1970s-era **Soviet architecture**, a prominent **bust of Lenin** and the **sports hall**. As in Barentsburg, there's a small shop in the **former hotel** selling a small selection of Soviet memorabilia and a bar serving up vodka shots.

Across Billefjorden to the east, **Nordenskjöldbreen** is a stunning glacier running as a broad front from the Svalbard interior to the fjord shoreline; most boat excursions from Longyearbyen draw near for photos. The boat journey itself from Longyearbyen is a stunning trip, passing striated cliffs and accompanied by puffins and fulmar.

❶ Getting There & Away

In summer, at least two Longyearbyen-based tour agencies offer 10-hour day cruises to Pyramiden (from Nkr1250). See p349 for further details.

In winter, snowmobile safaris between Longyearbyen and Pyramiden are possible (see p350).

Ny Ålesund

POP 30-130

Despite its inhospitable latitude (79°N), you'd be hard pressed to find a more awesome backdrop anywhere on earth than the scientific post of Ny Ålesund, 107km northwest of Longyearbyen. Founded in 1916 by the Kings Bay Kull Compani, Ny Ålesund likes to claim that it's the world's northernmost permanently inhabited civilian community (although you could make a case for three other equally minuscule spots in Russia and Canada).

Throughout much of the 20th century Kings Bay mined for coal. As many as 300 people once lived and worked here but, after the last of several lethal explosions resulted in 21 deaths, mining stopped in 1963. Ny Ålesund has since recycled itself as a prominent scientific post, with research stations of several nations, including Japan, France, the British Antarctic Survey and China (bizarrely in this land of polar bears and Arctic foxes, two marble lions stand watch over the Chinese quarters). There's a hardy year-round population of around 30 scientists, rising to 130 in summer (never more since that's the number of beds available) as researchers from about 15 countries fly in.

◉ Sights

There's a 1.5km trail with multilingual interpretive panels that takes you around the main sites of this tiny settlement.

In the early 20th century several polar explorers set off from Ny Ålesund, including the likes of Roald Amundsen, Lincoln Ellsworth, Admiral Byrd and Umberto Nobile. The **anchor pylon** was used by Nobile and Amundsen to launch the airship *Norge* on their successful flight over the pole to Alaska in 1926; it came in handy again two years later, when Nobile returned to launch the *Italia* on his ill-fated repeat attempt. You'll see **memorials** to these missions around the settlement.

Perhaps the most unusual sight is the stranded **steam locomotive** near the dock. In 1917 a narrow-gauge railway was constructed to connect the coalfields with the harbour and it remained in use until 1958. The restored locomotive is, naturally, the world's northernmost railway relic.

The town also supports a neat little **Mine Museum** (Gruvemuseum; donation suggested; ⊘24hr) in the old Tiedemann's Tabak (tobacco) shop, relating the coal-mining history of this area.

All nonprofessional visitors arrive in Ny Ålesund on tourist cruises and linger for an hour or two.

Around Ny Ålesund

KONGSFJORDEN

Ny Ålesund's backdrop, Kongsfjorden (the namesake for the Kings Bay Kull Compani) spectacularly contrasts bleak grey-brown shores with expansive white icefields. The distinctive Tre Kroner peaks, Dana (1175m), Svea (1226m) and Nora (1226m) – named in honour of Denmark, Sweden and Norway, respectively – jut from the ice and are among Svalbard's most recognisable landmarks.

BLOMSTRANDHALVØYA

Gravelly Blomstrandhalvøya was once a peninsula but, in the early 1990s, it was released from the icy grip on its northern end and it's now an island. In summer the name Blomstrand, or 'flower beach', would be appropriate, but it was in fact named for a Norwegian geologist. Ny London, at the southern end of the island, recalls one Ernest Mansfield of the Northern Exploration Company who attempted to quarry marble in 1911 only to discover that the stone had been rendered worthless by aeons of freezing and thawing. A couple of buildings and some forlorn machinery remain.

Magdalenefjord

The lovely blue-green bay of Magdalenefjord in Nordvest Spitsbergen, flanked by towering peaks and intimidating tidewater glaciers, is the most popular anchorage along Spitsbergen's western coast and is one of Svalbard's prettiest corners. In the 17th century, this area saw heavy Dutch whaling; at Graveneset, near the mouth of the fjord, you can still see the remains of two stoves used to boil the blubber. There are numerous protected graves of 17th- and mid-18th-century whalers.

Prins Karls Forlandet

On the west coast of Spitsbergen, the oddly shaped 86km-long island of Prins Karls Forlandet is a national park set aside to protect breeding walruses, seals and sea lions. The alpine northern reaches, which rise to Grampianfjellet (1084m), are connected to Saltfjellet (430m), at the southern end, by a long flat plain called Forlandsletta.

Krossfjorden

Thanks to Lillehöökbreen (its grand tidewater glacier) and several cultural relics, Krossfjorden also attracts quite a few cruise ships. At Ebeltoftbukta, near the mouth of the fjord, you can see several whalers' graves as well as a heap of leftover junk from a 1912 German telegraph office that was shifted wholesale to Ny Ålesund after only two years of operation. Opposite the entrance rise some crowded bird cliffs overlooking one of Svalbard's most verdant spots, with flowers, moss and even grasses.

Danskøya

One of the most intriguing sites in northwest Spitsbergen is Virgohamna, on the bleak, gravely island of Danskøya, where the remains of several broken dreams now lie scattered across the lonely beach. Among them are the ruins of three blubber stoves from a 17th-century whaling station, as well as eight stone-covered graves from the same era. You'll also find the remains of a cottage built by English adventurer Arnold Pike, who sailed north in his yacht *Siggen* and spent a winter subsisting on polar bears and reindeer.

The next adventurer at Virgohamna was Swedish engineer Salomon August Andrée, who in the summer of 1897 set off from Virgohamna in an airship, hoping to reach the North Pole. The fate of his expedition wasn't known until 1930, when sailors from a seal-hunting ship put ashore and stumbled across their last site on Kvitøya.

Then, in 1906, journalist Walter Wellman, who was sponsored by a US newspaper, attempted to reach the North Pole in an airship but failed. Next year, when he returned to try again, his ship was badly damaged in a storm. On his third attempt, in 1909, he floated to within 60km of the pole, met with technical problems and gave up for good; mainly because he'd heard that Robert Peary had already reached the pole anyway (although that claim is now largely discredited). All of the remaining junk (including dozens of rusted 44-gallon fuel drums) is protected. Erosion damage, caused by the few visitors who manage to get here, has been considerable, so do the right thing and stick strictly to the marked paths.

Moffen Island

Gravelly Moffen Island is known for its walrus population, though the 300m boat-exclusion zone around the island means that any views of these great beasts is distant at best.

Understand Norway

USA   NORWAY   UK

≈ 14 people

Norway Today

Crisis? What Crisis?

» Population: 4.67 million (2010)

» GDP per capita (2009): US$58,809

» Maternity/paternity leave on full pay: 46/10 weeks

» Life expectancy: 79.95 years

Ask most Norwegians how their country has weathered the global financial crisis and you're likely to be met with a guilty smile. Yes, growth rates stalled as world oil prices fell and the economy even contracted in 2009. And yet, the impact upon ordinary Norwegians has been minimal – unemployment in 2009 was just 3.2%, prices rose in the same period by an eminently reasonable 2.1% and the government's generous system of social welfare and other benefits remained intact. As a consequence, the average Norwegian has largely been insulated from the world's worst economic crisis in decades.

Independent & Apart

With such stability and prosperity at home, it's Norway's relationship with the rest of the world that dominates many public debates. For one thing, Norway continues to agonise over whether it should join the European Union (EU). Government-supported referenda on membership in 1972 and again in 1994 were narrowly defeated. And Norway looks increasingly likely to remain on the outside of the EU looking in. After a near 50-50 split for many years, opinion has hardened against membership – a series of opinion polls in mid-2010 found that just 25% of Norwegians favoured membership, with around two-thirds opposed. For now, the resistance to anyone else telling Norwegians how to live their lives – fostered during centuries of foreign occupation – seems to be winning the day.

Struggle for the Soul of Norway

When it comes to its hard-won national identity, Norway stands at something of a crossroads. Centuries of hardship forged a strong sense of self-reliance, while the fabulous oil wealth of the late 20th century nurtured

Top Books

The Ice Museum (Joanna Kavenna) Vividly captures our fascination with the Arctic North.

Rowing to Latitude (Jill Fredston) A journey by row boat along the length of Norway's coast.

Isles of the North (Ian Mitchell) A boat journey into the fjords, with musings on Norway's place among modern nations.

Fellowship of Ghosts (Paul Watkins) Follows the author's solo foot journeys through Norway's high country.

Conversations

» **Too many immigrants?** From 1.5% to 11.4% of the population in the past four decades.

» **Oil wealth** How to act as one of the world's richest countries?

» **The environment** Leading environmental activist versus leading producer of fossil fuels.

proportion of urban dwellers
(% of population)

if Norway were 100 people

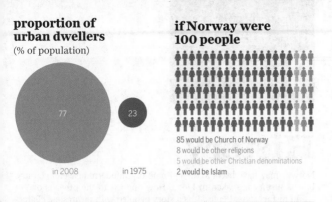

77 in 2008

23 in 1975

85 would be Church of Norway
8 would be other religions
5 would be other Christian denominations
2 would be Islam

the deeply held belief that Norway, as one of the richest countries on earth, had to serve as an example of a responsible and tolerant global citizen. But two issues in particular – the environment and immigration – have caused Norwegians to reassess how they see their country.

Norway's environmental policy is one of the world's most enlightened: new national parks are being added all the time, Norway is at the forefront of international efforts to forge agreements cutting greenhouse gas emissions and the government has promised to make Norway the first carbon-neutral country in the world. At the same time, Norway is a leading producer of fossil fuels (particularly oil) and has attracted significant international criticism for its stance on whaling. Shadowing this debate is the growing sense among many Norwegians that they are losing their connection with the land as the demographic make-up of the country shifts from a predominantly rural population of isolated farmsteads to one where three-quarters of the population now lives in urban areas.

High levels of foreign aid and Norway's important role in mediating international conflicts are a source of great pride to many Norwegians, but that self-image has become more complicated with the domestic rise of the Fremskrittspartiet (Progress Party). At parliamentary elections in 2005 and again in 2009, the party – which advocates a crackdown on immigration – polled around 22% of the vote. In the process it has easily become the second-largest party in the country.

That these issues are causing such angst serves as a reminder that, for perhaps the first time since the Viking era, Norway is negotiating its place in the world from a position of considerable strength.

» Area: 385,155 sq km
» Highest mountain: Galdhøpiggen (2469m)
» Number of national parks: 40
» Length of coastline: 25,148km
» Longest border: 1619km (Sweden)
» Shortest border: 196km (Russia)

Icons

Henrik Ibsen One of the world's best-loved playwrights.
Edvard Grieg Composer of Norway's classical soundtrack.
Edvard Munch The country's leading 20th-century painter.
Roald Amundsen Unrivalled explorer of the Arctic and Antarctic.

Fridtjof Nansen Explorer and architect of modern Norway.
Jan Garbarek Ground-breaking jazz saxophonist.

Dos & Don'ts

» **Do** take the time to talk with older Norwegians – it's amazing how far this country has come.

» **Don't** lecture Norwegians on whaling – they've heard it before.

» **Do** learn a few words in Norwegian – Norwegians appreciate the gesture.

History

Norway may have become the epitome of a modern, peaceful country, but its history is soaked in blood. How one led to the other is one of world history's great epics. It is a story peopled with picaresque characters and always revolving around recurring grand themes.

Before there were people in this land, Norway's story began with the great geological shifts and ice ages that formed one of Europe's most dramatic landscapes. Onto this terrain, at once forbidding and majestic, stepped the first and most enduring of Norwegian peoples, the forerunners of the modern Sami fleeing the icy wastes of Siberia.

But more than any other people, it was the Vikings who would come to dominate Norwegian history. Throughout their five centuries at the pinnacle of European power, their conquests extended across much of Europe, while at home enlightened and despotic kings, civil wars and battles between Norse gods and growing Christian influence produced some of the most fascinating sagas of Scandinavian history. The Vikings were a hard act to follow and centuries of decline – during much of which Norway was the restless vassal of its neighbours – cast a shadow over the Middle Ages in what would later become Norway.

Independence was hard-won and brought with it a flourishing cultural scene and growing national pride. Such events were, however, often overshadowed by desperate poverty and widespread emigration as Norwegians fled the depredations of home in search of a better life. WWII, and with it Nazi occupation, dealt a devastating blow to a country still reeling from the effects of the Great Depression. But the war also gave rise to stirring tales of Norwegian resistance that became an important pillar in forging a modern national identity.

The discovery of oil in the 1960s changed Norway forever. Suddenly transformed from an economic backwater into Europe's wealthiest country, Norway has never looked back and is now regarded as a model social

Little is known about the nomadic, hunter-gatherer Nøstvet-Økser people, who were most likely tall, blond-haired, blue-eyed and spoke a Germanic language, the predecessor of modern Scandinavian languages.

TIMELINE	12,000 BC	9000 BC	4000 BC
	The last ice age thaws and Norway takes on its present physical form with a new body of water separating Norway from northern Europe.	The hunting culture of the Komsa, the forerunner of the Sami, arrives in northern Scandinavia and the Komsa establish the first permanent settlements in Norway's Arctic North.	The earliest of the Unesco World Heritage–listed rock art is painted by Stone Age peoples close to modern Alta in Norway's far north, charting the region's human and natural history.

democracy and almost without peer in its willingness to use its oil wealth to take the best possible care of its citizens.

Darkness & Ice

Some of the most lasting impressions travellers carry with them after visiting Norway – a land of snow and ice, a bountiful coast, extreme climatic conditions and a thinly populated land – have been present here since the dawn of Scandinavian civilisation. Indeed, the human presence in Norway was for thousands of years overshadowed by Norway's geography and climate, which have strong claims to being the most enduring personalities of Norwegian history.

During the last ice age, Norway was barely inhabitable. But if Norway was less than hospitable, it was a paradise compared to northern Russia at the time and, as the ice began to melt, it was from the east that the first major, lasting migration to Norway took place when, around 11,000 years ago, the Komsa, who would later become the Sami (p404), arrived in Norway's Arctic North.

As the climate warmed and Norway became increasingly habitable, migrations of the Nøstvet-Økser people of central Europe began arriving along the southern Norwegian coast, drawn by relatively plentiful fishing, sealing and hunting. Wild reindeer also followed the retreating ice, moving north into the still-ice-bound interior, and the hunters that followed them were the first humans to traverse the Norwegian high country. Their presence was, however, restricted to itinerant, seasonal camps and there remained few human footholds in an otherwise empty land dominated by glaciers and frozen wastes.

Over the millennia that followed, settled cultures began to take root, to the extent that during the later years of the Roman Empire, Rome provided Norway with fabric, iron implements and pottery. The iron tools allowed farmland to be cleared of trees, larger boats were built with the aid of iron axes and a cooling climate saw the establishment of more permanent structures built from stone and turf. By the 5th century Norwegians had learned how to smelt their own iron from ore found in the southern Norwegian bogs. Norway's endless struggle to tame its wild landscape had begun.

Here Come the Vikings

Few historical people have captured the imagination quite like the Vikings. Immortalised in modern cartoons (*Asterix* and *Hägar the Horrible,* to name just a couple) and considered the most feared predators of ancient Europe, the Vikings may have disappeared from history, but as a seafaring nation with its face turned towards distant lands, they remain very much the forerunners of modern Norway. But who were these

---

Archaeo-logical Museums

» Bryggens Museum, Bergen

» Arkeologisk Museum, Stavanger

» Historical Museum, Oslo

» Museum of Natural History & Archaeology, Trondheim

» Alta Museum, Alta

The History of Norway – From the Ice Age to Today, by Øvind Stenersen and Ivar Libæk, provides more than enough historical detail for most travellers and is available at larger bookshops in Norway.

2500 BC	AD 787	793	871
The wonderfully named Battle-Axe, Boat-Axe and Funnel-Beaker people, named after the stone tools they used, enter southern Norway from Sweden. They traded amber for metals from mainland Europe.	The earliest account of Norse seafaring appears in the *Anglo Saxon Chronicle* for 787, describing how three ships came to Britain, piloted by sailors who were described as Northmen.	The dawn of the Viking age comes when Vikings plunder St Cuthbert's monastery on the island of Lindisfarne, off the coast of Northumberland in Britain.	Tønsberg in southern Norway is founded around this year, making it the oldest still-inhabited town in Norway. It later served as a royal court and an important trading town.

ancient warriors who took to their longboats and dominated Europe for five centuries?

Viking Sites

» Stiklestad
» Tønsberg
» Kaupang (Larvik)
» Eidfjord
» Kinsarvik
» Haugesund
» Karmøy island
» Balestrand
» Giske
» Leka
» Lindesnes

Conquest & Expansion

Under pressure from shrinking agricultural land caused by a growing population, settlers from Norway began arriving along the coast of the British Isles in the 780s. When the boats returned home to Norway with enticing trade goods and tales of poorly defended coastlines, the Vikings began laying plans to conquer the world. The first Viking raid took place on St Cuthbert's monastery on the island of Lindisfarne in 793. Soon the Vikings were spreading across Britain, Ireland and the rest of Europe with war on their minds and returning home with slaves *(thrall)* in their formidable, low Norse longboats.

The Vikings attacked in great fleets, terrorising, murdering, enslaving, assimilating or displacing local populations. Coastal regions of Britain, Ireland, France (Normandy was named for these 'Northmen'), Russia (as far east as the river Volga), Moorish Spain (Seville was raided in 844), and the Middle East (they even reached Baghdad) all came under the Viking sway. Well-defended Constantinople (Istanbul) proved a bridge too far – the Vikings attacked six times but never took the city. Such rare setbacks notwithstanding, the Viking raids transformed Scandinavia from an obscure backwater on Europe's northern fringe to an all-powerful empire.

For all of their destruction elsewhere, Vikings belonged very much to the shores from which they set out or sheltered on their raids. Viking raids increased standards of living at home. Emigration freed up farmland and fostered the emergence of a new merchant class, while captured slaves provided farm labour. Norwegian farmers also crossed the Atlantic to settle the Faroes, Iceland and Greenland during the 9th and 10th centuries. The world, it seemed, belonged to the Vikings.

The Haugelandet region of western Norway is considered by many to be the cradle of Viking culture and Karmøy island, south of Haugesund, has a Viking Festival in June (www.vikingfestivalen.no, in Norwegian). The website www.vikingkings.com covers the region's Viking history.

Harald Fair-Hair

Harald Hårfagre (Harald Fair-Hair), son of Hvaldan Svarte (Halvdan the Black), was more than the latest in a long line of great Viking names. While most Viking chieftains made their name in foreign conquest, Harald Fair-Hair was doing something that no other leader had managed before – he united the disparate warring tribes of the Viking nation.

Harald's greatest moment came in 872 at Hafrsfjord near Haugesund when he emerged victorious from one of world history's few civil wars to be decided at sea. When the dust settled, Norway had become a single country.

The reign of Harald Hårfagre was such an odd and entertaining time that it was recorded for posterity in the *Heimskringla,* the Norwegian

872

Harald Hårfagre (Harald Fair-Hair) fights his fellow Viking chieftains in the Battle of Hafrsfjord and unites Norway for the first time. Some 20,000 people flee to Iceland.

997

Trondheim is founded at the mouth of the Nid River and is the first major settlement in the country; it becomes the first capital of the fledgling kingdom.

MANFRED HOFER

» Exterior detail of Trondheim's Nidaros Cathedral (p246)

The main god who provided strength to the Viking cause was Odin (Oðinn), the 'All-Father' who was married to Frigg. Together they gave birth to a son, Thor (Þór), the God of Thunder. The Vikings believed that if they died on the battlefield, the all-powerful Odin would take them to a paradise by the name of Valhalla, where Viking men could fight all day and then be served by beautiful women.

Not surprisingly, it was considered far better for a Viking to die on the battlefield than in bed of old age and Vikings brought a reckless abandon to their battles that was extremely difficult for enemies to overcome – to die or to come away with loot, the Vikings seemed to say, was more or less the same. Equally unsurprising was the fact that the essential Viking values that emerged from their unique world view embodied a disregard for death, strength, skill in weapons, heroic courage and personal sacrifice.

But the Vikings were as much the sophisticates of the ancient world as they were its fearless warriors. Viking ships were revolutionary, fast, manoeuvrable vessels capable of withstanding torrid and often long ocean journeys. Longboats were over 30m long, had a solid keel, flexible hull, large, square sails and could travel at up to 12 knots (22km/h hour); they enabled the Vikings to launch and maintain a conquest that would go largely unchallenged for 200 years.

Perhaps the most curious aspect of Viking voyages, however, was the navigational tool they employed to travel through uncharted territory. Norse sagas mention a mysterious device known as a *solarsteinn* (sunstone), which allowed navigation even when the sky was overcast or the sun was below the horizon and celestial navigation was impossible.

It is now generally agreed that the *solarsteinn* was a crystal of cordierite, which is found around Scandinavia and has natural polarising qualities. When observed from below and rotated, light passing through the crystal is polarised blue when the long axis is pointed towards the source of the sunlight. Even today, jet planes flying over polar regions, where magnetic compasses are unsuitable, use a sky compass that determines the position of the sun by filtering sunlight through an artificial polarising lens.

kings' saga, by Icelander Snorre Sturluson. According to Snorre, Harald's unification of Norway was inspired by a woman who taunted the king by refusing to have relations with a man whose kingdom wasn't even as large as tiny Denmark. Through a series of confederations and trade agreements, he extended his rule as far north as what is now Trøndelag. His foreign policies were equally canny, and he even sent one of his sons, Håkon, to be reared in the court of King Athelstan of England. There is no record of whether the woman in question was sufficiently impressed. Harald died of plague at Avaldsnes on Karmøy island around 930.

The king who unified the country could do little about his own family, however. He had 10 wives and fathered a surfeit of heirs, thereby creating

c 1000	1024	1030	1049
Almost five centuries before Columbus, Leifur Eiríksson, son of Eiríkur Rauðe (Eric the Red), explores the North American coast, which he names Vinland, meaning the 'land of wine'.	Olav II founds the Church of Norway and establishes it as Norway's state religion throughout his realm, a situation that continues right to this day.	After being sent into exile by King Canute (Knut) of Denmark in 1028, King Olav II returns, only to be killed in Trøndelag at the Battle of Stiklestad.	Harald III (Harald Hardråde, or Harald 'Hard-Ruler'), half-brother of St Olav, founds Oslo and uses it as a base to launch far-ranging raids across the Mediterranean.

Viking Museums

» Viking Ship Museum, Oslo

» Lofotr Viking Museum, Vestvågøy, Lofoten

» Nordvegen Historiesenter, Karmøy island

» Vikingland, Spangereid

serious squabbles over succession. The one who rose above them all was Erik, his last child and only son with Ragnhild the Mighty, daughter of the Danish King Erik of Jutland. The ruthless Erik eliminated all of his legitimate brothers except Håkon (who was safe in England). Erik, whose reign was characterised by considerable ineptitude, then proceeded to squander his father's hard-won Norwegian confederation. When Håkon returned from England to sort out the mess as King Håkon den Gode (Håkon the Good), Erik was forced to flee to Britain where he took over the throne of York as King Erik Blood-Axe.

Christianity & the Viking Decline

The Vikings gave Norwegians their love of the sea and it was during the late Viking period that they bequeathed to them another of their most enduring national traits – strong roots in Christianity. However, this overturning of the Viking pantheon of gods did not come without a struggle.

King Håkon the Good, who had been baptised a Christian during his English upbringing, brought the new faith (as well as missionaries and a bishop) with him upon his return to Norway. Despite some early success, most Vikings remained loyal to Thor, Odin and Freyr. Although the missionaries were eventually able to replace the names of the gods with those of Catholic saints, the pagan practice of blood sacrifice continued unabated. When Håkon the Good was defeated and killed in 960, Norwegian Christianity all but disappeared.

Christianity in Norway was revived during the reign of King Olav Tryggvason (Olav I). Like any good Viking, Olav decided that only force would work to convert his countrymen to the 'truth'. Unfortunately for the king, his intended wife, Queen Sigrid of Sweden, refused to convert. Olav cancelled the marriage contract and Sigrid married the pagan king, Svein Forkbeard of Denmark. Together they orchestrated Olav's death in a great Baltic sea-battle, then took Norway as their own.

Christianity was finally cemented in Norway by King Olav Haraldsson, Olav II, who was also converted in England. Olav II and his Viking hordes allied themselves with King Ethelred and managed to save London from a Danish attack under King Svein Forkbeard by destroying London Bridge (from whence we derive the song 'London Bridge Is Falling Down'). Succeeding where his namesake had failed, Olav II spread Christianity with considerable success. In 1023 Olav built a stone cross in Voss, where it still stands, and in 1024 he founded the Church of Norway. After an invasion by King Canute (Knut) of Denmark in 1028, Olav II died during the Battle of Stiklestad in 1030. For Christians, this amounted to martyrdom and the king was canonised as a saint; the great Nidaros Cathedral in Trondheim stands as a memorial to St Olav and,

Explore North (www.explorenorth.com/vikings.html) is the ultimate site for wannabe Vikings, with extensive links to Viking history and sagas, Norse gods, Norse mythology and a delicious smattering of conspiracy theories.

1066	1261	1319	1349
The Viking age draws to a close after Harald III dies at the hands of King Harold of England at the Battle of Stamford Bridge in England.	Greenland joins the Kingdom of Norway, followed a year later by Iceland, reflecting Norway's growing influence over the affairs of Europe's far north.	Magnus becomes King of Sweden and unites Sweden and Norway. This ends Norwegian independence and the royal line of Harald Fair-Hair, and begins two centuries of decline.	Bubonic plague (the Black Death) arrives in Bergen and quickly spreads throughout the country, forever altering Norway's social fabric.

until the Protestant Reformation, the cathedral served as a destination for pilgrims from all over Europe (see the boxed text, p246). His most lasting legacy, however, was having forged an enduring identity for Norway as an independent kingdom.

Of the kings who followed, none distinguished themselves quite as infamously as Harald III (Harald Hardråde, or Harald 'Hard-Ruler'), half-brother of St Olav. Harald III raided throughout the Mediterranean, but it was a last hurrah for the Vikings. When he was killed during an ill-conceived raid in England in 1066, the Viking air of invincibility was broken.

No Longer Independent

The Vikings may have been fast disappearing into history, but Viking expansionism, along with the coming of Christianity, planted the seeds – of success, of decline – for what was to come. As Norway's sphere of international influence shrank, Norway's neighbours began to close in, leaving this one-time world power having to fight for its own independence.

Trouble Abroad, Trouble at Home

In 1107 Sigurd I led an expedition of 60 ships to the Holy Land. Three years later, he captured Sidon, in modern-day Lebanon. But by this stage foreign conquest had become a smokescreen for serious internal problems. Sigurd died in 1130 and the rest of the century was fraught with brutal civil wars over succession to the throne. The victorious King Sverre, a churchman-turned-warrior, paved the way for Norway's so-called 'Golden Age', which saw Bergen claim the title of national capital, driven by Norway's perennial ties to foreign lands and, in particular, trade between coastal towns and the German-based Hanseatic League (see p154). Perhaps drawn by Norway's economic boom, Greenland and Iceland voluntarily joined the Kingdom of Norway in 1261 and 1262, respectively.

But Norway's role as a world power was on the wane and Norway was turning inward. Håkon V built brick and stone forts, one at Vardø to protect the north from the Russians, and another at Akershus, in 1308, to defend Oslo harbour. The transfer of the national capital from Bergen to Oslo soon followed. When Håkon V's grandson Magnus united Norway with Sweden in 1319, Norway began a decline that would last for 200 years. Once-great Norway had become just another province of its neighbours.

In August 1349 the Black Death arrived in Norway on board an English ship via Bergen. The bubonic plague would eventually kill one-third of Europe's population. In Norway, land fell out of cultivation, towns were ruined, trading activities faltered and the national coffers decreased by

9999999The

The word 'Viking' derives from *vik*, an Old Norse word that referred to a bay or cove, a reference to Vikings' anchorages during and after raids.

According to some linguists, Viking gods gave their names to the days of the week in English – Tuesday (Tyr's Day), Wednesday (Odin's Day), Thursday (Thor's Day) and Friday (Freyr's Day).

GODS

HISTORY NO LONGER INDEPENDENT

1469	1537	1596	1612
The Orkney and Shetland islands, along with the Isle of Man, are sold to the Scots, bringing to an end centuries of Norwegian expansion.	The Reformation that sweeps across Europe reaches Norway, whereafter the incumbent Catholic faith is replaced with Lutheran Protestantism.	Willem Barents, a Dutch explorer searching for a northeast sea passage to Asia, becomes the first European to set foot on Svalbard. He names the archipelago Spitsbergen ('sharp mountains').	Commercial whaling begins on Svalbard, with English, Dutch, Norwegian, French and Danish fleets driving many whale and other marine species to the brink of extinction in the centuries that follow.

65%. In Norway, as much as 80% of the nobility perished. Because their peasant workforce had also been decimated, the survivors were forced to return to the land, forever changing the Norwegian power-base and planting the seeds for an egalitarianism that continues to define Norway to this day.

By 1387 Norway had lost control of Iceland and 10 years later, Queen Margaret of Denmark formed the Kalmar Union of Sweden, Denmark and Norway, with Eric of Pomerania as king. Margaret's neglect of Norway continued into the 15th century, when trade links with Iceland were broken and the Greenland colonies mysteriously disappeared without trace.

In 1469 Orkney and Shetland were pawned – supposedly a temporary measure – to the Scottish Crown by the Danish-Norwegian King Christian I, who had to raise money for his daughter's dowry. Just three years later the Scots annexed both island groups.

Buffeted by these winds of change, Norway had become a shadow of its former self. The only apparent constant was the country's staunch Christian faith. But even in the country's faith there were fundamental changes afoot. In 1537, the Reformation replaced the incumbent Catholic faith with Lutheran Protestantism and the transformation of the Norway of the Vikings was all but complete.

Denmark & Sweden – the Enemy

Talk to many Norwegians and you're likely to find that there's no love lost between them and their neighbours, Denmark and Sweden. Here's why.

A series of disputes between the Danish Union and the Swedish crown were played out on Norwegian soil. First came the Seven Years War (1563–70), followed by the Kalmar War (1611–14). Trondheim, for example, was repeatedly captured and recaptured by both sides and during the Kalmar War an invasion of Norway was mounted from Scotland (see the boxed text, p141).

In two further wars during the mid-17th century Norway lost a good portion of its territory to Sweden. The Great Nordic War with the expanding Swedish Empire was fought in the early 18th century and in 1716 the Swedes occupied Christiania (Oslo). The Swedes were finally defeated in 1720, ending over 150 years of warfare.

Despite attempts to re-establish trade with Greenland through the formation of Norwegian trading companies in Bergen in 1720, Danish trade restrictions scuppered the nascent economic independence. As a consequence, Norway was ill-equipped to weather the so-called 'Little Ice Age', from 1738 to 1742. The failure of crops ensured a period of famine and the death of one-third of Norwegian cattle, not to mention thousands of people.

Books about Vikings

» *A History of the Vikings*, Gwyn Jones

» *The Vikings*, Magnus Magnusson

» *The Oxford Illustrated History of the Vikings*, Peter Sawyer (Ed)

» *The Vikings*, Else Roesdahl

So ferocious were the Vikings that the word berserk comes from 'bare sark', which means 'bare shirt' and refers to the way that ancient, bare-chested Norsemen used to fight.

1720	1814	1861	1870s
After 150 years of conflict on Norwegian soil (the Seven Years War, the Kalmar War and the Great Nordic War) Sweden is finally defeated, although Danish and Swedish influence remains strong.	Norway is presented to Sweden in the so-called 'Union of the Crowns'. Disgruntled Norwegians draft their first constitution, an event still celebrated as Norway's first act of independence.	Fridtjof Nansen, an explorer, scientist, diplomat and winner of the Nobel Peace Prize, is born near Oslo (then called Christiania). He would become a symbol for Norway's growing international influence.	Emissaries from London gentlemen's clubs journey to Norway's western fjords to find blue ice for the clubs' drinks. Soon after, Thomas Cook begins the first tourist cruises into the fjords.

During the Napoleonic Wars, Britain blockaded Norway, causing the Danes to surrender on 14 January 1814. The subsequent Treaty of Kiel presented Norway to Sweden in a 'Union of the Crowns'. Tired of having their territory divided up by foreign kings, a contingent of farmers, businesspeople and politicians gathered at Eidsvoll Verk in April 1814 to draft a new constitution and elect a new Norwegian king. Sweden forced the new king, Christian Frederik, to yield and accept the Swedish choice of monarch, Karl Johan. War was averted by a compromise that provided for devolved Swedish power. Norway's constitution hadn't lasted long, but it did suggest that Norwegians had had enough.

The mystery behind the disappearance of the Greenland colonies is examined in Jared Diamond's *Collapse: How Societies Choose to Fail or Survive.*

Independent Norway

Norway may have spent much of the previous centuries as the subservient vassal of foreign occupiers and its days as a world power had long ago ended, but not all was doom and gloom. It took almost a century after their first constitution, not to mention nine centuries after Harald Fair-Hair first unified the country, but Norwegians were determined to once and for all become masters of their own destiny.

A Confident Start

During the 19th century, perhaps buoyed by the spirit of the 1814 constitution, Norwegians began to rediscover a sense of their own, independent cultural identity. This nascent cultural revival was most evident in a flowering of musical and artistic expression led by poet and playwright Henrik Ibsen (p409), composer Edvard Grieg (p411) and artist Edvard Munch (p413).

Language also began to play its part with the development of a standardised written form of Norwegian known as *landsmål* (or *Nynorsk*). Norway's first railway, from Oslo to Eidsvoll, was completed in 1854 and Norway began looking at increased international trade, particularly tied to its burgeoning fishing and whaling industries in the Arctic North.

Sweden and Visions of Norway: Politics and Culture 1814–1905, by H Arnold Barton, offers a detailed analysis of the enmity and uneasy neighbourliness between Norway and Sweden in the pivotal 19th century.

Norway was still extremely poor – between 1825 and 1925, over 750,000 Norwegians resettled in the USA and Canada – but the wave of national identity would not be stopped.

In 1905 a constitutional referendum was held. As expected, virtually no one in Norway favoured continued union with Sweden. The Swedish king, Oskar II, was forced to recognise Norwegian sovereignty, abdicate and reinstate a Norwegian constitutional monarchy, with Haakon VII on the throne. His descendants rule Norway to this day, with decisions on succession remaining under the authority of the *storting* (parliament). Oslo was declared the national capital of the Kingdom of Norway.

Newly independent Norway quickly set about showing the world that it was a worthy international citizen. In 1911 the Norwegian explorer

1895
Alfred Nobel's will decrees that the interest on his vast fortune be awarded each year 'to those who, during the preceding year, shall have conferred the greatest benefit on mankind'.

1905
Norwegians vote overwhelmingly for independence and against union with Sweden. Norway becomes independent, with its own constitutional monarchy.

» Nobel Peace Center (p47), Oslo

Roald Amundsen reached the South Pole. Two years later Norwegian women became among the first in Europe to be given the vote. Hydro-electric projects sprang up all around the country and prosperous new industries emerged to drive the increasingly healthy export economy.

Having emerged from WWI largely unscathed – Norway was neutral, although some Norwegian merchant vessels were sunk by the Germans – Norway grew in confidence. In 1920 the *storting* voted to join the newly formed League of Nations, a move that was opposed only by the Communist-inspired Labour Party that dominated the *storting* by 1927. The 1920s also brought new innovations, including the development of factory ships, which allowed processing of whales at sea and caused an

ROALD AMUNDSEN

The Norwegian explorer Roald Amundsen played a pivotal role in forging a proud sense of Norwegian identity in the early 20th century.

Born into a family of shipowners and captains in 1872 at Borge, near Sarpsborg in southern Norway, Amundsen sailed in 1897 to the Antarctic as first mate on the Belgian *Belgica* expedition. Their ship froze fast in the ice and became – unintentionally – the first expedition to overwinter in the Antarctic.

Amundsen then set his sights on the Northwest Passage and study of the Magnetic North Pole. The expedition, which set out from Oslo in June 1903, overwintered in a natural harbour on King William Island, which they named Gjøahavn. By August 1905 they emerged into waters that had been charted from the west, becoming the first vessel to navigate the Northwest Passage.

Amundsen dreamed of becoming the first man to reach the North Pole, but in April 1909 Robert Peary took that honour. In 1910 Amundsen headed instead for the South Pole. In January 1911, Amundsen's ship dropped anchor at Roosevelt Island, 60km closer to the South Pole than the base of Robert Falcon Scott's *Terra Nova* expedition. With four companions and four 13-dog sleds, Amundsen reached the South Pole on 14 December 1911, beating Scott by a month and three days.

In 1925 Amundsen launched a failed attempt to fly over the North Pole. He tried again the following year aboard the airship *Norge,* this time with Lincoln Ellsworth, Hjalmar Riiser-Larsen and the Italian explorer Umberto Nobile. They left Spitsbergen on 11 May 1926 and, 16 hours later, dropped the Norwegian, US and Italian flags on the North Pole. On 14 May they landed triumphantly at Teller, Alaska, having flown 5456km in 72 hours – the first ever flight between Europe and North America.

In May 1928 Nobile attempted another expedition in the airship *Italia* and, when it crashed in the Arctic, Amundsen joined the rescue. Although Nobile and his crew were subsequently rescued, Amundsen's last signals were received just three hours after take-off. His body has never been found.

1911	1913	1914	1940
Norwegian explorer Roald Amundsen becomes the first person to reach the South Pole, highlighting a period of famous Norwegian explorers going to the ends of the earth.	Norway introduces universal suffrage for women long before many other European countries and begins a tradition of gender equality that has become a hallmark of modern Norway.	Norway, Sweden and Denmark announce that they will remain neutral during WWI, thereby sparing Scandinavia the devastation that the war visited upon much of the rest of Europe.	On 9 April Nazi Germany invades Norway. King Haakon and the royal family flee into exile, first to the UK and then Washington, DC, where they remained throughout the war.

increase in whaling activities, especially around Svalbard and in the Antarctic; for more information on whaling, see p401.

Trouble, however, lay just around the corner. The Great Depression of the late 1920s and beyond almost brought Norway to its knees. By December 1932 there was 42% unemployment and farmers were hit especially hard by the economic downturn.

Norway at War

Norway had chosen a bad time to begin asserting its independence. The clouds of war were gathering in Europe and although Norway had been spared the ravages of WWI, it could not escape for long.

By the early 1930s fascism had begun to spread throughout Europe. Unlike during WWI, Norway found itself caught up in the violent convulsions sweeping Europe. In 1933 the former Norwegian defence minister Vidkun Quisling formed a Norwegian fascist party, the *Nasjonal Samling*. The Germans invaded Norway on 9 April 1940, prompting King Haakon and the royal family to flee into exile, while British, French, Polish and Norwegian forces fought a desperate rearguard action. For further insights into the Norwegian resistance to the Nazi occupation, see the boxed text on p51.

Six southern towns were burnt out and despite some Allied gains the British, who were out on a limb, abandoned Arctic Norway to its fate. In Oslo, the Germans established a puppet government under Vidkun Quisling, whose name thereafter entered the lexicon as a byword for those collaborators who betray their country.

Having spent centuries fighting for a country to call their own, the Norwegians didn't take lightly to German occupation. In particular, the Norwegian Resistance network distinguished itself in sabotaging German designs, often through the assistance of daring Shetland fishermen who smuggled arms across the sea to western Norway. Among the most memorable acts of defiance was the famous commando assault of February 1943 on the heavy water plant at Vemork, which was involved in the German development of an atomic bomb (see the boxed text, p111).

The Germans exacted bitter revenge on the local populace and among the civilian casualties were 630 Norwegian Jews who were sent to central European concentration camps. Serbian and Russian prisoners of war were coerced into slave labour on construction projects in Norway, and many perished from the cold and an inadequate diet. The high number of worker fatalities during the construction of the Arctic Highway through the Saltfjellet inspired its nickname, the *blodveien* (blood road).

Finnmark suffered particularly heavy destruction and casualties during the war. In Altafjorden and elsewhere, the Germans constructed submarine bases, which were used to attack convoys headed for Murmansk

WWII

The first Allied victory of WWII occurred in late May 1940 in Norway, when a British naval force retook Narvik and won control over this strategic iron ore port. It fell again to the Germans on 9 June.

1945	**1945**	**1949**	**1950s**
On 7 May the last foreign troops on Norwegian soil, the Russians, withdraw from Arctic Norway, following the devastation wrought across the country by the retreating German army.	Norway becomes a founding member of the UN. This membership would later provide a platform for Norwegian foreign policy, with Norway an important mediator in numerous international conflicts.	Norway joins NATO and aligns itself with the USA despite fears in the West that left-leaning Norway would turn towards the Soviet Union.	A Norwegian government commission declares that 'the chances of finding oil on the continental shelf off the Norwegian coast can be discounted'. How wrong they were.

HEADING INTO EXILE

When German forces invaded Norway in April 1940, King Haakon and the Norwegian government fled northwards from Oslo. They halted in Elverum and on 9 April the parliament met at the folk high school and issued the Elverum Mandate, giving the exiled government the authority to protect Norway's interests until the parliament could reconvene. When a German messenger arrived to impose the Nazis' version of 'protection' in the form of a new puppet government in Oslo, the king rejected the 'offer' before heading into exile. Two days later, Elverum became the first Norwegian town to suffer massive bombing by the Nazis and most of the town's old wooden buildings were levelled. By then the king had fled to Nybergsund (close to Trysil), which was also bombed, but he escaped into exile.

and Arkhangelsk in Russia, so as to disrupt the supply of armaments to the Russians.

In early 1945, with the Germans facing an escalating two-front war and seeking to delay the Russian advance into Finnmark, the German forces adopted a scorched-earth policy and devastated northern Norway, burning fields, forests, towns and villages. Shortly after the German surrender of Norway, Quisling was executed by firing squad and other collaborators were sent off to prison.

The Oil Years

Although there were initial fears in the postwar years that Norway would join the Eastern Bloc of Communist countries under the Soviet orbit – the Communist party made strong gains in postwar elections and even took part in coalition governments – the Iron Curtain remained firmly in place at the Russian border. More than that, Norway made a clear statement of intent in 1945 when it became a founding member of the UN. Ever conscious of its proximity to Russia, the country also abandoned its neutrality by joining NATO in 1949. Letting bygones be bygones, Norway joined with other Scandinavian countries to form the Nordic Council in 1952.

There was just one problem: Norway was broke and in desperate need of money for reconstruction, particularly in the Arctic North. At first, it appeared that the increasingly prosperous merchant navy and whaling fleet would provide a partial solution, but in truth Norway struggled through (postwar rationing continued until 1952) as best it could.

That would soon change in the most dramatic way possible. Oil was discovered in the North Sea in the late 1960s and the economy boomed, transforming Norway from one of Europe's poorest countries to one of

Books about WWII in Norway

» *Assault in Norway: Sabotaging the Nazi Nuclear Campaign*, Thomas Michael Gallagher

» *War and Innocence: A Young Girl's Life in Occupied Norway*, Hanna Aasvik Helmersen

» *The German Invasion of Norway, April 1940*, Geirr H Haarr

Late 1960s

Oil is discovered, transforming Norway into one of the richest countries in the world. Oil revenues have provided the basis for an all-encompassing system of social welfare and generous foreign aid.

1993

In defiance of international opinion and contrary to a 1986 moratorium, Norway resumes commercial whaling operations, thereby complicating its claims to be a model environmental citizen.

» Oil tanker docked at Stavanger (p188)

Modern Norway

Since oil transformed the Norwegian economy, successive socialist governments (and short-lived conservative ones) have used the windfalls (alongside high income taxes and service fees) to foster one of the most extensive social welfare systems in history, with free medical care and higher education, as well as generous pension and unemployment benefits. And there looks to be no end in sight for the era of government largesse – its rapidly rising oil fund for future generations has soared to nearly US$450 billion. It all adds up to what the government claims is the 'most egalitarian social democracy in Western Europe'.

Thanks in part to its oil wealth, Norway wields a level of influence on the international stage far out of proportion to its relatively small population. Its energetic participation in a range of international institutions, its pivotal involvement in peace processes from the Middle East to Sri Lanka and its role as a leading player in assisting refugees around the world, in particular, have won international plaudits.

At the same time, Norway remains, by choice, on the fringes of the continent that it inhabits and has yet to join the European Union. Casting an eye over Norwegian history, it's not difficult to understand why Norwegians remain wary of forming unions of any kind with other countries. Having narrowly voted against EU membership in 1972 and again in 1994 despite Norwegian governments pressing for a 'yes' vote, Norway remains on the outside looking in.

Travel Lit on Modern Norway

» *The Magnetic North: Notes from the Arctic Circle*, Sara Wheeler

» *True North: Travels in Arctic Norway*, Gavin Francis

1994	2001	2005	2009
Norwegians vote against joining the EU. The 'no' vote (52%) draws on the concerns of family farms, fishing interests and the perceived loss of national sovereignty that membership would supposedly bring.	A rare victory for a conservative-liberal coalition after the Labour-led government suffers a massive fall in its vote in national elections; no single party wins enough votes to form government.	A 'red-green' coalition wins parliamentary elections, overturning a conservative-led coalition government that had won power in 2001.	A centre-left coalition led by Jens Stoltenberg, who had led Labour to its 2001 election defeat, wins closely contested parliamentary elections.

Norwegian Life

Norway is consistently ranked among the most liveable countries in the world and it's not difficult to see why. Norway's famously generous cradle-to-grave welfare state (funded in part, it must be said, by high taxes) and civilised working conditions are backed by a seemingly inexhaustible stash of oil revenues saved up for future generations. But the erstwhile homogeneity of Norwegian culture is changing, if not rapidly then discernibly, with an increasingly multicultural society causing many to rethink Norwegian national identity.

In the nine years from 2001 to 2009, Norway ranked first seven times (including in 2009) on the UN Human Development Index, which ranks countries according to a range of quality-of-life indicators.

Work & Family Life

If government support for the family is your yardstick, Norway may be the best country in the world in which to have a family. From the early 1970s onwards, the foundation of Norway's family welfare system has been to provide 'a mother's wage', protecting a woman's right to remain at home without relying on her husband's income. Such measures remain in place, but the focus has broadened and now includes everything from paid leave (Norwegians are entitled to five weeks a year) to heavily subsidised childcare.

Perhaps because of these unparalleled levels of support, Norway has one of the highest fertility rates in the Western world (1.77 children per family). Another side effect is that the Norwegian workplace is extremely child-friendly. As one Norwegian mother told the BBC in 2006, 'There's just a completely different level of acceptance among employers here. It's not uncommon to put a telephone conference on hold because you can hear a baby crying in the background.' And according to the 2010 annual report of the NGO Save the Children, Norway was ranked as the best country in the world in which to have children.

There have nonetheless been changes in family demographics in recent years, with the average age (27.5) of first-time mothers increasing, a decline in marriage rates (5.5 per 1000 people get married each year), a rise in de facto relationships (over 50% of children are born outside wedlock, compared to 39% in 1990), and an increase in the number of single mothers (around one-quarter of children grow up in single-parent households).

A 2007 study found that Norway has more per-capita millionaires – 55,000, or one in every 85 Norwegians – than any other country in the world.

These new realities, most of which are protected under the welfare system, have begun a perceptible shift away from the traditional nuclear family, which has always provided the bedrock of Norwegian society. Partly this change is because of the greater choice that rising Norwegian incomes (US$58,809 per capita in 2009, the fifth highest in the world) have enabled, and partly because of a decline in churchgoing among the young. Perhaps the most noticeable impact has been not upon immediate family units – which have diversified rather than been replaced, and the double-income-two-kids model remains the norm – but on traditional, extended families whereby the requirement to care for elderly relatives seems to have transferred from family members to the state.

Norway has an ageing population, an official retirement age of 67, pensions guaranteed for the remainder of a person's life and an average life expectancy nudging 80 years. It does, however, have an advantage over other countries wondering how they'll meet their pension obligations as the pool of taxpayers shrinks: the Government Pension Fund.

Women in Norway

According to the UN's Gender-Related Development Index in 2009, Norway is the best place in the world to be a woman. In addition to the raft of beneficial social-welfare provisions, Norway has a female labour force participation rate of nearly 80%, well above the EU and Organisation for Economic Cooperation and Development (OECD) average; around 80% of married women with children under the age of six work in paid employment, although more than half of these work part-time. In the 1993 election all three party leaders were women, and, after the 2008 elections 39% of national MPs were women, the eighth highest in the world. Norwegian women have an average life expectancy of 82.7 years, one of the highest in the world.

In 2004 the government legislated that 44.2% of board members of companies would have to be women; this figure was officially reached in 2009 and Norway's female board participation rate is now easily the highest in the world.

Despite such positive statistics, there remain areas where Norwegian women are far from equal with their male counterparts. Women's real annual incomes represent just 77% (US$46,576) of those of their male counterparts (US$60,394), even though equal pay is mandated by law under gender-equality legislation. Just three of Norway's publicly listed countries have female CEOs. And domestic violence remains a serious

Although the marginal income tax rate is 28%, in practical terms this becomes around 36% for middle-income earners and 47.8% for high-income earners.

NORWEGIAN LIFE

SAVING FOR A RAINY DAY

Most countries with significant oil reserves look with concern towards the day when the oil runs out. Not so Norway.

Suddenly flush with oil money in the 1970s, Norway's government began by developing the country's infrastructure, after which the profits were used to pay off the country's debt, an aim achieved in 1995. Thus it was that in 1996, the government established the Norwegian Petroleum Fund. The aim? To safeguard the wellbeing of future generations of Norwegians, more specifically by putting aside enough money to pay for the health and pension costs of Norway's ageing population. The reserve fund, whose name was changed in 2006 to the Government Pension Fund, is now the largest public fund in Europe with a value of over US$449 billion. Some estimates suggest that the fund will swell to US$765 billion by 2014.

But this is not just any investment fund. For a start, the fund's managers may only invest outside Norway, a measure designed to avoid overheating the local economy. As such Norway has become one of the largest investors in the world. 'We basically own a slice of the world,' was how Henrik Syse, head of the fund's corporate governance department at Norwegian central bank, described it to the *International Herald Tribune* (IHT) in 2007.

The fund's managers are also bound by a strict ethical code when choosing where to invest. Companies (such as Wal-Mart) and countries (eg Myanmar) accused of human rights violations have been excluded from the fund as have mining and other companies accused of severe environmental damage. Discussing the policy of socially responsible investing, Gro Nystuen, a human rights lawyer who oversees the ethics council that vets the investments, told the IHT that 'Norwegians feel bad about having all this money. Our job is to make the Norwegian people feel less guilty.'

THE ECONOMICS OF CHILDBIRTH IN NORWAY

Paid maternity leave A compulsory six-week minimum (plus three weeks prior to birth), with full-pay provisions extending to 46 weeks (the longest in Europe) or 56 weeks on 80% pay.

Paid paternity leave A 10-week minimum that comes out of the 46 or 56 weeks allocated to the mother; if the weeks aren't taken, the weeks are lost to both parents.

Further leave entitlements Each parent is entitled to an additional one year's unpaid, job-protected leave (civil servants get three) or to work part-time on full pay for up to two years.

Government grants for children Government grants of over Nkr35,263 upon the birth of a child and family allowance income-support during the child's life.

problem; a 2005 study by the Norwegian Institute for Urban and Regional Research found that one in four Norwegian women experiences domestic violence in their lifetime.

When it comes to immigrant women in Norway, the government has been faced with a new set of controversies, especially relating to female circumcision. In 2007 Norway announced that it would stop families from travelling abroad if officials believe that the purpose of the trip is to circumcise a female family member. The move received considerable support in Norway after it was revealed that at least 185 girls from Norway had been circumcised in a Somali village.

Accessible yet serious-minded, Gender.no (www.gender.no) is easily the best resource on issues of gender equality in Norway.

Multiculturalism

Norway has become an increasingly multicultural society in recent years, even as Norway's complicated approach to immigration sends out numerous conflicting messages. Until recently, immigration was strictly controlled and only bona fide refugees (ie those who have been granted refugee status with the UN elsewhere), not asylum seekers, were admitted; around 10,000 asylum seekers applied for refugee status in Norway in 2010. Few nations contribute as much money to foreign aid and refugee programs as does Norway.

Norway was at last count home to 456,300 immigrants from 216 countries, plus 93,000 people born in Norway to immigrant parents, which together amount to 11.4% of the population (compared to 1.5% in 1970). More than half of Norway's immigrants come from non-Western countries, especially Pakistan, Somalia, Iraq, Iran, Bosnia and Kosovo, although the largest immigrant groups come from Poland, Sweden and Germany. In 2009 alone, 36,700 immigrants arrived in Norway. One-quarter of all immigrants have settled in Oslo, which is easily Norway's most multicultural city, with 27% of its population born outside Norway.

Although many non-Western immigrants came to Norway as refugees, a subtle shift has occurred from refugee-driven immigration to more family-reunion and labour immigrants (especially from Poland); this phenomenon has partly been driven by the often-acute labour shortages caused by Norway's almost nonexistent unemployment.

Norway has one of the highest percentages of well-educated immigrants in the world: 40% have received higher education, with little difference between Western and non-Western immigrants.

As in many European countries, Norway is involved in an often anguished debate over the country's cultural mix, with most Norwegians torn between traditional notions of fairness and the perception of a rapidly changing society. Norway's first racially motivated murder occurred in 2001 when a mixed-race youth was stabbed to death outside his Oslo home; 40,000 Norwegians took to the Oslo streets to protest. In 2005 the Fremskrittspartiet (Progress Party), which advocates far stricter limits on immigration, became the second-largest party in the Norwegian parliament; its characterisation of immigrants as responsible for increasing crime rates was denounced as xenophobic by all other political parties.

Statistics Norway revealed that a 2009 poll suggested that 29% of Norwegians agreed with the statement that 'most immigrants abuse the system of social benefits' and 33% agreed that 'most immigrants represent a source of insecurity in the country'. At the same time, 70% thought that 'most immigrants enrich the cultural life in Norway' and 89% said that 'all immigrants in Norway should have the same opportunities to have a job as Norwegians'.

Religion

As in other areas of Norwegian society, increasing immigration and other social changes are having an effect on the country's religious breakdown. Around 90% of Norway's population is Christian, with 85% nominally belonging to the Church of Norway. Although statistically small, Norway also has a growing Muslim population: approximately 3.5% (85% of whom live in Oslo).

Christianity in Norway dates back thousands of years and one of the country's earliest kings, Olav II, was canonised by the Catholic Church. However, modern Norwegian Christianity has been most influenced by German reformer Martin Luther, whose doctrines were adopted in Norway in 1537.

Today the Church of Norway is the national denomination of Protestant Evangelical Lutheranism and the Norwegian constitution states: 'All inhabitants of the Realm shall have the right to free exercise of their religion. The Evangelical-Lutheran religion shall remain the official religion of the State. The inhabitants professing it are bound to bring up their children in the same.'

The King of Norway is the official head of the Church. This power was dramatically exercised in 1961, when King Olav V appointed the country's first woman priest, and again in 1993, when King Harald V sanctioned the first female bishop. In the 1970s a bishop and quite a few priests quit after the *storting* (parliament), with royal sanction, passed a liberal abortion law. As many as 5000 Norwegians leave the official church annually.

For information on the Sami religion, see p405.

Sport
Winter Olympics

Skiing is etched deep in the Norwegian soul, not least because for thousands of years skis were the only practical means of winter transport in much of Norway. Not surprisingly, Norway is a leading winter-sports country and has won more medals at the Winter Olympics than any other country.

At the 1998 Winter Olympics, Norway finished second on the medal table, matching its 1994 medal tally when it was the host nation. The success turned to domination in 2002 when Norway topped the medal table, but no-one quite knows what happened in Torino in 2006, when Norway trailed in 13th with just two gold medals. As you can imagine, the sudden decline was reported as close to a national tragedy. A measure of national pride was restored in 2010, when Norway came fourth on the medals table with nine golds and 23 medals in total.

Among Norway's enduring Olympic legends are Sonja Henie, the Olympic figure-skating gold medallist who won gold in 1928, 1932 and 1936; speed-skater Johann Koss, who won three gold medals at the Viking Ship Arena in Hamar in 1994; and cross-country skier Bjørn Daehli who, at the 1998 Olympics, won his eighth gold medal, making him the most successful athlete in Winter Olympics history.

In 2004, the Norwegian prime minister Kjell Magne Bondevik rejected a plan to turn empty, disused churches into mosques, claiming that it was not 'the most natural' solution.

Education is compulsory (and has been since 1889!), with the public system heavily funded and private schools actively discouraged. Education, including university studies, is free. In 2008, 61% of university students were women, although 81% of professors were men.

Football

Football (soccer) is another hugely popular sport, with the domestic league season running from March to early November. Trondheim's Rosenberg is the most successful club in Norwegian history with 21 league titles, including 13 consecutive years from 1992 until 2004; the club again won the title in 2006 and 2009.

At a national level, the Norwegian men's football team climbed briefly to 2nd in FIFA's world rankings in 1993, but by August 2010 had fallen to 22nd, and the failure to qualify for the 2002, 2006 and 2010 World Cups has cast a pall of gloom over the sport in Norway. Ole Gunnar Solskjær, Tore Andre Flo and John Carew are among Norway's most famous football exports.

The Norwegian women's national team has strutted the world stage with much greater success, clinching the Women's World Cup in 1995 and the gold medal at the Sydney Olympics in 2000; the team came 4th at the 1999 and 2007 World Cups and had dropped to 7th in the world rankings by May 2010. Its best-known players are Heidi Støre, who played 151 times for Norway between 1980 and 1997; and Bente Nordby, the goalkeeper who saved US superstar Mia Hamm's penalty en route to a famous tournament victory in 1995.

The word 'slalom' derives from the Norwegian words *sla låm*, or 'slope track', which originally referred to a Nordic ski competition that wove over hill and dale, dodging thickets!

Norway's Landscape

Norway's geographical facts tell a story themselves. The Norwegian mainland stretches 2518km from Lindesnes in the south to Nordkapp in the Arctic North with a narrowest point of 6.3km wide. Norway also has the highest mountains in northern Europe and a landmass of 385,155 sq km (the fourth largest in Europe, behind France, Spain and Sweden). But these are merely the statistical signposts to landscapes of rare drama. Their secret lies in the sheer diversity of Norwegian landforms, from glacier-strewn high country and plunging fjords to the tundralike plains of the Arctic North.

The Coast

Seeming to wrap itself around Scandinavia like a protective shield from the freezing Arctic, Norway's coastline appears to have shattered under the strain, riven as it is with islands and fjords cutting deep fissures in-land. Geologists believe that the islands along Norway's far northern coast were once attached to the North American crustal plate – such is their resemblance to the landforms of eastern Greenland. Further north, Svalbard is geologically independent of the rest of Europe and sits on the Barents continental plate deep in the polar region.

In the North Sea lie two rift valleys that contain upper Jurassic shale bearing the extravagantly rich deposits of oil and gas.

Fjords

Norway's signature landscape, the fjords, ranks among the most aston-ishing natural landforms anywhere in the world. The Norwegian coast is riven with these inlets distinguished by plunging cliffs, isolated farms high on forested ledges and an abundance of ice-blue water extending deep into the Norwegian interior. Norway's network of fjords is so vast – and each fjord so rich in its own character – that you could spend months exploring the fjords and never grow tired of the sheer wonder and beauty of it all.

Norway's fjords are a relatively recent phenomenon in geological terms. Although Norwegian geological history stretches back 1.8 billion years, the fjords were not carved out until much later. During the glacial periods over this time, the elevated highland plateaus that ranged across central Norway subsided at least 700m due to an ice sheet up to 2km thick. The movement of this ice, driven by gravity down former river courses, gouged out the fjords and valleys and created the surrounding mountains by sharpening peaks and exposing high cliffs of bare rock. The fjords took on their present form when sea levels rose as the climate warmed following the last Ice Age (which ended around 10,000 years ago), flooding into the new valleys left behind by melting and retreating

NORWAY'S COAST

Geological history can seem to move at a speed indiscernible to the human eye, but Norway's coastline remains in a state of flux. In the early 1990s, Blom-strandhalvøya in northwestern Svalbard ceased to be a peninsula and became an island.

BIGGEST & HIGHEST

Jostedalsbreen (p211) is continental Europe's largest icecap.

Sognefjorden (p199), Norway's longest fjord at 203km (second only in the world to Greenland's Scoresby Sund), is 1308m deep, making it the world's second-deepest fjord (after Skelton Inlet in Antarctica). Hardangerfjord (p176) is 800m deep and is, at 179km, the second-longest fjord network in Norway and the third-longest in the world.

Galdhøpiggen (p147; 2469m) is the highest mountain in northern Europe.

Hardangervidda (p150), at 900m above sea level, is Europe's largest and highest plateau.

Utigårdsfossen, a glacial stream that flows into Nesdalen and Lovatnet from Jostedalsbreen (not readily accessible to tourists), is placed by some authorities as the third-highest waterfall in the world at 800m, including a single vertical drop of 600m. Other Norwegian waterfalls among the 10 highest in the world are Espelandsfossen (703m; Hardangerfjord); Mardalsfossen (655m; Eikesdal); and Tyssestrengene (646m in multiple cascades; p182), near Odda. Vøringsfossen (p180) is one of Norway's most visited natural landmarks.

glaciers. Sea levels are thought to have risen by as much as 100m, creating fjords whose waters can seem impossibly deep.

Not surprisingly Norway's fjords have many admirers. In 2005, Unesco inscribed Geirangerfjord and Nærøyfjord on their World Heritage List because they 'are classic, superbly developed fjords', which are 'among the most scenically outstanding fjord areas on the planet'. And then there are travellers who are drawn again and again to the water's edge or along a narrow trail hundreds of metres above the shoreline, to marvel at the silent, pristine drama of these remarkable cathedrals of ice and rock.

Glaciers

Perhaps it's their sheer scale or their evocation of a world inexorably in motion. Or maybe it's because glaciers have become a barometer for the health of the planet. Whatever the reason, few natural landforms inspire quite the same awe as glaciers. Ranking high among the standout natural highlights of the country, Norway's glaciers cover some 2600 sq km (close to 1% of mainland Norwegian territory and 60% of the Svalbard archipelago). But this is a far cry from the last Ice Age, when Norway was one vast icefield; the bulk of the ice melted about 8800 years ago.

Glacier Hikes

» Jotunheimen National Park
» Hardangerjøkulen glacier, Hardangervidda
» Folgefonna National Park
» Nigardsbreen
» Briksdalsbreen
» Bødalsbreen
» Saltfjellet-Svartisen National Park
» Lyngen Alps
» Svalbard

Not only are glaciers a stunning tourist attraction, but they also serve an important purpose in Norway's economy: 15% of Norway's electricity derives from river basins below glaciers.

Concerns about shrinking glaciers and ice sheets in the Arctic have taken on added urgency in recent years as the impact of global warming takes hold. Some of Norway's glaciers retreated by up to 2.5km in the 20th century, while glacial ice is also thinning at an alarming rate. In 2006 Norway experienced its fourth-hottest summer on record, following on from above-average temperatures in 2002 and 2003, thereby accelerating the melting of Norway's glaciers. Inland glaciers are considered to be at far greater risk than Norway's coastal glaciers and a few Norwegian glaciers have grown in recent decades – the thickness of the ice on the Nigardsbreen glacier grew by 13.8m from 1977 to 2007. Such stories are, however, the exception and do little to diminish the otherwise gloomy outlook.

Jostedalsbreen is mainland Europe's largest icecap and it feeds some of Norway's largest glaciers, among them Nigardsbreen, Briksdalsbreen and Bødalsbreen. Another spectacular example is Folgefonn, while central Norway's Jotunheimen National Park alone is home to 60 glaciers.

Arctic North

If the fjords have drama, Norway's Arctic North has an irrevocable sense of mystery. From Svalbard, almost equidistant from the North Pole and Norway's Nordkapp in the north of the mainland, to the expansively beautiful Arctic Highway (p270) that carries you from the south into Arctic Norway, Norway's far north is rich in phenomena that seem to spring from a child's imagination.

The first thing you'll likely notice is the endless horizon that never quite seems to frame a landscape of austere, cinematic beauty. In its most extreme form, this disorienting sense of a world without limit is known as Fata Morgana, whereby all sense of distance and perspective is lost. Or perhaps what you'll remember most is the astonishing night sky in winter when the weird and wonderful aurora borealis, also called the northern lights, can seem like an evocation of a colourful ghost story writ large. The midnight sun and seemingly endless polar night can be similarly disorienting, adding a strange magic to your Norwegian sojourn.

Another integral element in Arctic Norway's appeal is the soulful presence of the indigenous Sami people (p404), they of the reindeer herds and proud cultural traditions, for what could be more mysterious than a people who choose to live in such an inhospitable environment. Also part of Norway's Arctic mix is Svalbard, a lichen-strewn tundra landscape that s home to Europe's only population of polar bears (see the boxed text, p354) and other iconic wildlife species of the Arctic North. Put all of these elements together and Norway's Arctic takes on the quality of a frontier territory of the imagination.

The Aurora Borealis

There are few sights as mesmerising as an undulating aurora. Although these appear in many forms – pillars, streaks, wisps and haloes of vibrating light – they're most memorable when taking the form of pale curtains wafting on a gentle breeze. Most often, the Arctic aurora appears as

Glacier Museum
» Norwegian Glacier Museum, Fjærland

Written in 1986, *Arctic Dreams*, by Barry Lopez, is the enduring classic of Arctic landscapes, wildlife and peculiarly northern phenomena. It covers the entire Arctic, rather than simply Norway's Arctic territories, but there is no finer exploration of the Arctic.

NORWAY'S LANDSCAPE

FATA MORGANA

If the aurora inspires wonder, the Fata Morgana may prompt a visit to a psychiatrist. The clear and pure Arctic air ensures that distant features do not appear out of focus. As a result, depth perception becomes impossible and the world takes on a strangely two-dimensional aspect where distances are indeterminable. Early explorers meticulously laid down on maps and charts islands, headlands and mountain ranges that were never seen again. An amusing example of distance distortion, described in the enigmatic book *Arctic Dreams* by Barry Lopez, involves a Swedish explorer who was completing a description in his notebook of a craggy headland with two unusual symmetrical valley glaciers, when he discovered that he was actually looking at a walrus.

Fata Morganas are apparently caused by reflections off water, ice and snow, and when combined with temperature inversions, create the illusion of solid, well-defined features where there are none. On clear days off the outermost coasts of Lofoten, Vesterålen, northern Finnmark and Svalbard, you may well observe inverted mountains or nonexistent archipelagos of craggy islands resting on the horizon. It's difficult indeed to convince yourself, even with an accurate map, that they're not really there!

Also unsettling are the sightings of ships, large cities and forests where there could clearly be none. Normal visibility at sea is less than 18km, but in the Arctic, sightings of islands and features hundreds of kilometres distant are frequently reported.

MIDNIGHT SUN & POLAR NIGHT

Because the Earth is tilted on its axis, polar regions are constantly facing the sun at their respective summer solstices and are tilted away from it in the winter. The Arctic and Antarctic Circles, at 66° 33' north and south latitude respectively, are the southern and northern limits of constant daylight on their longest day of the year.

The northern half of mainland Norway, as well as Svalbard and Jan Mayen Island, lie north of the Arctic Circle but, even in southern Norway, the summer sun is never far below the horizon. Between late May and mid-August, nowhere in the country experiences true darkness and in Trondheim, for example, the first stars aren't visible until mid-August.

Conversely, winters here are dark, dreary and long, with only a few hours of twilight to break the long polar nights. In Svalbard, not even a twilight glow can be seen for over a month. During this period of darkness, many people suffer from SAD syndrome, or 'seasonal affective disorder'. Its effects may be minimised by using special solar-spectrum light bulbs for up to 45 minutes after waking up. Not surprisingly, most northern communities make a ritual of welcoming the sun the first time it peeks above the southern horizon.

TOWN/AREA	LATITUDE	MIDNIGHT SUN	POLAR NIGHT
Bodø	67° 18'	4 Jun–8 Jul	15 Dec–28 Dec
Svolvær	68° 15'	28 May–14 Jul	5 Dec–7 Jan
Narvik	68° 26'	27 May–15 Jul	4 Dec– 8 Jan
Tromsø	69° 42'	20 May–22 Jul	25 Nov–17 Jan
Alta	70° 00'	16 May–26 Jul	24 Nov–18 Jan
Hammerfest	70° 40'	16 May–27 Jul	21 Nov–21 Jan
Nordkapp	71° 11'	13 May–29 Jul	18 Nov–24 Jan
Longyearbyen	78° 12'	20 Apr–21 Aug	26 Oct–16 Feb

a faint green or light rose but, in periods of extreme activity, can change to yellow or crimson.

The visible aurora borealis, or northern lights, are caused by streams of charged particles from the sun, called the solar wind, which are directed by the earth's magnetic field towards the polar regions. Because the field curves downward in a halo surrounding the magnetic poles, the charged particles are drawn earthward. Their interaction with electrons in nitrogen and oxygen atoms in the upper atmosphere releases the energy creating the visible aurora. During periods of high activity, a single auroral storm can produce a trillion watts of electricity with a current of 1 million amps.

Northern Lights: The Science, Myth, and Wonder of Aurora Borealis by Calvin Hall et al combines hard science with historical legend and stunning photography to help unlock one of Norway's great mysteries.

The Inuit (Eskimos) call the lights *arsarnerit* ('to play with a ball'), as they were thought to be ancestors playing ball with a walrus skull. The Inuit also attach spiritual significance to the lights, and some believe that they represent the capering of unborn children; some consider them gifts from the dead to light the long polar nights and others see them as a storehouse of events, past and future. Norwegian folklore attributes the lights to old maids or dead maidens dancing and weaving. The lights were seen as a bad omen and a sign that God was angry, and people who mocked the superstition risked incurring the ire of God.

The best time of year to catch the northern lights in Norway is from October to March, although you may also see them as early as August. Oddly enough, Svalbard is actually too far north to catch the greatest activity.

High Country

If you think Norway is spectacular now, imagine what it was like 450 million years ago when the Caledonian Mountain Range, which ran along the length of Norway, was as high as the present-day Himalayas. With time, ice and water eroded them down to their current form of mountains and high plateaux (some capped with Europe's largest glaciers and icefields) that together cover more than half the Norwegian land mass – great news for tourists and adventure-seekers, less so for farmers, with less than 3% of Norwegian soil suitable for agriculture.

Norway's highest mountains are in the Jotunheimen National Park, where Galdhøpiggen soars to 2469m. Nearby Glittertind (2465m, and shrinking) was for a long time the king of the Norwegian mountains, but its melting glacier sees its summit retreat a little further every year.

The Arctic – The Complete Story, by Richard Sale, is arguably the best of recent books about the Arctic, with world-class photography and informative text.

Wildlife

Norway's wildlife may not match the numbers found in neighbouring Sweden and Finland – Norway's unique settlement pattern, which spreads the human population thinly, limits wildlife habitat and restricts numbers. But Norway more than compensates with its variety of iconic northern European species, from polar bears and Arctic fox in Svalbard to musk ox, reindeer and elk on the mainland. And in Norway's offshore waters, whales have survived the best efforts of hunters to drive them to extinction.

Land Mammals

Arctic Fox

Once prolific throughout Arctic regions, the Arctic fox may be Norway's most endangered land mammal. Numbers of Arctic fox have scarcely risen in the decades since it was officially protected in 1930; the species' greatest threat now comes from the encroachment of the much larger and more abundant red fox. Børgefjell National Park, north of Rørvik and just south of the Arctic Circle, is home to one of mainland Norway's few viable populations, although the species survives in more substantial numbers in Svalbard. A small population is believed to survive in the Dovrefjell-Sunndalsfjella National Park in central Norway and a tiny number have recently been reintroduced onto the Hardangervidda Plateau: Europe's southernmost Arctic fox population.

The Arctic fox is superbly adapted to harsh winter climates and is believed capable of surviving temperatures as low as minus 70°C thanks to its thick insulating layer of underfur. Almost perfectly white in winter, the Arctic fox can in summer have greyish-brown or smoky-grey fur. In Arctic regions, it inhabits the sea ice, often cleaning up the scraps left by polar-bear kills.

Musk Oxen & Elk

After being hunted to extinction in Norway almost two millennia ago, the downright prehistoric *moskus-okse* (musk oxen) were reintroduced into Dovrefjell-Sunndalsfjella National Park from Greenland in the 1940s and have since extended their range to the Femundsmarka National Park near Røros. Fewer than 100 are believed to survive in the two Norwegian herds, although their numbers remain more prolific in Greenland, Canada and Alaska; in North America, the Inuit word for the musk ox is *oomingmaq*, which means 'the animal with skin like a beard'.

Wherever it is found, the musk ox is one of the most soulful of all Arctic and sub-Arctic regions; in Barry Lopez' *Arctic Dreams*, the author quotes a Canadian musk ox biologist as saying: 'They are so crisp in the landscape. They stand out like no other animal, against the whites of winter or the colours of the summer tundra'. For more information on

Elk Safaris
» Oppdal
» Dombås
» Rjukan
» Evje

the species, and the best places to join a musk-ox safari in summer, see the boxed text, p140.

From the forests of the far south to southern Finnmark, *elg* (elk; moose in the USA), Europe's largest deer species, are fairly common, although given the Norwegian fondness for elk meat, they wisely tend to stay clear of people and roads.

Reindeer

Wild *reinsdyr* (reindeer) exist in large herds across central Norway, usually above the treeline and sometimes as high up as 2000m. The prime viewing areas are on the Hardangervidda Plateau, where you'll find Europe's largest herd (around 7000), but sightings are also possible in most national parks of central Norway, as well as the inland areas of Trøndelag. Unlike those further south, the reindeer of Finnmark in Norway's far north are domestic and owned by the Sami, who drive them to the coast at the start of summer, then back to the interior in winter. The smaller *svalbardrein* (Svalbard caribou or reindeer; see p354) is native only to Svalbard.

Other Land Mammals

Like many of Norway's larger mammal species, *bjørn* (brown bears) have been persecuted for centuries, and Norway's only permanent population is in Øvre Pasvik National Park in eastern Finnmark.

As in most places, *ulv* (wolves) aren't popular with farmers or reindeer herders and hunters, and only a few still exist in the country (around Hamar and in Finnmark).

A rare forest-dweller is the solitary lynx, which is northern Europe's only large cat.

Lemen (lemmings) occupy mountain areas through 30% of the country and stay mainly around 800m altitude in the south and lower in the north. They measure up to 10cm and have soft orange-brown and black fur, beady eyes, a short tail and prominent upper incisors. If you encounter a lemming in the mountains, it may become enraged, hiss, squeak and attempt to attack!

Other smaller mammal species that are more difficult to see include *hare* (Arctic hares), *pinnsvin* (hedgehogs; mainly in southern Trøndelag), *bever* (beavers; southern Norway), *grevling* (badgers), *oter* (otters), *jerv* (wolverines), *skogmår* (pine martens), *vesel* (weasels) and *røyskatt* (stoats).

Marine Mammals

Polar Bears

Isbjørn (polar bears), the world's largest land carnivore, are found in Norway only in Svalbard, spending much of their time on pack or drift ice. Since the ban on hunting came into force in 1973, their numbers have increased to between 3000 and 3500, although they remain extremely difficult to see unless you're on a cruise around Svalbard. Despite weighing up to 720kg and measuring up to 2.5m long, polar bears are swift and manoeuvrable, thanks to the hair on the soles of their feet, which facilitates movement over ice and snow and provides additional insulation.

A polar bear's diet consists mostly of seals, beached whales, fish and birds, and only rarely do they eat reindeer or other land mammals (including humans). Polar-bear milk contains 30% fat (the richest of any carnivorous land mammal), which allows newborn cubs to grow quickly and survive extremely cold temperatures.

For more information on polar bears, see the boxed text on p354.

POLAR BEARS

The World of the Polar Bear by Norbert Rosing is not one to take on your travels, but there's no finer photographic record of this remarkable species with informative accompanying text.

Polar Bears International (www.polarbears international.org) is dedicated to the polar bear, with educational information, details on threats and campaigns to save it, and great photos.

THE TRUTH ABOUT LEMMINGS

Few creatures have been so unjustly maligned as the humble lemming. We've all heard tales of countless lemmings diving off cliffs to their deaths in a ritual of mass suicide. Some people also maintain that their bite is fatal and that they spread disease.

All you need to know about lemmings? Actually, no. Firstly, although lemmings can behave aggressively and ferociously (sometimes even when neither threatened nor cornered), there's no evidence that their bite is any more dangerous than that of other rodents.

As for their self-destructive behaviour, lemmings are known for their periodic mass movements every five to 20 years, when a particularly prolific breeding season results in overpopulation. Thanks to the increased numbers, the vegetation is decimated and food sources grow scarce, forcing swarms of lemmings (the last plague was in 2001) to descend from the high country in search of other, less-crowded high ground. Most meet an undistinguished fate, squashed on roads or eaten by predators and domestic animals. Indeed, for a couple of years following a lemming population surge, there will also be an increase in the population of such predators as foxes, buzzards and owls.

Quite often, however, the swarms head for the sea, and often do face high cliffs. When the press of their numbers builds up near the back of the ranks, the leaders may be forced over the edge. Also, inclement weather when crossing fjords or lakes can result in mass drownings. As unpleasant as the phenomenon may be, particularly for the lemmings, there's no evidence to suggest that lemmings are prone to suicide.

Not all lemmings join the rush to near-certain death. The clever, more aggressive individuals who remain in the hills to guard their territories grow fat and happy, living through the winter under the snow and breeding the following year. Females as young as 15 days can become pregnant and most individuals give birth to at least two litters of five each year, thereby ensuring the survival of the species.

Whales

The seas around Norway are rich fishing grounds, due to the ideal summer conditions for the growth of plankton. This wealth of nutrients also attracts fish and baleen whales, which feed on the plankton, as well as other marine creatures that feed on the fish. Sadly, centuries of whaling in the North Atlantic and Arctic Oceans have reduced several whale species to perilously small populations. Apart from the minke whale, there's no sign that the numbers will ever recover in this area. Given this history, the variety of whale species in Norway's waters is astonishing.

US government scientists estimate that two-thirds of the world's polar bears (now between 20,000 and 25,000) will disappear by 2050 due to diminishing summer sea ice, and that the remainder could die out by the end of the 21st century.

Minkehval (minke whales), one of the few whale species that is not endangered, measure around 7m to 10m long and weigh between 5 and 10 tonnes. They're baleen whales, which means that they have plates of whalebone baleen rather than teeth, and migrate between the Azores area and Svalbard.

Between Ålesund and Varangerhalvøya, it's possible to see *knolhval* (humpback whales), baleen whales that measure up to 15m and weigh up to 30 tonnes. These are among the most acrobatic and most vocal of whales, producing deep songs that can be heard and recorded hundreds of kilometres away.

Spekkhogger (killer whales), or orcas, are the top sea predators and measure up to 7m and weigh around 5 tonnes. There are around 1500 off the coast of Norway, swimming in pods of two or three. They eat fish, seals, dolphins, porpoises and other whales (such as minke), which may be larger than themselves.

The long-finned *grindhval* (pilot whales), about 6m long, may swim in pods of up to several hundred and range as far north as Nordkapp. *Hvithval* (belugas), which are up to 4m long, are found mainly in the Arctic Ocean.

The grey and white *narhval* (narwhal), which grow up to 3.5m long, are best recognised by the peculiar 2.7m spiral ivory tusk that projects from the upper lip of the males. This tusk is in fact one of the whale's two teeth and was prized in medieval times. Narwhal live mainly in the Arctic Ocean and occasionally head upstream into freshwater.

The endangered *seihval* (sei whales), a baleen whale, swim off the coast of Finnmark and are named because their arrival corresponds with that of the *sei* (pollacks), which come to feast on the seasonal plankton. They can measure 18m and weigh up to 30 tonnes (calves measure 5m at birth). The annual migration takes the *sei* from the seas off northwest Africa and Portugal (winter) up to the Norwegian Sea and southern Barents Sea in summer.

Finhval (fin whales) measure 24m and can weigh 80 tonnes. These whales were a prime target after the Norwegian Svend Føyn developed the exploding harpoon in 1864 and unregulated whalers left only a few thousand in the North Atlantic. Fin whales are also migratory, wintering between Spain and southern Norway and spending summer in northern Norway.

Spermsetthval (sperm whales), which can measure 19m and weigh up to 50 tonnes, are characterised by their odd squarish profile. They subsist mainly on fish and squid and usually live in pods of 15 to 20. Their numbers were depleted by whalers seeking whale oil and the valuable spermaceti wax from their heads. The fish-rich shoals off Vesterålen attract quite a few sperm whales and they're often observed on boat tours.

The largest animal on earth, *blåhval* (blue whales), measure around 28m and weigh in at a staggering 110 tonnes. Although they can live to 80 years of age, 50 is more common. Heavily hunted for its oil, the species finally received protection, far too late, from the International Whaling Commission in 1967. Prior to 1864, there were between 6000 and 9000, but only a few hundred remain in the world's oceans (although some Norwegian estimates put the number at around 11,000). Recent evidence suggests that a few hardy blue whales are making a comeback in the northeast Atlantic.

Grønlandshval (bowhead whales), or Greenland right whales, were virtually annihilated by the end of the 19th century for their baleen, which was used in corsets, fans and whips, and because they are slow swimmers and float when dead. In 1679 Svalbard had around 25,000 bowheads, but only a handful remains and worldwide numbers are critically low.

To read about Norway's controversial stance on commercial whaling, see p401.

Other Marine Mammals

Norway's waters shelter reasonable populations of bottlenose, white-beaked, Atlantic white-sided and common dolphins.

Seals are also commonly seen near the seashore throughout Norway and some inland fjords. The main species include *steinkobbe* (harbour seals), *havert* (grey seals), *ringsel* (ringed seals), *grønlandssel* (harp seals), *klappmyss* (hooded seals) and *blåsel* (bearded seals).

The much larger *hvalross* (walruses), which in Norway live only in Svalbard, measure up to nearly 4m and weigh up to 1450kg; their elongated canine teeth can measure up to 1m long in males. Although once heavily hunted for their ivory and blubber, the Svalbard population has increased to around 1000 since they became a protected species in 1952.

Whale-Watching

» Stø

» Andenes

» Narvik

» Henningsvær

» Kabelvåg

WILDLIFE

Possibly the largest animal to ever inhabit the earth, the longest blue whale ever caught measured 33.58m; 50 people could fit on its tongue alone.

Marine Mammals of the North Atlantic by Carl Christian Kinze is an excellent field guide to 51 marine mammals, almost all of which are present in Norway.

Birds

Norway is an excellent destination for ornithologists. The greatest bird populations are found along the coastline, where millions of sea birds nest in cliff faces and feed on fish and other sea life. The most prolific species include terns, *havsule* (gannets), *alke* (razorbills), *lundefugl* (puffins), *lomvi* and *teist* (guillemots), *havhest* (fulmars), *krykkje* (kittiwakes), *tjuvjo* and *fjelljo* (skuas) and *alkekonge* (little auks).

The standout species among Norway's host of wading and water birds include the *storlom* (black-throated wading birds), *smålom* (red-throated divers; called 'loons' in North America), *horndykker* (horned grebes), *åkerrikse* (corncrakes) and Norway's national bird, the *fossekall* (dippers), which make their living by diving into mountain streams.

Norway is also home to at least four species of owls: *jordugle* (short-eared owls); *spurveugle* (pygmy owls); *snøugle* (snowy owls); and *hubro* (eagle owls).

The most dramatic of Norway's raptors is the lovely *havørn* (white-tailed eagle), the largest northern European raptor, with a wingspan of up to 2.5m; there are now at least 500 nesting pairs along the Nordland coast, Troms and Finnmark. Around the same number of *kongeørn* (golden eagles) inhabit higher mountain areas. The rare *fiskeørn* (ospreys) have a maximum population of 30 pairs and are seen only in heavily forested areas around Stabbursdalen and Øvre Pasvik National Parks, both in the far north.

Birdwatching Sites

» Femundsmarka National Park

» Fokstumyra marshes, Dovrefjell-Sunndalsfjella National Park

» Gjesvær

» Øvre Pasvik National Park

» Runde Island

» Stabbursnes

» Lovund Island

» Værøy

» Svalbard

National Parks

The Norwegian government's commitment to wilderness protection is impressive. At last count, Norway had 40 national parks (including seven in Svalbard where approximately 65% of the land falls within park boundaries). Ten new national parks have been created since 2003, with a further four new parks and three extensions to existing parks planned. Around 15% of the country lies within protected areas.

Further national park information is available at local tourist offices and from the Directorate for Nature Management (www.dirnat.no, www.norgesnasjonalparker.no, both in Norwegian) in Trondheim.

Guiding Philosophy

The focus of Norway's national parks is all about preservation, rather than on the managed interaction between humans and their environment, although a few interpretation centres do exist. In many cases, the parks don't protect any specific features and don't necessarily coincide with the incidence of spectacular natural landscapes or ecosystem boundaries. Instead, they attempt to protect remaining wilderness areas from development and many park boundaries simply follow contour lines around uninhabited areas.

Compared to their counterparts in the USA, Britain and elsewhere, Norwegian national parks are low profile and lack the traffic and over-developed tourist facilities that have turned parks in many countries into little more than transplanted (or seasonal) urban areas. Some parks, particularly Jotunheimen, are increasingly suffering from overuse, but in most parks erosion, pollution and distress to wildlife are kept to a minimum.

Park Restrictions

Regulations governing national parks, nature reserves and other protected areas are quite strict. In general, there are no restrictions on entry to the parks, nor are there any fees, but drivers must nearly always pay a toll to use access roads. Dumping rubbish, removing plant, mineral or fossil specimens, hunting or disturbing wildlife, and using motorised off-road vehicles are all prohibited.

MAJOR NATIONAL PARKS

NATIONAL PARK	FEATURES	SIZE (SQ KM)	ACTIVITIES	BEST TIME	PAGE NO
Ånderdalen	bogs, coastal pine & birch forests	125		Jul & Aug	
Børgefjell	alpine vegetation, Arctic fox	1447	birdwatching	Jun-Aug	p390
Breheimen	high country	1691	hiking	Jun-Aug	p143
Dovre	every Norwegian flora type present within its borders; highest elevation 1700m	289	hiking	Jun-Aug	p143
Dovrefjell-Sunndalsfjella	musk ox, reindeer, Snøhetta (2286m) highlands, Fokstu-myra marshes	1693	hiking, climbing, birdwatching, wildlife safaris	May-Sep	p140
Femundsmarka	glaciers, highlands, musk ox, reindeer	573	hiking, boat trips	mid-Jun–Aug	p137
Folgefonna	Glaciers, Folgefonna ice cap	545	glacier-hiking, summer skiing	May-Sep	p183
Forlandet	waterbird, seal & walrus breeding grounds	4647	birdwatching	Jul & Aug	p364
Hallingskarvet	wild reindeer	450	hiking	Jul & Aug	
Hardanger-vidda	vast upland plateau, largest wild reindeer herd in Europe	3422	nordic skiing, hiking	Jun-Aug	p150
Jostedals-breen	Jostedalsbreen icecap (487 sq km), glaciers	1310	hiking, ice-climbing, kiting, boat trips	Jun-Aug	p211
Jotunheimen	Norway's highest mountains, glaciers	1151	hiking	Jul & Aug	p147
Lierne	mountains, lynx, wolverine, bears	333	bird- and wildlife-watching	Jul & Aug	
Møysalen	Lofoton's last wilderness, Møysalen Peak (1262m)	51		Jul & Aug	
Nordvest Spitsbergen	Kongsbreen icefield, Mag-dalenefjord, archaeological sights, caribou & marine-mammal breeding grounds	9914	hiking, kayaking	Jul & Aug	p364
Øvre-Dividal	Arctic rhododendron & heather, wolverine	770	hiking, dog-sledding	year-round	
Øvre Pasvik	Norway's largest stand of virgin *taiga* forest, last Norwe-gian habitat of brown bear	119	hiking	year-round	p345
Rago	high peaks, plunging valleys & waterfalls	171	hiking	Jul & Aug	p278
Reinheimen	wild reindeer	1969	hiking	Jun-Aug	p143
Reisa	Reisa Gorge, waterfalls, wildlife	803	hiking	Jun-Aug	p350
Rondane	reindeer, Rondane massif, archaeological sites	963	hiking, wildlife safaris	Jun-Aug	p142
Saltfjellet-Svartisen	straddles Arctic Circle, up-land moors, icecaps, Sami archaeological sites	2102	hiking	Jul & Aug	p276
Sør Spitsber-gen	Norway's largest park, 65% ice coverage, sea-bird breed-ing grounds	13,282		Jul & Aug	
Stabbursdalen	world's northernmost pine forest	747	hiking	Jul & Aug	p336

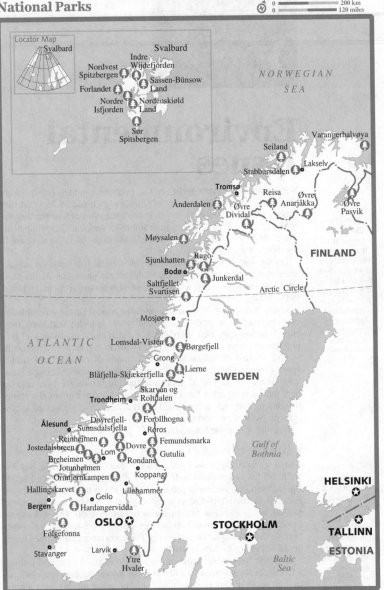

0   200 km
0   120 miles

Locator Map
Svalbard

Svalbard
Indre Wijdefjorden
Nordvest Spitzbergen
Sassen-Bünsow Land
Forlandet
Nordre Isfjorden
Nordenskiøld Land
Sør Spitsbergen

NORWEGIAN SEA

Varangerhalvøya
Seiland
Lakselv
Stabbursdalen
Tromsø
Reisa
Øvre Anarjåkka
Øvre Pasvik
Ånderdalen
Øvre Dividal

Møysalen

FINLAND

Sjunkhatten
Rago
Bodø
Junkerdal
Saltfjellet-Svartisen

Arctic Circle

Mosjøen

ATLANTIC OCEAN

Lomsdal-Visten
Børgefjell
Grong
Lierne
Blåfjella-Skjækerfjella
SWEDEN
Skarvan og Roltdalen
Trondheim
Dovrefjell-Sunnsdalsfjella
Forollhogna
Ålesund
Røros
Reinheimen
Femundsmarka
Jostedalsbreen
Lom
Dovre
Breheimen
Gutulia
Jotunheimen
Rondane
Ormtjernkampen
Koppang
Hallingskarvet
Lillehammer
Geilo
Bergen
Hardangervidda
Gulf of Bothnia
HELSINKI
OSLO
STOCKHOLM
Følgefonna
TALLINN
Stavanger
Larvik
ESTONIA
Ytre Hvaler
Baltic Sea

Environmental Issues

Norway and the environment are like everyone's model couple – from the outside, they seem like a perfect match even if you suspect that they conceal the occasional dark secret. Indeed, the story of how Norway has been acclaimed for promoting environmental sustainability while being one of the world's largest producers of fossil fuels (oil is the elephant in the room) is a fascinating tale.

On the one hand, the Norwegian government has made an unprecedented commitment to cut its greenhouse gas emissions. At the same time, Norway is one of the world's largest oil exporters and a major player in the fishing industry.

When it comes to Norway's micromanagement of the environment, there is much to be praised. Industrial waste is highly regulated, recycling is almost universal, there's little rubbish along roadsides and general tidiness takes a high priority in both urban and rural environments.

And yet loss of habitat has placed hundreds of plant and animal species on the endangered or threatened species lists. Although many animals are now protected, sport-hunting and fishing are more popular here than in most other European countries. Norway's unpopular stance on whaling and sealing has raised international ire and resulted in boycotts on Norwegian products.

In short, it's a complicated picture.

State of the Environment Norway (www.environment.no) is a comprehensive site covering everything from biodiversity and international agreements to statistics and Svalbard.

Climate Change

Global warming is by no means a solely Norwegian problem, but few countries have committed to doing as much about it as Norway. In 2007 the Norwegian government promised to 'be at the forefront of the international climate effort' and announced plans to become 'carbon neutral' and cut net greenhouse gas emissions to zero by 2050. This will mostly involve offsetting its annual carbon dioxide emissions by purchasing carbon credits on international markets. The government also agreed to cut actual emissions by 30% by 2030.

In 2009, Norway's annual emissions stood at 50.8 million tonnes, a fall of 5.4% compared to 2008 and the lowest figure since 1995. Although some of this reduction can, by the government's own admission, be attributed to the global financial crisis and reduced levels of industrial production, the longer-term downward trend is encouraging. Over 99% of Norway's electricity supplies come from renewable (primarily hydro power) sources, with fossil fuels accounting for just 0.4%. Norway also has targeted tax regimes on carbon dioxide emissions, and allocates billions of kroner to carbon dioxide capture and storage schemes and climate-related initiatives, both within Norway and overseas.

In the respected Environmental Performance Index for 2010, operated by the Yale Center for Environmental Law and Policy (http://epi.yale.edu), Norway ranked fifth out of 163 countries (down from second in 2008). Above Norway in the 2010 rankings were Iceland, Switzerland, Costa Rica and Sweden.

For all such good news, it is worth remembering that the average Norwegian emits 7.85 tonnes of greenhouse gases, twice the world average although in line with most other developed countries. Environmental groups have criticised Norway's promises on emissions as hypocritical, with Greenpeace arguing that 'Norway should take responsibility for the 500 million tonnes of emissions caused by its exports of oil and gas'.

Climate change in Norway is most evident in the worrying signs that its glaciers may be under threat (see p386). Norway has also been a leading international advocate for addressing the impact of climate change on Arctic ecosystems (from pollution to the threat posed to polar bears by retreating sea ice in Arctic waters). As ever, Norway's principled position on Arctic pollution is undermined by its production (if not consumption) of fossil fuels – the government's strict provisions protecting the environment in Svalbard have won praise, even as it continues to make exemptions for coal production on the archipelago.

Other touchstones of environmental health are more encouraging, with a detailed 2007 study of Arctic plant life on Svalbard by the University of Oslo (published in the prestigious journal *Science*) suggesting that the plants have proved more resilient than first thought, adapting and largely weathering the big climate swings of the past 20,000 years. The Svalbard Global Seed Vault (see the boxed text, p357) is also seen as an important resource in protecting biodiversity in the event of a large rise in global temperatures.

Glaciers & Climate Change – A Meteorologist's View by J Oerlemans can be a tad heavy-going, but it does tell you everything you need to know about why glaciers have become a cause célèbre for environmentalists across the world.

Commercial Fishing

Fishing and aquaculture (fish farming) remain the foundation of Norway's coastal economy, providing work for an estimated 28,000 people in the fishing fleet, and a host of secondary industries such as shipbuilding, fish feed, processing, packaging, fishing gear and the transportation of fish products. With an annual catch of around 2.5 to 3 million tonnes, Norway is the 10th-largest fishing nation in the world and one of the world's largest exporters of seafood.

A major factor in the success of Norwegian offshore fisheries has been the warm Gulf Stream waters entering the northern seas, although this varies from year to year. The larger the volume of warm water, the greater the growth of plankton in the far north and the greater the amounts of food available to fish and marine mammals.

And yet centuries of fishing have severely depleted fish stocks among species that were once the mainstays of the Norwegian economy.

In 2004, the fjords were voted first for environmental sustainability out of 115 major tourist destinations by *National Geographic Traveler* magazine. In 2009, the fjords again came out on top although this time with an even bigger margin and at the summit of 133 destinations.

A DANGEROUS ENVIRONMENTAL HAZARD – MOOSE FARTS

Global warming. Fossil fuels. Moose farts... Although it doesn't quite roll off the tongue as a serious threat to the environment, a moose with gas can actually be more dangerous to the environment than your average family car.

According to a report in London's *The Times* newspaper in August 2007, by doing nothing more than farting and belching every year a single adult moose releases the methane equivalent of 2100kg of carbon dioxide emissions, equal to about 13,000km of travel in a car. Or, to put it another way according to Reidar Andersen, the scientist at the Technical University in Trondheim who came up with this startling fact, 'shoot a moose and you have saved the equivalent of 36 flights between Oslo and Trondheim'. With an estimated 120,000 wild moose roaming the Norwegian wilds – the Norwegian authorities authorise an annual nationwide hunting quota of around 37,000 – that adds up to a disturbingly high output of methane, not to mention a heightened state of nervousness among otherwise innocent moose.

EMISSIONS

In 2007 Henriette Westhrins, the then State Secretary, Ministry of Environment, told Lonely Planet: 'Oil and gas extraction accounts for about one-fifth of our carbon dioxide emissions and just above one-fifth of our current GDP. Yes, that puts our emissions per person up above the EU average. But our policies eliminate any national feast of exorbitant consumption.'

Until about 25 years ago, deep-sea fishing in the area was pretty much a free-for-all. Ideal ocean conditions, wedded to the development of sonar, which located schools of herring and other commercially valuable fish, ensured that during the 1960s the Norwegian fishing community enjoyed particularly high catches. Such a bounty, however, was unsustainable, and by the late 1970s, herring stocks were nearly wiped out. In addition, overfishing depleted stocks of cod all across the North Atlantic.

Stung into action by the threat to tens of thousands of livelihoods, on 1 January 1977 Norway established a 200-nautical-mile offshore economic zone, which was extended to Svalbard later that year and to Jan Mayen in 1980. The country now has agreements with the EU, Russia, the Faroe Islands, Iceland, Greenland and Poland to set quotas. Three decades of conservation measures later, including strict quotas, the herring-fishery industry is recovering. Cod-fishing regulations are now in place, although it will be many years before the numbers return.

Despite these policies, a draft report by the World Wildlife Fund (WWF) in 1998 found that Norwegians place three or four times as much pressure on the environment as the average global citizen and were 'the most environmentally destructive people on earth', thanks largely to their consumption of marine fish; the national catch amounts to 250kg of fish per Norwegian per year, over 10 times the world average. The final report was later amended after claims by the Norwegian government that much of the data was either wrong or misinterpreted.

Henriette Westhrins, then State Secretary, Ministry of Environment, told us in 2007: 'We harvest about 2.5 million tonnes of marine life out of a world catch in the mid-80 millions. Yes, it is more than our share of the global population. This is, of course, because we have a very, very long coastline. Fish cross borders, so we have to cooperate with our neighbours in setting quotas. In particular cod, herring and mackerel have been overfished in the past, so sustainable quotas for all species are high on our list of priorities.'

It's fair to say that Norwegians usually view the critical depletion of fish stocks in Norwegian waters as much through the prism of economic self-interest as they see it as a strictly environmental concern. Throughout recorded history, the seas off the Norwegian coast have provided bountiful fishing opportunities and thereby providing a critical backbone to the Norwegian economy. Still Norway's second-largest export earner, it was one of the country's few commercial resources in the days before oil – an essential context to understanding many of Norway's environmental policies as they relate to fishing.

Fish Farming

The aquaculture industry, which has thrived for at least two decades and was born out of the depletion of wild-fish stocks, concentrates mainly on Atlantic salmon and trout, but there have also been experiments with Arctic char, halibut, catfish and scallops. Currently, fish farming amounts to around 500,000 tonnes of fish per annum, but the export of pen-raised salmon and trout constitutes 55% of the value of Norway's fish exports.

This ready-made alternative to ocean fishing does carry attendant and potentially serious consequences. The main drawback is that diseases in captive stock have spread to wild populations whenever fish escape from the pens, thereby threatening wild populations. Tightened government regulations have reduced escapes in recent years, but it remains an issue of major concern.

Sealing

Seal hunting, perhaps because of its shocking visual images, has been a lightning rod for condemnation by animal lovers and environmentalists around the world.

In Norway seal hunting has for decades been restricted to two species, the harp seal and hooded seal, although since 2007 the cull of hooded seals has been prohibited. The government's support for seal hunting – it provides funding for sealing vessels and sets an annual quota of between 30,000 and 47,000 seals – is mainly driven by the needs of the fishing community, which wishes to restrict the competition between fishing boats and marine mammals that depend on fish and eat up to 2.5kg per day. Seal meat is also considered a delicacy in many regions of coastal Norway.

Sealing occurs on a small scale, mainly for fur and meat, but it is argued that it's a cruel business. To mitigate protests, regulations limit seal hunters to only two tools: a rifle and a *hakapik,* or gaff; the former is for adult seals and the latter for pups (which may not be hunted while suckling). Hunters are also required to take courses and shooting tests before each sealing season. Such regulations notwithstanding, media reports in 2010 suggested that the injuring of young seals abandoned during the hunt was widespread.

Reports suggest that the Norwegian sealing industry may be in serious decline, with actual culls amounting to less than 10% of the allocated quota.

Whaling

No Norwegian environmental issue inspires more international fervour and emotion than that of renewed whaling in the North Atlantic.

The International Context

In 1986, as a result of worldwide campaigns expressing critical concern over the state of world whale populations, the International Whaling Commission (IWC) imposed a moratorium on whale hunting. Although it has largely held, two key elements in recent years have placed the moratorium under threat.

The first has been the decision by the three major whaling nations – Norway, Japan and Iceland – to either resume commercial whaling or, in the case of Japan and Iceland, to threaten to withdraw from the IWC and engage in a full-scale resumption of commercial whaling unless the moratorium is replaced by a management plan that allows some whaling.

The second development threatening world whale stocks is a concerted campaign that has seen nations with no history of whaling – including Mauritania, Ivory Coast, Grenada, Tuvalu and even landlocked Mongolia, San Marino and Mali – joining the commission. The result has seen a change from nine pro-whaling votes out of 55 in 2000 to an almost-50% split among its 88 members currently (a 75% majority is required to change IWC policy). Allegations that pro-whaling votes have been rewarded with development aid have not been denied by the Japanese.

Norway, for its part, sees the moratorium as unnecessary and outdated. It counters historical evidence indicating that whalers in this region hunted their prey to the verge of extinction (in the 17th century alone, Dutch whalers alone killed an estimated 60,000 whales in the waters off Svalbard), by claiming that modern whalers have a better and more informed perspective, that they adhere to a sensible quota system and now adopt more humane methods of killing. The Norwegians claim that they

ENVIRONMENTAL ISSUES

In 2005 Norway became the first country to announce a national geotourism program in accordance with National Geographic's Center for Sustainable Destinations. The scheme is built around 13 commitments, all of which focus on preserving not only the environment, but also on a country's diversity of cultural, historic and scenic assets, as well as stressing community involvement.

The International Whaling Commission (www.iwcoffice.org) is a largely dispassionate resource on whaling and the surrounding politics. There are also useful sections, such as the 'Status of Whales', with estimates for current whale populations.

support only traditional, family-owned operations and have no intention of returning to industrial whaling.

At a popular level, many Norwegians also feel that conservationists are mainly city folk who have an overly sentimental if unrealistic relationship with animals. Many also see threats not to the animals but to a traditional Norwegian industry and Norwegian freedom of action.

In addition to hunting, a major threat to Norwegian whales comes from chemical pollution, particularly the polychlorinated biphenyls (PCBs), which are suspected of damaging cetacean reproductive and immune systems, a phenomenon that has already led to numerous deaths from viral infections.

For a Norwegian perspective on whaling, stop by the Whaling Museum in Sandefjord, along Norway's southern coast. For more on whale species and populations in Norwegian waters, see p392.

Norway's Recent Practice

Follow the whaling debate at Greenpeace UK (www.greenpeace.org.uk), the Whale and Dolphin Conservation Society (www.wdcs.org), the High North Alliance (www.highnorth.no) and the Norwegian Ministry of Fisheries (www.regjeringen.no/en/dep/fkd.html?id=257).

Norway resumed commercial whaling of minke whales in 1993 in defiance of an international whaling ban but under its registered objection to the 1986 moratorium. While Norway supports the protection of threatened species, the government contends that minke whales, with a northeast Atlantic population of an allegedly estimated 100,000, can sustain a limited harvest. The Norwegian government, after a unanimous vote, issued a quota of 1052 in 2006, a 30% increase on the previous year's quota and more than half the number of minke whales Norway hunted every year before the moratorium was imposed. The quota dropped slightly in 2007 and 2008, but in late 2009, in the midst of complicated talks between pro- and anti-whaling nations, Norway announced a 45% increase in its minke-whale quota, from 885 in 2009 to 1286 in 2010; despite the quotas and Norway's planned increase, Norwegian whale hunters killed 484 minke whales in 2009, just over half their allocated quota. The increase has been condemned by international environmental groups such as Greenpeace and the Whale and Dolphin Conservation Society.

Japan and Norway resumed trading in whale meat in 2004 and it tends to be the export market that drives the industry rather than domestic consumption, although whale meat is openly sold in fish markets (especially Bergen) – a good moment to decide where you stand on the issue.

Forestry

Harpoon – Into the Heart of Whaling by Andrew Darby is an erudite (and unashamedly anti-whaling) account of whaling in all its manifestations, from the history of uncontrolled slaughter to the more complicated political debates of the present.

Forests cover an estimated 38% of mainland Norway, but forests set aside for cultivation account for around 25% of Norwegian territory. Government-protected wilderness areas account for less than 1% of Norway's forests, well below the international standard of 5%. More than 1000 forest-dwelling species are considered to be endangered and areas of old-growth forest are extremely rare.

One remaining stand of old-growth Norwegian forest that has caught the attention of environmentalists is Trillemarka-Rollagsfjell, about 100km west of Oslo and covering 205 sq km. Environmentalists have called on the Norwegian government to set aside the area as a protected reserve to shelter the endangered species that reside in the forest; among these species are the lesser spotted woodpecker, tree-toed woodpecker, Siberian jay and golden eagle, as well as threatened plant life.

Although no forestry operation can be entirely environmentally sound, Norway currently has one of the world's most sustainable forestry industries and much of the visible damage to the forests is due to agricultural clearing and timber overexploitation between the 17th and 20th centuries.

Numerous small forestry operations, mostly in eastern Norway, cut about 8.5 million cu metre annually. Clear-felling is practised in some areas but it's reasonably rare. In general, operations employ selective cutting to prevent soil erosion and unsightly landscape degradation. In addition, companies immediately re-seed the cuts, planting a total of around 50 million seedlings annually.

Wilderness Areas

Norway may have one of the lowest population densities in Europe, but due to its settlement pattern – which is unique in Europe, and favoured scattered farms over villages – even the most remote areas are inhabited and a large proportion of the population is rural-based.

As a result, and despite appearances, areas of true wilderness are rare in Norway. The natural world has been greatly altered by human activities and the landscape is criss-crossed by roads that connect remote homes, farmsteads and logging areas to more populated areas. All but a couple of the country's major rivers have been dammed for hydroelectric power; many Norwegian families own holiday homes beside lakes, around ski slopes or in areas of natural beauty; and even the wild-looking expanses of Finnmarksvidda and the huge peninsulas that jut into the Arctic Ocean serve as vast reindeer pastures. As a result, apart from the upland icefields and Norway's impressive network of national parks (see p395), real wilderness is limited to a few forested mountain areas along the Swedish border, scattered parts of Hardangervidda and most of Svalbard.

The Arctic: An Anthology, edited by Elizabeth Kolbert, brings together some of the most inspiring historical writings about the Arctic, with an emphasis on the exploration of Norwegian and other wilderness areas.

Recycling

Norwegians strongly support sorting of household waste for collection and recycling, and travellers are encouraged to do likewise. A mandatory deposit scheme for glass bottles and cans has been a success and about 96% of beer and soft-drink bottles are now returned. Supermarkets give money back for returned aluminium cans and plastic bottles (usually Nkr1 to Nkr1.50). There is also a prepaid recycling charge on automobiles sold in Norway, which ensures that they're turned into scrap metal rather than roadside eyesores when their life is over.

Since the early 1970s, however, the average annual level of household waste generated per person has nearly doubled to around 375kg, a rise that coincides with the golden years of Norway's oil-fuelled prosperity boom. Despite Norway's generally impressive environmental record, the reaction to this increase from governments and ordinary Norwegians was slow – by 1992, just 9% of household waste was recycled. However, the figures have since become a source of national pride: around 50% of household waste and two-thirds of industrial waste is now recycled, while Norway is a world leader when it comes to recycling electrical and electronics products. Methane from waste nonetheless still accounts for 7% of Norway's greenhouse gas emissions and Norwegians consume more than 130,000 tonnes of plastic packaging every year.

The Future History of the Arctic by Charles Emmerson is an engaging exploration of the politics of the Arctic with a particular focus on the big issues of energy security, environmental protection and the exploitation of the region's natural resources.

Norway's Sami

The formerly nomadic Sami people (once known as Lapps) are Norway's largest ethnic minority and can reasonably claim to be Norway's longest-standing residents – they have inhabited northern Scandinavia and northwestern Russia for millennia. Of the approximately 60,000 Sami, around 40,000 reside in Norway, primarily inhabiting the far northern region of Finnmark (scattered groups live in Nordland, Trøndelag and other regions of central Norway). The Sami, who refer to their traditional lands as Sápmi or Samiland, are also present in Sweden, Finland and Russia.

Sami History

Although it's believed that the Sami migrated to Norway from Siberia as early as 11,000 years ago, the oldest written reference to the Sami was penned by the Roman historian Tacitus in AD 98. In AD 555 the Greek Procopius referred to Scandinavia as Thule (the 'furthest north'), and its peoples as *skridfinns,* who hunted, herded reindeer and travelled about on skis. The medieval Icelandic sagas confirm trading between Nordic peoples and the Sami; the trader Ottar, who 'lived further north than any other Norseman', served in the court of English king Alfred the Great and wrote extensively about his native country and its indigenous peoples.

During medieval times, the Sami people lived by hunting and trapping in small communities known as *siida.* While the 17th- and 18th-century colonisation of the north by Nordic farmers presented conflicts with this system, many newcomers found that the Sami way of life was better suited to the local conditions and adopted their dress, diet and customs.

Around 1850, with Sami traditions coming under increasing threat from missionary activity, reforms were introduced, restricting the use of the Sami language in schools. From 1902 it became illegal to sell land to any person who couldn't speak Norwegian; this policy was enforced zealously and Sami culture seemed to be on the brink of extinction.

After WWII, however, official Norwegian government policy changed direction and began to promote internal multiculturalism. By the 1960s the Sami people's right to preserve and develop their own cultural values and language was enshrined across all government spectra. Increasingly, official policy viewed the Sami as Norwegian subjects but also an ethnic minority and separate people. Their legal status improved considerably and the government formed two committees: the Samekulturutvalget to deal with Sami cultural issues; and the Samerettsutvalget to determine the legal aspects of Sami status and resource ownership.

From 1979 to 1981, an increasingly bitter Sami protest in Oslo against a proposed dam on Sami traditional lands drew attention to the struggle for Sami rights – for more on this and on Sami traditional architecture, see p414. In 1988 the Norwegian government passed an enlightened constitutional amendment stating: 'It is the responsibility of the authorities of the State to create conditions enabling the Sami people to preserve and develop its language, culture and way of life.' It also provided for

To be officially considered Sami and (if 18 or over) be able to vote in elections for the Sami Parliament, a person must regard themselves as Sami, speak Sami as their first language or at least one of their parents, grandparents or great-grandparents must have spoken Sami as their first language.

The Sámi People: Traditions in Transition by Veli-Pekka Lehtola takes you on a journey through Sami history and is a study of how Sami culture has adapted to the needs of the modern world.

DIALECTS
1 South
2 Ume
3 Pite
4 Lule
5 North
6 Inari
7 Skolt
8 Kildin
9 Ter

NORWAY
SWEDEN
FINLAND
DENMARK
ESTONIA
RUSSIA

the creation of an elected 39-member Sami Parliament, Sameting (www.samediggi.no), to serve as an advisory body to bring Sami issues to the national parliament (similar bodies also exist in Finland and Sweden).

In early 1990 the government passed the Sami Language Act, which gave the Sami language and Norwegian equal status. Later the same year, Norway ratified the International Labour Organisation proposition No 169, which guaranteed the rights of indigenous and tribal peoples.

Although Sami rights are supported by most parties across the political spectrum, the Sami's struggle continues. The right-wing Fremskrittspartiet has called for the Sami Parliament to be abolished.

Reindeer herding, once the mainstay of the Sami economy, was successfully modernised in the 1980s and 1990s and is now a major capital earner. In addition to reindeer herding, modern Sami engage in fishing, agriculture, trade, small industry and the production of handicrafts. For more on Sami culture, see p347, and p411 for info on modern Sami music.

Sami Religion

Historically, Sami religious traditions were characterised mainly by a relationship to nature and its inherent godlike archetypes. In sites of special power, particularly prominent rock formations, people made offerings to their gods and ancestors to ensure success in hunting or other endeavours. Intervention and healing were affected by shamanic specialists, who used drums and small figures to launch themselves onto

Sami Sites

» Varanger Sami Museum, Varangerbotn

» Ceavccageadge, Mortensnes

» Sápmi Park, Karasjok

» Sami Parliament, Karasjok

» Sami National Museum, Karasjok

» Kautokeino Museum, Kautokeino

NILS MIKKEL SOMBY: SAMI REINDEER HERDER

Nils Mikkel Somby has spent his life in the rolling hill country above the Iešjokha River west of Karasjok. He continues to herd his family's 3000 reindeer and migrates with them to Nordkapp every April, returning around October.

It must be a tough life being a Sami. My mother was out herding reindeer on her own in winter when she was 10 and my father, who is 74, is still out herding every day.

There must have been many changes in the Sami way of life. In the old times, life for the Sami was very difficult. We had to do everything on skis or on foot and we had to be camped out in the mountains during the winter. Now we have cabins with heating. But if one thing has made Sami life easier, it is the snowmobile – we can use it to check on the reindeer, to bring supplies, and then return to our huts. So in that way, life is much better for us. But now there are too many rules, now many reindeer we can have and so on.

The winters must be very long. Life in winter is hard because of the cold and because it's always dark and you can only track the reindeer by looking for their footprints in the snow. But this is also my favourite time of the year. Can you see how beautiful it is here, with sun shining and no other people in sight?

And the next generation? The modern world needs so much, things like roads and resources from remote places. And with so many distractions for young Sami, it's difficult to keep our culture alive. Fifty years from now, I hope that there will still be Sami up here. I am not so sure.

out-of-body journeys to the ends of the earth in search of answers. As with nearly all indigenous peoples in the northern hemisphere, the bear, as the most powerful creature in nature, was considered a sacred animal.

Historically, another crucial element in the religious tradition was the singing of the *joik* (also spelt *yoik;* literally 'song of the plains'). So powerful was this personal mantra that early Christian missionaries considered it a threat and banned it as sinful. Although most modern Sami profess Christianity, elements of the old religion are making a comeback.

Sami Organisations

The first session of the Norwegian Sami Parliament (see p347) was held in 1989. The primary task of the parliament, which convenes in Karasjok and whose 43 representatives are elected from Sami communities all over Norway every four years, is to protect Sami language and culture.

The Norwegian Sami also belong to the Saami Council (www.saamicouncil .net), which was founded in 1956 to foster cooperation between political organisations in Norway, Sweden, Finland and Russia. In Tromsø in 1980, the Saami Council's political program adopted the following principles:

According to Norway's national statistics bureau, just under 10% (or around 3000) of Norway's Sami are involved in reindeer herding, primarily in the Finnmark region of Norway's far north, including roughly equal numbers of men and women.

We, the Sami, are one people, whose fellowship must not be divided by national boundaries. We have our own history, tradition, culture and language. We have inherited from our forebears a right to territories, water and our own economic activities. We have an inalienable right to preserve and develop our own economic activities and our communities, in accordance with our own circumstances and we will together safeguard our territories, natural resources and national heritage for future generations.

The Sami participate in the Arctic Council and the World Council of Indigenous Peoples, which encourages solidarity and promotes information exchange between indigenous peoples. The Sami University College (www.samiskhs.no) at Kautokeino was established as the Nordic Sami Institute in 1974 and promotes Sami language, culture and education, as well as research, economic activities and environmental protection.

Arts & Architecture

Arts

Like so many Norwegian forays onto the international stage, for more than two centuries Norway's contribution to international Western culture has been in inverse proportion to its size.

In the late 19th century and into the early 20th century, three figures – playwright Henrik Ibsen, composer Edvard Grieg and painter Edvard Munch – tower over Norway's cultural life like no others and their emergence came at a time when Norway was forging its path to independence and pushing the creative limits of a newly confident national identity. More than just artists, Ibsen, Grieg and Munch are an expression of the Norwegian soul. In the 20th century, three Norwegian writers – products of Norway's golden age of cultural expression, won the Nobel Prize for Literature.

Less decorated but of arguably similar cultural reach, the Norwegian contribution to contemporary music – especially jazz, electronica and heavy metal – has been considerable.

Literature

Medieval Norse Literature

Norwegian literature dates back over a thousand years to the sagas of the Vikings. The two mainstays of the genre are skaldic poetry (*skalds* – the metaphoric and alliterative works of Norwegian court poets in the 9th and 10th centuries) and eddic poetry (named after the *Edda,* the most important collection of medieval Icelandic literature). The latter, which combines Christian with pre-Christian elements, is the most extensive source of information on Norse mythology, but it wasn't written down until Snorre Sturluson recorded it in the 13th century, long after the Christianisation of both Norway and Iceland. Its subject matter includes the story of the origin, history and end of the world, instructions on writing poetry, and a series of disconnected aphorisms attributed to the god Oðinn. Apart from the *Edda* itself, there are three forms of eddic poetry: legendary sagas, heroes' sagas and didactic poetry.

Folk Tales

Nowhere else in Europe does a tradition of folk tales and legends survive to quite the extent it does in Norway. Although many of these tales have been committed to paper, their essence is that of an oral tradition that has passed down through the generations.

Norwegian folk tales, often drawing on the legends of medieval Norse literature, are populated by an impossibly rich imaginary cast of mythical characters. The antics of these fantasy characters, as well as the

The Prose Edda: Norse Mythology by Snorre Sturluson and Jesse L Bycock is the definitive collection of ancient Norse myths drawn from the Icelandic sagas first recorded by Sturluson.

THE TRUTH ABOUT TROLLS

The most Norwegian of Norway's supernatural beings is the troll, which emerged in Norway at the close of the last ice age. Trolls inhabit gloomy forests, moonlit lakes, deep fjords, snowy peaks and roaring waterfalls. They're creatures of shadow and darkness; any troll who is exposed to direct sunlight turns to stone.

Trolls, who can live for hundreds of years, come in all shapes and sizes, but nearly all have four fingers and toes on each hand and foot, as well as long, crooked noses and bushy tails. Some have multiple heads, with up to three eyes per head. They also have a strange predilection for harassing billy goats and a violent aversion to church bells. Despite having a short fuse and being decidedly cranky, they're generally kind to humans.

Among the better-known trolls is the Nokken, a slimy creature who lives in mountain ponds, and the Huldra, a stunning temptress who seduces young men before dragging them into the woods (unless they can first drag her to a church). There are even lucky trolls who grant wishes to fishermen who treat them nicely.

A larger version of the troll was the giant, and according to legend, the world was created from the body of the giant Ymir of Jotunheimen (home of the giants), after his death at the hand of the Norse god Oðinn.

princesses and farm boys that managed to outwit them, are as essentially Norwegian as the fjords and Vikings. But it is only due to the work of Peter Asbjörnsen and Jörgen Moe in the early 1800s that they were ever written down at all. Inspired by the popular work of the Grimm brothers, the two men began with what they knew best: the folk tales told in the woods and valleys surrounding Oslo. Comic, cruel, moralistic, ribald and popular from the moment they were published, these stories set the tone for some of Norway's greatest authors, including Henrik Ibsen and Bjørnstjerne Bjørnson.

The tales, most often illustrated with the distinct sketches of Erik Werenskiold and ending with the words 'Snipp. Snapp. Snute. Så er eventyret ute' (a Norwegian rhyme signifying 'The End'), remain popular and easy to find.

Mythical Creatures

In addition to trolls, elves, which normally live by streams in the deepest forests, come in both good and bad varieties. They only emerge at night, and it's said that the sites of their nocturnal festivities and dances are marked by luxuriant rings of grass. Other elusive creatures include the frightening draugen, a headless fisherman who foretells drownings with a haunting wail; and the vetter (wights), who serve as the guardian spirits of the wildest coastlines. Serpents also existed in Viking mythology, and at least one is still with us today – the mysterious Selma the Serpent (see the boxed text, p117).

Natural Phenomena

The valleys in western and northern Norway are rich sources of folk tales, sagas and myths, many of them explaining curious geographic features.

In one story, a lonely island-dwelling giantess shouted across the water to a giant named Blåmann (Blue Man) on the mainland, asking him to marry her. He agreed, provided she brought the island along with her. Sadly, by the time she'd packed, the sun rose and she turned to stone, as did Blåmann, who'd stayed out too long waiting for her. The island became known as Gygrøy (Giantess Island), but local fisherfolk renamed it Landegode (Good Land), lest the giantess take offence. Landegode's distinctive profile is a familiar landmark on the ferry between Bodø and Kjerringøy, while poor old Blåmann is now an icecap.

Another legend involves Hestmannen (the Horseman), who attempted to shoot the princess Lekamøya with an arrow when she wouldn't marry him. Her father, the king of Sømna, threw down his hat as a distraction, and the result was Torghatten, a hat-shaped peak that looks as if it's been pierced through, on Torget island south of Brønnøysund. Hestmannen himself is a knobbed peak on the island of Hestmanna, located further north near Mo i Rana.

The Golden Age

The late 19th and early 20th centuries were the golden age of Norwegian literature. Although most of the attention centres on Henrik Ibsen, it was Bjørnstjerne Bjørnson (1832–1910) who in 1903 became the first Norwegian writer to win the Nobel Prize for Literature. Best known for *Trust and Trial* (1857), Bjørnson's work included vignettes of rural life (for which he was accused of romanticising the lot of rural Norwegians). His home at Aulestad (p129) is open to visitors.

Henrik Ibsen Sites

» Ibsen Museum, Oslo

» Ibsenhuset Museum, Grimstad

» Henrik Ibsenmuseet, Skien

» National Theatre, Oslo

Knut Hamsun (1859–1952) won the Nobel Prize for Literature in 1920. His greatest novels include *Hunger* (1890), *Mysteries* (1892) and *The Growth of the Soil* (1917). Hamsun's elitism, his appreciation of Germanic values and his idealisation of rural life led him to side with the Nazis in WWII, forever darkening his reputation with Norwegians. Only now is he being recognised as belonging to the tradition of Dostoevsky and Joyce.

Sigrid Undset (1882–1949) became the third of Norway's Nobel Literature laureates in 1928 and is regarded as the most significant female writer in Norwegian literature. Undset began by writing about the plight of poor and middle-class women; between 1920 and 1922 she published the *Kristin Lavransdatter* trilogy, which was set in 14th-century Scandinavia and was later turned into a film (see the boxed text, p414). Her former home in Lillehammer (p125) is open to the public.

Contemporary Literature

One of the best-known modern Norwegian writers is Jan Kjærstad (b 1953), whose *The Seducer* (2003) combines the necessary recipe for a bestseller – a thriller with a love affair and a whiff of celebrity – with

CULTURAL ICON: HENRIK IBSEN

Born in Skien in southern Norway, Henrik Johan Ibsen (1828–1906) became known internationally as 'the father of modern drama', but to Norwegians he was the conscience of a nation. Norwegians are extremely proud of Ibsen, but from 1864 until 1891 he lived in disenchanted exile, decrying the small-mindedness of the Norwegian society of the day. In 1863 he wrote *The Pretenders*, which takes place in 13th-century Norway with King Håkon Håkonsson expressing anachronistic dreams of national unity. The enormously popular *Peer Gynt* (1867) was Ibsen's international breakthrough. In this enduring epic, an ageing hero returns to his Norwegian roots after wandering the world and is forced to face his own soul.

His other best-known plays include *The Doll's House* (1879), the highly provocative *Ghosts* (1881), *An Enemy of the People* (1882), *Hedda Gabler* (1890) and, his last drama, the semi-autobiographical *When We Dead Awaken* (1899).

Throughout his life, Ibsen was always more than a chronicler of Norwegian society and saw himself as the very reflection of 19th-century Norwegians: 'He who wishes to understand me must know Norway. The magnificent but severe natural environment surrounding people up there in the north forces them to keep to their own. That is why they become introspective and serious, they brood and doubt – and they often lose faith. There, the long, dark winters come with their thick fogs enveloping the houses – oh, how they long for the sun!'

seriously good writing. It won the 1999 Nordic Prize for Literature among other international prizes.

Other Norwegian winners of the prestigious Nordic Prize include Per Petterson (b 1952), who won in 2009 and whose works include *Out Stealing Horses, To Siberia* and *I Curse the River of Time*; and Lars Saabye Christensen (b 1953), whose novel *Beatles* was hugely popular in Norway.

Another increasingly world-renowned author is Jostein Gaarder (b 1952), whose first bestselling novel, *Sophie's World* (1991), sold over 15 million copies worldwide. Other Gaarder works include *The Solitaire Mystery* and *The Christmas Mystery*, which are similarly written in the voice of a child protagonist, and his 2010 work *The Castle in the Pyrenees*.

Other popular and well-known novelists include Erik Fosnes Hansen (b 1965), Ingvar Ambjørnsen (b 1956), Erlend Loe (b 1969) and Dag Solstad (b 1941); the latter is the only Norwegian author to win the Norwegian Literary Critics' Award three times. Herbjørg Wassmo (b 1942) has also won numerous international prizes, and her 1989 *Dina's Book,* set in 1840s Norway, was turned into a film called *I am Dina* (2002), starring Gerard Depardieu. Her acclaimed *The House with the Blind Glass Windows* is set in and after WWII. In the crime fiction genre, Gunnar Staalesen and Karin Fossum have devoted international followings.

Another name to catch international headlines is journalist Åsne Seierstad, whose *The Bookseller of Kabul* was a runaway international success, although it was hugely controversial. The Kabul family, portrayed somewhat unflatteringly in the book, sued her in European courts and, in a landmark July 2010 ruling, Seierstad and her publisher were found guilty of defamation and 'negligent journalistic practices'; the court awarded punitive damages against the author and her publishers, who were also required to pay legal costs. Seierstad has promised to appeal, while other members of the Afghan family with whom she stayed in 2002 have threatened to launch separate legal actions against her. Seierstad's more recent works include *A Hundred and One Days,* a first-hand account of the fall of Saddam Hussein, and *Angel of Grozny: Inside Chechnya*.

For more on Norway's active literary scene, visit Oslo's Litteraturhuset (see the boxed text, p71).

Music

Classical Music

The 19th century was an extraordinarily rich time for Norwegian music. It was at this time that Edvard Grieg, who is regarded as one of history's greatest composers, emerged. Of arguably equal importance was the virtuoso violinist Ole Bull, known throughout Europe as the 'Nordic Paganini'. Bull is credited with critically encouraging the careers of Edvard Grieg and Henrik Ibsen, bringing the Hardanger folk fiddlers to Bergen concert halls and reviving Europe-wide interest in Norwegian folk music.

There are fine philharmonic orchestras in Oslo, Bergen (dating from 1765), Trondheim and Stavanger; the Norwegian Opera Company (established in 1958) is based in Oslo. In addition to Grieg, watch out for works by his contemporaries Halfdan Kierulf and Johan Svendsen, or more recent composers such as David Monrad Johansen, Geirr Tveitt, Fartein Valen, Pauline Hall and Ketil Bjørnstad (www.ketilbjornstad.com). Modern Norwegian compositions often bear unmistakable traces of folk-music roots.

Folk Music

Folk music is another central pillar of Norwegian music, and the Hardanger fiddle – which derives its distinctive sound from four or five sympathetic strings stretched out beneath the usual four strings – is one of Europe's best-loved folk instruments.

Edvard Grieg Experiences

» Troldhaugen, Bergen

» Open-air concerts, Bergen

» Grieghallen, Bergen

Music from Norway (www.musicfromnorway.com/default.aspx) is a thorough overview of Norwegian music, with biographies and informative summaries of the most popular musical forms as well as album releases and concert tours.

CULTURAL ICON: EDVARD GRIEG

Norway's renowned composer Edvard Grieg (1843–1907) was so disappointed with his first symphony that he scrawled across the score that it must never be performed! Thankfully, his wishes were ignored. Grieg was greatly influenced by Norway's folk music and melodies and his first great signature work, *Piano Concerto in A minor*, has come to represent Norway as no other work before or since.

Two years after the concerto, Grieg, encouraged by luminaries such as Franz Liszt, collaborated with Bjørnstjerne Bjørnson, setting the latter's poetry and writing to music. The results – *Before a Southern Convent*, *Bergliot* and *Sigurd Jorsalfar* – established Grieg as the musical voice of Norway. This was followed by a project with Henrik Ibsen, setting to music Ibsen's wonderful novel *Peer Gynt*. The score found international acclaim and became Grieg's – and Norway's – best-remembered classical work.

By 1885 Grieg had developed a formidable repertoire (including *Ballad in G minor*, *The Mountain Thrall*, *Norwegian Dances for Piano* and the *Holberg Suite*), and he and his wife Nina moved into the coastal home at Troldhaugen (p161), close to Bergen, from which he set off on numerous concert tours of Europe. According to his biographer, Aimer Grøvald, it was impossible to listen to Grieg without sensing a light, fresh breeze from the blue waters, a glimpse of grand glaciers and a recollection of the mountains of western Norway's fjords.

ARTS & ARCHITECTURE ARTS

Some of the hottest folk acts include Tore Bruvoll and Jon Anders Halvorsen, who perform traditional Telemark songs *(Nattsang)*; the live Norwegian performances of Bukkene Bruse (heavy on the Hardanger fiddle; *Spel*); Rusk's impressively wide repertoire of music from southeastern Norway *(Rusk)*; Sigrid Moldestad and Liv Merete Kroken, who bring classical training to bear on the traditional fiddle *(Spindel)*; and Sinikka Langeland, whose *Runoja* draws on ancient runic music.

In 2009 Norwegian folk music shot into the international arena when Alexander Rybak, a Norwegian composer, fiddler and pianist of Belorussian descent won the Eurovision Song Contest with 'Fairytale', a song he composed himself and which draws deeply on Norwegian folk traditions. He was accompanied by the modern folk dance troupe Frikar. His debut album *Fairytales* reached number one on the Norwegian and Russian charts and the top 20 in seven other European countries.

In recent years, folk music has also taken a somewhat unexpected turn with the fusion genre of folk-rock bringing traditional folk music to a younger audience. Both Gåte and Odd Nordstoga in particular have won plaudits for their unlikely but successful combination of folk music with heavy metal.

For a wonderful overview of traditional Norwegian folk music, the 2007 CD *Norway: Traditional Music* excavates long-lost music from the vaults of Norwegian Public Radio.

Sami Music

The haunting music of the Sami people of northern Norway is also enjoying a revival. Recent Sami artists such as Aulu Gaup, Sofis Jannock, Mari Boine Persen and Nils Aslak Valkeapää have performed, recorded and popularised traditional and modern versions of the traditional *joik* (personal songs). Boine in particular has enjoyed international air-time and her distinctive sound blends folk-rock with *joik* roots. For more on Sami history and culture, see p404.

Fiddling for Norway: Revival and Identity, by Chris Goertzen, looks at the revival of folk-fiddling in Norway, the history of Norwegian folk music and its influence on the world folk-music scene.

Contemporary Music

Modern Norwegian music is about far more than A-ha – yes, they're still around and released their ninth studio album *Foot of the Mountain* in 2009 – with Norwegian artists excelling at everything from jazz and electronica to that peculiarly Norwegian obsession, black metal.

Jazz

If the country's jazz festivals (see p19) are any indication, Norway has a thriving jazz scene, with world-class festivals held throughout the year and all over the country.

Jazz saxophonist Jan Garbarek is one of the most enduring Norwegian jazz personalities and is one of the biggest names on the international stage, quite apart from his fame within Norway. His work draws on classical, folk and world-music influences and he has recorded 30 albums, some including collaborations with renowned artists across a range of genres. His 1994 *Officium*, with its echoes of Gregorian chants, did well in the pop charts across Europe, while his 2005 *In Praise of Dreams* received a Grammy nomination. His daughter, Anja Garbarek, is seen as one of the most exciting and innovative performers on the Norwegian jazz scene, bringing pop and electronica into the mix.

Other well-known performers include the pianist Bugge Wesseltoft, saxophonist Trygve Seim, accordion player Frode Haltli, drummer Jon Christensen, guitarist Terje Rypdal, percussionist Paal Nilssen-Love, bassist Ingebrigt Håker Flaten, trumpeter Nils Petter Molvaer, and female jazz singers Solveig Slettahjell, Sidsel Endresen and Karin Krog. Supersilent, the Christian Wallumrod Ensemble and the cutting-edge Jaga Jazzist rank among Norway's best-loved jazz groups. Jazzbasen (www.jazzbasen.no/index_eng.html), the internet's true home of Norwegian jazz, covers festivals and has an extensive list of jazz artists to watch out for.

Electronica

Norway is at once one of Europe's most prolific producers and most devoted fans of electronica. Although much of the energy surrounding Norwegian electronica has shifted to Oslo in recent years, the so-called Bergen Wave was largely responsible for putting Norway on the world electronica circuit in the first years of the 21st century. Röyksopp (www.royksopp.com) in particular took the international electronica scene by storm with its debut album *Melody A.M.* in 2001 and the group has never really left the dance-floor charts since. The Bergen Wave was not just about electronica; it also produced internationally acclaimed bands Kings of Convenience (www.kingsofconvenience.com) and Ephemera (www.ephemera.no).

In recent years Oslo has taken up the electronica mantle with *Sunkissed*, produced by Oslo label Small Town Super Sound (www.smalltownsupersound.com) and spun by G-Ha and Olanskii – although the fuss has died down a little since its 2007 release, it remains quite simply the hottest thing to hit Norwegian dance music since Röyksopp.

Other well-known electronica acts include Kim Hiortøy, Magnet (aka Even Johansen; www.homeofmagnet.com), Bjørn Torske, Bassdiver, Frost, Ralph Myerz and the Jack Herren Band, Xploding Plastix, Icon of Coil, Det Svenska Folket and Palace of Pleasure.

Metal

Metal is another genre that Norway has taken to heart and, again, Bergen tends to be the home city for much of the action, although it's a nationwide phenomenon. Two venues famous throughout Europe are Hulen (p169), an almost mythical venue among European heavy and indie rock fans; and Garage (p169), another iconic rock-heavy venue.

Although traditional heavy metal is popular, Norway is particularly known for its black-metal scene which, for a time in the early 1990s, became famous for its anti-Christian, Satanist philosophy. A handful of members of black-metal bands were involved in the burning down of churches such as the Fantoft Stave Church in Lom – see p162.

Jazz Festivals

» Polar Jazz, Longyearbyen
» Vossajazz, Voss
» May Jazz, Stavanger
» Night Jazz (Nattjazz), Bergen
» Kongsberg Jazz, Kongsberg
» Moldejazz, Molde
» Canal Street Jazz & Blues, Arendal
» International Jazz, Oslo
» Silda Jazz, Haugesund
» Lillehammer Jazz, Lillehammer

CULTURAL ICON: EDVARD MUNCH

Edvard Munch (1863–1944), Norway's most-renowned painter, was a tortured soul: his mother and elder sister died of tuberculosis and his younger sister suffered from mental illness from an early age. Munch's first great work, *The Sick Child*, was a portrait of his sister Sophie shortly before her death. In 1890 he produced the haunting *Night*, depicting a lonely figure in a dark window. The following year he finished *Melancholy* and began sketches of what would become his best-known work, *The Scream*, which graphically represents Munch's own inner torment.

In 1892 Munch buried himself in a cycle of angst-ridden, atmospheric themes collectively entitled *Frieze of Life – A Poem about Life, Love and Death*. Beyond the canvas, his obsession with darkness and doom cast a long shadow over his life. Alcoholism, chronic emotional instability and a tragic love affair culminated in the 1907 work *Death of Marat*, and, a year later, he checked into a Copenhagen mental-health clinic for eight months.

After leaving the clinic, Munch settled on the coast at Kragerø. It became clear that Munch's postclinic work was to be altogether different, dominated by a sunnier, more hopeful disposition dedicated to humans in harmony with their landscape.

Among the better-known (or notorious) Norwegian black-metal bands are Darkthrone, Mayhem, Emperor, Enslaved, Gorgoroth, Satyricon and Arcturus. The Norwegian Black Metal site (www.norsksvartmetall.com) has everything you ever wanted to know about Norway's own genre of metal.

Painting & Sculpture

Nineteenth-century Norway gave birth to two extraordinary talents: painter Edvard Munch and sculptor Gustav Vigeland (see p55).

During the early 20th century, the Impressionist Henri Matisse inspired several ardently decorative Norwegian artists such as Axel Revold, Per Krohg, Alf Rolfsen and Henrik Sørensen, known collectively as the 'fresco brothers'. During the postwar years, the brooding forests of Jakob Weidemann, the constructivist paintings of Gunnar S Gundersen, and the literal (nonfigurative) sculptures of Arnold Haukeland and Åse Texmon Rygh dominated the visual arts scene.

Of the crop of contemporary Norwegian artists, Olav Jensen, Anne Dolven, Ørnulf Opdahl, Bjørn Tufta, Håvard Vikhagen, Odd Nerdrum and Anders Kjær have all created a minor stir with their return to abstract and expressionist forms. Their works often feature harsh depictions of the Norwegian landscape. Norwegian sculptors who've distinguished themselves include Bård Breivik, Per Inge Bjørlo and Per Barclay.

Cinema

Norway has a small but internationally respected film industry. Pioneering the industry's claims to international recognition were the Oscar-nominated Nils Gaup and Arne Skouen. Other directors to catch the eye include Marius Holst, Berit Nesheim, Anja Breien and Jens Lien.

The only Norwegian feature film to win an Academy Award was Thor Heyerdahl's *Kon-Tiki* for Best Documentary Feature in 1951. In 2006 *The Danish Poet*, which was directed by Norway's Torill Kove and narrated by Liv Ullmann, won the Oscar for Best Animated Short Film, and became the second Norwegian production to receive an Academy Award.

The Norwegian film industry's own version of the Hollywood spectacular is the Amanda Awards, which has been running since 1985 and which is held during Haugesund's Norwegian Film Festival in August.

Of the movies filmed in Norway, *Black Eyes*, by Russian director Nikita Michalkhov, was set in the spectacular landscapes around Kjerringøy

Best Art Galleries

» National Gallery, Oslo

» Munch Museum, Oslo

» Bergen Kunst Museum, Bergen

» Rogaland Art Museum, Stavanger

» National Museum of Contemporary Art, Oslo

» Astrup Fearnley Museum, Oslo

» Henie-Onstad Art Centre, Oslo

Film Festivals

» Kosmorama, Trondheim – April

» Norwegian Film Festival, Haugesund – August

» Bergen International Film Festival – October

TOP NORWEGIAN FILMS

» *Nine Lives* (1957; director Arne Skouen) Oscar-nominated tale of a soldier on the stormy northern coast of Norway during the German occupation; has twice won awards for best Norwegian film of all time.

» *Pinchcliffe Grand Prix* (1975; director Ivo Caprino) Animated feature and still Norway's biggest box-office success.

» *Wives* (1985; director Anja Breien) One of the most-acclaimed Norwegian movies of all time.

» *The Pathfinder* (1987; director Nils Gaup) Based on a medieval legend and presented in the Sami language.

» *Frida* (1991; director Berit Nesheim) A searing portrayal of adolescence.

» *Cross My Heart and Hope to Die* (1994; director Marius Holst) A 1995 Berlin Festival winner for its depiction of childhood conflicts in Oslo.

» *Kristin Lavransdatter* (1995; director Liv Ullmann) Based on the novel by Sigrid Undset and set in 14th-century Norway.

» *The Bothersome Man* (2006; director Jens Lien) An absurdist fable set in a love-less and claustrophobic IKEA-world.

» *The Kautokeino Rebellion* (2008; director Nils Gaup) Recreates the 1852 Sami uprising in Kautokeino with a soundtrack dominated by Sami musician Mari Boine Persen.

» *Max Manus* (2009; directors Joachim Rønning and Espen Sandberg) Big-budget movie that depicts the eponymous Norwegian Resistance fighter.

in Nordland, while Caspar Wrede's *One Day in the Life of Ivan Denisovich* was filmed in Røros.

Architecture

Norway's architects have clearly been inspired by the country's dramatic landscapes, while recognising the need to build structures capable of withstanding the harsh dictates of Norway's climate. The results are often stunning: from rustic turf-roofed houses, whose design dates back almost two millennia, to Norway's signature stave churches, soaring religious architecture, and creative adaptations of Sami symbols and some Arctic landforms. While the rural sense of style revels in its rustic charm, Norway's urban architecture strives for a more modern aesthetic, with clean lines and minimalism all the rage.

Architectural Highlights

» Oslo Opera House, Oslo

» Arctic Cathedral, Tromsø

» Art nouveau, Ålesund

» Bryggen area, Bergen

» Heddal Stave Church, Notodden

» Miners' cottages, Røros

» Nidaros Cathedral, Trondheim

» Sami Parliament, Karasjok

» Stave church, Urnes

Traditional Architecture

Timber and stone are the mainstays of traditional Norwegian architecture; nowhere is this more evident than in the delightful former mining village of Røros, where many of the colourful timber houses date back to the 17th and 18th centuries. For an overview of Norwegian architectural styles down through the centuries, it's worth making a detour to Lillehammer to visit Maihaugen (p124), or any of the excellent folk museums dotted around the country.

Sami Architecture

In the far north, where both wood and stone were in short supply, the early nomadic Sami ingeniously built their homes out of turf, which provided excellent insulation against the cold. The temporary shelter that the Sami used on their travels is popularly known as the *lavvo* (although it has different names in various Sami dialects). Less vertical (and hence more stable in the winds of the high Arctic) than the North American teepee, the *lavvo* was held aloft by a tripod of three notched poles with a cover of reindeer skins (and later canvas).

The *lavvo* formed at once a centrepiece of Sami life and a refuge from the elements – during and after the devastation wrought by Germany's WWII occupation of northern Norway, the *lavvo* became the primary Sami dwelling for a time. The *lavvo* also holds considerable modern symbolism for the Sami: in the early 1980s, the Oslo police bulldozed a Sami *lavvo* that had been set up outside Norway's parliament building to protest against a proposed dam that would have inundated Sami herding lands. These events provided a catalyst for a reassessment of Sami rights and which led indirectly to the foundation of the Sami parliament. These days, the *lavvo* is occasionally used as a temporary shelter for Sami, but is more often a tourist attraction for those eager to experience Sami culture. The stunning modern Sami Parliament building in Karasjok was inspired by the traditional *lavvo* form.

Stave Churches

If Norway can be said to have made one stand-out contribution to world architecture, it is undoubtedly the stave church. Seemingly conceived by a whimsical child-like imagination, the stave church is an ingenious adaptation to Norway's unique local conditions. Originally dating from the late Viking era, these ornately worked houses of worship are among the oldest surviving wooden buildings on earth, albeit heavily restored. Named for their vertical supporting posts, these churches are also distinguished by detailed carved designs, dragon-headed gables resembling the prows of classic Viking ships and by their undeniably beautiful, almost Asian, forms. Of the 500 to 600 that were originally built, only about 20 of the 28 that remain retain many of their original components.

Contemporary Architecture

Due to the need to rebuild quickly after WWII, Norway's architecture was primarily governed by functionalist necessity (the style is often called *funkis* in the local vernacular) rather than any coherent sense of style. Nowhere is this exemplified more than in the 1950, red-brick Oslo Rådhus. As the style evolved, functionality was wedded to other concerns, such as recognising the importance of aesthetics in urban renewal (for example in Oslo's Grünerløkka district), and ensured that architecture once again sat in harmony with the country's environment and history.

It is with the latter concept that Norway's architects have excelled, especially in the Arctic North. Tromsø's Arctic Cathedral, designed by Jan Inge Hovig in 1964, mimics Norway's glacial crevasses and auroral curtains. Another beautiful example is the Sami Parliament in Karasjok, where Arctic building materials (birch, pine and oak) lend the place a sturdy authenticity, while the use of lights to replicate the Arctic night sky and the structure's resemblance to a Sami *lavvo* are extraordinary. The creative interpretation of historical Norwegian shapes also finds expression at the Viking Ship Sports Arena in Hamar, while Oslo's landmark new opera house powerfully evokes a fjord-side glacier and is easily the most exciting example of contemporary architecture to emerge in Norway during the last decade.

Folk Museums

» Maihaugen, Lillehammer

» Norwegian Folk Museum, Oslo

» Setesdalsmuseet, Setesdalen

» Hardanger Folk Museum, Utne

» Romsdalmuseet, Molde

» Sverresborg Trøndelag Folkemuseum, Trondheim

ARTS & ARCHITECTURE ARCHITECTURE

Architecture buffs will find much to enjoy in *Made in Norway: Norwegian Architecture Today* by Ingerid Helsing Almaas. It takes a detailed look at 30 projects completed by Norwegian architects since 2007 and has interviews with some of the leading lights.

Norwegian Cuisine

Norwegian food *can* be excellent. Abundant seafood and local specialities such as reindeer are undoubtedly the highlights, and most medium-sized towns have fine restaurants in which to eat. The only problem (and it's a significant one) is that prices are prohibitive, meaning that a full meal in a restaurant may become something of a luxury item for all but those on expense accounts. What this does is push many visitors into eating fast-food meals in order to save money, at least at lunchtime, with pizzas, hot dogs and hamburgers a recurring theme. As a result, you may end up leaving Norway pretty uninspired by its food. It's not only foreign visitors who feel the pinch – it's often claimed, backed by authoritative research surveys, that Pizza Grandiosa, a brand of frozen pizza, is in fact Norway's national dish.

Striking a balance between eating well and staying solvent requires a clever strategy. For a start, most Norwegian hotels and some hostels offer generous buffet breakfasts ensuring that you'll rarely start the day on an empty stomach; if you take full advantage, you'll need only a light meal for lunch. Some hotels also lay on lavish dinner buffets in the evening – they're generally expensive, but excellent if it's your main meal of the day. Another key is to think in kroner and avoid converting the Norwegian price into your home currency, otherwise you really might wind up emaciated.

Food

Meat

Norwegians love their meat and some of the most memorable meals for carnivores will involve Norway's signature species. Roast reindeer *(reinsdyrstek)* is something every nonvegetarian visitor to Norway should try at least once; despite its cost (starting from around Nkr275 and often much higher), you'll likely order it again as it's one of the tastier red meats. If you're fortunate enough to be invited to a Sami wedding, you might also come across a traditional reindeer stew *(bidos)*. Another popular local meat is elk *(elg)*, which comes in a variety of forms, including as a steak or burger.

Other meat-based dishes that Norwegian chefs excel at preparing include *bankebiff* (slices/chunks of beef simmered in gravy), *dyrestek* (roast venison) and *lammebog* (shoulder of lamb). Not surprisingly given the Norwegian climate, meats are often cured, one variety of which is *spekemat* (cured lamb, beef, pork or reindeer, often served with scrambled eggs). Further dishes include *kjøttpålegg* (cold meat cuts), *fårikål* (lamb in cabbage stew), *syltelabb* (boiled, salt-cured pig's trotter), *lapskaus* (thick stew of diced meat, potatoes, onions and other vegetables) and *pytt i panne* (eggs with diced potato and meat).

The Norwegian Kitchen by K Innli (ed) brings together more than 350 favourite recipes of members of the Association of Norwegian Chefs.

Surprisingly few Norwegian restaurants offer the kind of meals that Norwegians eat at home, or at least used to when their mothers and grandmothers cooked for them. One such dish is traditional Norwegian meatballs served with mushy peas, mashed potatoes and wild-berry jam. One place worthy of special mention where this and other traditional dishes dominate the menu is Pingvinen (p166) in Bergen.

Seafood

One Norwegian contribution to international cuisine that you shouldn't miss is salmon (*laks;* grilled or smoked, in which case it's called *røyke-laks*). Where other Norwegian foods may quickly empty your wallet without adequate compensation for taste, salmon remains blissfully cheap, although this applies only to farmed salmon; wild salmon is considerably more expensive. The quality is consistently top-notch. An excellent salmon dish, *gravat laks*, is made by marinating salmon in sugar, salt, brandy and dill and serving it in a creamy sauce.

Other Norwegian freshwater seafood specialities that are recommended include brown trout (only in the south), perch, Arctic char, Arctic grayling, bream, tench and eel.

The most common ocean fish and seafood that you're likely to eat are cod (*torsk* or *bacalao;* often dried), boiled or fresh shrimps, sprat, haddock, mackerel, capelin, sand eel, ling, ocean perch and coalfish. The ugly but inexplicably lovable catfish is, sadly, rather delicious, as is the blenny. Herring (once the fish of the poor masses and now served pickled in onions, mustard or tomato sauce) is still served in some places, but it's becoming rarer while wild stocks recover. Norwegians are also huge fans of *fiskesuppe,* a thin, creamy, fish-flavoured soup.

Other dishes to watch out for include *fiskebolle* (fish balls), *fiske-grateng* (fish casserole), *gaffelbitar* (salt- and sugar-cured sprat/herring fillets), *klippfisk* (salted and dried cod), *sildesalat* (salad with slices of herring, cucumber, onions etc) and *spekeslid* (salted herring, often served with pickled beetroot, potatoes and cabbage).

Other Specialities

Potatoes feature prominently in nearly every Norwegian meal and most restaurants serve boiled, roasted or fried potatoes with just about every dish. Other vegetables that turn up with sometimes monotonous regularity are cabbage, turnip, carrot, swede (rutabaga), cauliflower and broccoli.

Norwegian National Recipes: An Inspiring Journey in the Culinary History of Norway by Arne Brimi can be hard to track down, but there's no finer study of Norwegian food covering all regions and it's written by one of Norway's premier chefs.

In 2008 Norwegian chefs topped the medal table in an international cooking competition known unofficially as the 'culinary Olympics' and involving 32 countries (which didn't, perhaps significantly, include France or Spain).

TRAVEL YOUR TASTEBUDS

Norway has its share of strong-tasting culinary oddities that the brave among you may wish to try:

» whale steak (*hvalbiff*) – a reasonably common sight on restaurant menus and in harbourside markets (eg in Bergen); eating it is an act of defiance to your environmental credentials

» brown cheese – *Gudbrandsdalsost* is made from the whey of goat's and/or cow's milk and has a slightly sweet flavour despite its off-putting caramel-coloured appearance

» reconstituted cod, mackerel or saithe balls – more common in homes than restaurants and something of a staple for older folk

» cod tongues – these are hugely popular in Lofoten and, strangely enough, nowhere else

» fermented trout – some Norwegians swear by it, but some Lonely Planet authors are happy to leave them to it

The country's main fruit-growing region is around Hardangerfjord, where strawberries, plums, cherries, apples and other orchard fruits proliferate. The most popular edible wild berries include strawberries, blackcurrants, red currants and raspberries; blueberries (huckleberries), which grow on open uplands; blue, swamp-loving bilberries; red high-bush and low-bush cranberries; and muskeg crowberries. The lovely amber-coloured *moltebær* (cloudberries) are highly prized and considered a delicacy. They grow one per stalk on open swampy ground and in Norway some cloudberry patches are zealously guarded. Warm cloudberry jam with ice cream is simply fantastic!

Norwegian cheeses have come to international attention as a result of the mild but tasty Jarlsberg, a white cheese first produced in 1860 on the Jarlsberg estate in Tønsberg.

One scheme worth watching out for in northern Norway is the Arctic Menu (see the boxed text, p275), an attempt by an association of restaurants to revive interest in local ingredients and recipes.

Vegetarian & Vegan Food

Norwegians are not the most vegetarian of people. That said, most restaurants offer some vegetarian options. Sometimes this may just be a cheese-and-onion omelette or a pasta with cream sauce, but increasingly you'll find creative salads (although vegans won't appreciate the widespread use of cheese) and a range of crepes or pancakes to add some variety to your diet. The predominance of potatoes on most Norwegian restaurant menus almost always provides a fall-back option.

In general, the rule is that the larger the town, the wider your choices of vegetarian fare. In Oslo, Bergen, Stavanger and Trondheim, you'll find plenty of European-style cafes with a range of vegetarian choices and even vegetarian restaurants. Tapas restaurants are a recurring theme in larger towns and most have vegetable-only options. Pizza restaurants also always have at least one vegetarian dish.

> The website of Arne Brimi (www. brimiland.no, in Norwegian), arguably Norway's most celebrated chef, may appear only in Norwegian for now, although expect that to change as his international reputation grows.

Drinks

Hot Drinks

If Norway has a national drink, it's coffee. In fact, coffee is drunk in such staggering quantities that one can only wonder how people can remain so calm under the influence of so much caffeine. Most Norwegians drink

---

FOOD IN A TUBE

A Parisian orders a cafe au lait, a Londoner kippers. In New York it might be a bagel, in Tokyo rice. Comfort food or culture shock, they're all breakfast, and for Norwegians it comes in a tube.

The question mark at hotel breakfast buffets, and nothing to do with dental hygiene, cream cheese and *kaviar* (sugar-cured and smoked cod roe cream) packaged in tubes have been Norwegian favourites for decades. There are two especially popular Norwegian brands: the Trondheim-based Mills, best known for its *kaviar*, and the older Kavli in Bergen. A dairy established in 1893, Kavli began exporting cheese to the US in the early 1920s and launched its first tube of Primula cream cheese in 1924 – quite the groundbreaking event in the cheese-processing world. It now produces bacon, ham, salami, shrimp, tomato, mexicana and jalapeño flavoured cheeses, all packaged in the familiar tubes.

Though both spreads are good alone and part of a well-rounded Norwegian *frokost* (breakfast), *kaviar* is especially popular coupled with Norvegia cheese or a few slices of boiled egg.

The national spirit, aquavit (or *akevitt*) is a potent dose of Norwegian culture made from potatoes and caraway liquor. The name is derived from the Latin *aqua vitae,* the 'living waters'. Although caraway is an essential ingredient, various modern distilleries augment the spicy flavour with any combination of orange, coriander (cilantro), anise, fennel, sugar and salt! The confection is aged for three to five years in 500L oak barrels that have previously been used to age sherry.

Perhaps the most esteemed version of this libation is *linje aquavit,* or 'line aquavit', which first referred to stores that had crossed the equator. In the early days, ships carried oak barrels of aquavit abroad to trade, but the unsold barrels were returned to Norway and offered for sale. When it was discovered that the product had improved with age and travel, these leftovers became highly prized commodities. Today, bottles of *linje aquavit* bear the name of the ship involved, its route and the amount of time the barrels have aged at sea.

it black and strong, but foreigners requiring milk and/or sugar are normally indulged.

Teas and infusions are also available all over the country, as are the usual range of fizzy drinks and mineral water; they're much cheaper in supermarkets.

Alcoholic Drinks

Beer is not far behind coffee in the popularity stakes. It's available in bulk at eminently reasonable prices from the beer outlets of Vinmonopolet (see the boxed text, p420), the only place, outside of bars and restaurants, where wine and spirits may be purchased.

Beer is commonly sold in bars in 400mL (from Nkr60) or 500mL (from Nkr70) glasses (about 30% and 15% less than a British pint, respectively). The standard Norwegian beer is pils lager, with an alcohol content of around 4%, and it's still brewed in accordance with the 16th-century German purity law. The most popular brands are the lagers Ringsnes in the south and Mack in the north. Munkholm is a fairly pleasant alcohol-free beer. Note that when friends go out drinking, people generally buy their own drinks rather than rounds, which is scarcely surprising given the prices.

Roots web (www.rootsweb. com/~wgnorway/ recipe.html) has easy-to-follow recipes of traditional Norwegian foods passed down through generations of people of Norwegian descent.

Norway has no wine-growing tradition of its own, but Norwegians increasingly drink wine with meals. According to one study, wine makes up one-third of Norway's alcohol intake, compared to just 12% in 1974. Quality restaurants increasingly offer extensive wine lists with wines from across Europe (especially Spain, France, Germany and Italy) and sometimes further afield (Australia, Chile, South Africa and California). In some cities (especially Bergen and Oslo), wine bars are all the rage.

Eating in Norway

Habits & Customs

The Norwegian day starts with coffee (always!), a boiled egg and some sort of bread or dry crispbread (normally Ryvita) topped with cheese, cucumber, tomato and a type of pickled herring.

For lunch, most people opt for a sandwich or a slice of bread topped with sardines, shrimp, ham, olives, cucumber or egg. In the midafternoon Norwegians often break for coffee and one of the highlights of the day, waffles with cream and jam. Unlike the firm Belgian waffles, which are better known abroad, Norwegian waffles are flower-shaped, soft and often strongly flavoured with cardamom.

RECIPES

THE TROUBLE WITH ALCOHOL

Norway must be one of few countries in the world where the population actually voted *for* prohibition (in a 1919 referendum)! The ban on alcohol remained in force until 1927, by which time half the Norwegian population was involved either in smuggling or illegally distilling home brew, including no doubt many who had voted in favour of the ban. The state monopoly system (state alcohol outlets are called Vinmonopolet, or fondly known as just 'pole') emerged as an alternative method of restricting alcohol, but even today it seems to have had little effect on the amount of illegal distilling that continues. If you're offered any homemade swill, remember that the effects can be diabolical!

Alcohol sales are strictly controlled and a few towns have even implemented virtual prohibition. In some places, drinking beer in public incurs a hefty fine and/or prison time, although we're yet to hear of any tourist doing time for enjoying a quiet pint.

Norway's official attitude towards alcohol borders on paranoia, especially as alcohol consumption by Norwegians is among the lowest in Europe, although whether this is because of the strict laws or in spite of them it's difficult to tell. Yes, Norwegian alcohol consumption has increased from 3.4L per person per week in 1960 to 6.2L in recent years, but these figures are still barely more than half the consumption levels in Germany or the UK. That said, there is a disturbing recent phenomenon whereby average alcohol consumption (and binge drinking) among Norwegian 15- to 20-year-olds has increased dramatically. As one young bartender explained to us, prohibitive bar prices for drinks forces many young Norwegians to buy alcohol in bulk from Vinmonopolet outlets, drink at home ('foreplay' according to the local vernacular) until midnight when they go out to drink in bars.

The main meal is eaten between 4pm and 6pm. Usually the only hot meal of the day, it normally includes a meat, seafood or pasta dish, with boiled potatoes, a scoop of vegetables and perhaps even a small salad or green garnish. Note that Norwegians often take full advantage of long summer days and eat out considerably later.

Costs, Opening Hours & Listing Order

Throughout this guidebook, the order of restaurant listings follows the author's preference, and each place to eat is accompanied by one of the following symbols.

€ <Nkr125 per main course per person
€€ Nkr125 to Nkr200 per main course per person
€€€ >Nkr200 per main course per person

Authentic Nor-wegian Cooking by Astrid Karlsen Scott has an emphasis on the practical and has been endorsed by none other than Ingrid Espelid, the Betty Crocker or Delia Smith of Norway.

Although lunch is usually served from noon to 3pm and dinner from 6pm to 11pm, many restaurants (and their kitchens) remain open from noon to 11pm. Only significant exceptions to these rules are noted in the restaurant listings throughout this book.

Where to Eat & Drink

Hotel breakfasts in Norway often consist of a gargantuan buffet that is dominated by continental-style choices, with a few hot dishes (usually bacon, eggs and/or sausages) and some Scandinavian options (such as pickled herrings) thrown in. If you're staying somewhere where break-fast is not included, your best bet is a bakery where bread, pastries, sand-wiches and bagels are well priced.

If you love fresh fish, any of Norway's fish markets are fabulous places to eat; buy what you want as a takeaway and find a quiet vantage point alongside the water.

Norwegians love to eat out and just about every town in Norway has at least one sit-down restaurant. Although it's more usual to eat a light lunch and save the main meal for dinner, many Norwegian restaurants, especially in larger towns, serve cheaper lunch specials (often around Nkr79). These are often filling and well sized for those wanting more than a sandwich. Sometimes these are signed as a *dagens rett* (daily special).

Cheap Eats

If you're trying to save a bit of money, shop in supermarkets, Norway's last bastion of reasonable prices. Aside from the usual packaged foods, some supermarkets have reasonably priced delicatessens where you can pick up salads or grilled chickens. These delicatessens also sell smoked or cured meats that make an excellent filling for a sandwich or roll. If you buy your bread from a bakery and the rest of the items from a supermarket, you'll end up saving bucket loads of krone over the course of your trip. Major supermarket chains that you'll find across the country include Rimi, Spar, Co-op and Rema 1000.

Salads and other snacks are also available from convenience stores and petrol stations. Your standard snack for a quick lunch is usually a *pølse* (hot dog), of which you'll find various varieties; garnish and sauce cost no extra and if you buy a drink with it you'll often pay just Nkr35 to Nkr50. Petrol stations also often have a small choice of paninis and rolls that are similarly priced and far more healthy. *Gatekjøkken* (food wagons or kiosks) also serve hot dogs, burgers, chips, pizza slices and the like, and the better ones will also offer fish and chips and a range of sandwiches.

If you're by the coast, fish markets are often well priced and those that receive large numbers of tourists usually have a range of ready-to-go snacks, such as fish balls or takeaway platters of salmon and other fishy wonders.

Pizzas feature prominently in the local diet. Peppe's Pizza is Norway's standout pizza chain with creative pizzas (from Nkr159) that are a cut above the rest and servings large enough for two; its lunchtime buffets are even better value. Another similar chain is Dolly Dimple's.

Celebrations

Food is central to Norwegian celebrations and this is particularly true at Christmas, when special dishes include *rømmegrøt* (a delicious sour-cream variant on porridge); *rupa* (ptarmigan or grouse); *lutefisk* (a glutinous dish of dried cod or stockfish treated in lye solution that's definitely an acquired taste and extremely popular among Norwegians living overseas); *pinneribbe* (mutton ribs steamed over birch or juniper branches); and pork roast, which stems from the Viking tradition of sacrificing a pig at Yuletide. Raisin buns and a variety of sweet biscuits, including *strull, krumkake* and *goro*, are what children get excited about.

The almost-universal Christmas drink is *gløgg,* which roughly translates as 'grog', but is far more exciting in reality, blending cinnamon, raisins, almonds, ginger, cloves, cardamom and other spices with juice, which may or may not be fermented. Many people also imbibe *julaøl,* or 'holiday beer', which dates from the Viking days, when it was associated with pagan sacrifices; as with the *lutefisk,* not all foreigners fully appreciate it. Die-hard alcohol fans celebrate the season with generous quantities of Norway's own potato power brew, aquavit (see the boxed text, p419).

Fish Markets
» Bergen
» Stavanger
» Kristiansand
» Trondheim
» Narvik

Every Thursday from September to May, many Bergen restaurants serve *raspeballer,* a powerful traditional meal with salted meat, potatoes and mashed turnip – an acquired taste perhaps, but hearty winter food.

Survival Guide

Directory A-Z

Accommodation

Norway offers a wide range of accommodation, from camping, hostels and pensions to international-standard hotels. You'll pay a lot more for what you get compared with other countries, but standards are high. Most hotels have wi-fi access for those with laptops; see p430 for more details.

Reservations

Although it's rare that you arrive in a town to find that all of the accommodation is full – festivals are an exception – it's always advisable to book in advance to ensure that you get the accommodation of your choice; the hotel you'd like to stay in may have rooms, but the only available ones probably have a view of the back wall rather than the fjord.

Most places in Norway accept phone or email reservations (you'll often have to leave a credit-card number for the latter). Many hostels are normally happy to book beds at your next destination for a small fee (around Nkr20). Note that popular hostels in Oslo and Bergen are often heavily booked in summer.

Many tourist offices can help you find accommodation, usually for a fee of around Nkr50; apart from in some larger tourist offices, this service usually operates only if you're physically present in the tourist office and not for advance bookings.

Seasons

The main tourist season runs from around the middle of June to the middle of August. Unusually, although this is the high season, it's also when accommodation prices are at their lowest and many hotels offer their best deals. In some areas, the season begins in mid-May and/or hangs on until mid-September.

Winter, particularly in northern Norway where travellers come for activities such as snowmobiling and dog-sledding, is also a popular time to visit although, unlike in summer, prices rarely drop as a consequence. Some hotels and the overwhelming majority of campsites close during the winter months, while that rare breed, ice hotels – there are examples in Kirkenes and Alta – only open in winter.

Prices

Throughout this guidebook, the order of accommodation listings is by author preference, and each place to stay is accompanied by one of the following symbols (the price relates to a double room with private bathroom and, unless stated otherwise, includes breakfast):

€ <Nkr750 per double room
€€ Nkr750-1400 per double room
€€€ >Nkr1400 per double room

Prices at Norwegian hotels vary widely throughout the year and prices given throughout this book are for the tourist high season from mid-June to mid-August; in a few places, discounted high-season prices apply in July only, while in others it can seem as if there are as many different prices as there are days in the year. The sometime exception to this general rule is the southern Norwegian coast, where beach resorts raise their prices to cash in on the school-holiday influx.

During the rest of the year, the assumption seems to be that the only people travelling are those doing so for business and on expense accounts, and prices can soar accordingly (by as much as 40%). The exception is weekends (usually Friday and Saturday nights, but sometimes also Sunday) when, year-round, prices can drop to their much more reasonable summer rates. If you're travelling outside the summer months, ask the hotel about special offers to see if discounts are available.

Prices for single rooms are generally not much less than (and certainly significantly more than half of) the rates for double rooms. And remember that if you're making inquiries in advance about prices, they're often quoted *per person* for double rooms, so always check.

Staying within a tight budget is difficult in Norway, and you'll either need to stay at campsites (in a tent or a simple cabin), hostel or guesthouse; within the budget category, it's rare that you'll have your own private bathroom. A handy source of information (and discounts) for budget travellers is **VIP Backpackers** (☎90 62 16 44; www.vipbackpackers.no).

In the midrange and top-end categories, rooms are usually very comfortable and almost always have a private bathroom.

Accommodation Types

BED & BREAKFASTS
Some places operate as B&Bs, where prices (usually with shared bathrooms) start from single/double Nkr350/500 and can go up to Nkr650/900. These options can be tracked down through **Bed & Breakfast Norway** (www.bbnorway.com), which has extensive online listings for B&Bs throughout Norway; it also sells *The Norway Bed & Breakfast Book*, with listings throughout the country.

CAMPING
Norway has more than 1000 campsites. Tent space ordinarily costs from Nkr90 at basic campsites up to Nkr200 for those with better facilities or in popular or expensive areas, such as Oslo and Bergen. Quoted prices usually include your car, motorcycle or caravan. A per-person charge is also added in some places; electricity often costs a few kroner extra and almost all places charge Nkr10 for showers.

Most campsites can also rent simple cabins with cooking facilities, starting at around Nkr350 for a very basic two- or four-bed bunkhouse. Bring a sleeping bag, as linen and blankets are provided only at an extra charge

(anywhere from Nkr50 to Nkr100).

Unless you opt for a more expensive deluxe cabin with shower and toilet facilities (Nkr750 to Nkr1200), you'll also have to pay for showers and washing water (there are a few exceptions). Normally, cabin occupants must clean their cabin before leaving or pay an additional cleaning charge (around Nkr150).

Note that although a few complexes remain open year-round, tent and caravan sites are closed in the off-season (normally early September to mid-May).

For a comprehensive list of Norwegian campsites, pick up a copy of the free *Camping* (available at some tourist offices and campsites); it has hundreds of listings but most entries are in Norwegian. Otherwise, visit the following:
NAF Camp (www.nafcamp.no)
Norsk Camping (www.camping.no)

DNT & OTHER MOUNTAIN HUTS
Den Norske Turistforening (DNT; Norwegian Mountain Touring Club; ☎22 82 28 22; www.turistforeningen.no; Storgata 7, Oslo) maintains a network of 460 mountain huts or cabins located a day's hike apart along the country's 20,000km of well-marked and maintained wilderness hiking routes. Of these, over 400 have beds for sleeping, with the remainder reserved for eating, rest stops or emergency shelter.

DNT huts range from unstaffed huts with two beds to large staffed lodges with more than 100 beds and renowned standards of service. At both types of huts, DNT members receive significant discounts.

For details of becoming a DNT member, see p30.

Most DNT huts are open from 16 February to 14 October. Staffed DNT lodges also open from the Saturday before Palm Sunday until Easter Monday, but staffed huts along the Oslo–Bergen railway and a few others open for the cross-country ski season as early as late February. DNT can provide lists of opening dates for each hut.

Members/nonmembers who prefer to camp outside the huts and use the facilities will pay Nkr50/60.

There are also numerous private hikers' huts and lodges peppered around most mountain areas, but not all are open to the public. Some offer DNT members a discount.

Unstaffed DNT Huts
All unstaffed huts offer cooking facilities, but in most places you must have your own sleeping bag or hostel-style sleeping sheet; sleeping sheets are often sold or included in the price at staffed huts. Staffed lodges don't normally have cooking facilities for guests, but a self-service section with cooking facilities is available at some lodges when unstaffed.

For unstaffed huts, you must pick up keys (Nkr125 to Nkr175 deposit) in advance from a DNT office or a staffed hut. To pay, fill out a Once-Only Authorisation slip and leave either cash or a valid credit-card number in the box provided. There are two classes of unstaffed huts. Self-service chalets are stocked with blankets and pillows and have wood stoves, firewood, gas cookers and a wide range of tinned or freeze-dried food supplies for

BOOK YOUR STAY ONLINE

For more accommodation reviews by Lonely Planet authors, check out hotels.lonelyplanet.com/Norway. You'll find independent reviews, as well as recommendations on the best places to stay. Best of all, you can book online.

sale (on the honour system). At other unstaffed huts, users must carry in their own food. In unstaffed huts, DNT members/nonmembers pay Nkr185/285 for a bed.

Staffed DNT Huts

At staffed huts, which are concentrated in the south, you can simply turn up and pay your fees. In compliance with international mountain hospitality, no one is turned away, even if there's only floor space left; DNT members over 50 years of age are guaranteed a bed, even if it means displacing a younger hiker! Huts tend to be packed at Easter and consistently busy throughout summer.

For the full range of options at staffed huts, and prices, see the DNT website.

GUESTHOUSES & PENSIONS

Many towns have *pensjonat* (pensions) and *gjestehus* (guesthouses) and some, especially the latter, are family-run and offer a far more intimate option than the hostel or hotel experience.

Prices for a single/double with a shared bathroom usually start at Nkr450/700 but can cost significantly more; linen and/or breakfast will only be included at the higher-priced places.

HOSTELS

In Norway, reasonably priced hostels (*vandrerhjem*) offer a dorm bed for the night, plus use of communal facilities that usually include a self-catering kitchen (you're advised to take your own cooking and eating utensils), internet access and bathrooms. Some also have single or double rooms with either shared or private bathroom facilities, but these often represent poor value.

While some hostels have quite comfortable lodge-style facilities and are open year-round, some are used for school accommodation except during summer months and others are the cheaper wing of a hotel; occasionally prices work out more expensive than a cabin or budget hotel. In most hostels, guests must still bring their own

sleeping sheet and pillowcase, although most hire sleeping sheets for a one-off fee (starting from Nkr50) regardless of the number of nights.

Most hostels have two- to six-bed rooms and beds cost from Nkr170 to Nkr370. The higher-priced hostels usually include a buffet breakfast, while other places may charge from Nkr50 to Nkr100 for breakfast. Some also provide a good-value evening meal for around Nkr125.

Although not all Norwegian hostels belong to the **Hostelling International** (HI; www.hihostels.com) network, many do. Where applicable, prices listed in this book are those for non-HI members; members pay 15% less. Check the HI website to find its office in your home country so that you can join and qualify for members' prices in Norway (although some Norwegian hostels will let you take out membership when you check in). The Norwegian hostelling association, **Norske Vandrerhjem** (☑23 12 45 10; www.hihostels .no), is HI-affiliated.

Several hostel guides are available, including HI's annually updated Europe guide, while Norske Vandrerhjem publishes the free *Hostels in Norway*, which contains a full listing of hostels and updated prices for the 77 hostels on its books; it's available from hostels and some tourist offices.

HOTELS

Norway's hotels are generally modern and excellent, although those with anything approaching character are pretty thin on the ground. Aside from individual exceptions, it's always worth checking out the worthwhile **De Historiske** (☑55 31 67 60; www.dehistoriske.no) network, which links Norway's most historic old hotels and restaurants. The quality on offer is consistently high, every hotel is architecturally distinguished and many are family-run. Admittedly, they

---

can be expensive, but are almost always worth it.

Otherwise, comfortable nationwide chain hotels are the norm and the rooms can all start to look the same after a while, whether you're sleeping in Oslo or Kirkenes. The advantage of these chains or hotel networks, however, is that many offer hotel passes, which can entitle you to a free night if you use the chain enough times; some passes only operate in summer. The main nationwide chains (whose discounts sometimes also apply in other Scandinavian countries) include the following:

Best Western (www.best western.no) Best Western Rewards system operates at the 28 Best Western hotels in Norway, in addition to occasional summer deals.

Choice Hotels (www.choice. no) Covering Clarion, Quality and Comfort Hotels, the Nordic Choice Club can add up to free nights if you stay in enough member hotels. In some Comfort Hotels, you get a light evening buffet included in the price.

Fjord Pass (www.fjordpass. no) Probably the pick (and certainly the broadest) of the hotel passes, the Fjord Pass costs Nkr120 (valid for two adults and any children under 15) and is available at 170 hotels, guesthouses, cabins and apartments year-round; no free nights, but the discounts on nightly rates are considerable. Works best if you book in advance through its website, rather than simply turning up and hoping for a discount.

Rica Hotels (www.rica.no) Free 'loyalty program' earns points that can translate into free nights (between every six and 10 nights) at around 90 Rica hotels in Norway and Sweden.

Thon Hotels (www.thon hotels.com) Another program with free membership that qualifies you for discounts or free nights.

PRIVATE HOMES

Tourist offices in some towns have lists of private rooms, which are among the cheapest places to stay. In some cases, they allow you to stay with a Norwegian family. Prices vary, but you'll rarely have to pay more than Nkr350/450 for a single/ double; breakfast isn't normally included. Showers sometimes cost Nkr10 extra.

Along highways, you'll occasionally see *rom* signs, indicating informal accommodation typically costing from Nkr250 to Nkr400 per room (without breakfast); those who bring their own sheets or sleeping bags may get a discount.

SUMMER HOMES & CABINS

Most tourist offices in popular holiday areas keep lists of private huts, cabins and summer homes that are rented out to holidaymakers when the owners aren't using them; these arrangements sometimes also apply in the ski season. The price for a week's rental starts from around Nkr1400 for a simple place in the off-season to around Nkr15,000 for the most elaborate chalet in midsummer. Most cabins sleep at least four people, and some accommodate as many as 12; if you have a group, it can be an economical option. Advance booking is normally required, and you'll probably have to pay a deposit of around Nkr750 or 20% of the total fee, whichever is less.

Two privately run Danish agencies that act as clearing houses for hundreds of self-catering cabins and chalets in Norway:

Dansommer (☑in Denmark 39 14 33 00; www.dansommer. com)

Novasol (☑in Denmark 39 14 55 55; www.novasol.com)

Business Hours

Reviews in this guidebook won't list business hours

unless they differ from the following standards. These standard opening hours are for high season (mid-June to mid-September) and tend to decrease outside that time. The opening hours for attractions and tourist offices are listed throughout the book.

Banks 8.15am to 3pm Monday to Wednesday and Friday, 8.15am to 5pm Thursday

Central Post Offices 8am to 8pm Monday to Friday, 9am to 6pm Saturday; otherwise 9am to 5pm Monday to Friday, 10am to 2pm Saturday

Restaurants noon to 3pm, 6pm to 11pm

Shops 10am to 5pm Monday to Wednesday and Friday, 10am to 7pm Thursday, 10am to 2pm Saturday

Supermarkets 9am to 9pm Monday to Friday, 9am to 6pm Saturday

Customs Regulations

Alcohol and tobacco are extremely expensive in Norway. To at least get you started, it's worth importing your duty-free allotment: 1L of spirits and 1L of wine (or 2L of wine), plus 2L of beer per person. Note that drinks with an alcohol content of over 60% may be treated as narcotics! You're also allowed to import 200 cigarettes duty-free. Importation of fresh food and controlled drugs is prohibited.

Svalbard is a duty-free zone and many items are considerably cheaper there than in mainland Norway as they're subject to neither VAT or customs duties.

Discount Cards

In addition to the following, a Hostelling International membership card will get you a 15% discount at youth hostels – see p426.

Senior Cards

Honnør (senior) discounts are available to those aged 67 years or over for admission to museums, public pools, transport etc. The discounted price usually amounts to 75% of the full price. You don't require a special card, but those who look particularly youthful may, apart from enjoying the compliment, need proof of their age to qualify.

Student Cards

Discounts (usually 75% of the normal fee) are available for students. You will need some kind of identification (eg an International Student Identity Card; www.isic.org) to prove student status. Not accepted everywhere. Some travellers have reported being refused access with their normal university cards (unless it's from a Norwegian university), so the ISIC card is a good investment. It can provide discounts on many forms of transport (including airlines, international ferries and local public transport) and in some internet cafes, reduced or free admission to museums and sights, and cheap meals in some student restaurants.

Embassies & Consulates

Australia The nearest Australian embassy is in Copenhagen; contact the British embassy in an emergency.

Canada (☎22 99 53 00; www. canada.no; 4th fl, Wergelandsveien 7, Oslo)

Denmark (☎22 54 08 00; www.amboslo.um.dk; Olav Kyrres gate 7, Oslo)

Finland (☎22 12 49 00; www. finland.no; Thomas Heftyes gate 1, Oslo)

France (☎22 28 46 00; www. ambafrance-no.org; Drammensveien 69, Oslo)

Germany (☎22 27 54 00; www.oslo.diplo.de; Oscars gate 45, Oslo)

Ireland (☎22 01 72 00; www. embassyofireland.no; Håkon VII's gate 1, Oslo)

Japan (☎22 99 16 00; www. no.emb-japan.go.jp; Wergelandsveien 15, Oslo)

Netherlands (☎23 33 36 00; www.netherlands-embassy. no; Oscars gate 29, Oslo)

New Zealand The British embassy handles consular affairs; the nearest New Zealand embassy is in The Hague.

Russia (☎22 55 32 78; www. norway.mid.ru; Drammensveien 74, Oslo)

Sweden (☎24 11 42 00; www. sverigesambassad.no; Nobelsgata 16, Oslo)

UK (☎23 13 27 00; http:// ukinnorway.fco.gov.uk; Thomas Heftyes gate 8, Oslo)

USA (☎22 44 85 50; www. usa.no; Henrik Ibsens gate 48, Oslo) A new embassy is being built in the Oslo district of Huseby. Check the website for updates.

Electricity

The electricity current in Norway is 220V, 50Hz.

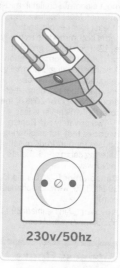

230v/50hz

Gay & Lesbian Travellers

Norwegians are generally tolerant of alternative lifestyles – a 2008 Gallup poll found that 58% of Norwegians supported extending equal marriage rights to homosexual partnerships. On 1 January 2009 Norway became the sixth country in the world to legalise same-sex marriage when its parliament passed a gender-neutral marriage law. The new law replaced the existing right to form 'registered partnerships' and granted full rights to church weddings, adoption and artificial insemination to married couples regardless of their sexual orientation.

All of that said, public displays of affection are not common practice, except perhaps in some areas of Oslo. Oslo is generally the easiest place to be gay in Norway, although even here there have been occasional recent attacks on gay couples holding hands, especially in the central-eastern areas of the capital. You're most likely to encounter difficulties wherever conservative religious views predominate, whether among newly arrived Muslim immigrant communities or among devoutly Lutheran communities in rural areas.

Oslo has the liveliest gay scene (see the boxed text, p66), and it's worth stopping by Use-It (p73), also in Oslo, where you can pick up its excellent annual *Streetwise* booklet, which has a 'Gay Guide' section.

Organisations & Websites

Global Gayz (www.global gayz.com) The Norway page has some interesting background information and practical information.

Landsforeningen for Lesbisk og Homofil frigjøring (LLH; ☎23 10 39 39; www.llh. no, in Norwegian; Valkyriegaten

15, Oslo) The Norwegian National Association of Lesbian and Gay Liberation.

Night Tours (www.night tours.com/oslo/) A guide to the Oslo night.

Visit Oslo (www.visitoslo. com) Click on 'Gay Olso' for some useful links.

Health

Norway is, in general, a very healthy place and no special precautions are necessary when visiting. The biggest risks are likely to be viral infections in winter, sunburn and insect bites in summer, and foot blisters from too much hiking. If you do fall ill while in Norway you will be very well looked after as health care is excellent.

Most medications are available in Norway, but may go by a different name than at home, so be sure to have the generic name, as well as the brand name. If carrying syringes or needles, be sure to have a physician's letter documenting their medical necessity.

Recommended Vaccinations

The World Health Organization (WHO) recommends that all travellers should be covered for diphtheria, tetanus, measles, mumps, rubella and polio, regardless of their destination.

Availability & Cost of Health Care

Good health care is readily available in Norway, and for minor, self-limiting illnesses, pharmacists can dispense valuable advice and over-the-counter medication. They can also advise when more specialised help is required. The standard of dental care is usually good; however, it is sensible to have a dental check-up before a long trip. Remember that, like almost everything else, medical care can be prohibitively expen-

sive in Norway and insurance is a must.

Water

Tap water is always safe to drink in Norway, but it's wise to beware of drinking from streams, as even the clearest and most inviting water may harbour giardia and other parasites. For extended hikes where you must rely on natural water, the simplest way of purifying water is to boil it thoroughly. Vigorous boiling should be satisfactory; however, at high altitude water boils at a lower temperature, so germs are less likely to be killed. Boil it for longer in these environments (up to 10 minutes).

If you cannot boil water it should be treated chemically. Chlorine tablets (Puritabs, Steritabs or other brands) will kill many pathogens, but not giardia and amoebic cysts. Iodine is more effective in purifying water and is available in tablet form (such as Potable Aqua). Follow the directions carefully and remember that too much iodine can be harmful.

Hypothermia & Frostbite

Norway's perilously cold winters require that you take the proper precautions if travelling at this time. Even on a hot day in the mountains, the weather can change rapidly – carry waterproof garments and warm layers, and inform others of your route.

Hypothermia starts with shivering, loss of judgment and clumsiness. Unless rewarming occurs, the sufferer deteriorates into apathy, confusion and coma. Prevent further heat loss by seeking shelter, warm dry clothing, hot sweet drinks and shared body warmth. Acute hypothermia follows a sudden drop of temperature over a short time. Chronic hypothermia is caused by a gradual loss of temperature over hours.

Frostbite is caused by freezing and subsequent damage to bodily extremities. It is dependent on wind-chill, temperature and length of exposure. Frostbite starts as frostnip (white, numb areas of skin) from which complete recovery is expected with rewarming. As frostbite develops, the skin blisters and becomes black. Loss of damaged tissue eventually occurs. Wear adequate clothing, stay dry, keep well hydrated and ensure you have adequate calorie intake to prevent frostbite. Treatment involves rapid rewarming. Avoid refreezing and rubbing the affected areas.

Insect Bites & Stings

In northern Norway, the greatest nuisances are the plagues of blackflies and mosquitoes that swarm out of tundra bogs and lakes in summer. Fortunately, malaria is unknown, but the mental risks can't be underestimated, as people have literally been driven insane by the ravenous hordes. Midsummer is the worst, and regular mosquito coils and repellents are scarcely effective; hikers must cover exposed skin and may even need head nets to keep the little buggers from making kamikaze attacks on eyes, nose, ears and throat. If you're camping, a tent with mosquito netting is essential.

Most people get used to the mosquito bites after a few days as their bodies adjust and the itching and swelling become less severe. An antihistamine cream should help alleviate the symptoms. Use a DEET-based insect repellent.

Rabies

Rabies, caused by a bite or scratch by an infected mammal, is found in Svalbard and (occasionally) in eastern Finnmark. Dogs are a noted carrier, but cats, foxes and bats can also be infected. Any bite, scratch or even lick from a warm-blooded, furry animal should be cleaned immediately and thoroughly. Scrub with soap and running water, and then apply alcohol or iodine solution. If you've been infected by a rabid animal, medical help should be sought immediately.

Insurance

A travel-insurance policy to cover theft, loss, medical problems and cancellation or delays to your travel arrangements (due to illness, ticket loss, industrial action etc) is a good idea. Paying for your ticket with a credit card can often provide limited travel-accident insurance and you may be able to reclaim the payment if the operator doesn't deliver.

Note that some policies specifically exclude 'dangerous activities' such as motorcycling, skiing, mountaineering, snowmobiling or even hiking. Make sure the policy covers ambulances and an emergency flight home. A policy that pays doctors or hospitals directly may be preferable to one where you pay on the spot and claim later. If you have to claim later, make sure you keep all documentation.

In Norway, EU citizens may be required to pay a service fee for emergency medical treatment, but presentation of an E111 form will certainly expedite matters and minimise the amount of paperwork involved. Inquire about these at your national health service or travel agent well in advance.

Worldwide travel insurance is available at lonelyplanet.com/travel_services. You can buy, extend and claim online anytime – even if you're on the road.

For details of car insurance, see p442.

Internet Access

For useful Norwegian travel-related websites see p15.

Internet Cafes

Good cybercafes that last the distance are increasingly hard to find; ask at the local tourist office. Prices per hour range from Nkr40 to Nkr75; students sometimes receive a discount.

Public Libraries & Tourist Offices

The scarcity of internet cafes is compensated for by having free internet access available in most municipal libraries (biblioteket). As it's a popular service, you may have to reserve a time slot earlier in the day; in busier places, you may be restricted to a half-hour slot. Internet access is also available at some tourist offices around the country; it's sometimes free but there's usually a small fee.

Wi-Fi

Widely available at most hotels and in some cafes and restaurants; generally (but not always) free. Connection speed often varies from room to room in hotels, so always ask when you check in. Hotels offering wi-fi are indicated throughout this book with an icon (🛜). If they have a public-access computer terminal, the icon is @. Airports have wi-fi but generally charge around Nkr60 for the first hour.

Language Courses

Learning Norwegian is possible at the following places in Oslo:

Berlitz Language Services (☎23 00 33 60; www.berlitz.no; 7th fl, Akersgata 16; 0158 Oslo)

Folkeuniversitetet Oslo (☎22 47 60 00; www.fuoslo.no; 5th fl, Torggata 7, Oslo)

International Summer School, University of Oslo (☎22 85 63 85; www.summerschool.uio.no; 6th fl, Gaustadalléen 25, Oslo)

Oslo Adult Education (Oslo Voksenopplæring; ☎23 47 00 00; www.english.oslovo.no; Karoline Kristiansens vei 8, 0603 Oslo)

Maps

In addition to the city and town maps throughout this guidebook, most local tourist offices distribute user-friendly and free town plans.

Country Maps

Bilkart over Norge (1:1,000,000) by Nortrabooks is one of the best maps of Norway for general travellers. It includes useful topographic shading and depicts the entire country on one sheet. Michelin Norway – 752 (1:1,250,000) is also good although the last update was in January 2007 and the font size can be a problem. **Statens Kartverk** (www.statkart.no), Norway's official mapping authority, covers the country in 21 sheets at a scale of 1:250,000.

Hiking Maps

Den Norske Turistforening (DNT; Norwegian Mountain Touring Club; ☎22 82 28 22; www.turistforeningen.no; Storgata 7, Oslo) is the best source of hiking maps. Hikers can pick up topographic sheets at any DNT office, although the offices in larger cities have a wider selection beyond the local area. National-park centres and nearby tourist offices are good sources for the excellent Turkart or Statens Kartverk hiking maps.

Road Maps

The best road maps are the Cappelens series, which are sold in Norwegian bookshops. There are three maps at 1:335,000 scale: No 1 Sør-Norge Sør, No 2 Sør-Norge

Nord and *No 3 Møre og Trøndelag*. Northern Norway is covered in two sheets at 1:400,000 scale: *No 4 Nordland og Sør-Troms* and *No 5 Troms og Finnmark*. The *Veiatlas Norge* (Norwegian Road Atlas), published by Statens Kartverk, is revised every two years.

Money

The most convenient way to bring your money is in the form of a debit or credit card, with some extra cash for use in case of an emergency. You'll find information on exchange rates and costs on p14.

ATMs

'Mini-Banks' (the Norwegian name for ATMs) are widespread and most accept major credit cards as well as Cirrus, Visa Electron and/or Plus bank cards, although check with your bank before leaving about which banks charge the lowest withdrawal fees.

Changing Money

Don't assume that all banks will change money and in some places you may need to shop around to find one that does. Rates at post offices and tourist offices are generally poorer than at banks, but can be convenient for small amounts outside banking hours.

Credit & Debit Cards

Visa, Eurocard, MasterCard, Diners Club and American Express cards are widely accepted throughout Norway; not all places accept debit cards. If your card is lost or stolen in Norway, report it immediately:
American Express (☏80 06 81 00)
Diners Club (☏21 01 50 00)
Eurocard (☏21 01 52 22)
MasterCard (☏21 01 52 22)
Visa (☏81 50 05 00)

Currency

The Norwegian krone is most often represented either as Nkr (preceding the number, as in this book), NOK (preceding the number) or simply kr (following the amount). One Norwegian krone (Nkr1) equals 100 øre.

Taxes & Refunds

For goods that cost more than Nkr315 at shops displaying the 'Global Refund Tax Free Shopping' logo, you're entitled to a 'Refund Cheque' for the 25% MVA (the equivalent of value-added or sales tax). At the point of sale, you fill out the cheque with your name, address and passport number, and then, at your departure point from the country, you present your sealed goods, passport and Refund Cheque to collect the refund; ferry passengers normally collect their refund from the purser during limited hours once the boat has sailed.

For more information, pick up the *How to Shop Tax Free* brochure from most tourist offices and some tourist shops, which explains the procedure and lists border crossings at which refunds can be collected, or visit www.globalrefund.no.

Tipping

Service charges and tips are included in restaurant bills and taxi fares and tipping on a North American scale is not expected. It is, however, customary to round up the bill. If the service has been particularly helpful, feel free to leave more.

Travellers Cheques

Post offices, some tourist offices and banks accept all brands of travellers cheques, which command a better exchange rate than cash by about 2% (but this may be cancelled out by commission fees).

Photography

Although few Norwegians are camera-shy, you should always ask permission in Sami areas, where you may encounter some camera sensitivity, as well as in villages where whaling is a mainstay (people may be concerned that the photos will be used against them in the media).

For comprehensive advice on taking terrific photos, check out *Lonely Planet's Guide to Travel Photography* by Richard I'Anson.

Public Holidays

New Year's Day (Nyttårsdag) 1 January
Maundy Thursday (Skjærtorsdag) March/April
Good Friday (Langfredag) March/April
Easter Monday (Annen Påskedag) March/April
Labour Day (Første Mai, Arbeidsdag) 1 May
Constitution Day (Nasjonaldag) 17 May
Ascension Day (Kristi Himmelfartsdag) May/June, 40th day after Easter
Whit Monday (Annen Pinsedag) May/June, 8th Monday after Easter
Christmas Day (Første Juledag) 25 December
Boxing Day (Annen Juledag) 26 December

Safe Travel

Your personal belongings are safer in Norway than in most people's home countries, and the cities – even east Oslo, which has a relatively poor reputation – are reasonably safe at all hours of the night. However, don't become blasé about security: be careful near the nightclubs in the Rosenkrantz gate area of Oslo and beware of pickpockets around the Torget area of Bergen. Normally, the greatest nuisance value will come

CHRISTMAS IN NORWAY

Christmas, or *jul*, is a wonderful time to be in Norway. The name *jul* is derived from *joulu* or *lol*, a pagan fertility feast that was celebrated all over Europe in pre-Christian times and synchronised nicely with the holiday to honour the birth of Christ. Currently, most people celebrate between Christmas Eve and Epiphany, or 12th night, although some continue until the Feast of St Canute (the 20th day of Christmas).

A Christmas tree is a requisite part of the decor in most homes, and gifts are exchanged on Christmas Eve. In the countryside, sheaves of oats known as *julenek* are mounted on a pole and left out for the birds. In gratitude for past blessings, a bowl of porridge is also left out for the *nisse*, the gnome that historically brought good fortune to farmers. This concept has now been merged with the international tradition of Santa Claus in the personage of Jule-nissen, whom Norwegians believe makes his home in Drøbak, south of Oslo: there's a Santa Crossing road sign there to prove it!

For a rundown on traditional Christmas foods, turn to p421, while more information on this special time of the year in Norway is contained in the free *Christmas in Norway* brochure available from some tourist offices.

SIM card, these can be purchased from any 7-Eleven store and some Narvesen kiosks. However, as the connection instructions are entirely in Norwegian, you're better off purchasing the card from any Telehuset outlet, where they'll help you connect on the spot. SIM cards start from Nkr200, which includes Nkr100 worth of calls.

There are three main service providers:

NetCom (www.netcom.no, in Norwegian)
Network Norway (www.networknorway.no, in Norwegian) Operates as Mobile Norway.
Telenor Mobil (www.telenor.com)

Phone Codes

All Norwegian phone numbers have eight digits. Numbers starting with '800' usually indicate a toll-free number, while those beginning with '9' are mobile (cell) phone numbers. There are no local area codes (these are incorporated into listed numbers).

Directory assistance ☏180 (calls cost Nkr9 per minute)
International access code ☏00
Norway country code ☏47

Phonecards

International calls can be prohibitively expensive. Although there are Telekort

from drug addicts, drunks and/or beggars (mainly in Oslo) who can spot a naive tourist a block away. Oslo and other larger cities suffer from a growing drug problem. Although dope may be readily available in places, it isn't legal.

If you're planning on hiking out into the Norwegian wilds, remember that Norway's weather can, even in summer, change rapidly. For more information, see p30.

nasty surprise when your next bill arrives; although agreements between European countries have substantially reduced calling costs in recent years, prices remain high.

If you wish to use your mobile, but with a Norwegian SIM card, check with your network before leaving home as some phones sold by some networks are blocked from using other carriers. If your phone will accept a foreign

Telephone
Mobile Phones

There aren't too many places where you can't get GSM mobile access with coverage for close to 90% of the country. This doesn't, of course, apply to wilderness areas and the hiking trails of most national parks.

If you want to use your home-country mobile in Norway, always check with your carrier about the cost of roaming charges to avoid a

GOVERNMENT TRAVEL ADVICE

The following government websites offer travel advisories and information for travellers:

Australian Department of Foreign Affairs & Trade (www.smartraveller.gov.au)
Canadian Department of Foreign Affairs & International Trade (www.voyage.gc.ca)
French Ministere des Affaires Etrangeres Europeennes (www.diplomatie.gouv.fr/fr/conseils-aux -voyageurs_909/index.html)
New Zealand Ministry of Foreign Affairs & Trade (www.mft.govt.nz/travel)
UK Foreign & Commonwealth Office (www.fco.gov.uk)
US Department of State (www.travel.state.gov)

(Telenor phonecards), they're increasingly hard to find (ask for the cards at post offices and Narvesen kiosks), as are card and coin phones. Your best bet is to go for one of the phonecards issued by private companies. Usually costing Nkr100, they allow you to make over six hours' worth of calls using a scratch PIN number on the back and a local access number. The only drawback is that they, too, can be difficult to find – some kiosks sell them, but the easiest place to look is an 'ethnic' grocery store.

For international calls, internet-connected calls (eg www.skype.com) are the way to go, although unfortunately if you're not travelling with a laptop, few internet cafes are Skype-enabled. You cannot make phone calls from municipal library computers.

Time

Note that when telling the time, Norwegians use 'half' as signifying *half before* rather than half past. Always double-check unless you want to be an hour late! Although the 24-hour clock is used in some official situations, you'll find people generally use the 12-hour clock in everyday conversation.

Norway shares the same time zone as most of Western Europe (GMT/UTC plus one hour during winter, and GMT/UTC plus two hours during the daylight-saving period). Daylight saving starts on the last Sunday in March and finishes on the last Sunday in October.

Note the following time differences:

Australia During the Australian winter (Norwegian summer), subtract eight hours from Australian Eastern Standard Time to get Norwegian time; during the Australian summer, subtract 10 hours.

Finland One hour ahead of Norway.

Russia Two hours ahead of Norway.
Sweden & Denmark Same time as Norway.
UK & Ireland One hour behind Norway.
USA Norwegian time is USA Eastern Time plus six hours and USA Pacific Time plus nine hours.

Toilets

Most towns (and many roadside stops) have public facilities. However, at some shopping malls, train stations, bus terminals and even some (but not many) restaurants you may have to pay up to Nkr10.

Tourist Information

It's impossible to speak highly enough of tourist offices in Norway. Most serve as one-stop clearing houses for general information and bookings for accommodation and activities. Nearly every city and town has its own tourist office and most tourist offices in reasonably sized towns or major tourist areas publish comprehensive booklets giving the complete, up-to-date low-down on their town.

Offices in smaller towns may be open only during peak summer months, while in cities they're open year-round but with shorter hours in the off-season. Opening hours and contact details are listed under each city throughout the book.

Tourist offices operate under a variety of names – *turistkontor* and *reiseliv* are among the most common – but all have the information symbol (i) prominently displayed outside and are easy to identify and find.

For general info on travelling in Norway, contact the **Norwegian Tourist Board** (Norges Turistråd; ☑22 00 25 00; www.visitnorway.com; PO Box 448, Sentrum, N-0158 Oslo).

Travellers with Disabilities

Norway is generally well set up for travellers with disabilities and all newly constructed public buildings are required by law to have wheelchair access. That said, like in most countries, the situation remains a work-in-progress. As a result, anyone with special needs should plan ahead.

Most Norwegian tourist offices carry lists of wheelchair-accessible hotels and hostels, but your best bet is to contact the Norwegian Association for the Disabled (see below). Nearly all street crossings are equipped with either a ramp or a very low kerb (curb), and crossing signals produce an audible signal – longer beeps when it's safe to cross and shorter beeps when the signal is about to change.

Most (but not all) trains have carriages with space for wheelchair users and many public buildings have wheelchair-accessible toilets.

Organisations & Tours

Access-able Travel Source (www.access-able.com) US information portal with 25 listings for Norway.

Accessible Travel & Leisure (☑01452-729739; www.accessibletravel.co.uk; Avionics House, Naas Lane, Quedgeley, Gloucester GL2 2SN, UK) Claims to be the biggest UK travel agent dealing with travel for the disabled and encourages the disabled to travel independently.

Flying Wheels Travel (☑507-451 5006; www.flyingwheelstravel.com; 143 W Bridge St, Owatonna, MN 55060, USA) Runs hosted six-day 'Highlights of Norway' tours as well as helping to organise independent travel in Scandinavia.

Norwegian Association for the Disabled (Norges Handikapforbund; ☑24 10 24 00;

www.nhf.no; Schweigaards gate 12, Grønland, Oslo) For information on disabled travel and sites of special interest to disabled travellers in Norway.

Society for Accessible Travel & Hospitality (212-447 7284; www.sath.org; 347 Fifth Ave, Ste 605, New York, NY 10016, USA) Although largely concentrated on the USA, this organisation can provide general information.

Visas

Norway is one of 25 member countries of the Schengen Convention, under which 22 EU countries (all but Bulgaria, Cyprus, Ireland, Romania and the UK) plus Iceland, Norway and Switzerland have abolished checks at common borders; Cyprus has signed the Schengen agreement, but full membership has been postponed until sometime in 2011 at the earliest. For more information on entering Norway, see p435.

The visa situation for entering Norway is as follows:

Citizens of Denmark, Finland, Iceland and Sweden No visa or passport required.

Citizens or residents of other EU & Schengen countries No visa required.

Citizens or residents of Australia, Canada, Israel, Japan, New Zealand and the USA No visa required for tourist visits of up to 90 days.

Other countries Check with a Norwegian embassy or consulate.

To work or study in Norway A special visa may be required – contact a Norwegian embassy or consulate before travel.

Women Travellers

Women travellers will have few worries in Norway, and sober Norwegian men are normally the very picture of decorum. While alcohol-impaired men may become tiresome or obnoxious, they're probably no different from the same breed you'll encounter in your home country.

Women who have been attacked or abused can contact the **Krisesenter** (23 01 03 41; www.krisesenter.com) in Oslo or dial 112 nationwide.

Of the general websites dedicated to women travellers, **Journeywoman** (www.journeywoman.com) is outstanding. There's also a women's page on Lonely Planet's **Thorn Tree** (www.lonelyplanet.com).

Work

In order to work in Norway, knowledge of basic Norwegian is required at the very least. As a member of the European Economic Area (EEA), Norway grants citizens of other EEA countries the right to look for work for a three-month period without obtaining a permit; those who find work have the right to remain in Norway for the duration of their employment. For other foreigners, it's very difficult and an application for a work permit must be made through the Norwegian embassy or consulate in your home country before entering Norway.

For help with looking for work, the best places to start are the **Norwegian Labour & Welfare Organisation** (800 33 166; www.nav.no), which produces a number of useful free online PDF booklets, including *Living & Working in Norway* (which has a section entitled 'How to Find a Job in Norway'); or Use-It (p73).

Transport

GETTING THERE & AWAY

Norway is well linked to other European countries by air. There are also regular bus and rail services to Norway from neighbouring Sweden and Finland (from where there are connections further afield to Europe), with less regular (and more complicated) services to/from Russia. Regular car and passenger ferries also connect southern Norwegian ports with Denmark, Sweden and Germany.

Flights, tours and rail tickets can be booked online at www.lonelyplanet.com/travel_services.

Entering Norway

Crossing most borders into Norway is usually hassle-free. That's particularly the case if you're arriving by road where, in some cases, you may not even realise that you've crossed the border.

If you're from a non-Western country expect that you and your baggage will come under greater scrutiny than other travellers at airports and some of the staffed border crossings; this also applies for all travellers crossing by land into Norway from Russia. Also, if you're arriving in Norway from a non-EU or non-Schengen country, expect your papers to be checked carefully.

For visa requirements info, see p434.

Passport

All travellers – other than citizens of Denmark, Iceland, Sweden and Finland – require a valid passport to enter Norway.

Air

Airports & Airlines

For a full list of Norwegian airports, visit www.avinor.no; the page for each airport has comprehensive information. The main international Norwegian airports are Gardermoen (Oslo), Flesland (Bergen), Sola (Stavanger), Tromsø, Værnes (Trondheim), Vigra (Ålesund), Karmøy (Haugesund), Kjevik (Kristiansand) and Torp (Sandefjord).

Dozens of international airlines fly to/from Norwegian airports. Airlines that use Norway as their primary base include the following:

Norwegian (www.norwegian.com) Low-cost airline.

SAS (www.sas.no)

Widerøe (www.wideroe.no) A subsidiary of SAS.

Land

Norway shares land borders with Sweden, Finland and Russia.

For almost all international bus services to/from Norway, the main operator is **Eurolines Scandinavia** (www.eurolines.nu), which acts

---

CLIMATE CHANGE & TRAVEL

Every form of transport that relies on carbon-based fuel generates CO_2, the main cause of human-induced climate change. Modern travel is dependent on aeroplanes, which might use less fuel per kilometre per person than most cars but travel much greater distances. The altitude at which aircraft emit gases (including CO_2) and particles also contributes to their climate change impact. Many websites offer 'carbon calculators' that allow people to estimate the carbon emissions generated by their journey and, for those who wish to do so, to offset the impact of the greenhouse gases emitted with contributions to portfolios of climate-friendly initiatives throughout the world. Lonely Planet offsets the carbon footprint of all staff and author travel.

as a feeder for national companies. **Nor-Way Bussekspress** (www.nor-way.no) also has a reasonable range of international routes.

Train travel is possible between Oslo and Stockholm, Gothenburg, Malmö and Hamburg, with less frequent services to northern and central Swedish cities from Narvik and Trondheim.

Finland
BUS
Buses run between northern Norway and northern Finland, with most cross-border services operated by the Finnish company **Eskelisen Lapin Linjat** (☑016-342 2160; www. eskelisen-lapinlinjat.com).

CAR & MOTORCYCLE
The E8 highway extends from Tornio, in Finland, to Tromsø, and secondary highways connect Finland with the northern Sami towns of Karasjok and Kautokeino. Regular buses serve all three routes.

Russia
Russia has a short border with Norway and buses run twice daily between Kirkenes in Norway and Murmansk in Russia (one way/return Nkr350/Nkr600, five hours). Once in Murmansk, trains connect to St Petersburg and the rest of the Russian rail network.

To cross the border, you'll need a Russian visa, which must usually be applied for and issued in your country of residence.

FINLAND–NORWAY BUSES

Options for bus travel between Finland and Norway include the following (some in summer only).

FROM	TO	FARE	DURATION (HR)
Rovaniemi	Alta	€97	10
Rovaniemi	Karasjok	€76.30	7
Rovaniemi	Tromsø	€103.20	8-10
Rovaniemi	Vadsø	€100.80	8
Saariselkä	Kirkenes	€54.30	3

Sweden
BUS
Swebus Express (☑0200 218 218; www.swebusexpress. se) has the largest (and cheapest) buses between Oslo and Swedish cities. **GoByBus** (www.gobybus.se, in Swedish and Norwegian) is also worth checking out.

Among the numerous cross-border services along the long land frontier between Sweden and Norway, there are twice-daily services between Narvik and Riksgränsen (one hour), on the border, and Kiruna (three hours).

There are also less frequent services between Bodø and Skellefteå, and along the Blå Vägen, or 'Blue Highway', between Mo i Rana and Umeå.

TRAIN
Rail services between Sweden and Norway are operated by **Norwegian Railways** (NSB; ☑81 50 08 88; www.nsb. no) or **Swedish Railways** (SJ; ☑in Sweden 0771-75 75 99; www.sj.se).

It's worth noting that some of the Stockholm–Oslo services require a change of train in the Swedish city of Karlstad.

It's also possible to travel from Trondheim to Sweden via Storlien and Östersund, although you'll need to change trains at the border.

Sea
Ferry connections are possible between Norway and Denmark, Germany, Iceland, the Faroe Islands and Sweden; sadly the ferry services between the UK and Norwegian ports have been discontinued. Most ferry operators offer package deals that include taking a car and passengers, and most lines offer substantial discounts for seniors, students and children. Taking a bicycle incurs a small extra fee.

If you're travelling by international ferry, consider picking up your maximum duty-free alcohol allowance on the boat.

Denmark
The following companies operate ferries between Norway and Denmark.
Color Line (☑in Denmark 99 56 19 77, in Norway 22 94 42 00; www.colorline.com;)
DFDS Seaways (☑in Denmark 33 42 30 00, in Nor-

SWEDEN–NORWAY BUSES

Buses operate from Oslo to the following Swedish destinations.

FROM	FARE	DURATION (HR)	FREQUENCY (PER DAY)
Gothenburg (Göteborg)	from Skr158	3¾	5
Malmö	from Skr248	8	2-4
Stockholm	from Skr283	8-13	around 5

SWEDEN–NORWAY TRAINS

Train services between Sweden and Norway include the following.

FROM	TO	FARE	DURATION (HR)	FREQUENCY (PER DAY)	OPERATOR
Gothenburg (Göteborg)	Oslo	Nkr199-484	4	up to 3	Norwegian Railways
Malmö	Oslo	from Skr401	7½	1	Swedish Railways
Stockholm	Oslo	from Skr314	6-7½	up to 3	Swedish Railways
Stockholm	Narvik	from Skr782	18-20	1-2	Swedish Railways

way 21 62 13 40; www.dfds
seaways.com)
Fjord Line (☎in Denmark 97
96 30 00, in Norway 51 46 40
99; www.fjordline.com)
Stena Line (☎in Norway
02010; www.stenaline.no)

Germany & Sweden

Color Line (☎in Germany
0431-7300 300, in Norway 81 00
08 11, in Sweden 0526-62000;
www.colorline.com) also connects Norway with Germany
and Sweden. Check the website for different fare and
accommodation types. From
Oslo to Kiel in Germany there
are seven weekly departures
(from €174.50, 20 hours),
while ferries from Sandefjord
to Strömstad in Sweden

depart up to 20 times weekly
(from €22, 2½ hours).

Tours

Given the expenses involved
in Norwegian travel, it may
be worth looking into an
organised tour. For details of
some Norwegian operators,
see p445, while international
operators with an activities
focus are covered on p35.

Some of the more repu-
table international operators
include the following:
Arctic Experience (www.
arctic-experience.co.uk) UK
operator with a handful of
winter and summer trips.
Bentours International
(www.bentours.com.au) One
of the few Australian travel

agencies specialising in
Scandinavia, with organised
tours and options for independent travellers.
Brekke Tours (www.brekke
tours.com) US company
with excellent escorted and
independent tours.
Grand Nord Grand Large
(www.gngl.com, in French)
French company with
cruises and hiking in Svalbard and Lofoten, among
other destinations.
Nordic Experience (www.
nordicexperience.co.uk) UK-
based company with a wide
range of well-run, year-round
tours.
Scanam World Tours
(www.scandinaviantravel.com)
US operator with cruises
and shorter upmarket tours.

DENMARK–NORWAY FERRIES

Ferry services between Denmark and Norway include the following. Fares are for high
season (mid-June to mid-August); at other times, fares can be half the high-season price
but departures are much less frequent. Depending on the route, there are a range of
prices and accommodation types and, in most cases, you can transport your car; check
the company websites for the latest fares.

FROM	TO	FARE PER PERSON	DURATION (HR)	WEEKLY DEPARTURES	FERRY OPERATOR
Copenhagen	Oslo	from €112	16½	7	DFDS Seaways
Fredrikshavn	Oslo	from €29	12	7	Stena Line
Hirtshals	Bergen	from €30	19½	3	Fjord Line
Hirtshals	Kristiansand	from €39	2¼-3¼	up to 14	Color Line & Fjord Line
Hirtshals	Larvik	from €49.50	3¾	up to 14	Color Line
Hirtshals	Stavanger	from €72	12	4	Fjord Line

RAIL PASSES

In addition to the websites listed below, details about rail passes can also be found at www.railpass.com.

InterRail Passes

InterRail (www.interrail.net) passes are available to people who have lived in Europe for six months or more. They can be bought at most major stations and student travel outlets, as well as online.

InterRail has a Global Pass encompassing 30 countries that comes in four versions, ranging from five days of travel made within 10 days to a full month's travel. These in turn come in three prices: adult 1st class, adult 2nd class and youth 2nd class. The one-month pass costs, respectively, €792/528/352; children (aged four to 11 years) travel for half the cost of the adult fare. Youth passes are for people aged 12 to 25. Children aged three and under travel for free.

The InterRail one-country pass for Norway can be used for three, four, six or eight days in one month. For the eight-day pass you pay €310/155/202 per adult/child/youth.

Eurail Passes

Eurail (www.eurail.com) passes are for those who've been in Europe for less than six months and are supposed to be bought outside Europe. They're available from leading travel agencies and online.

Eurail Global Passes are good for travel in 21 European countries (not including the UK); forget it if you intend to travel mainly in Norway. Passes are valid for 10 or 15 days within a two-month period, 15 or 21 consecutive days, or for one, two or three months.

The Eurail Select Pass provides between five and 15 days of unlimited travel within a two-month period in three to five bordering countries (from a total of 19 possible countries). As with Global Passes, those aged 26 and over pay for a 1st-class pass, while those aged under 26 can get a cheaper 2nd-class pass.

Eurail also offers a Norway national pass, a two-country regional pass (Norway and Sweden) and a Scandinavia Rail Pass (valid for travel in Norway, Sweden, Finland and Denmark). For these passes, you choose from between three and 10 days' train travel in a one- or two-month period. The adult eight-day national pass (valid for one month) costs €292. Regional passes come in three versions: 1st-class adult, 2nd-class adult saver (for two or more adults travelling together) and 2nd-class youth.

Scantours (www.scantours.com) US company with an extensive range of short tours in Norway.

Taber Holidays (www.taber hols.co.uk) Year-round tours from the UK.

GETTING AROUND

Norway has an extremely efficient public transport system and its trains, buses and ferries are often timed to link with each other. The handy *NSB Togruter*, available free at most train stations, details rail timetables and includes information on connecting buses. Boat and bus departures vary with the season and the day (services on Saturday are particularly sparse, although less so in the summer high season), so pick up the latest *ruteplan* (timetables) from regional tourist offices.

Rail lines reach as far north as Bodø (you can also reach Narvik by rail from Sweden); further north you're limited to buses and ferries. A fine alternative to land travel is the Hurtigruten coastal ferry, which calls in at every sizable port between Bergen and Kirkenes.

One thing that you should always watch out for, whether you're travelling by bus, train or air, are cheaper *minipris* tickets; they're usually available only if you book early and/or over the internet.

Air

Due to the time and distances involved in overland travel, even budget travellers may want to consider a segment or two by air. The major Norwegian domestic routes are quite competitive, meaning that it is possible (if you're flexible about departure dates and book early) to travel for little more than the equivalent train fare.

Keep an eye out for *minipris* return tickets, which can cost just 10% more than full-fare one-way tickets. In addition, spouses (including gay partners), children aged two to 15, travellers aged under 26, students and senior citizens over 67 years of age may be eligible for significant discounts on some routes – always ask.

Airlines in Norway

Four airlines fly domestic routes:

DOT LT (☎75 58 37 77; www.flydot.no) Small planes with flights to Oslo from Røros and Fagernes.

Norwegian (☎81 52 18 15; www.norwegian.com) Low-cost airline with an extensive network throughout the country.

SAS (☎91 50 54 00; www.sas.no) The largest route network on mainland Norway and the only flights to Longyearbyen (Svalbard).

Widerøe (☎81 00 12 00; www.wideroe.no) A subsidiary of SAS with smaller planes and a handful of flights to smaller regional airports.

Bicycle

Given Norway's great distances, hilly terrain and narrow roads, only serious cyclists engage in extensive cycle touring, but those who do rave about the experience.

Assuming that you've steeled yourself for the challenge of ascending mountain after mountain, the long-distance cyclist's biggest headache will be tunnels (see the boxed text, p443), and there are thousands of them. Most of these, especially in the western fjords, are closed to nonmotorised traffic; in many (although not all) cases there are outdoor bike paths running parallel to the tunnels. If no such path exists, alternative routes may involve a few days' pedalling around a long fjord or over a high mountain pass.

Rural buses, express ferries and nonexpress trains carry bikes for various addi-

tional fees (around Nkr120), but express trains don't allow them at all and international trains treat them as excess baggage (Nkr275). Nor-Way Bussekspress charges a child's fare to transport a bicycle!

Our favourite cycling routes are covered in the boxed text on p29.

The Norwegian government takes cycling seriously enough to have developed an official **Cycling Strategy** (www.sykkelby.no), among the primary goals of which is to increase cycling in larger Norwegian cities.

Hire

Some tourist offices, hostels and camping grounds rent out bicycles to guests, while bicycle shops (sykkelbutikken) are another good place to ask. Rental usually starts at around Nkr60 for an hour and is rarely more than Nkr300 per day, although prices drop if you rent for a few days.

Boat

Norway's excellent system of ferries connects otherwise inaccessible, isolated communities with an extensive network of car ferries crisscrossing the fjords; express boats link the country's offshore islands to the mainland. Most ferries accommodate motor vehicles, but express coastal services normally take only foot passengers and cyclists, as do the lake steamers.

Highway ferries are subsidised and therefore aren't overly expensive (at least in a Norwegian context), but long queues and delays are possible at popular crossings in summer. They do, however, run deep into the night, especially in summer, and some run around the clock, although departures in the middle of the night are less frequent. Details on schedules and prices for vehicle

ferries and lake steamers are provided in the timetables published by the Norwegian Tourist Board, or *Rutebok for Norge*. Tourist offices can also provide timetables for local ferries.

Canal Trips

Southern Norway's Telemark region has an extensive network of canals, rivers and lakes. There are regular ferry services or you can travel using your own boat. See the boxed text on p112 for details.

Hurtigruten Coastal Ferry

For more than a century, Norway's legendary **Hurtigruten coastal ferry** (☎81 00 30 30; www.hurtigruten.com) has served as a lifeline linking coastal towns and villages and it's now one of the most popular ways to explore Norway. Year in, year out, one of 11 Hurtigruten ferries heads north from Bergen every night of the year, pulling into 35 ports on its six-day journey to Kirkenes, where it then turns around and heads back south. The return journey takes 11 days and covers a distance of 5200km. In agreeable weather (which is by no means guaranteed) the fjord and mountain scenery along the way is nothing short of spectacular. Most of the ships are modern, others are showing their age; the oldest ship dates from 1956, but all were substantially remodelled in the 1990s.

Onboard, meals are served in the dining room and you can buy snacks and light meals in the cafeteria.

FARES

Long-haul Hurtigruten trips can be booked online, while all tickets can be purchased from most Norwegian travel agencies. The Hurtigruten website carries a full list of international sales agents. You can also purchase tickets through **Fjord Tours** (☎81 56 82 22; www.fjordtours.no).

THE HURTIGRUTEN – SLOW TRAVEL?

Although the Hurtigruten route is a marvellous journey, some travellers are keen to emphasise that it's more useful as a means of getting from one town to the next than it is for sightseeing at towns along the route, as the ferry usually only stops in ports for 15 to 60 minutes and these times can be cut shorter if the ferry is behind schedule. As one traveller noted: 'There was only one stop which gave any opportunity to visit a town, Trondheim, but that was at 6am till 9.30am... The attitude of the ship was geared to meeting the route times.' It is important to keep in mind that even though the majority of passengers are tourists, the Hurtigruten is a regular ferry service not a tour.

Summer fares, which run from mid-April to mid-September, are considerably more expensive than winter prices. Prices depend on the type of cabin, which range from those without a view to supremely comfortable suites. Sample fares (per person in a twin-bedded cabin):

Bergen–Kirkenes–Bergen From Nkr9506 (November to February) up to Nkr14,056 (June and July).

Bergen–Kirkenes Nkr6654 to Nkr9839.

Kirkenes–Bergen Nkr5228 to Nkr7731.

It is also possible, of course, to book shorter legs, although you'll probably need to do this once in Norway; the Hurtigruten website makes shorter-haul bookings near-on impossible. Cars can also be carried for an extra fee. Children aged four to 16, students, and seniors over the age of 67 all receive a 50% discount, as do accompanying spouses and people aged 16 to 25. Ask also about cheaper, 21-day coastal passes if you're aged between 16 and 26 years.

EXCURSIONS

It's possible to break up the trip with shore excursions, especially if you're travelling the entire route. The excursions, which are organised by the shipping company, may only be available on either

northbound or southbound routes – there are 24 northbound and 15 southbound excursions, although many are seasonal and not available year-round. Options range from city tours, cruises deep into the interior fjord network, a bus up to Nordkapp or a trip to the Russian border from Kirkenes to activities such as dog-sledding and snowmobiling. The Hurtigruten website has a full list, with prices.

These excursions offer fairly good value but, in a few cases, you'll miss segments of the coastal scenery.

Yacht

Exploring the Norwegian coastline aboard your own yacht is one of life's more pleasurable experiences, although harsh weather conditions may restrict how far north you go. Almost every town along Norway's southern coast has an excellent *gjestehavn* (guest harbour) where the facilities include showers, toilets, electricity and laundries as a bare minimum, while some offer bicycle hire and wireless internet. Standard mooring fees generally range from Nkr120 to Nkr175 per 24 hours.

Bus

Buses on Norway's extensive long-distance bus network

are comfortable and make a habit of running on time.

Nor-Way Bussekspress (✆81 54 44 44; www.nor-way.no) operates the largest network of express buses in Norway, with routes connecting most towns and cities. There are also a number of independent long-distance companies that provide similar prices and levels of service.

Considerably cheaper are buses operated by **Lavprisekspressen** (✆67 98 04 80; www.lavprisekspressen.no, in Norwegian), which sells tickets over the internet. Its buses run along the coast between Oslo and Stavanger (via Kristiansand and most towns in between) and along two north–south corridors linking Oslo with Trondheim. If you're online at the right moment, fares between Oslo and Trondheim can cost as little as Nkr49, and even its more expensive tickets are often significantly cheaper than those of its competitors.

In northern Norway, there are several Togbuss (train–bus) routes, while elsewhere there's a host of local buses, most of which are confined to a single *fylke* (county). Most local and some long-distance bus schedules are drastically reduced everywhere in Norway on Saturday, Sunday and in the low season (usually mid-August to mid-June).

To get a complete listing of bus timetables (and some prices) throughout the country, pick up a copy of the free *Rutehefte* from any reasonably sized bus station and some tourist offices. All bus stations and tourist offices have smaller timetables for the relevant routes passing through town.

Costs & Reservations

Advance reservations are rarely required in Norway and Nor-Way Bussekspress even has a 'Seat Guarantee – No Reservation' belief in its ability to get you where you want to get to at the time of your choosing. That said, you're more likely to find cheaper fares the earlier you book.

Buying tickets over the internet is usually the best way to get the cheapest fare, and online bookings are often the only option for Lavpriseks-spressen buses. Tickets are also sold on most buses or in advance at the bus station, and fares are based on the distance travelled, averaging around Nkr175 for the first 100km. Some bus companies quote bus fares excluding any ferry costs, so always check.

Many bus companies offer student, child, senior and family discounts of 25% to 50%, so it pays to ask when purchasing. Groups (including two people travelling together) may also be eligible for discounts.

In northern Norway, holders of InterRail and Eurail passes (see the boxed text, p438) are also often eligible for discounts on some routes.

In summer, special *mini-pris* tickets are frequently offered for some of the more popular long-distance services if you book early.

Car & Motorcycle

There are no special requirements for bringing your car to Norway. For details on ferry services to Norway from other European countries, see p436. Main highways, such as the E16 from Oslo to Bergen and the entire E6 from Oslo to Kirkenes, are open year-round; the same cannot be said for smaller, often more scenic mountain roads that generally only open from June to September, snow conditions permitting. **Vegmeld-ingssentralen** (☎175), Statens Vegvesen's 24-hour Road User Information Centre, provides up-to-date advice on road closures and conditions throughout the country.

Automobile Associations

By reciprocal agreement, members affiliated with AIT (Alliance Internationale de Tourisme) national automobile associations are eligible for 24-hour breakdown recovery assistance from the **Norges Automobil-Forbund** (NAF; ☎08505, 92 60 85 05; www.naf.no). NAF patrols ply the main roads from mid-June to mid-August. Emergency phones can be found along motorways, in tunnels and at certain mountain passes.

Driving Licence

Short-term visitors may hire a car with only their home country's driving licence. Ask your automobile association for a *lettre de recommendation* (letter of introduction), which entitles you to services offered by affiliated organisations in Norway, usually free of charge. These services may include touring maps and information, help with breakdowns, technical and legal advice etc.

Fuel

Leaded and unleaded petrol and diesel are available at most petrol stations. Although prices fluctuate in keeping with international oil prices, prevailing prices at the time of research ranged from around Nkr11 per litre up to Nkr13. Diesel usually costs around Nkr1 per litre less. You can pay with major credit cards at most service stations.

In towns, petrol stations may be open until 10pm or midnight, but there are some 24-hour services. In rural areas, many stations close in the early evening and don't open at all on weekends. Some have unstaffed 24-hour automatic pumps operated with credit cards.

A word of warning for those driving a diesel vehicle: don't fill up at the pump labelled '*augiftsfri diesel*', which is strictly for boats, tractors etc.

Hire

Norwegian car hire is costly and geared mainly to the business traveller. Walk-in rates for a compact car with 200km per day free start typically approach Nkr1000 per day (including VAT, but insurance starts at Nkr60 per day extra), although per-day rates drop the longer you rent.

In summer, always ask about special offers, as you may be able to get the smallest car (eg VW Polo) for a three- to five-day period for Nkr500 per day with 50km free, or Nkr600 per day with 200km free; each extra kilometre costs Nkr2.50, which quickly adds up. Some major rental agencies also offer weekend rates, which allow you to pick up a car after noon on Friday and keep it until 10am on Monday for around Nkr1200 – be sure it includes unlimited kilometres.

If you'll be using the car for a while, you should seriously consider hiring your car in Sweden and either return it there afterwards, or negotiate a slightly more expensive one-way deal. This is possible through the following online rental agencies, which act as clearing houses for cheap rates from major companies and offer a host of pick-up and drop-off options in Norway and across Europe.

Auto Europe (www.auto-europe.com) US-based operator.

Autos Abroad (www.autos abroad.com) UK-based operator.

Ideamerge (www.ideamerge. com) Information on the Renault company's car-leasing plan, motor-home rental and much more.

The following multinational car rental agencies operate in Norway:

Avis (☎81 56 30 44; www. avis.no, in Norwegian)

Bislet Bilutleie (☎22 60 00 00; www.bislet.no)

Budget (☎81 56 06 00; www. budget.no, in Norwegian)

Europcar (☎67 16 58 20; www.europcar.no, in Norwegian)

	Ålesund	Alta	Bergen	Bodø	Florø	Hammerfest	Harstad	Kautokeino	Kirkenes	Kristiansand	Kristiansund	Lillehammer	Narvik	Odda	Oslo	Røros	Stavanger	Tromsø
Alta	1701																	
Bergen	384	2071																
Bodø	1008	814	1378															
Florø	201	1970	248	1277														
Hammerfest	1845	144	2215	959	2114													
Harstad	1186	557	1556	300	1455	701												
Kautokeino	1827	131	2197	941	2096	276	684											
Kirkenes	2215	519	2585	1329	2484	498	1072	451										
Kristiansand	811	2226	492	1533	652	2370	1711	2352	2740									
Kristiansund	142	1609	517	916	329	1753	1094	1735	2123	867								
Lillehammer	382	1756	439	1063	466	1900	1241	1882	2270	473	396							
Narvik	1190	511	1560	304	1459	655	119	637	1025	1715	1098	1245						
Odda	416	2064	159	1371	320	2208	1549	2190	2578	333	549	362	1553					
Oslo	533	1909	478	1216	512	2053	1394	2035	2423	322	562	168	1398	357				
Røros	401	1569	635	876	535	1713	1054	1695	2083	704	327	263	1058	624	382			
Stavanger	603	2251	179	1558	426	2395	1736	2377	2765	245	736	587	1740	187	453	836		
Tromsø	1440	290	1810	554	1709	435	296	417	805	1965	1348	1495	250	1803	1648	1308	1990	
Trondheim	287	1414	657	721	556	1558	899	1540	1928	812	195	342	903	650	495	155	837	1153

Hertz (☎67 16 80 00; www.hertz.no)

Rent-a-Wreck (☎81 52 20 50; www.rent-a-wreck.no)

SixT (☎81 52 24 66; www.sixt.no)

Insurance

Third-party car insurance (unlimited cover for personal injury and Nkr1,000,000 for property damage) is compulsory and, if you're bringing a vehicle from abroad, you'll have fewer headaches with an insurance company Green Card. Ensure that your vehicle is insured for ferry crossings.

If you're renting, it's worth paying extra for comprehensive insurance – in the case of even a small accident, the difference between having to pay Nkr1000 and Nkr8000 is considerable.

Road Conditions

If Norway were Nepal they'd have built a road to the top of (or underneath) Mt Everest. There are roads that can inspire nothing but profound admiration for the engineering expertise involved. The longest tunnels link adjacent valleys, while shorter tunnels drill through rocky impediments to straighten routes. To get an idea of just how hard-won were Norway's roads and tunnels through the mountains, visit the Norwegian Museum of Road History in Hunderfossen, outside Lillehammer.

Most tunnels are lit and many longer ones have exhaust fans to remove fumes, while others are lined with padded insulation to absorb both fumes and sound. Motorcyclists must be wary of fumes in longer tunnels and may want to avoid them where possible.

We do, however, have two complaints. For all their considerable expertise in road-building, Norway's transport authorities seem incapable of understanding the frustration of sitting behind a slow vehicle for an hour or more. More overtaking lanes, please!

And when you've spent four hours going just 200km along a major, though single-lane, highway, it's galling to say the least to have to pay a toll (up to Nkr150) for the privilege.

Road Hazards

Older roads and mountain routes are likely to be narrow, with multiple hairpin bends and very steep gradients. Although most areas are accessible by car (and very often tour bus), some of the less-used routes have poor or untarred surfaces only suitable for 4WD vehicles, and some seemingly normal roads can narrow sharply with very little warning. On some mountain roads, caravans and campervans are forbidden or advisable only for experienced drivers, as it may be necessary to reverse in order to allow approaching traffic to pass. Restricted roads for caravans are outlined on a map published by **Vegdirektoratet** (☏02030; www.vegvesen.no); its website also has a handy route planner.

If you're expecting snowy or icy conditions, use studded tyres or carry snow chains.

Road Rules

For more detail than you probably need, there's a downloadable PDF of Norway's road rules on the website for **Vegdirektoratet** (www.vegvesen.no); follow the links to 'Traffic', then 'Traffic Rules'.

Blood-alcohol limit The limit is 0.02%. Mobile breath-testing stations are reasonably common, and violators are subject to severe fines and/or imprisonment. Because establishments serving alcohol may legally share liability in the case of an accident, you may not be served even a small glass of beer if the server or bartender knows you're driving.

Foreign vehicles Should bear an oval-shaped nationality sticker on the back. UK-registered vehicles must carry a vehicle registration document (Form V5), or a Certificate of Registration (Form V379), available from the DVLA in the UK. For vehicles not registered in the driver's name, you'll require written permission from the registered owner.

Headlights The use of dipped headlights (including on motorcycles) is required at all times and right-hand-drive vehicles must (in theory) have beam deflectors affixed to their headlight in order to avoid blinding oncoming traffic.

Legal driving age for cars 18 years.

Legal driving age for motorcycles & scooters Ranges from 16 to 21 (depending on the motorcycle's power). A licence is required.

Motorcycle parking Motorcycles may not be parked on the pavement (sidewalk) and are subject to the same parking regulations as cars.

Red warning triangles Compulsory in all vehicles for use in the event of breakdown.

Roundabouts (traffic circles) Give way to cars coming from the right, which are liable to shoot across your bows 'like a troll from a box', as one Norwegian told us.

Side of the road Drive on the right side.

Speed limits The national speed limit is 80km/h on the open road, but pass a house or place of business and the limit drops to 70km/h or even 60km/h. Through villages limits range from 50km/h to 60km/h and, in residential areas, the limit is 30km/h. A few roads have segments allowing 90km/h, and you can drive at 100km/h on a small part of the E6 – bliss! The speed limit for caravans (and cars pulling trailers) is usually 10km/h less than for cars.

TUNNELS IN NORWAY

In November 2000 the world's longest road tunnel, from Lærdal to Aurland (24.51km long, 7.59km longer than the St Gotthard tunnel in Switzerland), was completed at a total cost of Nkr1082 million. There are no tolls to use the tunnel as it was paid for entirely by the national government. The two-lane tunnel, part of the vital E16 road connecting Oslo and Bergen, reduces the difficulties of winter driving and replaces the lengthy Gudvangen–Lærdal ferry route. It was drilled through very hard pre-Cambrian gneiss, with over 1400m of overhead rock at one point. There's a treatment plant for dust and nitrogen dioxide in the tunnel, 34 gigantic ventilation fans, emergency phones every 500m and three bizarre 'galleries' with blue lighting to 'liven up' the 20-minute trip.

Motorists should tune into NRK radio when driving through the tunnel (yes, there are transmitters inside!) in case of emergency.

Norway has three out of the 10 longest road tunnels in the world; in addition to Lærdal, they are Gudvangentunnelen in Sogn og Fjordane (11.43km, also on the E16) and Folgefonntunnelen in Hardanger (11.15km, on Rv551 and passing beneath the Folgefonn icecap).

Norway also has a number of undersea tunnels, which typically bore over 200m below the sea bed; Eiksundtunnelen (7.76km long, connecting Eika island to the mainland in Møre og Romsdal) is the world's deepest undersea tunnel at 287m below sea level. Other long undersea tunnels include Bømlafjordtunnel (7.89km long, in southwestern Norway, connecting Føyno island), Oslofjordtunnelen (7.2km, on the Rv23, south of Oslo) and Nordkapptunnelen (6.87km, on the E69 and connecting Magerøya Island to the mainland).

ROAD TOLLS & SPEED CAMERAS

Road Tolls

Around one-quarter of Norway's road construction budget comes from road tolls, and new segments of highway and even some not-so-recently built tunnels and bridges must be paid off in user tolls. Either way, you'll soon become accustomed to the ominous 'Bomstasjon – Toll Plaza' signs.

Apart from some smaller country roads, most of Norway's toll stations are automated. If you're driving a Norwegian rental car, they'll be fitted with an automatic sensor – after you return your car, the hire company adds up the accumulated tolls and then charges it to your credit card.

If, however, you're driving a foreign-registered car (including some rental cars from other countries), you're expected to either register your credit card in advance online at www.autopass.no (whereupon you pay a Nkr200 deposit) and the tolls are later deducted. The alternative is to stop at one of the pay stations (sometimes the first petrol station after the toll station) to pay the fee there. If you don't pay, the authorities will attempt to track you down once you return to your home country (often as much as six months later) and you'll be expected to pay both the toll and a penalty fee of Nkr300. Motorcycles are usually exempt from the tolls, but check at the nearest pay station.

Speed Cameras

The lethargy-inspiring national speed limits may seem laborious by your home standards, but avoid the temptation to drive faster as they're taken very seriously. Mobile police units lurk at the side of the roads. Watch for signs designating *Automatisk Trafikkontrol*, which means that there's a speed camera ahead; these big and ugly grey boxes have no mercy at all – you'll be nabbed for even 5km/h over the limit. Fines range from Nkr1000 to well over Nkr10,000.

If you're in a rental car, the fine will be deducted from your credit card. If you're in a foreign-registered vehicle, you may be tracked back to your home country.

Road Signs

Most road signs are international, but a white M on a blue background indicates a passing place on a single-track road (the 'm' stands for *møteplass*). Others worth watching out for:

All Stans Forbudt (No Stopping)

Enveiskjøring (One Way)

Kjøring Forbudt (Driving Prohibited or Do Not Enter)

Parkering Forbudt (No Parking)

Rekverk Mangler (Guardrail Missing)

Vehicle Ferries

While travelling along the scenic but mountainous and fjord-studded west coast may be spectacular, it also requires numerous ferry crossings that can prove time-consuming and costly. For a complete list of ferry schedules and fares, get hold of the Nkr225 *Rutebok for Norge*, a phone-book-sized transport guide sold in bookshops and larger Narvesen kiosks. Otherwise, order directly from **Norsk Reiseinformasjon** (☎22 47 73 40; www.reiseinfo.no, in Norwegian; Karl Johans gate 12a, 0154 Oslo), or download it at www.rutebok.no.

Hitching

Hitching isn't entirely safe and we don't recommend it. Travellers who decide to hitch should understand they're taking a potentially serious risk. People who choose to hitch will be safer if they travel in pairs and let someone know where they're planning to go.

If you're determined to hitch, you'll find Norwegians generally friendly, and they understand that not all foreigners enjoy an expense-account budget or earn Norwegian salaries. Your chances of success are better on main highways, but you still may wait for hours in bad weather. One approach is to ask for rides from truck drivers at ferry terminals and petrol stations; that way, you'll normally have a place to keep warm and dry while you wait.

Local Transport

Bus

Nearly every town in Norway supports a network of local buses, which circulate around the town centre and also connect it with outlying areas. In many smaller towns, the local bus terminal is adjacent to the train station, ferry quay and/or long-distance bus terminal. Fares range from Nkr18 to Nkr30 per ride. Day- or multitrip tickets are also available.

Taxi

Taxis are best hailed around taxi ranks, but you can also reserve one by phone; hotels and tourist offices always have the numbers for local companies. If you're phoning for a taxi immediately, remember that charges begin at the moment the call is taken. Daytime fares, which apply from 6am to 7pm on weekdays and from 6am to 3pm on Saturday, cost from around Nkr40 at flagfall (more in larger cities), plus Nkr15 to Nkr25 per kilometre. Weekday evening fares are 22% higher, and in the early morning, on Saturday afternoon and evening, and on Sunday, they're 30% higher. On holidays, you'll pay 45% more. In some places, you may find 'maxi-taxis', which can carry up to eight passengers for about the same price.

Tours

Norway has some outstanding local tours that enable you to make the most of limited time and which save the hassle of having to arrange your own transport. In every tourist office you'll find an exhaustive collection of leaflets, folders and brochures outlining their offerings in the immediate area. Aside from the myriad local tours, the following are of interest:

Den Norske Turistforening (DNT; Norwegian Mountain Touring Club; ☑ 22 82 28 22; www.turistforeningen. no) Organises hundreds of year-round adventure trips in the Norwegian mountains, including cycling, fishing, hiking, skiing, glacier hiking, rock and ice-climbing, family activities, hut-to-hut trekking, Svalbard tours, and so on.

Fjord Tours (☑ 81 56 82 22; www.fjordtours.no) Operates the year-round Norway in a Nutshell tour, organised through travel agencies, NSB rail services and tourist offices around southern and western Norway. Itineraries vary, but most involve a one- or two-day excursion taking in the rail line between Bergen or Oslo and Myrdal, the Flåmsbana line to Flåm, a cruise along Nærøyfjord to Gudvangen, a bus to Voss, and then rail trips to Bergen or to Oslo on the overnight train. The itineraries can be taken in whole or in part. It also offers similar deals in Sognefjord, Hardanger, Geiranger and Lysefjord, and a Hurtigruten-focused trip. Check the website for prices.

Fjord1 (☑ 55 90 70 70; www. fjord1.no) A range of tours and ferries in the fjord region.

Norway Fjord Cruise (☑ 57 65 69 99; www.fjord cruise.no) A range of boat cruises throughout the country, including Lofoten, Sognefjord, Hardangerfjord and Svalbard.

For more information on touring the western fjords, see the boxed texts on p164 and p178.

Train

Norwegian State Railways (Norges Statsbaner; NSB; ☑ 81 50 08 88, press 9 for English; www.nsb.no) operates an excellent, though limited, system of lines connecting Oslo with Stavanger, Bergen, Åndalsnes, Trondheim, Fauske and Bodø; lines also connect Sweden with Oslo, Trondheim and Narvik. Most train stations offer luggage lockers for Nkr40 to Nkr75

NATIONAL TOURIST ROUTES

The Norwegian Public Roads Administration has 18 specially designated roads (covering 1850km) known as 'National Tourist Routes' (www.turistveg.no/index. asp?lang=eng), each one passing through signature Norwegian landscapes. The plan is to set up regular lookouts and information points along these pre-existing routes. Of most interest to visitors of this scheme is the easy identification of some of Norway's most scenic routes, and help in planning and making the most of your trip along Norway's most picturesque drives.

Of the 18 roads, some of our favourites:

» Sognefjellet Road (Rv55; p147)

» Rv86 and Rv862 on the island of Senja (p324)

» Kystriksveien coastal route between Stokkvågen, west of Mo i Rana, and Storvik, south of Bodø (p285)

» E10 through Lofoten (p291)

» West coast road through Vesterålen from Risøyhamn to Andenes (see the boxed text, p308)

» Gamle Strynefjellsvegen between Grotli in Oppland and Videseter in Sogn og Fjordane (Rv258; see the boxed text, p219)

» Trollstigen (p223), south of Åndalsnes

» Atlantic Ocean Road (see the boxed text, p238)

» Two routes through Hardanger from Halne in the east to Steinsdalfossen (Rv7; p176) and Jondal (Rv550; p183) in the west

MINIPRIS – A TRAVELLER'S BEST FRIEND

If you plan to travel on longer routes by train through Norway and know your itinerary in advance, the following information will save you hundreds of kroner. On every route, for every departure, Norwegian State Railways sets aside a limited number of tickets known as *minipris*. Those who book the earliest can get just about any route for just Nkr199. Once those are exhausted, the next batch of *minipris* tickets goes for Nkr299 and so on. These tickets cannot be purchased at ticket counters and must instead be bought over the internet (www.nsb.no) or in ticket-vending machines at train stations. Remember that *minipris* tickets may only be purchased in advance (minimum one day), reservations are non-refundable and cannot be changed once purchased. In peak seasons (especially from mid-June to mid-August) on popular routes, you may need to book up to three weeks in advance to get the cheapest fares. That said, the savings are considerable, often as much as 75% off the full fare.

and many also have baggage storage rooms.

Most long-distance day trains have 1st- and 2nd-class seats and a buffet car or refreshment trolley service. Public phones can be found in all express trains and most intercity trains. Doors are wide and there's space for bulky luggage, such as backpacks or skis.

Reservations sometimes cost an additional Nkr50 and are mandatory on some long-distance routes.

Classes & Costs

On long-distance trains, 2nd-class carriages provide comfortable reclining seats with footrests. First-class carriages, which cost 50% more, offer marginally more space and often a food trol-ley, but they're generally not worth the extra expense.

Travelling by train in Norway is (like everything else) expensive. Indeed, the fact that it often costs less to fly than it does to catch a train puts a dint in Norway's impressive environmental credentials. However, if you learn how to work the *minipris* system, or the train passes (see the boxed text, p438), train travel suddenly becomes affordable. And think of the scenery...

There's a 50% discount on rail travel for people aged 67 and older, for disabled travellers and for children aged between four and 15; children under four travel free. Students get discounts of between 25% and 40%.

On long-distance overnight routes, sleeper compartments (you pay for the whole two-bed compartment) are additional to the standard fares.

Train Passes

For details of rail passes that can be used in Norway (but which should be bought before you arrive in the country), see the boxed text on p438. Eurail has a pass that includes only Norway.

Language

WANT MORE?

For in-depth language information and handy phrases, check out Lonely Planet's *Scandinavian Phrasebook*. You'll find it at **shop.lonelyplanet. com**, or you can buy Lonely Planet's iPhone phrasebooks at the Apple App Store.

The official language of Norway is Norwegian, which belongs to the North Germanic (or Scandinavian) group of languages.

There are two official written forms of Norwegian, known as *Bokmål* (literally 'book language') and *Nynorsk* (or 'new Norwegian'). They are actually quite similar and understood by all speakers. Both varieties are written standards, and are used in written communication (in schools, administration and the media), whereas the spoken language has numerous local dialects. *Bokmål* is predominant in the cities, while *Nynorsk* is more common in the western fjords and the central mountains. It's estimated that out of the five million speakers of Norwegian around 85% use *Bokmål* and about 15% use *Nynorsk*. In this chapter we've used *Bokmål* only.

In northern Norway, around 20,000 people speak Sami, a language of the Finno-Ugric group. It's related to Finnish, Estonian and Hungarian. There are three distinct Sami dialects in Norway – Fell Sami (also called Eastern or Northern Sami), Central Sami and South Sami. Fell Sami is considered the standard Sami language. Most Sami speakers can also communicate in Norwegian.

Pronunciation

Most Norwegian sounds have equivalents in English, and if you read our coloured pronunciation guides as if they were English, you'll be understood. Length is a distinctive feature of Norwegian vowels, as each vowel can be either long or short. Generally, they're long when followed by one consonant and short when followed by two or more conso-

nants. Note that the eu in the pronunciation guides is like the 'ur' in 'nurse', and that ew is pronounced like the 'ee' in 'see' but with pursed lips.

Most Norwegian words have stress on the first syllable, and sometimes there's more than one stressed syllable in a word. In our pronunciation guides the stressed syllables are indicated with italics.

BASICS

Hello.	God dag.	go·daag
Goodbye.	Ha det.	haa·de
Yes.	Ja.	yaa
No.	Nei.	ney
Thank you.	Takk.	tak
Please.	Vær så snill.	veyr saw snil
You're welcome.	Ingen årsak.	ing·en awr·saak
Excuse me.	Unnskyld.	ewn·shewl
Sorry.	Beklager.	bey·klaa·geyr

How are you?
Hvordan har du det?   vor·dan haar doo de

Fine, thanks. And you?
Bra, takk. Og du?   braa tak aw doo

What's your name?
Hva heter du?   vaa hey·ter doo

My name is ...
Jeg heter ...   yai hay·ter ...

Do you speak English?
Snakker du engelsk?   sna·ker doo eyng·elsk

I don't understand.
Jeg forstår ikke.   yai fawr·stawr i·key

ACCOMMODATION

Do you have a ... room?	Finnes det et ...?	fi·nes de et ...
single	enkeltrom	eyn·kelt·rom
double	dobbeltrom	daw·belt·rom

How much is it per night/person?
Hvor mye koster det pr dag/person? — vor mew·e kaws·ter de peyr daag/peyr·son

campsite	campingplass	keym·ping·plas
guesthouse	gjestgiveri	yest·gi·ve·ree
hotel	hotell	hoo·tel
youth hostel	ungdoms-herberge	ong·dawms·heyr·beyrg

air-con	luftkjøling	luft·sheu·ling
bathroom	bad	baad
window	vindu	vin·du

DIRECTIONS

Where is ...?
Hvor er ...? — vor ayr ...

What is the address?
Hva er adressen? — va ayr aa·dre·seyn

Could you write it down, please?
Kan du skrive det? — kan doo skree·ve de

Can you show me (on the map)?
Kan du vise meg (på kartet)? — kan du vee·se ma (paw kar·te)

at the corner	på hjørne	paw yeur·ney
at the traffic lights	i lyskrysset	ee lews·krew·sey
behind	bak	baak
far	langt	laangt
in front of	foran	faw·ran
left	venstre	vens·trey
near (to)	nær	neyr
next to	ved siden av	vey see·den aav
opposite	ovenfor	aw·ven·fawr
right	høyre	hoy·rey
straight ahead	rett fram	ret fram

EATING & DRINKING

A table for (four), please.
Et bord til (fire), takk. — et bawr til (fee·re) tak

What would you recommend?
Hva vil du anbefale? — va vil doo an·be·fa·le

What does it include?
Hva inkluderer det? — va in·kloo·dey·re de

SAMI

Although written Fell Sami includes several accented letters, it still doesn't accurately represent the spoken language – even some Sami people find the written language difficult to learn. For example, giitu (thanks) is pronounced gheech·too – the strongly aspirated 'h' is not written.

Hello.	Buorre beaivi.
Hello.	Ipmel atti. (reply)
Goodbye.	Mana dearvan. (to person leaving)
Goodbye.	Báze dearvan. (to person staying)
Thank you.	Giitu.
You're welcome.	Leage buorre.
Yes.	De lea.
No.	Li.
How are you?	Mot manna?
I'm fine.	Buorre dat manna.

1	okta
2	guokte
3	golbma
4	njeallje
5	vihta
6	guhta
7	cieza
8	gávcci
9	ovcci
10	logi

I don't eat (meat).
Jeg spise ikke (kjøtt). — yai (spi·se) i·key (sheut)

Cheers!
Skål! — skawl

I'd like the bill, please.
Kan jeg få regningen, takk. — kan yai faw rai·ning·en tak

Key Words

bar	bar	bar
bottle	flaske	flas·ke
breakfast	frokost	fro·kost
cold	kald	kal
cup	kopp	kawp
dinner	middag	mi·da
food	mat	maat

grapes	druer	droo·er
mushroom	sopp	sop
onion	løk	leuk
orange	appelsin	aa·pel·sin
pineapple	ananas	aa·naa·nas
potato	potet	po·tet
strawberries	jordbær	yor·bar
tomato	tomat	too·maat
vegetable	grønnsak	greun·sak

Signs

Åpen	Open
Damer	Women
Forbudt	Prohibited
Herrer	Men
Informasjon	Information
Inngang	Entrance
Stengt	Closed
Toaletter	Toilets
Utgang	Exit

fork	gaffel	ga·fel
glass	glass	glas
grocery store	matbutikk	maat·boo·tik
hot (warm)	het	heyt
knife	kniv	kniv
lunch	lunsj	loonsh
market	marked	mar·ked
menu	meny	me·new
restaurant	restaurant	res·tu·rang
spoon	skje	shai
vegetarian	vegetariansk	ve·ge·ta·ree·ansk
with/without	med/uten	mey/u·ten

Other

butter	smør	smeur
cake	kake	ka·ke
casserole	gryterett	grew·te·ret
cheese	ost	ost
chocolate	sjokolade	sho·kaa·laa·de
cold buffet	koldtbord	kolt·bawr
cream	fløte	fleu·te
eggs	egg	eg
ice cream	is	ees
jam	syltetøy	sewl·te·toy
nuts	nøtter	neu·ter
pancake	pannekake	pa·ne·kaa·ke
pâté	postei	po·stai
salad	salat	sa·lat
sugar	sukker	soo·ker
sweetbread	brissel	bri·sel

Meat & Fish

beef	oksekjøtt	ook·se·sheut
chicken	kylling	chew·ling
cod	torsk	tawshk
fish	fisk	fisk
hake	lysing	lew·sing
halibut	hellefisk	he·le·fisk
ham	skinke	shin·ke
herring	sild	seel
lamb	sauekjøtt	sow·e·sheut
mackerel	makrell	ma·krel
meat	kjøtt	sheut
pork	svinekjøtt	svee·ne·sheut
sardine	brisling	brees·ling
sausage	pølse	peul·se
shrimp	reker	rey·ker
tuna	tunfisk	tun·fisk

Drinks

beer	øl	eul
coffee	kaffe	kaa·fe
(orange) juice	(appelsin)jus	(a·pel·seen·)joos
milk	melk	melk
red wine	rødvin	reu·veen
soft drink	brus	broos
tea	te	te
(mineral) water	(mineral)vann	(mi·ne·ral·)van
white wine	hvitvin	veet·veen

Fruit & Vegetables

apple	eple	ep·le
banana	banan	baa·naan
fruit	frukt	frookt

EMERGENCIES

Help!	
Hjelp!	yelp
Go away!	
Forsvinn!	fawr·svin
I'm lost.	
Jeg har gått meg vill.	yai har gawt mai vil
There's been an accident.	
Det har skjedd en ulykke.	de har shed en oo·lew·ke

Call ...!	Ring ...!	ring ...
a doctor	en lege	en le·ge
the police	politiet	po·lee·tee·ay

I'm ill.
Jeg er syk.　　　　yai er sewk

It hurts here.
Det gjør vondt her.　　de yeur·vont heyr

I'm allergic to (antibiotics).
Jeg er allergisk mot　　yai eyr a·ler·gisk mot
(antibiotika).　　　　(an·ti·bi·o·ti·ka)

SHOPPING & SERVICES

I'm looking for ...
Jeg leter etter ...　　yai ley·ter e·ter ...

May I look at it?
Kan jeg få se på det?　kan yai faw se paw de

I don't like it.
Det liker jeg ikke.　　de lee·ker yai i·key

How much is it?
Hvor mye koster det?　vor mew·e kaws·ter de

That's too expensive.
Det er for dyrt.　　　de eyr fawr dewrt

What's your lowest price?
Hva er din absolutt　　va eyr deen ab·saw·lut
laveste pris?　　　　la·ves·te prees

There's a mistake in the bill.
Det er en feil på　　　de eyr en fail paw
regningen.　　　　　rai·ning·en

ATM	minibank	mee·ni·bank
credit card	kredittkort	kre·dit·kawrt
internet cafe	Internettkafé	in·ter·net·ka·fe
post office	postkontor	pawst·kawn·tawr
mobile phone	mobiltelefon	mo·beel·te·le·fon
tourist office	turist- informasjon	tu·reest· in·fawr·ma·shawn

TIME & DATES

What time is it?
Hva er klokka?　　　vaa eyr klaw·ka

It's (two) o'clock.
Klokka er (to).　　　klaw·ka eyr (taw)

Question Words		
How?	Hvordan?	vor·dan
What?	Hva?	vaa
When?	Når?	nawr
Where?	Hvor?	vor
Which?	Hvilken?	veel·keyn
Who?	Hvem?	vem
Why?	Hvorfor?	vor·fawr

Half past (one).
Halv (to).　　　　　haal (taw)
(lit: half (two))

in the morning
om formiddagen　　awm fawr·mi·dan

in the afternoon
om ettermiddagen　　awm e·ter·mi·dan

in the evening
om kvelden　　　　awm kve·len

yesterday	i går	ee gawr
today	i dag	ee daag
tomorrow	i morgen	ee maw·ren

Monday	mandag	maan·daa
Tuesday	tirsdag	teers·daa
Wednesday	onsdag	awns·daa
Thursday	torsdag	tawrs·daa
Friday	fredag	frey·daa
Saturday	lørdag	leu·daa
Sunday	søndag	seun·daa

January	januar	yaa·nu·aar
February	februar	fe·broo·aar
March	mars	maars
April	april	aa·preel
May	mai	mai
June	juni	yoo·nee
July	juli	yoo·lee
August	august	ow·goost
September	september	sep·tem·ber
October	oktober	awk·taw·ber
November	november	naw·veym·ber
December	desember	de·seym·ber

TRANSPORT

Public Transport

boat	båt	bawt
bus	buss	bus
plane	fly	flew
taxi	drosje	draw·shey
train	tåg	tawg

1st class	førsteklasse	feur·ste·kla·se
economy class	økonomi- klasse	eu·ko·no·mi· kla·se
one-way ticket	enveisbillett	en·veys·bee·let
return ticket	returbillett	re·toor·bee·let

Numbers

1	*en*	en
2	*to*	taw
3	*tre*	trey
4	*fire*	fee·re
5	*fem*	fem
6	*seks*	seks
7	*sju*	shoo
8	*åtte*	aw·te
9	*ni*	nee
10	*ti*	tee
20	*tjue*	shoo·e
30	*tretti*	trey·tee
40	*førti*	feur·tee
50	*femti*	fem·tee
60	*seksti*	seks·tee
70	*sytti*	sew·tee
80	*åtti*	aw·tee
90	*nitti*	nee·tee
100	*hundre*	hun·dre
1000	*tusen*	tu·sen

I want to go to …
Jeg skal til …   yai skaal til …

At what time does it arrive/leave?
Når ankommer/   nawr an·kaw·mer/
går den?   gawr den

Does it stop at (Majorstua)?
Stopper denne på   staw·per dey·ne paw
(Majorstua)?   (maa·yoor·stu·a)

Please tell me when we get to (Oslo).
Kan du si fra når vi   kan doo see fraa nawr vee
kommer til (Oslo)?   kaw·mer til (os·law)

Please stop here.
Vær så snill å stoppe   veyr saw snil aw sto·pe
her.   heyr

first	*første*	feur·ste
last	*siste*	si·ste
next	*neste*	ne·ste

baggage claim	*bagasjeskranke*	ba·gaa·shes·kran·ke
bus stop	*busstopp*	bus·stawp
cancelled	*avbestillt*	av·be·stilt
delayed	*forsinket*	fawr·sin·ket
left-luggage office	*gjenglemt bagasjeskranke*	yen·glemt ba·gaa·shes·kran·ke
reservation	*reservasjon*	re·ser·va·shawn
train station	*stasjon*	staa·shawn

Driving & Cycling

I'd like to hire a …	*Jeg vil gjerne leie en …*	yai vil yer·ne lai·e·en …
4WD	*fire-hjulstrekk*	fee·re·hyools·trek
bicycle	*sykkel*	sew·kel
car	*bil*	beel
motorcycle	*motor-sykkel*	maw·tor·sew·kel
child seat	*barnesete*	bar·na·se·te
diesel	*diesel*	dee·sel
mechanic	*verksted*	verk·stey
petrol/gas	*bensin*	ben·seen
service station	*bensin-stasjon*	ben·seen·staa·shawn

Is this the road to (Gol)?
Er dette veien til (Gol)?   eyr de·tey vai·en til (gol)

(How long) Can I park here?
(Hvor lenge) Kan bilen   (vor leng·e) kan bee·len
min stå her?   min staw her

I have a flat tyre.
Jeg har punktert.   yai haar poonk·tert

I've run out of petrol.
Jeg har gått tom for   yai haar gawt tawm fawr
bensin.   ben·seen

I've had an accident.
Jeg har vært i en   yai haar veyrt ee en
ulykke.   oo·lew·ke

GLOSSARY

You may encounter some of the following terms and abbreviations during your travels in Norway. Note that although the letters ø and å fall at the end of the Norwegian alphabet, we have in-cluded them under 'o' and 'a' respectively to make things easier for non-Norwegian-speaking readers.

allemannsretten – 'every man's right'; a tradition/law allowing universal access to private property (with some restrictions), public lands and wilderness areas

apótek – pharmacy

Arctic Menu – scheme to encourage the use of the region's natural ingredients in food served by restaurants

arête – a sharp ridge between two valley glaciers

arsarnerit – name given by Inuit (Eskimos) to aurora borealis

aurora borealis – northern lights

automatisk trafikkontrol – speed camera

bakke – hill

berg – mountain

bibliotek – library

billett – ticket

bilutleie – car-hire company

blodveien – literally 'blood road'; nickname given to the Arctic Highway during construction due to the high number of worker fatalities

bokhandel – bookshop

bro, bru – bridge

brygge – quay, wharf

bryggeri – brewery

bukt, bukta – bay

bunad – the Norwegian national costume; each region has its own version

by – town

calving – the breaking off of icebergs from tidewater glaciers

cirque – an amphitheatre scoured out by a glacier

crevasse – a fissure in moving ice, which may be hidden under snow

dal – valley

DNT – Den Norske Turistforening (Norwegian Mountain Touring Club)

domkirke – cathedral

dressin – rail bikes or bicycles on bogies

elg – elk (moose)

elv, elva – river

Fata Morgana – Arctic phenomenon whereby distant features do not appear out of focus

fell, fjall, fjell – mountain

festning – fort, fortress

fiskeskrue – fish press

fjord – drowned glacial valley

fonn – glacial icefield

forening – club, association

foss – waterfall

friluft – outdoor, open-air

Fv – Fylkesvei; county road

fylke – county

fyr – lighthouse

galleriet – gallery, shopping arcade

gamla, gamle, gammel – old

gamlebyen – the 'old town'

gamma, gammen – Sami tent or turf hut, sometimes partially underground

gård, gard – farm, courtyard

gata, gate – street (often abbreviated to g or gt)

gatekjøkken – literally 'street kitchen'; street kiosk/stall/grill

gjestehavn – 'guest harbour'; the area of a port town where visiting boats and yachts moor

gjestehus – guesthouse

gravlund – cemetery

grønlandssel – harp seal

gruva, gruve – mine

hage – garden

halvøya – peninsula

Hanseatic League – association of German traders that dominated trade in Bergen from the 12th to 16th centuries

hav – ocean

havn – harbour

honnør – senior citizen

Hurtigruten – literally 'the Express Route'; a system of coastal steamers plying the route between Bergen and Kirkenes

hus – house

hval – whale

hvalross – walrus

hytte – cabin, hut or chalet

hytteutleie – hut-hire company

ice floe – a flat chunk of floating sea ice or small iceberg

icecap, icefield – a stable zone of accumulated and

compressed snow and ice, and a source of valley glaciers; an icecap generally covers a larger area than an icefield

isbjørn – polar bear

jernbanestasjon – train station

jerv – wolverine

joik – 'song of the plains'; religious Sami tradition

jul – Christmas

kai, kaia – quay

kart – map

kerk, kirke, kirkja, kirkje – church

kort – card

krambua – general store

krone – Norwegian currency unit

kulturhus – a large complex containing cinemas, public library, museums etc

kvadraturen – the square grid pattern of streets measuring six long blocks by nine shorter blocks

kyst – coast

landsmål – Norwegian dialect

lavvo, lavvu – tepee; Sami tent dwelling

legevakten – clinic

lemen – lemming

libris – books; indicates a bookshop

lundefugl – puffin

magasin – department store

marka – the forested hills around Oslo

mil – Norwegian mile measuring 10km

minipris – cheaper fares, usually for transport

MOMS – Value Added Tax/sales tax

moskus-okse – musk oxen

M/S – motorskip or motor ship; designates ship names

museet – museum

MVA – see *MOMS*

nasjonalpark – national park

navvy – railway worker

nord – north

nordlys – northern lights (aurora borealis)

Norge – Norway

Norges Turistråd – Norwegian Tourist Board, formerly NORTRA

Norsk – Norwegian

Norway in a Nutshell – a range of tours that give high-speed travellers a glimpse of the best of Norway in one or two days

NSB – Norges Statsbaner (Norwegian State Railways)

ny – new

Nynorsk – see *landsmål*

og – and

øst – east

oter – otter

øvre – upper

øy – island

pack ice – floating ice formed by frozen seawater, often creating an impenetrable barrier to navigation

pensjonat – pension, guesthouse

plass – plaza, square

polarsirkelen – Arctic Circle; latitude 66°33'N

Pomor – Russian trading and fishing community from the White Sea, which prospered in northern Norway in the 17th century

rådhus – town hall

reinsdyr – reindeer

reiseliv – local tourist office

riksdaler – old Norwegian currency

rom – signs on roads indicating private rooms/cabins for rent

rorbu – cabin/fishing hut

rutebilstasjon – bus terminal

ruteplan – transport timetable

Rv – Riksvei; national highway

schøtstue – large assembly room where employees of the Hanseatic League met and ate

sentrum – town centre

siida – small Sami communities or bands that hunted and trapped together

sild – herring

sjø – sea

sjøhus – fishing bunkhouse on the docks; many are now available for tourist accommodation

skalds – metaphoric and alliterative works of Norwegian court poets in the 9th and 10th centuries

skerries – offshore archipelago of small rocky islets

skog – forest

sla låm – slope track

slott – castle, palace

snø – snow

solarsteinn –Viking navigational tool used when the sky was overcast or the sun below the horizon

sør – south

spekkhogger – killer whale (orca)

stabbur – raised storehouse

stasjon – station

Statens Kartverk – State Mapping Agency

stavkirke – stave church

steinkobbe – harbour seal

storting – parliament

strand – beach

stuer – trading firm

sund – sound, strait

Sverige – Sweden

sykkel – bicycle

sykkelutleie – bicycle-hire company

taiga – marshy forest

tårn – tower

teater – theatre

telekort – Telenor phone cards

tog – train

togbuss – bus services in Romsdalen and Nordland run by NSB to connect railheads with other popular destinations

torget, torvet – town square

turistkontor – tourist office

ulv – wolf

utleie – hire company

vandrerhjem – youth hostel

vann, vannet, vatn, vatnet – lake

veg, vei – road (often abbreviated to v or vn)

vest – west

vetter – mythical Norwegian guardian spirits of the wildest coastline

vidda, vidde – plateau

Vinmonopolet – government-run shop selling wine and liquor

yoik – see *joik*

behind the scenes

SEND US YOUR FEEDBACK

We love to hear from travellers – your comments keep us on our toes and help make our books better. Our well-travelled team reads every word on what you loved or loathed about this book. Although we cannot reply individually to postal submissions, we always guarantee that your feedback goes straight to the appropriate authors, in time for the next edition. Each person who sends us information is thanked in the next edition – and the most useful submissions are rewarded with a free book.

Visit **lonelyplanet.com/contact** to submit your updates and suggestions or to ask for help. Our award-winning website also features inspirational travel stories, news and discussions.

Note: We may edit, reproduce and incorporate your comments in Lonely Planet products such as guidebooks, websites and digital products, so let us know if you don't want your comments reproduced or your name acknowledged. For a copy of our privacy policy visit lonelyplanet.com/privacy.

OUR READERS

Many thanks to the travellers who used the last edition and wrote to us with helpful hints, useful advice and interesting anecdotes:

Jarl Aanestad, Jennifer Ablett, Marthe Edwarda Bang, E Bell, Bjarke, Cheryl Braunstein, Elisabeth Cato, Wai-chung Chan, Monica DeVold, Ana Felicio, Werner Furrer, Sue & Laurence Hayward, Simone Hilson, Emiel Hoogendijk, Vidar Hovlid, Anders Jeppsson, Thomas van Luijtelaar, Coco Manson, Andre Marcoux, Gyri Midtveit, Berit Nereng, Per Persson, Carol Peterson, Jennifer Pike, Amy Prendergast, Bill Rowntree, Richard Scholes, Pernille Skårbrevik, Marijana Sostaric, Rimco Spanjer, Lea Steder, Mary Steele, Peter Strachan, Christian Stranger-Johannessen, John Taylor, Jonathan Vessey, Guy Voets, Zvi Weizman, Tim Wodskou, Xiang Xin, Agnes van Zundert

AUTHOR THANKS

Anthony Ham

Just about every Norwegian I met was a friendly and unfailingly helpful ambassador for their country – there are too many to name, but I am deeply grateful to all of them. Thanks to my co-authors, Miles, a long-standing companion of the road, and Stuart. At Lonely Planet a big thank you to Carolyn Boicos and Simon Williamson, whose wise editing improved the book. This book is dedicated to Marina and our two girls Carlota and Valentina (who was born not long after I returned home from Norway) – one day we'll explore Svalbard together.

Stuart Butler

In Oslo I would like to thank Linn Saxrud Johansen at the tourist office, Hanne Mårds, Franco Villalba, Alex Belov and Petra Mikulasova for nightlife advice, and Sugaal Rashid and Issak Abdi for pointing me to the best African restaurants. Away from the big city, thanks to Ari Olsen at Kragerø tourist office and Amkristin at the Arendal tourist office. Thanks also to Anthony, Miles, Jo, Anna and all the other Lonely Planet in-housers. Finally, and most importantly, thanks to my wife Heather and to my baby son Jake, who giggled his way up and down many a Norwegian mountain.

Miles Roddis

My chapters are for Eric Parkinson, who enjoys the wild outdoors. As always, huge thanks to Ingrid, who drove the breadth and nearly the length of Norway. Also to Hilde Glomstad for hospitality, Trondheim tips and an unforgettable afternoon of berry and mushroom picking. Major thanks too to Knut

Hansfold, a sparky spokesperson for his native Tromsø and the north, for ideas and for kindly reading through my final text. Helpful tourist office staff are, alas, too numerous to mention by name. Well informed and many as articulate in English as I am, they were a delight to relate to.

Climate map data adapted from Peel MC, Finlayson BL & McMahon TA (2007) 'Updated World Map of the Köppen-Geiger Climate Classification', *Hydrology and Earth System Sciences*, 11, 163344.

Cover photograph: Lillehammer, Norway, Per-Andre Hoffman/Getty. Many of the images in this guide are available for licensing from Lonely Planet Images: www.lonelyplanet images.com.

BEHIND THE SCENES

THIS BOOK

This 5th edition of Lonely Planet's *Norway* guidebook was coordinated by Anthony Ham, who also coordinated the previous two editions. He was assisted by co-authors Miles Roddis, who also worked on the previous two editions, and Stuart Butler, who wrote the Oslo and Southern Norway chapters for this edition.

This guidebook was commissioned in Lonely Planet's London office, and produced by the following:

Commissioning Editors Jo Potts, Anna Tyler

Coordinating Editor Carolyn Boicos

Coordinating Cartographer Valeska Cañas

Coordinating Layout Designer Jacqui Saunders

Managing Editors Imogen Bannister, Liz Heynes

Senior Editors Helen Christinis, Susan Paterson

Managing Cartographers Alison Lyall, Herman So

Managing Layout Designer Jane Hart

Assisting Editors Jackey Coyle, Jessica Crouch, Cathryn Game, Beth Hall, Simon Williamson

Assisting Cartographers Xavier Di Toro, Brendan Streager

Assisting Layout Designer Nicholas Colicchia

Cover Research Sabrina Dalbesio

Internal Image Research Rebecca Skinner

Language Content Branislava Vladisavljevic

Thanks to Mark Adams, David Connolly, Melanie Dankel, Stefanie Di Trocchio, Janine Eberle, Joshua Geoghegan, Mark Germanchis, Michelle Glynn, Lauren Hunt, Laura Jane, David Kemp, Yvonne Kirk, Lisa Knights, Nic Lehman, John Mazzocchi, Wayne Murphy, Trent Paton, Adrian Persoglia, Piers Pickard, Kirsten Rawlings, Lachlan Ross, Michael Ruff, Julie Sheridan, Laura Stansfeld, John Taufa, Sam Trafford, Gerard Walker, Juan Winata, Emily Wolman, Nick Wood

index

how to use this book

These symbols will help you find the listings you want:

- ◉ Sights
- 🏃 Activities
- 🍃 Courses
- 👆 Tours
- 🎊 Festivals & Events
- 🛏 Sleeping
- 🍴 Eating
- 🍷 Drinking
- ⭐ Entertainment
- 🔒 Shopping
- ℹ Information/ Transport

Look out for these icons:

TOP CHOICE — Our author's recommendation

FREE — No payment required

🌿 — A green or sustainable option

Our authors have nominated these places as demonstrating a strong commitment to sustainability – for example by supporting local communities and producers, operating in an environmentally friendly way, or supporting conservation projects.

These symbols give you the vital information for each listing:

- ☎ Telephone Numbers
- ⊙ Opening Hours
- Ⓟ Parking
- ⊖ Nonsmoking
- ✳ Air-Conditioning
- @ Internet Access
- 🛜 Wi-Fi Access
- 🏊 Swimming Pool
- 🥗 Vegetarian Selection
- 📖 English-Language Menu
- 👪 Family-Friendly
- 🐾 Pet-Friendly
- 🚌 Bus
- ⛴ Ferry
- Ⓜ Metro
- Ⓢ Subway
- ⊖ London Tube
- 🚋 Tram
- 🚆 Train

Reviews are organised by author preference.

Map Legend

Sights
- ❷ Beach
- ❹ Buddhist
- ❸ Castle
- ❶ Christian
- Ⓦ Hindu
- ❻ Islamic
- ❾ Jewish
- ❶ Monument
- ⊕ Museum/Gallery
- ❽ Ruin
- ❾ Winery/Vineyard
- ❽ Zoo
- ◉ Other Sight

Activities, Courses & Tours
- ⊜ Diving/Snorkelling
- ❺ Canoeing/Kayaking
- ❶ Skiing
- ❶ Surfing
- ❸ Swimming/Pool
- ❹ Walking
- ❺ Windsurfing
- • Other Activity/ Course/Tour

Sleeping
- ⊜ Sleeping
- ❺ Camping

Eating
- ❽ Eating

Drinking
- ❾ Drinking
- ❾ Cafe

Entertainment
- ⊙ Entertainment

Shopping
- ⊙ Shopping

Information
- ❸ Bank
- ❺ Embassy/ Consulate
- ⊕ Hospital/Medical
- ⊚ Internet
- ❾ Police
- ❸ Post Office
- ❽ Telephone
- ❶ Toilet
- ❶ Tourist Information
- • Other Information

Transport
- ❹ Airport
- ❽ Border Crossing
- ❷ Bus
- ⊕ Cable Car/ Funicular
- ⊜ Cycling
- ⊖ Ferry
- Ⓜ Metro
- ⊕ Monorail
- Ⓟ Parking
- ⊜ Petrol Station
- ⊜ Taxi
- ⊕ Train/Railway
- ⊕ Tram
- • Other Transport

Routes
- Tollway
- Freeway
- Primary
- Secondary
- Tertiary
- Lane
- Unsealed Road
- Plaza/Mall
- Steps
-)=== Tunnel
- Pedestrian Overpass
- Walking Tour
- Walking Tour Detour
- Path

Geographic
- ⊕ Hut/Shelter
- ❺ Lighthouse
- ❸ Lookout
- ▲ Mountain/Volcano
- ❸ Oasis
- ❸ Park
-)(Pass
- ⊕ Picnic Area
- ❸ Waterfall

Population
- ❸ Capital (National)
- ◉ Capital (State/Province)
- • City/Large Town
- • Town/Village

Boundaries
- ––– International
- ---- State/Province
- — Disputed
- – – Regional/Suburb
- Marine Park
- Cliff
- Wall

Hydrography
- River, Creek
- Intermittent River
- Swamp/Mangrove
- Reef
- Canal
- Water
- Dry/Salt/ Intermittent Lake
- Glacier

Areas
- Beach/Desert
- + + + Cemetery (Christian)
- × × × Cemetery (Other)
- Park/Forest
- Sportsground
- Sight (Building)
- Top Sight (Building)

OUR STORY

A beat-up old car, a few dollars in the pocket and a sense of adventure. In 1972 that's all Tony and Maureen Wheeler needed for the trip of a lifetime – across Europe and Asia overland to Australia. It took several months, and at the end – broke but inspired – they sat at their kitchen table writing and stapling together their first travel guide, *Across Asia on the Cheap*. Within a week they'd sold 1500 copies. Lonely Planet was born.

Today, Lonely Planet has offices in Melbourne, London and Oakland, with more than 600 staff and writers. We share Tony's belief that 'a great guidebook should do three things: inform, educate and amuse'.

OUR WRITERS

Anthony Ham

Coordinating Author, Central Norway, Bergen & the Southwestern Fjords, Svalbard Anthony fell in love with Norway the first time he laid eyes on it and there aren't many places in Norway he hasn't been, from Lindesnes in the south to the remote fjords of Svalbard in the far north. His true passion is the Arctic North, whether dog-sledding and spending time with the Sami around Karasjok or, for this edition of the guide, drawing near to glaciers and scouring the horizon for polar bears in the glorious wilderness of Svalbard. When he's not travelling for Lonely Planet to the Arctic (or, his other great love, the Sahara), he lives in Madrid and writes and photographs for magazines and newspapers around the world.

Read more about Anthony at:
lonelyplanet.com/members/anthonyham

Stuart Butler

Oslo, Southern Norway Hailing from southwest England, Stuart grew up surrounded by both the sea and stories of travel and adventure. By his late teens he had managed to combine the two into a life spent travelling to the remoter coastlines of the globe in search of unknown surf spots. It was this that first led him, in a frozen November, to the far north of Norway where he surfed almost within the shadow of Nordkapp. Fortunately, the very short days meant he didn't have to spend long in the water. He now lives in the much warmer southwest of France, but has returned to hike in the beautiful mountains of Norway a number of times.

Miles Roddis

The Western Fjords, Trondelag, Nordland, the Far North A distant camping holiday in Finland, an even more distant Swedish girlfriend, and a need to refresh his northern European roots: such are the three pulls that draw Miles back to Scandinavia. He heads for the sheer, unrivalled majesty of Norway's central fjords and journeys beyond the Arctic Circle, exploring offshore islands and relishing the space and emptiness of the far north. Based for more than 20 years in Valencia, Spain, he and his wife, Ingrid, have explored the lands north of Sognefjord for the last three editions of this guidebook.

Published by Lonely Planet Publications Pty Ltd
ABN 36 005 607 983
5th edition – May 2011
ISBN 978 1 74179 330 7
© Lonely Planet 2011   Photographs © as indicated 2011
10 9 8 7 6 5 4
Printed in China